Kant
and the
Claims of Knowledge

This book offers a radically new account of the development and structure of the central arguments of Kant's *Critique of Pure Reason*: the defense of the objective validity of such categories as substance, causation, and independent existence. Paul Guyer makes far more extensive use than any other commentator of historical materials from the years leading up to the publication of the *Critique* and surrounding its revision, and he shows that the work which has come down to us is the result of some striking and only partially resolved theoretical tensions. Kant had originally intended to demonstrate the validity of the categories by exploiting what he called "analogies of appearance" between the structure of self-knowledge and our knowledge of objects. The idea of a separate "transcendental deduction," independent from the analysis of the necessary conditions of *empirical* judgments, arose only shortly before publication of the *Critique* in 1781, and distorted much of Kant's original inspiration. Part of what led Kant to present this deduction separately was his invention of a new pattern of argument – very different from the "transcendental arguments" attributed by recent interpreters to Kant – depending on initial claims to *necessary* truth. This new form of argument forced Kant's defense of the categories into a far more idealistic framework than was otherwise necessary, although the original impetus to realism reappeared in his brief "Refutation of Idealism" in 1787.

This book thus provides a detailed study of the grounds which motivated Kant to realism as well as to idealism, presenting a picture of Kant as a more torn but therefore even more profound philosopher than we have come to accept in recent decades.

Kant
and the
Claims of Knowledge

PAUL GUYER

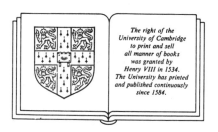

The right of the
University of Cambridge
to print and sell
all manner of books
was granted by
Henry VIII in 1534.
The University has printed
and published continuously
since 1584.

CAMBRIDGE UNIVERSITY PRESS

CAMBRIDGE

NEW YORK   NEW ROCHELLE   MELBOURNE   SYDNEY

Published by the Press Syndicate of the University of Cambridge
The Pitt Building, Trumpington Street, Cambridge CB2 1RP
32 East 57th Street, New York, NY 10022, USA
10 Stamford Road, Oakleigh, Melbourne 3166, Australia

First published 1987

Printed in the United States of America

Library of Congress Cataloging-in-Publication Data
Guyer, Paul, 1948–
Kant and the claims of knowledge.
Includes indexes.
1. Kant, Immanuel, 1724–1804 – Contributions in theory of knowledge.
2. Knowledge, Theory of. I. Title.
B2799.K7G88   1988   121'.092'4   87–878

British Library Cataloguing in Publication Data
Guyer, Paul
Kant and the claims of knowledge.
1. Kant, Immanuel – Knowledge, Theory of
I. Title
121'.092'4   B2799.K7

ISBN 0 521 33192 7 hard covers
ISBN 0 521 33772 0 paperback

FOR PAMELA

Contents

vii

CONTENTS

Acknowledgments

This book has been in preparation for a long time. Work expressly intended for it began in 1978–9: During that year I enjoyed the support of a National Endowment for the Humanities Fellowship for Independent Study and Research and was able to begin the study, especially of Kant's *Nachlass*, that resulted in my articles "Kant's Tactics in the Transcendental Deduction" (*Philosophical Topics* 12 [1981]:157–99, reprinted in J. N. Mohanty and Robert W. Shahan, eds., *Essays on Kant's Critique of Pure Reason* [Norman: University of Oklahoma Press, 1982]) and "Kant's Intentions in the Refutation of Idealism" (*Philosophical Review* 92 [1983]:329–83). These articles form the basis of parts II and IV of the present work, respectively, although in the first case in particular the material has been very much revised and expanded. (Some of the new material in part II also appears as "The Failure of the B-Deduction," *Southern Journal of Philosophy* 25, Supplement [1987]: 67–84.) A John Simon Guggenheim Memorial Fellowship for 1982–3, as well as generous support from both the University of Illinois at Chicago and the University of Pennsylvania, enabled me to draft the earliest version of the material that appears here as parts I and III as well as a sketch of part V. Much of the material in part V was first drafted during 1984, some of it for presentation at the March 1985 meeting in San Francisco of the Pacific Division of the American Philosophical Association, under the title "The Rehabilitation of Transcendental Idealism?" I am very grateful to the National Endowment for the Humanities and the Guggenheim Foundation for their patient support of this work, and I thank the editors of the publications mentioned for permission to reuse some of the material which they first published.

But I have really been at work on this book since I began studying Kant, so it is a much harder task to acknowledge and thank the many individuals who have helped and influenced me over the years. Nevertheless, some attempt is required. As a student, I was fortunate to be able to work on Kant with Stanley Cavell, Robert Nozick, Charles Parsons, John Cooper, John Rawls, Frederick Olafson, Nelson Goodman, and, chronologically last but hardly least, Dieter Henrich. Although I was never his student, I have also enjoyed the generous support and encouragement of Lewis White Beck from a very early stage. I hope that the present work repays in some small degree the confidence as well as patience of all these men. Since I began my own teaching career, I have continued to learn from many colleagues at my own and other institutions; even the most incomplete list would certainly include Annette Baier, Alexander Nehamas, Carl Posy, the late Gareth Evans, Ralf Meerbote, Rolf-Peter Horstmann, Anthony Brueckner, John Biro, Christopher Swoyer, Akheel Bilgrami, Allen Wood, Thomas Ricketts, William Harper, Michael Williams, Frederick Beiser, Stephen Hudson, Robert Fogelin, and Joseph Margolis. Michael Friedman has given me many useful comments, especially on material for part V, and I am grateful to Manley Thompson and Patricia Kitcher for reading and commenting on the whole of the penultimate draft of the work.

As already suggested, the material in this book originated in the five separate sections represented by its five parts. The book is by no means meant to be a systematic commentary on the *Critique of Pure Reason*: It goes to Kantian sources well beyond the *Critique* on many issues but also ignores many standard issues within the *Critique*. But I trust this work will not read like five monographs bound together. The division into chapters is an artifact of the final round of revision, but I hope it will nevertheless facilitate the reader's study of what has become a rather larger book than I had originally planned.

P.G.

Philadelphia

Note on sources

Quotations from the *Critique of Pure Reason* are based on the German edition by Raymund Schmidt (Hamburg: Felix Meiner Verlag, 1926); translations from the *Critique* are my own, although naturally influenced by the translation by Norman Kemp Smith, *Immanuel Kant's Critique of Pure Reason*, 2nd ed. (London: Macmillan, 1933). As is customary, citations from the *Critique* are located by the pagination of the first edition of 1781 (A) and/or the second edition of 1787 (B): A citation to A or B alone means that the passage quoted appeared only in that edition; a citation to both A and B means that the passage appeared in both editions. All other quotations from Kant are from *Kants gesammelte Schriften, herausgegeben von der Deutschen* [formerly *Königlichen Preussischen*] *Akademie der Wissenschaften*, 29 volumes (Berlin: Walter de Gruyter [and predecessors], 1902–). Citations are located by a short title, if necessary, or, in the case of items from Kant's *Handschriftliche Nachlass*, by the letter R (for *Reflexion*), followed by the number assigned in the *Akademie* edition; the volume and page number in the *Akademie* edition then follows. All translations from German are my own unless otherwise indicated. Translations from Kant's *Habilitationsschrift, Principiorum primorum cognitionis metaphysicae nova delucidatio* (abbreviated *Nova Delucidatio*) are from F. E. England, *Kant's Concept of God* (London: Allen & Unwin, 1932). Translations from Kant's inaugural dissertation of 1770, *De mundi sensibilis atque intelligibilis forma et principiis* (abbreviated ID), are by G. B. Kerferd, taken from G. B. Kerferd and D. E. Walford, *Kant: Selected Pre-Critical Writings and Correspondence with Beck* (Manchester: Manchester University Press, 1968). Bibliographic information for all other works cited is supplied in the notes.

1. What is an object?

2. In what does the relation of a determination of the soul to something else consist?

3. What is the ground of agreement?

4. By what means do we distinguish what is related to the object and what to the subject?

(R 4286, 17:496)

All determination in time can take place only according to an *a priori* principle, that is [a principle] such that each thing succeeds something preceding it according to a rule.

(R 5214, 18:120)

Introduction

In the preface which he wrote for the second edition of the *Critique of Pure Reason* in 1787, Immanuel Kant drew a famous analogy between his own theoretical philosophy and the revolution in astronomy inaugurated by Nicolaus Copernicus. Previously, he wrote, metaphysics – in this, presumably, like all other sciences – had proceeded on the simple assumption that "all of our knowledge must conform to objects." On this assumption, however, all of metaphysics's efforts toward its aim – quite unlike that of other sciences – of "determining something" about objects "*a priori* through concepts, whereby our knowledge may be amplified" had "gone for naught." Faced with this failure, Kant decided to follow the "primary idea of Copernicus" and effect a radical change in the point of view from which metaphysics was conducted. Instead of continuing in the vain attempt to discover through ordinary experience universal and necessary truths which do not merely display the concepts we have already adopted but show us what sort of concepts we must adopt and how they must be put together to begin with – for only such truths are *a priori* yet amplify our knowledge – Kant would for once "try whether we might not succeed better in the tasks of metaphysics if we assumed that objects must conform to our knowledge" (B xvi). Tacit in this description of his experiment is the assumption that even if the experience of objects cannot directly yield universal and necessary but informative truths about them, the character of our own cognitive constitution – comprising both the "constitution of our faculty of intuition," by means of which we are given our data about objects, and the rules of the faculty of understanding, "which are in me even before I am given objects" but in accord with which I must form all my judgments about objects (B xvii) – can somehow be made to yield nontrivial universal and necessary truths that must apply to the objects on which we exercise these capacities.

Other philosophers, of course, had also asserted that we must reflect on our own cognitive constitution before venturing too much speculation about the nature of objects. Most famously, John Locke – the only major philosopher Kant mentions by name in either of his prefaces for the two editions of the *Critique* (in the first-edition preface at A ix) – had also proposed "to enquire into the Original, Certainty, and Extent of humane Knowledge; together, with the Grounds and Degrees of Belief, Opinion, and Assent" and by means of such an inquiry – to be conducted by a "Historical, plain Method" – to give an "Account of the Ways, whereby

I

our Understandings come to attain those Notions of Things we have."[1] Locke's reflection on human understanding did lead him to degrade some of our ideas as misleading (for instance, like every other modern from Galileo and Hobbes on, he argued that there are no qualities in external objects resembling our ideas of color, taste, and smell) and to the pessimistic conclusion that our prospects for discovery of the necessary connections in the real inner constitutions of external objects are extremely limited. But he certainly did not arrive at any wholesale rejection of the picture of reality which, he thought, could filter through the screen set up by our crude senses and intellect. Yet though Kant thought he had a better method for examining our cognitive constitution than the "Historical, plain Method" of Locke, which he scornfully rejected as mere "physiology" (A ix) that could only "sensualize" all "concepts of the understanding" (A 271 / B 327), he himself utterly degraded all of the results so painfully attained by his own revolutionary method. From the apparently innocuous assumption that "objects must conform to our knowledge," Kant seems to have arrived at the bizarre conclusion that space and time, the indispensable forms for all of our representations of objects, "are only forms of sensible intuition," and thus that these indispensable features of human knowledge, as well as all of the additional concepts that we formulate in terms of them, "are only conditions of the existence of things as appearances," which cannot yield us any knowledge of "objects as things in themselves" (B xxv–xxvi). What could Kant's new Copernican method be, that it should be so superior to Locke's yet yield such decidedly inferior results?

There are really two questions here. How does Kant propose to discover the indispensable features of our cognitive constitution to which any objects that we might know "must conform"? Yet why does he seem to conclude that the objects which at least appear to conform to these indispensable requirements of our own cognition actually do not possess, just as they are "in themselves," the very properties required by this conformity?

The images Kant employs in his prefaces give us no clues to these mysteries. Associating himself with the scientific revolution, Kant appeals first to Francis Bacon and then to such genuine scientific pioneers as Galileo, Torricelli (who invented the barometer), and his countryman the chemist G. E. Stahl (who theorized about oxidation and, unfortunately, phlogiston as well). These men realized that "reason has insight only into what it brings forth according to its own design," and thus that "nature must be forced to answer reason's questions" (B xiii). But there are two problems here. First, this little lesson in scientific method contains no unequivocal clue to a new method in metaphysics. These scientists had learned that a purely inductive accumulation of observations could yield no particular theory and that experiments must instead be designed to test particular hypotheses. But they had no special method for the formulation of the hypotheses to be tested: These could be arrived at by the idealization of observation, by the construction of purely mathematical models, or for that matter by inspired guesswork. Once the hypotheses were put to the test of controlled experimentation, it made no difference how they had themselves been discovered. But in philosophy – precisely because Kant rejected Locke's "physiological" or empirical method for the study of the mind itself – it would make all the difference in the world what method was used to discover the constitution of the mind itself. Second, and perhaps even more obvious, the hypothetical yet experimental method pioneered by Galileo and the others introduced no general gap between appearance and reality at all. Nature would answer only the specific questions we asked her, to be sure, but her answers would be truthful, and from the fact that we have to design the experiments we put to her, it certainly does not follow that we determine what answers will result. Reason must produce our experimental tests for nature; it does not produce nature itself. Yet Kant seems to take his philosophical method to imply the opposite: We do not merely ask nature certain questions, it seems, but we instead impose upon her certain answers – to which we also know she does not really conform! Why should this be so?

Kant's own comparison of his venture with that of Copernicus makes this second problem even plainer. Since "the explanation of the heavenly motions did not go well when he assumed that the whole host of stars revolved around the observer," Kant writes, Copernicus tried "whether it might not go better if he let the observer revolve, and on the contrary, left the stars at rest" (B xvi–xvii). Likewise, he suggests, his procedure too will change the position of the observer, the human subject of knowledge itself. Although from a purely geometrical point of view the resulting image will be more Ptolemaic than Copernican – the knowing subject will be placed at the center of the realm of objects, rather than vice versa – the philosopher, like the astronomer, will dare, "in a manner contrary to the senses yet true, to seek the observed motions not in the objects of the heavens but in their observer" (B xxii). But why should such a procedure yield any gap between the results it produces and the true nature of reality? To be sure, the Copernican model of the solar system introduces a distinction between the solar and planetary motions we on earth appear to see and the motions which, according to the theory, actually take place; it was the apparent rather than real motions, after all, that gave rise to the Ptolemaic image of the geocentric universe. But two points must be noted about this particular gap between appearance and reality. First, on the Copernican model of the solar system the true motions of the planets are hardly unknown; on the contrary, it is nothing less than accepting the heliocentric hypothesis about the planetary motions which leads to the characterization of the rising and setting of the sun and the erratic epicycles of the planets as merely apparent motions. In the absence of their contrast to the true motions, there would be no reason to call what we observe apparent. Second, it is even misleading to call what we observe "mere appearances," if by that it is suggested that there is anything illusory or even unreliable about them. On

3

the contrary, just as (as Thomas Reid suggested in 1764) "a circle seen obliquely" really "will appear an ellipse, and a square, a rhombus,"[2] so the rising and setting of the sun and apparently nonorbital motions of the planets are exactly what we should see if the Copernican hypothesis is right. They are thus hardly illusions themselves, and they certainly give us no reason to impugn the Copernican claims about the true motions of the heavenly bodies. So our question still stands: Why should Kant's use of a Copernican method in metaphysics give rise to an unbridgeable chasm between appearance and reality which that method does not produce in science itself?

Many writers today think that Kant never intended to deny anything about the real nature of things. On this view, Kant's "transcendental idealism" – for so he names his metaphysical conclusion – is meant only to restrict the philosophical (and for that matter scientific) claims we make about objects to those objects we are capable of experiencing, as they appear to beings constituted as we are. Kant certainly makes statements which, at least if taken in isolation, can bear this interpretation. Thus the statement already quoted, that space and time are only forms of sensibility, continues by saying that "we can therefore have knowledge of no object as a thing in itself but only insofar as it is an object of sensible intuition, that is, an appearance" (B xxvi). At another place he states that "we may well say that space comprehends all things that may appear to us externally but not all things in themselves, whether they are intuited or not, or by whatever subject they might be intuited" (A 27 / B 43). Such formulations suggest a restriction on the scope of the claims we are to derive by discovery of the indispensable conditions of our own cognition: We may assert that they hold of all the objects we are capable of experiencing but not of whatever other objects there might be, if there are any others. But such remarks fail to prove that these conditions do not genuinely characterize those objects to which they do apply. Unfortunately, we shall find ample evidence that Kant does not confine himself to this anodyne interpretation of his ambiguous statement that objects must "conform" to our knowledge; there are many places where he plainly asserts that space and time, and all that depends on them, cannot genuinely characterize those objects which we experience as in space and time (thus, A 26 / B 42 – a page *before* the apparently weaker formulation).

Other writers, however, have not shied away from recognizing the real import of transcendental idealism's contrast between appearances and things as they are in themselves and have also been puzzled by Kant's inference from the very fact that space and time are necessary conditions for our representation of any objects to the conclusion that these conditions cannot possibly represent inherent features of the objects represented. Thus one author has recently said, "Surely it is only because we are able to represent the world that we are able to get to know anything about it at all. Representation is a necessary means to knowledge, not an obstacle." This view is so natural, it seems, that Kant's inference that "our knowledge is drastically limited" can be explained only by his further supposition "of a contrasting cognition of reality that does not involve representations" and to which our method of representation, necessary as it may be for creatures like us, is inferior.[3] Or, as another writer puts it, in Kant's many arguments for the conclusion that "things cannot really be as they are given in experience as being" there is "always the secret reference to the conception of things as they would be revealed to be, if we could have access to them as they in themselves are. What they appear to be is condemned as appearance because it fails to square with such a conception."[4] And the source of this contrasting conception is not far to seek: Kant's degradation of the very features of our cognition which he has discovered to be necessary for us is held to follow from his continuing attachment to the theological ideal of divine knowledge independent of all space and time – knowledge, indeed, which cannot fail to be right for the very reason that the existence of its object is utterly dependent upon the divine conception of it. To be sure, Kant explicitly rejects the supposition that our own "intuition is itself the ground of things"[5] and always alleges that the idea of an "intellectual intuition," in which the mere thought and the actual experience of an object utterly coincide, is only a possibility. But, it is supposed, theology retains such a grasp over Kant that even the bare possibility of an alternative to our own means for representing objects leads him to downgrade the latter to mere appearance after all.[6] In the end, then, these contemporary commentators conclude, Kant's transcendental idealism just rests on a more pessimistic theology than was entertained by his great predecessors: Whereas Descartes's God would give us everything we might want to know and Locke's would give us less but certainly not deceive us about what he does let us see, for Kant the mere possibility of a divine alternative to our own way of representing objects is indeed an obstacle to any insight at all into the nature of independent reality.

There is something to this story, but it is far from the whole truth, or even the philosophically most important part of it. Neither of these two contemporary views about Kant can be straightforwardly accepted. Kant's assumption that "objects must conform to our knowledge" is profoundly ambivalent: Part of him inclines to the realistic assumption that we succeed in knowing objects which really conform to our conditions for representing them – though we must always look to ourselves first in order to discover what these conditions are – and part of him inclines to the view that things as they are in themselves cannot possibly have those very properties that they must appear to have. But the latter view – and thus Kant's metaphysical ambivalence as a whole – is far from an accidental inheritance or residue from the religious tradition in which he grew up. Instead, Kant's transcendental idealism is a direct result of one of his methods (indeed, for much of the vital decade of the 1780s his preferred method) for discovering necessary conditions of our cognition. In other words, the method and the metaphysics of Kant's Copernican revolution are not two separate puzzles but are intimately connected. In fact, Kant employs two radically different

5

methods for his investigation of our cognitive constitution. In one mood, he simply assumes that we know certain propositions as universal and necessary truths; he then argues that such claims to knowledge of necessary truth can be explained only by our antecedent possession of certain conceptions and capacities which we must, in turn, be able to impose upon a reality which does not itself, even contingently, conform to these conditions – for even the contingent conformity of reality to our *a priori* conceptions would undermine their claim to truly universal necessity. In his other mood, Kant makes no initial claims to our knowledge of necessary truth but painstakingly displays principles that we must adopt in order to confirm even contingent empirical judgments. In this mood, he suggests no special reasons to suppose that when we successfully claim empirical knowledge, reality is not much as we claim it to be. Kant's ambivalence about the metaphysics of reality, in the end, is part and parcel of his ambivalence about the proper method for the critical philosophy.

This claim will seem shocking to many. To be sure, Kant does describe what he calls a "regressive" or "analytical" method for his critical philosophy, which is characterized precisely by the initial assumption that certain informative knowledge-claims – the foundations of mathematics and physics – are indeed universally and necessarily true. He then displays *a priori* forms for sensing and conceptualizing objects which are alleged to be the only conditions under which such synthetic *a priori* – to use Kant's terms – claims to knowledge can be valid. But this method is supposed to be confined to the *Prolegomena to Any Future Metaphysics*, Kant's "popularization" of his system (see 4:263). The *Critique of Pure Reason,* by contrast, is supposed to employ a "synthetic method,"[7] which would apparently be characterized by the very absence of any initial claim to universal and necessary truth among its premises – although, of course, synthetic *a priori* knowledge is the desired conclusion of this method. But we shall see that such a distinction, even though suggested by Kant himself, simply was not sustained. The *Critique of Pure Reason* is permeated by "transcendental proofs" (A 786 / B 814) that do not merely "yield an *a priori* synthetic cognition" (A 782 / B810) but actually presuppose a valid claim to universal and necessary truth and then deny the property at issue to things as they are in themselves, independent of their cognitive relation to us, by a simple argument: Although features we impose on our representations of objects can be considered necessarily true of those representations, they could be at best contingently true of other objects – but such contingent truth would undercut the very claim to necessary truth from which the argument began. Here Kant's transcendental method and his transcendental idealism go hand in hand.

This style of argument, to be sure, is not the only method Kant employs. On the contrary, we shall see that in the great creative period of the 1770s, when Kant was fermenting the must of ideas that became the *Critique of Pure Reason,* his first strategy was to derive the pure categories of the understanding[8] from the necessary conditions for the "exposition of appearances" or "determination of the ground on which the connection of" even subjective representations depends (R 4674, 17:643). Such an exposition amounts to nothing less than the ordering of both subjective representations as such and the objective states of affairs in a "unitary time in which all things and all states of things have their determinate position" (R 4673, 17:636-7). Kant's idea is that although our judgments about such temporal positions are themselves merely empirical judgments, there are nevertheless "rules of perception" by means of which "the objects of the senses" – and even sensory representations themselves – "are determinable in time" (R 4681, 17:666). Such rules would constitute necessary and universal but informative – therefore synthetic *a priori* – conditions for cognition, without themselves being derived from any antecedently assumed universal and necessary truths – and they would themselves require no immediate inference to transcendental idealism.

This strategy and the arguments by which he ultimately accomplished it represent Kant's most enduring contribution to theoretical philosophy. Kant was initially far from clear on the details of these arguments; if he had been, it would not have taken another dozen years and two quite different versions of the *Critique* for him to present his views. And even when these two editions of the *Critique* were finally finished (or almost – see this volume, Part IV), what Kant had created was not a single theory but an uneasy combination of very different arguments. Like every other philosopher, whether brought up on a diet of Wolffian rationalism or not, Kant was concerned that his ideas appear consistent and systematic, and so he presented the two kinds of argument that have just been described as if they formed two stages of a single argument: first, a transcendental deduction of the pure concepts of understanding (as well as pure forms of sensibility), and then an application of these to yield principles of empirical knowledge, in particular principles for the empirical judgment of temporal relations. But the actual contents of the *Critique* do not fit this model. Instead, the work offers a transcendental deduction (indeed, a variety of deductions) starting from a claim to necessary truth and ultimately leading to a disclaimer of knowledge of independent reality, but also offers a quite independent examination of the necessary conditions of empirical knowledge-claims which implies no disclaimer of insight into reality at all. To sort out these different claims to knowledge, as well as to assess Kant's metaphysical disclaimer, will be the fundamental task of this book; thus the title, *Kant and the Claims of Knowledge*.

I
Kant's early view

I

The problem of objective validity

The emergence of a problem

Though Kant coined his name for the problem of synthetic *a priori* knowledge only well into his career, he criticized from the outset the rationalist assumption that the *a priori* knowledge characteristic of general and special metaphysics could be derived from analysis according to laws of logic alone. Thus his earliest purely philosophical writings, the *New Exposition of the First Principles of Metaphysical Knowledge* (the *Nova Delucidatio*) of 1755 and *The Only Possible Proof of the Existence of God* of 1762, argue that sufficient reasons for the determinations of real objects could not be established just by the analyses of what are in fact merely concepts of possible objects in accord with the laws of identity and noncontradiction alone, but that there must also be an explanation of the logically contingent limitation of real possibilities to some subset of the formally consistent conceptions of objects.[1] These works thus first express Kant's most fundamental claim that all analysis presupposes synthesis (e.g., B 133–4n), and therefore that analysis alone can never be the basis of knowledge, metaphysical or otherwise.[2] But only more gradually did it become clear to Kant that if the basic laws of metaphysics were *synthetic* – not true by logic alone, and thus not true of all possible objects of logical thought whatever – a special account would have to be given of how these principles could be known *a priori* and yet also be known to be true of objects, independent of our mere thought of them. Only gradually, in other words, did Kant realize that the problem of synthetic *a priori* knowledge included a problem of *objective validity*: the problem of how representations which must somehow be connected with the nature of the cognitive subject itself, in order to be known *a priori*, can also provide insight into objects which exist independently of this subject of knowledge.

To be sure, a germ of Kant's eventual solution to this problem of objective validity was present in his first treatment of the problem of the synthetic *a priori*. The *Nova Delucidatio* of 1755, in which Kant first argued that analysis presupposes synthesis, also included a remarkable anticipation of what was eventually to be the decisive argument in Kant's solution to the problem of objective validity three decades later, the "Refutation of Idealism" added to the *Critique of Pure Reason* in 1787. In the 1755 work Kant contended that

the mind, namely, is subject through means of internal sense to internal changes;

11

since these changes cannot . . . arise from its own nature considered in isolation and apart from a connection with other things, those other things must be present outside the mind, and the mind must be connected with them in a mutual relation.

(*Nova Delucidatio,* 2:411–12)

But though this comment anticipated Kant's later solution, it was not yet offered in response to the problem of objective validity. Kant was here offering an argument intended only to revise the logic and ontology of Leibnizo-Wolffianism. That is, Kant was arguing that the principle of sufficient reason is a principle logically independent of the principles of analysis – the laws of identity and noncontradiction. But he also argued that in order to explain the successions of states that occur in substances undergoing change, this principle itself requires a physical influx, or real influence, between substances, rather than merely a preestablished harmony without genuine interaction. But at this point in his own career, at which, to borrow his later words, "the proud name of Ontology" had not yet given way "to the modest title of a mere Analytic of pure understanding" (A 247 / B 303), Kant understood this as a dispute within ontology; it did not yet reflect a concern with an epistemological problem about the objective validity of synthetic *a priori* knowledge. From the outset of his career, Kant's rejection of preestablished harmony in favor of real interaction reflected his Newtonian rather than Leibnizian conception of the content of empirical and metaphysical knowledge, but Kant did not equally early question the epistemological confidence engendered by the supposition that every substance represents the entire universe of independent substances from its own point of view.[3]

The epistemological problem of objective validity seems to have become central to Kant's conception of the task of theoretical philosophy only in the years of intellectual ferment surrounding the publication of his inaugural dissertation, *On the Form and Principles of the Sensible and Intellectual World,* in 1770, and particularly in the years from 1769 to 1772. Within this period, the problem seems to have presented itself to Kant in two distinct stages. First, there arose the problem with respect to the objective validity of the representations of space and time which is first addressed in the dissertation. This problem arose at least partially as a result of Kant's realization that the absolute space which he required, in 1768, to solve the physical problem of incongruent counterparts could not be metaphysically understood as an entity ontologically independent of ourselves, as Newton had understood it, for that would be a "fabrication of the reason" (ID, §15.D, 2:404), or an absurd, "self-subsisting *Unding*" (A 39 / B 56). Absolute space could be only our own all-encompassing system of spatial representation. Kant thought he had solved this first problem with the theory of the transcendental idealism of space and time which he then advanced, though not yet with that name. As he put it a few years later, "*Spatium absolutum, this riddle of philosophers,* is something entirely correct, but not *reale,* rather *ideale*" (R 4673 [1774], 17:639).[4] As we shall subsequently see, however, the problem became a difficult one, and it was not until 1787 or after that Kant clearly asked how we can reconcile the thesis that our *a priori* knowledge of absolute space and time has subjective origins with the premise concerning the objective validity of our judgments about independent objects in space and time. The second problem of this period, that concerning the objective validity of the intelligible rather than sensible forms and principles – that is, the problem of what Kant would later call the categories and the principles of judgment, rather than that of the pure intuitions of space and time – was neither evident in nor addressed by the inaugural dissertation. It seems rather to have been first formulated by Kant only as an indirect result of reflection upon objections to this dissertation raised by a number of leading figures, but especially by J. H. Lambert, and first announced in Kant's famous letter to his disciple Marcus Herz in 1772.

The basic form of the problem announced in 1772 is of course well known. Kant discovered that the "key to the whole secret" of metaphysics required an answer to the question "On what basis rests the relation to the object of that which, in ourselves, we call representation?", in the case in which this representation is neither a mere *effect* of the causal agency of the object, as it is in the case of our ordinary empirical intuitions and concepts of objects, which are grounded in their stimulation of our passive or receptive senses, nor itself the *cause* of the represented object, as it is in the case of the actual creation of objects from their mere representation by the divine intellect or *intellectus archetypus*. That is, metaphysics requires an explanation of the possibility of "intellectual representations" of outer objects or "axioms of reason concerning these objects [which] agree with them, without this agreement being permitted to derive assistance from experience" (10:131).[5] The very formulation of this problem reveals an underlying assumption of the objective validity of these "intellectual representations" that constitutes a key constraint on any solution, although this constraint may not always have been clear to Kant himself and certainly has not always been clear to his interpreters. It will be worth pausing for a brief analysis of the theory of the inaugural dissertation and of the import of this objection to it.

The dissertation begins by drawing a profoundly antirationalist distinction between merely *conceiving* of something by means of an "abstract notion of the intellect" and actually *following up* such a notion through the "sensitive faculty of knowledge," that is, representing " the same notion to oneself in the concrete by a distinct intuition." Thus, Kant holds, there is a difference between, on the one hand, merely forming the concept of a simple part which would be the ultimate result of a completed analysis, or forming a concept of a complete whole which would be the result of a completed synthesis, and, on the other, arriving at a concrete intuition of a simple part or a complete whole "under the laws of intuitive cognition" and "in a finite assignable period of time" (ID, §1, 2:387–8).[6] Such a distinction, of course, is the basis for Kant's entire critique of rationalist metaphysics in the "Transcendental Dialectic" of the *Critique of Pure Reason*. But Kant does

13

not go on to insist on the necessary interaction of conceiving and intuiting for *any* cognition, which is so characteristic of the later *Critique*, and which is the most enduring aspect of its dual revolution against both the rationalist "intellectualization" of knowledge as well as its Lockean "sensualization" (cf. A 271 / B 327). Instead, Kant advances a theory in which the faculty of *intuiting* objects functions independently of any other faculty to provide a system for the representation of external objects, and in which an ability to *conceive* of objects – in Kant's later terminology, the understanding as a faculty of concepts – has no clearly demarcated function at all.

The last claim may seem surprising. As ordinarily understood, the inaugural dissertation posits the same two faculties which figure in Kant's later model of empirical knowledge, namely, sensibility and understanding, but describes them not as working together for the production of empirical though merely phenomenal knowledge but rather as fulfilling two distinct functions, of different epistemic dignity: Sensibility, by itself, is supposed to represent things merely as they appear, and the understanding, by itself, is supposed to know them as they really are. But this common interpretation is somewhat misleading. Such a conception is not entirely absent from the dissertation, but in general what Kant distinguishes as sensitive and intellectual cognition in this work corresponds more closely to what he later classified as the faculties of sensibility and *reason,* in that they do not furnish different representations, with different epistemic value, of a single set of objects but rather furnish representations of quite distinct sets of objects. And the functions of the later faculty of *understanding* barely appear in the theory of the dissertation at all, being emphasized only in a (profoundly revealing) afterthought. But, we shall see, the very reason why the function of the understanding was overlooked also reveals a fundamental fact about the underlying intention of Kant's approach to the problem of objective validity.

Kant's opening comment on the different roles of intuiting and conceiving in analysis and synthesis is followed by a "distinction between sensibles and intelligibles in general" (Section II), with subsequent discussions of the principles of form in the sensible and intelligible worlds respectively (Sections III and IV), and finally a diagnosis of the results of confusing the two kinds of principles (Section V). Most of the details of these discussions will not concern us here, but several points are vital for present purposes. Kant begins by distinguishing *sensibility,* "the *receptivity* of a subject by which it is possible for the subject's own representative state to be affected in some definite way by the presence of some object," from *intelligence* or rationality, the *active* "*faculty* of a subject by which it has the power to represent things which cannot by their own quality come before the senses of the subject" (ID, §3, 2:392). This distinction between a "receptivity" and an active "faculty" or "power" leads to a fundamental, and perhaps fatal, step. It seems to be built into Kant's very idea of a passive rather than active mode of representation that its content is *necessarily* reflective of the constitution of the patient *rather* than the agent, of the cognitive subject *rather* than the object.[7] As Kant says in the next section of the dissertation,

> ... Whatever in cognition is sensitive is dependent upon the special character of the subject to the extent that the subject is capable of this or that modification by the presence of objects, and these modifications can differ in different cases according to variations in the subjects ...

Consequently it is clear that things which are thought sensitively are representations of things *as they appear*, but things which are intellectual are representations of things *as they are*.   (ID, §4, 2:392)

Paradoxically, Kant appears to think that a passive reception of an external stimulus reveals more about the constitution of the *mind* than of the object, whereas an active creation of a representation better reflects the independent fact than the mere nature of the mind.[8] Yet this paradoxical assertion without argument represents Kant's introduction of his basic distinction between things as they appear and things as they are in themselves. The vital concern for our present interest, however, is not the justifiability of Kant's thesis but its content, and here we must recognize two facts. First, Kant is somewhat ambivalent about which objects are being classified as appearances and which are being classified as things as they are. Second, however he intends to draw this distinction, in all cases the objects represented are clearly conceived to be objects which exist quite independently of the representations of them. Let us consider these two points in order.

The absence of the understanding

The sentence last quoted from §4 of the dissertation certainly makes it sound as though the distinction between the objects of sensibility and the intellect – sensibles and intelligibles, or, as Kant also names them, phenomena and noumena (§3) – is essentially an epistemological distinction between representations of objects but not any ontological distinction between kinds of objects. That is, Kant seems to be distinguishing between the mere appearance and the actual nature of a single set of objects: Sensibility represents the mere appearance of the very same objects the actuality of which is represented by the intellect. Kant's opening statement in §3 seems at least compatible with such a reading: "Things which cannot by their own quality come before the senses of [the] subject" could be understood, at least in the present context, as things which *can* come before the senses by virtue of a quality or qualities lent by the subject rather than derived from their own nature. As it turns out, however, this would be a partially correct but partially misleading account of Kant's subsequent discussion of the objects of the intellect. It is correct in that Kant does indeed advocate that phenomena are appearances of objects which do exist independently of any representation of them, but it is misleading insofar as it suggests that Kant focuses on the role of the intellect in conceiving of the *same* objects which are intuited by sensibility. Instead, Kant virtually ignores any possible role for the intellect in the cognition of the objects of sensibility – though this is precisely the crucial function of the faculty of understanding in his later scheme. Instead, Kant chiefly considers an alleged use of the intellect for the cognition of objects which do not manifest themselves to sensibility in any form, whether direct or indirect, whatever.

Kant's theory of the intellect in the inaugural dissertation is presented by means of two distinctions. The first of these is the distinction between the *logical* and *real* use of the intellect. The logical use is the content-indifferent use of the intellect to subordinate concepts to one another, "no matter what the source from which they are given, ... in accordance with the principle of contradiction." As Kant says, this "logical use of the intellect is common to all the sciences" (§5, 2:393). The "real" use of the intellect, however, is that use, unique to metaphysics (§8, 2:395) rather than common to all the sciences, by which *special* concepts, "whether of things or relations, *are given*" (§5, 2:393). Thus, the logical use of the intellect may be exercised on "even the most general empirical laws," but the concepts which provide the content for such use will remain "none the less sensual" (*loc. cit.*). In the case of the real use of the intellect, however, the "concepts whether of objects or relations are given by the very nature of the intellect and they have not been abstracted from any use of the senses, nor do they contain any form of sensitive cognition" (§4, 2:394).

It is only when Kant introduces a second distinction concerning the use of the intellect, however, that the main concern of the dissertation's theory of intelligibles becomes obvious. The "use of things intellectual," he says, apparently referring only to the real use, "is preeminently two-fold": There is an *elenctic* use, "of value negatively," by means of which things "conceived sensitively" are kept away from noumena, but there is also a *dogmatic* use, in accordance with which "the general principles of the pure intellect, such as are displayed in ontology or in rational psychology, issue into some exemplar [which is] only to be conceived by the pure intellect and which is a common measure for all other things in so far as they are realities" (§9, 2:395–6). This distinction between elenctic and dogmatic uses of the intellect obviously foreshadows Kant's later distinction between negative and positive conceptions of noumena (e.g., B 307). But what is important to note here is not merely that Kant admits the dogmatic use of the intellect, whereas he later rejects the positive conception of a noumenon;[9] we must also recognize that the "exemplar" which provides the content for the dogmatic use of the intellect, and is thus the paradigmatic object of intellectual rather than sensitive cognition in the theory of the dissertation, has nothing to do with the objects which appear to us through the senses even as they are in themselves. Instead, the proper objects of intellectual cognition are objects which are entirely distinct from the objects of empirical knowledge considered from any point of view. The exemplar of intellectual cognition is noumenal perfection, which, taken in either a theoretical or practical sense respectively, is either God or moral perfection. The basic content of intellectual cognition, in other words, is not knowledge of the noumenal nature of the same objects which also appear phenomenally; it is moral philosophy and rational theology (§9, 2:396). The special objects of this intellectual cognition are not, of course, entirely without relation to ordinary empirical objects – God is, after all, their cause, and the concept of moral perfection provides a standard for judging them – but the objects of the concepts given by the real use of the intellect are not those things in themselves which merely appear to us as phenomena. Those objects do not seem to have a special place in the scheme of the inaugural dissertation at all.

Such, at least, is the initial impression created by Kant's opening section on the distinction between the sensible and intelligible. And in fact the only modification of this position which the continuation of Kant's argument suggests is not significant. Section III, "On the Principles of the Form of the Sensible World," a preliminary (though in some ways more perspicuous) version of the later "Transcendental Aesthetic" of the *Critique,* opens by excluding immaterial substances as well as the cause of the world from the embrace of the form of the sensible world, which "is limited to *things actual* in so far as they are thought capable of *falling under the senses*" (§13, 2:398). This contrast suggests that the positive content of the theoretical and practical dogmatic use of the intellect includes the soul as well as God and the ideal of a maximum of moral perfection (cf. §9, 2:396). But this still does not suggest that the "real" use of the intellect uses concepts in any way analogous to Kant's later concepts of pure understanding to provide noumenal knowledge *of the objects of appearance.* The real use of the intellect is not concerned with the objects of ordinary empirical knowledge as they appear *or* as they are in themselves.

An apparently more significant modification may be suggested when Kant comes to discuss "the principle of the form of the intelligible world," following his discussion of space and time as the form of the sensible world. In this section the problem to be solved by the intellect is the question, "*What is the principle upon which this relation of all substances itself rests, a relation which when seen intuitively is called space?*" (§16, 2:407). To solve this question the intellect must "make clear how it is possible that *several substances should be in mutual interaction*" (*loc. cit.*). The principle of intellectual cognition does this, in a way which Kant claims differs not only from the standard theories of physical influx and occasionalism but also from the theory of preestablished harmony (though the difference is not easy to detect) by representing the "*world, in its own essence,*" as a whole "*composed of mere contingents*" (§19, 2:408) which are all derived "*from one entity*" and which therefore, rather than being members of a mere heap "whose causes are alien to any mutual relation" instead enjoy "UNITY *in the conjunction of substances in the universe* [as] *a consequence of the dependence of all from one*" who is not merely *creator* but also *architect* (§20, 2:408).

Kant's claim is that a relation *among* contingents is possible only if there is a relation *between* them all, on the one hand, and a single cause of them all, on the other. This claim presupposes that the "real" use of the intellect does provide some noumenal knowledge of the *same* objects which appear to us phenomenally in the form of space and time, for the relation of the mutual dependence of contingents upon a single necessary cause is supposed to be the same "*relation which when seen intuitively is called space.*" But the positive content of this dogmatic use of the intellect is still very limited. Though a number of ideas corresponding to the later categories are employed here (Kant's theory of a general harmony [§22, 2:409] invokes the concepts of substance, interaction, causation, and of the modalities of necessity and contingency), the propositional content of our noumenal knowledge of phenomena on this account is confined to a single thesis: that the objects which appear to us phenomenally are, metaphysically, contingents dependent upon a common cause for their mutual relation. And this is more a claim about an ontologically distinct object to which ordinary objects are related than a noumenal insight into the real nature of those objects themselves.

Basically, the idea of a faculty of understanding which uses pure concepts in empirical knowledge is simply *missing* from the inaugural dissertation. The real use of the intellect provides knowledge of objects such as God, the soul, and moral perfection, which are not objects of sensible cognition at all, not even through a distorting lens of appearance, and adds at most a single thesis about the *relation* of ordinary objects, as contingents, to their common cause. Aside from this, Kant's supposition seems to be that the forms of sensible cognition need to be supplemented only by the *logical* use of intellect in order to arrive at even the most general kinds of empirical knowledge; the dissertation's opening distinction between intuiting and conceiving in analysis and synthesis is not followed by an argument that *each* of these functions is necessary and only the two together sufficient for empirical knowledge. Essentially, the dissertation has no theory of the role of *concepts* in empirical knowledge at all.

So it remains, until, incredibly, Kant adds the heart of his later theory of understanding as an afterthought to the final section of the inaugural dissertation. This final section, "on the method of metaphysics concerning things sensitive and things intellectual" (2:410), which as a whole anticipates the first *Critique*'s "Transcendental Dialectic" rather than its "Transcendental Analytic," prescribes a method for avoiding the contamination of intellectual concepts with the limitations of sensibility by exposing three "subreptic axioms" that can lead to such contamination. These are the axioms:

1. The same sensitive conditions under which alone the *intuition* of an object is possible is the condition of the *possibility* itself of the *object;*
2. The same sensitive condition under which alone *the things given can be collated with one another to form the intellectual concept of the object* is also the condition of the possibility itself of the object;

18

3. The same sensitive condition under which some *object* met with can *alone be subsumed under a given intellectual concept* is also the condition of the possibility itself of the object. (§26, 2:413)

If we *reject* reasoning based on these axioms, Kant tells us, we shall discover that most of the puzzles which have burdened the progress of metaphysics like the "stone of Sisyphus" (§23, 2:411) "vanish like smoke" (§27, 2:415). Then, with as little argument as fanfare, Kant adds the remarkable claim that there are certain other principles which have a "great affinity" to these "subreptic principles" but which clearly have a *positive* value. Kant lists three of these principles. Two of them correspond to the most vital of his later principles of judgment and to the first and second analogies of experience. The third corresponds most closely to the general principle of the systematicity of empirical knowledge adumbrated in the treatment of regulative ideas in the *Critique of Pure Reason* and then argued for more fully in the *Critique of Judgment*.[10] The first principle that Kant mentions is that "*all things in the universe take place in accordance with the order of nature,*" a principle of the universal determination of events by efficient causation that clearly anticipates the principle of his later second analogy. The third principle that Kant lists is that "*no matter at all comes into being or passes away,*" the principle held to schematize the objective validity of the concept of substance in his later first analogy. And the second principle that Kant mentions is a vague "*leaning towards unity which is proper for the philosophical spirit.*" This is clearly a higher-order principle applying to empirical laws rather than empirical objects themselves, since Kant claims that one instance of it is a variation of Ockham's razor, concerning principles rather than entities: "*Principles are not to be multiplied beyond what is absolutely necessary*" (§30, 2:418). Kant calls these three principles, so casually introduced, "principles of convenience."

This imprecise title seems to reflect Kant's uncertainty about the source and function of these principles. On the one hand, he gives a description of them which appears to anticipate his later strategy for demonstrating the objective validity of concepts and principles by showing them to be conditions for the possibility of experience: The principles are "rules of judging," he says, "to which we gladly submit ourselves and to which we cling as axioms, for the sole reason that *if we depart from them scarcely any judgment about a given object would be permitted to our intellect*" (2:418). This indeed makes it sound as though, first, the intellect does have a definite role to play in the judgment of empirical objects and, second, the intellect functions by supplying the concepts employed in these principles some basis for their universal applicability. But Kant provides no argument whatever for such a claim, and other remarks in the same paragraph seem to withdraw at least the suggestion that these principles are strictly necessary for judgment of objects, if not the intimation that they have their source in the faculty of intellect. Thus, Kant says of these principles in general that they rest "on the laws of intellectual cognition itself, namely the conditions under which it seems to the intellect easy and practicable to use its own perspicacity," which seems weaker than the suggestion that they are in some way actually *necessary* for the judgment of objects. And he says about his second principle, the principle of unity or simplicity, that we "give our vote [to it] not because either by reason or experience we clearly see a causal unity in the world, but we pursue that very unity driven on by our intellect which seems to itself to have been successful in the explanation of phenomena only to the degree that it has received permission to descend from the same principle to the very large number of things grounded." This is a thoroughly confusing statement: It begins by *denying* to the principle of convenience a source in either experience or reason, but it then goes on to say that the principle is both *derived* from the intellect and *accepted* by it on the basis of the intellect's own past success when using it.

The dissertation thus concludes with a return to its opening hint of a connection between conception and intuition. Its final thought is that there must be some concepts and principles that are more closely connected to the intellect than to the forms of sensitive cognition, and that are nevertheless requisite for the empirical knowledge of phenomena, which has otherwise seemed to be grounded in those forms of sensitive cognition alone. But this afterthought is both vaguely formulated and entirely undefended. It is obvious that reflection on the results of the dissertation could have suggested to any careful reader, including its own author, that there was more of a problem here than this casual treatment revealed. As we shall see, Kant – though not even his most perspicacious readers – soon did become aware of the profundity of the problem so lightly glossed over here, and most of his effort in the "silent decade" between this work and the appearance of the first edition of the *Critique of Pure Reason* in 1781, and even for the decade beyond that, may be seen as an effort to defend the assertions so casually tossed off here.

Ontological realism

But before we turn to the beginning of Kant's efforts to solve the fundamental problem hidden for now by his "principles of convenience," we must note one feature about the underlying assumptions of the inaugural dissertation which constitutes an essential constraint on any intended solution of this problem. As I noted earlier, Section III of the dissertation anticipates Kant's later "Transcendental Aesthetic." Space and time are argued to be presupposed by all empirical representations of particulars, and are thus themselves *forms of intuition*, and they are also argued to be themselves singular, thus *pure intuitions*. Metaphysical difficulties with both the absolute and relational conceptions of space and time are then raised, and epistemological problems with the relational conception are hinted at (cf. §15.D, 2:404),[11] from all of which it is concluded that space and time are not themselves real features or relations of objects.

Time is not something objective and real, nor is it a substance or an accident or a relation, but it is the subjective condition necessary by the nature of the human mind for coordinating with each other by a fixed law whatsoever things are sensible.

(§14.5, 2:400)

Space is not something objective and real, nor is it a substance or an accident, or a relation, but it is *subjective* and ideal and proceeds from the nature of the mind by unchanging law, as a schema for coordinating with each other absolutely all things externally sensed. (§15.D, 2:403)

But it is crucial to notice that although he is denying the reality of space and time and of spatial and temporal form, Kant does not imply that there is any way in which the existence of the objects perceived in space and time is ideal or dependent upon the "nature of the human mind." Rather, his assumption is that it is precisely mind-independent objects which come before the mind by means of these ideal and mind-dependent forms. As Kant put it four years later, although of course using the term "understanding," which was not yet in currency in 1770,

The understanding must acknowledge that there are in general things which correspond to the sensibility; therefore the *ideality of space* is nothing more than *the distinction between sensibility and what is posited by means of it,* by means of the understanding and what is thereby thought. By means of ideality the reality of bodies (certain beings, which correspond to them) and certain properties is not denied ... (R 4673, 17:639–40)

As we have already noted, when Kant comes to consider the intellectual principle upon which the relation of all substances as noumena or objects of the intellect rests, he says that it is this *"relation which when seen intuitively is called space"* (§16, 2:407). Since there is no suggestion whatever that the objects of the intellect are in any way dependent upon the human mind, which is not an *intellectus archetypus*, this clearly suggests that although space as the form of intuition for sensitive knowledge is ideal, the objects of sensitive knowledge are not.

Perhaps even better evidence for the ontological position intended by the inaugural dissertation is furnished by this claim, which precedes the detailed discussion of space and time:

Now although phenomena are properly species of things and are not ideas, nor do they express the internal and absolute quality of objects, none the less cognition of them is most veridical. For first of all, in as much as they are sensual concepts or apprehensions, they are witnesses, as being things caused, to the presence of an object, and this is opposed to idealism. (§11, 2:397)

Here Kant clearly claims that the thesis that the forms of intuition are ideal, that they represent appearances (it is in this sense that "species" is used here) rather than things as they really are, is not equivalent to and does not imply idealism about the things represented. Again, there is no suggestion that the *ideality* of space and time in any way impugns the *reality* of the things represented in and by these ideal forms. Of course Kant later came

21

to have the gravest doubts about the force of the causal argument used here. These doubts certainly led him to waver from the combination of idealism about form together with realism about existence just described until he discovered an alternative form of argument which allowed him to return to his original position. But the point, for the moment, is just that the position which Kant originally adopted was a form of realism about the existence, if not the forms, of objects in space and time and that when he came to raise a problem about the objective validity of the "principles of convenience," or of what he eventually described as the pure concepts of the understanding, it was precisely the problem of how they could be known *a priori* to apply to objects *so understood*: how principles rooted in the organization of our own thought could necessarily apply to objects which exist independently of our thought of them.

This is just what we shall see if we now return to the famous letter of 1772. In the fall of 1770, Kant received comments on the inaugural dissertation from three of the most famous savants of the German republic of letters: J. H. Lambert, J. G. Sulzer, and Moses Mendelssohn. Each of these writers responded with consternation to Kant's thesis concerning the ideality of time. Lambert put the point in a broad form: "*If changes are real, so is time. . . . Since I cannot deny reality to change,* until I am convinced to the contrary, I am still unable to say that time and thus space as well are both merely expedients for the benefit of human representations" (10:102).[12] This leaves open the possibility that change is somehow real, even though not intrinsically temporal. But Mendelssohn raised a more difficult objection:

There are several reasons why I cannot persuade myself that time should be something merely subjective. Succession is, after all, at least a necessary condition of the representation of finite minds. Now finite minds are not merely subjects but also objects of representations, both of God and of their fellow-minds. Consequently succession is also to be regarded as something objective. (10:110)[13]

Mendelssohn surely weakened his case by bringing in God (a fact which Kant was not to miss), but his basic point was clear enough: Even if temporal succession is just the form in which nontemporal objects appear to human minds, still it must really characterize *those minds themselves* and cannot be just an appearance of the mind to itself.

Six months later Kant asked his intermediary in Berlin, his former student Marcus Herz, to apologize for his procrastination in answering these letters from such "honest people"; his excuse, he said, was that the letters from Lambert and Mendelssohn had led him "into a long chain of researches" which had to be completed before these writers could be answered (letter of 7 June 1771, 10:116–17).[14] But what is remarkable is that Kant's "long chain of researches" does not seem to have concerned the problem of the ideality of time at all,[15] for Kant apparently never wavered from this position. Although he did attempt to supply more arguments for the point than were included in the dissertation, he does not seem to have begun thinking of them until some years after 1771. Instead, Kant's next letter to Herz, the famous letter of February 1772, revealed that he had been thinking about a problem which none of his correspondents of 1770 had even raised: the necessity of what are now for the first time called "pure concepts of the understanding" (10:125) rather than mere "principles of convenience" for conceiving of the very same objects given to us by the forms of sensitive cognition, and the difficulty of explaining how such concepts can be known *a priori* and yet be objectively valid.

As we saw at the outset of this chapter, the problem which Kant announced to his disciple in 1772 was this: "On what basis rests the relation to the object of that which, in ourselves, we call representation?" Two accounts were excluded. In the case of the "pure concepts of the understanding" the representations could not be caused by their objects, as is the empirical content (but not, as Kant had argued by 1770, the form) of sensible, passive representations; yet the objects could not be related to the pure concepts simply by being their effect, or by the concepts being the cause. The reason for the latter exclusion is self-evident: To think that our pure concepts literally caused their objects would be to think of ourselves as, like the *intellectus archetypus*, creating objects simply by conceiving of them, and that would be as baseless as it was heretical. The reason for the former exclusion is not, in fact, made clear at first, but eventually emerges. The problem is that these pure concepts furnish "axioms of pure reason concerning" their objects, that the understanding "construct[s] for itself entirely *a priori* concepts of things, with which the things are necessarily in agreement" (10:130–1). That is, because its principles are known to be true *a priori*, the understanding must draw them up, out of its own resources, independently of experience, yet the objects of experiences *necessarily*, rather than accidentally, agree with these principles (10:126). Since the objects do not cause the principles nor the principles the objects, some third account must be found to explain necessary rather than contingent agreement between representation and object. That is the task which must be accomplished before *The Limits of Sensibility and Reason* can be published (10:124). Kant optimistically expected to publish such a work in a few months; of course, the *Critique of Pure Reason* actually appeared only after another decade of labor.

But what is vital to see is that this is a problem only on the very supposition that the objects to which the pure concepts of the understanding will be applied are conceived to exist independently of the human mind, or on the supposition that the human intellect is not an *intellectus archetypus*. If these concepts, although subjective because *a priori*, are not at least intended to be used with reference to objects existing quite independently of us and our representations, there is no philosophical problem here; there would be only a question of adding some to the list of representations which the mind can employ in its own constructions. Indeed, Kant makes precisely this point by distinguishing the case of the pure concepts of the understanding from that of the concepts of magnitude, the objects for which we can always construct for ourselves. In that case, there is no puzzle about agreement; it is only because the concepts of the understanding, though they must have a source within the mind if they are to be known *a priori,* are intended to be used to know objects that exist independently of them that there arises "an obscurity with respect to the faculty of our understanding: whence comes the agreement with things" (10:131).

Thus, Kant's problem of 1772, as well as his theory of 1770, suggest that there is at least some sense in which his ontology is to be *realism* and that the newly discovered need for a justification of what first seemed to be mere "principles of convenience" must take place within a framework which is realistic in the requisite sense. Of course, evidence about intentions is just that, and the possibility must be left open for the discovery that the only way to solve the problem is by revising its original conception. But such a solution would be a Pyrrhic victory. Some have felt that only such a dissolution of realism could make a solution to the problem of the objective validity of *a priori* intuitions and concepts possible. Thus, DeVleeschauwer writes: "One of the actual conditions of the problem is incompatible with the future deduction, namely, the thing in itself."[16] But I shall argue that even though Kant was clearly tempted to achieve such a victory, he was never completely happy with it. Thus, although the denial of realism dominates the first edition of the *Critique of Pure Reason,* Kant's original allegiance to realism returned to the fore in the second edition's "Refutation of Idealism." To be sure, only in the several years after 1787 did Kant actually consider how to reconcile realism and *a priori* knowledge, and even then he was obviously unable to settle into a stable realist solution to his epistemological problem. But we shall see at the very least that his purely Pyrrhic concession to idealism was only a temporary expedient.

2
The transcendental theory of experience: 1774–1775

Little more than three years after his famous letter to Marcus Herz, a great deal of Kant's eventual solution to the problem of the *a priori* but objective validity of the categories was already in place. These three years must have been a period of intense thought, but little of what Kant may have written during them has survived. Fortunately, however, some evidence of Kant's ideas at this point is preserved for us in a number of fascinating fragments. Several of these are marginalia in a copy of Baumgarten's *Metaphysica* which Kant used for many years, beginning in 1767. (For that reason the marginalia have been dated only loosely.) But the bulk of them are a set of closely related separate sheets (so-called *lose Blätter*) known as the *Duisburg Nachlass,* which have been assigned to the years 1774 and 1775 with some certainty.[1] These documents provide fundamental insight into both the strategies and the problems of the eventual *Critique* by virtue of both their similarities to and their differences from the published work and are revealing in what they leave obscure as well as in what they make clear. They furnish indispensable evidence for the objectives and assumptions underlying the *Critique of Pure Reason.*

These materials suggest the following conclusions. The fundamental idea of 1774–5 is that certain rules can be shown to be necessary conditions for thinking of objects, as opposed to merely having sensations. But there is an underlying ambivalence on Kant's part as to how these rules are to be derived which is never really resolved, even in the *Critique* of 1781. Kant is not sure whether these rules should be derived directly from the concept of an object of experience, which by definition stands in contrast to a merely subjective form of consciousness, or whether there are rules for self-consciousness itself which are epistemologically prior to rules for objectivity yet which also imply the latter, as rules of the medium through which all objects must be represented. Second, although Kant is not initially equivocal about what we may call the force of these rules, he subsequently also becomes so. That is, to the initial position that these are conditional rules which must be satisfied if experience is to be possible but which the mind itself may not have the power to enforce under all circumstances, Kant gravitates toward the position that they are instead rules which the mind can literally impose upon its objects regardless of the circumstances and are therefore valid under all circumstances, and, for that reason, might be called absolute. These two ambivalences, the first surviving into Kant's thought in the 1780s and the second becoming prominent only during that period, are in large part responsible for the profoundly suggestive but equally confusing diversity of arguments found in the "Transcendental Analytic" of the *Critique of Pure Reason* – arguments which have lent themselves to deeply diverging interpretations precisely because they reflect deeply divergent theoretical strategies.

Kant might be thought to have resolved the first of these ambivalences – whether to begin the deduction of the objective validity of the categories from the *concept of an object* or from the *conditions of self-consciousness* – in the second-edition version of the transcendental deduction. We shall see, however, that even if he intended that text to found the objective validity of the categories unequivocally upon necessary conditions for any form of self-consciousness whatever, he did not succeed. Although the "Refutation of Idealism" of 1787 does introduce an argument which derives *a priori* knowledge of objects from conditions of self-consciousness, even then Kant's casual insertion of this argument as a mere "postulate of empirical knowledge," and its apparently subsidiary significance in comparison to the official deduction of the categories, reflects his continuing uncertainty as to the most promising basis for his defense of the objective validity of the categories.

In the second case of ambivalence – whether the categories of the understanding are merely necessary conditions for experience or rules that we can actually impose upon it – Kant's "transcendental idealism" of 1781, especially his conceptions of transcendental synthesis and transcendental affinity, first asserts the unequivocal view that we can impose our categories on any data of sensibility whatever (though it may be natural to associate such a view about categories with the similar view about forms of intuition apparently already adopted by 1770). This conclusion follows from an assumption, initially unexceptionable but ultimately unjustifiable, which is noticeable because of its absence from the *Duisburg Nachlass*. It is the assumption, not merely that there are conditions for the possibility of empirical consciousness which may be known *a priori*, but that there is also a unity of consciousness which is itself known to obtain *a priori*. This requires the further supposition that the conditions for this knowledge of the unity of consciousness must therefore not merely be known *a priori* but must also in some sense be *imposed* on the contents of consciousness, a thesis which is one of the linchpins of transcendental idealism. Precisely because it omits this assumption, the *Duisburg Nachlass* can be read to promise a theory of the *a priori* conditions of *empirical* knowledge which need not lead to the metaphysics of transcendental idealism but which can be seen to be fulfilled by the argument finally suggested in the "Refutation of Idealism" of 1787 and after. Thus, this last argument represents a withdrawal from the unequivocal idealism of 1781 – the Pyrrhic victory over the problem of objective validity referred to in the preceding chapter. But Kant's unrevised republication of many other parts of the first edition of the *Critique* means that he remained ambivalent about the ontological import as well as the argumentative strategy for his solution to the problem of objective validity.

That the *Duisburg Nachlass* attempts to provide a theory of the *a priori* conditions of empirical knowledge is also suggested by the fact that although it contains a clear conception of the *task* to be satisfied by a transcendental deduction of the categories, it does not suggest the distinction later made in the *Critique* between such a transcendental deduction of the categories and the separate arguments for the principles of *judgment*. Instead, it makes the role of the categories in the determination of the *temporal structure of experience* – what in the *Critique* is the special concern of the chapter on the principles of judgment – central throughout. In the *Duisburg Nachlass*, the categories are to be justified by their role in determining the temporal structure of experience, which is to say by their role in the justification of claims to empirical knowledge. In fact, not yet insisting on the existence of twelve categories and at least four separate types of argument on behalf of their objective validity, the *Duisburg Nachlass* attempts to show only that the three relational categories of substance, causation, and composition and/or interaction are the conceptual (rather than intuitional) conditions of the possibility of experience. The interpretation of the *Critique of Pure Reason* to be defended in this book holds that the distinction between the "Analytic of Concepts" and the "Analytic of Principles" – that is, an initial defense of pure categories of the understanding, followed by a further argument for them in their "schematized" or temporally significant form – is artificial, and that the only part of even the "Analytic of Principles" which is really compelling is the theory of time-determination outlined in the "Analogies of Experience" as supplemented by the "Refutation of Idealism." What is striking about the *Duisburg Nachlass* is that it suggests that such an interpretation reconstructs exactly the kind of argument which Kant himself intended in his initial conception of his solution to the problem of the objective validity of the categories.

Synthetic judgment and the possibility of experience

In a note in his copy of Baumgarten's *Metaphysica* written after the letter to Herz of February 1772 but before 1776, Kant took a number of important steps beyond the formulation of his problem of metaphysics contained in that letter. In this note he provides his first clear identification of the problem of synthetic *a priori* judgment as lying in the objective validity of the concepts employed in such judgment. He also makes his first clear suggestion that this problem is to be solved by discovery of the conditions which make experience possible. Just at the point where he should have turned from the conditions furnished by sensibility to those furnished by the understanding, however, this fragment comes to an abrupt halt.

27

Kant begins by maintaining that knowledge of an object does not consist in the mere occurrence of representations of it; rather, we know an object only insofar as we think or say that two predicates are connected. More precisely, cognition of any object *x* requires that we add to some predicate *a*, which we take to designate some property or properties of *x* and by means of which we intend to refer to *x*, this predicate *a* thus being called the "logical subject" of our judgment, another predicate *b*. Alternatively, Kant suggests, all cognition of objects may be thought of as issuing in claims of identity between the subjects of distinct monadic predications: They assert that some particular *x* which is *a* is identical with (*einerley mit*) the *x* which is *b*. However, the predicates *a* and *b* may be connected in a variety of ways: *b* may "already lie in" or be "involved" in the concept which is expressed by *a*, or it may belong to *x* without being "included" in *a*. In the first case the connection between *b* and *a* can be discovered by analysis, and the judgment "The *x* which is *a* is also *b*" will be an analytic judgment; in the second case, *b* will have to be "added" to *a* or connected to it by means of a synthesis, and the resultant judgment will be a synthetic judgment. Now, Kant says, judgments which are analytic can be understood *a priori*; and, contrapositively, those judgments which can be justified only *a posteriori* – thus, all empirical judgments – must be synthetic. "However," he continues, "there are judgments the validity of which seems to be established *a priori*, which nevertheless seem synthetic, as for example 'Everything which can change has a cause.'" And this leads to the first form of his famous question "Whence comes one to these judgments? From where do we undertake to associate one concept with another concept of the very same object, when no observation and experience indicates this?" (R 4634, 17:616–17).

In the next paragraph, Kant makes both the motivation and the force of his question even clearer:

We therefore possess *a posteriori* judgments, which are synthetic, but also *a priori* judgments, which are nevertheless synthetic and which cannot be derived from any experience, since they contain a true universality and therefore necessity just as much as pure concepts [*lauter Begriffe*] do, which cannot have been created out of experience. These concepts may come to us from wherever they will; from whence do we take their connection[?] Is it from revelations, prejudices, etc. [?]

(R 4634, 17:617)

Begging what might seem a large question indeed, Kant here assumes that these connections among concepts or judgments are universal and necessary and must therefore be known *a priori* rather than *a posteriori*, and he asks what the source of such *a priori* knowledge can be. It is clearly *not* to be any such revelation or prejudice as he ironically mentions.

Kant next provides the form of his answer to this question, as well as some remarks on the force to be assigned to it:

If certain concepts are not contained in us otherwise than as that by means of which experience is made possible from our side, then, prior to all experience and yet with complete validity, they may be asserted of everything that can ever come before us. They are valid then, to be sure, not of things in general, but yet of everything which can ever be given to us through experience, since they contain the conditions by means of which these experiences are possible. Such propositions will therefore contain the conditions of the possibility not of things but of experience. However, things which cannot be given to us by any experience are nothing for us; therefore we can very well use such propositions as universal from a practical point of view, only not as principles of speculation concerning objects in general.

(R 4634, 17:618)

If concepts can be shown not just to be found in us independent of any experience but also to be conditions of the possibility of experience, then they can be inferred to be valid of all objects that are given to us by experience, although in a relative or restricted sense: That is, such concepts cannot be held to be absolutely valid of all things in general but just of those things that are capable of being experienced by us. For all practical purposes, of course, those are all the things we care about – but note, for all *practical* purposes. There is no suggestion that any metaphysical conse- quence can be drawn from the fact of any object's conformity to the conditions which make it possible for us to experience it. That is, although Kant denies that the conditions of experience "from our side" can also be maintained to be conditions of the possibility of all things in general, he does not suggest that they do not correctly characterize those things which we do experience as those things really are. There may be some things which the nature of our own constitution prevents us from experiencing at all, but there is nothing in the mere idea of conditions of experience "from our side" which automatically implies that objects which we experi- ence by means of such conditions are other than as we experience them to be.

As we shall see later, Kant did not always abide by this fundamental restriction; what must be noted now, however, is that although this reflection contains the mature formulation of Kant's problem of objective validity and the first prominent occurrence of his formula for solving it, it does not cast much light on how Kant thinks we discover what are the conditions which make experience possible, on how they make experience possible, or on the significance of the obscure remark that these conditions are what make experience possible "from our side." For although Kant goes on to make the important claim that an analysis of experience in general tells us that "in every experience there is something by means of which an object is given to us and something by means of which it is thought," his remarks on the latter topic are as obscure as they could be. The conditions by means of which objects of experience are given to us are clear enough, for here Kant's view is already worked out in 1770: Objects appear to us by means of sensibility, and the conditions on the possibility of their appearance are none other than the forms of space and time, on the one hand, and the actual occurrence of sensation on the other. But what are the conditions which make it possible for objects to be thought rather than

29

given, the conditions which will solve the problem of 1772? On this, Kant has only the following parenthetical remark to make:

(When we place something in space and time, we act; when we place it next to and after another, we synthesize [*verknüpfen*]. These acts are only means to bring these places into being [*iene stellen zu stande zu bringen*], but they can be considered separately; if we take the same thing several times or set it next to another in the same act, this is a sort of action, by means of which we set something in accord with the rule of appearances, whereby this positing must have its own special rule, which is different from the conditions of the form as it is posited in respect of appearance.)

(R 4634, 17:619)

But this last claim, though something like it must be necessary to carry through Kant's new program, is a mystery. What must be provided are rules for the thinking of an object which are *distinct* from the rules by which the appearances of objects are given, and the suggestion is apparently that it is rules for the action of the mind in positing objects which will constitute these new conditions for the experience of objects "from our side." But since Kant says only that appearances are to be connected by these acts of the mind in spatial and temporal juxtaposition, which is all that he mentions, why should we think that any rules other than the geometrical and chronometrical rules which would be given by the forms of space and time themselves should be required? Why are rules of thought, distinct from the rules of sensibility imposed directly on all sensation by the forms of intuition themselves, also conditions of the possibility of experience? Clearly Kant thinks that the necessity of such rules of thought does follow from his reference to our "actions" of positing objects in space and time, but why he thinks so is obscure.

Perhaps by anticipating later lines of thought one might suppose that the answer to this question is already contained in the opening moves of this argument. By emphasizing the judgmental nature of cognition, that is, Kant might have meant to suggest that cognition must therefore abide by certain characteristic forms or functions of judgment – "functions" insofar as there are invariant ways of connecting one predicate to another, regardless of specific differences in the content of those predicates – and that it is these which furnish rules for positing objects which are distinct from those given by the mere forms of sensibility. But such a simple argument is precluded by another reflection from the same period. On the back of a letter from November 1773, Kant wrote:

First there must be certain titles of thought [*Titel des Denkens*], under which appearances in themselves are brought: e.g., whether they are to be regarded as magnitude or as ground or as whole or merely as reality (figure is no reality). On this account I cannot regard whatever I want in appearance as subject or whatever I want either as subject or predicate; rather it is determined as subject [or] respectively as ground. What sort of a logical function therefore is really valid of one appearance with regard to another, whether that of magnitude or of subject, therefore which function of judgment. For otherwise we could use logical functions

30

arbitrarily, without establishing or perceiving that the object is more suited to one than to the other. Therefore one can[not] think an appearance without bringing it under a title of thinking in general, thus determining an object for it.

(R 4672, 17:635–6)

Kant's argument is that thinking of an object does indeed require connecting representations of appearance by means of logical functions of judgment, which are simply the available forms for judgmental connection, but that these forms themselves are not sufficient for the determinate connection of appearances. They do not tell us which appearances should be assigned to which functions, what sorts of appearances should be treated as subjects and which should be taken to represent only properties of subjects expressible by predicates. But only when we know this do we have any rules for the determinate thought of objects. Yet, Kant clearly supposes, there must be some special rules or "titles of thought" for making such determinations – the mere idea of applying logical functions of judgment to empirical contents of sensibility does not determine how the latter should be carved up to represent objects. So R 4672 suggests that something other than the merely logical functions of judgment themselves must constitute the rules for the acts of the mind, contemplated at the end of R 4634, which are in turn distinct from the mere forms of space and time.

This conclusion suggests a fundamental constraint on a successful interpretation of Kant's eventual argument for the objective validity of the categories: It cannot proceed by reference to the logical form of judgments alone, but instead requires independent *conceptual* as well as *intuitional* conditions on the employment of the merely logical forms of judgment. We shall later see that several prominent lines of thought in Kant's published work of the 1780s fail precisely because they do not satisfy this constraint. More important now, however, is the fact that we still do not know how the Kant of the 1770s expected to derive the objective validity of the categories from the conditions of the possibility of experience. It is only when we turn to the *Duisburg Nachlass* of 1774–5 that further light is shed upon this question. Here we clearly find Kant attempting to explain why thinking of an object requires rules distinct from those for merely being given the appearances of the object. But we also find that he alternates between two different accounts of the sources of these distinct rules, though in the end perhaps he does suggest a way of uniting these two accounts into one.

R 4675, the item written on the back of the letter of 20 May 1775, is a document of remarkable interest. After sketching some general ideas, to which we shall return shortly, Kant for the first time clearly distinguished between understanding and reason and named the new discipline of "transcendental logic" to deal with the former:

All of our cognitions are differentiated according to the matter (content, object) or the form. As far as the latter is concerned, it is either intuition or concept. The former is of the object, insofar as it is given; the latter, so far as it is thought. The faculty of intuition is sensibility, that of thinking is understanding (that of thinking *a priori*, without an object being given, is reason). Understanding is thereby set in opposition to both sensibility and reason. The perfection of cognition according to intuition is aesthetic, according to concepts is logical. Intuition is either of the object (*apprehensio*) or of our self; the latter (*apperceptio*) figures in all cognitions, even those of understanding and reason.

Transcendental logic deals with cognitions of the understanding according to the content, but without determination in respect of the manner in which objects are given. (R 4675, 17:650–1)

By this last suggestion that "transcendental logic" has something to do with the content of knowledge although not with the purely intuitional aspect of knowledge – the way in which objects are given – Kant reveals that he is indeed contemplating a new discipline, the rules for which will not be derived from the merely formal structure of judgments, let alone from the rules of inference governing the "logical use of the intellect" as understood in the inaugural dissertation of 1770. The moral of R 4672 seems to be heeded in this definition. And although Kant's new distinction between understanding and reason is hardly expansive on this subject, it is suggestive: If reason is an ability to think *a priori* without any object being given (thus possibly a faculty the speculative use of which may give rise to dialectical illusion, in Kant's later terminology), then one may suppose, by contrast, that understanding is a faculty of thinking *a priori* about objects that *are* given. That is, it is essential to the notion of the understanding, as opposed to the idea of intellect characteristic of the inaugural dissertation, that the concepts of the understanding must be used in conjunction with intuitions, rather than apart from or instead of them – even if these concepts are themselves *a priori*.

Finally, Kant casually introduces a conception of *apperception* which represents a radical departure from the concept associated with the same name by his predecessors, although it will take him years to clarify the significance of this new concept. In Leibniz and even in the the *Philosophische Versuche* of J. N. Tetens, published a year after the composition of the present note, the French word *appercepcion* and the German *Apperzeption* mean only an explicit perception, a representation of an objective state of affairs or stimulus which is sufficiently clear and distinct to come to consciousness. But there is no suggestion that a reference to the self which has such a perception is any part of the intentional content of such an apperception.[2] Kant's formulation, however, suggests that the self is in some way the intentional object of an *apperceptio*; an apperception is essentially – not just indirectly or accidentally – a presentation of the self. Further, contrary to what some of Kant's own remarks elsewhere may seem to suggest, Kant's definition of apperception in R 4675 suggests that it is not just a *concept* of the self but essentially is or involves some *intuition* of the self; indeed, only because this is so can Kant's further remark that apperception is relevant "even" to cognitions of the understanding appear to be synthetic rather than analytic, substantive rather than tautologous.

32

But just how apperception is relevant to the cognitions of the understanding will take years to emerge.

Still, the present paragraph suggests no answer to the question with which we began: Why must there be rules for thinking of objects which can be derived neither from the mere forms of sensibility nor from the purely logical functions of judgment, and what is the source of these rules? However, on the next page of R 4675 Kant gives us the further hint that the special rules for thinking of objects derive from the conditions for thinking of objects *in time*:

(If *x*, which is the objective condition of *a*, is at the same time the subjective condition of *b*, there then arises a synthetic proposition, which is only true restrictively [*restrictive*]. E.g., all existence belongs to a substance, everything which happens [is] a member of a series, everything which is simultaneous is in a whole the parts of which reciprocally determine themselves.) *x*, the time wherein it is determined what happens, is the subjective condition [for what] in the concept of the understanding is to be thought of only as consequence from a ground. The subjective condition signifies the condition of specifying a concept of understanding corresponding to this relationship. Such principles are not axioms. There are no actual anticipations of appearance. One finds them confirmed through experiences, since the laws of experience become possible thereby. Other appearances yield no laws. They have no evidence, since it is not the appearances but experiences which become possible through them. Synthesis of thinking and appearance.

The subjective conditions of appearance, which can be cognized *a priori*, are space and time: intuitions.

The subjective condition of empirical knowledge is apprehension in time in general and therefore according to the conditions of inner sense in general.

The subjective condition of rational knowledge is the construction [*crossed out:* in time] by means of the condition of apprehension in general.

The general relation of sensibility to understanding and to reason is either that through which [sensibility] is given *a priori*, thus the sensible condition of intuition; second, the sensible condition of judgment in general about that which is given; finally, the sensible condition of the *a priori* concept. The *a priori* rules, which enunciate these conditions, contain in general the relation of the subjective to the objective. Either that of the subjective, through which the objective is given, or that through which it can be thought as given in general (as object) or determined *a priori*.

Everything which is given is thought under the universal conditions of apprehension. Therefore the subjective universal of apprehension [is] the condition of the objective universal of intellection. (R 4675, 17:652–3)

Kant's mention of only the three concepts of substance, series, and a whole of reciprocally related members is of great significance, as is his claim that the principles yielded by the subjective conditions for making such concepts of the understanding specific are not "axioms" or "actual anticipations." But what is most important in this passage is its suggestion that there is a fundamental distinction between time (and space) as mere forms of intuitions and the subjective conditions of apprehension *in* time or the construction of objects in it. It is apparently the latter conditions which will furnish us with the desired universal conditions for the "intellection" of objects and, in fact, for concepts of the understanding corresponding to and supplementing such purely logical conceptions as that of the relation of ground to consequence. Although his reason is not yet clear, Kant is clearly suggesting that determining the position in time of things which happen depends upon conditions beyond those yielded by the formal structure of time alone, and that these are the rules by which objects can be thought as opposed to being merely given, thus the conditions which make experience possible.

The same idea is made even clearer in further notes in the *Duisburg Nachlass*. The basic contention is asserted in R 4680:

Everything which happens is, on account of the determination of its concept among the appearances, that is, in respect of the possibility of experience, represented as contained under a rule, the relation to which is expressed through a concept of the understanding. In the appearance *x* therefore, in which *a* is a concept, in addition to that which is thought through *a* conditions of its specification must also be contained, which make necessary a rule whose function is expressed by *b*. *a* cannot be specifically determined in the time in which it occurs except by means of a rule. Therefore no experience of *a* takes place without a rule. Therefore the principle of sufficient reason is a *principium* of the rule of experience, namely to order it.

The proposition, that everything which follows something in time follows something else in accord with a rule or that in respect of its succession a rule obtains, *does not lie* in the specification of the concept *a* of occurrence or contingency, for there only the *appearance* is meant. (Even the appearance is only an existence according to a rule of time.) The ordering of appearances according to relations of space and time requires a rule, just as appearance itself requires a form.

(17:665)

That appearances have temporal (and spatial) form depends only on the forms of sensibility, but to determine the precise place of any appearance *in* time – to see it as a determinate existence or event – requires a rule by which at least its occurrence at that time can be related to other states of affairs at preceding times. The conditions for the "ordering of appearance" in relations of space and time are clearly to furnish the rules of understanding necessary for thinking of objects, and these rules are clearly not identical to the spatial and temporal forms of appearances themselves.

The same general point is made in R 4681 by means of the suggestion that perception has special conditions because perception is the determination of something in time; and it is precisely making determinate its temporal position which constitutes *thinking*, rather than merely *being given* an object:

A reality is always attached to a point in time and to that which determines it . . . (condition of perception) . . .

If there were not something at all times, therefore something permanent, *stabile,* there would be no fixed point or determination of the point in time, therefore no perception, that is, determination of something in time.

If there were not something which invariably preceded an occurrence, then

34

among the many things which precede it there would be nothing according to which that which occurs belongs in a series; it would have no determinate place in the series.

By means of the rules of perception, the objects of the senses are determinable in time; in intuition they are merely given as appearances. According to these rules an order is found which is quite other than that in which the object is given.

(R 4681, 17:665–6)

For some reason (to be sure, not yet stated), merely being given in the intuitional form of time is not sufficient for the assignment of a determinate position in a unique temporal ordering of events. Such an assignment, Kant momentously suggests, requires that a particular state of affairs be associated both with something which endures and with something which invariably precedes it, that is, presumably, which characteristically precedes events of its type.

The same claim is made in the next reflection by means of the distinction between appearance and experience, rather than that between appearance and perception, and its implications are made more explicit:

The concept: what happens, is a determination of sensibility, but by means of the understanding, in that something is set in the time-order [*Zeitfolge*]. This cannot happen except in relation to something which precedes it. Accordingly the rule that what happens is determined through something which precedes it asserts nothing other ... than that the determination of the place of an existence in time must happen through the understanding, therefore according to a rule.

Reality is that, by means of which something is an object of perception. "In every reality there is a relation of the accident to the substance" therefore says as much as: The determination of an existence in time in general can come about only by means of something which is in all time.

The analogies of appearance mean this much: If I were not able to determine every relation in time by means of a universal condition of relation in time, I would not be able to refer any appearance to its place.

The concepts substance, ground, and whole therefore serve only to refer every reality in appearance to its place, insofar as each represents a function or dimension of time, in which the object that is perceived should be determined and experience be made out of appearance. (R 4682, 17:668–9)

Experience itself is nothing other than the determination of the temporal position of the realities which are indeterminately given in mere appearance. These rules of the understanding that are the conditions of the possibility of experience going beyond the mere forms of intuition, as well as beyond the merely logical functions of judgment, then, would be the rules or relations that allow the temporal position of such objects to be made determinate. Without demonstration, Kant states that the three concepts of substance, ground, and whole are necessary and sufficient to formulate the necessary rules. And for reasons equally obscure, he calls the procedures for time-determination "analogies," though here he speaks of "analogies of appearance" rather than "analogies of experience" as he later will. All of these claims need justification, but surely the most pressing

35

question concerns the basic assumption of Kant's emerging argument. Why does time-determination require rules for the understanding, in addition to the mere forms of sensibility? Even if we concede that assignment or recognition of temporal position is distinct from the merely passive reception of data in a temporal stream of raw experience, why should such an act require any distinctive rules?

The last of the *Duisburg* fragments casts some light on this question. Kant's thesis is that perception or experience requires that representations or mere appearances of objects be assigned to determinate points in a unique temporal ordering. "Time is unique," he writes, and "in it all things and all states of things have their determinate place" (R 4673, 17:636–7). He also asserts, however, that even though appearances are given as temporal – that is, given in time – their being so given does not determine their unique position – that is, suffice for us to recognize the specific times at which they are given. But why should this be so, if, as the inaugural dissertation had already argued, the mere structure of time itself *does* imply that "all things which are sensible, no matter how, cannot be thought unless either as simultaneous or as placed one after another, and so as enfolded, as it were, by a period of unique time and related to one another by a determinate position" (ID, §14.7, 2:402)? An initial answer is hinted at in R 4684:

How can one know what more is contained in a thing in general which is not given to the senses beside what is actually thought in its concept a[?] But since one time, in which something happens, is not to be distinguished from another time, the sequence [*Folge*] can be determined only by means of a rule, and therefore we can represent to ourselves more in the sensible condition than is thought in a. ... We therefore represent the object to ourselves through an analogy of construction, namely that it allows of being constructed in inner sense, namely that as something always follows something else, so, when something happens, it follows something else ...

In analytic judgments the predicate really goes with the concept a, in synthetic judgments with the object of the concept, since the predicate is not contained in the concept. But the object which corresponds to a concept has certain conditions for the realization of this concept, that is, position *in concreto*. ... Now the condition for all concepts is sensible; therefore when the concept is also sensible, but universal as well, it must be considered in its concreteness. ... If the concept signifies not pure but empirical intuition, that is, experience, then the x contains the condition of relative position (a) in space and time, i.e., the condition of determining something universally therein. (R 4684, 17:670–1)

Here Kant links his concern with synthetic *a priori* judgment with his emerging theory of time-determination. Synthetic judgments require that the subject-concept be supplemented by an appeal to intuition, in order to yield a nontautologous connection with the predicate. The act in which subject and predicate are linked in intuition is generically called "construction." In the case of the mathematical objects of pure *a priori* knowledge, the formal structure of pure intuition alone is sufficient to yield the rules which must be followed in such construction. But this is precisely because in these cases a determinate position of the object of knowledge *in* space and/or time is irrelevant: The construction of a triangle involved in a proof in euclidean geometry does not yield a triangle located at some unique and particular point in real space, and even if (as Kant sometimes suggests) the result of an arithmetical operation depends upon the structure of a synthesis in time, it employs only general features of the structure of time and does not involve the determinate position of any item in a unique temporal ordering of all events. In the case of empirical knowledge, however, the "intellection of appearance" which yields the result that, "for example, something exists, something happens" (17:671) involves a "construction" which is not merely constrained by the general structure of the forms of sensibility but must also yield knowledge of the determinate position in space and time of the object so constructed. It is this additional feature of the synthetic knowledge of empirical objects, or propositions about them, which requires *a priori* rules for the understanding as well as for sensibility. And now Kant finally hints why: Although determining the position of an object or its state in time requires assigning it to some unique point in the unique succession of moments which constitutes the whole of time, there is no intrinsic difference between one moment of time and another. There is thus nothing about any moment of time itself which can determine that a particular state of affairs should be uniquely associated with *it*. The basis for such determinations must therefore lie in something other than the formal structure of time itself.

In other words, Kant grounds his deduction of the rules of understanding from the conditions of time-determination on the premise that there is nothing about points of time themselves which is unique and sufficient to determine the occurrence of events. This premise, which asserts the indiscernibility of the moments of time as such, comes straight from Leibniz. Kant, however, draws a totally different conclusion from this premise than Leibniz did. Leibniz assumed the principle of sufficient reason, derived from it the identity of indiscernibles, and then concluded from the indiscernibility of moments of time that time could not be a genuine property of objects. But though Kant was already committed to the ideality of time, this was on the basis of an argument about *a priori* knowledge, and not on the basis of Leibniz's premise. Kant used Leibniz's premise only to explain the inadequacy of the *formal* structure of time for empirical knowledge. That is, he does not argue that what the structure of time itself does not make determinate – namely, temporal position – does not exist, but only that it requires additional rules to make this determinate. In fact, it will be precisely the necessity of such rules which grounds the applicability of the principle of sufficient reason to empirical objects and events for Kant. The *principium rationis* is not an ontological principle with ontological implications, but an epistemological principle grounded in the conditions necessary for determining the time-order of empirical objects and events. Further, these rules by means of which the principle of sufficient reason is applied will be diametrically opposed to the spirit of Leibniz's philosophy, which requires the uniqueness of the underlying constituents of reality, because these rules will turn out to require the repeatability of types of events: Only insofar as individual events can be subsumed under universal rules dictating the sequence of particular types of events, Kant is to argue, can the position of any particular event in time be made determinate:

[The] *Principium rationis* is the principle of the determination of things in the time-order [*Zeitfolge*]; for this cannot be determined through time, but time must be determined in the understanding through the rule of the existence of appearances. *Principium* of the possibility of experience.

Therefore it is not possible to determine the place of things in time without the presupposition of this principle, through which the course of appearances is first made uniform. ... (R 5202, 18:116)

From a Leibnizian premise Kant will ultimately deduce a profoundly anti-Leibnizian conclusion.

At this stage, however, Kant's argument is radically incomplete. First, though the Leibnizian premise now offers some explanation of why the formal structure of time is inadequate for time-determination, it is itself terribly abstract; a more concrete – and better motivated – premise might be desired. Second, even granted that the uniformity of the moments of time dictated by the structure of pure intuition means that this structure itself is inadequate to fix the determinate position of objects or events in time, the question remains, why should some additional sort of rules be needed to accomplish this? Why should not just that which differentiates empirical knowledge of ordinary objects from *a priori* knowledge of mathematical objects – namely, the matter or content furnished by sensation – suffice for this purpose? After all, the Leibnizian requirement of nonidentity of discernibles is satisfied by any form of variety, yet sensation clearly introduces a source of variety into experience that is lacking in the forms of intuition themselves, as well as in the diverse but abstract objects of mathematics which may be constructed in accordance with those forms alone. Why should the mere variety of sensations that will be given in the experience of empirical objects be insufficient to make determinate which objects or events are being experienced where and when?

Answering this question preoccupied Kant for fifteen more years after 1775. Unfortunately, at the very beginning of his attempt to demonstrate that rules distinct from both the rules of mathematics and the rules of logic are required for time-determination, a fundamental ambivalence about the appropriate premise for such a demonstration emerged in Kant's thought. We shall see that although Kant eventually deployed a methodological distinction which might have allowed him to resolve this ambivalence in principle, in practice he never really resolved this uncertainty about the best starting point for the deduction of the categories.

Kant's fundamental ambivalence

In the reflections just considered Kant began by asking how two logically independent predicates a and b could be judged *a priori* to be connected in a single object x when neither the form of intuition nor the logical form of judgment alone could require such a connection. In particular, Kant asked what could determine that one concept, a, should function as the subject and another, b, as the predicate, when no such particular assignment could be determined by the purely logical requirement that there be both a subject and a predicate in every judgment. Kant then began to suggest that the necessity of determining the temporal order of objects and their states could lead to rules for making such connections. But thus far we have not seen why any special rules are required for making these determinations, or why the mere occurrence of sensations in the pure form of time is not enough. What seems to have been the next stage of Kant's thought is the idea that there is some extralogical content in or constraint on the *unity of a subject,* from which the necessity of the desired rules for thinking of objects could be derived. But at this stage Kant's thought then seems to have proceeded down two at least sometimes independent paths, the difference between which may have been masked by a fundamental ambiguity in the conception of a subject, and thus in Kant's idea of the unity of a subject. In some instances Kant seems to have in mind what we could call the *grammatical* subject of a judgment – that is, precisely its intended *object of reference* – and to assume that there must be some fundamental, though extralogical, content built into the notion of an *object* of judgment. In other cases, Kant seems to consider as the basis of his argument what we might call the *cognitive* subject – that is, an agent who makes a judgment – and to assume that there are rules inherent in the structure of the *thinker* which would also carry over (in a manner that could be described in a variety of ways) to any thought of an object of knowledge. Kant's failure to decide between, perhaps even clearly to distinguish between, these two concepts of the subject and the two argumentative strategies they suggest leads to confusion in the *Duisburg Nachlass.* I will also argue that this confusion leads to an unresolved multiplicity of arguments in the alleged heart of the *Critique of Pure Reason,* namely the transcendental deduction of the categories itself.

In certain sketches of his emerging argument, Kant's use of the term "subject" seems to be simply ambiguous, hovering between these two quite distinct senses:

x is therefore the determinable (object), which I think through the concept a, and b is its determination (or the manner of determining it). In mathematics x is the construction of a; in experience [x is] the *concretum*; in respect of an inhering representation or thought in general x is the function of thinking in general in the subject [*die function des Denkens Uberhaupt im Subjekte*], therefore the (real) concept is determined altogether: 1. through the subject, 2. in respect of succession through the ground, 3. in respect of coexistence through composition.

(R 4674, 17:645–6)

Another passage is similarly obscure:

If, however, *a* and *b* are not identical ... and *x* is not quite determinately thought through the concept of *a*, then *a* and *b* are not in a logical but a real relation of combination. ... Therefore their relation is not determined by means of the concepts themselves but by means of *x*, of which *a* contains the designation. How are such syntheses possible? *x* must be a *datum* of sensibility, in which a synthesis, that is, a relation of coordination, takes place; for this contains more than is thought through its concept *a* and is the representation of *a in concreto*. Now there are three cases where a transcendental subject is sensible and yields a relation of concepts: Either it is the intuition of *a* or the appearance of *a* or ... the empirical cognition. In the first case the relation of $a:b$ follows from the construction $a = x$. In the second from the condition of the intellection of *a*; in the third it is drawn from observation. The first two syntheses are *a priori*. ... For in the second case *a* signifies a universal sensible condition of perception, but *x* the condition of the subject in general, in which the relation of all perception is determinable. ... So *a* will signify the universal of perception, *x* the sensible condition of the subject (*substratum*), in which the perception is to obtain its place. Consequently the condition of disposition. *b* finally [is] the universal function of the mind [*des Gemueths* (sic)], which is to determine the place of *a* in *x*, therefore the exponent of the relation of perceptions [*crossed out*: in the mind, to one another], thus it is to determine their place according to a rule.   (R 4676, 17:654–5)

In the first of these passages, and in at least the beginning of the second, it is simply not possible to tell whether Kant means to refer to the grammatical subject of a judgment or to the cognitive subject which has or makes the judgment, and it is therefore not possible to tell whether he means to suggest that the derivation of the objective validity of the key concepts of the understanding is to proceed by the demonstration that there are, after all, certain extralogical constraints built into the idea of an object of knowledge, or rather that it is to proceed by showing that there are certain rules for the ordering of perceptions in the cognitive subject, with which rules the objects presented by those perceptions must also accord in some suitable manner. In neither case, it should be clear, would Kant intend that it is either the pure form of intuition alone or the purely logical concept of an object which would yield the desired rule; pure intuition alone, both passages make clear, yields only the *a priori* construction of mathematical but not empirical objects, and pure analysis of the concept of an object has already been argued to yield no satisfactory result. Rather, what is being offered as the suitable basis for the argument is the condition for the determination of the subject *in concreto*, which can mean only the determination of the subject in intuition, that is, *in* time (and space). But what is left unclear is whether it is supposed to be the general ideal of making determinate the temporal position and relations of an object of knowledge which somehow implies the objective validity of certain rules, or whether it is supposed to be the case that there are conditions requisite for the determinate temporal orderings of perceptions as such in the history of the perceiver which will also imply the validity of certain rules for the objects of such perceptions.

To be sure, the switch from the ambiguous word "subject" to the clearly mental term "mind" could suggest that it is the latter form of argument that Kant intends, that what he is doing is merely first introducing in more abstract (and, unfortunately, ambiguous) but then in more specific terms a single argument that the conditions for a determinate temporal ordering of perceptions as the states of a single perceiving and thinking subject also imply objectively valid rules for the objects of such a subject's perceptions. But it does not seem justifiable to interpret Kant's intention in such an unequivocal way. Kant reveals his hesitation in the very sentence in which he switches from "subject" to "mind" by then crossing out the words which most unequivocally suggest that the "relation of perceptions," the conditions for which will determine the general conditions for the "intellection" of an object, is their relation *in the mind to one another.* Moreover, the *Duisburg Nachlass* also includes self-contained sketches of each of the two thoroughly independent lines of argument allowed by the ambiguity of the term "subject." In some passages, Kant argues to the objective validity of the categories from premises which clearly already include the supposition that cognition has an objective content, by simply connecting the categories with the conditions for thinking of objects in time. In others, he tries to begin with a supposition that the unity of the mind as a temporally extended whole requires certain rules, which, as conditions for the determinate thought of the mind itself, also place constraints on the thought of external objects. We shall now look more closely at these two types of argument, which will continue to characterize Kant's attempts at a deduction of the objective validity of the categories throughout his publications of the 1780s.

Titles of the understanding

In several extended reflections, Kant presents arguments the basic premise of which is that knowledge does have objective content, and the primary further contention of which is that such knowledge requires rules which are required neither by pure intuition nor by mere logic but by the very concept of an object of knowledge itself. In some of these passages Kant also seems to suggest that the only available source for such rules is apperception or self-consciousness and the rules which are characteristic of it, and this produces entanglements, but even these passages do not attempt to use the fact that apperception itself requires rules to *justify* the initial assumptions that we do have knowledge of objects and that any such knowledge requires some nonformal and extralogical rules. Thus that the conception of objects for knowledge requires such rules remains the fundamental assumption throughout these arguments.

We may begin with a note in which Kant does in fact begin by attempting to derive the fundamental categories of substance, causation, and interaction from the conditions under which the cognitive subject can experience an object:

An object [*ein Gegenstand*] of the senses is that only which affects *my senses,* thus which acts and is substance. Therefore the category of substance is fundamental. Every beginning of a state of the representation is always a transition from a previous one, for otherwise we would not perceive that it had begun. Therefore, since the same subject is always valid for one object as well as for the other and since the boundary is common to both, the one which precedes belongs to what follows as that which determines it. In the unity of the mind a whole is possible only insofar as the mind reciprocally determines one partial representation from another and comprehends all together in one action which is valid of them all.

(R 4679, 17:663)

Kant begins to argue for the key feature of the characterization of objects from a consideration about how they affect the epistemic subject: Our perceptions are effects which must have active causes, but activity is the criterion of substance,[3] therefore our perceptions must have objects which are substances. Then Kant intimates another claim about the knower which will ultimately be of great importance – namely, that the occurrence of events or changes can be perceived only by means of a contrast to a prior state of affairs – but this is here developed only by the inexplicable inference that since there is a common boundary between a preceding state of affairs and the succeeding one, the former must determine the latter. This is hardly a satisfactory deduction of the objective necessity of causation. Finally, Kant makes the equally obscure suggestion that the unity of the mind requires that its objects be reciprocally related, as it were by a single action. This paragraph stakes out the claim which Kant will ultimately succeed in mining: It asserts that the unified experience of the cognitive subject, even regarded merely as such, is possible only if that experience is regarded as representing a world of enduring substances thoroughly determined by laws of causation and interaction. But Kant hardly explains why the "unity of the mind" should require such constraints on the objects of its representations.

Perhaps just because starting from essential characteristics of the mind is leading to such obscure connections, Kant suddenly changes tack and begins a deduction of the categories of substance, causation, and interaction directly from conditions for thinking of objects, without any further reference to the conditions for representing the unity of the mind:

The mere apprehension already reveals that behind the appearance there must be a substance, a cause of the juxtaposition; only the observation and estimation must indicate which is the subject, etc. Where there is an action, there is a substance, e.g., by the light it becomes warm; but whether the light is a substance flows not from the apprehension but from the exposition of appearance. That something is represented as having happened is sufficient to regard it as an effect, for the apprehension of it is indeed an effect, which takes place in the mind.

The intellectual functions therefore make a beginning with apprehension, but only specification gives us the rule of the application of this concept; therefore determinate rules of synthesis can be given only through experience, but the general norms thereof are given *a priori.*

42

Empirical intuition is appearance.

Appearance of which one is conscious is perception.

Every perception must be brought under a title of the understanding, for otherwise it yields no concept, and nothing is thought thereby. By means of these concepts we make use of the appearances, or rather the concepts indicate the way in which we are to employ the appearances as material for thought. 1. the intuition in general for magnitude, 2. the sensation, in order to determine the real relation in the appearance. We say: the stone weighs [something], the wood falls, the body moves itself, that is, it acts, thus it is substance. The field is plowed, the meadow dried out, the glass broken: These are effects, which are related to a cause. The wall is strong, the wax soft, the gold dense: These are connections in that which is composite. Without these sorts of concepts the appearances would be separated and would not belong to one another. Even if they had the same relations to one another in space or time, these would not be determined from the objects of appearance but would merely be placed next to one another.

Experience is perception that is understood. But we understand it [only] if we represent it to ourselves under a title of understanding. Experience is a specification of the concepts of the understanding through given appearances. Appearances are the matter or the substrate.

Experiences are therefore possible only by means of the presupposition that all appearances belong under titles of the understanding; that is, in all mere intuition there is magnitude, in all appearance substance and accident[, i]n the alteration of these cause and effect, in the whole of them interaction. Therefore these propositions are valid of all objects of experience. The very same propositions also hold of the mind in respect of the generation of its own representations and are moments of *genesis*. Under the title of apperception, however, must all appearances be brought, so that they are just as constructed according to intuition as ... [*breaks off*]

However, the conditions of subsumption under these concepts are derived from the sensible relations, which stand in analogy with the acts of understanding and belong to inner sense, therefore apperception ... [*breaks off*]

(R 4679, 17:663–4)

Here, Kant offers a clear pattern for his basic argument for the central categories as "titles" for understanding objects and then suggests a relation between such rules for thinking of objects and further rules for representing the unity of the mind, or apperception, which clearly makes the former primary and the latter analogical.

First, the basic argument proceeds from the assumption that "experience is perception which is understood." That is, it is premised that we can judge that our representations have independent objects, and the only question is what concepts are required to make these judgments. The argument is, then, that the forms of intuition alone suffice to dictate that objects will be represented as having determinate magnitudes, but additional "titles of the understanding" dictate that such objects must be conceived as substances having accidents, standing in relations of cause and effect, and involved in reciprocal interaction with other such objects as well. That is, only by means of the concepts of substance, cause and effect, and composition or interaction can we use mere empirical intuition, to which the pure forms of intuition add no more than the requirement of

43

determinate magnitude, to think of such more determinate objects as plowed fields, dense gold, and so on. Kant clearly believes that without such rules appearances would be juxtaposed with each other but would not be determined by objects or represent determinate objects, although he offers no explanation of why just *these* concepts – substance, causation, and interaction – are required in order to transform mere appearance into the thought of objects. But he does make clear the supposition that the necessity of these concepts arises directly from the conception of an object, rather than from the conditions of the unity of the cognitive subject. These "titles of the understanding" are simply the necessary and sufficient general conditions for determinate knowledge of empirical objects: Such objects are made determinate only if they are seen as determinate magnitudes instantiating some specific assignment of accidents to a substance, some specific relations of cause and effect, and some specific form of composition or interaction.[4] The understanding supplies these general concepts, and sensation lends them specific content.

Indeed, this passage suggests that the rules for the unity of objects are logically prior to any conditions for the unity of the mind. Contrary to the initial paragraph of the reflection, the remainder does not suggest that the unity of the mind is the model or source for the unity of objects but clearly holds that the rules for conceiving of objects are also, and perhaps derivatively, the rules for conceiving of the "generation" of representations in the mind. Since representations are "generated" in the mind successively, there are thus rules for making determinate the succession of representations in the mind; thus the rules for objects are in some sense the rules for the unity of the mind as well. Indeed, the last and incomplete paragraph suggests that there is an analogy between the sensible relations of objects of experience and relations in inner sense, so that *the mind itself is understood in analogy to the way we understand other objects.* These rules do not directly derive their validity from their role in representing the unity of mind but from their role in thinking of objects. They are then applied to the mind, as a subsidiary case, simply because they are our only rules for thinking of things in general.

Thus, one of Kant's initial strategies for the deduction of the fundamental "titles of the understanding" is an argument in which the knowledge of objects is primary and the validity of certain rules for self-consciousness itself is a consequence, but not a premise, of the argument. Obviously, there are two pressing problems with such an argument. First, beginning with the assumption that we know objects through the titles of understanding might seem to beg the very problem of objective validity raised in the letter to Marcus Herz: that the concepts of the intellect make connection to independent objects is precisely the point at issue. Second, the connection between "perception which is understood" and the specific categories of substance, causation, and interaction is asserted rather than demonstrated.

Kant may be seen as attempting to redress at least the second of these problems on or about 20 May 1775, though in so doing he may also be making his first step toward changing his initial assumption that the three categories are directly derived from the conception of an object of knowledge:

Something is posited [as] outside us only so far as its representation constitutes persistence and a particular point of relation.

If my representation succeeds something, its object would not also succeed it unless its representation were determined as a consequence of something, which cannot happen except by means of a general law. Or there must be a general law that all consequences are determined by something antecedent; otherwise I could not set any succession of objects against a succession of representation. For in order to set objects against my representations it is always requisite that the representation be determined according to a general law, for the object consists precisely in the universally valid point.

Just so I would not represent anything as outside me and therefore make appearance into (objective) experience if the representations did not relate to something which is parallel to my I, through which I refer them from myself to another subject. Likewise if manifold representations did not determine each other according to a general law. The three relations in the mind therefore require three analogies of appearance, in order to transform the *subjective functions* of the mind into objective ones and thereby make them into concepts of the understanding which give reality to the appearances.   (R 4675, 17:648)

Kant begins with a more informative argument than we have yet encountered. He makes it clear that to have knowledge of objects is precisely to contrast something to mere representations, mere modifications of the mind, and he claims that this contrast can be made only through determination according to a universally valid law: "The object consists precisely in the universally valid point." Then he adds further content to this consideration by bringing in the temporal form of intuition: If our representations are given to us successively, so that any knowledge of objects must include knowledge of the determinate order of the temporal succession of their states, then the contrast required for objective knowledge will be between a universally valid succession of objects and their states and the mere succession of our representations. It can thus be inferred that the rules for representing a determinate succession of objects and their states are indeed the indispensable rules for the exposition of experience. So, as both the initial sentence of this quotation as well as the first sentence of its third paragraph suggest, at least the concept of external objects as persisting parallel to our succession of representations but as also themselves changing in accord with general laws, rather than merely in accord with the perhaps arbitrary succession of our own representations, will be requisite for representing objects of experience at all.

This is indeed a promissory note for the argument Kant later developed in the *Critique of Pure Reason*'s "Analogies of Experience." But instead of trying to spell out such a derivation of the rules for objects and then showing how the mind itself may be understood in analogy with external objects, Kant here begins to shift his ground. For he proceeds as if the argument thus far showed only the need for some as yet undetermined rules for thinking of objects and then suggests that the source of these rules is some antecedent knowledge of rules for the mind which are transformed by analogy into rules for objects. Here Kant takes it as self-evident that we must think of objects, but then suggests that these rules can be derived only by conceiving of something "parallel" to the mind, organized according to rules analogous to the other rules, themselves known unproblematically, that organize our knowledge of the mind itself. The rules for the exposition of appearances as objects are obviously described as "analogies of appearance" because they are derived by analogy *from* the rules for the mind.

The same shifting of ground appears in R 4681, where Kant similarly starts off by suggesting that it is from the concept of knowledge of the object that the need for rules of thought arises but that it is in the structure of the mind itself that the rules have their source:

Nothing synthetic can be objectively valid except that which is the condition through which something is given as an object or through which something that is given is thought as an object. An object is thought only insofar as it stands under a rule of appearance, and the receptivity of the rule is that which makes the appearance objective; therefore it is not the appearances which stand under a rule, rather the *objects* which are their ground. They are expounded [*exponiert*] according to this rule.

Without such rules of perception no experiences could be made, since the latter are the titles of appearances, just as sensible concepts are the titles of intuitions.

Rules of presumption as estimation of appearances provisional to determining judgments.

One can, to be sure, see much which appears but understand nothing, unless it is brought under concepts of the understanding and by means of these into relation to a rule; this is the assumption through the understanding.

Synthesis contains the relation of appearances not in the perception but in the concept. That all relation in perception equally presupposes a relation in concept shows that the mind contains in itself the universal and sufficient source of synthesis and that all appearances are exponible in it. . . .

We perceive something only by being conscious of our apprehension, consequently of existence in our inner sense, thus as belonging to one of the three relations in the mind. All observation demands a rule.

The intellectual [aspect] of perception goes to the power of inner sense. The analogies of observation go to the thoroughgoing perception or the thoroughly determinate perception.

All connections are made through the mind, and the mind connects nothing objectively except what is necessarily determined from its *correlato;* otherwise the representations would indeed be conjoined but not connected [*zusammengestellt, aber nicht verknüpft*], to be sure in perception but not in concept.

Only that which is capable of a fixed ground rule in the mind do we call object. Therefore estimations must precede objective judgments. For everything else, which does not assume such ground rules, is nothing for us and cannot be perceived. Since perception demands a conjugation according to a universal ground. (R 4681, 17:657–9)

Like R 4679, this passage clearly begins by simply assuming that there are objectively valid and synthetic cognitions which must be known by means of rules, just since it is rules which make cognition objective. The difference between there merely being appearances, or merely having representations, and knowing objects is simply being able to submit appearances to rules, and no question is raised that we do know objects. But like R 4675, this passage also seems to suggest that though the application of the rules is to objects, the source of the rules is the self. The idea seems to be that the self is the source of all rules for synthesis, because all cognition involves acts of apprehension, which are themselves actual states of the self. The passage also suggests that there are determinate rules – indeed, "three relations in the mind" – by which *mental states as such* are linked, that is, by which their own order in the mind, independent of what they may represent, is determined. Because these rules govern our representations, that is, our encounters with objects, it seems, they must also govern the objects themselves. But the primary requirement is that perception be rule-governed, and only to satisfy *that*, it is beginning to seem, must objects also be rule-governed. In other words, Kant's account of the source of the rules for objects begins to suggest an alternative account of the need for these rules.

It would be premature to try to assess the ultimate potential of an approach to the problem of objective validity on which Kant was to work for another dozen years. But a few conclusions are now in order. All three of the reflections we have just considered run the risk of begging the question of 1772 by simply assuming that knowledge of objects must be governed by universal rules or, as Kant said in R 4679, "general norms." The danger of this may be one of the forces pushing Kant toward the idea that the mind itself is rule-governed, as in R 4681, for in this way the rule-governedness of our representations of objects can itself be explained. However, R 4675 has come the closest of these passages to lending some content to the general idea of rules for objects by suggesting that some particular types of rules may be needed to ground a *contrast between the temporal succession of our representations and the temporal succession of objects*. And if the categories of substance, causation, and interaction which Kant wants to derive are not derived from the necessity of this contrast – a contrast deriving from the conception of the object, and one the necessity of which may become less apparent if we just assume that the representation of mental life itself must be rule-governed – the question may then reappear, Whence these particular rules? In other words, as R 4681 pushes us toward Kant's alternative tactic of directly deriving rules for objects from rules for the mind, the question of how he is going to establish that the representation of the mind itself must be rule-governed will become more pressing.

Functions of apperception

Kant's most general statements of the strategy of deriving rules for objects of thought from the rules of thought itself are contained in the ambivalent fragment R 4675, which also suggested the strategy of beginning with knowledge of objects. This fragment concludes with the claim, "Everything which is given is thought under the general conditions of apprehension. Therefore the subjective universal of apprehension is the objective universal of intellection" (17:653). Earlier on the same piece of paper, Kant had already written that "the condition of all apperception is the unity of the thinking subject. From that flows the connection of the manifold according to a rule and in a whole, since the unity of the function must suffice for subordination as well as coordination" (17:651). These two remarks together suggest an argument that a recognition of the unity of the self is the condition of self-consciousness (apperception); that this requires that "the manifold" – that is, apparently, the manifold *states of the self* – be rule-governed both in subordination and coordination (whatever that means); and then that these rules for the organization of what are regarded from a subjective point of view as the representational states of the self will also have to be involved, in some way, in the "intellection" of the objects represented by these states. In Cartesian terms, one might put it, the inference is that rules which govern the relations of thoughts as formal realities will also govern relations inherent in the objective reality of those thoughts, that is, in what they represent.

Putting Kant's point this way, however, means that we must ask not only what he means by "subordination" and "coordination" in the unity of the thinking subject and why he supposes that these require rules, but also why it should be assumed that any rules there might be for the connection of representations as such must also be constraints on the *contents* of these representations. In fact, these are the two fundamental questions throughout Kant's efforts to construct a transcendental theory of experience which are not really answered until he makes his final attempts at the refutation of idealism. For the moment, however, we may see that he attempts to shed some light on the first of these questions by reminding us that the unity of the thinking subject must be a unity of temporally diverse elements. Thus R 4673, written a year before the notes of the *Duisburg Nachlass,* includes, among several other claims about time, the statement

1. Time [is] unitary. Which says as much as: I can intuit all objects only in myself and in the representations to be found in my single subject, and all possible objects of my intuition are related to each other according to the special form of this intuition;

and

4. In [time] all things and all conditions of things have their determinate place. For they must have their determinate relation to all other objects of intuition which can be given in the unity of inner sense. (17:636–7)

In other words, the unity of the cognitive subject is the unity of a determinate and unique ordering of items in inner sense, the form of which is temporal. Thus we can at least infer that subordination and coordination, as well as the rules on which they depend, must have something to do with the temporal ordering of the states of the self. And it will then be rules by which the subordination and coordination of items in time can be accomplished which apply, as it were, transitively to the objects of intuition and representation as well.

The same idea seems to be the basis for the final paragraphs of R 4674. Here Kant claims that there is a "threefold dimension of synthesis," because

there are three functions of apperception, which are to be met with in all thought of our condition in general and to which all appearance must on that account conform, since no synthesis [would] lie in appearance in itself if the mind did not add such or make it out of the *datis* of appearance. The mind is therefore the original of such a synthesis through original and not derivative thinking.

That is, there are three dimensions to the synthetic thought of objects, because there are three basic dimensions to self-consciousness. And the reason there are three dimensions to self-consciousness is that

... apperception is the perception of oneself as a thinking subject in general. Apperception is the consciousness of thinking, that is, of representations, as they are placed [*gesetzt*] in the mind. Here there are three exponents: 1. the relation to the subject, 2. the relation of succession among one another, 3. of composition.
(17:646–7)

Kant's underlying idea appears to be that there are three main rules for the organization of representations into self-consciousness – that is, the representation of a unitary subject – and thus three main forms of rules for thinking of the objects of representations as well, *because the temporal structure of consciousness or inner sense requires this.* That is, to think of representations which are given temporally as the representations of a single thinking subject, one must (1) ascribe each of them individually to the subject – "the relation to the subject"; (2) think of each of them as standing in some particular relation of succession to any other – "the relation of succession among one another"; and (3) think of them all collectively as belonging to this single subject – "the composition." This much seems to flow from the idea of being self-conscious of a single subject with a manifold of states, when the form in which that manifold ("*in concreto,*" to use the term by which Kant indicates that the conclusion follows from combining the concept of a unitary self with the form of intuition in which its constituents are given, and not from a mere analysis of the concept) is temporal succession. This is made even clearer in R 4676:

If something is apprehended, it is taken up in the functions of apperception. I am, I think, thoughts are in me. These are collectively relations, which, to be sure, do not give rules of appearance but which make it such that all appearances are represented as contained under rules. The I constitutes the substratum for a rule in general, and apprehension relates every appearance to it.

For the origination of a rule three things are required: 1. *x* as the datum for a rule (object of sensibility or rather sensibly real representation). 2. *a* the *aptitudo* for the rule or the condition, through which it is related in general to a rule. 3. *b* the exponent of the rule.

Now if a norm for a rule of appearances in general or experiences is to arise – e.g., everything which exists is in substance – then *x* is sensation in general as the specif[ication] of reality. By means of being represented as reality it becomes the material for a rule, or sensation becomes capable of a rule, and *a* is only a function of the apprehension of appearance as given in general. Now since everything must be given in time, which therefore comprehends everything, *b* is an act of apperception, namely the consciousness of the subject, which apperceives [itself] as that which is given in the whole time [and] is necessarily connected with [*b*], for otherwise the sensation would not be represented as belonging to me.　　　(R 4676, 17:656)

This passage tries to establish the transcendental theory of experience by arguing that the interpretation of any particular sensation (*x*) as an object of experience requires that it be governed by both the general functions of appearance as given – that is, the rules of sensibility – and by the rule that an act of apperception represent its particular object as part of its representation of a unified self. The representation of a unified self, in turn, is identified with the consciousness of the self in the whole of the time through which it has experience: Apperception is clearly the consciousness of the identity of the self through time.[5] It is thus suggested that thought must be governed by some rules which are identical *neither* to the mere rules of sensibility *nor* to the mere rules of formal logic; these will be the extralogical rules which constitute the content of the transcendental theory of experience and which will apply both to representations as such and to their objects.

But can an argument of this sort yield anything more than the general rule that all representations must be "represented as belonging to me" in the "whole time" in which I exist, spelled out at most by the "three exponents" of R 4674? And can it yield anything more about the objects of representation than the general requirements which allegedly correspond to these three exponents, namely the general rules that objects be assigned (1) accidents ascribed to substances, (2) states which succeed one another in time, and (3) some sort of composition or interaction? In particular, can the present sort of argument yield the conclusion that some further rules are needed to instantiate or apply these general rules – for instance, the law of cause and effect, to ground determinations of succession? The first paragraph of the last extract seems to suggest that the purely general rules which can be derived from the realization that apperception is perception of the self in time – the rules that particular thoughts be ascribed to a single self ("I am"), that they be regarded as particular events which succeed others ("I think"), and that they be collectively ascribed to the same self ("Thoughts are in me") – are not themselves identical to the rules by which such ascriptions can be made but are rather conditions, the satisfaction of which requires that appearances be represented as contained under some other rules. But what these other rules are, let alone why they are required, is not explained. Why objects must be subsumed under laws of cause and effect in order for thoughts to be represented as successive, for instance, is far from clear – though this is precisely what Kant must ultimately explain.

Do any of Kant's other sketches of the connection between apperception and rules from 1775 tell us anything more about what these rules must be? Unfortunately, although they clarify certain other points, they do not throw further light on this question. We see this in both R 4677 and R 4678:

Everything which is *thought* as an object of perception stands under a rule of apperception, self-perception.

(Experience in general. Either intuition or sensation.)

Appearance is made objective by means of being brought under a title of self-perception. And therefore the original relations of apprehension are the conditions of the perception of (real) relations in appearance, and indeed just insofar as one says that an appearance belongs thereunder is it determined by a universal and represented as objective, that is, thought. When one represents it by means of an isolated perception rather than as belonging under the functions of self-sensation it is called mere sensation. We can determine this just as *a priori* from the functions of perception in respect of the objective, that is, the conditions which are independent of the individual relations of the senses, as we can in respect of the relations of space and time. The mind must have a faculty for apprehending, and its functions are just as necessary for perception as is the receptivity of appearances.

If we intuited intellectually, no title of apprehension would be needed to represent an object to oneself. For the object would not even appear then. Now, the appearance must be subordinated to a function by means of which the mind disposes over it, and indeed to a universal condition of this function, for otherwise nothing universal would be found therein.   (R 4677, 17:658)

The first two sentences of this make it clear that Kant is indeed attempting the strategy of deriving the necessity of rules for thinking of objects from the idea of apperception rather than from the idea of perceiving an object itself. And the last paragraph also reinforces a number of points we have already observed. First, by asserting that the "titles" of apprehension would not apply to objects if we had intellectual rather than sensible intuition of them, Kant may suggest that although the rules he is seeking cannot be derived *from* the forms of sensible intuition alone, they are needed to form determinate thoughts of the objects given *by* sensible intuitions – that is, to think objects which are concretely given in time. Second, the distinction between a "function" and a "universal condition" *of* such a function, in the second sentence of this paragraph, again suggests that Kant thinks there is some distinction between the mere requirements that a succession of separate thoughts be both severally and jointly ascribed to a single self and the rules or conditions applying to objects *by which* such ascriptions can actually be accomplished. But again, he does not suggest how the transition to these more specific rules is to be made. The thought is confirmed that the rule-governedness of the *objects* of experience is not simply to be taken as a given but is rather to be derived from the rule-governedness of apperception itself, but again, details are not forthcoming.

Nor does the last of Kant's unequivocal attempts to derive the conditions of objective validity from the conditions for the unity of the mind resolve this question:

> That in the soul there is a *principium* of disposition as well as of affection. That the appearances can have no other order and cannot otherwise belong to the unity of the faculty of representation, except insofar as they are in accord with the common *principio* of disposition. For all appearances with their thoroughgoing determination must yet possess unity in the mind, consequently must be subject to such conditions through which the unity of representation is possible. The unity of apprehension is necessarily connected with the unity of the intuition of space and time, for without the former the latter would yield no real representation.
>
> The principles of exposition must be determined on the one hand by the laws of apprehension, on the other by the unity of the faculty of understanding. They are the standard for observation and are not borrowed from perceptions but are the ground thereof ...
>
> Pure thinking (*a priori*), but in relation to experiences, that is, to objects of the senses, contains principles which contain the origin of all experiences, that is, that which is thoroughly determined for all experiences.   (R 4678, 17:660)

Here Kant attempts to secure the inference from the conditions for the unity of representations in the mind to conditions on the objects of representations precisely by saying that it is *appearances* and not just *representations* which are subject to the "*principio* of disposition" – for where there are appearances, there are things which appear. And Kant again emphasizes that the unity of "exposition" or experience has a twofold foundation, requiring the laws of both apprehension and understanding, thus making clear that the rules of thought he is deriving from apperception are not identical to the laws of the pure forms of sensibility. But again, Kant fails to shed any further light on the specific nature of the rules required for thinking of either the unity of self or of objects represented by the representational states of the self.

So Kant's earliest attempts to effect a deduction of the fundamental categories of understanding from the phenomenon of apperception or self-perception leave us with hints but also questions. These fragmentary arguments make clear that, at least in Kant's initial conception of his argument, the temporality of self-consciousness, the fact that the contents of the self are presented only in a succession of moments by inner sense, is the crucial premise of his argument. It thus seems fairly clear that it is by virtue of its temporality that the fact of apperception can be hoped to yield more information about the conditions for the possibility of experience than either the pure forms of intuition or the pure functions of the logic of judgment yield by themselves. But it remains unclear what more specific than the very general requirements that a succession of thoughts be ascribed both individually and collectively to a single self can be derived from this notion of apperception. In other words, it remains unclear what rules these sorts of self-ascription of experiences are supposed to require, or indeed why they should be thought to require any sort of rule at all. Further, it remains unclear precisely what inferences should be drawn from rules for apperception to rules for the objects of experiences: Do the rules for apperception necessarily apply to the *contents* as well as to the relationships of representations among themselves? And if so, in precisely what form?

Indeed, does the unity of self-perception even require that its component elements also be interpreted as representing independent objects? Kant clearly assumes that thought must always represent such objects, but is it apperception which requires the representation of objects independent from the self, or does Kant just assume that thought is always about objects distinct from the self, although cognition of such objects is additionally subject to any special conditions for thinking of the self as well? The fragments of 1774 and 1775 suggest no clear answer to this question, and indeed we shall see that Kant remains ambivalent on this profoundly important question until well into the 1780s. Indeed, this is one of the two fundamental ambivalences of the transcendental deduction of the categories.

Restriction or imposition?

The texts of 1774 and 1775 suggest one strategy of deriving rules for objects from the rules for apperception, as well as another of deriving them directly from the concept of objectivity itself, but they do not choose between these strategies. Another question they leave unresolved is that of the precise modality which Kant intends to ascribe to rules for objects. Must they apply to any representations we could conceivably have, or do they apply only under certain conditions? This is obscure, in turn, because Kant leaves obscure the exact source of the requirement of conformity which is to obtain between our laws for representing objects and the objects that in fact we represent – the reason why these objects conform to these rules.

As we have just seen, Kant's ideas for the transcendental theory of experience, especially his second strategy, turn on the assumption that there must be some conformity between the rules for apperception and the objects represented by the various states comprised in one's unitary consciousness. He has said, for instance, that the "three functions of apperception" to which "all thought of our own condition in general" must conform are also rules "to which all appearances must conform" (R 4674, 17:646–7), and that "all appearance with its thoroughgoing determination must yet possess unity in the mind, consequently be subject to such conditions by means of which the unity of representations is possible" (R 4678, 17:660). The contrast in this passage between "appearance" (*Erscheinung*) and "representation" (*Vorstellung*) makes it particularly clear that there is supposed to be conformity between subjective states and the objective states which they represent. But what is the force of the "must" in these assertions? In just what sense is it necessary that this conformity obtain?

Here too Kant leaves room for ambivalence, though tension on this issue does not become inescapable until the 1780s. Some comments from the 1770s do suggest that there is an absolute or unconditional necessity that this conformity obtain, a necessity that the conformity obtain regardless of what else might be true of the contents of appearance; the possibility of the organization of appearances according to the rules in question is somehow guaranteed. Such a position is suggested, for example, when Kant remarks that "the mind contains the universal and sufficient source of synthesis in itself, and all appearances are exponible in it" (R 4681, 17:667), or when he writes that from the condition of the unity of the thinking subject there "flows the connection of the manifold according to a rule and in a whole, since the unity of the function must suffice for its subordination as well as its coordination" (R 4675, 17:651). Passages such as these make it sound as if the mind cannot fail to discover the necessary conformity in the objects of its representations, for it itself is, or possesses, the sufficient condition for the existence of this conformity. And though this might seem a remarkable position to adopt, we can understand why Kant might have held it. Long before 1775, after all, certainly already in 1770, he was inclined to treat the intellect, unlike the sensibility, as an active rather than a passive power, and an active power would naturally be in a position to impose its own requirements on its objects. Furthermore, Kant often seems to suppose that there is no connection or relation in objects considered apart from our perception of them, for relations can be constructed only by the mind, and this might suggest that there can be nothing in them to oppose the mind's active power to combine any given representations according to its own principles. Thus Kant continues the last remark from R 4674 by saying that appearances must conform to the functions of apperception "because no synthesis in itself lies in them," and therefore there would be none "if the mind did not add it or make it out of the data" given to it (17:647). It is for this reason that he asserts that the mind is itself the "original" (*Urbild*) of all connection, through its "orginal" (*ursprüngliche*), rather than "derivative" (*abgeleitete*), power of thought.

But the claim that the mind itself can always ensure that the conditions necessary for the possibility of experience, even of its own self-consciousness, obtain – which is precisely what the present suggestion implies – is remarkably strong, and in most of the passages from the 1770s Kant rejects such a strong view. The key evidence of this more restrained view is this statement in R 4678:

The *principium* of *analysis*: a rule of thought in general. The principles of thinking, so far as it is restricted [*restringiert*] through the condition of the subject or determined to the subject, are not principles [*Grundsätze*] but rather restrictions [*restrictionen*]. (1. Of the possibility of empirical *synthesis* in general.) Cognition is determined to an object *a priori* when it 1. goes to the condition through which an object is given [*above the line*: construction], and the cognition represents this only through concepts of appearance. 2. when it [concerns] appearance, insofar as this contains the conditions for making a concept of it. 3. when it concerns apprehension in general, insofar as it contains the condition of perception as well as of intellection, that is, the agreement of appearances among each other and with the unity of the mind, consequently with the exposition [of them].

(R 4678, 17:661)

In this passage, Kant seems to suggest that there is a *conditional* or *hypothetical* necessity that the objects of experience conform to the rules under which a unified experience or "exposition" of them, and indeed under which a unified self-consciousness itself, is possible. That is, he does not suggest that the mind is such that it can always ensure that experience is possible, but rather that it is so constituted that experience will be possible only if the objects of experience, as a matter of fact, conform to the requisite conditions. Here the idea would be that representations may be combined into a unified self-consciousness only if their contents permit of organization according to the requisite conditions. This seems to be what Kant is saying when he says that the principles of synthesis are restrictions rather than *Grundsätze*: they restrict the possibility of synthesis to certain conditions, without implying that we can ourselves ensure that those conditions will be fulfilled under all circumstances. The same point seems to be made when Kant more precisely contrasts synthesis in pure intuition – that is, the construction of a (mathematical) object, which is always possible for us – with the synthesis of appearances, where it appears to be the case that the appearances must contain the conditions under which we can form concepts of them, if we are to give a successful exposition of them.

These two positions on necessity suggest, of course, two quite different metaphysical pictures of the relation between mind and reality. On the view that conformity is always guaranteed, it is natural to explain this as guaranteed by the mind's ability to impose its rules on a pliable or formless material, or at the very least on a material any instrinsic form of which is inaccessible to the mind and can be replaced by a form of the mind's own making. On the conditional view of the necessity of the rules of thought, it is possible to think that we can know in advance of successful experience what objects must be like if we are to experience them but that we have no special power to make objects be like that, thus to make experience possible. On this view, in other words, the conditions of the possibility of experience are, if anything, the limits of our mental powers rather than the products of them.

Such an ambivalence would not be resolved by the kind of comment which is usually associated with the *Critique of Pure Reason* but which is already present in the *Duisburg Nachlass*. In R 4681, at the end of the page in which he says that the mind is the "universal and sufficient source of all synthesis," Kant also adds that "only that which is capable of persistent principles in the mind do we call 'object'. ... For everything else, which does not assume such principles, is nothing for us and cannot be perceived" (17:668; cf. A 116). This sort of remark, that objects which do not conform to the principles of the possibility of experience are "nothing for us," implies that for some reason the case of nonconformity is one which should not concern us. But for what reason: because such a case cannot arise? or because, although such a case can arise, if it does occur self-consciousness itself will be impossible, and therefore a subject will literally find it impossible to worry about such a case (*de re*)? The former reason would be the natural consequence of the absolute necessity of conformity of objects to the conditions of the possibility of experience, yet the latter would be consistent with the merely conditional necessity of this conformity – and the present remark hardly requires interpretation one way rather than the other.

Nevertheless, it would be surprising if Kant were to have clearly insisted upon the absolute necessity of conformity to the conditions of the possibility of experience, for, both in notes from 1775 and indeed throughout the whole period of the later 1760s through the mid-1770s, Kant defends precisely the general view that the principles of human knowledge yield *conditional* rather than absolute necessities. In R 4683, for instance, Kant clearly rejects the idea that any synthetic proposition can be ascribed unconditional necessity: "A synthetic proposition which is valid of all things in general, and especially one the subject of which is a pure concept of the understanding, is false. Unless it is not to be absolutely valid objectively [*objective schlechthin gelten soll*], but only under the subjective restriction of the use of reason" (17:669). But the full import of this remark can be appreciated only against a wider background of reflections reaching back into the 1760s.

Throughout this period, Kant insists that we should not confuse the necessary features of our thought with features which are intrinsically necessary to the objects of our thought. Thus a note from 1769 already announces the key to the transcendental theory of experience. It says that "the nature of our understanding entails that nothing contingent is thinkable according to its rules without a connection with grounds, and that a succession (according to time) cannot be thought with a ground, nor an occurrence of something without being in connection to its ground" – but also admonishes us that

it does not follow that that which must be judged according to the laws of our understanding is true if it concerns such things as our understanding is not, according to the arrangement for its use, determined to judge.

We borrow the law of sufficient reason from corporeal appearances, but if we want to make it universal and apply it to things which are elevated above the idea of our understanding, then we confuse the idea of absolute incomprehensibility for us with that of intrinsic impossibility. (R 3922, 17:346–7)

Yet if incomprehensibility does not imply absolute impossibility, then it follows, by contraposition, that comprehensibility does not imply the absolute necessity of the satisfaction of the conditions which make for that comprehensibility. A similar sentiment appears in Kant's lectures in the latter half of the 1770s, where he is recorded as having said that "the subjective hindrances of incomprehensibility are essentially different from the objective hindrances of impossibility" (*Metaphysik L 1*, 28:271).

The more specific expression of Kant's general standpoint during this time employs three different distinctions, although Kant's own terminology does not always make this clear. Two of these distinctions are logical in nature, and the third draws a line between what we would now call epistemological and ontological claims. The logical distinctions are, first, a distinction concerning the *extension* of a claim of necessity, whether it is valid of all objects or only of some. Thus what Kant sometimes means by asserting or denying that a proposition is absolutely – *schlechthin* – necessary is that it is, or is not, true of all possible objects (this might be his meaning in, for instance, R 4683). Second, however, and more typically, Kant has in mind the logical distinction between something which holds only given a prior supposition, or which holds subject to that condition, and something which holds without any condition, or unconditionally. This seems to be the sense of the contrast that Kant draws between absolute and hypothetical necessity (see, e.g., R 4030 [1769?], 17:390–1), or between necessity which is unconditional and that which is conditioned. He expresses this second contrast with the opposing terms *unbedingt* and *bedingt* (e.g., R 3717 [1763–8], 17:260) and the terms *conditional* and *absolut* or *ohne condition* (see, e.g., R 5181, 18:110–11). Finally, Kant draws a third contrast between what we might call the epistemological claim that some rule is a necessary condition of our thought, on the one hand, and the ontological claim that some rule is an inherently necessary feature of the object we are thinking about, on the other, by contrasting *subjective* and *objective* necessity. Thus he says that "the highest principle of human reason is either: that which expresses the condition under which alone we can cognize things by means of our reason, or: under which alone things are possible; subjective, objective" (R 4386, [1771? 1773–5?], 17:528). Kant then expresses the constraint he wants to place on legitimate assertions of necessity by saying both that they are subjective rather than objective and by maintaining that, except in one special case, they are always conditional rather than absolute.

Thus, as early as the mid-sixties Kant suggests both of these restrictions, writing that "metaphysics treats only the subject dogmatically, but the object in respect of synthetic judgments problematically" (R 3716, 17:259) and also that "all necessity and contingency which we can represent to ourselves is conditional. The unconditional is thought problematically. Absolutely contingent (e.g., free action) and absolutely necessary can neither of them be thought" (R 3717, 17:260). The first of these statements claims that metaphysics delivers subjective but not objective necessity; the second, that it yields conditional but not absolute necessities. Metaphysics can tell us how we are cognitively constituted, and so how objects must be constituted if we are to successfully cognize them, but not how objects must be constituted *tout court*. It can tell us that one object must be if some other one is, but not, apparently, that any object simply exists necessarily.

The claim that the necessities of metaphysics are subjective rather than objective, which encapsulates Kant's fundamental departure from the deepest assumption of his predecessors,[6] is what most concerns us now. This claim is defended in many notes. For instance, one fragment from 1769 says:

> The representation of all things is really the representation of our own condition and the relation of one representation to another by means of our inner laws. The impossibility of separating concepts or of their connection without all laws of our understanding is merely subjective; equally so the possibility. . . . The *axiomata* (*synthetica*) of philosophy concern merely the relation of what can be known only subjectively according to the laws of our understanding.
>
> (R 3929, 17:351–2; cf. R 3931, 17:353, and R 3935, 17:354)

Or even more clearly: "Metaphysics is a science of the laws of pure human reason and therefore subjective" (R 3952, 17:362). And the implication of this is nicely put in one more note from this same year:

> Therefore when I say: a principle is subjective, that is, it contains the *conditiones* under which alone we can judge by means of our reason according to laws of experience, this does not mean that our reason must assume this law in the objects; for it does not even concern them; therefore one can say neither that it is false nor that is true.
>
> (R 3954, 17:363; see also R 3977, 17:373)

Statements of the same form can be found in the immediate period of the *Duisburg Nachlass*. Thus, the remains of the general period 1773–6 commence with this:

> The *analysis* of pure reason yields nothing except clarity in the representations which we already have.
>
> The synthetic propositions concern the conditions of judgments according to pure reason and are subjective. Therefore pure reason cannot teach us to know objects except in application to the senses.
>
> (R 4626, 17:613)

Finally, Kant insists that this general principle of the merely subjective – epistemic but not ontological – validity of the general principles of metaphysics must be maintained, even though what these principles require is precisely that the connections among the individual objects and events of our experience be seen as thoroughly necessitated by universal laws:

> The *principium contingentiae* means that nothing really exists as absolutely contingent, that is, that its existence must be objectively cognized as determined, if it is determined subjectively in perception. – Everything is necessary, either absolutely or hypothetically, but even so, nothing is unrestrictedly [*schlechterdings*] necessary, rather only in relation to the possibility of the objects of experience.
>
> (R 5914, 18:383, late 1770s or early 1780s)

In other words, the most general conclusion of the transcendental theory of experience itself, that objective states of affairs must be distinguished from subjective ones precisely by being seen as necessitated by laws in a way that the latter are not, is to be interpreted only as a subjective law restricting the conditions under which we can know objects. This is not to be confused with an *ontological* claim that it is necessary without any restriction that objects conform to the conditions of the possibility of experience – that is, to this requirement of thoroughgoing necessitation. That conformity itself remains contingent. *If* experience is to be possible, its several objects must stand in necessary connections, but *that* experience is possible is not itself something which can be known to be necessarily true.

So Kant does draw a general distinction between epistemological necessity and ontological necessity prior to the publication of the *Critique*. What about the *logical* distinction between that which is necessary only subject to a prior condition and that which is necessary without any such presupposition? Kant's transcendental theory of experience is precisely that all objects of experience must be considered necessary in the former, conditional sense: Laws of causation and interaction function precisely to make one object or state of affairs necessary, given the occurrence of some other. However, Kant also holds that to prevent an infinite regress in experience we must add to such conditional necessity at least the idea of some *one* thing which is absolutely necessary. But even here Kant refrains from ascribing ontological significance to this necessity, that is, he refrains from making a law of our thought into a genuine necessary truth about objects valid independently of our thought about them. From the time of the *Only Possible Proof* (1762) onward, Kant never entirely gave up the idea that one must at least *think,* if not know, that there is an absolutely necessary being, if one is ever to come to an end in thinking of the chain of things that are merely conditionally or hypothetically necessary. Thus, this pair of notes from 1769 states the requirement of the concept of a necessary being to terminate our chains of reasoning about hypothetical necessities, but even then it also reiterates the ontological restriction on such a claim of absolute necessity:

One should think of something absolutely [*schlechthin*] necessary, since everything which is, is necessary, but not everything can be hypothetically necessary. But one cannot think anything absolutely necessary. One must think of the world as limited, but one also cannot think these limits. (R 3937, 17:355)

and:

Besides those conditions without which objects cannot be, there are in our reason further conditions without which we cannot think certain objects through reason, even though these conditions are not determinations of the objects themselves. These *conditiones* are therefore subjective, and their concepts signify nothing in the object. All synthetic judgments of pure reason are accordingly subjective, and the concepts themselves signify [only] relations of acts of reason to themselves.

(R 3938, 17:355)

Other passages from the same period make it even clearer that the restriction on the modality of any ontological claim applies even to the postulation of an absolutely necessary being as the ground and termination of all conditional necessities. Thus,

> The intrinsically necessary is absolutely necessary (*omnimode*), but we cannot have insight into intrinsic necessity on account of the omission of the determinate conditions. Only our concept of necessity requires also that of a ground and, indeed, a universal ground, and one understands this also in the idea of thoroughgoing necessity, but this is only a relational concept in the subordination of ideas and is logically conditional. ... (R 3888, 17:328)

Or,

> All absolute necessity is either of judgments or of things [*Sachen*]. The former, as logical, is always a conditional necessity of the predicate. The necessity of things which we can know is always conditional, for in itself we can always suspend the thing, since where we affirm nothing we contradict nothing through its negation. The concept of the necessary is in the first place a concept given through reason, since through it alone is something made determinate. Absolute necessity is a limiting-concept [*Grenzbegriff*], since without it there would be no *completudo* in the series of the contingent. But this limiting-concept is itself problematic and cannot be cognized *a priori* through reason, since it is a *conceptus terminator* ...
> (R 4033, 17:391–2; see also R 4034, 17:392, and R 4039, 17:393–4)

And finally, closer to the period of the *Duisburg Nachlass*, this lapidary conclusion:

> The transcendental concept [of God] is necessary, not the transcendental proof. ... The necessity of the divine existence as a necessary hypothesis either of the mere concept of the possible or of experiences in this world, as well as the hypothesis of morality. Absolute necessity cannot be proved.
> (The proof of the existence of God is not apodictic, rather hypothetical *sub hypothesi logica* and *practica*.) (R 4580, 17:600)

Let us now draw some conclusions from these reflections. Throughout the later 1760s and the 1770s, Kant was emphatic that metaphysics could not yield claims of absolute necessity. It could not claim that any of the conditions it imposed upon *the experience of* ordinary objects, that is, finite objects in space and time rather than God, were intrinsically necessary to any of those objects themselves. Even when reason's (or rationalism's) abhorrence of infinite regresses itself led to the idea of an absolutely necessary being numerically distinct from the objects of ordinary experience – a ground of the world, rather than an object in the world – Kant was not willing to admit a theoretical assertion that such an absolutely necessary being exists. (At least not on speculative grounds – the reference to a practical hypothesis in R 4580 obviously prepares the way for Kant's theory of God as a postulate of practical reason which was to be developed in his later writings in moral philosophy.) All claims of necessity were, in Kant's view, subject to conditions. For instance, particular claims of, for example, causal connection are always conditional on some prior state of affairs (see, e.g., R 4598, 17:599–600), and general claims that objects conform to the requirements of the possibility of our experience are also subject to a condition – the condition, presumably, *that we do in fact experience them.* Kant's general position on necessity would thus militate against reading very much into a remark such as his description of the mind as the "universal and sufficient source of synthesis" in R 4681 and would instead suggest that the position of R 4678, that the conditions of the possibility of experience are restrictions on what we can experience but not absolute principles, was Kant's considered position in 1775.

Thus, although its language leaves room for confusion, it might seem that the transcendental theory of experience of the *Duisburg Nachlass* does not contain an ambivalent stance on the necessity of the laws of thought after all. In spite of several infelicitous expressions, it seems to be Kant's intention just to discover what conditions the objects which cause our empirical intuitions must satisfy *when and if* we are capable of a unified experience of them and/or of ourselves. But he need not offer any explanation, let alone guarantee, that these objects *must* conform to such conditions, apart from the hypothesis that we do in fact experience them. The surprise is rather that in the *Critique of Pure Reason* Kant suddenly departs from the strictures on the status of metaphysical necessities that he earlier advanced and forcefully insists on an absolute necessity to the objective validity of the categories that can be explained only by the assumption that the mind actually imposes its rules on an otherwise formless reality. The question then must be, what premise *absent* from his earlier transcendental theory of experience leads Kant to this alternative metaphysical conclusion? Although the metaphysics of imposition is compatible with the theory of intuition that Kant held from 1770 onward and is permitted by the language used in the theory of categories in the *Duisburg Nachlass,* it would seem to be precluded by Kant's explicit views on modality. Something must thus be added to lead to the stronger conclusion. The addition, we shall see, was a new interpretation of the premise from which Kant deduced the objective validity of the categories. In particular, it was the new assumption that what Kant comes to call the "transcendental unity of apperception" is not merely a ground for *a priori* knowledge of the objective validity of the categories but is *itself* something known *a priori* to obtain under all possible circumstances of representational activity. That is, Kant will actually assume not merely that experience has necessary conditions but that it *is* itself necessary – and this will introduce an absolute necessity which can ground the absolute necessity of applying categories to objects, thus imposing them on such objects. In the 1770s, however, such a line of thought remained a hidden possibility.

Analogies of experience

We have now seen that in the central period of the 1770s Kant was clearly ambivalent about the proper premise for a transcendental theory of experience and that he at least left room for ambivalence about the metaphysical force of such a theory. We shall see that in his mature transcendental deduction of the categories the former ambivalence remained unresolved, and the latter blossomed. Before we turn directly to the transcendental deduction of the 1780s, however, a few further lessons will be drawn from the texts of the mid-1770s. In particular, it will be noted that the *Duisburg Nachlass* suggests certain conclusions about the meaning of the title of the "Analogies of Experience" of the later *Critique of Pure Reason* and about the role or function of these "analogies" in Kant's mature theory of experience.

First, we have seen that Kant's efforts at a transcendental theory of experience of 1774 and 1775 have treated the perception of objects, as well as self-perception, as a matter of the "exposition" or determination of the temporal order of empirical intuitions; in other words, the transcendental theory of experience, in either of its two fundamental forms, is essentially a theory of time-determination. This suggests that the theory of time-determination developed in the *Critique*'s "Analogies of Experience" and "Refutation of Idealism" does not merely represent the application of Kant's transcendental deduction of the categories to the special case of empirical or even scientific knowledge but instead reflects the historical origin of Kant's deduction of the categories. Indeed, Kant's original conception of the transcendental theory of experience not only contains no distinction between the transcendental deduction of the categories and the proofs of the principles of empirical knowledge, no distinction between a more general theory of the categories and a more specific theory of time-determination; it also virtually consists of the analogies of experience alone. As we saw, the theory of the *Duisburg Nachlass* suggested that objects of perception must have a determinate magnitude, thereby anticipating the *Critique*'s "Axioms of Intuition," but the theory also suggested that this principle derived directly from the forms of intuition rather than from the laws of the understanding; the content of the latter seemed to be exhausted by the principles of substance, causation, and interaction. Of course, it would be a historical fallacy to argue that because the analogies of experience exhausted Kant's first attempt at a theory of experience, they are the only significant part of his final theory. Nevertheless, there are profound gaps between the *Critique of Pure Reason*'s theory of time-determination and much else in its "Transcendental Analytic" that may indeed be explained by the realization that Kant's theory of time-determination was his original inspiration.

The second point I will discuss here is that Kant's published justification for calling the principles of time-determination "analogies" is not only strained but also incomplete, because it includes a distorted account of only one of at least three different reasons which Kant had for conceiving of these principles as analogies.

We may begin on the first point with a reminder of some results already established. We have seen that although by the middle of the 1770s Kant had a clear conception of the task to be performed by a transcendental deduction of the categories, he did not make his later distinction between separate arguments for pure concepts of the understanding and for principles of experience. Instead, we have seen that Kant clearly intended that the task of a transcendental deduction of the categories be accomplished by a transcendental theory of time-determination. Though Kant was ambivalent about exactly how the argument should proceed, each of his strategies attempted to go directly from some characterization of experience as an "exposition" of temporally given intuitions to the proposition that objects must be interacting substances with law-governed successions of states, without any intervening deduction of nontemporal categories. There is, for instance, no deduction of the logical relation of "ground and consequence" prior to the deduction of the relation of cause and effect. Any suggestion that the categories could successfully be deduced without use of their function in time-determination is absent. Whether Kant supposed that the primary premise of the transcendental theory of experience was that objects must be ordered in the whole of time or that the states of the self must be so ordered, in either case the underlying assumption of his argument was precisely that the fundamental task of the understanding is the ordering – the "exposition" – of events in a unique temporal order.[7]

In other words, Kant's transcendental theory of experience of 1774–5 was virtually identical with his attempt to show that the objective validity of the concepts of substance, causation, and interaction is the necessary condition of time-determination – that is, his theory was identical with the program of the "Analogies of Experience" and the "Refutation of Idealism." We shall now examine more evidence that this is so, even though Kant does use classifications in this period which may initially seem to anticipate the remainder of the program of the "Principles of Judgment" of the published *Critique*.

We can begin with some suggestive remarks omitted from my earlier quotations from the *Duisburg Nachlass*. One comes from R 4675, where, it will be remembered, Kant argued that the very idea of an object of experience implies the idea of something "parallel to my I" but that the conception of this object is cast in terms borrowed from my representation of the unity of myself. Kant had put this point pregnantly by writing that "the three relations in the mind therefore require three analogies of appearance in order to transform the *subjective functions* of the mind into objective ones, and thereby to make them into concepts of the understanding which give reality to appearances." Breaking the argument off, Kant then went on to make the following comments:

This is all grounded on conditions of experience; consequently it is not necessary and is also not understood as such; rather it is *analoga* of axioms which take place *a priori* but only as anticipations of all laws of experience in general.

Everything which happens is *a priori connex*; everything which is simultaneous is *comitative connex*; everything which is, is *inhaesive connex*.

The axioms have a primitive certainty, the analogies a derivative certainty, the petitions an adopted certainty. The derivative certainty from the nature of our thinking in general not as appearances, rather as actions of the subject, which thought, so far as it is to yield an object, must be in a substance, determined through a ground, and connected with the whole of the faculty of representations. It is therefore derived from the subjectively real conditions of thinking in general.

(R 4675, 17:648–9)

We may now also note that in R 4681, between the claim that the mind contains the "universal and sufficient source of synthesis in itself" and the further argument that all perception takes place through apprehension, which is itself, however, governed by the laws of inner sense, Kant had included the following list of unexplained titles and assertions:

principia of perception.

Ground rule [*Grundsätze*] of observation or of the exposition of appearances in general.

There are presumptions of experience.

Analogies of understanding.

Axioms of intuitions, analogies of understanding, petitions of reason.

(R 4681, 17:667)

These remarks suggest that the theory of time-determination exhausts the essential content of the principles of judgment precisely by placing a reference to "analogies" in a position which would have to correspond to that of the whole "Analytic of Concepts" itself, in a listing of the three main divisions of the *Critique of Pure Reason*'s "Doctrine of Elements."

This statement may seem surprising, for it could certainly seem as though the list "axioms of intuitions, analogies of understanding, petitions of reason" anticipates Kant's later division of the "Principles of Judgment" into the "Axioms of Intuition," the "Anticipations of Perceptions," the "Analogies of Experience," and the "Postulates of Empirical Thought."[8] But to assume so would be a mistake. In fact, the "axioms of intuitions," which are said in R 4675 to have a "primitive certainty," clearly refer to the axioms directly derivable from the *forms of intuition,* or to the synthetic *a priori* results of mathematics, which are grounded not in the published "Axioms of Intuition" but by the "Transcendental Aesthetic." The "anticipations of all laws of experience" (R 4675, 17:649) do not describe anything different from the "*analoga* of axioms" but are another title for them. The "petitions of reason" which, after all, have only an "adopted certainty," have nothing to do with the later postulates of empirical thought but rather are clearly nothing but the "subreptic axioms" of 1770, or the fallacious inferences based on them – that is, the subject of the later "Transcendental Dialectic." But this means that if one divides the *Critique*'s "Doctrine of Elements" into the "Aesthetic," "Analytic," and "Dialectic," such phrases as "analogies of understanding" or "analogies of

64

appearance" *must subsume the whole of the originally intended content of the "Transcendental Analytic."* In other words, as Kant originally understood his task, the statement of these analogies and the presentation of the argument in their behalf are all that is necessary to accomplish the explanation and proof of the objective validity of the categories.

The same conclusion follows from a fragment even closer in date to the composition of the *Critique* than the ones we have so far considered. In this note, from between 1776 and 1778, Kant first briefly lists the contradictions that arise if we make unrestricted use of such concepts as infinity, ground, freedom, and necessity (in other words, he gives a quick sketch of the later "Antinomies") and then continues:

> But if these concepts are taken only according to the conditions of apprehension, they are limited to objects of the senses and also have only a restricted meaning, for instance, everything that happens has a first cause in some particular ordering, or rather the *axiomata* are not transcendent but hold only as anticipations. So that they hold only of the data of the senses, insofar as these can be understood. For instance, what happens has a ground, since without a rule according to which it is given according to laws of sensibility, one would not think any object by means of the representation.
>
> The *principium contradictionis* contains the *conditiones* of thought in general. The *anticipationes,* which affirm the *conditiones* of apprehension of the concepts of the understanding (e.g., in every substance there is *aliquid perdurabile,* or a substance endures forever), contains the conditions (*postulata*) of understanding, and these are always true in respect of the sensible conditions. (R 5263, 18:136)

The only one of Kant's later *titles* for the principles of judgment which is not employed here is none other than "Analogies of Experience," but the only *principles* which Kant is talking about here are of course the principles of substance and causation. Kant refers to these principles as "axioms" (*axiomata*), though, as we shall shortly see, he also has a contrast to make between the principles of empirical knowledge and the genuine axioms of pure mathematics (e.g., R 4675). He suggests that the principles of substance and causation do not directly describe transcendent reality but rather anticipate the course of ordinary experience – though again we shall soon see that Kant also has a qualification to make here. Finally, Kant says that these principles can also be called "postulates," because they state the conditions under which the understanding can be employed. Presumably he has in mind that they are analogous to postulates in mathematics, in that they are neither definitions nor theorems but rather presuppositions which are necessary for theorems to hold of their objects (in mathematics, on the Kantian conception, one postulates that an object can be constructed which will satisfy a definition and ensuing theorems). It is clear, then, that although in the 1770s Kant had already used all of the titles which he was later to use to organize the "Principles of Judgment," he used them all in reference to a single set of principles – the three principles of substance, causation, and interaction.

This is, of course, an indirect way of arriving at the conclusion that it is the proof of the objective validity of the three categories of substance, causation, and interaction alone which constitutes the essential objective of the transcendental deduction. But Kant also states this directly. One marginal note from the mid-1770s says:

We have three categories and their predicaments: first, of position (being and not-being); 2. of *respectus*. 3. of *completudinis*. The first is, whether something is or not; the second, what there is respective of something else or not; the third, how much of a thing is together, &c. *Quaeitas, Qualitas, quantitas propositionis.*

(R 4715, 17:684-5)

This makes one point and suggests another. First, it virtually asserts that there are only three categories – substance, consequence, and composition – and that other general forms of concepts would merely be "predicaments" of these. Second, Kant's final words in Latin seem to imply that these three categories are sufficient to correspond to the basic *logical* dimensions of propositions, which are also three in number. In other words, he seems to imply that following his later "clue" of deriving the basic forms of the concepts of objects from the basic "logical functions" of judgments (the so-called metaphysical deduction) would produce the same result as is derived from taking the theory of time-determination as the key to the transcendental theory of experience – that is, not the twelve categories propounded in the *Critique of Pure Reason* but the three vital categories of substance, causation, and interaction.

Many of the notes of the *Duisburg Nachlass* suggest the same conclusion. R 4675's claim that "everything which happens, is *a priori connex*; everything which is simultaneous, is *comitative connex*; everything which is, is *inhaesive connex*" (17:649) suggests that the three concepts of inherence in a substance, connection with a prior event, and concomitance or interaction with concomitant events are sufficient for the determination of experience. The same conclusion seems implicit in this paragraph from R 4682: "The understanding cannot determine anything in the sensibility except by means of a universal action. For example, origination through a general condition of succession. Existence through a subject of all existence. Simultaneity [*zusammenseyn*] through a universal unity" (17:670). In spite of this passage's intimation of a fallacious inference from the necessity of all existence pertaining to some substance or other to that of all existence pertaining to some one substance (see also R 4675, 17:650, lines 20–3), its general point is clear enough: The concepts of inherence in a substance, succession according to a rule, and interaction are sufficient to provide the conceptual framework for the determination or "exposition" of appearances. The same assumption is evident in Kant's more extensive arguments in R 4679, R 4681, and R 4682 and is, moreover, explicitly asserted in one crucial passage:

We think everything to ourselves by means of predicates; therefore there is always a relation to x. In judgments, however, there is a relation of $a:b$, which are both related to x. a and b in x, x by means of $a:b$, finally $a + b = x$.

66

The absolute predicate in general is reality ...
Determinate predicates (relation-predicates) which are real concern only relations. Of these there are three. According to the three relations in judgment.

(R 4676, 17:657)

Here Kant's thought appears to be that the idea of reality is not itself a
particular form of judgment or a category, since it is presupposed by all
thought whatever (the "absolute predicate") and that there are then only
three *real concepts,* corresponding to the three *relational* forms of judgment.

Thus, whether Kant's argument is that the structure of apperception is
indirectly necessary for objects, because the experience of objects must be
structured and its structure must be borrowed from apperception, or rather
that it is *directly* necessary, just because apperception itself must be
structured, his conclusion seems to be the same: There are only three real
categories for objects, because there are just three basic forms of relation or
functions for thinking of apperception. There are "three sorts of concepts
for objects as appearances" or a "threefold dimension of synthesis,"
because there are "three functions of apperception" (R 4674, 17:646) or
because "we perceive something only by means of being conscious of our
apprehension ... as belonging to one of the three relations in the mind"
(R 4681, 17:667–8). This is so, in turn, Kant has claimed (though, of
course, not yet convincingly argued) because the temporal unity of self-
consciousness has three dimensions. Thus, Kant's conception in 1775 is
t.̀at there are only three basic categories for the understanding. Again, as
witn the distinction between the "Transcendental Deduction" and the
"Analytic of Judgment," the absence of Kant's later list of *twelve* rather
than three categories, and of the *four* subdivisions rather than one
subdivision of the "Analytic of Judgment," does not itself imply that the
later expansion is ill conceived. But it does again suggest that the original
inspiration for Kant's transcendental theory of experience is his theory of
time-determination.

I now turn to the meaning of the phrase "analogies of experience." The
material we have been examining suggests that Kant had at least three
different motivations for using this name.

(1) First, Kant clearly called the basic principles of understanding
"analogies" because they are *derived by an analogy* between the organization of the mind itself and the organization of its objects. As we have seen,
the Kant of the 1770s was ambivalent about the direction of this analogy.
That is, sometimes he thought that the fundamental act of the understanding is to draw analogies *from* the unity of the mind *to* the unity of objects:
"The three relations in the mind therefore require three analogies of
appearance, in order to transform the *subjective functions* of the mind into
objective ones" (R 4675; 17:648; see also R 4674, 17:646–7), and "the
sensible relations ... stand in analogy to the acts of understanding"
(R 4679, 17:664). But sometimes Kant conceived of the analogy as
operating in the opposite direction: The mind itself is conceived of in
analogy *to* our conception of objects; the propositions that there are

substance, cause and effect, and interaction in every whole "are valid of all objects of experience, [and] the very same propositions are also valid of the mind in respect of the generation of its own representations" (loc. cit.). However, whatever the details, Kant's most basic idea was that we must conceive of two orders of existence, self and objects, that we have only one set of rules for so doing, and thus the basic nature of thought itself, most generally expressed, must be to construct analogies or parallels between one realm and the other. As Kant most obscurely put this point at this stage of his development, "The mind can be conscious of itself only through the appearances which correspond to its dynamic functions, and of the appearances only by means of its dynamic functions" (R 4686, 17:675). The obscurity of this remark suggests that working out the details of how knowledge of objects can depend upon knowledge of the mind whereas knowledge of the mind also requires knowledge of objects will not be easy, but the very fact that the "analogies" constitute the heart of Kant's novel transcendental theory of experience, the addition to his philosophy needed to solve the new problem of 1772, also suggests that working out the difficulties of this parallelism will likewise be the discovery of the key to Kant's theory of knowledge.

Second, by calling the principles of experience "analogies," Kant also meant to connote something about their status as well as about their origin: They are not exactly axioms, but "*analoga* of axioms" (R 4675, 17:649). Here, in fact, two ideas seem to have been before Kant's mind. One is that these rules do not hold with the same degree of assurance as genuine axioms or genuine necessary truths do; there is some element of contingency in their validity. The other idea is that they do not hold with the same degree of specificity as a genuine axiom does: A genuine axiom determines one particular solution for any given problem, but an analogue of an axiom only "anticipates" a concrete law of experience; that is, it sets some general guideline which experience might fulfill with some degree of variety. As Kant will later put it, particular causal laws cannot be known *a priori*.

(2) Kant's terminology for making the first of these two points varies. Sometimes he calls the analogies mere "presumptions." Sometimes he contrasts them, informally titled "ground rules" (*Grundsätze*), with more formally titled "*principia*" (as in R 4681). Sometimes he says rather that they are a species of *Grundsätze* but one which does not possess the same degree of "evidence" as another species, namely axioms proper, does. What could these remarks mean? One suggestion may be found in R 4674, where Kant explains the claim that the rules of experience are not genuine axioms by saying that "actual anticipations of appearance are not to be had. One finds [these principles] confirmed by experience, since laws of experience become possible through them" (17:652). (Note here that Kant suggests that the word "anticipations" should not be used of principles of experience at all, so far is he from arriving at the classification of principles of experience in the *Critique*.) And this, in turn, suggests the remark of R 4678, that "the principles of thought" are not "*Grundsätze*" at all but

"restrictions" (17:661). In other words, one of the points of calling the basic principles of experience mere "analogies" or "*analoga* of axioms" might be precisely to deny that they are principles that the mind can impose on objects and, rather, to suggest that they are principles to which objects must conform if they – the objects – are to permit our minds to experience them. Thus, we might suggest that Kant's very choice of the term "analogies" reveals at least some original inclination to the "restriction" rather than "imposition" model of the mind, the view that its rules must be conditional rather than absolute, thus that only some premise not yet introduced into the arguments of the *Duisburg Nachlass* could force him to the imposition view. This is at least suggested by Kant's remark that the principles of experience must *await experience* for their confirmation.

(3) Finally, Kant's derivation of the name "analogies" from such an expression as "*analoga* of axioms" also suggests that the basic principles of understanding differ from those of sensibility in their specificity: They are not determinate rules for the construction of objects in the same way that the laws of pure intuition are, but are only analogues of such rules. As Kant puts it, "The presumption is no anticipation, because it does not determine but only says that something is determinable according to a certain given exponent [and] a rule yet to be found" (R 4677, 17:659). That is, if these rules were genuine axioms for the construction of objects, they would be satisfied by only one solution in any given case, and the solution could be fully determined by the rule and the data which are given. But this is not the case with the principles of experience, which tell us only what *kinds* of connection to search for in the determination of experience; therefore they are only analogues of genuine axioms in this sense as well. Thus Kant concludes: "Therefore we represent the object to ourselves by means of an *analogon* of construction," and "Therefore the analogies of understanding have no evidence. They are, to be sure, constitutive, but not directly objective" (R 4684, 17:670, 672).

This last of the three reasons for calling the principles of understanding analogies, which is the one to which Kant gives least prominence in the course of the *Duisburg Nachlass,* is the only reason Kant mentions to explain the title of the "Analogies of Experience" in the *Critique* itself, and even then his statement of the point is strained. The *Critique* explains that these principles are analogies because with them "from three given members we can obtain *a priori* knowledge . . . of the relation to a fourth," though, to be sure – and here is the difference which he notes between analogies in philosophy and in mathematics – "not the fourth member itself. The relation yields, however, a rule for seeking the fourth member in experience, and a mark whereby it can be detected" (A 179–80 / B 222). Kant's published explanation of the title, in other words, is that just as in a mathematical analogy, where the values for three quantities determine the value of the fourth, so, in the case of his philosophical analogies, determinations of some states of affairs will, if not uniquely determine the missing existent, at least send one looking in the right direction. This account is not very different in spirit from the third aspect of the account of 1775 which we are considering but, as put, it is farfetched. There is no account of why in the philosophical case there are *four* facts, *three* of which are already known, and even if one could detect an allusion to Hume's account of *causal* reasoning in this picture (from a past experience of two successive items, the mind forms an inclination to leap from a third like the first of the past two to a fourth like the second), it would be difficult indeed to relate the content of the *first* and *third* analogies of experience to this mathematical model. But, more important, this account obscures the locus of the analogy Kant is talking about. For, as originally put, Kant's claim does *not* mean that there is any use of analogy *in* the process of finding a *particular* causal explanation of some state of affairs – that causal connections can be discovered only when three things are already known, just as the missing numerator of a fraction can be discovered only when we are given its denominator and another fraction with which to compare it. Rather, Kant intends only the more general point that there is some analogy, but not strict isomorphism, between the construction of mathematical objects and the search for empirical laws in general: namely, that the latter (contrary to empiricist assumptions) is just as rule-governed as the former, although the rules do *not* yield the same degree of specificity – that is, unique solutions.

We now have before us the outlines of Kant's transcendental theory of experience in its initial form – essentially, promissory notes for demonstrating that the concepts of substance, causation, and interaction are the necessary conditions for temporally determinate experience of external objects and/or of self-consciousness itself, conditions to which objects clearly must conform if experience is to take place but which the mind may or may not have the power actively to impose upon the raw data of sensibility that come to it. We will now examine the transformation of these ideas into the *Critique of Pure Reason* as that evolved through its two editions in 1781 and 1787. We shall see that Kant's original ideas suffered a complicated fate. On the one hand, his original ideas about time-determination were subordinated to a more complicated, but not more persuasive, general theory of judgment. On the other hand, the original theory of time-determination was eventually more fully developed into a two-staged theory expounded in the "Analogies of Experience" and the "Refutation of Idealism" first published in 1787 and perfected in the following years.

II

The transcendental deduction from 1781 to 1787

3
The real premises of the deduction

We have now seen that Kant's initial attempts to deduce the objective validity of the categories of the understanding from a transcendental theory of experience were characterized by a fundamental ambivalence about the conception of experience to be assumed, and that they left room for uncertainty about the type of necessity to be assigned to the conditions of the possibility of such experience. We will now see that Kant continued in some confusion about the best premise for a transcendental deduction throughout the 1780s, but also that he took an unprecedented turn to the strong view that the mind actually imposes conformity to the conditions necessary for its experience on objects, and is not just restricted by those conditions to the experience of objects which do as a matter of fact conform to them. Yet even this view, especially predominant in the first version of the transcendental deduction in 1781, was not asserted unequivocally. Because of these uncertainties, it was inevitable that the deduction, which should have been the keystone to the triumphal arch of the *Critique of Pure Reason*, never amounted to more than a disjointed summary of significantly different strategies.[1] Moreover, none of these strategies is free from serious problems, and in the end the "key to metaphysics" which Kant had been promising since 1772 (10:130) remains little more than another promissory note for the theory of time-determination eventually worked out in the "Analogies of Experience" but completed only by the "Refutation of Idealism," which was first added to the text of the *Critique* in 1787 and perfected only in the next half-dozen years.

A plethora of premises

Kant's thought clearly continued to be ambivalent during the period between the composition of the *Duisburg Nachlass* and the publication of the *Critique*. Thus, this note from between 1776 and 1778 introduces characteristic language of the *Critique* yet obviously fails to distinguish between two different strategies for the deduction of the categories:

In the case of whatever is passive or is given, apprehension must not merely be found but must also be necessitated, in order to represent it as given: That is, the particular apprehension must be determined through the universal. The universal is the relation to the other [apprehensions] and to the whole state. Something is considered as given by being distinguished from what is arbitrary and is considered as something only by being subsumed under the categories. It must therefore be

73

represented according to a rule, for appearance thereby to become experience and for the mind to grasp it as one of its acts of *self-consciouness*, wherein, as in space and time, all data are to be found. The unity of the mind is the condition of thinking, and the subordination of every particular under the universal is the condition of possibility for associating a given representation with others by means of an act. Even if the rule does not leap to the eye, one must still represent the object as in accordance with a rule in order to conceive that it represents something, that is, which has a certain place and function among its other determinations ...

(R 5203, 18:116)

First Kant suggests that it is basically in order to conceive of representations as giving an independent object of experience, as opposed to being merely arbitrary states of mind, that their apprehension must be regarded as determined by some form of universal law. But then he immediately goes on to suggest that it is, rather, the mind's own requirement for an internally unified connection of its several acts which requires that the contents of its act be submitted to rules; the subordination of particular representations under universals is the condition of the possibility of the mind's representation of its own unified action, and *for that reason* also true of its objects.

Therefore, although Kant's exposition is continuous, it clearly intimates distinct arguments beginning from distinct premises. It is also clear, of course, that neither of the arguments that Kant intimates is terribly convincing. As the promised "key to metaphysics," the apparently analytic proposition that the conception of an object is the conception of something rule-governed as opposed to something arbitrary comes perilously close to begging the question of objective validity, and it certainly does not suggest how the objective validity of the particular categories of substance, causation, and interaction is to be derived. The second argument, the mere claim that the consciousness of the unity of the self requires recognition that some form of rules links all of its contents, is simply opaque – at least its truth could hardly have been obvious to Kant's Leibnizian readers, who understood apperception simply as clear perception of the *contents* of consciousness, without any reference to any special unification or organization of consciousness as such, and, moreover, assumed that there could easily be perception without any awareness or "apperception" at all. Thus apperception, in their sense, was hardly an ineliminable condition for the possibility of experience.[2] Even such a transitional figure as Tetens, whom Kant was reading when he wrote this note, understood apperception or self-consciousness as being constituted essentially by the contrast between the undifferentiated feeling of the self and the organized, therefore rule-governed representation of the differentiation of distinct objects from one another.[3] Tetens understood it, that is, in a manner akin to Kant's first argument, which turns on the simple contrast between the objective as rule-governed and the subjective as arbitrary. Had Kant's bare assertion that consciousness of the unity of the self requires a rule-governed connection of its states (even if they are regarded as merely subjective states) been published, his contemporaries could only have been completely stumped.

These observations suggest what would be required to resolve the ambivalent strategy for the transcendental theory of experience which emerged in the *Duisburg Nachlass*. To prevent the question of objective validity from simply being begged, the rule-governed representation of objects must indeed be shown to be a condition of the possibility of the recognition of the unity of the self, and not just taken for granted. But it must also be shown why the self requires any *rules* merely to represent its own unity, let alone rules linking its own states and their change to an independent world of enduring objects governed by laws of action and interaction. Unfortunately, no single argument unequivocally executing such a strategy can be found anywhere in the numerous versions of a transcendental deduction of the categories which Kant wrote during the years from 1781 to 1787. To be sure, Kant wrote as if his work on the deduction were governed by an unequivocal conception of its proper premise and method. Thus, he enunciated a general principle for this deduction in emphatic and apparently unambiguous language, included in both editions of the *Critique*: "The transcendental deduction of all *a priori* concepts has . . . a principle according to which the whole enquiry must be directed, namely, that they must be recognized as *a priori* conditions of the possibility of experience" (A 94 / B 126), precisely because "the *a priori* conditions of a possible experience in general are at the same time conditions of the possibility of objects of experience" (A 111). But this apparently unequivocal statement of Kant's intended strategy masks the fact that Kant used a number of distinct tactics in both his published and unpublished attempts at the transcendental deduction. In fact, each of the two main ideas invoked in Kant's ringing statement is ambiguous, reflecting the ambivalences of his original transcendental theory of experience. Neither the concept of experience, which is to be its premise, nor the conception of displaying the conditions of the possibility of this experience, which is to furnish the method for a transcendental deduction, is univocal. The combination of these two fundamental ambiguities yields the possibility of four crucially different methods for attempting to achieve the strategic objective of the transcendental deduction. What we shall now see is that Kant's various versions include clear attempts to use each of the first three of these methods but that the premises explicitly or tacitly assumed in each of these three attempts undercut any promise of success for them. On the contrary, the fourth method, which is not only the sole method for the transcendental deduction which exploits the original insight of the transcendental theory of experience but also the only one with a promise of success, is no more than hinted at in the actual texts of the deductions from the 1780s. It is, however, precisely the strategy which Kant does exploit in the theory of time-determination contained in the "Analogies of Experience" and the "Refutation of Idealism."

The reader should clearly understand that the assessment of the transcendental deduction to be expounded in the following chapters departs radically from what is currently in danger of becoming the received interpretation. According to this view,[4] Kant's deduction is founded on an unequivocal conception of the transcendental unity of apperception which is expressed by the unexceptionable and analytic principle that in any manifold of representations or data which can furnish the material for a single complex thought, each of the several representations constituting the manifold must be capable of being individually ascribed to the single self which is also to think the whole. But since, as Kant learned from Hume, there is no direct or immediate presentation of a continuing self in the content of any single representation,[5] even the mere self-ascription of the several representations which is required by this principle of apperception must be founded in some sort of combination among these representations. But any combination of representations is nothing other than a judgment which links them. Thus, the mere possibility of linking several representations in the apperception of a single self guarantees the possibility of making judgments about them. But judgments can and must be made in only a determinate number of forms, which are revealed by the logical description of judgmental structure and which are also associated with certain concepts necessary to fit such judgments to representations. These concepts are nothing other than the categories. Hence the mere possibility of apperception ensures the objective validity of the categories by means of the two fundamental assumptions that all apperception implies the combination of representations and that any combination of representations must employ judgments with determinate logical form.

To be sure, advocates of this interpretation will concede that such an abstract argument obviously requires a variety of supplementations in order to achieve all the goals of the transcendental deduction. Of course, the argument requires both an analysis of the logical forms of judgment and a correlation of those logical forms with more object-oriented categories, and it is de rigueur to criticize both Kant's hidebound, prequantificational logic and his arbitrary correlations between the syntactical features of propositions and the more semantical categories necessary to apply such logical forms to representations.[6] More important, it is obvious that the abstract conception of representation employed in the general argument has to be fleshed out with the specifically spatiotemporal nature of human experience in order to yield adequate content to the categories,[7] to prove that the categories apply to genuine external objects (or have "objective reality") and not just to abstract objects of merely possibly true judgments ("objective validity"),[8] or even to confirm what is merely assumed in the more abstract argument – that the actual contents of human experience really are manifold and thus must be linked by the judgmental forms of a discursive intellect.[9] Nevertheless, the advocates of this interpretation all share the conviction that Kant has discovered an unimpeachable connection between apperception or the ascription of individual representations to a continuing self and the subsumability of such representations to judg-

76

ments, and that by means of his emphasis on the determinacy of the logical forms of judgment and the application of such forms to the determinate structure of human intuitions, he has at least shown how to make a start on the proof of the objective validity of the categories.

In what follows, I will argue that this encouraging interpretation seriously misdescribes what Kant supplied in the name of a transcendental deduction of the categories. To be sure, he suggests a general connection between the combinatory nature of human understanding, the logical structure of judgments, and special categories needed to ensure that such logical structures can be used in application to the spatiotemporal materials of human intuition. This connection is most clearly put in what Kant calls "The Clue to the Discovery of All Pure Concepts of the Understanding" (A 76–83 / B 102–9) (which Kant subsequently refers to as the "*metaphysical deduction*" [B 159]), although this passage makes no appeal to the concept of apperception to confirm the underlying claim that all human thought requires a combination of representations. This might then suggest that the work remaining to be done in the transcendental deduction is simply to establish a connection between apperception and judgment in general, on the one hand, and between the conceptual forms of judgment and the forms of human intuition on the other. This is exactly what most contemporary commentators see as the two steps of the transcendental deduction, especially as structured in the second edition of the *Critique*.[10] Plausible as such an argument would be, however, it is simply not what Kant provides in any of the texts of the transcendental deduction. In particular, whether Kant appeals to the general concept of judgments about objects or to the specific concept of apperception in order to establish the synthetic or combinatorial nature of human consciousness – two alternative strategies which Kant does not successfully integrate – we shall see that he does not simply infer from the *judgmental form* of such combination (or its expression) to the application of the categories to the objects of such judgments. Instead, Kant's inferences are always from what he takes to be the *necessary truth* of synthetic judgments about either ordinary objects or the unity of self to the existence of some *a priori* ground for such necessity, which *a priori* ground is only retrospectively identified with the categories associated with the merely logical form of judgments. In other words, what Kant himself explicitly recognized as a transcendental deduction always assumes a *synthetic but necessary truth* for its premise, a fact which is simply omitted from most contemporary reconstructions of his argument.[11] This foundation of Kant's own preferred strategies for the transcendental deduction on assumptions of necessary truth may make Kant's own argument a far less attractive model for a general form of "transcendental argument" than has recently been supposed. We shall also see, however, that the one strategy which is only hinted at in the official texts of the deduction but which is subsequently developed in the "Analogies" and "Refutation of Idealism" – that is, the strategy of demonstrating that the categories are the necessary conditions of empirical time-determinations –

is free from any explicit or tacit assumption that the judgments grounded by the categories are necessary truths and from the concomitant inference of the apriority of the categories directly from the necessity of those judgments.

The true character of Kant's own premises for all forms of the transcendental deduction separate from the theory of time-determination may well be masked by the ambiguity of some of Kant's explicit characterizations of the method of a transcendental deduction of the conditions of the possibility of experience. Kant clearly defines a transcendental "proof" as one which discovers the *a priori* conditions of the possibility of experience (A 782–3 / B 810–11). However, he equally clearly allows room for two different assumptions about the kind of premises which such a proof must have. On the one hand, in attempting to explain the distinction between a "metaphysical exposition" and a "transcendental exposition" which he introduces into the "Transcendental Aesthetic" in his revisions of 1787, Kant says that " a transcendental exposition [is] the explanation of a concept, as a principle from which the possibility of other *a priori* synthetic knowledge can be understood" (B 40). This explicit reference to other synthetic *a priori* knowledge suggests not merely that a transcendental deduction produces some *a priori* knowledge, but rather that (A) a transcendental deduction is the display of the conditions of the possibility of some knowledge-claim which is itself a claim to synthetic *a priori* knowledge. Thus, in the case at hand in the "Transcendental Aesthetic," Kant's argument seems to be that the existence of an *a priori* intuition of space is the condition of the possibility of the *antecedently accepted supposition* that geometry is "a body of *a priori* synthetic knowledge" (B 41). That is, the transcendental exposition of space does not *conclude* that geometry is a form of synthetic *a priori* knowledge; it *presupposes* that, and then argues only the additional claim that space must be a pure form of intuition in order for us to have such synthetic *a priori* knowledge. But on the other hand, in his general statement entitled "The Principles of Any Transcendental Deduction" (§13), which precedes the text of the deduction, Kant simply says that such a deduction is "the explanation of the manner in which concepts can . . . relate *a priori* to their objects" (A 85 / B 117). This distinguishes a transcendental deduction from a merely empirical one by the fact that it produces synthetic *a priori* knowledge, but it does not clearly imply that such a proof *presupposes* any knowledge which is itself synthetic *a priori*. Perhaps even more clearly, Kant's statement in the "Doctrine of Method" that the "proofs of transcendental synthetic propositions" proceed "by showing that experience itself, and therefore the object of experience, would be impossible" without "the possibility of arriving synthetically and *a priori* at some knowledge of things which was not contained in the concepts of them" (A 782–3 / B 810–11) does not imply that such a proof begins by *assuming* any premise which is itself a claim to synthetic *a priori* knowledge. These definitions leave open the possibility (B) that a transcendental deduction is an argument which shows that *a priori* knowledge of the validity of certain categories is a condition of the possibility of some other knowledge which may itself be *a posteriori* rather than *a priori*. Thus, whether Kant's initial conception of experience itself involves a reference to objects or only to the mere representations of a cognitive subject, alternative tactics for a transcendental deduction would seem to be possible, depending on whether or not any *a priori* knowledge about such experience is presupposed by the argument. In fact, we shall see, Kant's own conception of a transcendental deduction always involves a premise which is at least tacitly, if not explicitly, a claim to synthetic *a priori* knowledge. Although only a proof that even empirical judgments have *a priori* conditions might seem like a compelling deduction of such conditions to us, the hard fact is that Kant himself no more than hints at the possibility of a transcendental deduction with such a premise in the official texts of the deduction and instead relegates the exploitation of such a premise – though only such a premise was contemplated in the original transcendental theory of experience – to the subsequent "Analytic of Principles."

Second, Kant's conception of experience itself is indeed ambiguous. Unlike the ambivalence of his conception of the method of a transcendental deduction, this ambivalence cannot be displayed by a single contrast between two explicit definitions; instead, it is revealed by Kant's ambivalent use of each of a number of related terms, such as, of course, "experience" itself, but also "unity of consciousness" and even "apperception." This ambivalence makes it unclear whether such a statement as this – "All experience does indeed contain, in addition to the intuition of the senses through which something is given, a concept of an object as being thereby given" (A 93 / B 126) – is intended as (I) a definition or other sort of *premise* somehow evident from the very concept of experience itself, from which the deduction can *begin,* or rather as (II) a synthetic claim representing the *conclusion* of an argument beginning with some weaker, more purely subjective conception of experience not immediately and analytically understood to require the representation of objects external to and independent of our experience of them. That is, on such a conception, experience might be discovered to be subject to internal constraints which might ultimately require the representation of external objects by means of certain determinate concepts, but the representation of such objects would not be part of the meaning of such a conception of experience. In polemical terms, this makes it unclear whether Kant intends his transcendental deduction to answer an empiricist who concedes the possibility of valid judgments about objects distinct from himself and questions only whether any *a priori* knowledge of such objects is required by those judgments, or to answer a skeptic who, to be sure, concedes the possibility of judgments about his own states but does not recognize that knowledge of objects, let alone *a priori* knowledge of objects, is a condition of the possibility of experience in this weaker sense. Thus, whereas some authors have argued that Kant's deduction can be understood as an unequivocal argument against an empiricist, and thus that it has no antiskeptical intentions,[12] others simply take it for granted that Kant's argument is explicitly intended as a refutation of skepticism.[13] Such confusion about the strategic objectives of the transcendental deduction is a necessary concomitant of Kant's ambivalence about what to include in the concept of experience from which it begins. As we saw, Kant's letter to Herz made it clear in 1772 that the task of a deduction of the objective validity of the categories was to show that the categories could be known *a priori* yet could also be known to apply to objects independent of our representations of them. But whether the completion of this project required only that these *a priori* categories be shown to apply to such objects, or also that it be proved that there really are such objects, was not clarified during the course of the 1780s.

Some might protest that much of this ambivalence can be resolved by the distinction between *synthetic* and *analytic* methods which Kant introduced in the *Prolegomena to Any Future Metaphysics,* the book he published two years after the first edition of the *Critique* as both popularization and defense of it. The latter method, which is illustrated by nothing other than the argument from the synthetic but *a priori* truth of geometry and pure natural science to the existence of the *a priori* forms of intuition and conceptualization which explain such synthetic *a priori* knowledge, would appear to differ from the synthetic method of deduction precisely by its use of an assumption of objective and even *a priori* knowledge which the synthetic method forgoes. But this distinction resolves nothing. This is partly for the crude but inescapable fact that the second edition of the *Critique* incorporates the *Prolegomena*'s argument about geometry as its very "transcendental exposition" of the concept of space,[14] thus completely belying the suggestion that the two works have a different method, or at least that Kant understands the difference between the two methods. But more important, even if the *Critique* is understood to forswear appeal to a specific body of synthetic *a priori* knowledge in a special science such as geometry, that does not mean that is "synthetic" method must forgo a general assumption that we have knowledge of external objects and even that such knowledge is in some sense comprised of necessary truths. And it is yet more obvious that even if the synthetic method of the *Critique* means that it must start from an assumption only of self-knowledge as contrasted to knowledge of objects – which Kant by no means says – this hardly implies that such self-knowledge does not comprise a synthetic *a priori* premise for any further deduction. Thus, the methodological comment in the *Prolegomena* hardly precludes the methodological confusions which we shall find in the *Critique.*[15] An examination of key terms in the *Critique* will put this beyond doubt.

Let us begin with the concept of experience. On the one hand, Kant sometimes clearly defines the very concept of experience as including a reference to objects. For instance, the revised "Analogies of Experience" of 1787 begins by stating that "experience is an empirical knowledge, that is, a knowledge which determines an object through perceptions" (B 218). In light of a definition like this, it would seem that Kant can intend the deduction only as an argument of type I, which shows that some *a priori* knowledge of objects is a condition of the possibility of any judgment about them at all but which assumes from the outset that experience is knowledge of objects. Only two sentences later, however, Kant uses the term "experience" in what is clearly a more subjective sense. Here he says that in "experience indeed perceptions come together only in accidental order, so that no necessity determining their connection is or can be revealed in the perceptions themselves" (B 219); this equates experience with the mere *occurrence* of perceptual states, rather than with any *judgment* that perceptions represent an object. Indeed, as Lewis White Beck has pointed out,[16] this ambiguity is present in the very first lines of the *Critique*, for it is only by means of such an equivocation that Kant could even construct such a statement as "There can be no doubt that all our knowledge begins with experience. For [otherwise] how should our faculty of knowledge . . . work up the raw materials of our sensible impressions into that knowledge of objects which is called experience?" (B 1). Unless Kant first used "experience" to mean merely the raw materials, the subjective states which are the data for all judgment and which may or may not be determined to represent objects, but then subsequently used the term precisely to connote knowledge of objects as opposed to the merely subjective materials of potential claims to knowledge, this passage would not even make sense. But if Kant does use "experience" in this systematically ambiguous way,[17] then the definition of a transcendental deduction as a proof that certain concepts are the conditions of the possibility of experience is obviously ambiguous, wavering between, on the one hand, a conception which assumes that we have knowledge of objects and merely determines the necessary conditions thereof and one, on the other, which shows instead that knowledge of objects, which requires the employment of certain categories, is itself a necessary condition of some form of self-consciousness.

Nor do any of the other phrases which Kant characteristically employs at crucial points in his description or exposition of the transcendental deduction automatically resolve this ambivalence. Sometimes Kant argues that *a priori* knowledge of the categories is a condition of the possibility of the "unity of consciousness," yet this phrase too can connote either the connection among representations by virtue of which they represent an *object* or else the mere fact that several states of mind *as such* are recognized to constitute a manifold of *representations,* whether or not this manifold is also understood to represent an object existing independently of the apprehension of it. So, for example, after first introducing the concept of "transcendental apperception" as a "consciousness of self" at A 107, Kant says that "there can be in us no cognitions, no connection of one cognition with another, without that unity of consciousness which precedes all data of intuition." This suggests that the "unity of consciousness" is a consciousness of a connection that representational states have even regarded merely as such, whether or not they are taken to constitute experience of an object (see also A 108). But on the preceding two pages Kant also identifies "the formal unity of consciousness" as "the unity which the object makes necessary ... in the synthesis of the manifold of representations" and which is "generated in accordance with a rule by means of such a function of synthesis as makes the reproduction of the manifold *a priori* necessary and renders possible a concept in which it is united" (A 105), and he equates the "synthetic unity of consciousness" with the "necessary reproduction" of a manifold of representations produced by a "rule for synthesis" yielded by such a concept as the "concept of a body" (A 106). In these premises, there is no suggestion that unity of consciousness involves any representation of the connection of representations *in the subject,* but rather only that connection by means of which representations can represent "something that has to be distinct from all our representations." (To be sure, Kant then goes on to argue that the necessary numerical identity of the self somehow yields the "transcendental condition" for the necessity of the connection of representations which represent an object distinct from the self [A 106–7], but that is not because the unity of consciousness in the representation of an object is analytically equivalent to the unity of self-consciousness. Indeed, if it were, the transcendental deduction's objective of yielding *synthetic a priori* knowledge would be jeopardized.)

Some of Kant's notes from the period of the *Critique* also suggest this thoroughly objective interpretation of such phrases. This one does so programmatically:

1. *Unity of the object,* to which the manifold is related, that is, concept. Unity of consciousness.

2. Agreement of the manifold with the object according to rules, that is, *truth.*

3. The connection of all rules from a single concept, that is, from *principles,* that is, *perfection.* (R 5745, 18:342)

The last point in this wonderful note suggests Kant's program for replacing objective teleology with the regulative ideal of the systematicity of scientific laws,[18] and the second suggests his program for replacing agreement with rules for correspondence with objects as the criterion (although not the *meaning* of truth); but what is crucial here is the first point, which *equates* unity of consciousness with the "unity of the object." Another note from the early 1780s uses both "experience" and "unity of consciousness" in this sense, so clearly presupposing valid reference to independent objects of thought:

Space and time are themselves nothing other than forms of the combination [*Zusammensetzung*] of objects of sensation; thus, if one there canceled all combination, nothing would remain. Now the unity of consciousness in this combination, so far as it is considered (as) universal, is the concept of the understanding, and this unity belongs to experience as objective cognition; therefore *a priori* concepts of the understanding are also required for the possibility of experience. Something must therefore precede even experience,* whereby it itself becomes possible, but in [experience] alone must all *a priori* cognition have its reality.

*(For the logical form of the understanding in judgments must yet precede, and the appearances (as mere representations) must be regarded as determined in respect of each one of these forms; otherwise no experience can arise therefrom. In place of the word[s] *objects of the senses*, we can also put the word experience.)

(R 5926, 18:388)

The interpretation of "unity of consciousness" as well as "experience" itself as equivalent in meaning to "object of the senses" obviously suggests a deduction of the categories which presupposes that we are conscious of objects and confines its actual argument to the demonstration that the categories are the necessary conditions of such consciousness (though of course even that relatively confined assignment may be difficult enough). Yet it is equally clear that A 107 also suggests the alternative strategy, that consciousness of the unity of the self somehow requires consciousness of objects to begin with.

The term "apperception" is also used in a systematically ambiguous way. Thus, as we just saw, the concept of transcendental apperception is officially introduced as a "consciousness of self" (A 107), and "original apperception" is explicitly described (at A 113, for example) as a "transcendental representation" of "self-consciousness," from which, indeed, "numerical identity is inseparable" and which "is *a priori* certain." This suggests that some claim, indeed an *a priori* claim, about the identity of the self in its different subjective states is the premise of the deduction. Similarly unequivocal references to the self appear in Kant's notes for his anthropology lectures from the period 1783–4:

Sense is either internal or external; only one sense is called internal, and thereby apperception is understood. But this is not a sense; rather, by means of it we are conscious of the representations of outer as well as inner senses. It is only the relation of all representations to their common subject, not to the object.

The form of inner sense is time. The form of apperception is the formal unity in consciousness in general. . . .   (R 224, 15:85)

These comments obviously suggest that apperception is our consciousness of the unified connection of various representations *to the subject* rather than to any external object they might represent. This would in turn suggest that the strategy for any deduction of the necessary conditions of the unity of apperception would have to be that of showing that knowledge of objects ruled by the categories is somehow a condition of the possibility of a form of self-consciousness which is not itself analytically equivalent to such knowledge of objects.

But even before his, as it were, formal introduction of the term "apperception" in the *Critique* at A 107, Kant has already used it without any obvious reference to the self. Thus in discussing the rule by which we construct a triangle, Kant says that "this unity of rule determines all the manifold and limits it to the conditions which make unity of apperception possible"; this suggests that the unity of apperception is that form of connection among representations by which an *object* is represented.

Similarly, §18 of the second-edition text of the deduction equates the "transcendental unity of apperception" with an objective, as opposed to subjective, unity (B 139). Kant suggests that this just means that apperception is rule-governed, as opposed to arbitrary self-consciousness. When he then claims, however, in §19, that this difference is precisely that between (1) that kind of relation among representations by which an object distinct from those representations is presented, and (2) a relation of representations that presents merely "the state of the subject," he is either failing to state his argument for this conclusion or else just equating the objective unity of apperception with the unity by means of which a manifold of representations is distinguished as representing an independent object (B 142).[19] Finally, in as late a work as the draft for the essay on the "real progress" of metaphysics, probably written in 1793,[20] Kant also uses the term "apperception" without any reference to consciousness of the self as such. Here he argues that "determination of objects" always requires the composition (*Zusammensetzung*) of mere intuitions, and thus a "concept of composition" as well as a form of intuition, and then that since such a concept cannot be abstracted from mere empirical intuitions of objects, it must be *a priori* (20:271). He then simply says that "there may be as many *a priori* concepts in the understanding" as there are "modes of synthetic unity of the apperception of the manifold given in intuition,"[21] but there is no suggestion that apperception is an explicit consciousness of the self, as opposed to the unity involved in consciousness of an object as such.

Thus, even though he can clearly contrast apperception as ascription to the subject with apperception as ascription to an object, as in R 5224, Kant also sometimes equates apperception with knowledge of objects or with a strong sense of "experience" equivalent to knowledge of objects. In places where he does so, he is clearly tempted to suggest a strategy for the transcendental deduction that presupposes the possibility of making judgments about objects, but he actually argues merely that such judgments about objects are possible only given *a priori* knowledge of the objective validity of the categories.

Kant can thus gloss his claim that "the categories . . . are nothing but the conditions of thought in a possible experience" with an explanation that "the possibility, indeed the necessity, of these categories rests on the relation in which our entire sensibility, and with it all possible appearances, stand to original apperception" (A 111), without resolving his fundamental ambivalence about the appropriate tactic for the transcendental deduction, for the term "apperception" is just as ambiguous as the word "experience" itself. Further evidence for Kant's equivocal usage will appear as we go through his texts in detail in the next two chapters. But it should be clear by now that Kant is attracted to two different types of argument. On the one hand, Kant sometimes argues for the categories as conditions for the possibility of at least a certain form of self-consciousness *as well as* of the consciousness of objects, without first *equating* these two conceptions, and in at least some versions of his argument the reference to self-consciousness is indispensable. Thus the sentence following that just quoted, in which he links the categories with "original apperception," continues: "In original apperception everything must necessarily conform to the conditions of the thoroughgoing unity of self-consciousness, that is, to the universal functions of synthesis, namely of that synthesis according to concepts in which alone apperception can demonstrate *a priori* its complete and necessary identity" (A 111–12). But, on the other hand, Kant is also sometimes content to argue only that the possibility of judgments about objects requires *a priori* knowledge of the categories, even to label as a "complete deduction of the categories" an argument which maintains only this[22] without mentioning apperception at all, and in such arguments he is satisfied to treat the possibility of apperception as identical to the possibility of judgments about objects.

If we combine the alternative styles of argument allowed by the ambiguity of such terms as "experience" and even "apperception" itself with Kant's failure to explain clearly whether or not a transcendental deduction requires a premise which already claims synthetic *a priori* knowledge, we see at once that *four* tactics are available, at least in principle, for a proof that *a priori* knowledge of the objective validity of the categories is a condition of the possibility of experience. In all cases, of course, the existence of experience itself must be assumed. But experience may be equated with knowledge of objects given by perception and then, depending on whether or not it is also assumed that any claim to knowledge of objects already involves *some* form of synthetic *a priori* knowledge, the deduction may take either of two forms:

IA: Judgments about empirical objects are possible, and these actually contain some synthetic *a priori* knowledge which implies the *further a priori* knowledge of the categories.

or

IB: Judgments about empirical objects are possible, and although these do not themselves *assert* any claims to *a priori* knowledge, they do *presuppose a priori* knowledge of the categories.

Alternatively, experience may be understood merely subjectively – that is, equated with the possibility (cf. B 131–2) of apperception as a form of mere *self*-consciousness, rather than consciousness of objects other than the self. In that case, Kant's remaining ambivalence about the kind of premise requisite for a transcendental proof yields these two possible forms of argument:

IIA: The possibility of apperception as *itself* a kind of synthetic *a priori* knowledge implies *a priori* knowledge of the objective validity of the categories, that is, *a priori* knowledge of their application to objects regarded as distinct from the self.

and

IIB: The possibility of apperception even as a form of merely *empirical* knowledge of the self nevertheless implies *a priori* knowledge of the application of the categories to objects regarded as existing independently of the self.

In the next two chapters we shall see that Kant's attempts at a transcendental deduction throughout the 1780s clearly include arguments intended to be of forms IA, IB, and IIA – although his attempt to execute method IB – that is, an argument that even empirical knowledge of objects involves *a priori* conditions – quickly collapses into an argument which, like IA and IIA, really assumes from the outset the possibility of some synthetic *a priori* knowledge. Indeed, on at least some occasion Kant describes each of these tactics as the unique method of the deduction. We shall also see, however, that tactics IA and IIA contain an outright assumption of a claim to knowledge of necessary truth that is too strong to furnish the premise for a compelling proof against either skeptic or empiricist that we can know *a priori* that the extralogical concepts of substance, causation, and interaction apply to objects understood to exist independently of our representations of them, and that Kant's attempt to exploit strategy IB, although it does not involve an initial assumption of necessary truth, quickly introduces one by fallacious inference. This leaves only the possibility that an argument of type IIB – that is, a proof that even empirical knowledge of the self has *a priori* conditions – can ultimately be regarded as a plausible tactic for accomplishing the objectives of the transcendental deduction. But although such a method is none other than that first intimated in the *Duisburg Nachlass* and finally developed in the theory of time-determination in the "Analogies of Exprience" and the "Refutation of Idealism," it must be clear that Kant barely hints at it in the official text of the deduction and does not, in fact, seem to regard it as offering a genuine transcendental deduction.

The implications of the present schema for the classification of Kant's tactics for the transcendental deduction can be emphasized by contrasting the present interpretation with the most significant work on the deduction in the last decade, Dieter Henrich's *Identität und Objektivität*. Henrich argues that Kant's texts contain *two* different kinds of deduction, which he calls the "objectivity" deduction and the "identity" deduction. This obviously corresponds to my distinction between type I and II deductions: that is, between deductions of the categories which presuppose that we have knowledge of external objects, and deductions which additionally attempt to argue that knowledge of objects is itself a necessary condition of some form of the unity of apperception or self-consciousness. However, Henrich does not draw my distinction between A and B: that is, between deductions which argue for *a priori* knowledge of the categories only on the basis of some prior claim to *a priori* knowledge, and those which assume only empirical claims to knowledge. Thus, his interpretation does not reveal the unfortunate fact that many of Kant's efforts at an "objectivity" deduction reach their conclusion by simply equating empirical knowledge of objects with some claim to necessary truth. Moreover, where Henrich's interpretation does recognize an explicit claim to necessary truth as the premise of the deduction – in his most favored version of the "identity" deduction, which assumes "Cartesian certainty" of the unity of apperception,[23] a version of what I call tactic IIA – it does not acknowledge the philosophical problems involved. Thus Henrich does not concede that method IIB, although a form of "identity" deduction which is not unequivocally recognized as a transcendental deduction by Kant, offers Kant's only chance for accomplishing the objective of the transcendental deduction.[24]

The deduction and time-determination

In spite of Kant's hesitation about using an argument with no initial claim to necessary truth as a transcendental deduction, several pieces of evidence put it beyond doubt that Kant sometimes recognized at least that the deduction could not succeed without acknowledgment of the temporality of experience. A pair of sketches of the deduction, apparently from the period in which Kant was reflecting on the initial criticisms of the *Critique* and preparing the *Prolegomena to Any Future Metaphysics* as his reply (1782–3), clearly suggest that providing a unique ordering of representations in time is the fundamental task of the understanding and thus the basic function of its *a priori* categories. First, this programmatic note:

> The *quaestio facti* is, in what manner one has first come into possession of a concept; the *qvaestio iuris*, with what right one possesses and uses it.
> The universality and necessity in the use of the pure concepts of the understanding betray their origin and that it must be either entirely unreliable and false or else nonempirical.
> In the pure sensibility, the pure imagination, and the pure apperception lies *a priori*[25] the ground of the possibility of all empirical knowledge and of the synthesis according to concepts, which has objective reality. . . .
> All representations, from wherever they may come, are yet in the end modifications of the inner sense, and their unity must be regarded from this point of view. To receptivity to them corresponds a spontaneity of *synthesis*. . . .
> (R 5636, 18:267–8)

This irrefutably indicates that the role of the active synthesis of the understanding is to provide representations with a unique temporal ordering, although the reference to "inner sense" expresses *only* the temporality of the representations and their unity and does *not* unequivocally imply that in such a synthesis the representations are *regarded as* states of the self rather than representations of objects. Nor does this passage explain why any special rules are necessary for the spontaneous synthesis of the understanding which grounds the unity of representation in time. Kant's next note also falls short of providing such an explanation, though it does explicitly assert that it is by means of the categories that the understanding accomplishes its fundamental task of time-determination:

(Key – through the nature of synthetic *a priori* judgments.)

Were space not given *a priori* in our subject as the form of its (sensible) intuition, and [were not] objects outside us given in this form alone, no synthetic propositions, which at the same time hold of real external objects, would be possible *a priori*. For should we derive the representations from the objects as they are given in themselves, then everything would rest on experience, and no *a priori* synthesis together with necessity of judgments would be valid, at least not objectively. Were time not given subjectively and therefore *a priori* as the form of inner sense (and an understanding, to compare it), then apperception would not cognize *a priori* the relation in the existence of the manifold, for in itself time is no object of perception; apperception would, to be sure, determine the succession and coexistence of representations, but not the place of objects in time; thus it could not constitute any experience, unless it had rules of the time which is determinable in the object, but these it cannot take from the object.

I ask everyone, from whence he [would] derive the mathematical and necessary (synthetic) propositions about things in space, if space were not already the condition in us *a priori* of the possibility of the empirical representation of objects, through which these can be given to us. We determine *a priori* the manifold of appearance according to existence by means of the categories. I ask: From where should this synthesis be derived, if time, the condition of the possibility of all perception, did not lie [in us] *a priori* and if the rules of the determination of all existence in this time ... prior to all perception did not flow from the subjective constitution of our sensibility, on which everything objective rests.

(R 5637, 18:271–2)

In this case, Kant does resolve his underlying ambivalence in favor of the view (I) that rules are required to *contrast* experience of objects to non-rule-governed, merely subjective consciousness, but what is important for us now is only his explicit assertion that the rules of the understanding have their fundamental employment in the task of determining temporal relations. And what is even more intriguing, though we are far from ready to explore the significance of it at this point, is Kant's suggestion that this role for rules of the understanding is somehow required by the fact that time is not itself an "object of perception."

A marginal comment which Kant added to his own copy of the first edition of the *Critique* (thus presumably before the appearance of the second edition in 1787) also emphasizes that the fundamental task of the understanding is connected with time-determination: "The synthetic unity of apperception in relation to the transcendental power of imagination is the pure understanding. This transcendental power is that which determines all appearances in general in relation to time, according to rules which are valid *a priori*" (*Loses Blatt* B 12, 23:18). But we do not need to rely solely on texts external to the *Critique* for evidence of Kant's ultimate recognition that the transcendental deduction must revolve on the necessary conditions for time-determination. At least once in the *Critique* itself Kant also suggests that any successful tactic for the transcendental deduction must turn on the temporality of experience. In both editions of the book, Kant makes it explicit that all aspects of his campaign are to be governed by the single underlying premise that any form of knowledge whatsoever involves a connection of diverse representations and that such a connection requires a mental act of combination: thus, "knowledge is a whole in which representations stand compared and connected," so that "if each representation were completely foreign to every other, standing apart in isolation, no such thing as knowledge would ever arise" (A 97); similarly, "the combination (*conjunctio*) of a manifold in general can never come to us through the senses, and cannot, therefore, be already contained in the pure form of a sensible intuition," for "it is an act of spontaneity," and therefore "all combination – whether we are conscious of it or not, whether it is a combination of the manifold of intuition, empirical or nonempirical, or of various concepts – is an act of understanding" (B 129–30). But in the first edition Kant also makes it clear that the combination which is essential to knowledge, whether of the subjective or of the objective, must ultimately be understood as *determination of temporal relations*: Since it is *by time* that the diverse representations are separated – "for each representation, *insofar as it is contained in a single moment,* can never be anything but absolute unity" – it is therefore *in time* that all representations "must be ordered, connected, and brought into relation" (A 99).

These statements do indeed reveal the basis of what is ultimately Kant's only successful strategy for completing the task he set himself in 1772 and first tried to accomplish in 1774 and 1775. But, crucial as they are, the unequivocal evidence of these few statements cannot obscure the fact that Kant does indeed attempt a variety of tactics for his deduction. Many if not most of these methods make no use of the temporality of experience at all, and even when Kant does place temporality in its central role, he is not immediately clear whether he should begin with the temporal relations of objects as opposed to subjective consciousness or rather with the temporality of self-consciousness itself. The explanation of this fact is not obvious. On the one hand, Kant may simply have been tempted by tactics for the deduction which appeared to be a great deal simpler as well as more compelling than the theory of time-determination; on the other, he may well have been driven to seek these alternative tactics by the undeniable fact that although he was persuaded of the centrality of time-determination almost from the outset of his search for a proof of the objective validity of the categories, he did not even begin to develop a theory of time-determination that could accomplish such a fundamental task until he was well into his revisions of the *Critique* for the edition of 1787 – and by this time he could not very readily retract his other suggestions for the argument. But whatever the explanation for Kant's multiplicity of tactics, the evidence for it is ample. In the next two chapters, we shall consider Kant's attempts to accomplish the goals of the deduction by methods IA,

IB, and IIA. In the subsequent two parts of the book, parts III and IV, we shall consider his actual execution of the suggested method IIB, the theory that empirical time-determinations, even merely subjective ones, have *a priori* conditions.

4

The deduction from knowledge of objects

In this chapter, we shall consider versions of the deduction which assume (I) the possibility of knowledge of objects from the outset and which attempt to show only that such knowledge presupposes *a priori* knowledge of the categories – arguments, if you will, targeted at empiricists but not at skeptics. Such arguments can initially be divided into those (A) which assume some claim to synthetic *a priori* knowledge from the outset and those (B) which ostensibly do not – although we shall also see that Kant's actual execution of strategy IB involves an early and fallacious introduction of a necessarily true premise.

Among the three styles of argument that we shall examine under the rubric IA, only one follows the model of the transcendental exposition of space (B 40–1) by postulating a specific body of synthetic *a priori* knowledge (indeed, the *same* body of knowledge, that is, geometry) which can be shown to have further *a priori* conditions (although, in this case, pure concepts rather than pure intuitions). But in the other two types of argument to be considered under this rubric – namely, Kant's deductions of the categories from the concept of *judgment* (IA.ii) and from the very concept of an *object* itself (IA.iii) – the assumption that judgment or knowledge of objects is *universal* and *necessary* and therefore involves an *a priori* element is so quickly introduced that it seems best to regard these as arguments in which Kant explicitly assumes that even empirical knowledge has a synthetic *a priori* component which can be furnished only by the categories.

In the course of this chapter, it will become obvious that arguments which make an outright assumption that we can claim knowledge of synthetic but necessary truths must have little force against an empiricist, and of course an argument (such as IB) which illegitimately assumes a necessarily true premise will fare even worse. Thus, Kant's tactics for a proof of the objective validity of *a priori* categories must fall back upon the general strategy (II) of showing that some form of self-consciousness requires knowledge of objects, which knowledge, in turn, requires such categories; hence, Kant's refutation of empiricism must be embedded in his refutation of skepticism. But in the next chapter we shall also see that Kant's attempt to derive the *a priori* but objective validity of the categories from the *a priori* certainty of apperception is also subject to serious objection. In the end, then, Kant's only hope for attaining the objective of the deduction is strategy IIB, showing that even empirical knowledge of the temporal determination of the self requires *a priori* knowledge of the categories – that strategy which lies closest to the original inspiration of the transcendental theory of experience in the *Duisburg Nachlass* but which Kant is least willing, in the 1780s, to acknowledge as the method of the transcendental deduction.

IA: *A priori* knowledge of objects

We begin with those versions of the deduction in which Kant assumes both that we have knowledge of objects and that such knowledge has an *a priori* component, and in which he really tries to argue only for the identification of the categories with this component. As I have mentioned, the first of these three forms of argument alone may seem to fit this description immediately, but Kant's transcendental deductions from the concept of judgment and from the concept of an object, to which by far the bulk of his texts on the transcendental deduction are devoted, will quickly be seen to have a substantially similar form.

IA.i: Categories and the pure manifold of intuition

Precisely because it does assume that empirical knowledge of objects contains an *a priori* component which is clearly distinct from *a priori* knowledge of the categories themselves but which yet requires the addition of the categories to this other *a priori* element in order to achieve complete knowledge of objects, this first argument may avoid the charge of *petitio principii* which will threaten the next two, but it may do this only at the cost of failing to establish any genuine connection between premise and conclusion at all. This argument is suggested in "The Synthesis of Reproduction in Imagination," a section of the first-edition text of the transcendental deduction. Kant states that as part of the combination of the manifold, which, by his underlying assumption, is necessary to produce any knowledge, reproduction of relevant past representations is required, and "this law of reproduction presupposes that appearances are themselves subject to ... certain rules" (A 100).[1] By the arguments of the "Transcendental Aesthetic," the manifold to be reproduced even in the case of empirical objects includes pure *a priori* intuitions. But if such intuitions are included among those which must be reproduced, then the rules according to which this synthesis of reproduction takes place must also be *a priori*, Although the argument is not brought to a conclusion, it seems obvious that Kant means to suggest that such *a priori* rules can be only the categories. Thus:

For if we can show that even our purest *a priori* intuitions yield no knowledge, save insofar as they contain a combination of the manifold such as renders a thorough-going synthesis of representations possible, then this synthesis of imagination is likewise grounded, antecedently to all experience, upon *a priori* principles, and we must assume a pure transcendental synthesis of imagination as conditioning the very possibility of all experience.

(A 101)

But the problem with such an argument is obvious. Even if the underlying assumption that the reproduction of a manifold of representations requires *some kind of rules* is conceded – indeed even if for some reason we concede that such reproduction must require rules known *a priori* – the question pressed in our examination of the *Duisburg Nachlass* immediately arises: Why should our *a priori* knowledge of the geometry or temporal topology of empirical objects – which is surely the only *a priori* knowledge, and thus form of combination, which can be derived from the "Transcendental Aesthetic" – require any *a priori* rules *other* than those of geometry and the corresponding mathematics of time themselves? And of course there is no mention of substance, causation, or interaction in these. To take the examples with which Kant himself follows the passage just quoted, what could the *a priori* rules needed "to draw a line in thought ... or even to represent to myself some particular number" (A 102) possibly have to do with *a priori* concepts, for instance, of substance and causation? The answer appears to be: nothing. Although it will ultimately be of great importance for Kant to argue that empirical determination of unique positions in space and time requires the categories in spite of our *a priori* knowledge from pure intuition alone that each empirical object must have a unique position as a part of the single whole of space or time,[2] the present argument fails to suggest an adequate basis for the assumption that the "transcendental synthesis of the imagination" required for the construction of pure rather than empirical objects of intuition must be guided by the categories, as opposed to purely mathematical axioms derivable from acquaintance with the pure forms of intuition alone.

Kant must have recognized the inadequacy of such an argument, tempting only in its simplicity, for we do not find it repeated in the *Critique*. Indeed, the obvious inadequacy of such a deduction could easily make its very ascription to Kant, based as it is on a few lines of text ripped out of context, seem quite unjustifiable. But there is independent evidence of Kant's temptation by such an argument. A note from the early 1780s – which, since it begins with an attempt to properly define the nature of Kant's "putative idealism," must be from the period in 1782–3 when he was grappling with the charges of subjective idealism that called forth the *Prolegomena*[3] – includes this paragraph as its whole reprise of the deduction, indeed of the "Transcendental Analytic":

For judgments, concepts are required, and for the concepts intuitions. The concepts, insofar as they apply to *a priori* intuitions, cannot originate through the individual empirical consciousness of the manifold; otherwise they would not be concepts of the connection of the intuition; rather they are possible only through the connection of the intuition in an apperception by means of the unity of the synthesis thereof. And therein consist the *a priori* concepts.   (R 5642, 18:280)

This could just mean that *any* act of combination entails the use of *a priori* concepts, an argument which, as we shall see, Kant does make elsewhere, but the statement that *a priori* concepts for connection are required *insofar* as it is *a priori* intuitions which must be combined suggests that in Kant's view *a priori* intuitions clearly require *a priori* concepts for their synthesis. But then of course the question again arises, why should these concepts be the categories instead of just the concepts of geometry or chronometry themselves?

Even in Kant's own notes, expositions of this type of argument are not common. Far more frequent are arguments which do not attempt to derive the *a priori* validity of the categories from our *a priori* intuition of the *form* of all objects, empirical as well as pure, but rather arguments which assume that we have knowledge of objects, not just meaningless sequences of representations, and then attempt to derive a role for categories known *a priori* from the necessity and universality contained in the very concept of a *judgment* or even of an *object* itself.

IA.ii: Categories and the concept of judgment

The tactic for the deduction in which Kant obviously felt the most confidence in the years immediately following the publication of the first edition of the *Critique,* and which clearly continued to enjoy much of his confidence even at the time of the second edition, is the argument that the very idea of *judgment* itself implies knowledge of a *necessary and universal* connection, which can be explained only by the supposition that we have *a priori* knowledge of the categories in terms of which such judgments are made. Particular versions of such an argument assert that a judgment is a connection among representations which is necessary and therefore universal as well, or universally valid and therefore necessary as well, or simply both necessarily and universally valid, and that this is so even in the case of a judgment concerning an empirical object. From the unquestioned assumption that no amount of purely empirical evidence ever justifies a genuine claim of universality and necessity,[4] it then follows that it cannot be the particular *contents* of empirical judgments which account for these characteristics. So it follows that there must be something which is known *a priori* even about empirical objects, in order to account for the universality and necessity of empirical judgments, and that this must be some sort of rule or rules valid for both such objects and such judgments independently of their content. From here it is only a short step to *a priori* knowledge of the categories.

The preface to the *Metaphysical Foundations of Natural Science,* which was written while Kant still smarted from the sting of the initial criticisms of the *Critique,* especially the charge that the deduction, which "should have been the clearest" part of the work, was instead the "most obscure" (4:474n), tries to remedy the situation with the bold assertion that "the problem as to *how* experience is possible by means of those categories . . .

can be solved almost by a single conclusion from the precisely determined definition of a judgment in general (an act by which given representations first become cognitions of an object)" (4:475n). Kant also gives the concept of judgment itself a very prominent role in the versions of the deduction included in the *Prolegomena* and the second edition of the *Critique*. But of course most of these expositions weave together a number of separable considerations. Perhaps the clearest versions of the deduction directly from the concept of judgment can be found in several of Kant's sketches from the period 1783–4.

The first of these is a long sketch (R 5923) which Kant wrote in these years with the explicit title "Deduction of Pure Cognitions *A Priori*" – and which, interestingly enough, he inscribed in his interleaved copy of Baumgarten's *Metaphysica* next to the paragraph on *causa et causatum* (§307).[5] Kant begins his argument with a firm contrast between the connection inherent in experience as knowledge of objects and the absence of any special form of connection which (in a deduction of the general type I) is assumed to be characteristic of the manifold of representations, regarded as mere modifications of our subjective state. Indeed, this passage is exceptionally good evidence for Kant's attraction to the weak or "regressive" strategy for the deduction beginning from a conception of experience itself which already includes a claim to the objectivity of knowlege: "But the consciousness of perceptions relates all representations only to our self as modifications of our condition; they are therefore separated among themselves, and in particular they are not cognitions of any particular thing, and are not related to any object. They are therefore not yet experience." In a passage of this kind, the reference to the self serves to explain only the *disconnection* of representations which must be rectified by the synthetic efforts of the understanding, culminating in the making of judgments; the *unity* of self-consciousness as such plays no role whatever in the argument. Following this contrast between genuine experience and merely subjective modifications of the self, Kant then asserts that the connection which noncognitive subjective states lack is precisely the kind of connection asserted by a *judgment*:

If we question logic as to what can count as knowledge in general, then a concept is a representation which is related to an object and designates it, and when we connect ... one concept with another in a judgment, we think something of the object that is designated through a given concept – that is, we cognize it when we judge about it. All knowledge, thus that of experience also, consists of judgments. ... Therefore experience is possible only through judgments.

But such judgments cannot be grounded on passively received empirical intuitions alone. Even though "perceptions, to be sure, constitute the empirical materials" of such judgments, "the relation of these [judgments] to an object, and knowledge of the latter through perception, cannot depend upon empirical consciousness alone"; for a judgment, Kant assumes, always asserts a *necessary connection*: "But the form of every judgment consists in the objective unity of consciousness of the given concepts, that is, in the consciousness that these *must* belong to one another, and on that account designate an object, in the (complete) representation of which they are always to be found." Since such universality cannot be grounded in the empirical content of the judgment, it can be explained only by the assumption that there are rules in accordance with which such judgments, regardless of their content, must be made, and clearly, though Kant does not spell this out, rules which are independent of any "material" of empirical intuition must be capable of being known *a priori*. In addition, Kant plainly supposes that these rules must derive from the "moments of the understanding" itself, that is, the categories:

But this necessity of connection is not a representation of empirical origin; rather it presupposes a rule which must be given *a priori,* that is, unity of consciousness which takes place *a priori.* This unity of consciousness is contained in the moments of the understanding in judgment, and only that is an object in relation to which unity of the consciousness of the manifold of representation is thought *a priori.*
(R 5923, 18:385-7)

From the unstated assumption that we do indeed experience empirical objects to be contrasted with our own states of mind, and from the stated assumption that judgments about even empirical objects assert genuinely necessary connections, Kant infers that such judgments must presuppose rules known *a priori,* which must obviously be grounded in some "moments" or categories inherent in our understanding itself.

Another note written in the same interleaved pages varies the argument by emphasizing the *universality* rather than the necessity of judgment and also by explicitly introducing the term "category" (though by means of a definition which is much too comprehensive), but the basic idea remains the same. After noting that synthetic *a priori* judgments always concern appearances, rather than things in themselves, because synthetic judgments always require intuitions (refining and defending his conception of transcendental idealism is never far from his thoughts in this period), Kant goes on to write:

[A] category is the representation of the relation of the manifold of intuition to a universal consciousness (to the universality of consciousness, which is really objective). The relation of representations to the universality of consciousness, consequently the transformation of empirical and particular unity of consciousness, which is merely subjective, into a consciousness which is universal and objective, belongs to logic. This unity of consciousness, insofar as it is universal and can be represented *a priori,* is the pure concept of the understanding. This can therefore be nothing other than the universal of the unity of consciousness, which constitutes the objective validity of a judgment.
(R 5927, 18:388-9)

As we shall see in our examination of Kant's next variant of tactic IA, Kant goes on from here to introduce the deduction from the concept of an object; it is certainly unclear whether it is in the concept of an object or a judgment that he supposes the ultimate basis of the claim to universality and necessity lies. But confining ourselves to this one paragraph, we see that Kant clearly equates the *objective* validity of a judgment with its claim to *universal* validity – though he leaves it equally unclear whether by such "universality" he means that a predicate applies to all members of some class of *objects* to which the particular object of the judgment belongs, or rather that the judgment must be accepted by all *cognitive subjects* who consider it.[6] But in any case Kant takes it as evident that no claim to universal validity can be grounded in the empirical content of consciousness itself. It must depend instead on a category. Our knowledge of the objective validity of any judgment requires *a priori* knowledge of the validity of a category for the object of the judgment, regardless of the empirical content of its intuition.

We may now consider a version of the deduction from the conception of judgment itself that Kant actually published, namely that of the *Prolegomena to Any Future Metaphysics*. To fully understand both this argument and that of the second-edition text of the deduction, however, we must now pause to consider a section of the *Critique* which was mentioned in Chapter 3 but not considered at any length, the so-called metaphysical deduction of the categories. This argument needs to be briefly expounded only so that we can be clear about the questions it leaves unanswered. In this section, Kant defines a judgment as the "mediate knowledge of an object," or a "function of the understanding" by means of which an object is represented by the connection of one concept which subsumes it by virtue of one of its properties with other concepts also subsuming it (A 68 / B 93). "All judgments are accordingly functions of unity among our representations, since, namely, instead of an immediate representation [i.e., an intuition] a *higher* representation, which subsumes this [representation] and others, is used for cognition of the object, and many possible cognitions are thereby drawn together into one" (A 69 / B 94). Whatever else is true of it, then, all genuine knowledge, as opposed to mere occurrence or possession of intuition, is expressed in or constituted by judgments. Kant then asserts that there are certain *logical forms* within which all judgments must be cast, or, as we might say using language of a later day, there is a unique set of possibilities for the logical syntax of any judgment. These logical forms are derived from traditional Aristotelian logic and are tabulated by Kant in the *Critique*'s table of the "Logical Functions of Judgment" (A 70 / B 95).[7] According to this table, each judgment must be formed by means of (1) a specific "quantity": It may be universal, particular, or singular; (2) a "quality": It may be affirmative, negative, or what Kant calls "infinite"; (3) a "relation": It may be a hypothetical, categorical, or disjunctive judgment; and finally, what Kant calls (4) a "modality": The judgment may be problematic, assertoric, or apodictic; that is, assert a possibility, actuality, or necessity.[8] Thus, a particular judgment might affirm (quality) that a particular predicate may (modality) characterize (relation) all (quantity) objects to which some other predicate applies, or affirm that if a judgment of the first form is true then some other judgment is also true (the hypothetical relation) or not (the disjunctive relation), and so on. Each judgment has some logical form representing one of the possible permutations of the twelve items in the table of the logical functions of judgment. Then, Kant argues, there must also be some special concepts by means of which the *objects* of such judgments are conceived, in order for these logical or syntactical forms of judgment actually to yield judgments about objects. The diverse contents of empirical intuition must be combined to yield knowledge of objects; such knowledge must be expressed by judgments; so the combination must take place in a way that permits judgments with their characteristic logical forms to be asserted of the objects or the "synthesis of representations." And this, Kant claims, will be possible only if "the same understanding, through the same operations by which in concepts, by means of analytical unity, it produced the logical form of a judgment, also introduces a transcendental content into its representations, by means of the synthetic unity of the manifold in intuition in general" (A 79 / B 105). In order to do this, Kant then concludes, the understanding must organize the combinations of representations which it synthesizes with certain *categories* corresponding to the *logical forms* of judgment; the *concepts of objects* must take certain forms if the logical forms of judgment are to apply to them. Thus Kant generates his famous "Table of Categories," which is a list of the possible forms of properties, relations, and status of objects by virtue of which judgments with the logical forms previously tabulated can be asserted of the objects. Here Kant claims, then, that it is by virtue of the unity, plurality, or totality of a group of objects that universal, particular, or singular judgments can be made; reality, negation, or limitation in objects which allows affirmative, negative, and infinite judgments to be made; relations of inherence and subsistence, causality and dependence, or community among objects or their properties which permit categorical, hypothetical, or disjunctive judgments to be made; and objective possibility, existence, and necessity, or their opposites, which permit problematic, assertoric, and apodictic judgments to be made (A 80 / B106).

Kant's argument appears straightforward enough but is widely recognized to raise serious questions about our *a priori* knowledge of the objective validity of the categories. First, even if we grant the soundness of Kant's logic and thus concede the correctness and the uniqueness of his tabulation of logical forms, why should we assume that *all* of the logical forms which judgments about empirical objects in particular might take must in fact be used? Most obviously, of course, why should we assume that we must be able to make hypothetical as well as categorical judgments, and thus have a *priori* knowledge of the objective validity of the vital category of cause and effect? Second, what is the basis for Kant's correlation of the categories to the logical functions of judgment? In some cases, to be sure, his correlations seem unimpeachable; thus, it is hard to see how we could make judgments about "all" and "some" unless we could divide the contents of our experience into discrete objects – that is, unless we could experience both unity and plurality. But in other cases, the connection is less obvious: In particular, it is hard to see why we should be able to make hypothetical – that is, "if ... then _____" – judgments only if we can detect *causal* connections among objects, and disjunctive judgments – that is, "either ... or _____" judgments – only if objects *interact*. To put this point in the terms suggested by my earlier discussion of the *Duisburg Nachlass,* how does Kant intend to make the transition from the logical forms of judgment to the *extralogical* concepts with which the categories have been identified? Or, since Kant had *contrasted* purely *logical* relations of opposition or dependence with *real* relations of opposition or causation at least since 1763 (see the essay on *Negative Quantities* of that year[9]), why should it suddenly seem obvious that it is only on the basis of the real relations which Kant has now correlated with them that the logical functions of relation should be applicable to empirical objects? This is to say, of course, that it is hard to see how the metaphysical deduction can advance Kant's arguments with respect to the very categories with which he is really most concerned. And it is equally hard to see how the metaphysical deduction could yield more than the hypothetical conclusion that if we do make judgments about empirical objects they must be conceived in certain ways, and thus yield the categorical and antiskeptical conclusion that we in fact can make judgments about such objects.

We have seen that Kant was uncertain about the antiskeptical intentions of the deduction and thus might not have seen the last of these points as a problem. But even if it is not this point which is to be resolved by the addition of a transcendental to the metaphysical deduction,[10] it would certainly seem natural to suppose that the transcendental deduction is intended to resolve the other issues left open by the metaphysical one, and thus that it is intended to demonstrate precisely that all of the objective categories properly correlated with the logical functions of judgment must be used if experience is to be possible at all. What we shall now see, however, is that in those versions of the transcendental deduction apparently most closely connected with the metaphysical one – namely, the deduction from the concept of judgment itself – Kant does not pursue these issues. Instead, he presents precisely the entirely independent argument that we have already encountered that any judgment's claim to universal and necessary validity implies *a priori* grounds, which are only retrospectively identified with the categories which the metaphysical deduction is assumed to have adequately correlated with the logical functions of judgment.

This pattern of argument is evident in both the *Prolegomena* and in the heart of the transcendental deduction in the second edition of the *Critique.* The argument of the *Prolegomena* proceeds in the following way. The most fundamental premise of this argument is obviously the strong notion of experience that already assumes knowledge of objects: "Experience consists in the synthetic connection of appearances (perceptions) in one consciousness, insofar as this is necessary" (§22, 4:305). But Kant tries to

99

exploit this fundamental assumption by specific implications of the concept of judgment, and so he introduces a notorious distinction between "judgments of experience" and mere "judgments of perception" (§18, 4:298). Kant characterizes the latter as "judgments which hold only for ourselves, that is, for our subject," and thus as judgments which convey nothing more than a report of subjective state, but he also describes them as judgments which require "only the logical connection of perceptions in a thinking subject." A judgment of experience, however, possesses a "new relation, namely to an object," and is not understood merely to report the subjective condition of the particular subject entertaining it; rather we intend such a judgment "to be valid for ourselves at all times and also for everyone else as well." Kant then interprets this as the intention that "all judgments [of experience] concerning the same object must agree among themselves," and so concludes that "the objective validity of the judgment of experience signifies nothing other than its necessary universal validity," or that "objective validity and necessary universal validity (for everyone) are equivalent concepts" (§19, 4:298).[11] Any such claim to universal and necessary validity, however, as a claim to *a priori* knowledge, goes beyond mere empirical intuition and instead requires "special *concepts originally generated in the understanding*" (§18), and, although Kant does not clearly spell this out, since these concepts are not involved in the merely "logical connections of perceptions" which are judgments of perception, they must be *other than* any merely logical concepts. Thus extralogical categories, conceptions of real rather than logical form, must be known *a priori*. The categories are not, in fact, just the necessary conditions of the logical form of empirical judgments but are rather "the condition of universal validity of empirical judgments" (§19). It is from the conception of judgments of experience *as universal and necessary* that the need for categories is deduced, and not from the more neutral idea suggested by the metaphysical deduction that certain special concepts of objects may be needed in order to subsume them under the logical functions of judgment.

The question of the transition from this general call for categories to the specific notions of substance, causation, and interaction thus still remains, but before considering that, a general observation about this argument is required. It must be noted that Kant's argument turns on the contrast between merely subjective reports of "sensible conditions" (§19, 4:299) – how I happen to be affected now, or even how many people may usually happen to be affected in some perceptual circumstance[12] – and objectively valid reports about what must be the case. His argument also rests on the additional claim that although the logical forms of judgment can be employed in the former, they do not suffice for the latter; that is why extralogical categories are required. It is often asked how the initial distinction is to be reconciled with Kant's view that the unity of apperception, thus apparently any form of self-consciousness itself, entails the use of the categories. How can judgments of perception express any form of self-consciousness, yet not use the categories? Commentators have gone to great lengths to answer this question,[13] but the obvious answer is that the notion of judgments of perception cannot be reconciled with the assumption that categories figure in any form of self-consciousness at all, precisely because this notion is an expression of Kant's type I premise that there is a fundamental contrast between self-consciousness and objective experience, rather than of his distinct type II premise that the use of the categories is ultimately a necessary condition of self-consciousness itself. The difficulties that all commentators have experienced in trying to reconcile the distinction between judgments of perception and experience with Kant's notion of the categorial basis of the transcendental unity of apperception, in other words, is additional evidence for Kant's fundamental ambivalence about the proper premise for the transcendental deduction. The distinction is not to be reconciled with a deduction based on the categorial basis of all apperception, but only superseded by it. We shall soon see that even when a version of the distinction reappears in the second-edition text of the deduction, in spite of Kant's clear attempt to begin that argument from assumptions about self-consciousness alone, this is evidence only of Kant's continuing confusion about his two quite distinct strategies for the deduction.

That Kant's contrast between the logical forms which suffice to formulate judgments of perception and the categories which are necessary for objectivity (that is, universally and necessarily valid judgments of experience) is vital to this tactic should be evident from the way in which Kant finally attempts to justify the introduction of such specific categories as cause and effect. Kant's completion of the argument of the *Prolegomena*, to which we now return, depends on the following claim:

Quite another judgment must therefore precede before experience can arise from perception. The given intuition must be subsumed under a concept, which determines the form of judgment in general in respect of the intuition, connects the empirical consciousness of the latter in a consciousness in general, and thereby procures universal validity for empirical judgments; such a concept is an *a priori* concept of the understanding, which does nothing except merely determine in general the manner in which an intuition can serve for judgments.

(§20, 4:300)

The crucial clause is Kant's statement that the form of judgment must be determined *in respect of the intuition*; this presumably suggests that *something about the form of intuition,* the way in which the empirical material is given to us, limits the way in which the purely logical functions of judgment can be applied or the conditions under which they can be used. The same implication is suggested by the example that Kant gives:

The judgment: "The air is elastic" becomes universally valid, and thereby finally a judgment of experience, only because certain judgments precede it which subsume the intuition of the air under the concept of cause and effect and thereby determine the perceptions not merely with respect to one another in my subject but with respect to the form of judgment in general (here the hypothetical) ...   (301)

Something about the form of intuition determines that it is only by the use of the category of cause and effect that the logical form of the hypothetical judgment can be applied to empirical objects; the logical form itself does not suffice to imply the category of cause and effect.

Such a suggestion is consistent with Kant's original conclusion, re-iterated in the argument of the *Prolegomena,* that some extralogical considerations are required to justify the categories. Unfortunately, nothing beyond these obscure hints is offered to explain what it is about the form of intuition that determines that it is through the category of cause and effect alone that the logical form of the hypothetical judgment can find empirical employment. We are given a profound clue, perhaps, a hint to reverse the usual interpretation of the procedure which Kant calls "schematism" and look, not for forms of intuition entailed by the logical functions of judgment, but rather for special forms or relations in intuition which alone *justify* the use of certain logical forms of judgment. But we are not given an argument which proves that it is indeed the category of cause and effect alone that allows the empirical use of the hypothetical form of judgment, or an argument directly on behalf of any other category. The transcendental deduction in the *Prolegomena* assumes a strong conception of experience and exploits a definition of one form of judgment as the assertion of a necessary and universal connection, but even with that it falls short of showing how the deduction of particular categories is to be achieved (the problem that should have been left after the metaphysical deduction).

At this point, it would be natural to turn to the second-edition text of the deduction, which, in spite of a quite different beginning, lapses into an argument not very different from that of the *Prolegomena.* But since in this version of his argument Kant intertwines the roles of the conception of judgment and the concept of an object itself so closely as to make their separation artificial, it will be best if we now turn to the third version of tactic IA, in which the concept of an object is the fundamental premise – even if the character of Kant's argument in the text of the deduction from the second edition in the end makes this distinction somewhat artificial.

IA.iii: Categories and the concept of an object

Sometimes Kant attempted the at least superficially distinct alternative of deriving the universal and necessary validity claimed even by empirical judgments from the concept of an *object* of judgment rather than from the conception of judgment itself; such an argument, of course, would have at least the tactical advantage of avoiding the contradiction that seems to arise when the definition of any judgment as a claim to universal and necessary validity is juxtaposed with the *Prolegomena*'s distinction between judgments of experience and of perception, since it would not render incoherent the concept of a judgment of perception, which claims neither universality and necessity nor objectivity. In this form of argument, Kant does not merely define the object as, for instance, "that in the concept of which the manifold of a given intuition is *united*" (B 137); rather, he conceives of an object as that in virtue of which the several representations constituting such a manifold are *necessarily* connected.[14] Thoughts along these lines are clearly expounded in Kant's notes and are exploited at several points in the exposition of the *Critique* itself. One clear passage is in a note from the crucial period 1783–4 (part of which was already quoted in my discussion of the ambivalence of Kant's use of the phrase "unity of consciousness"):

The manifold, insofar as it is to be represented as belonging necessarily to a consciousness (or also to the unity of consciousness in general), is thought through the concept of an object: The object is always a something in general. Its determination rests solely on the unity of the manifold of its intuition, and indeed on the universally valid unity of the consciousness of it.

[Thus] two parts of cognition occur *a priori.* 1. Intuitions, 2. Unity of the consciousness of the manifold of intuitions (even of the empirical [manifold]). This unity of consciousness constitutes the form of experience as objective empirical cognition.   (R 5927, 18:389)

Here a certain conception of the object itself is placed at the foundation of Kant's thought. Representation of any kind of object, pure or empirical, requires representation of necessary connections; therefore any cognition which is to be both empirical yet objective requires such connections; therefore experience requires necessary connections. But of course any representation of necessary connection requires an *a priori* basis; therefore unity of consciousness of even the empirical manifold of intuitions, not just a pure manifold, requires an *a priori* foundation. And as the earlier part of R 5927 has already argued, this must be one or more of the categories, for only a "category is the representation of the connection of the manifold of intuition to a universal consciousness (to a universality of consciousness, which is genuinely objective)" (18:388).

Another note, which may have been written at the same time but which may also have been written even earlier in the 1780s, likewise emphasizes that the function of the conception of an object is to express the necessary connection of the individual items of intuition. Thus, if it is conceded that there is such a thing as knowledge of objects at all, Kant's argument will entail, it must also be conceded that there is, knowledge of necessary and universal connections and an *a priori* basis for such connections, thus *a priori* concepts as well as intuitions. This note is lengthy, but it reveals a great deal about the assumptions really at work in Kant's thought and is well worth considering in its entirety:

In all synthetic *a priori* cognition there must be thought first [an] *a priori* intuition, second [an] *a priori* concept of the synthesis of the manifold. On this are grounded the principles of synthetic cognition in general. For these contain nothing but the conditions under which alone certain intuitions can be brought under concepts of their synthesis. The latter are called *categories*.

(We can sense something, without thinking it[;] the question arises, whether we cannot also think without sensing. (*a priori*.) But we can also intuit, without sensing. Now should we think without sensing, then this must be related to that [i.e., pure] intuition.)

Intuition is immediate relation of the power of representation to a particular [*einzeln*] object. [A] concept [is] the representation of it through a mark that is common to it and others. Intuition belongs to the senses, [a] concept [to] the understanding.

Concepts of the synthesis of the manifolds of possible intuitions are nothing other than the connection which the representations in one consciousness (can) have (so far as they are necessary in respect of an intuition), only thought synthetically, that is, that to one ... something *else* is connected brings forth the consciousness of the representation of *one* object.

In the representation of an object, which should contain the manifold of its intuition, the synthetic unity of the latter is necessary. The representation of this necessary unity, under which all the manifold of the intuition must stand, is, if there is to be cognition of an object of intuition, the foundation of synthetic cognitions in general and must itself obtain *a priori*.

Something, which is *determined* in respect of the functions of judgment, is the object, and this determination is determination of the object. ... The categories are therefore concepts of the determination of the objects of our cognition in general, so far as intuitions are given for that. [They are] therefore principles for making from appearance experience, which is purely objective, that is universally valid empirical cognition, since therefore the synthesis must be determined *a priori*, for it would otherwise not be necessary and universal. For we know an object only as a something in general, of which the given intuitions are only predicates. Now how these can be the predicates of a third thing cannot be known through their comparison, rather through the manner in which the consciousness of the manifold in general can be regarded as necessarily connected in one consciousness. In the representation of an object the manifold is unified. All intuitions are only representations; the object, to which they are related, lies in the understanding.

A synthesis can never be cognized as necessary and therefore *a priori* from the representations, which are to be connected synthetically, but only from the relation of these to a third concept, in which and in relation to which this connection is necessary. This third concept is that of an object in general, which is thought precisely through this synthetic necessary unity and which is determined in regard to the logical functions of such unity. For only by this means does the manifold of representations first become objective, that is, cognition, and appearance become empirical cognition.

That something is determined objectively cannot be cognized *a posteriori*, without determining it objectively according to an *a priori* rule; for everything which is determined objectively must allow itself to be determined *a priori* from the concept of the object, not indeed as far as the matter is concerned, but yet concerning the form of the connection. Through these very same representations through which the concept of an object is made determinate, the representations are, conversely, objectively determined.   (R 5643, 18:282–4)

A great deal about the assumptions by which Kant was tempted and the arguments he was trying to make is revealed by this document. In the first paragraph Kant indicates the assumption he had made since the time of the *Duisburg Nachlass* that there must be a source of synthetic *a priori* knowledge in addition to what may be found in the pure forms of intuition alone. In the obscure second paragraph,[15] however, Kant may intimate an argument, analogous to the obscure argument discussed earlier in this chapter as tactic IA.i, according to which it is the task of synthesizing a pure manifold as such which requires this additional *a priori* foundation, and only for that reason that the synthesis of empirical manifolds also requires this foundation. The third paragraph gives a useful exposition of Kant's conception of the difference between an intuition and a concept, emphasizing that an intuition is characterized by the two criteria that it is an immediate representation of a particular or of a singular item.[16] The main argument of the note, however, commences in the third and fourth paragraphs, where Kant asserts that the unity of consciousness which is required for synthesis is consciousness of the *necessary* connection of representations, and that this is identical to the connection of separate representations in the representation of an object: To represent an object is precisely to think that its manifold representations are necessarily conjoined as they are. In the next paragraph of the note, Kant vaguely alludes to the connection between the categories and the logical functions of judgment, but the main point of the paragraph is to argue that because the predicates of an object, or the representations of them, must be recognized to have a necessary connection, they must have an *a priori* rather than empirical basis. Thus knowledge of an object can never arise from a mere "comparison" of several representations of it – an obvious swipe at the inductive empiricism of Hume – but must be grounded in an *a priori* concept or form for the unification of a manifold of representations. Thus, as the penultimate paragraph makes explicit, even empirical cognition requires *a priori* concepts, not (as he had argued in the last passage I discussed) because the synthesis of a pure manifold does, but because the claim to objectivity is equivalent to a claim to universal and necessary validity in the connection of representations, and such a claim must always have an *a priori* basis. Of course, as the final paragraph emphasizes, it is only the form and not the matter of empirical knowledge which is *a priori*, and this leads Kant to conclude with the elegant statement that the pure concepts of the understanding must be made determinate – in the sense of being made specific – by having empirical representations subsumed under them, whereas at the same time such representations must be made determinate – in the sense of representing a particular object – by being connected in accordance with these categories or *a priori* forms for the connection of intuitions, which Kant again tries to specify by means of an allusion to the logical functions of judgment. But throughout all of this it must be kept in mind that what is alleged to require the existence of categories known *a priori* is not just that the representation of an object is the representation of a *connection* among the manifold of its representations, but the fact that an object is represented by a *necessary connection* of individual representations presenting its diverse predicates. Or, to put the same point in another way, in spite of his allusions to the logical functions of judgment, Kant is not arguing that because there are only a determinate number of ways to connect manifolds of representation it is therefore necessary that any manifold be connected in one of these ways; rather, he is arguing that because in order to represent an object a manifold must display a necessary connection, there must therefore be some determinate ways of connecting manifolds, which modes of connection must therefore be known *a priori*.

The concept of an object of knowledge is similarly exploited in the dense expositions of the transcendental deduction of the categories in the two editions of the *Critique*. Indeed, inferences like those which Kant made explicit in his notes appear even in arguments that start off from quite different premises, suggesting that the conception of an object as the locus of necessary connections had an irresistible attraction for Kant. In the first edition, Kant's tendency to equate objectivity with the necessary connection of predicates shows up in his preliminary exposition of the deduction, that is, his exposition of the "threefold synthesis which must necessarily be found in all knowledge" (A 97), especially in the section entitled "The Synthesis of Recognition in a Concept" (A 103–10). The discussion of the threefold synthesis begins with the fundamental and unexceptionable premise that any form of knowledge is a whole in which representations are connected. This is apparently meant to display the places where *a priori* rules may enter into empirical knowledge by first showing what kinds of combinatory act the mind must be able to perform; the rules governing these forms of combinations should then be introduced. However, Kant leaps to the desired conclusion of the objective validity of categories known *a priori* at several points in his argument.

We already saw him do so in his discussion of the mere "Synthesis of Apprehension in Intuition"; in "The Synthesis of Recognition in a Concept" he leaps to his conclusion by the express introduction of a strong definition of "an object of representations" (A 104). The section begins by asserting the uncontroversial but also *conditional* necessity that *if* the successive apprehension and reproduction of some particular representations are to furnish any knowledge at all, there must be some sense in which these representations can be regarded as representations of some single object (A 103): *If* they are to represent *that* object, then it is indeed necessary that they be connected in a certain way. But this would be true even if the concept of this object were thoroughly empirical and *a posteriori*; that the concept of an object must be *a priori* or have an *a priori* element will follow only if there is some stronger sense in which knowledge of an object is knowledge of necessary connections.

Kant leaps to the same conclusion as he continues the preliminary exposition of the deduction. In order to clarify what he means by the "expression of an object of representations," he writes:

We find, however, that our thought of the relation of all cognition to its object carries with it something of necessity, since namely this relation is regarded as that which is contrary to our cognitions being haphazard or arbitrary, and rather

DEDUCTION FROM KNOWLEDGE OF OBJECTS

determines them *a priori* in particular ways, since, insofar as they are to be related to an object, they must also necessarily agree among themselves in relation to this, i.e., they must have that kind of unity which constitutes the concept of an object.

(A 104–5)

To be sure, any claim to objectivity implies some kind of contrast between an entirely arbitrary and subjective association of impressions, on the one hand, and something more orderly, less subject to whim or accident, on the other, but Kant simply leaps to the conclusion that the kind of necessity implied by such a claim to objectivity is one that must be known on the basis of some synthetic *a priori* principle. The same assumption is made a page later:

All cognition requires a concept, ... but a concept is always, as regards its form, something universal, which serves as a rule. So the concept of body serves our cognition of external appearances as a rule by means of the unity of the manifold which is thought through it. But it can be a rule of intuitions only if it represents the necessary reproduction of the manifold of given intuitions, thus the synthetic unity in the consciousness of them. Thus in the case of the perception of something outside us, the concept of body makes the representation of extension, and with it impenetrability, form, etc., necessary.

A transcendental condition always lies at the basis of all necessity. Therefore there must be found a transcendental ground of the unity of consciousness in the synthesis of the manifolds of all our intuitions, thus also of the concepts of objects in general, consequently also of all objects of experience ...   (A 105–6)

Likewise,

Unity of synthesis according to empirical concepts would be entirely contingent, and, if it were not grounded on a transcendental ground of unity, it would be possible for a crowd of appearances to fill our soul without experience ever being able to arise from it.   (A 111)

Of course a genuine insight lies behind this claim. In idle fancy we can put predicates together any way we like, and thus dream of, say, extended but fully interpenetrable bodies, but if we are to claim knowledge of an object, then there are constraints on how we can represent them – certain predicates must be put together, and others must not be. But such necessities might be analytical consequences of the particular concept we wish to employ: We must put together extension and impenetrability *if* we wish correctly to designate something a body, but not necessarily if we are willing to call it something else. Or such rules might just express the implications of the regularities we have discovered in our empirical acquaintance with the world. It would certainly take considerable further argument to prove that claims to objective necessity are synthetic yet genuinely necessary truths in any sense requiring a "transcendental" ground for the explanation of our knowledge of them.

Kant may obscure this gap in his deduction by choosing as his most prominent example of the kind of object of which several representations are seen as successive representations a mathematical object; since such an object may be constructed entirely in pure intuition, it may well seem obvious that the rules for its synthesis can only be known *a priori*. "Thus we think of a triangle as an object by being conscious of the combination of three straight lines according to a rule, according to which such an intuition can always be presented" (A 105). But if we take as our example an ordinary empirical object, it is not immediately apparent why the rules which connect its several representations into the representation of a whole must themselves be known *a priori*. For instance, the concept of my computer keyboard seems to connect a variety of intuitions – empirical intuitions of beige and brown colors, clicking sounds, a disposition suddenly to generate nonsensical strings of *y*'s, and so on – into the representation of a single object, which would indeed not be a representation of *that* kind of object – a computer keyboard – unless it linked *those* kinds of empirical intuitions in *that* kind of connection; yet it nevertheless appears to be a thoroughly empirical concept. Thus, when Kant asks, "What is an object?" and then answers by saying, "That, the representation of which is the sum of several representations belonging to it: [e.g.,] The plate is round, warm, pewter, etc." (R 6350, 18:676), it is not immediately obvious that any special *a priori* form for linking such empirical predicates or empirical intuitions of properties should be required.[17] It is only when Kant assumes that there is some stronger sense in which it is necessary that the representations of an object are connected in the way they are that an inference to *a priori* forms of connection appears plausible. An analytical connection among the several predicates of the concept "plate" or "computer keyboard" – that is, a conventional definition of the concept – would suffice for me to know that if I am to represent a plate or a keyboard, then I must represent those various predicates, but this would not require *a priori* knowledge of any rules of synthesis without further explanation. If there were some stronger kind of necessity that my empirical intuitions be synthesized in the way in which they are when such a concept is applicable, perhaps the basis for an inference to such rules would be evident. But here Kant appears to rely only on his own definition of an object as the expression of a necessary connection. To an empiricist who assumes that we have empirical knowledge of objects but does not equate such knowledge with a claim to necessary truth, such an argument can seem only to beg the question of the objective validity of *a priori* concepts.

However, the most striking evidence of Kant's temptation to execute the deduction by a simple inference from the conception of objectivity itself lies in the revised exposition of the deduction which Kant supplied for the second edition of the *Critique*. Since here the distinction between a deduction from the concept of the object and that from the conception of judgment collapses, this version will also allow us to conclude the discussion of tactic IA. These claims may seem surprising, since the second-edition text of the deduction begins with remarks about the transcendental unity of apperception which seem more clearly than any of Kant's other texts to identify this concept, and thus the chief premise of Kant's argument, with the unity of *self*-consciousness rather than the representation of an object. In spite of this initial promise, however, Kant effects his goal in this version of the deduction by nothing other than a direct exploitation of a strong conception of objectivity itself.

In what follows, I shall expound Kant's argument in five steps, in order to display its character clearly.

(1) Since Kant ultimately suggests at least three different arguments based on the opening claims of the second-edition text, I shall have to recur to these initial steps several times. It will therefore save time later if I now expound them somewhat more thoroughly than the immediate context might itself require. Kant opens the new exposition by asserting the premise that "the combination (*conjunctio*) of a manifold in general can never come to us through the senses, and therefore also cannot already be contained in the pure form of sensible intuition; for it is an act of the spontaneity of the power of representation" (§15, B 129–30). Thus, representation of an object requires the passive apprehension of the several representations in a manifold as well as some active synthesis of this manifold into a whole. However, Kant also claims – in what is obviously intended as a brief reprise of the threefold synthesis of the first-edition deduction – that "the concept of combination" requires, in addition to the passive apprehension of the manifold and the *act* of synthesizing it, a "*concept* of the unity of the manifold" (emphasis added) which "cannot arise out of the combination" but which rather "by its addition to the representation of the manifold first makes the concept of the combination possible" and which "therefore precedes *a priori* all concepts of combination" (B 130–1). These last conclusions are clearly meant to justify the inference that there must be *a priori* categories which apply to all manifolds of representation independently of whatever *empirical concepts* may be found to apply to them, but Kant immediately creates problems for himself by going on to say that the *a priori* representation of combination which precedes the act of combination precedes all *categories* (B 131). This certainly raises a problem about what this *a priori* concept of unity distinct from all categories is supposed to be, and what unique role the categories themselves will then have left to play, in addition to that fulfilled by this underlying concept of unity. But the more pressing problem with Kant's opening argument is the question of why any representation of unity must *precede* the synthesis of the manifold or act of combining it into a whole at all. Supposing that the several constituents of a manifold are temporally discrete (as the fundamental premise of the deduction at A 99 would entail, though this premise is not reiterated in the new exposition), and therefore must be successively apprehended, why should a subsequent reproduction of them all in a single, complex representation not suffice for a representation of their combination? Whence arises the requirement that some additional *concept* of unity is required which must precede such an act of synthetic reproduction and make it possible? Surely nothing in this first

paragraph (§15) explains this inference; it is thus by no means apparent why the requirement of an *act* of combination should entail the existence of any special *rules* of combination which are known *a priori*.

It must nevertheless be recognized that the opaque inference of §15 surely represents Kant's most basic level of thought. Indeed, Kant often employed the inference directly from an act of combination to *a priori* rules as the whole of a transcendental deduction, whether of the categories or even of the forms of intuition. That is, apart from any special implications of the concept either of self-knowledge or of knowledge of objects, Kant clearly believed that the basic fact that all concepts of synthesis require an *a priori* framework for their organization is sufficient to undermine the empiricist assumption that all concepts are abstracted from experience – whether that assumption takes the form of the Humean account of the idea of causation or, for that matter, of the Leibnizian theory of space and time as relations abstracted from the (indistinct) experience of objects. Thus, the underlying argument of the "Transcendental Aesthetic" is clearly meant to be accepted independently of the further details of the metaphysical and transcendental expositions of space and time: "Since that in which sensations can alone be ordered and arranged in certain forms cannot itself be another sensation, so is the matter of all appearance, to be sure, given to us only *a posteriori,* but its form must lie ready *a priori* for it all in the mind, and thereby be capable of being considered in abstraction from all sensation" (A 20 / B 34). It is not even conceivable that the manner in which sensations are connected is determined in the act of combining them; some template for their combination must be employed by any such act of combination. Similarly, there are numerous passages in which Kant seems willing to ground the whole transcendental deduction of the categories on the basic idea of §15 without many further steps. In the bluntest – and earliest – form of this kind of argument, Kant just assumes that there must be rules by which the mind performs its act of combining representations into connected wholes of knowledge, without actually arguing that combination requires laws. He also just assumes that because there are such rules, we can know them *a priori* without proving that the mind's operations must be transparent. An argument of this form is to be found in a marginal note in Kant's copy of Baumgarten, from the same period as the *Duisburg Nachlass*:

The empirical laws a *priori* contain the conditions of apprehension and conception (together with those of intellection). We can connect nothing in the appearances and thus give them a real form except by connecting them to one another, through one another, and with one another and except insofar as the appearance determines the mind to this activity. Therefore something is possible as an object of experience only insofar as it appears subject to the laws of apprehension; that is, if its appearance is to be whole, then it must hang together according to the laws of apprehension. Just as nothing can appear except in the universal whole of space and time, so nothing can become experience except insofar as it is connected with other things by the universal laws of the activities of the mind. Therefore nothing happens accidentally, that is, without being subject to a universal rule in respect to something with which it is connected (whether or not the latter also appears). For we can encounter the ground of a particular connection in an object only insofar as the object contains something which can be subsumed under a universal rule of connection. Ground and consequent, namely, are not mere apprehensions, but inferences or universal actions of transition.

Everything which is given to us through experience must be capable of being cognized *a priori*, that it, its possibility must be capable of being known from the laws of sensibility or understanding in relation to which the experiences can also occur. That it can be cognized *a priori* means: that it has an object and is not merely a subjective modification. (R 5216, 18:121)

Kant's initial, contradictory description of what is apparently a single set of laws as both "empirical" and "*a priori*" is obviously an infelicity; he clearly means that there are *a priori* laws underlying empirical knowledge-claims and thus any empirical generalizations. But his initial confusion might be seen as revealing the underlying problem: He just assumes that because knowledge requires a combination of representations, thus an act of combination as well as apprehension, which of course has its own laws, there must be "universal laws of the activities of the mind" by which such combination is effected. Kant's reference to the combination of representations "to," "through," and "with" one another makes it clear that he has in mind the basic categories of object and property, causation, and interaction, but there is no explanation of why in fact any act of combination requires rules, let alone why just these forms of combination are dictated by the fact that combination does arise from an "activity" of the mind.

In a more subtle form of argument, which comes closer than usual to connecting the transcendental with the metaphysical deduction, Kant tries to rectify these problems by emphasizing the need for *expression* of acts of combination. This is intended to allow him to derive both the *necessity* of a *priori* rules for such connections and their *identity* from the *forms for the expression* of acts of combination – which are, of course, nothing but the logical functions of judgment. Such an argument has an initial similarity to tactic IA.ii, so evident in the *Prolegomena* and in such notes as R 5923, but differs vitally in attempting to infer the necessity of *a priori* concepts from the permissible *forms* for the expression of empirical judgments, rather than from the alleged *necessity* of what are nevertheless supposed to be empirical judgments. Such an argument may be found in this note (R 5934), also from the period of the *Prolegomena*, which was written during the interval between the publication of the first and second editions of the *Critique*: "Experience is knowledge of that which is object of sensation *a posteriori*. Sensations yield, however, no knowledge; therefore something must be added to them if experience is to be possible. [But] to *a priori* representations only *a priori* representations from concepts can be added, and this can be only connection (synthesis), insofar as it is determined *a priori*."

In other words, if sensations both exhaust the sphere of the *a posteriori* and yet are insufficient to constitute experience or knowledge of objects, what must be added to them can come only from the realm of the *a priori*. Kant then introduces the concept of judgment in order to specify the identity of this *a priori* element:

The general principle of possible experience is therefore: *All perceptions are determined *a priori* in respect of their connection in one consciousness (for consciousness is unity, in which alone the connection of all perception is possible, and if it is to be knowledge of an object, it must be determined *a priori*). The objective unity of the consciousness of different representations is the form of judgment. Therefore all perceptions, so far as they are to constitute experience, stand under the formal conditions of judgment in general, and the determination of them through this function is the concept of the understanding.

(R 5934, 18:393)

The deduction is then completed by the addition of two further propositions to this argument. First, attaching this claim to the asterisk in the note just quoted, Kant identifies the "formal conditions of judgments" with the categories: "*All appearances are, in respect to their connection, determinable *a priori* in accord with the unity of consciousness in all judgments in general, that is, they stand under categories." Then, in another note from the same period, he also asserts that *all* the categories identified as forms of judgment must apply to the objects of the understanding: "For the logical form of understanding in judgments must yet precede [experience], and the appearances (as mere representations) must be regarded as determined in respect of every one of these forms, for otherwise no experience can arise" (R 5926, 18:388). Thus Kant attempts first to argue that there really must be an *a priori* element in the knowledge of objects, just insofar as that knowledge requires a combination at all, and then tries to specify that element by equating combination with judgment and the *a priori* element of the former with all the *a priori* forms of the latter.

Of course, the first stage of this argument is not much more persuasive than an outright assumption of the existence of some laws by which the mind performs its operations. Nevertheless, Kant was doubtless gripped by the apparent self-evidence of such an assumption. Not only does he suggest it in subsequent passages of the second-edition text of the deduction:

... Combination does not, however, lie in the objects, and cannot be borrowed from them, and so, through perception, first taken up in the understanding. On the contrary, it is an affair of the understanding alone, which itself is nothing but the faculty of combining *a priori* ... (B 134–5)

He also continues to offer it as a self-sufficient strategy for the deduction even after the publication of the second edition of the *Critique*. Thus, in the essay on the real progress of metaphysics, this is what he offers as the *nervus probandi* of any deduction of the objective validity of *a priori* categories:

Now the representation of something composite, as such, is not a mere intuition, but requires the concept of a composition, so far as it is applied to the intuition in space and time. This concept therefore (together with that of its contrary, the simple) is not a concept which is derived from intuitions, as a partial representation contained in them, but is rather a fundamental concept [*Grundbegriff*], to be sure *a priori*, ultimately the only *a priori* fundamental concept, which, original in the understanding, lies at the ground of all concepts of objects of the senses.

(*Real Progress*, 20:271)

Here Kant identifies the *a priori* concepts of the composite and the simple as the *a priori* concepts which must be employed in any act of combining pure or empirical intuitions and which are thus self-evidently the *a priori* categories for all synthetic cognition. By thus resolving the problem about the identity of the most fundamental *a priori* concepts, however, Kant also makes even more pressing the problem of the connection between these *a priori* concepts and the specific categories which are supposed to be linked with the judgmental form of knowledge of objects and/or of the self. Although Kant's commitment to the argument that all acts of combination presuppose *a priori* concepts is clearly profound, the matter of how this fundamental insight is to be connected to any of his specific strategies for accomplishing the transcendental deduction remains profoundly obscure. Precisely the same problem is evident in Kant's letter to J. S. Beck of 16 October 1792:

In my judgment everything comes to this: That, since in the empirical concept of the *composite* the composition is not given by means of the mere intuition and its apprehension but can be represented only through the *self-active connection* of the manifold in the intuition, and indeed in a consciousness in general (which is not, in turn, empirical), this connection and the function thereof must stand in the mind under *a priori* rules, which constitute the pure thought of an object in general (the pure concept of the understanding under which the apprehension of the manifold must stand insofar as it constitutes *one* intuition, and which also constitutes the condition of all possible empirical knowledge of the composite (or what belongs to it) ... which is asserted through those principles. According to the common conception, the representation of the composite as such comes with the representation of the manifold which is apprehended *as given,* and it accordingly does not belong – as yet it must – entirely to spontaneity, and so on. (11:376)

In other words, even after he had completed his major work in theoretical philosophy, Kant was still content to represent the gist of his theory as its opposition to the "common conception" that combination is simply given in perception, and thus implies that the deduction rests chiefly on the premise that combination is an active function of the mind which necessarily proceeds according to laws of combination which can be known *a priori.*

However, an inference from the premise that the mind must perform an act of synthesis to the conclusion that there are *a priori* concepts of the understanding requires two still ungrounded assumptions. First, it assumes that what the mind must add to *a posteriori* representations to constitute knowledge is indeed *another* representation of some sort, and not just its own *act* of combination. Second, it assumes that the division into *a posteriori* and *a priori* is exhaustive, so that if this additional representation is not the former, it can be only the latter – and not, for instance, just arbitrary or invented. All of this is a fair amount to assume.

The second paragraph quoted from R 5934 might seem to suggest the argument that since the connection of representations takes place *in judgment,* the former must be governed by the forms or structures available for the latter. This would indeed be different from the *Prolegomena*'s argument that since judgments have necessary and universal validity they must imply the *a priori* validity of certain concepts. It would not assume the judgments must claim necessity, but only that they have certain internal structures which must be employed in any act of mental combination at all, since there is no alternative to them or to judgments as the form of expression for such acts. It should be noted in particular that the present form of argument does not depend on claiming any unconditional necessity *that* judgments be made. Further, the suggested argument claims only the conditional necessity that *if* experience is to take place (that is, if combination of representations is to occur), it must take the form of judgment, and thus that *if* it is to take place it must take on the specific forms of judgment. We shall see, however, that as Kant continues from this basic thought in the second edition he does not attempt to develop such an argument, free of the initial assumption that empirical judgments are a form of necessary truth, let alone pursue the special promise of a direct connection between apperception and the synthetic nature of all thought. Instead, although Kant next introduces the concept of apperception into the revised argument of the deduction, he actually makes no legitimate use of it. Instead, he immediately relapses into a form of the deduction from the conceptions of object and judgment that is not significantly different from that offered in the *Prolegomena.*

This will seem a shocking statement to most readers, so I shall make my claim clear. Of course, the next section of the revised deduction (§16) introduces the concept of *"pure apperception"* or the *"transcendental* unity of apperception." In so doing, Kant appears to intend to apply the result of §15 by showing us that if *any* consciousness of combination requires an *a priori* concept of unity, then since *self*-consciousness itself is actually consciousness of a combination, even mere self-consciousness requires an *a priori* concept of unity. Kant's alternative tactic of deducing the objective validity of the categories from the conditions of self-consciousness, rather than from a conception of experience which already includes relation to objects, is supposed to be grounded in this inference, of course, but if the argument must depend upon Kant's unexplained inference that any act of combination must be preceded by some *a priori* concept of unity, it will be in trouble from the outset. However, it is also possible that the concept of the transcendental unity of apperception could be used to make good the deficiency of the preceding section. If Kant could show that any synthesis of a manifold of representations, whatever else may be true of it, presupposes self-consciousness of the items in the manifold, that this self-consciousness involves a combination of these items, and that because of some *special feature of self-consciousness* such a combination requires some *a priori* rule or rules of its own, he would have an argument for the conclusion which is only asserted in §15. In fact, Kant seems to proceed in §16 and the next three sections as if at least tacitly recognizing that an independent argument must be derived from the special case of apperception to support the claim of §15. But in spite of this promising start, Kant's argument in §17 through §19 collapses into the crude tactic of deriving *a priori* categories directly from the supposed necessity of objective truth, and thus in the end completely bypasses any special promise of the conditions of a unified self-consciousness.

(2) Section 16 begins with Kant's famous claim – his epistemological substitute, if you will, for Descartes's ontological foundation "*cogito ergo sum*" – that "the *I think* must be capable of accompanying all of my representations; for otherwise something would be represented in me which could not even be thought" (B 132). By this Kant apparently means to argue that whatever else might be thought to be necessarily true of any synthesis of representation, it must certainly be admitted that any conditions which have to be satisfied for the consciousness of individual representations as such *as one's own* will have to be included among the conditions of synthesis. Unless one has several data of a manifold, there is obviously no way one can achieve a synthetic representation of the manifold, and Kant obviously assumes that this implies that one cannot synthesize a manifold of representations unless one can severally recognize its members as one's own. We shall subsequently see that this apparently obvious inference is far from innocuous, but Kant must clearly accept it in order to introduce his premise that I can *have* no representation to which I cannot attach the "I think," that is, *recognize* as my own. Thus, because this apparently necessary ability to recognize any of one's representations as one's own clearly must obtain independently of success in performing any more particular synthesis on them, and in that sense must precede all further synthesis, Kant also calls it *original apperception*. Further, because (as Kant intends to show) there are in fact rules which can be known *a priori* to be necessary conditions of the possibility of the combination which is involved in original apperception, and which are thus *a priori* rules for all other syntheses as well, Kant names "the unity of this apperception the *transcendental* unity of apperception" (B 132).[18] Thus, Kant now apparently intends to argue that there is a combination implicit in this fact of original apperception and that this combination does indeed require *a priori* rules.

That even the minimal form of self-consciousness expressed by asserting "I think ..." of some particular representation involves an act of combination or synthesis is easy enough for Kant to show. He says that "the manifold representations, which are given in a particular intuition, would not all be *my* representations, if they did not all belong to one self-consciousness" (B 132); "Only insofar as I can comprehend the manifold [of representations in the case of a given intuition] in one consciousness do I call them all *my* representations" (B 134). Kant even goes so far as to say that this principle is a "necessary, thus analytic proposition" (B 135), apparently meaning that it follows from the very concept of a self that to recognize a single representation as one's own is just – or at least – to recognize it as belonging to the whole collection of representations which are also severally called one's own. Whether such a conclusion follows from any concept of the self may be questionable; much more questionable, as we shall see, is whether Kant in fact restricts himself to a purely analytic interpretation of his proposition. But in any case such an analytic proposition seems sufficiently self-evident as a starting point for a powerful argument. It seems hard to deny, that is, that an entirely isolated consciousness "which accompanies different representations" would be "in itself diverse and without relation to the identity of the subject," or that "this thoroughgoing identity of the apperception of a manifold given in intuition contains a synthesis of representations, and is possible only through consciousness of this synthesis" (B 133). I convey nothing by calling an individual representation "mine" unless by that I mean that it belongs together with others which are also mine. Thus I must be conscious of my representations as constituting some kind of group, and not just be successively conscious of each in isolation from the others.

Now Kant also adds that "as my representations ... [they] must also necessarily conform to the condition, under which alone they *can* stand together in a universal self-consciousness, for they would not otherwise thoroughly belong to me" (B 132–3). From this, he claims, "Much will follow." Obviously, what will follow is that the conditions of belonging to self-consciousness must be satisfied by any synthesis whatever and will thus provide necessary conditions on the synthetic representations of objects as well. But now two questions arise. In addition to the obvious question – What *is* the condition required if several representations are to belong to consciousness of a single self? – there is also a deeper question: *Why* should we assume that there *is* any such condition? As before, why is the mere *reproduction* of several representations originally apprehended successively not sufficient to constitute them as a collection?

The last two paragraphs of §16 contain hints in another direction (see IIA in chapter 5), but for present purposes we may regard Kant's argument as continuing in §17. Kant begins by reiterating the preceding conclusion, stating that the principle "that all the manifold of intuition should be subject to conditions of the original synthetic unity of apperception" is indeed the "supreme principle" governing the role of the understanding in all synthesis (B 136). That is, whatever else might be required for synthesis of manifolds of intuition by the understanding, whatever is required for the recognition of the items in those manifolds as merely belonging to a single self is indispensable. This in turn means that whatever is required for the combination of representations in a unified self-consciousness is required for any further synthesis of them, "for without that, nothing can be thought or cognized by their means, since the given representations would not have the act of apperception, *I think,* in common, and thus would not be grasped together in a single self-consciousness" (B 137). But what is required for this indispensable recognition that a manifold of representations comprises states of a single self?

(3) It is precisely at this point that Kant's attempt to exploit the Archimedean point of apperception collapses into the deduction from the concepts of object and/or judgment that we have been considering. For Kant now introduces the concept of an object into his argument, but instead of using independently discovered conditions on the unity of apperception to discover necessary conditions for cognition of objects, as his argument to this point suggests he will, he just uses first the concept of an object and then the concept of objective judgment to provide the necessary conditions of apperception itself. This reduces the new deduction to the kind of argument offered in the *Prolegomena* and notes from 1783–4, and indeed to a version which is no more persuasive than those, in spite of its avoidance of the particularly problematic concept of a "judgment of perception."

Kant first defines the faculty of understanding, which has thus far simply been conceived as the faculty of *combination,* as the *"faculty of knowledge,"* where knowledge "consists in the determinate relation of given representations to an object" and an *"object* is that in the concept of which the manifold of a given intuition is *united"* (B 137). Now these comments could either imply a stipulative redefinition of "object" which does away with its ordinary connotations of externality and independence and simply identifies it with whatever concept of unity serves to express the combination of a manifold, or else, as the argument thus far suggests should now be done, introduce a conception of the object as a concept of the unity of the manifold which must at least *include* those conditions which are required for the unified self-consiousness of the manifold as such. In the latter case, Kant would be guilty of mistaking a merely necessary for a sufficient condition when he next asserts that "the unity of consciousness is that which *alone* constitutes the relation of representations to an object, thus their objective validity" (emphasis added). But this is of no matter, for in either case Kant's maneuver would produce information about the necessary constituents of the concept of an object only if necessary conditions for the unity of merely subjective consciousness of the manifold had already been displayed. Yet this is exactly what is still missing, and instead of now providing an independent argument for any such conditions, Kant next just identifies them with necessary conditions for knowledge of objects derived directly from the concept of object and/or judgment. This renders the argument of §17, indeed the progress of the whole new deduction, circular: It sets out to derive the conditions for knowledge of objects from the conditions for self-consciousness, but instead just identifies the latter with the former.[19] Thus, although §17 sets out to argue that the conditions for the unity of consciousness should reveal necessary conditions for knowledge of objects as well, in §18 Kant just identifies the transcendental unity of apperception with knowledge of objects and in §19 he then introduces the *a priori* constituents of knowledge of objects in identifying knowledge of objects with judgments claiming universal and necessary validity, the possibility of which is, in turn, explained in §20 by *a priori* knowledge of the logical functions of judgment.

In §18, Kant creates the appearance of continuity but in fact simply redefines the notion of the transcendental unity of apperception that was introduced in §16. Thus, he now introduces a distinction between the *"objective"* and *"subjective* unity of consciouness."* By the former, the earlier notion of an original or transcendental unity of consciousness seems to be intended, but in fact this new distinction simply contrasts the subjective unity of consciousness, as the mere material or *"determination of inner sense,* through which the manifold of intuition for a . . . connection is empirically given" (B 139), with the objective knowledge that may be made of such material. In other words, if by his new distinction Kant meant to distinguish only between the merely "diverse," that is, successive, "empirical consciousness' of the several representations in a manifold, on the one hand, and apperception as the recognition that those representations constitute states of a single self-consciousness, on the other, then he would be remaining within the framework of §16, though certainly introducing a source of confusion by renaming the recognition of the unity of self-consciousness "objective." But Kant is not contrasting the raw materials of consciousness with explicit self-consciousness at all. Instead, he is identifying the merely "empirical" or "subjective unity of consciousness," which should be the raw material for apperception, with subjective states which are self-ascribed but which are not taken to represent an object, as in the case of a mere association of ideas or other idiosyncrasy (as when, for instance, "one person connects the representation of a certain word with one thing, someone else with another thing" [B 140]), and he is identifying the "transcendental" or "objective unity of consciousness" not with the inescapable recognition of one's possession of one's own representations – which is present in what he here calls the subjective unity of consciousness, whether that is idiosyncratic or not – but instead with that unity "through which all of the manifold given in an intuition is united in the concept of an object" (B 139). But this just equates the transcendental unity of apperception with knowledge of objects by fiat, instead of demonstrating a synthetic connection between them (in either direction). That is, Kant does not develop an argument that self-consciousness as such has special *a priori* conditions which also apply to objects, or even show that self-consciousness as such requires knowledge of objects, whatever the source of the latter. Instead, he just *dismisses* the question of "whether I can become empirically conscious of the manifold as simultaneous or successive" as resting on mere "circumstances or empirical conditions" and falls back on a contrast between rule-governed knowledge of objects and an entirely *conditionless* conception of self-consciousness. For all practical purposes, this distinction is identical to the *Prolegomena*'s distinction between judgments of experience and judgments of perception, and the second-edition deduction's opening suggestion that there is a unity to consciousness, independent of its empirical content, which unity must have its own rules, is simply transmuted into the outright assumption that we are entitled to claim knowledge of objects, with all that such knowledge may entail. Thus, although it is only the conditions for empirical consciousness of the simultaneity or successiveness of the manifold which will ultimately yield the *a priori* constituents of knowledge of objects, for now the possibility of such an argument is foreclosed.[20]

(4) Thus, §19 continues in the same vein: Section 18 having identified the transcendental unity of apperception with knowledge of objects, Kant now defines *judgment* precisely as a claim to *knowledge of an object,* where such a claim is in turn nothing other than the claim that several predicates *"necessarily* belong *to one another."* A "judgment is nothing but the manner in which to bring given cognitions to the objective unity of consciousness"; its copula is simply the means "by which to distinguish the objective unity of given representations from the subjective" (B 141–2). A judgment does this, even in the case of empirical judgment, by claiming the *"necessary unity"* of subject and predicate. As in the *Prolegomena,* Kant identifies "a relation which is *objectively valid,"* that is, an assertion that "two representations are connected in the object ... and not merely conjoined in perception (however often this might be repeated)," with a claim to knowledge of *necessity* that can be sustained only by *a priori* knowledge.

To be sure, in expounding his argument in §19, Kant remarks that he "does not indeed want to say that these representations *necessarily* belong *to one another* in the empirical intuition, but rather that they belong to one another *in virtue of the necessary unity* of apperception in the synthesis of intuitions, that is, according to principles of the objective determination of all representations" (B 142). This could be taken to mean that empirical judgments are not themselves to be understood as necessary truths – which would certainly be healthy – but are to be understood only as somehow necessarily incorporating certain conditions on the unity of apperception itself. But this concession does not really affect the structure of Kant's argument. For since Kant has already identified the unity of apperception with knowledge of objects and completes the present argument precisely by interpreting such knowledge as knowledge of necessary connections, it is best to read the remark to mean only that necessity is not yielded by the passive apprehension of empirical intuition and must be added by the understanding or faculty of apperception. Evidence of Kant's recognition that empirical judgments are not themselves necessary truths is best sought elsewhere (especially at §26, B 165), for such a recognition is quite incompatible with the present argument.

(5) In §20, finally, Kant introduces the categories into the argument. He

says that the "act of the understanding" which produces the "original synthetic unity of apperception" now shown to have been necessary – but also simply identified with knowledge of necessary connections in objects – is the "logical function of judgment." "All the manifold, insofar as it is given in a single empirical intuition, is therefore *determined* in respect of one of the logical functions for judging," and these are "nothing other than the *categories*" (B 143). This, of course, absolutely violates Kant's original constraint that the categories cannot merely be identified with the logical functions of judgment, though they must stand in some kind of connection with the latter which may well serve as a clue to their discovery. Even the *Prolegomena* avoided the outright identification of the categories with the logical functions of judgment.

Basically, though, the argument of the second-edition text of the deduction, up to §20, like the argument of the *Prolegomena,* collapses into the assertion that empirical judgments of objects are actually *claims of necessity* which imply *a priori* knowledge of categories. And this means, of course, that the argument is open to the same kind of objections as the argument of the *Prolegomena.* Even leaving aside the unsatisfactory details of Kant's inference from knowledge of necessary connection to the categories, the basic problems about his claim that empirical knowledge involves necessary connections possible only on *a priori* foundations remain. On the one hand, on what basis can he exclude the possibility that the necessary connections claimed are analytic rather than synthetic? How can he exclude the possibility, for instance, that when I assert that a body "*must* be heavy," rather than just asserting that "if I support a body, I feel an impression of weight" (B 142), I am actually asserting nothing more than the conditional necessity that (because, say, of the definition of a body) *if* I am correct in describing what I am feeling as a "body," it must be heavy? To be sure, Kant has stated that although such an analysis may apply to the case of the assertion "All bodies are extended," it does not apply to the assertion "All bodies are heavy," claiming that the predicate "heavy" is "something quite different from anything that I think in the mere concept of body in general" (A 7 / B 11). That was just an introductory statement, however; where is the argument for it? Or, on the other hand, even if we concede that such an empirical judgment does go beyond mere concepts, where is the argument that a claim to knowledge of empirical objects *is* in fact anything more than the assertion that certain perceptions are "usually conjoined in this manner" (*Prolegomena,* §20, 4:301n)? If Kant had succeeded in showing that self-consciousness itself contains necessary connections which are perforce carried over into knowledge of empirical objects, this question would have become moot. But since §17 reversed this connection, reducing the necessity in apperception to the necessity in knowledge of objects, the question remains, and the conclusion is unavoidable that Kant merely asserts his interpretation of the objective validity of empirical knowledge without argument. In the end, tactic IA, though clearly often Kant's most favored version of the deduction, rests upon a conception of the nature of empirical knowledge that no empiricist, let alone skeptic, is likely to countenance. Even in Kant's time, a claim to necessary truth could not have been a promising place at which to *begin* a transcendental deduction.

IB: *A priori* conditions for empirical knowledge

We may now consider passages in which, although Kant does not attempt to justify the initial assumption that we are indeed entitled to claim empirical knowledge of external objects, he also does not seem to make an initial assumption that such judgments contain explicit claims to universal and necessary validity, but instead appears to intend to show that there are *a priori* conditions necessary for empirical judgments about objects. Under this general description I shall examine two different types of argument. The first of these, like Kant's argument from the pure manifolds of intuition (IA.i), is made in passing in his discussion of the threefold synthesis in the first-edition text of the deduction. The problem with this argument, however, is not that it leaves unclear why the categories, as opposed to pure mathematical concepts, should be required, which was the problem with (IA.i), but rather that it quickly but fallaciously introduces a claim to necessary truth, and thus collapses into the basic form of arguments IA.ii and iii. The second form of argument that we shall consider does not contain this fallacy but instead returns to the original promise of the metaphysical deduction and attempts to show that the objects of judgment must be made determinate in order to allow the logical functions of judgment to be used in making predications about them. Here the problem will be that Kant simply fails to make much progress in getting past the unresolved problems of that original "clue."

Argument IB.i: The necessary synthesis of reproduction

Kant intimates a simple but fallacious argument for the objective validity of *a priori* categories in his account of the second of the three syntheses described in the preliminaries to the first-edition text of the deduction, "The Synthesis of Reproduction in Imagination." Kant begins with the unexceptionable assumption – and indeed ultimately vital premise – that since all knowledge requires, indeed in one sense consists in, a combination of a manifold of representations which, as has been pointed out at A 99, are always temporally diverse and thus successive, it is a necessary condition for knowledge of an object that one's *present* representation of the object, which is not in itself a manifold, be able to bring about "a transition of the mind" to an actual manifold, that is, to one or more of the other – and past – representations constituting the manifold of the intuition of the object. This follows from the premise which Kant has said will be "quite fundamental" in all that follows, namely the claim that "every intuition contains in itself a manifold which can be represented as a manifold only insofar as the mind distinguishes the time in the sequence of one impression upon another; for each representation, *insofar as it is contained in a single moment,* can never be anything but absolute unity" (A 99). But though it is indeed this premise which will ultimately provide the key to the objective validity of the categories, at this point Kant leaps to a hasty conclusion. He says that this "law of reproduction" in turn "presupposes that appearances are themselves actually subject to such a rule, and that in the manifold of these representations a coexistence or sequence takes place in conformity with certain rules" (A 100). This claim is to be grounded in the fact that if the raw data of experience did not contain orderly sequences of representations, then the imagination might not be able to exercise its essential power of reproducing past representations on being stimulated by a present one:

... without that, our empirical imagination would never be able to do what is in accord with its capacity and would therefore remain hidden within the mind as a dead and in itself unknown faculty. If cinnabar were once red, once black, once light, once heavy, if a person were once altered into this animal form, once into that one, if on the longest day the land were once covered with fruit, once with ice and snow, then my empirical imagination could never find occasion to make the transition in thought from the representation of red color to that of heavy cinnabar, or ... unless a certain rule obtained, to which the appearances are already in themselves subjected, no empirical synthesis of reproduction would be able to take place.   (A 100–1)

From this it can correctly be inferred that if it is contingent whether or not our senses present us with repeated patterns of representations, it is also contingent whether or not we can ever reproduce the patterns of representations which are required for the knowledge of an object; if experience is an incoherent stream of unrepeated juxtapositions, no rcpeated patterns of representations will be able to be recalled from it. But Kant assumes that the only alternative to this unattractive possibility is that "there must therefore be something which, as the *a priori* ground of a necessary synthetic unity of appearances, makes their reproduction possible," namely *a priori* principles which ground the "transcendental synthesis of imagination" (A 101). Thus from the premise that if it is contingent that the data of intuition are orderly, it is also contingent that we can reproduce them, he concludes that it is in fact necessary that they are orderly. Unfortunately, this result would follow only if it were also in fact necessary that such reproduction take place. Yet there is no way in which Kant's premise shows such reproduction to be necessary except in the strictly relative or conditional sense that it must take place *if* empirical knowledge is to be had. Kant stumbles on the very distinction between conditional and absolute necessity which he had earlier been at such pains to draw.

A slight formalization of Kant's inference will make the fallacy apparent. We may certainly grant the initial assumption that to be able to reproduce representations requires being aware of a regularity among these representations. But to reach the conclusion that there is some sense in which the reproducibility of the representations is itself necessary, that is, necessary in a sense explicable only by the supposition of *a priori* knowledge, we would have to add not just the *conditional* that

(1) it is necessary that if I am to experience an object, then I must be aware of a regularity among the representations of it,

but the stronger claim that

(2) if I am to experience an object, then I must be aware of a necessary regularity among the representations of it.

Yet 2 is neither logically equivalent to point 1 nor a consequence of Kant's evidence, which, though undeniable, is also conditional (and, presumably, just an empirical fact as well), namely his observation that if cinnabar were sometimes red, sometimes black, and so on, then the empirical imagination would not have occasion to reproduce any empirical regularities. Nothing Kant says seems to establish more than point 1, the conditional necessity that if I am to know an object, then there had better *in fact* be some regularity among the representations of it which I can experience. So although at one level Kant's argument infers a requirement of necessary connection rather than just postulating one, it also turns on a clearly undefended assumption that this necessity is absolute rather than conditional. Kant's inference to the existence of *a priori* knowledge requires not just the conditional necessity 1, but an unconditional necessity which we can express by detaching the consequent of 2 and asserting simply that

(3) I am aware of a necessary regularity among the representations of objects.

But this, of course, cannot be detached from 1 without fallacy.[21]

Now there is of course a way in which we could reach something like 3 by a valid inference. If we were to add to 1 the additional premise that

(4) it is necessary that I experience objects,

we might make the regularity of experience itself an unconditional necessity. For this would be equivalent to using the unexceptionable rule of modal inference that if p implies q and p is necessary, then q is also necessary, to infer from 4 and 1 that

(5) it is necessary that I am aware of regularity among the representations I have.

We could then perhaps introduce 3, namely my awareness of necessary connections, as the only possible explanation of 5.[22] But surely neither a skeptic who questions the existence of empirical knowledge nor even an empiricist who accepts its existence but questions whether there is any *a priori* basis for empirical knowledge could be imagined to concede a supposition that it is in any sense *necessary* that we experience objects, let alone the supposition that it is *necessary* that there be regularity in experience. Even the empiricist would concede only the *actuality* of empirical knowledge, which leaves empirical knowledge and the conditions necessary for it to occur contingent rather than necessary. And all that can be inferred from the contingent occurrence of empirical knowledge is, once again, 1: the conditional necessity that *if* empirical knowledge is possible, then it must also be possible to reproduce the raw data of intuition.

Thus argument IB.i is fallacious. Kant can infer that reproducibility is a condition of the possibility of knowledge of objects but not that *necessary* reproducibility, and therefore *a priori* principles from which such a necessity could flow, is such a condition. The unconditional claim to necessity could be established only if Kant could derive it from *some other* necessity; this suggests that Kant would have to demonstrate 4, or that it *is* necessary that I have experience of objects. And this in turn suggests that the argument of the deduction cannot succeed while it confines itself to the examination of what is necessary *if* we are to experience objects – it must find something with respect to which such experience can itself be seen to be not just possible but necessary. This suggestion of such a direction, as well as the evidence it provides for Kant's difficulty in handling the topic of necessity itself, are in the end the main reasons for considering argument IB.i. Thus, this argument allows us to see that the strategy with which Kant apparently began the second-edition deduction – that is, the idea that the unity of self-consciousness itself might require knowledge of objects without itself being equivalent to it – could provide a way to establish 4, and thus 3. As we saw, however, even in the second edition Kant was quickly diverted from that direction. What is worse, we shall shortly see that when Kant does attempt to exploit the potential of the transcendental unity of apperception within the confines of the official transcendental deduction, he offers an argument remarkably similar to the profoundly flawed tactic we have just described. But before we turn to that, we should consider Kant's most direct attempt to pursue the metaphysical deduction's "clue" that empirical judgments may have necessary forms without themselves asserting necessary truths.

Argument IB.ii: The determinate use of forms of judgment

Kant's most elaborate attempt to exploit the metaphysical deduction's "clue" of the logical functions of judgment appears in neither version of the *Critique* itself but is transcribed in a set of student lecture notes from the period between the two editions of the *Critique,* more specifically from the winter semester of 1784–5, or the period in which Kant was placing all his hopes on a deduction directly from the concept of judgment (as he announced in the preface to the *Metaphysical Foundations of Natural Science* of the following year). Without equating all, and thus even empirical judgments with assertions of necessity, this argument attempts to show that the manifold of intuition must be combined according to certain distinct rules, if the results of such combination are to be capable of expression through the logical functions of judgment. Successful execution of such a tactic would avoid the problem of Kant's underlying direct assumption that combination must have *a priori* laws (IA.iii), as well as the problem inherent in his direct equation between categories and logical functions of judgment, namely that this equation directly contravenes the fundamental constraint on a transcendental deduction which Kant had already established in the 1770s. Yet this argument also leaves unresolved all of the original problems of the metaphysical deduction.

Since this argument from 1784–5 is as little known as it is fascinating, it will be necessary to quote it at length. As is often the case, Kant's introduction of the transcendental deduction to his classroom came when he arrived at Baumgarten's discussion of ground and consequence, and the passage I want to consider begins with one of Kant's clearest rejections of Hume's treatment of causation. This marvelous page provides further evidence of the close connection which Kant saw between the transcendental deduction and the problem of causation, which will be considered later. Here we need consider only Kant's more general argument:

We want herewith at once to examine the possibility of synthetic a priori *cognitions.* All of our cognition consists of judgments, and these must have an object; mere intuition is not cognition. If I say that this or that pertains to some thing, I cognize it, it is therefore related to the object, and this is at once a judgment, which yet consists of concepts. Now in respect of the concepts which we take from the senses, it is arbitrary which form for judging we want to use; for example, I can make the representation of body into one or many or all bodies. I can say that this thing is a body [but] also say that it is not a body, that the body is extended, [but] also that which is extended is a body. But now if my sensible representations are to be related to an object, and my judgments about an object [*Gegenstand*] of the senses are to be related to that object [*Object*], then the form of judgment can no longer be indifferent. For all of our representations are to be regarded merely as predicates for possible judgments in regard to an object, which is regarded merely as a something in general, and which must be made determinate in all judgments which are to be made of this something. In regard to the object, which form of judgment I should judge according to must also be made determinate; for example, the representation of body contains a great deal but is determined only through its predicate: [E.g.,] in thinking of a massive house, [I must think that] a wall encloses an empty space, etc. The representations are related as predicates to something in general, and in regard to the object is it determined in what ways these predicates can be predicated of it. But I cannot here consider the subject also as a predicate, rather only as a subject – Experience is the relation of empirical representations of sense to the object. Cognition is a concept of the object through given representations. To all experiences there also belongs a relation of these representations of sense to the object, and in order to relate my representations to the object the form of judgment must be made determinate. Those concepts which contain the determination of an object in general in another form are called pure concepts of the understanding, and these first make experience possible, for through these our sensible representations are related to objects, [and] this makes our representations cognitions of objects. Experience is therefore really an empirically objective representation and becomes possible only through such concepts, for there can be no individual object which does not stand under one of the categories: For example, body must be represented as a multiplicity [*Vielheit*], because it is composed out of several parts, but one can use this concept affirmatively or negatively. But if I want to designate *one* body, then the form must be determinate. Our experience is an entirely new product of our power of cognition from sensible impressions and representations according to those rules by which an object is determined in regard to its predicates. The relation of cause and effect is therefore a cognition of reason through which experience is possible. Without connection between that which happens and ... the consequence, there can be no experience, and both must be made determinate; this alone is that through which our appearances can be related to an object. Our pure concepts of the understanding contain only the form of judgments. If we want to make them universally valid, [then] the representation is determined through one or the other of the forms of judgment; for example, I can myself think of motion and rest in succession, but if I say: "The motion follows on the rest," then it is determined in the object and must be valid for everyone ...

(Metaphysik Volckmann, 28:404–6)

In the last sentence of this passage, and in what follows, Kant lapses into the argument of the *Prolegomena,* according to which there must be, as he puts it here, a "principle of universal validity of representations," just because "my representation of the object must be universally valid" (28:406). But prior to that relapse, something perhaps only subtly but also crucially different is suggested. In these lines, Kant does not simply infer that there must be an *a priori* basis for claims to necessity nor just assert that the logical functions of judgment are the only available forms for any act of mental combination. Instead, he suggests that although, as far as the mere logical forms of judgment themselves are concerned, they could be applied in any (logically consistent) manner whatever to representations regarded merely as such (here he parallels the *Prolegomena*'s conception of a "judgment of perception"), knowledge of an object requires that representations be connected in some *determinate* manner. This requires that something *in the object,* or in the way in which representations are connected in the representation of an object, must determine *which* of the logical functions of judgment is to be used to express a judgment about the object. In other words, this argument shares Kant's general assumption that the logical functions of judgment are the only forms in which judgments – for that matter, any judgments, whether objectively valid or not – can be expressed, but it does not equate the categories with these forms of judgment. Instead, it argues that there must be *distinct* concepts which organize representations so as to make the use of one logical function of judgment rather than another, in respect to those representations, nonarbitrary. If I am not aiming for determinate knowledge of an object, then it makes no difference whether I think of body as one or many, but if I am aiming for determinate knowledge, then *something in the object* must determine that I must use the plural rather than singular form of judgment. For instance, if I am merely thinking to myself, then it makes no difference how I apply the hypothetical form of judgment, but if I am aiming for determinate knowledge of an object, then it must be the relation of cause and effect *in the object* which determines that I must employ the logical function of ground and consequence. It is not because we are entitled to claim knowledge of necessary truths that we must have some *a priori* foundation for our claim; it is because there are only certain kinds of concepts of objects which can make it determinate which logical functions of judgment we are to use in expressing judgments about those objects that we can know *a priori* that those concepts must be valid of whatever objects we can judge at all.

This argument, so reminiscent of some of the original considerations of the *Duisburg Nachlass,* though written a decade later, does not rest on an outright claim that empirical judgments are in any sense themselves necessary truths, nor does it require an ungrounded supposition that it is in any sense necessary that we have experience or make empirical judgments. And though it does accept the completeness of the tabulation of the logical functions of judgment, it does not simply postulate that there are laws for the mental act of combination which can be known *a priori* because of the transparency of thought. Nevertheless, there are definitely problems with the argument; it clearly makes little progress beyond the original ideas of ten years before. This may explain why Kant continued to press alternative tactics for the deduction and even why he did not give such an argument the prominence in the text of the *Critique* which the "clue" of the metaphysical deduction might otherwise have suggested.

First, the meaning of the premise that the function of knowledge of an object is to make the connection of representations "determinate" is not fully spelled out. As we have seen before, Kant is entitled to some kind of contrast between the entirely arbitrary connections which are permissible in idle fancy and the constraints in our ideas which are imposed upon them by the requirement that they veridically represent a particular object. But what more can be said? No direct equation of determinacy with universal and necessary validity, as opposed to merely subjective validity, can be invoked; this would just return the argument to the level of the *Prolegomena.* So Kant must have some other way to show that the requirement of determinacy must be linked to a representation of an object distinct from any sequence of representations and cannot be accommodated by some construction on the latter alone. Unless it can be shown that application of the categories to objects distinct from representations, though not *identical* to a distinction between arbitrary and nonarbitrary sequences of representations as such, is nevertheless a necessary condition for making that distinction, the link between determinacy and objectivity remains opaque. But no such result is demonstrated in the present argument.

Second, what is the criterion for the identification of any particular category as the only ground for the use of a particular form of judgment? Kant clearly supposes that although the logical form of judgment itself does not dictate that we judge that bodies are many instead of one, there is something about the experience of body which requires that we judge precisely this. What is it? Similarly, what is it about experience that requires us to link antecedent and subsequent events as causes and effects if we are to find any employment for the logical function of ground and consequence? As in the *Prolegomena,* Kant leaves obscure the method for discovering the categories as conditions for the application of logical functions of judgment. We see only that we cannot go directly from the logical functions of judgment to rules for connecting empirical intuitions for subsumption under the former, but we are not told what the method for discovering the objectively valid categories of the understanding is. This leaves Kant where he was ten years earlier.

Finally, the most serious problem about the metaphysical deduction also remains. Even if we waive the worry about the gap between logical and ontological concepts – for example, between the logical concept of a ground and the substantive concept of a cause (although recognition of this difference was one of Kant's deepest insights) – an equally serious problem remains. This is that although Kant undoubtedly supposes that it is not possible for us to use just *some* of the functions of judgment but that it is necessary to use them *all,*[23] it is by no means obvious how this could be established by the present argument. Even if the fact that knowledge of an object does indeed require a combination of representations did imply that it must employ *some* form of judgment, it would imply neither that any individual cognition must involve *all* the forms of judgment nor that for each form of judgment there must be *some* cognition which employs it. And when we consider Kant's particular, indeed consuming interest in the categories of causation and interaction – those two categories the demonstrated objective validity of which will overwhelm both Leibniz and Hume in a single blow – the significance of this problem immediately becomes apparent. For it is clearly Kant's view that use of the categorical form of judgment suffices to formulate what we might call atomic judgments – that is, judgments which link particular representations which are not themselves judgments – and that the hypothetical and disjunctive forms of judgment link only other judgments, not particular representations themselves (A 73 / B 98). Yet the general concept of combination, unless supplemented by further constraints on the nature of empirical intuition, would appear to require only the connection of particular representations for the formulation of judgments about objects. The possibility of empirical knowledge understood as combination of representations would thus seem to be secured by the use of the categorical form of judgment and its associated category of inherence and subsistence alone. Even if it should seem *possible* to use the hypothetical and disjunctive form of judgment – and the categories of causality and dependence and community which are allegedly required to apply them – it is not obvious why it should be *necessary* to guarantee the possibility of cognition as thus far described. But if this is so, then it is not obvious how any form of transcendental deduction in which the tabulation of the logical functions of judgment plays a central role, even if not an exclusive one, can establish that the vital relational categories are necessary conditions for the possibility of any experience or combination at all.[24] Some additional basis is required to show that the logical functions of ground and consequence and disjunction *must* have determinate applications in experience. But of course what provides this additional information might suffice for the justification of the relational categories and render the argument from the logical functions of judgment otiose (as in the case of cause and effect) or irrelevant (as in the case of interaction).

Fundamental questions are thus left unanswered by Kant's attempts to deduce the objective validity of the categories directly from an initial assumption of either *a priori* or empirical knowledge of objects. It is now time to see whether Kant fares any better with the alternative strategy of deducing the necessity of knowledge itself as well as its *a priori* conditions from a more minimal assumption about self-knowledge, rather than from knowledge of objects.

5

The deduction and apperception

Through much of the 1780s, especially in the period between the two editions of the *Critique,* Kant placed his chief hopes for a deduction of the categories in the argument directly from the concepts of object and/or judgment, which can but seem to us to beg his most fundamental questions: the need for knowledge of objects at all, as well as the difference between mere logical functions of judgment and the genuine categories of substance, causation, and interaction. But in each of the two editions of the *Critique* Kant does also attempt to deduce our *a priori* knowledge of the objective validity of the categories from a conception of apperception as a cognitively significant form of self-consciousness which is not, at least immediately, simply identified with judgments about objects claiming necessary truth. For all its potential importance, Kant's treatment of apperception and its necessary conditions is much more condensed than one might have expected after his initial investigations of it in the 1770s, and much too brief for his purposes. Some take this as evidence that Kant was simply more interested in the polemical applications of his "critical philosophy" than in its own foundations.[1] But there is an alternative explanation for Kant's surprisingly – and disappointingly – brief treatment of apperception. This is just that after his initial explorations of the conditions of apperception, in the mid-1770s, he discovered what he thought was a simple but powerful argument from what he took to be our *a priori* knowledge of the necessary unity or identity of the self throughout all of our experiences to the need for an *a priori* synthesis of the manifold of intuition, conducted in accord with *a priori* concepts. Such an argument would not require a detailed exposition of the structure of self-consciousness or a detailed examination of the role which the alleged conditions of its possibility play in bringing it about. With such a promising proof to supplement his in any case considerable confidence in the deduction of the categories from the conceptions of object and judgment, Kant obviously felt it was not necessary to linger over the conditions of empirical claims to self-knowledge in the transcendental deduction. Thus the *Duisburg Nachlass*'s original conception of apperception as knowledge of the position of one's own perceptions in time could be touched upon in passing in the official exposition of the deduction and relegated to a subsequent passage of the *Critique* – indeed, to one added only in the second edition, the "Refutation of Idealism."

IIA: *A priori* knowledge of the unity of the self

We shall now consider the argument from *a priori* knowledge of self-identity to *a priori* knowledge of the categories which Kant thought he had discovered. Before turning to its details, however, we should note that this newly discovered argument is also clearly connected with Kant's departure from his previous caution about the force of the laws of thought. With this new argument in hand, Kant leaves behind the view that conditions of the possibility of experience merely *restrict* the occurrence of experience to circumstances in which the given manifold of intuition happens to comply with these conditions, and instead gravitates toward the view that the conditions of possible experience are rules which the mind *imposes* on any possible manifold. That is, hand in hand with his new argument from the *a priori* certainty of apperception goes Kant's newly firm view, "however exaggerated, however absurd it may sound," that "the understanding is itself the source of the laws of nature" (A 127). For such a view – the view that the mind can impose an "affinity" on all appearances which guarantees that they must be "associable in themselves and subjected to universal rules of thoroughgoing connection" (A 122) – is the only possible explanation of the premise of this new argument, the assumption that unity of apperception is *a priori* certain or guaranteed to obtain under all possible circumstances. Only if we can be sure that we can impose the conditions necessary for apperception on any possible experiences can we be sure that apperception will be possible.

Perhaps this profoundly counterintuitive consequence should have shaken Kant's confidence in his new argument. Perhaps because this counterintuitive result coincided with what he had already deduced from his theory of space and time, it did not. Nevertheless, although Kant's assumption of the necessity of the transcendental unity of apperception may seem self-evident – "indeed an identical, and therefore analytic, proposition," as Kant describes it (B 135) – it is not. In fact, if the transcendental unity of apperception is interpreted as the mere tautology that "the manifold representations, which are given in a particular intuition, would not all be *my* representations, if they did not all belong to one self-consciousness" (B 132) – as Kant suggests it should be – then it asserts a merely conditional necessity that I must synthesize my several representations if I am to be conscious of them all, but cannot suffice to imply the existence of any absolutely necessary connection among them that can be explained only by an *a priori* synthesis according to *a priori* concepts. Yet if the unity of apperception is understood as an *a priori* but nontautologous certainty, which is what is required to make its dependence on the occurrence of any particular kind of synthesis apparent, then the assumption that we have *a priori* knowledge of the identity of the self can only seem deeply questionable. In light of this dilemma, Kant's project of an easy deduction of the categories directly from *a priori* knowledge of the identity of the self can seem no more promising than his simple deduction from his conceptions of objectivity and judgment. The only method that will remain for a successful attainment of the strategic objective of the deduction, the proof that the necessary conditions for the possibility of experience are also necessary conditions for the objects of experience, is the more arduous exposition of the structure of self-consciousness as empirical knowledge of the determinate relations of representations in time, accompanied by a demonstration that the objective validity of the categories of relation is the necessary condition for determinate, *empirical* judgment of such relations. An argument of this form, from the possibility of empirical knowledge of the unity of the self, rather than from the necessity of *a priori* knowledge of the unity of the self, would be tactic IIB in my scheme. But such an argument, we shall see, is no more than hinted at in the official texts of the deduction; indeed, it is only in the second-edition text that it is hinted at all. No such argument is actually provided until Kant completes his theory of objective and subjective time-determination in the "Analogies of Experience" and the "Refutation of Idealism," but even then it is presented as if it were a mere application of results already accomplished in the transcendental deduction. In Kant's own mind, an argument for *a priori* conditions of knowledge that does not itself employ an already certain yet synthetic *a priori* claim to knowledge as its premise may well not have qualified as a genuine transcendental deduction. But what new idea could have led him to depart so far from the kind of argument about apperception as empirical self-knowledge which he originally considered as the foundation of the transcendental theory of experience?

Apperception and a priori *synthesis*

Kant introduces the topic of apperception into his expositions of the deduction in two different ways. In the preliminary exposition of the deduction in the first edition, as we have already seen (argument IA.iii), Kant first argues that because knowledge of an object involves a claim to necessity, it requires a "transcendental ground" (A 104–6); he then adds, in a further step that we did not consider earlier, that the only available candidate for such a ground is transcendental apperception: "Now this original and transcendental condition is none other than the *transcendental apperception*" (A 106–7). In the "systematic" exposition of the deduction in the first edition (A 115), however, as well as in the second-edition text, Kant simply begins with the assertion that "the 'I think' must be capable of accompanying all my representations; for otherwise something would be represented in me which could not be thought at all" (B 131–2), or "At the ground of all empirical consciousness lies pure apperception, that is, the thoroughgoing identity of the self in all possible representations" (A 116). But once the ubiquitous validity of transcendental apperception is introduced, Kant basically proceeds the same way. Except for those central paragraphs of the second-edition text (§§17–20) where he simply reduces apperception to knowledge of objects (IA.iii), Kant proceeds essentially

133

just by construing the possibility of adding "I think" to any representation as an expression of a necessary *synthetic* truth which requires an *a priori* synthesis, obviously conducted according to *a priori* rules, for its explanation. The real premise of his primary argument from apperception is that "we are conscious *a priori* of the thoroughgoing identity of the self in regard to all representations which can ever belong to our cognition, as a necessary condition of the possibility of all representations. ... This principle is certain *a priori*" (A 116).

This statement must seem surprising in face of Kant's twice-repeated assertion that the "principle of the necessary unity of apperception is itself ... an analytic proposition" (B 135; see also B 138). However, Kant's argument actually depends on the truth of his equally clear statement in the first edition that "the synthetic proposition: that all the various *empirical consciousness* must be combined in a single self-consciousness, is the *absolutely* first *and synthetic* [my emphasis] principle of our thought in general" (A 117n). Only the assumption of a synthetic necessary truth that all representations must be combined into a single self-consciousness will explain the kind of argument that Kant offers.[2]

We can see how Kant's argument actually works right from the start, so it is worth having the whole of his first exposition of it before us. After his preliminary claim that knowledge of objects requires knowledge of necessary connections, Kant exploits his introduction of apperception thus:

Now, this original and transcendental condition is none other than the *transcendental apperception*. Consciousness of the self according to the determinations of our condition in inner perception is merely empirical, always changeable, can yield no fixed or enduring self in this stream of inner appearances and is customarily called *inner sense* or *empirical apperception*. That which should *necessarily* be represented as numerically identical cannot be thought as such by means of empirical data. There must be a condition which precedes all experience, and which makes this itself possible, which makes such a transcendental presupposition valid.

Now, no cognitions can take place in us, no connection and unity of them among one another, without that unity of consciousness which precedes all data of intuitions and in relation to which all representation of objects is alone possible. This pure original, inalterable consciousness I shall now name *transcendental apperception*. That it deserves this name is clear from this: that even the most pure objective unity, namely that of the *a priori* concepts (space and time), is possible only through the relation of intuitions to it. The numerical unity of this apperception therefore lies *a priori* at the ground of all concepts, just as the manifoldness of space and time lies at the ground of intuitions of sensibility.

But this very transcendental unity of apperception constitutes from all possible appearances which can ever come together in one experience a connection of all these representations according to laws. For this unity of consciousness would be impossible if in its cognition of the manifold the mind could not become conscious of the identity of function by means of which it connects them synthetically in one cognition. Therefore the universal and necessary consciousness of the identity of itself is also a consciousness of an equally necessary unity of the synthesis of all appearances according to concepts, that is, according to rules which do not merely make them necessarily reproducible but which also determine an object for their intuition, that is, the concept of something in which they are necessarily connected: For the mind could not possibly think the identity of itself in the manifoldness of its representations, indeed think this *a priori*, if it did not have before its eyes the identity of its action, which submits all synthesis of apprehension (which is empirical) to a transcendental unity and first makes possible its connection according to *a priori* rules. (A 106–8)

The argument begins from the premise that independently of – or as Kant puts it, prior to – my acquaintance with any of the individual items in the changing flux of empirical consciousness – the raw data of experience – and prior to whatever particular connections or determinations of objective significance I might make, I am aware that these changing states must "*necessarily* be represented" as states of a numerically identical self. I therefore have *a priori* certainty of my numerical identity in all these states. As Kant reiterates his premise, "All possible appearances belong, as representations, to the whole possible self-consciousness. But from this, as a transcendental representation, numerical identity is inseparable, and certain *a priori*, because nothing can enter into cognition except by means of this original apperception" (A 113). Then his argument is that because (1) we are certain of such a connection – collective possession by a numerically identical self – among our representations, which is independent of their particular empirical content and thus of whatever particular empirical syntheses we may perform upon them, yet because (2) such a connection, like any other connection, presupposes a synthesis of its diverse elements, (3) there must therefore be a transcendental synthesis of all possible items of consciousness independent of all ordinary empirical cognition, indeed preceding all such experience. It is for this reason that the "original and necessary consciousness of the identity of the self" is also a recognition of an "equally necessary unity of the synthesis of all appearances according to ... rules" (A 108). The unity of all representations in one consciousness which is independent of their empirical content has to be grounded in a synthesis which is likewise independent of merely empirical conditions. And of course (4) such an *a priori* synthesis can proceed only according to *a priori* rules; thus the mind's *a priori* certainty of its numerical identity is taken to ground its *a priori* knowledge of the validity of fundamental rules of synthesis for any possible data of experience.

Other writers have tried to defend Kant from my view that he posits an act of transcendental synthesis, as opposed merely to (empirical) acts of synthesis which are guided by *a priori* rules.[3] Kant certainly says things which suggest such a "weakened" but sensible conception of transcendental synthesis: For example, "There is indeed a transcendental synthesis, ... which, however, concerns nothing more than the conditions under which the perception of a thing in general can belong to possible experience" (A 719 / B 747), and "Transcendental propositions ... contain only the rule according to which a certain synthetic unity of that which cannot be represented by *a priori* intuitions ([that is, the unity of] perceptions) would be sought empirically" (A 720-1 / B 748-9). I do not mean to deny that Kant offers such a notion of transcendental synthesis; indeed, such a notion is required by his ultimate theory of time-determination. But it is crucial to see that in his exposition of the transcendental deduction he *derives* the existence of *a priori* rules for self-consciousness from an independent guarantee that all of one's representations can be combined in the representation of a single self regardless of their empirical content, rather than directly showing that *empirical* knowledge of the self can be acquired only through the use of certain special concepts. It is in this sense that his argument depends upon the postulation of a special act of *a priori* synthesis distinct from whatever merely empirical syntheses are conducted in accord with *a priori* rules. Of course he supposes that such empirical syntheses *are* constrained by *a priori* rules, but the very existence and validity of such rules is itself derived from the postulation of an *a priori*, "transcendental" synthesis of all of the self's representations.

The same inference from *a priori* knowledge of the identity of the self in its diverse representations to the existence of an *a priori* synthesis of all possible manifolds of representation is also evident in Kant's two chief "systematic" expositions of the deduction from apperception. It is unmistakable in the crucial paragraph in the first edition:

We are conscious *a priori* of the complete identity of the self in regard to all representations which can ever belong to our knowledge, as a necessary condition of the possibility of all representations (since these can represent something in me only in that they belong to one consciousness together with all others, they must therefore be capable of being connected therein). This principle is certain *a priori* and may be called the *transcendental principle of the unity* of all the manifold of our representations (therefore also in intuition). Now the unity of the manifold in one subject is synthetic: Pure apperception therefore yields a principle of the synthetic unity of the manifold in all possible intuition.

But this synthetic unity presupposes or includes a synthesis, and if the former is to be *a priori*, the synthesis must also be *a priori*. (A 116-18)

It is precisely in reference to this passage that Kant offers his one explicit acknowledgment that the principle of apperception is in fact a synthetic proposition (A 117n). And even though he claims in the second edition that the principle of apperception is merely analytic, the fundamental argument which he offers there, before simply relapsing into his deduction from the concept of the object, is identical to that just presented:

The thought that the representations given in intuition all belong to *me* accordingly means that I unite them in one self-consciousness, or can at least so unite them, and although this thought is not itself the consciousness of the *synthesis* of the representations, it presupposes the possibility of that synthesis; that is, only because I can grasp the manifold of intuitions in a single consciousness do I call them all together *my* representations, for otherwise I would have a self as diversely colored as [all] the representations I have of which I am conscious. Synthetic unity of the manifold of all intuitions, as generated *a priori*, is therefore the ground of the identity of apperception itself, which precedes *a priori* all *my* determinate thought.

(B 134)

This passage makes the nature of Kant's argument particularly clear. The premise that several representations must be grasped in a single act of consciousness in order to constitute a recognition of them as several states of a single self is indisputable. It is the premise (which Kant clearly shares with Hume) that there is no impression of selfhood in any single representation. Since this is so, only some form of connection among several representations could possibly suffice to ground self-consciousness of them.[4] But if this were interpreted as a merely analytical proposition, as Kant indeed suggests in the next paragraph (B 135), then it would merely express a conditional necessity that *if* self-consciousness is to occur, then there had better be *some* connection discerned or created among the several representations. It would not imply that a unified self-consciousness of any particular set of mental states that happens to be given to a subject must be possible, therefore that there must be any synthesis – let alone a particular form of synthesis – that can be performed on any given mental states. It would not directly imply even that *if* self-consciousness of some particular mental states is possible there is a particular form of synthesis performed upon them. Rather, the conclusion which Kant attempts to draw from the present argument would follow only if its premise is understood to be that there is an unconditional necessity that self-consciousness of any given mental states is possible – this is what is certain *a priori* – and that the guarantee of this possibility requires the occurrence of an *a priori* synthesis of any possible representations, or at least a synthesis in some sense independent of the eventual results of empirical cognition.

In considering the difficulties inherent in such an argument, it will help if we have a slightly formalized version of it before us. We may interpret Kant to be arguing in the following manner. He begins with the premise

(1) We have *a priori* knowledge that whatever diverse (therefore temporally successive) representations we may have will be recognizable as states of our numerically identical selves.

This knowledge must be independent of whatever empirical objective content may eventually be ascribed to particular representations; this is what our *a priori* certainty of our numerical identity in all possible representations amounts to. Further, this *a priori* certainty also means that although we may not become conscious of our possession of any given mental states, there can be no representations at all of which we could not become conscious as our own, and thus which are not subject to a thoroughgoing synthesis with all other mental states, independent of the particular empirical content of any of them. Then, since knowledge of any sort of whole requires recognition of a connection among the elements of a manifold (A 97), this means that

(2) We know that there are connections among our representations.

But in fact, since according to 1 we have *a priori* knowledge of the numerical identity of the self possessing all of our possible representations, the operative lemma must really be

(3) We know *a priori* that there are connections among all our representations sufficient to ground the recognition of self-consciousness, independent of the particular content of any of those representations.

Again, only if some connections among our representations can be known to hold independently of their empirical content can these conditions ground our *a priori* certainty of our possession of all of our possible representations. Then, because all knowledge of a combination requires an *act* of combination or synthesis (B 129–30), 2 means that

(4) We know that we perform a synthesis upon all our representations;

and given 3, this entails that

(5) We know that we perform an *a prior* synthesis upon all our representations.

Now, in the versions of the argument we have been considering thus far, Kant basically stops here, contenting himself with the identification of any such *a priori* synthesis with an act of the "productive imagination" and/or "pure understanding" which is self-evidently governed by "pure *a priori* cognitions" "in" the understanding, or categories (e.g., A 119). In at least one place, however, Kant suggests a more elaborate conclusion to the argument. The preliminary exposition of the deduction in the first edition reaches its essential conclusion with these words:

All possible appearances belong, as representations, to the whole possible consciousness. But from this, as a transcendental representation, numerical identity is inseparable and *a priori* certain, since nothing can come to our knowledge except by means of this original apperception. Now, since this identity must necessarily enter into the synthesis of all the manifold of appearances, so far as the synthesis is to be empirical knowledge, the appearances are subject to *a priori* conditions, with which the synthesis of their apprehension must be in complete accordance. Now, however, the representation of a universal condition, according to which a particular manifold ... can be posited, is called a *rule,* and if it *must* be so posited, a *law.* Therefore all appearances stand in a thoroughgoing connection according to necessary laws, and thus in a *transcendental affinity,* of which the *empirical* is a mere consequence. (A113–14)

With the possible exception of the final reference to a "transcendental affinity" which seems numerically distinct from "empirical" affinity, this passage might be read to express the "weakened" recognition that since I cannot actually perform any kind of synthesis upon my empirical intuitions prior to their actual occurrence, and therefore in complete independence of their empirical content, the *a priori* certainty of transcendental apperception had better be secured by postulating *a priori* laws governing the synthesis of empirically given intuitions, rather than by postulating a separate *a priori* synthesis of them. On this account, since a literal interpretation of 5 must be rejected because of the reasonable assumption that we cannot actually *perform* a synthesis upon any representations before their actual occurrence, 5 would have to be replaced with something more like this:

(5′) There are certain concepts which we know *a priori* can be used to connect any of our representations, and which indeed suffice to connect them into a unified whole.

And since, of course, we cannot know anything about the specific *content* of our particular representations independent of their actual occurrence, these *a priori* concepts must concern some features of the *structure* or *relations* of those representations, although obviously not the same features of struc-ture or relations imposed by the forms of intuition.[5] The only candidate for such a role would be the categories; therefore, the deduction could be concluded with something like this:

(6) We know *a priori* that the categories apply to all our representations and therefore to what is represented by them.

Thus it would finally be established that what is a necessary condition of experience, in a subjective sense, namely the unity of consciousness, is also a condition of the possibility of the objects of experience. But even in this more refined form, Kant's argument would still depend upon the assump-tion of *a priori* certainty of the numerical identity of the self with respect to whatever representations one might be given.

Problems with Kant's argument

A more complicated presentation of Kant's argument could undoubtedly be offered, but this reconstruction displays its fundamental premise in sufficient detail for the kinds of criticisms I now wish to make. The keys to Kant's argument are the claims (1) that we have *a priori* certainty of our continuing identity in different states and (4) that such knowledge requires a unique synthesis. However, there are two serious problems with these claims. First, there is no reason to think that claim 1, the assumption that we have some kind of synthetic yet *a priori* certainty of our numerical identity, is true. Second, the very reason for accepting anything like 4, namely, that consciousness of one's own continuing identity in different representational states requires judgment or a synthesis according to any specific rules, is precisely what undermines any assumption that conscious-ness of the numerical identity of the self can be known *a priori* in any sense except as a trivially *analytic* proposition that *if* several representations are known to belong to a single self, then they must be known to be connected to each other.

Problem 1. As I have said, the first edition's characterization of the principle of apperception as synthetic (A 117n), rather than the second edition's description of it as merely "identical and therefore analytic" (B 135), is clearly required to get the present argument off the ground. For it should now be obvious that if we were to interpret the principle of apperception as strictly analytic, the most that would follow from it is that *if* I am conscious of my continuing identity with respect to several different representations, then there must be *some* synthesis by which I can connect them. But it would not follow that I must know independently of the occurrence and content of any particular representations that I *shall be* conscious of my identity with respect to them, and therefore that I *can* synthesize them. *A fortiori,* it does not follow that there is any specific kind of synthesis – a synthesis according to any particular rules – that I can perform on them. In other words, if Kant's claim that "all *my* representations in any given intuition must be subject to that condition under which alone I can ascribe them to the identical self as *my* representations" (B 138) is taken analytically, it can imply only what might be called in current terminology the *de dicto* necessity that *if* I call several representations "one and all *my* representations," *then* I must "apprehend them as constituting *one* intuition" (B 135). That does not imply, however, that I can know independently of the occurrence of any given representations the *de re* necessity that I shall be able to recognize *them* as one and all my representations. Thus it does not imply that I can know *a priori* that I synthesize them, *a fortiori* that I synthesize them according to certain rules. What Kant requires is not an analytic claim that if I call several representations mine I must see them as representations of a single self (an explication, as it were, of what it *means* to call them "mine"), but a synthetic claim asserting the *de re* necessity that, *whatever* representations I have, I *can* call them mine and thus ascribe them to myself as representations of a single self. Only *a priori* certainty of this synthetic proposition would require *a priori* knowledge of any synthesis of them.

It must be recognized, however, that this assertion of *a priori* knowledge of the identity of the self in all its representations is profoundly questionable. Why should Kant have felt entitled to suppose that any such synthetic proposition can be known *a priori* and with certainty? Clearly gripped by the principle, Kant does not argue for it at any length, but he does briefly describe two considerations in support of it and at least suggest a third. Though none of these arguments is ultimately persuasive, the third has at least initial plausibility.

(*a*) Kant's most explicit support for claim 1, our alleged *a priori* certainty of our continuing numerical identity in all possible representational states, is the claim that any representation which could not be ascribed to a continuing, identical self would not concern us in any fashion whatever. Thus the systematic exposition of the deduction in the first edition supports its statement of claim 1 ("We are conscious *a priori* of the complete identity of the self . . .") with the explanation that "all intuitions are nothing to us, and do not in the least concern us, unless they can be taken up into consciousness, whether they influence it directly or indirectly" (A 116), or that "without its relation to an at least possible consciousness, appearance would never be able to be an object of knowledge for us, and would therefore be nothing for us, and since it has no objective reality in itself, but exists only in cognition, it would be nothing at all" (A 120). In the second edition, Kant immediately follows his first assertion of the universal possibility of apperception with the same kind of claim: "The *I think* must be *able* to accompany all my representations; for otherwise something would be represented in me which could not be thought at all, which is as much as to say that the representation would be either impossible or at least nothing to me" (B 131–2). The supposition seems to be that unless I am conscious of the occurrence of a representation, I have no basis to suppose that it even exists, yet to be conscious of a representation is just to ascribe it to an identical self along with all the other representations of which one is also conscious. A nonconscious representation is a contradiction, or at least something which could never be known to exist.

Kant's claim sounds plausible on first hearing, just as does Locke's similar contention against the theory of innate ideas – which Kant could easily have had in mind – that "to imprint anything on the Mind without the Mind's perceiving it, seems to me hardly intelligible."[6] But Kant's statement of the point in the second edition reveals a fatal ambiguity in the claim: It could mean either that I cannot actually *have* a representation without being aware of it, or else just that I cannot be *aware* of any representation without recognizing its connection to my identical self. The latter claim, however, would not follow from the former, unless Kant simply *equates* consciousness with cognition – which he may suggest in the quotation from A 120 but which would clearly beg the question of the deduction from apperception as surely as does the equation of apperception with knowledge of objects in §17 of the second edition. That is, it may well be true that a representation can *exist* only as a modification of consciousness or change in mental state, but this does not itself imply that I must be able to *recognize* every modification of my consciousness as such or self-consciously *ascribe it to myself as mine*. In other words, the plausibility of Kant's claim depends on its expression *in the first person*. Leaving aside assumptions about what is necessary for me *to say* I am in a given state, there is no reason why I cannot *be* in a representational state which I yet cannot *say* I am in.[7] Thus, circumstances can easily be imagined in which, say, only another person's report about my utterances or other outward behavior could convince me that I must have had a mental state which I did not in fact recognize as such or ascribe to myself. Hypnotic trances, talking during sleep, and the like are common enough occurrences which would imply nonself-conscious representations for all but the most convinced behaviorist. Of course, the representations I am inferred to have had in such cases would not have existed at all unless they existed *in* me, but this does not seem to mean that they must be part of my self-consciousness, capable of being ascribed to my identical self *by* me.

To be sure, representational states of which I am not actually conscious might be "nothing to me" when it comes to explicit claims of knowledge, in the sense that I could not justifiably use representations of which I had never been conscious to support my empirical judgments on any other subjects. In an epistemological analogue to the evidentiary exclusion of hearsay (see *Anthropology*, §2, 7:129), I could not include such representations among my data for an empirical knowledge-claim to be grounded in my empirical intuitions. But this concession does not help Kant's argument. It does not imply that there is an absolute or *de re* necessity that any possible representation, regardless of its empirical content, be synthesized. It therefore does not imply the existence of an *a priori* synthesis, which is the premise for Kant's inference of the *a priori* validity of the categories. It implies only the conditional necessity that any representation which is *in fact* ascribed to my identical self must also have some discernible connection to other representations also so ascribed. But a conclusion like this, though it is indeed reminiscent of Kant's merely analytical interpretation of the principle of apperception, does not suffice to imply that there is any synthesis of the manifold other than the empirical synthesis which occurs when in fact a given representation is indeed successfully associated with some others, or that there are any special concepts, known *a priori,* by means of which synthesis must be performed. What is indisputable in Kant's claim – that representations of which we are not aware (in at least some fashion) are not available for ordinary epistemological purposes – is too weak to support the conclusion which Kant tries to draw from the principle of apperception.

It is interesting to note that several years after he completed the second edition of the *Critique,* Kant himself acknowledged, at least indirectly, that the mere occurrence of consciousness does not automatically ensure recognition of self-consciousness. This acknowledgment comes in yet another of Kant's revealing letters to Marcus Herz. Discussing, in this letter of May 1789, the need for rules in thinking of objects as well as intuitions for perceiving them, Kant emphasizes with regard to the former that

... only under these conditions, therefore, can we have experience of objects; and consequently, if intuition (of objects of appearance) did not agree with these conditions, objects would be nothing for us, that is, not objects of *knowledge* at all; we should have knowledge neither of ourselves nor of other things ...

Thus, he shortly continues,

... All *data* of the senses for a possible cognition would never, without those conditions, represent objects. They would not even reach that unity of consciousness that is necessary for knowledge of myself (as object of inner sense). I would not even be able to know that I have [such data]; consequently for me, as a knowing being, they would be absolutely nothing. They could still (if I imagine myself to be an animal) carry on their play in an orderly fashion, as representations connected according to empirical laws of association, and thus even have an influence on my feeling and desire, without my being aware of them (assuming that I am even conscious of each individual representation, but not of their relation to the unity of representation of their object, by means of the synthetic unity of their apperception). This might be so without my knowing the slightest thing thereby, not even what my own condition is. (11:51–2)

In these remarks, Kant distinguishes precisely between the conditions for the mere *occurrence* of a multiplicity of representations and the conditions for *recognizing* that one has such data. One might have to imagine oneself into the position of an unself-conscious animal in order to be gripped by this distinction, for the obvious reason that our ordinary, first-person conception of our own condition is precisely that of self-consciousness and not mere consciousness without synthesis, but the implication seems clear that the latter is no absolute impossibility. This means that *a priori* rules for the understanding might be deduced from the conditions of experience of objects, as the first paragraph suggests, or even from the conditions for "knowledge of myself (as object of inner sense)" as the second paragraph promises, but not from any necessity that all consciousness also be self-conscious.[8]

At this point, one might interject that the thought of conscious but not self-conscious animals is hardly necessary to suggest that apperception is not an absolutely necessary concomitant of any form of representation whatever. After all, Kant must have been familiar with the Leibnizian contrast between *petite perceptions* and apperception, so prominent in the *New Essays* which Kant carefully studied after their publication in 1765. Of course, Kant was aware of Leibniz's distinction, and in his anthropological description of human cognition he appealed to obvious examples to illustrate it – for example, a musician who can make decisions about "a host of ideas" "in a matter of seconds" without having individual consciousness of them (*Anthropology*, §5, 7:136). But two points must be noted about Kant's use of Leibniz's distinction. First, Kant carefully describes the distinction as one between *clear* and *obscure* perceptions, rather than as one between *conscious* and *unconscious* perceptions, so that even the recognition of the distinction does not commit him to the supposition that there can be any representations inexorably barred from the reach of apperception. Second, Kant is also careful to insist that the "theory of obscure ideas belongs only to ... physiological ... anthropology," which shows us the "passive side of man, as the plaything of sensations" (7:136). Thus, the obscurity of some sensations can be ignored in the theoretical consideration of apperception, precisely because the active rather than passive nature of the latter is the antidote for obscurity: There is no hint that there is anything in the obscurity of sensations which can bar the otherwise guaranteed possibility of apperception. If anything, Kant turns the Leibnizian distinction between perception and apperception into another illustration of his own conception of empirical intuition as the merely passive material for the active "self-consciousness of reflection" achieved by the mind's activity on such material (see *Anthropology*, §4, 7:134n). Or Kant accepts Leibniz's distinction between perception and apperception as one between two *aspects* of self-consciousness, but not as one between *instances* of mere consciousness as opposed to instances of self-consciousness.

This said, however, the reason for Kant's complete certainty about the impossibility of perception without apperception remains obscure.

(*b*) In his argument for an objective affinity of all appearances, that is, a ground "on which rests the possibility, indeed the necessity of a law which extends itself to all appearances" – which is a consequence of the *a priori* synthesis of apperception and the very point in Kant's mature work where his commitment to the view, earlier rejected, that the laws of the intellect are literally *imposed* on the data for knowledge is most clearly revealed – Kant employs a variant of the argument just considered. What he wants to exclude is precisely the contingency which would reduce the principle of apperception to a merely conditional necessity, namely the possibility that though appearances must indeed fit into a connected whole if self-consciousness is to occur, it is nevertheless "something entirely accidental that appearances do lend themselves to a connected whole of human cognition" (A 121). That such a whole is in itself something accidental, or, to put it less dramatically, something which we cannot ourselves guarantee or automatically impose on the manifolds of intuition that we are given, would indeed be the case if it were at all possible that "much empirical consciousness [could] arise in my mind, but in a state of separation, and without belonging to a consciousness of myself." However, Kant argues, such an obstacle to the thoroughgoing affinity of all appearances is entirely "impossible": "Only because I assign all perceptions to a single consciousness (that of original apperception) can I say of all perceptions that I am conscious of them" (A 122). Unfortunately, however, although this may be true, it again expresses a merely conditional necessity which cannot suffice to support the claim of objective affinity or the guaranteed possibility of an *a priori* synthesis of apperception. For by predicating his argument on the assumption of representations of which I *can say* that I am conscious, Kant restricts it to just those representations for which self-consciousness and its concomitant consciousness of a connection are already conceded. There is, to be sure, a *de dicto* necessity that whatever representations I can *call* my own be connected into a synthetic whole of self-consciousness. But this leaves entirely unproved what must be defended to ground the postulation of objective affinity, namely, the *de re* necessity that *all* of my representations must be capable of being ascribed to my identical self. Thus, his appeal to the necessary conditions for *saying* that I am conscious of any representations begs Kant's question.

(*c*) There is, however, another consideration that appears to have persuaded Kant of our *a priori* certainty of the numerical identity of the self in all its possible representations. Although this argument is never as clearly stated as arguments *a* and *b*, it appears to have worked on Kant at a deeper level. It also, at least initially, appears much more powerful. This argument is intimated in the second-edition text of the deduction when Kant states that my consciousness of the identity of my apperception of my manifold must *precede* my *determinate* thought of the manifold (B 134) and that my representation of the unity of the manifold "first makes possible" any *particular* combination of it (B 130-1). A clearer expression of the underlying assumption that makes the truth of even the synthetic proposition of apperception seem so self-evident to Kant, however, may be found in a version of the transcendental deduction that is included along with Kant's marginalia from his own copy of the first edition of the *Critique*, and thus must date from the period between the two editions, but which is entirely different from all the simple deductions from the concept of an object and/or a judgment which we find in that period. The first paragraph of this note was quoted earlier, but now we can appreciate the rest of the argument:

The pure synthesis of imagination is the ground of the possibility of the empirical synthesis in apprehension, therefore also of perception. It is possible *a priori* and brings forth nothing except forms. The transcendental synthesis of imagination concerns only the unity of apperception in the synthesis of the manifold in general through the imagination. Thereby a concept of the object in general is thought according to the different kinds of transcendental synthesis. The synthesis takes place in time.

No appearances concern me at all insofar as they are [only] in the senses, but rather as they can at least be met with in apperception. But they can be met with in the latter only by means of the synthesis of apprehension, that is, the imagination, but this must accord with the absolute unity of apperception; therefore all appearances are elements of a possible cognition only insofar as they stand under the transcendental unity of the synthesis of imagination. Now the categories are nothing other than the representations of something (appearance) in general insofar as it is represented through the transcendental synthesis of imagination[.] Therefore all appearances as elements of a possible cognition (experience) stand under the categories.

All appearances are nothing for us unless they are taken up into consciousness. Therefore their relation to possible cognition is nothing but their relationship to consciousness. But all connection of the manifold of intuition is nothing unless it is taken up into the unity of apperception, thus every cognition which is possible in itself belongs to a possible cognition only by belonging together with all other possible cognitions in a relation to one apperception.

(*Loses Blatt* B 12, 23:18-19)

For any empirical intuition to be recognized as even a candidate for the empirical knowledge of some determinate object, it must already be regarded as subsumed under the unity of apperception, or as an intuition experienced by the same self which has a variety of other intuitions: Self-consciousness of representations is a condition even of "possible cognition" or their use for any possible empirical knowledge. That is, Kant suggests, whatever the outcome of my empirical investigation of any particular manifold, and thus whether I discover that it does or does not lend itself to any particular claim of empirical knowledge, I must at least *know* that I possess the different representations the empirically objective content of which I propose to investigate. It is for this reason that the unity of apperception must *precede* or *first make possible* all my determinate thought (B 131, 134). So, apparently avoiding begging the question as in arguments *a* and *b* by confining himself to the case of those representations which are in fact fit for empirical knowledge – that is, avoiding the outright assumption of an absolute necessity that all my representations are indeed fit for self-consciousness – Kant is nevertheless able to argue that my knowledge of my common possession of these representations must be independent of the outcome of any empirical investigation of them or of any synthesis according to merely empirical concepts. Thus the unity of my apperception of all the representations which figure in my empirical knowledge must be certain *a priori*, even if there is no *de re* necessity that all states of consciousness also be self-conscious. Yet since even this unity of apperception is genuinely synthetic, it requires a synthesis which is *a priori* and independent of the particular empirical syntheses which presuppose it. This is the "pure synthesis of imagination" which is the ground or precondition of any "empirical synthesis in apprehension."

The assumption that even the candidacy of any representation for empirical knowledge presupposes that it already be assigned to the unity of apperception seems to be the deepest reason for Kant's assertion of the *a priori* certainty of apperception.[9] And even if the Leibnizian distinction between perception and apperception might have suggested an exception to this assumption, it can hardly be doubted that either the skeptics or empiricists against whom the transcendental deduction is aimed would have shared it – again, recall Locke's mocking insistence that the possibility of something's being "imprinted" on the mind without one's recognizing it is "hardly intelligible." Nevertheless, this assumption still does not yield a philosophically sound argument for the premise which Kant requires to ground his direct inference from apperception to *a priori* synthesis, and thus to *a priori* categories. This is because Kant has failed to establish that I must in fact *know* – *a fortiori*, be certain – that I have really had all of a putative series of representations through some period of my continued existence in order to investigate their possible empirical significance. He therefore has not shown it to be necessary that any rule-governed synthesis of my representations be performed prior to or other than that which eventually yields empirical knowledge of their objective significance. To be sure, during the time in which I am performing any such investigation, it must obviously *seem* to me that I have had certain representations or made the observations that I am investigating. It is thus obviously necessary that some *psychological* reproduction of the manifold – or, as Kant would say, "empirical synthesis of reproduction" (A 101) or "subjective and *empirical* ... *association*" (A 121) – must take place whenever I investigate its empirical significance. But unless Kant can exclude *a priori* the possibility that one of the results of my investigation could be the very *rejection* of the supposition that I actually had one or more of the representations the possible empirical connections of which I am investigating, he cannot prove that certainty of my possession of any particular representations really is presupposed by any empirical investigation of them. Yet certainly I can easily imagine that I might often be able to make empirical sense of my manifold of representations only by rejecting my initial assumption that I did indeed ever have all the representations I initially ascribe to myself. For instance, I might be able to make sense of the observations I have recorded in a lab book only if I admit that one of my notes describes an observation I never could have made, thus a representation I never could have had. Unless Kant can exclude such a possibility, he cannot directly show that *a priori* certainty of apperception, as opposed to mere empirical reproduction, is a necessary condition of empirical knowledge, thus that transcendental apperception as he actually understands it (at, e.g., A 106, A 113, and A 116) exists. Thus the conditions of the possibility of conducting any empirical synthesis at all – what Kant ultimately appeals to in support of his argument from *a priori* apperception – do not include *a priori* certainty of the numerical identity of the self with regard to any putative representations it may consider.[10]

Problem 2. Why Kant's support for premise 1 should be open to criticism of this sort may become even clearer if we now consider the possible reasons for his adherence to claim 4, the supposition that knowledge that several different representations belong to my identical self requires a rule-governed synthesis of these representations. We return to the question that has been haunting us throughout: Why should mere self-consciousness of a manifold of representations require a synthesis of it according to rules? Obviously, Kant agrees with Hume that there is nothing in the content of any particular representation considered by itself which can represent its possession by a self, *a fortiori* a continuing self. But he also sees clearly what Hume did not, that in the absence of any internal mark of selfhood, possession by a single self can be represented only by some kind of relation among the several representations which are ascribed to such a self, thus a combination or synthesis of representations. This much progress over Hume is evident at the start of the second-edition text of the deduction:

... The empirical consciousness, which accompanies diverse representations, is in itself scattered and without relation to the identity of the subject. This relation comes about, not merely if I accompany each representation with consciousness, but only if I *conjoin* one representation with another and am conscious of the synthesis of them. Only because I can unite a manifold of given representations in *one consciousness*, therefore, is it possible for me to represent the *identity of the consciousness in these representations* itself. (B 133)

Only if I recognize some relation among my representations *other* than that of possession by my continuing self, which is what must be established, can I recognize my common possession of them. But how can Kant take the further step and show that there must be something *a priori* about this synthesis? Why should the mere empirical reproduction of a manifold of representations be insufficient to allow me to recognize that they all belong to me? We have seen that the need for rules cannot be inferred directly from *a priori* certainty of such recognition, since that certainty does not appear to exist. The only alternative is that there is some condition for even merely empirical or *a posteriori* ascriptions of representations to a continuing or identical self which requires the use of certain rules.

In fact, such a condition follows from the fact about the temporality of consciousness which Kant claimed to be the premise of the deduction even in his first exposition of it but then seemed to ignore in all that followed (A 99). It may indeed seem puzzling that we should need any special rules for the representation of a connected manifold of our own representations if we are thinking of the self-ascription of a *single present* representation: *That* seems to be as good a case of criterionless knowledge as we could ever imagine. From that we might easily be tempted to leap to the conclusion that we do not need any special rules or criteria for the self-ascription of any *manifold* of representations either. Just as I simply *have* my present representation, and need no rules to judge *that* it is mine, so, it would seem, I am directly acquainted with any *manifold* of my representations, and could not possibly require any rules to judge that the whole manifold is mine either. However, what is on Kant's account the fundamental premise of his whole deduction is precisely the assumption that I am *not* immediately acquainted with any *manifold* of representations insofar as I think of our representational state as "contained in a single moment," but can instead think of a manifold *as a manifold* only if I first represent a "sequence of one impression upon another." Now, Kant's immediate reason for mentioning this premise is his argument that the *unity* of a representation also requires that there be at least several moments of an apprehension for a manifold of representations to be available for cognitive connection. But his statement that "intuition ... does indeed offer a manifold, but a manifold which can never be represented as a manifold, *and as contained in a single representation*" without a synthesis also implies that at any given time *my representation of a manifold of representation* is not itself a *manifold of representations* but rather a *single representation* which must be *interpreted* or *judged* to *represent* a diversity or manifold of representations.[11] And then the further argument could be made that I can provide such an interpretation only by the use of a *rule* from which I can deduce that, given its content, a present representation can be understood *only* as the representation of a sequence of previous representations. If we assume no *a priori* constraints upon the internal complexity of any representation regarded simply as a presently occurrent mental state, then the mere contents of a present representation itself cannot dictate that it be interpreted as a representation of several temporally diverse representations, although this is what we need in order to interpret it as representing a manifold of representations at all. Only if we synthesize the content of the representation according to rules requiring us to interpret it as representing the "sequence of one impression upon another" can we interpret it as a manifold at all. Although the successive *occurrence* of intuitions ultimately

148

provides all the *material* for a manifold of intuition, it cannot itself provide the *recognition* of a manifold, and *a fortiori* knowledge of the possession of this by an identical self, unless its present state is interpreted in the light of some rules sufficient to introduce into it an interpretation of temporal diversity.[12]

An argument of this form, which does not assume any *a priori* certainty of the unity of apperception but assumes only that the self-ascription of representations is an empirical possibility, could finally show why a synthesis according to rules should be necessary to represent the identity of the self in its manifold of representations, for it would show that the rule-governed interpretation of one's mental state is necessary to represent even the diversity, as well as the connection, of the manifold of representations itself. But such an argument is not merely independent of the assumption of the *a priori* certainty of numerical identity; it also undermines it, or at least undermines anything like argument *c* in behalf of premise 1. For as soon as we see that my representation of a manifold requires the *interpretation* of my present representational state as representing a temporal diversity of states, we also see that there is no reason why an *error* in such interpretation should not be possible – why some feature of my present state should not be interpreted as representing a past representation which in fact never occurred at all or which, if it did occur, was not mine. If we picture the manifold of representations as somehow all before us at once – which I strongly suspect is the customary though tacit assumption in the interpretation of Kant's argument – then there would seem to be no possibility of error in determining their common possession by ourselves. There would thus seem to be *a priori* certainty about the unity of apperception, though a certainty that has no need for rules of synthesis to determine that the manifold of representations belongs to the identical self. But if we need to interpret our present representational states in order even to see them as representing a manifold of representaions, then we can understand why we must apply some such rules in order to interpret features of our present states as representing members of a temporally extended manifold of states, but also why it should not be impossible to err in this interpretation. What might otherwise appear to be just the curious fallibility of memory claims would be seen to be in fact an intrinsic liability of any representation of a manifold whatsoever, and the same consideration which would finally show why rules are necessary for the recognition of the unity even of mere self-consciousness would also undercut Kant's assumption of the *a priori* certainty of the transcendental unity of apperception.

IIB: *A priori* conditions of empirical self-knowledge

Kant clearly did not recognize that the premise of the argument just described – namely, that the representation of a manifold is a representation of a temporal diversity of states which requires an act of interpretation of my present representational state – also undermines the *a priori* certainty of apperception. For he clearly placed his hopes for a deduction from apperception on the argument from its *a priori* certainty, and the hints at the possibility of an argument from empirical self-consciousness which we may find in the published texts of the deduction were not intended as an *alternative* strategy by Kant himself when he wrote these texts. This means that if the various deductions of forms IA, IB, and IIA are open to the objections we have considered, Kant does not accomplish the mission of the transcendental deduction in the texts meant to do so and can do so, if at all, only in later parts of his text. Given what Kant himself has told us is the key to all that follows (A 99), we could expect this mission to be accomplished only in the theory of time-determination offered in the "Analogies of Experience" and the "Refutation of Idealism." Nevertheless, Kant's original conception of the method for a transcendental theory of experience may have been responsible for certain hints at these subsequent arguments in the official exposition of the newly invented transcendental deduction. At the same time, Kant's confidence in his new idea that there could be a transcendental deduction directly from the *a priori* certainty of apperception also led him to downplay these hints.

As we saw in Chapter 2, the connotation of a determinate knowledge of the temporal order of subjective states had been a part of the sense of at least some of Kant's uses of the term "apperception" since the 1770s. Recall that in the *Duisburg Nachlass* Kant wrote that "apperception is the consciousness of thinking, that is, of representations, as they are positioned [*gesetzt*] in the mind. There are three exponents [of this position]: 1. the relationship to the subject; 2. the relation of succession to one another; 3. the synthesis [*Zusammennehmung*]" (R 4674, 17:647). By using the temporal term "succession," Kant implied there that apperception involves an awareness of the temporal succession of representations, and thus that the conditions for determining such a succession are necessary conditions for the consciousness of apperception itself. Another passage made it even clearer both that such a determination involves the application of a rule and that it is a necessary condition of regarding even subjective states as belonging to a single subject: "Now since everything must be given in time, which therefore includes everything in itself, the [use of a rule] is an *actus* of apperception, namely the consciousness of the subject which apperceives [itself] as that which is given in the whole time, [and] is necessarily connected with [the use of a rule], for otherwise the sensation would not be represented as belonging to me" (R 4674, 17:656). Thus Kant long had in the back of his mind the view that both ascribing any particular sensation to a particular moment in even the subjective experience of the subject and representing the continuity of that experience – representing the subject as "that which is given in the whole time" – require the use of certain rules. Finally, there were several passages which both linked "apperception" with "self-perception" (*Selbstwahrnehmung*) and defined "perception" as involving temporal position, thus implying that the "relations of apperception" which are to be determined by synthesis according to categories are precisely the determinate relations of subjective states in time. "Perception is position in inner sense in general and resolves into sensations according to relations of apperception of self-consciousness, according to which we become conscious of our own existence" (R 4677, 17:658–9). The style was dense but implied that the kind of consciousness of our own existence with which Kant is concerned is consciousness of the existence of our different states in time. These remarks were little more than promissory notes, however, and did little to explain the need for rules to achieve temporal self-consciousness. Yet when Kant finally has the opportunity to expand on them in the second-edition text of the deduction, he also does less than we would hope to exploit the hint which, as we have now seen, lies in the key premise at A 99.

Still, the hints are there. In §25 of the second-edition text, Kant emphasizes that intuition as well as mere thought are required for self-knowledge but also reveals the assumption that such intuition must be *made determinate*:

Now in order to *know* ourselves, there is required in addition to the act of thought, which brings the manifold of every possible intuition to the unity of apperception, a determinate mode of intuition, whereby this manifold is given; it therefore follows that . . . the determination of my existence can take place only in conformity with the form of inner sense, according to the special mode in which the manifold which I combine is given in inner intuition. (B 157–8)

Thus, no self-knowledge is possible without the presentation of a manifold of states of the self in the form of inner sense – which is, of course, temporal. But Kant also precedes this statement with the statement in §24 that although intuition is a necessary condition of knowledge, its mere occurrence is not a sufficient condition thereof, precisely because intuition can be made *determinate* only in judgment:

Inner sense . . . contains the mere form of intuition, but without combination of the manifold in it, and therefore so far contains no *determinate* intuition, which is possible only through the consciousness of the determination of the manifold by the transcendental act of imagination (synthetic influence of the understanding upon inner sense). (B 154)

However, judgment according to certain rules is required to make the intuition of time determinate. At least Kant so assumes in his next assertion:

. . . We cannot obtain for ourselves a representation of time, except under the image of a line, which we draw, and . . . by this mode of depicting it alone could we know the singleness of its dimension; and similarly . . . for all inner perceptions we must derive the determination of lengths of time or of points of time from the changes which are exhibited to us in outer sense. . . . The determinations of inner sense have therefore to be arranged as appearances in time in precisely the same manner in which we arrange those of outer sense in space. (B 156)

To make determinate judgments about the temporal succession of subjective states at all, which is presupposed even by empirical knowledge that my continuing self actually has a manifold of representations, I must link those representations in some way to objects in space which are capable of both continued existence and yet determinate changes. Only thus can I determine that my present state actually represents a "sequence of one impression upon another." Yet to make such connections requires precisely that I make judgments about the continued existence of objects regarded as distinct from mere modifications of inner sense and judge the changes of such objects. What can this be but to apply the concepts of inherence and subsistence to things regarded as objects in a strong sense and to apply to such objects the further dynamic categories of causality and dependence and perhaps even reciprocity of action? Thus, making the temporal judgments presupposed by any self-knowledge requires the use of the categories, and it is at least necessary that *if* I make the former, then I must use the latter.

Yet although the second-edition text of the deduction *asserts* such connections, it hardly *argues* them. Indeed, Kant mentions these connections for an explicit purpose quite different from the basic task of deducing the objective validity of the categories, namely to prove that the temporal knowledge of subjective states, since it depends on knowledge of objects in space, must be, like the latter, knowledge of mere appearances rather than of things in themselves. Nor is Kant as willing to accept the exclusive identification of apperception with the "self-perception" of temporally successive states an he was in the *Duisburg Nachlass*; the opening line of §25 still seems to insist that even the mere knowledge "that I am" already involves the "original synthetic unity of apperception" (B 157) and its *a priori* rules, implying that the determinate self-knowledge discussed in §24 must not be *identical* to the transcendental apperception which is the ground of the transcendental deduction, but something additional to it.

Both the these problems must have the same source, namely that Kant was persuaded by the argument from *a priori* certainty of apperception that we have examined as argument IIA and thus thought that an analysis of the conditions of merely empirical self-knowledge, though that of course involves the categories and can thus furnish an additional proof of them, required basically only the application of a point already proved.

This will also explain why Kant's discussion of the conditions of time-determination in the "Analogies of Experience," and even his final proof in the "Refutation of Idealism" that any determination of the temporal relation of subjective states presupposes these objective time-determinations, take the guise of the "schematism" understood as a mere *application* of the categories already deduced, in spite of the fact that we have seen – beginning with our examination of the *Prolegomena* – that what Kant requires is nothing less than a proof that the categories are the only candidates for applying the logical functions of judgment to empirical intuitions. nevertheless, we shall eventually see that, although only after many detours and, indeed, not until after the publication of the second edition of the *Critique,* Kant did finally attempt to construct self-sufficient arguments demonstrating that the representation of a merely subjective manifold as temporally successive requires the categorical concepts of substance and causation. He thus did ultimately attempt to execute strategy IIB, though it will take us most of the rest of this book to see this.

One point about the interpretation of Kant's eventual development of argument IIB in his theory of time-determination can be made here, however, since it follows from considerations which have been advanced in the present chapter. Kant's strategy for deriving the necessity of categories from the conditions presupposed by any empirical knowledge at all will be grounded on the premise that the synthesis which produces such knowledge presupposes a manifold, but that this manifold must be a temporally diverse one; yet since we are never actually in possession of such a manifold at any moment, we can represent it only by interpreting our present representation as a representation of temporally diverse representations according to certain rules. Since reference to such a manifold is also presupposed by any informative reference to an identical self, the use of such rules is also a necessary condition of any judgment of the identity of the self. A moment's reflection, however, must persuade us that it cannot be synthesis according to such rules which first *generates* any consciousness of time at all, that is, the psychological or "empirical" condition in which it merely *seems* to us that we are aware of a succession of different representational states. The metaphysical conception of an understanding which does not itself act in time but which generates temporal order out of a diversity which is itself both atemporal and also preconscious verges on unintelligibility, or at least requires the refuge of transcendental idealism (B 155–6). More important, however, the causal laws about the behavior of objects by which we make the temporal interpretation of our own experience (according to B 156) are themselves laws which must be inductively confirmed in time and so cannot be first used to generate any consciousness of time at all. It is, however, perfectly intelligible to suppose that causal *beliefs,* like the *beliefs* about our own states which they can and must be used to confirm, can be *transformed into knowledge* within time. That is, although a transcendental *psychology* which explains how consciousness of time is *produced* would be completely incoherent, a transcendental *epistemology* which displays the necessary conditions for the confirmation of judgments about temporal order is perfectly plausible. So if we interpret Kant's theory not as a theory of the psychological genesis of temporal consciousness but as an epistemological theory of the confirmation of temporal knowledge, it will at least be intelligible.

On this account, of course, the metaphysics of Kant's theory of transcendental affinity will not be acceptable. Instead, Kant will be forced to return to the conservatism of the *Duisburg Nachlass*: The principles of thought which Kant's argument will finally produce will not be able to be thought of as "foundations" imposed on all experience by the form of consciousness itself, but will instead have to be regarded as "restrictions" on those cases of consciousness which do in fact count as cognitive judgments (cf. R 4678, 17:661). This is because Kant's theory of time-determination will not be able to require us to postulate psychological processes which in every case of consciousness at all must employ or instantiate the rules we need for the synthesis of determinate temporal relations; it will only be able to describe conditions which experience must meet if we are to be capable of determinate self-consciousness. Of course, such a return to Kant's original position on the force of the laws of thought is precisely what we should expect from the substitution of a theory of the conditions for empirical self-consciousness for the argument from the *a priori* certainty of apperception, since it is only the latter which really gave Kant reason to depart from his original restrictions on claims to necessity. Without the assumption of *a priori* certainty of apperception, Kant will have no need to postulate transcendental syntheses taking place whether we know it or not, or before we know anything at all; he will have ground to claim only that when empirical judgments of apperception can in fact be justified, certain rules must be employed. On the argument by which their objective validity will finally be deduced, since we neither have an *a priori* guarantee for our judgments of self-knowledge nor need one in order to undertake empirical synthesis, the categories will not have to be supposed to be implemented in any act of synthesis except empirical synthesis itself.

Given the little that was accomplished by all of the explicit tactics of the transcendental deduction of the 1780s, what Kant should have done next was demonstrate that the categories are the only means by which determinate judgments can be made about even the intuitions of inner sense. This would be a fit task to be described as the "Schematism of the Pure Concepts of the Understanding." Given his own assumption that he had already succeeded in deducing the categories from the metaphysical and transcendental deductions, Kant offered something at least apparently different under this rubric. We must now pause to examine this before we can consider Kant's explicit exposition of the theory of time-determination.

III
The principles of empirical knowledge

6

The schematism and system of principles

What is the schematism?

In his original transcendental theory of experience, Kant tried to demonstrate the objective validity of *a priori* categories of the understanding by directly demonstrating the role of the concepts of substance, causation, and interaction in the temporal organization of experience. For the *Critique of Pure Reason,* however, he attempted to separate the pure concepts of the understanding from the principles of temporal determination. The metaphysical deduction purported to derive the categories from the logical functions of judgment alone, and even though the premise that "all our knowledge is ... subject to time" was placed at the head of the transcendental deduction in the first edition (A 99), this claim had no obvious role in the three methods for a transcendental deduction to which Kant devoted most of his effort during the 1780s. It had an explicit role only in the suggestion that the objective application of the categories is the necessary condition for making determinate empirical judgments even about inner sense or empirical self-consciousness. But since such an argument was barely hinted at in the final sections of the second-edition text, the major work of Kant's transcendental deduction remained to be done even after the chapter officially devoted to it.

Of course this is not how the author of the *Critique* explicitly saw his position at the end of the transcendental deduction. Kant naturally thought that he had already demonstrated that the pure concepts of the understanding, first identified with the help of the logical functions of judgment, must be employed in all pure as well as empirical knowledge, and he therefore assumed that the fundamental task remaining for the constructive part of his theoretical philosophy was merely the application of these concepts, or the display of the principles of empirical judgment generated by the application of these categories to intuitions formed as ours are. We shall see, however, that Kant does not confine himself to such a modest program, and that the chapter entitled "The Schematism of the Pure Concepts of the Understanding" and the following chapter, "The System of All Principles of Pure Understanding," really do contain the basic materials for his only successful deduction of the categories. Since it is precisely these chapters which develop the arguments – or analogies – first intimated in the transcendental theory of experience of 1774–5, this is what we should expect.

In fact, the "Schematism" and "Principles" chapters offer a two-stage theory of time-determination which ultimately demonstrates the claim of Kant's original transcendental theory of experience: Just as was suggested by numerous passages in the *Duisburg Nachlass* (e.g., R 4672, R 4679), the objective validity of the category of magnitude and then chiefly of the relational categories is the necessary condition of empirical knowledge or determinate intuition of inner as well as outer sense. At the first stage of this theory Kant assumes that we do have knowledge about the temporal relations of objects distinct from our own representations of them and directly argues only that certain principles – namely, the principles that the objectively real is ultimately composed of permanent substances of determinate magnitude, and that these all stand in relations of causation and interaction – are the necessary conditions for the possibility of such empirical knowledge, or experience in a strong sense. As the second stage of his theory, however, Kant tries to argue that such empirical knowledge, and therefore the principles which are its necessary conditions, are the necessary conditions of the possibility of experience, even in the weaker sense of determinate knowledge of the temporal relations of subjective states as such. This second stage of the argument is the special task of the "Refutation of Idealism" that was inserted into the system of principles in the second edition of the *Critique,* although the argument of this refutation was not expounded with any satisfactory degree of clarity before 1790.

Kant creates a sense of obscurity when he writes that "this schematism of our understanding, in its application to appearances and their mere form, is an art concealed in the depths of the human soul, whose real modes of activity nature is hardly likely ever to allow us to discover and to have open to our gaze" (A 141 / B 180–1). Such pessimism seems unwarranted by the official program for the chapter. On Kant's account, the objective validity of the pure categories of the understanding is supposed to have been established already, although their content has been described only indirectly by their correlation to purely logical features of the structure of *judgments.* They thus far, therefore, describe only indirectly any features of the *objects* of judgments. The chief objective of the schematism must therefore be to show exactly how these categories can be instantiated or manifested in our sensible intuition of objects. So, to give the categories sufficient content for their empirical use, temporal and/or spatial correlates must be found for what have thus far remained purely logical properties and relations of judgments.[1] Such correlates will be the transcendental schemata of the pure categories.

As a subsidiary point, Kant also employs the concept of a schema to dissolve the problem of abstract ideas which Berkeley pressed against Locke, the problem of how we can have an abstract idea of, for example, a triangle which is yet not an idea of a right nor an obtuse nor an acute triangle (A 141 / B 180). By so doing Kant does not mean to invoke a *general* theory of schematism according to which between all concepts and the objects to which they apply there must lie some *third thing* as an intermediary – though this is the aim that some commentators have ascribed to him and then ridiculed. Jonathan Bennett, for instance, says that "Kant seeks to answer the following suspect question: 'Given that I possess a concept, how can I apply it to its instances?'"[2] But Kant does not raise his question in a form suspect because of its generality. First, he does not recognize a question about the applicability of concepts as a *logical* question at all, for if *logic* "sought to give general instructions how we are to subsume under . . . rules, that is, to distinguish whether something does or does not come under them, that could be only by means of another rule" (A 133 / B 172), and an infinite and vicious regress would instantly arise (see also *Critique of Judgment*, 5:169). In fact, Kant does not think that there *is* any real problem about the application of concepts in the case of two main classes of concepts which we *ordinarily* employ, namely the pure sensible concepts of mathematics and the empirical concepts of natural science and ordinary life, for his view of such concepts is that they basically *are* rules for applying predicates to particular objects or their images, and thus virtually identical to schemata. Kant's empiricist predecessors ran into difficulties, of course, by attempting to analyze these sorts of concepts as *images* rather than as rules or schemata, but these difficulties were of their own making.[3] From Kant's point of view, there is a *real* problem about schematism, and a need for a genuine intermediary between concept and object, only in the case of the *special* concepts which concern transcendental philosophy, that is, the *pure* concepts of the understanding. It is only because the content of these is initially specified in merely logical terms that a special theory is needed to specify further "the sensible condition under which alone the pure concepts of the understanding can be employed" (A 136 / B 175).

Nevertheless, we can understand why Kant may have felt uneasy about his conception of the schematism. For one thing, according to his original conception of the transcendental theory of experience, the categories of relation – the categories that were chiefly at stake – were linked to the sensible conditions of time-determination from the start. On such a conception a separate schematism would indeed have been otiose, because the categories were never purely logical at all. Second, though some of Kant's arguments from the mid-1780s (the arguments from the *Prolegomena* and *Metaphysik Volckmann* considered in Chapter 4) did suggest the need for something like a schematism, they seemed to call for something rather different from what the *Critique* supplies: not a simple *derivation* of special forms of intuition from logical functions of judgment, but rather a *proof* that certain relations in intuition are the only available candidates for the application of these logical functions. Finally, as we shall see in the last section of this chapter, there is the peculiar fact that Kant seems to recommence the argument for the principles of judgment in the second chapter of the "Analytic of Principles," as if the "Schematism" chapter did not precede it. All of this suggests that the schematism was inserted into the organization of the *Critique* (perhaps at quite a late date in the book's composition, since there seems to be little anticipation of it in any of Kant's surviving notes), without a very clear conception of the proper structure for his transcendental deduction at its deepest level. In other words, the deepest mystery about the schematism is just the general mystery of why Kant ever departed from his original conception of the direct deduction of the categories from the conditions of time-determination and thus separated the task of the schematism from that of the transcendental deduction itself. Here we can only appeal to the answer which chapters 4 and 5 have offered – namely, that Kant's invention of the deduction directly from the apriority of judgment, and even more that of the deduction from the *a priori* certainty of apperception, led him to reconceive of the theory of time-determination as a merely subsidiary part of his theory of knowledge, separated from the transcendental deduction itself. Once so separated, the theory of time-determination – and thus Kant's real proof of the objective validity of the categories – could indeed be reinstated into the program of the *Critique* only by the artifice of the schematism.

Whatever the programmatic necessity of separate chapters on the schematism and the system of principles, however, the content of these pages is of profound importance. The chapter on the schematism shows the way around the empiricist problem of abstract concepts in general and resolves Hume's particular problem about the impression – that is, empirical manifestations – of the especially problematic concepts of causation and of externality itself. But more important, by their emphasis on both the ubiquity of time as the form of inner sense and on the need for *a priori* rules for time-determination, the two chapters create the conceptual space into which Kant's solution to the problem of objective validity by his refutation of idealism is eventually inserted.

This significance is revealed by the course of Kant's exposition in these two chapters. To be sure, he begins his exposition of the schematism as if assuming that the categories have already been identified by the metaphysical deduction and shown to have objective validity by the transcendental deduction, so that only a problem about how categories identified through logic can be applied to intuitions remains to be solved. Thus he writes:

The *Analytic of Principles* will accordingly be merely a canon for the *faculty of judgment,* which teaches it to apply to appearances the concepts of the understanding which contain the conditions for rules *a priori.* On this ground, although I take as my theme the actual *principles of understanding,* I will employ the title of a *doctrine of the faculty of judgment* as more accurately designating this task.

(A 132 / B 171)

But as he proceeds, Kant's exposition begins to take on the form of a new *deduction* of objectively valid principles for experience in which the supposition that the categories have already been identified and justified plays almost no role at all, or in which the prior deduction of the categories functions as little more than a "clue" (compare A 218 / B 265 with A 66 / B 91). And this is just to say that Kant's original conception of a transcendental theory of experience, on which the task for a transcendental deduction was identified by an abstract discussion of synthetic *a priori* judgments but was solved only by the theory of time-determination implied by the "analogies of appearance," resurfaces in the course of the "Schematism" and "System of All Principles of Pure Understanding." The separation of these chapters from the official transcendental deduction in the architectonic of the *Critique* may reflect Kant's ambivalence about the best form for his argument but even then does not entirely suppress the original springs of his theory.

The underlying structure of Kant's argument becomes particularly clear in the introductory sections of the "System of All Principles." Here, with only the most cursory of references to the preceding "Schematism" (A 148/ B 187), Kant poses the problem of a principle for synthetic judgments (as opposed to the law of noncontradiction, which can ground only analytic judgments [A 150–3 / B 189–93]) almost as though it had not yet been addressed and then suggests that the principle can be discovered by the recognition that "the possibility of experience is, then, what gives objective reality to all our *a priori* cognitions" (A 156 / B 195). This remark might be taken to mean just that although the categories have already been shown to be necessary if we are to be able to think of objects, they must still be shown to be capable of being applied to our sensible intuition.[4] Kant also suggests that the task of showing the relation between "the synthesis of imagination and the necessary unity of this synthesis in transcendental apperception," on the one hand, and "a possible empirical knowledge in general," on the other, remains to be accomplished (A 158 / B 197). And this almost suggests that the separate steps of the schematism and the transcendental deduction itself had not already been traversed. In any case, Kant's exposition of the proofs of the several principles of pure understanding makes little reference to the prior results of the separate transcendental deduction and is conducted as though it is in these proofs that the task of demonstrating the objective reality of the *a priori* concepts of the understanding is first being broached. And so it would be, on Kant's original conception of the transcendental theory of experience.

This tension between the official architectonic of the *Critique* and the continuing grasp of a transcendental theory of experience on Kant's earlier model is most evident in Kant's general discussion of the schematism and principles of understanding and in the discussion of the first two classes of principles, the axioms of intuition and the anticipations of perception. These will be my subjects in this and the following chapter, and in these chapters it may therefore sometimes seem as though I have digressed from the subject of Kant's theory of time-determination. In the subsequent discussions of the analogies of experience and the refutation of idealism, however, Kant's fundamental theory will return to full view as he proceeds virtually without reference to the earlier architectonic.

Intuitions, schemata, and concepts

The primary task of the schematism on Kant's official program is set out in the introduction to the "Analytic of Principles" and then clarified in the opening pages of the "Schematism" itself. In the first passage, Kant points out that *in general* there is neither a need for nor a possibility of the discovery of rules for the *application* of concepts in addition to the concepts themselves. "Mother wit," or a talent for judgment, is needed to apply ordinary concepts to their objects, but to suppose that any rules besides those furnished by the concepts themselves (and by general logic – that is, the logic of consistency [cf. A 59 / B 83–4]) are needed to apply them is to open up a vicious regress: If rules were needed to apply concepts, which are themselves rules, then further rules might be needed to apply those, and so on ad infinitum (A 133–4 / B 172–3; see also *Critique of Judgment,* 5:169). But in the case of *pure* concepts of the understanding, the story is different, for here there is both the need and the possibility for principles of judgment which function in the application of these concepts and which have content in addition to the content of the pure concepts themselves. Kant begins by stressing the possibility of such principles, but then also suggests why they are needed:

Transcendental philosophy has the peculiarity that in addition to the rule (or rather the universal condition for rules) which is given in the pure concept of the understanding, it can also display *a priori* the instance to which the rule is to be applied. The ground of the advantage which in this respect it has over all other didactical sciences (with the exception of mathematics) lies precisely in this: that it deals with concepts which are to relate to their objects *a priori,* the objective validity of which thus cannot be shown *a posteriori,* for that would leave quite untouched the former dignity; rather transcendental philosophy must also show under what conditions objects can be given in accord with its concepts, in universal but sufficient characteristics; otherwise they would be without all content, thus mere logical forms and not pure concepts of the understanding. (A 135–6 / B 174–5)

The initial explanation of the possibility of *a priori* specification of the application of pure concepts is merely promissory, but the concluding account of the need for this is clear: The pure concepts of the understanding must be supplemented with additional principles because at this stage of the argument these concepts are merely logical forms and have not yet been cast in terms of properties or relations that can actually be manifested by objects as they are given to us through the forms of sensibility. Although their role in judgments of objectivity or in the unity of apperception has, officially, already been demonstrated, the categories have thus far been specified only as *correlates* of the forms of *judgment* – that is, as forms which the concepts of objects must embody if the propositional forms countenanced and required by general logic are to be applicable to them. But this means that the *only* content thus far assigned to the categories is that derivable from the *logical* forms and relations characteristic of judgments. So before the categories can be used for the knowledge of the self and/or objects, they must be associated with some sorts of principles directly instantiable in objects of experience as presented by our forms of sensibility.[5] Thus, the "Schematism of Pure Understanding" must "treat of the sensible condition under which alone pure concepts of understanding can be employed" (A 136 / B 175). Or, to use the terms of my discussion of the *Duisburg Nachlass:* On the official account, the argument of the *Critique* has thus far shown that there must *be* some extralogical principles of understanding, but has not yet *described* them extralogically.

This point is expanded upon in the discussion of "homogeneity" in the opening paragraphs of the "Schematism" chapter. Here Kant states that "in all subsumptions of an object under a concept the representation of the object must be *homogeneous* with the concept, that is, the concept must contain something which is represented in the object that is to be subsumed under it" (A 137 / B 176). Two points must immediately be made about this statement. First, Kant is not addressing a problem in the theory of perception, or asserting that there must be some special way in which a property of an object is also present in the representation of the object; he is not reverting to a medieval theory of sensible species, for instance. Rather, he is simply assuming that there is some way in which *properties* of objects are represented by *predicates* or marks which can be entertained in thought and is only pointing out that for an object to be properly denoted by a given concept, that concept must include such a predicate – that is, one suitable to designate some significant feature of the object. Second, Kant is not saying that there is in general any problem about how objects may be subsumed under concepts or about how objects and concepts are "homogeneous"; in general, concepts subsume objects precisely by including predicates which designate properties of objects as they are given in experience. Both of these points are evident in Kant's illustration of his opening claim:[6] "Thus the empirical concept of a *plate* is homogeneous with the pure empirical [concept] of a *circle,* in that the roundness which is thought in the former can be intuited in the latter" (A 137 / B 176). This says that there is no problem about how a concept such as *plate* can apply to objects of our actual experience, because that concept includes in it a predicate or mark – circularity – which itself represents a form that can be given by pure intuition and *a fortiori* in actual empirical intuition. The empirical concept is not itself round, as a plate is – the concept and the plate are not homogeneous in this sense – but the concept of a plate includes the concept of a property which can actually be intuited, namely circularity. When concepts include predicates for properties that can actually be intuited, there is no problem about their homogeneity with the objects to be subsumed under them, and no need for any special schematism.

Another way in which Kant denies that there is a general problem about schematism is precisely by suggesting that ordinary empirical concepts are their own schemata. This is the first part of his dissolution of the empiricists' problem about general concepts. Berkeley was puzzled by the contrast between the specificity of a particular object or a particular image

163

of a particular object and the generality of class concepts of such things.[7] Kant thinks that there is no puzzle about this gap, for it is just the gap between an instance and a rule or schema for the correct identification of this instance. This solves the problem, because there is no further gap between such a schema and an empirical concept. The empirical concept is not an image, but it also does not need to be schematized, because it is already "immediately related to the schema of the imagination, as a rule for the determination of our intuition, according to some general concept," its content being exhausted by such a rule. Thus, for instance, "The concept *dog* signifies a rule according to which my imagination can delineate the figure of a four-footed animal in general, without being limited to any single particular figure which experience offers me or even to such a possible image as I could represent *in concreto*" (A 141 / B 180).[8] The rule by which the reproductive imagination *represents* a dog or the understanding *recognizes* an object presented to it as a dog is just the rule that anything which displays four-footedness (and of course a number of other similarly sensible properties, such as certain characteristics of dentition, musculature, and so on) is to be called a "dog," and this rule is precisely the rule signified by the concept *dog*. In other words, the rule which functions as a schema *is* the concept signified by the expression "dog."[9] So there is no problem about the homogeneity of the empirical concept *dog* with either actually perceived dogs or particular mental pictures of them. Of course, the property of, for instance, four-footedness which is included in the general empirical concept *dog* is not itself fully *determinate* – it does not specify whether the four feet are covered with smooth or wiry fur, nor whether they are little or big – but it *is* a property which can actually be intuited in the case of a particular dog or be read off of a particular image of a dog, whether that dog be a mastiff or a terrier.[10] In this way the empirical concept *dog* is its own schema and is also homogeneous with the object to be subsumed under it. Empirical concepts *are* rules or schemata which tell us to predicate a certain title of a particular object, just in case certain sensible properties indeterminately specified in the rule are actually, and of course determinately, instantiated by that particular object.

That there may be a gap between a concrete particular such as a drawing in the sand and an abstract rule for the proper construction or classification of the particular, which can be filled only by good judgment or mother wit, but that there is no gap between such a rule or schema and a concept, also solves the problem of abstraction in the other case about which Berkeley was vexed, namely the case of mathematical concepts such as *triangle*.[11] Here too Kant argues that it is a mistake to confuse the concept of such a thing with any particular image, for the concept *is*, rather, a rule, though in this case a rule which tells us how to *construct* rather than just correctly *classify* the particular. Thus, we have the rule that an "image of the number five" may be furnished by "five points set alongside one another" (A 140 / B 179), and any particular triangle or image of a triangle will of course be, as Berkeley insisted, either scalene or right or obtuse. But since on Kant's

164

view "it is schemata, not images of objects, which underlie our pure sensible concepts" (A 141 / B 180), the content of a concept such as *triangle* does not have to be *derived* from any such particular, the details of which must somehow be ignored to make it generally applicable (but without a rule telling one which details to ignore, for such a rule would be, or presuppose, a concept as conceived by Kant after all). Rather, like an empirical concept, a mathematical concept *is* a schema or rule, a "representation of a universal procedure of imagination in providing an image for a concept" (A 140 / B 180). The schema of number is "the representation of a method whereby a multiplicity, for instance a thousand, may be represented in an image in conformity with a certain concept"; the schema of a triangle "is a rule of synthesis of the imagination, n respect to pure figures in space" (A 141 / B 180) – a rule or method which tells us how to enclose a plane with three straight lines, as well as to call the figure so produced a "triangle," although certainly not a rule which informs us how to tell whether a line is straight, or straight enough (Plato's problem). Thus the concepts *number* and *triangle* are also such rules, not images of any sort.

The thesis that there is an "immediate relation" between pure and empirical concepts and their schemata thus dissolves the problem of abstraction in the kinds of case which Berkeley pressed against Locke. But Kant clearly believes that there is a problem of abstraction in the special case of the homogeneity of pure concepts of the understanding with their objects. Since the only content which has been provided for these concepts thus far is derived from the *logical* forms and relations suggested by the "functions of judgment," these concepts are "quite heterogeneous from empirical intuitions, and indeed from all sensible intuitions" (A 137 / B 176) (pure as well as empirical). And it should now be obvious what Kant means. He does not mean that pure concepts are not identical to actual perceptions of empirical objects or to actual constructions of mathematical ones in pure imagination, for no concepts are ever identical to things such as that. Rather, the problem is that the *content* of the pure concepts of the understanding does not include any predicates which do directly designate any properties of pure or empirical intuition; they are not yet rules which can be satisfied by objects of intuition. Although being four-footed or triangular is something that may be *both* thought in a concept and directly presented in the appropriate kind of intuition, being *real* or *a ground of a consequence* – that is, possessing the property which is the objective correlate of the logical function of affirmation or the logical relation of antecedent to consequent – is not the kind of property that is directly presented in pure or empirical intuition. Thus for these concepts, but *only* for these, "there must be some third thing, which is homogeneous on the one hand with the category, and on the other hand with the appearance, and which thus makes possible the application of the former to the latter" (A 138 / B 177).

Thus, although Kant brushes aside Berkeley's problem of abstraction for empirical and mathematical concepts, he most certainly believes that

Hume has discovered a genuine problem of abstraction for higher-order concepts such as the concept of causation and the concept of external object itself – but also that he can solve it by means of his concept of a schema. Precisely to illustrate the heterogeneity of pure concepts of the understanding and all intuitions, Kant asserts that no one would say that a category such as causality "could be intuited through sense itself and is contained in the appearance" (A 137–8 / B 176–7). Of course, this is exactly what Hume presupposed when he went looking for some *impression* of necessary connection to furnish the missing element (or "sensory component") in our *idea* of causation, or for some *impression* of existence, in addition to our impressions of the particular properties of external objects, to account for our *belief* in objects beyond our impressions. That is, Hume assumed that concepts such as causality and externality *do* directly connote properties which are presented in empirical intuition and then became skeptical about them when he could find no such impressions. Kant's view is that such skepticism arises from nothing less than the failure to realize that pure concepts of the understanding need to be schematized, although other concepts already are. Kant's thesis that there is a problem about the homogeneity of pure concepts of the understanding, which, however, can be solved by the schematism of these concepts, is nothing other than the conclusion of one who "first tried whether Hume's objection could not be put into a general form, and [who] found that the concept of the connection of cause and effect was by no means the only concept by which the understanding thinks the connection of things *a priori*" (*Prolegomena*, 4:260).

Categories, appearances, and time

Let us now see what Kant's solution to the problem of homogeneity is in the one case in which such a problem arises.

The transcendental deduction is supposed to have established that the categories apply to all appearances whatever that can enter into a thoroughgoing unity of consciousness; they are thus known *a priori* to apply to all appearances. But their content is derived from logical relations which are not directly exemplified by the sensible form of appearances. What is required to make the categories homogeneous with appearances is some aspect of those appearances which, first, holds of them *universally*, so that by its means the categories can indeed be made applicable to *all* appearances; which, second, can be known *a priori*, so that the *a priori* applicability of the categories can be preserved; and which, finally, contains sufficient *diversity* so that the different logical properties and relations from which the categories are (allegedly) derived can *all* be assigned an interpretation by means of this intermediary. If such a medium can be found, and if it is possible to differentiate within it properties or relations that can be both associated with the logical import of the categories and exemplified in actual appearances, these properties or relations can function as the schemata of the categories: rules by which actual appearances can be subsumed under the categories, in spite of the originally merely logical meaning of the latter.

Kant's candidate for such an aspect of appearances is nothing other than *time* itself. In nominating time for this role, Kant emphasizes the apriority and the universality of this form of sensation:

The concept of the understanding contains pure synthetic unity of the manifold in general. Time, as the formal condition of the manifold of inner sense, thus of the connection of all representations, contains an *a priori* manifold in pure intuition. Now a transcendental time-determination is homogeneous with the *category* (which constitutes its unity) insofar as it is *universal* and rests on an *a priori* rule. But it is, on the contrary, homogeneous with the *appearance* insofar as *time* is contained in every empirical representation of the manifold. Thus an application of the category to appearances becomes possible by means of the transcendental time-determination which, as the schema of the concept of the understanding, mediates the subsumption of the [appearance] under the [category].

(A 138–9 / B 177–8)

Temporality is an aspect of the form of all appearances, so if the categories are applied to appearances through time they will be applicable to all appearances. Further, (something about) the determinations of time can be known *a priori,* so if the categories are applied to appearances through time, then the conditions for the applicability of the categories, and not just their logical import, can be known *a priori.* These two claims are explicit in Kant's statement. What is not explicit, but what also seems intended by Kant's exposition, is the third point, that time permits of a *variety* of "transcendental time-determinations," and thus allows for the schematiza- tion of the *variety* of the categories – each category can be associated with a *different* transcendental time-determination. This, of course, becomes more obvious a few pages later, when Kant catalogs a variety of transcen- dental determinations of time and explicitly associates them with the several categories.

Before we can proceed to the list of transcendental time-determinations, however, we must pause over the first step in Kant's argument. For this requires careful statement if it is not to conflict with the larger argument to which the theory of the schematism must ultimately be seen as just the introduction. The assumption on which the thesis that the schemata of the categories must be transcendental determinations of *time* most obviously turns is that since all appearances in outer sense are also appearances in inner sense, but not vice versa, determinations of time *but not of space* are universally valid of all appearances. Therefore the schemata of the categories must be temporal but not spatial determinations.[12] But this conclusion itself is also part of a larger argument, the next main step of which will be that time *is not itself directly or immediately perceived,* or, perhaps more intelligibly, that particular temporal relations are not directly perceived. Instead, Kant will argue, the particular determination of what temporal relation any given appearance does instantiate itself depends on

cognizance of some *spatial* relation – even though spatial relations themselves are also not always directly perceived, and recognition of them in
turn may depend upon knowledge of dynamic relations among objects in
space.[13] Thus, though the *contents* of the transcendental schemata of the
categories are supplied by the several transcendental determinations of
time, the *use* of these schemata – and thus of the categories themselves –
requires *objects in space*. The spatiality of objects of appearances will be the
ultimate condition for the objective validity of the categories, even if it does
not figure in the actual schematization of them.

And this suggests an even deeper reason for the temporality of the
schemata than the fact that time is ubiquitous in a way that space is not.
The fact that the use of the categories begins with schema which are purely
temporal provides a vital premise for the antiskeptical conclusion of Kant's
ultimate theory of experience. By beginning with the premise that the
categories can be interpreted in the purely temporal forms of inner sense,
but then arguing that the determinate temporal relations of subjective
states thus called for can be judged only if those states are also linked to
independent objects in space, Kant can show that the categories can be
given empirical *sense* in terms of knowledge which even the skeptic must
concede – knowledge of the temporal structure of subjective states
themselves – but that they can be *used* only if knowledge of external reality
is also conceded. So by restricting the content of the schemata to temporal
relations and only subsequently showing that their use requires knowledge
of spatial relations as well, Kant does nothing less than prepare the way for
his ultimate refutation of skepticism, or as he calls it, problematic idealism.

The existence of this larger argument is not suggested in the "Schematism" itself but becomes apparent only in the succeeding chapter, "System
of All Principles." Indeed, the premise that time itself is not directly
perceived and the conclusion that spatiality is therefore indispensable to
the actual use of the categories even once they have been furnished with
their schemata are not given due emphasis until the second edition of the
Critique.[14] Further, the ultimate *basis* for this premise, as well as its
ultimate *consequence* – a certain form of realism – are not fully clarified until
Kant's further elaboration of the refutation of idealism after 1787. To
understand the ultimate significance of the schematism, however, we must
recognize that its restriction of the schemata to transcendental determinations of time tacitly expresses the premise of this larger argument.

The remark that "time cannot be perceived in itself" does occur in the
first edition of the first analogy of experience (A 183), and a similar remark
about the impossibility of the apprehension of empty time is also to be
found in that edition's version of the second analogy (A 192). It is only in
the second edition, however, that this doctrine is obviously placed in the
position of a premise for the extended argument of the whole "Analytic of
Principles." First it is centrally placed in the paragraph on the general
method of proof for the analogies which Kant included in the second
edition:

168

But since experience is a cognition of objects through perceptions, in it the relation in the existence of the manifold must be represented not as it is [merely] juxtaposed in time but as it is objectively in time, yet since time itself cannot be perceived, the determination of the existence of objects in time can occur only by means of their connection in time in general, thus only through concepts which connect [them] *a priori*. (B 219)

Next, the statement that "time cannot by itself be perceived" is clearly placed as a prominent premise in the new opening paragraph added to the discussion of each of the three analogies in the second edition (B 225, 233, 257). Finally, in the "General Note on the System of the Principles," also added to the second edition, Kant includes a general statement which makes explicit the complex view that the *temporal* schemata, which are the conditions of the applicability of the categories themselves, have their own conditions of application in *spatial* relations: "It is a . . . noteworthy fact, that in order to understand the possibility of things in conformity with the categories, and so to demonstrate the *objective* reality of the latter, we need, not merely intuitions, but intuitions that are in all cases *outer intuitions*" (B 291). To "understand the possibility of things in conformity with the categories" is precisely to understand the homogeneity of the categories with appearances, so Kant is now saying that *outer* intuitions are a *condition* of the solution to the problem of homogeneity, though he is *not* saying that spatial rather than temporal relations constitute the *content* of the schemata. Rather, what he goes on to suggest is that in order to render the temporal relations which constitute the schemata of the categories actually *determinable* in inner sense, empirical judgments about the latter must in turn be grounded in intuitions of outer sense (B 292).

Kant also uses this "General Note" to illustrate the doctrine for the one vital principle of experience other than the analogies – the principle that all objects of experience must have a determinate magnitude. "Similarly," he says, "it can easily be shown that the possibility of things as *quantities,* and therefore the objective reality of [the category of] quantity, can be exhibited only in outer intuition, and that only through the mediation of outer intuitions can it be applied also to inner sense" (B 293). We shall see later how direct Kant attempts to make the connection between determinate magnitude and spatiality in some of his versions of the refutation of idealism. For the moment, however, we need to see only that it is at least Kant's program to construct a general argument, applying to all the categories, that though the only universal schemata or conditions of application available to give objective reality to the categories are temporal determinations, temporal determinations themselves can be cognized only with the assistance of spatial intuitions.

But what does the claim that time itself cannot be perceived mean? One element of its meaning is suggested by a passage already included in the first edition. In a recapitulation of the argument of the second analogy about halfway through its exposition, Kant explains that the understanding is required for the possibility of experience not because it merely *clarifies* information given by the senses (as the rationalists would have it) but because it is required to *determine* the "time-order" of "appearances and their existence." And the reason for this is that "this determination of the position" of appearances in time "cannot be derived from the relation of appearances to absolute time (for that is no object of perception), rather the opposite: The appearances must determine for one another their positions in time and make this position in the time-order necessary" (A 200 / B 245). Kant does not mean here to retract his theory of the forms of intuition by implying that perception is *given* without temporal *form;* he is not denying that there is some aspect of the temporality of experience – the appearance of successiveness itself – which can be regarded as immediately given, in at least some contexts. Rather, using concepts central to the classical debate in the physics of his time, he is suggesting that although all perception may very well *occur* temporally, determinate positions and relations in time – which are required to represent the logical relations originally intended by the categories – cannot be *cognized* by means of any simple relationship which can be directly recognized to obtain between any individual representation and some straightforward representation of the absolute passage of time itself. Individual appearances do not come with their correct temporal position labeled on them, nor do we have access to some measure of absolute temporal position (a digital timer forever ticking away at the border of our consciousness) by which the temporal position of any given appearance can be determined without further ado. Instead, the determinate temporal positions of appearances must be worked out by the use both of the categories and of some form of intuition which apparently can be given immediately. The only candidate for that, of course, is space – although, again, Kant's ultimate position is certainly not that *all* relations among objects in space are themselves immediately given. Dynamic interactions among objects are required because, although spatial extension (unlike temporal succession) actually exists in one moment and can therefore be the object of a single representation, *position* in absolute space (and thus the spatial relation between even simultaneously existing objects, which cannot, however, be simultaneously perceived) can be perceived no more directly than position in absolute time.

These claims should seem surprising. For Kant's theory of the pure forms of intuition makes it seem natural to suppose, and the argument for the analogies indeed seems to presuppose, that there *is* one temporal relationship which is directly given: Consciousness of the *successiveness* of distinct appearances or perceptions of them *does* seem to be given without any additional mediation or foundation. In Kant's own words, "In the synthesis of appearances the manifold of representations is always successive" (A 198 / B 243). In other words, it seems obvious that each representation comes to consciousness self-evidently marked as subsequent to the one preceding it and as prior to the next one.

One might think of arguing that this assumption itself entails that further considerations are required to properly assign appearances their temporal positions, because there are *more* relations that objects and even experiences of them may have in time than succession alone. Further, supposing that the necessity of the contrast between experience of the self and of objects has already been established (by some version of the transcendental deduction), at this point one might also assume that *objects* may have temporal relations which differ from the temporal relations that *representations* of those objects have. So one might quickly conclude that even if the successiveness of representations of objects is directly given in perception, the determination of the *full* panoply of *objective* temporal relations must indeed require something going beyond that aspect of temporality which is apparently immediately perceived, namely successiveness. In other words, even if the successiveness of representations is directly perceived, since there are more transcendental determinations of time than succession, and since there are objective as well as subjective determinations of time, intuitions other than those of inner sense alone are therefore required to deploy all the schemata which are in turn necessary to apply all the categories to objects.

But though such a conclusion does suggest the strategy for the first stage of Kant's larger theory of time-determination, it fails to capture the ultimate implication of Kant's claim that time itself cannot be perceived. The argument just outlined supposes that at least the *succession* of representations in inner sense as such *is known* without any foundation beyond the mere apprehension of these states themselves, and suggests that the appeal to outer sense is necessary only to ground cognition of *other* time-determinations, or the time-determinations of objects *other* than representations as such. And indeed the argument of the "Analogies of Experience" will proceed on precisely such suppositions. But, we shall see, the whole argument of the "Analytic of Principles" involves two stages, and the second stage of this argument will turn on a deeper idea about the imperceptibility of time itself than the account just given has employed. To be sure, Kant will first argue that to differentiate all other temporal determinations from the successiveness of inner sense, the principles of judgment are required, and in demonstrating this he will proceed as though knowledge of the successiveness of the various states of inner sense itself did not have any epistemic conditions of its own. But he will then argue that even determinate knowledge of the succession of states in inner sense has its own conditions, of which knowledge of the independent existence of objects in space is the most basic. In fact, even the key argument of the analogies, the argument for the universal objective validity of the concept of causation, cannot succeed without this further step. For what the fundamental premise of Kant's transcendental theory of experience – the thesis of A 99 that insofar as it is contained in a single moment, each representation can be nothing but absolute unity – implies is precisely that although, of course, the manifold of subjective states *occurs* or *is given* successively, *knowledge* at any particular time *that* any particular succession of such states *has occurred* must be based on *the single representational state available at that time.* And this means that an *interpretation* of that state is necessary for the mind to determine the sequence of one impression upon another (as Kant puts it). In other words, the several members of a succession of states are indeed immediately perceived in succession, but there is nothing which counts as *immediate perception of the succession.* This is the ultimate reason why knowledge of the determinate instantiation of the temporal schemata of the categories requires spatial intuition, and indeed the only ground from which it can ultimately be argued that the categories have objective validity as required by the problem of 1772, namely, application to objects which exist independently of our representations of them but which our representations are suited to represent.

The transcendental time-determinations

All of this lies beneath the surface of Kant's exposition of the schematism, however, which itself turns directly from the ubiquity and apriority of time as a form of intuition to the further point that time must yield an adequate *variety* of relationships to schematize all of the categories on Kant's official list. In spite of what might have been hoped, given his argument in the *Prolegomena* or *Metaphysik Volckmann*, Kant's official procedure at this point is to derive that there is a variety of transcendental time-determinations, and what this variety is, *from* the list of categories. These categories, of course, fall under the general headings of *quantity, quality, relation, and modality,* and in accord with these Kant divides the transcendental determinations of time into those relating "the categories to the *time-series*, the *time-content,* the *time-order,* and lastly to the *scope of time* in respect of all possible objects" (A 145 / B 184–5).

The meaning of these titles will become more apparent as we consider Kant's attempt to subsume the schemata under these headings – but so will the problems inherent in Kant's official program. Given the assumption that the categories are first derived from the logical functions of judgment and only subsequently associated with their transcendental schemata, there are two kinds of problem which could arise for any particular schema. First, it could turn out that the category to which the schema is supposed to be related is not itself legitimately derived. Second, it could turn out that the schema has not in fact been shown to be the unique and indispensable condition for the homogeneity or objective validity of the relevant category. As we consider Kant's list of the schemata and then his arguments for the principles of judgment themselves, we shall see that what survives these two hurdles is primarily the three analogies of experience – which is to say, the substance of Kant's original transcendental theory of experience. But we shall also see that it is precisely in his argument for these analogies that Kant's official stance that the derivation of the categories precedes their schematism begins to fade, and it is there that his original supposition that the analogies of experience might be derived *directly* as the conditions of

172

the possibility of experience, without an independent argument for the categories, begins to surface again.

Kant begins his catalog of the transcendental schemata with a schema for the concept of *magnitude*. The image of the magnitude of *external* objects is space, he says, and that of *all* objects of the senses, since all objects (whether spatial or not) must be presented through inner sense, is time. But this is not where the temporality of the schema of magnitude enters the argument. Instead, Kant suggests that the common, underlying schema for representing either spatial or temporal magnitude is *number,* and he then intimates that number itself qualifies as a transcendental *time-*determination, because time is involved in arriving at any particular assignment of numerical magnitude: A number is "a representation which comprises the successive addition of homogeneous units" (A 142–3 / B 182; see also *Prolegomena* §10, 4:283). This claim immediately confronts us with the two types of problem that we have just been prepared to expect. First, although it seems natural to assume that recognizing the *logical* quantities – one, some, all – which are subsumed under the categorical heading of *quantity* requires being able to *count* in numbers, one might at least look for some argument that, for instance, a geometrical recognition of the subdivision of spatial regions – as in Venn diagrams – is inadequate for a satisfactory application of the concepts of logical quantity. Thus, it is not as obvious as it should be that there is a unique relationship between logical quantity and number. More important, however, it is hardly clear that number is an essentially temporal phenomenon, even if the *act* of counting always takes place in time. Thus it is unclear that the category of number should have a temporal schema. Kant sometimes seems to recognize this and to deny the thesis that there is an essential connection between number and temporally extended counting.[15] We shall see that Kant also suggests a less than clear connection between time and counting in his eventual refutation of idealism. But there Kant will assume the ability to count moments of time and will instead try to argue that there is a necessary connection between the ability to count in general and the representation of *space*. Although there will certainly be problems in that argument, it does not make the supposition that *number* itself is essentially temporal. This assertion is certainly difficult to entertain in our post-Fregean epoch, where number is linked to timeless relationships of sets.

Next, turning to the categories of *quality,* reality and negation (the third member of the official triad, limitation, is not even mentioned), Kant argues that the basis for the ascription or denial of reality to objects in time is sensation – that sensation, we might say, is what provides the basis for our judgments about the actual contents of time (the "time-content"). He then insists that there is a continuity of magnitude, down to nothingness (no upper bound is mentioned) for all sensation and concludes from this that "the schema of a reality, as the quantity of something insofar as it fills time, is just this continuous and uniform production of that reality in time"

(A 143 / B 182–3). Here, Kant's suggestion that sensation is the ultimate basis for empirical judgments of being (or nonbeing) seems indisputable, and thus the fact that we fill time (or do not) with objects or events judged to exist (or not) on the basis of sensation seems clear enough; but the further step of the argument, the tacit inference from the *continuity* of time to the *continuity* of sensation, is both questionable in itself and also apparently abjured in Kant's later discussion of the "Anticipations of Perception." So that continuously variable sensation is the only possible schema for the category of reality is not obvious.

Kant then turns to the three relational categories, or to the specific forms of *time-order*, and argues that the three categories of substance, cause, and community or reciprocity are to be made homogeneous with the forms of sensibility by means of the three temporal determinations of "the permanence of the real in time," "succession according to a rule," and "coexistence according to a universal rule" (A 143–4 / B 183–4). These three schemata are of course the three analogies of experience which Kant had identified as early as 1775, and their discussion constitutes the heart of the "Analytic of Principles." I will reserve all comment on them for later.

Finally, to clarify the obscure idea of the "*scope of time* in respect of all possible objects," Kant tries to associate three different time-determinations with the three modal categories of possibility, actuality, and necessity. "The schema of possibility is the agreement of the synthesis of different representations with the conditions of time in general"; "the schema of actuality is existence in some determinate time"; and that of necessity "is existence of an object at all times." Here, the schematization of actuality alone seems unproblematic. First, the temporal constraint on *possibility* by which Kant illustrates his schematization of that category – "Opposites, for instance, cannot exist in the same thing at the same time, but only the one after the other" (A 144 / B 184) – is indeed part of Kant's proposal for the meaningful use of the concept of possibility. It is, however, only *part* of the conditions for that use, and here the restriction of the conditions of possibility to the temporal form of intuition, as opposed to the forms of intuition in general, seems particularly troublesome. The anti-skeptical justification for restricting the schemata to temporal forms seems more plausible in the case of actuality than of possibility, since it is the former rather than the latter which is the skeptic's target. And second, the schema for necessity which Kant gives here – existence at all possible times (A 145 / B 184) – although obviously derived from the traditional conception of a necessary being, for whose nonexistence there can never be a sufficient reason and which must therefore exist at all times, is exactly the kind of conception of necessity which Kant's later discussion of the concept in the "Postulates of Empirical Thought" will undercut: The only empirically significant sense of necessity which that argument will countenance is sufficiently determined occurrence *within* the temporal series of phenomenal events, or "material necessity in existence" which can be known "only comparatively *a priori* relative to another previously given existence" (A 227 / B 279). The traditional notion of a necessary being can therefore be modeled only as a being existing out of time altogether, which is of course just to use the category of necessity for an idea of reason, rather than for any empirical knowledge at all. Thus Kant seems to have no justification for equating the schema of necessity with existence at all times.[16]

The problems with the schematization of the several categories will be considered in more detail in the next four chapters. But what they will show is that only in the case of the three relational categories does there seem to be a genuine possibility that any persuasive connection can be drawn between the logical relations officially providing the basis for the categories and distinct relations or determinations of time. Given the almost exclusive emphasis on the relational categories in Kant's original conception of the transcendental theory of experience, in which the thesis that objects must have determinate magnitude was derived directly from the forms of intuition, and the "titles of the understanding" were invoked primarily to demonstrate the necessity of using the concepts of substance, causation, and composition, this should come as no surprise. The generalization of the theory of schematism beyond the categories of substance and causation, questioned by Hume, and the category of interaction or composition, which was questioned by Leibniz, to the remainder of Kant's list of twelve is required by his attempt to provide a separate transcendental deduction of the logically derived categories prior to establishing their precise role in empirical time-determination. But since this separate transcendental deduction is flawed, it only is to be expected that the schematization of the categories other than the relational ones should also present problems.

And even in the case of the relational categories, where Kant's arguments for his schemata do seem most promising, this will not be because these schemata are obviously the necessary and unique conditions for the application of previously identified categories. Kant's argument will succeed precisely because these schemata can be linked with the possibility of experience understood as the "exposition" or time-determination of appearances, without reference to the textually prior but historically subsequent metaphysical and transcendental deductions of the categories. This is just what Kant promised in his original sketches of a transcendental theory of experience and intimated in the *Prolegomena* and *Metaphysik Volckmann,* when he at least suggested that the temporal structure of experience might show which logical forms are necessary for expressing judgments about it, rather than vice versa. But it is also in fact something we find in notes from the period of the composition of the *Critique* and which is, after all, hinted at in the published text. So, as we now leave the "Schematism," it will be illuminating to consider the evidence of Kant's continuing attachment to his original conception of the significance of time-determination rather than to his official assignment of its position in the architectonic of the *Critique.*

The reemergence of Kant's original argument

Let us consider again the remarkable note which Kant wrote on or shortly after 22 March 1780, thus shortly before he began the final composition of the *Critique*, in which he sketched his "key" to the entire problem of the "nature of synthetic *a priori* judgment" (R 5637, 18:271). On the conception of his argument expounded in this key, all such judgments are founded directly in our intuition of space, on the one hand (judgments founded thus are the synthetic *a priori* judgments of mathematics, of course) or in the conditions of the empirical determination of objects in time, on the other (judgments grounded in this way are the nonmathematical "necessary (synthetic) propositions of things"). This argument assumes that we have knowledge of objects, and not just of subjective representations, but it also makes clear that it is the idea of principles of time-determination which is the key to the nature of synthetic *a priori* judgments even on this assumption:

Key – through the nature of synthetic *a priori* judgments . . .

Were time not given subjectively and therefore *a priori* as the form of inner sense (and an understanding, to compare it), then apperception would not cognize *a priori* the relation in the existence of the manifold, for in itself time is no object of perception; apperception would indeed determine the succession and coexistence of representations, but not the place of objects in time, thus it could not constitute any experience, unless it had rules of the time which is determinable in the object; but these it cannot take from the object.

I ask everyone, from whence he [would] derive the mathematical and necessary (synthetic) propositions about things in space, if space were not already the condition in us *a priori* of the possibility of the empirical representation of objects, through which these can be given to us. We determine *a priori* the manifold of appearance according to existence by means of the categories. I ask: from where should this synthesis be derived, if time, the condition of the possibility of all perception, did not lie [in us] *a priori* and if this rule of the determination of all existence in this time . . . did not flow from the subjective constitution of our sensibility . . . (R 5637, 18:271–2)

In the first step of this argument, the categories are prominently mentioned. But what is noteworthy is that they are not invoked as the *premise* for the argument for *a priori* rules of time-determination. On the contrary, the necessary existence of *a priori* rules for time-determination in determinations of existence is clearly suggested to be the basis for the *a priori* validity of the categories themselves. Just as the intuition of space is the ultimate basis for *a priori* judgments about the mere form of appearances – that is, mathematical judgments – so the possibility of objective time-determination is held to be the basis of all nonmathematical – dynamical or existential – judgments about objects, and of the categories themselves. As late as March 1780, therefore, Kant could basically suggest that the categories should be derived from the transcendental schemata of time-determination rather than the latter from the former.

To be sure, the argument just sketched assumes that no rules whatever are needed for *subjective* determinations of the succession and coexistence of representations as such, and instead proceeds as if *a priori* rules of time-determination were required only for judgments about the temporal positions and relations of objects as contrasted to the representations of them. That is, this passage reflects Kant's weaker tactic of simply assuming knowledge of objects, and thus hints only at the first but not the second stage of Kant's eventual theory of time-determination. But that only reflects what we saw in Chapter 4, namely that Kant's general tendency in the early part of the 1780s was to rest on this object-presupposing tactic, and that it was not until 1787 and after that he returned to seriously exploit the possibility of that tactic, just hinted at in the *Duisburg Nachlass,* which would derive the rules for objects from the conditions of *self*-knowledge.

The same general contrast between the official progress of Kant's exposition and its underlying impetus surfaces when we turn from the "Schematism" to the opening section of the chapter "System of All Principles of Pure Understanding" itself. This chapter begins with only the most general sort of use of the results of the prior transcendental deduction. Moreover, the quality of arguments offered in behalf of the four classes of principles which Kant now introduces varies greatly, and so does the degree to which these arguments adhere to the model of the schematism. The distinction of these principles into two classes which Kant draws is also very poorly argued. This too suggests that the articulation of Kant's argument into the mature architectonic with its separate deduction, schematism, and principles was a late and not very well digested accretion to his thought.

Particular problems concerning Kant's division of the principles into two separate classes can be deferred until the next chapter. All that need concern us now is the more general character of Kant's argument in the introduction to the chapter. In accord with Kant's official program, the section opens by suggesting that now that it has been shown under what conditions the *categories* can be applied to objects of sensible intuition, it remains only to catalog the *principles,* or actual synthetic *a priori* judgments, which may be reached by realizing that the universal applicability of the categories themselves implies the universal validity of the schemata by means of which they may be applied:

In the preceding chapter we have evaluated the transcendental faculty of judgment only according to the universal conditions under which alone the pure concepts of the understanding can suitably be used for synthetic judgments. Now our job is to exhibit in systematic connection the judgments which the understanding can really make *a priori* under this critical provision, for which, without a doubt, our table of categories must provide us with natural and secure guidance. For it is just by means of the relation of these categories to possible experience that all pure cognition of the understanding must be constituted, and on account of the relation of which to sensibility in general that all transcendental principles of the use of the understanding can be displayed completely and in a system. (A 148 / B 187–8)

The thought of this paragraph – that the schemata may be derived from the categories by the addition of the sensible form of inner sense, and that principles asserting the universal applicability of these schemata then follow from the universal validity of the categories themselves – is certainly in accord with Kant's initial program for the "Analytic of Principles" as a whole:

This transcendental doctrine of the faculty of judgment will now contain two chapters: the first, which treats of the sensible conditions under which alone the pure concepts of the understanding can be employed, that is, the schematism of the pure understanding; and the second, which [concerns] those synthetic judgments which under these *a priori* conditions flow from pure concepts of the understanding, and which underlie all other *a priori* knowledge, that is, of the principles of pure understanding. (A 136 / B 175)

But all of this formal division of labor very quickly fades from view. For Kant next proceeds to raise the problem of discovering a basis for synthetic as opposed to analytic judgments in a way that is virtually continuous with the discussion of this issue in the introduction to the whole *Critique* (A 6–10 / B 10–14). He then claims that this problem can be solved by an appeal to the conditions of the possibility of experience in a way which hardly differs from the original statement of the principle of the transcendental deduction itself (see A 94 / B 126). In other words, Kant writes as if the deduction of the categories, let alone their schematism, had not even intervened. With respect to analytic judgments, he writes, "The *principle of contradiction* must be recognized as being the universal and completely sufficient *principle of all analytic knowledge*" (A 151 / B 191), but in the case of "synthetic judgments I am to proceed beyond the given concept in order to think in connection with it something entirely different from what is thought in it, which is a relation neither of identity nor of contradiction" (A 154 / B 193–4). Instead, he continues, "an intermediary" (*ein Drittes*) – just like the "unknown = X" of the introduction (B 13) – is needed to establish a synthetic connection between the two nonidentical or noncontradictory concepts. And then, just as in the opening movements of the transcendental deduction itself, both the general claim that "the possibility of experience is therefore that which gives objective reality to all our *a priori* cognitions" (A 156 / B 194; cf. A 94 / B 126) and the more specific claim that "there is only one whole in which all our representations are contained, namely inner sense, and its *a priori* form, time" (A 155 / B 194; again, see also A 99) are adduced as the basis for the solution of the problem of this intermediary for synthetic judgments. In other words, Kant now writes as if the argument for the principles must go back to the very foundations of the deduction itself – as if it must restart the argument of the deduction – rather than just apply the conclusions already reached in the deduction and the schematism.

Perhaps this overstates the point. When he comes to the central paragraph of this introduction to the principles, Kant does not write as

178

though there had been no transcendental deduction at all. But he certainly does write as though the deduction had established at most the very general point that experience or empirical knowledge requires *the concept of an object,* and as if the schematism had added only the equally general point that this must be the concept of an object capable of being given by means of the kind of sensibility we possess:

> The possibility of experience is therefore that which gives objective reality to all our *a priori* cognitions. Now experience rests on the synthetic unity of appearances, that is, on a synthesis according to concepts of the object of appearances in general, without which it would not even be cognition but a rhapsody of perceptions, which would not fit together in any context according to rules of a thoroughly connected (possible) consciousness, thus neither according to the transcendental and necessary unity of apperception. Experience therefore has principles of its form [which] lie at its ground, namely universal rules of unity in the synthesis of appearances, the objective reality of which as necessary conditions of experience, indeed even of its possibility, can always be proved ...   (A 156–7 / B 195–6)

> The highest principle of all synthetic judgments is therefore: Every object stands under the necessary conditions of the synthetic unity of the manifold of intuition in a possible experience.
>   In such a way synthetic *a priori* judgments are possible, if we relate the formal conditions of *a priori* intuition, the synthesis of imagination, and the necessary unity of the latter in a transcendental apperception, to possible empirical knowledge in general, and say: The conditions of the *possibility of experience* in general are at the same time the conditions of the *possibility of the objects of experience,* and therefore have objective validity in a synthetic *a priori* judgment.
>   (A 158 / B 197)

If we are to read the last of these paragraphs as asserting more than a mere tautology, then perhaps we should see Kant as presupposing and building upon the results of a prior deduction of the categories, at least to the extent that it is the deduction which shows that any form of experience, even in the weakest sense, requires interpretation as experience *of objects,* and which also shows that *concepts* are necessary for such an interpretation.[17] Then the argument for the principles could be seen as determining what the general forms of the concepts of objects are, and, in light of the universal applicability of these general forms, expressing them by means of principles rather than mere concepts. But even on this reading no use or mention is made of the specific categories – in spite of the fact that the argument is supposed to provide us with "natural and secure guidance." In other words, the metaphysical deduction is ignored completely, and no more than the very general result that experience requires the concept of an object is borrowed from the transcendental deduction, for it is now strictly assumptions about the structure of time rather than about the structure of judgments which guide the argument. The actual course of the "Analytic of Principles" has much more to do with the list "time-series, time-content, time-order, and the scope of time" than it does with the division of the logical functions of judgment.

Finally, that the connection between the "Analytic of Principles" and the transcendental deduction is not what Kant's official program requires but what his original conception of the transcendental theory of experience suggests also emerges in his peroration to the discussion of the analogies of experience themselves, for this too emphasizes a direct connection between "rules of synthetic unity *a priori*" and the "determinations of appearances in time," while confining the categories to what is hardly more than an honorific mention. The first paragraph of this concluding section of the published argument derives the threefold division of the analogies not from the three categories of relation – as should be the case if the real role of the categories in Kant's argument were anything like their official role – but from what are treated as if they were simply the three basic aspects of the structure of time itself:

These, then, are the three analogies of experience. They are nothing other than principles of the determination of the existence of appearances in time, according to all its three modes, [namely] the relation to time itself, as a magnitude (the magnitude of time, that is, duration), the relation in time, as a series (successive), finally also in it as a sum of existence (simultaneous). This unity of time-determination is through and through dynamic, that is, time is not regarded as that wherein experience immediately determines the position of every existence, which is impossible because absolute time is no object of perception with which appearances could be compared; rather the rule of understanding, through which alone the existence of appearance can require synthetic unity according to time-relations, determines for each appearance its place in time, thus *a priori* and validly for each and every time. (A 215 / B 262)

Here the suggestion is that we can make determinations that objects endure and succeed or coexist with one another in time, but that we cannot make such determinations on the basis of any perception of absolute time, so we must have some rule or rules of the understanding applying to objects in time – and thus "through and through dynamic" – by means of which to make such determinations. There is no suggestion that we know that we can make just these three forms of time-determination *because* we *independently* know that there are three categories of relation, or that we must be able to make these three kinds of time-determination *because* only thus will we be able to use or lend objective reality to such categories. There is in fact no mention of categories at all. Kant goes directly from the modes of time which have to be determined because of the structure of time itself and the possible relations among objects in it to the existence of principles of the understanding, without either an advance road map or a detour.

Again, this conclusion may be a bit overstated, for in the next, and concluding, paragraph of the discussion of the analogies the categories are mentioned after all. Still, they are once again described only as a "clue" and not as an indispensable stage of the argument for the analogies. And the basis of the argument remains a direct appeal to the "possibility of experience as a knowledge wherein all objects must in the end be capable of being given to us" – an appeal indeed made as if it were for the first time, that is, as if it had not already been employed in a separate transcendental deduction:

> Concerning the method of proof, however, of which we have made use in the case of these transcendental laws of nature, and its peculiarity, a comment is to be made which must also be very important as a prescription for every other attempt to prove *a priori* propositions which are intellectual but also synthetic. If we had attempted to prove these analogies dogmatically, that is, from concepts, ... all the effort would have been entirely in vain. For one cannot go from one object and its existence to the existence of another or its manner of existence by means of mere concepts of these things, no matter how these concepts are analyzed. So what alternative remained? The possibility of experience, as a cognition wherein all objects must in the end be capable of being given to us, if their representation is to have objective reality for us. In this medium, the essential form of which consists in the synthetic unity of the apperception of all appearances, we found *a priori* conditions of the thoroughgoing and necessary time-determination of all existence in appearance, without which even the empirical time-determination would be impossible, and we found rules of synthetic unity *a priori,* by means of which we could anticipate experience. In the absence of this method, and in the folly of trying to prove dogmatically synthetic propositions which the empirical use of the understanding has recommended as its principles, a proof has often but always vainly been sought for the proposition of sufficient reason. And no one has even thought of the other two analogies, because the clue of the categories was lacking, which alone uncovers and makes noticeable every gap of understanding, in concepts as well as principles. (A 216–18 / B 263–5)

Here the categories are treated as a useful *check* on the completeness of the derivation of the *a priori* principles of judgment from the conditions of time-determination. But it is not insisted that the objective validity of the categories themselves is a *premise* in the argument from the general need for time-determination to these specific principles. So by the time Kant concludes his detailed treatment of the analogies of experience, which are officially supposed to be principles *flowing from* the prior schematization of the categories, the official position that there are categories which have to be, and have been, proved to be objectively valid and which then had to be schematized, all prior to the argument for the analogies, has, if not quite dropped away, been markedly weakened.

Thus, Kant prepares us to reverse the direction of his schematism and to derive the categories of the understanding from the principles of time-determination, rather than vice versa. Before we can finally consider Kant's mature theory of time-determination, however, we must pause over the last roadblock which he puts in our way, the discussions of the first two principles of empirical knowledge, to which he gives the tongue-twisting titles "Axioms of Intuition" and "Anticipations of Perception."

7
Axioms and anticipations

Mathematical and dynamical principles

Beyond the principles of logic and the synthetic *a priori* propositions of pure mathematics, Kant's original transcendental theory of experience assumed that the forms of intuition sufficed to entail that external objects would have a determinate magnitude, and appealed to the "titles of the understanding" only to establish the *a priori* application of the concepts of substance, causation, and interaction to such independently existent external objects. In other words, the theory anticipated only Kant's mature analogies of experience and refutation of idealism, even if it did not yet include any detailed anticipation of the arguments which Kant eventually produced. At this early stage of his thought, as we saw in Part I, Kant did not yet separate the transcendental deduction of these principles from the demonstration of their role in time-determination or the "exposition" of appearances. When Kant did introduce the conception of a separate transcendental deduction, as we saw in Part II, he created a gap between the categories, which are most closely connected with the logical functions of judgment, and the principles of time-determination – although, as we also saw, his attempts to derive the categories from the logical functions of judgment while also showing them to have extralogical content were of dubious success. In the last chapter, we saw that Kant attempted to use the theory of the schematism to close the gap between categories and time-determination that had been opened by his insertion of a separate transcendental deduction. Thus, in his discussion of the schematism Kant argued that although the categories were derived from the logical functions of judgment, they could be applied to objects only in the form of transcendental determinations of time. Further, Kant argued, just as there were four groups of categories – quantity, quality, relation, and modality – so there are also four aspects of time-determination – the *time-series*, the *time-content*, the *time-order*, and the *scope of time* (A 145 / B 184) – which yield schemata for the four classes of categories. Added to the lack of any textual evidence for a separate deduction and schematism in Kant's original plans, the clumsiness of this machinery suggests a late accretion to his thought which, however, obscured but did not suppress the underlying impetus of the real key to his theory of knowledge, the theory of time-determination.

In the present chapter, the impression of a poor fit between Kant's

183

underlying insight and his official program will be further confirmed by an examination of the first two principles of experience, which Kant labels the "Axioms of Intuition" and "Anticipations of Perception." On the one hand, these principles have only a weak connection with the categories derived from the logical functions of judgment and thus belie the pretense of a separate transcendental deduction resting on a conception of judgment which is independent of the idea of the "exposition" of appearances in empirical knowledge. On the other hand, however, these principles also fail to fulfill, at least very persuasively, the promise of the schematism to link only transcendental determinations *of time* to the categories. In these ways they clearly display tension between Kant's official program and his underlying concern with time-determination. Nevertheless, a careful examination of these principles will repay our efforts. First, just because these principles are not very persuasively argued at all, they confirm the view that Kant's arguments lose their grip precisely as they become distant from the theory of time-determination, and thereby confirm that the latter is indeed the real basis of Kant's epistemology. But at the same time, a clear grasp of these principles will help us avoid some common errors in the subsequent interpretation of Kant's principles of time-determination. In particular, the recognition that Kant's theory of measurement is offered in the discussion of the axioms of intuition will aid us in avoiding the mistaken supposition that the *first analogy* of experience rests on an argument about the *measurement* of temporal durations. Second, recognition of the kind of ontological *realism* clearly presupposed in the discussion of the anticipations of perception will point the way to the realist framework for the interpretation of Kant's theory of time-determination ultimately revealed by the refutation of idealism.

Before I can turn to these issues, however, I must comment on Kant's general classification of the principles of judgment. Corresponding to the four aspects of time-determination produced by the schematism, Kant divides the principles into four classes, reflected in the headings "Axioms of Intuition," "Anticipations of Perception," "Analogies of Experience," and "Postulates of Empirical Thought in General" (A 161 / B201). In spite of their plural titles, each of the first two of these headings in fact subsumes only a single principle. The principle entitled "Axioms of Intuition" – which, however, Kant denies is itself an "axiom" – is that all intuitions, and therefore all appearances of objects, can be assigned an extensive magnitude, that is, a number representing a sum of *separate* parts, though these parts themselves need not always be *discrete* but may also be separated only by *limits*. The principle entitled "Anticipations of Perception" is that sensations, and the reality or matter in empirical objects which is imputed to objects as the cause of our sensations (see A 168 / B 210), can be assigned an intensive magnitude or degree – that is, a numerical measure constituted of units which correspond to an instance of a qualitatively similar sensation with some particular intensity but which do not correspond to any actual *parts* of the given sensation, and therefore – although here Kant wavers – to parts of the objects of empirical intuitions. Under the rubric "Analogies of Experience," however, Kant does subsume three separate theses – although it will be a central contention of the following chapters that both the intended *use* and the only possible *deduction* of these principles are interdependent. These are the three principles that "in all changes of appearances substance is permanent" (B 223), that "all alterations take place in conformity with the law of cause and effect" (B 232), and that "all substances, so far as they coexist, stand in thoroughgoing communication, that is, in mutual interaction" (A 211). Finally, Kant provides three "Postulates of Empirical Thought." These consist of the claims that the (empirically) possible is "that which agrees with the formal conditions of experience"; the (empirically) actual is "that which is bound up with the material conditions of experience"; and the (empirically) necessary is "that which in its connection with the actual is determined in accordance with universal conditions of experience" (A 218 / B 265–6). These do not introduce any new principles for empirical judgment at all but rather use the principles already described to give sensible meaning to the logical concepts of modality, that is, possibility, actuality, and necessity. They are indeed schemata as officially defined – sensible applications for logical concepts – but precisely because they do not yield any additional principles of judgment, they provide additional evidence that the arguments for such principles proceed independently of the metaphysical and transcendental deductions of the categories, rather than in dependence upon the latter. However, because the "Refutation of Idealism" was inserted into the discussion of the schema of actuality in the second edition of the *Critique,* this section of the text is of great substantive if not architectonic significance.

As we saw in Part I, such a fourfold division of principles of empirical knowledge was not part of Kant's original theory of experience; instead, in the 1770s Kant used the terms "analogies," "anticipations," and "postulates" coextensively and *denied* that any of these were genuine "axioms." Further evidence that Kant had not used this new division of principles long enough to work out all its problems is found when we turn from the four sets of principles just listed to the two larger groups into which Kant also divided them. Kant calls the axioms of intuition and the anticipations of perception "mathematical" principles, and the analogies of experience and the postulates of empirical thought "dynamical" principles. There is a general reason why the former principles are called mathematical, which is unexceptionable, and which does indeed go back several years in Kant's thinking prior to the *Critique.* But Kant also gives two specific reasons for holding these principles to be mathematical and the others dynamical, and one consequence of this classification, none of which can withstand scrutiny.

Kant's general reason for calling the principles ascribing extensive and intensive magnitudes to objects "mathematical" is that it is by means of these principles that pure mathematics gains its purchase *on* empirical objects. That mathematical statements interpreted as descriptions of pure intuitions alone do not constitute any actual knowledge is a position which Kant states – or overstates – in the introductory discussion of the principle of all synthetic judgments:

Although we know so much *a priori* in synthetic judgments about space in general or about the figures which the productive imagination draws in it that we really require no experience for this, yet this knowledge would be nothing at all, an occupation with a mere fantasy, if space were not to be regarded as the condition of the appearances which constitute the matter for external experience; therefore those pure synthetic judgments relate, though only mediately, to possible experience or rather to its possibility itself, and on this alone is grounded the objective validity of their synthesis. (A 157 / B 196)

On this account, the *only* mathematical knowledge at all is knowledge of *empirical* objects *by means of* mathematical judgments. To prove that any particular part of mathematics actually furnishes knowledge at all would therefore require proof that it has empirical application. Sometimes, however, Kant makes a less extreme claim by distinguishing between *pure* and *applied* mathematics and arguing only that the cognitive value *of the latter* depends upon a proof that empirical objects must indeed instantiate specific parts of pure mathematics. One note from the period 1776 to 1778 asserts the distinction between pure and applied mathematics: "In mathematics one may well make the division into *pure* and *applied* mathematics, for the objects of experience do not provide any *principia mathematica*, rather the latter are only applied to the former ..." (R 4993, 18:54). Another note from the late 1770s (or possibly the early 1780s) then distinguishes the epistemological justifications for the two forms of mathematics. Pure mathematics consists of synthetic judgments which are justified by appeal to pure intuition alone, but the justification of any applied mathematics requires the additional principles that actual *appearances* are extensive and intensive magnitudes:

Principium of possibility of mathematics as a synthetic cognition *a priori*. It is synthesis in *a priori* intuition, that is, space and time. Pure mathematics.
   Principium of mathematical cognition of appearances: All appearances have as intuitions their extensive magnitude and as sensation their degree. For (as far as the latter is concerned) every sensation arises from nonbeing, since it is a modification. Therefore through alteration. All alteration however proceeds from o to a through infinitely many small steps. (R 5585, 18:241)

The problem of Kant's connection of intensive magnitude with the continuity of alteration will concern us later; what concerns us now is only the claim that the cognitive value of applied mathematics – or even of mathematics in general, if Kant is not committed to the distinction between pure and applied – depends upon the applicability of intensive and extensive measures *to appearances*. It is because they ground this application for mathematics that Kant calls the axioms of intuition and anticipations of perception "mathematical." They are not propositions *in* mathematics themselves – that is, they are not themselves propositions of, for instance, number theory or geometry – but they are principles which guarantee the empirical employment *of* mathematics:

> Therefore I do not reckon among my principles those of mathematics, but certainly those on which the possibility and *a priori* objective validity of the former are grounded, and which are thus to be regarded as the principle [*Principium*] of these [mathematical] principles [*Grundsätze*],[1] and which proceed from *concepts* to intuition, but not from *intuition* to concepts.　　　　(A 160 / B 199)

That they ground applied mathematics or the empirical use of mathematics in general seems an adequate reason for calling the theses of the axioms and anticipations "mathematical."[2] However, there are problems not just with the suggestion that these principles are themselves in any way derived from the categories, as the final clause of the last quotation implies, but also with the further claims in support of the division between mathematical and dynamical principles which Kant offers. Finally, the central conclusion which Kant draws from this distinction also fails to follow.

First, Kant says that the mathematical principles are concerned with the "mere intuition of an appearance in general," whereas the dynamical principles are concerned with its "existence" (A 160 / B 199). Mathematical principles are concerned "with appearances and the synthesis of their empirical intuition," whereas dynamical principles are concerned "with the *existence* of such appearances and their *relation* to one another in respect of their existence" (A 178 / B 220). But this claim is belied by Kant's very statement of the principle of the anticipations of perception. It is plausible to read the principle of the axioms of intuition as the assertion that because of the nature of space and time as the pure forms of intuition, the empirical representation *of* any empirical object must have some extensive magnitude. But it is very difficult *not* to read the thesis of the anticipations of perception as asserting that the appearance, in the sense of the empirical object which *corresponds* to a sensation (see A 20 / B 34), possesses a degree of reality measurable as an intensive magnitude. Yet this is surely a claim about the *existence* of an empirical object as opposed to one about the mere *intuition* of the object. Thus it does not seem that the anticipations of perceptions should be counted as a mathematical principle as so described.

Second, Kant says that

> ... the principles of mathematical employment are unconditionally, that is, apodictically necessary, but those of the dynamical employment [of the synthesis of understanding] have, to be sure, the character of an *a priori* necessity, but only under the condition of empirical thought in an experience; thus they carry [this necessity] only mediately and indirectly and consequently do not contain this immediate evidence ...　　　　(A 160 / B 199–200)

That is, there is a difference in epistemological status between the two groups of principles. But this claim is undermined by the very reason Kant supplied for the existence of the mathematical principles. These conditions for the employment *of* mathematics were required precisely because the immediate insight into the truth and certainty of propositions of pure mathematics which is yielded by *a priori* intuition is not enough to justify *applied* mathematics. For this reason an additional claim about the nature of our *empirical* intuition – or experience – is required. But then there is certainly no obvious epistemological difference between the mathematical and the dynamical principles; in both cases their certainty seems to depend upon claims about the nature of our empirical rather than *a priori* intuition.

Perhaps the best evidence of difficulty in Kant's classification of the principles of judgment, however, is that the chief consequence which Kant draws from his division of these principles into mathematical and dynamical does not logically follow from it. Kant claims that the mathematical principles are "constitutive" but that the dynamical principles are only "regulative." The former are constitutive because "the way that something is apprehended in appearance is *a priori* determined in such a way that the rule of its synthesis at the same time yields this *a priori* intuition in every empirical intuition that lies before us," whereas (this is supposed to be a contrast) "the existence of appearances cannot be known *a priori,* and although ... we can infer to some existence, we do not cognize this determinately" (A 178 / B 220–1). The analogies of experience, in particular, which are concerned with time-relations, are merely regulative, because "if one perception is given in a time-relation to some other (although undetermined) perception, then there is to be no thought of axioms or anticipations; rather it cannot be said *a priori* which other ... perception is necessarily connected with the first but only that its existence is connected in this mode of time" (A 179 / B 222). That is, a principle such as that of universal causation is merely regulative because it is indeterminate: For any given event it tells us that there is some cause or other, but not what that cause is. That awaits empirical discovery. Since the mathematical principles are constitutive rather than regulative, however, they must not be affected by the same indeterminacy.

But the example by which Kant means to substantiate this claim undermines it instead. To show us how the mathematical principles justify the use of "numerical magnitudes and ... the determination of appearance as magnitude," the exposition of the anticipations includes the contention that one can, "for instance, determine *a priori,* that is, construct, the degree of the sensation of sunlight by composing it out of 200,000 illuminations of the moon" (A 178–9 / B 221). But this example shows only that the principle of intensive magnitude, an allegedly constitutive principle, is also indeterminate and therefore regulative in exactly the same way as the principle of causation. The principle tells me that I can assign *some* definite degree to the intensity of my sensation of sunlight, and thus to the real which it represents, namely sunlight itself, by measuring it with *some* unit based on *some* (in this case surely less intense) sensation of light. But the discovery that the sensation of sunlight is in fact 200,000 times as intense as the sensation of moonlight – as opposed to 199,000 or 201,000 times as intense, or for that matter, twice as intense – is as little *a priori* as is, say, the discovery that the crystals of sodium chloride have the form of a cube rather than of some other permissible polyhedron. The geometry of the cube may be entirely *a priori*, but surely the discovery that some particular chemical is described by that geometry is not. In other words, the mere fact that the mathematical principles offer a general justification for the application of certain branches of mathematics to empirical objects, whether solid geometry or real numbers, hardly makes those principles themselves any less indeterminate than the dynamical principles and thus fails to justify the claim that these principles are constitutive rather than regulative. To the extent that any of these principles are valid, they are all certainly regulative in the sense defined.

In light of this kind of confusion, it is revealing to discover that even *after* he published the *Critique*, the organization of his "System of Principles" was not well settled in Kant's mind. One of the comments that Kant wrote in his own copy of the first edition of the *Critique* undermines the distinction between mathematical and dynamical principles that we have just been examining. Kant gives a little table:

1. Axioms of Intuition. *Formal.*
   pure mathematics – *pura*
   applied [mathematics] – *dynamik.*
2. Anticipations of Perception. *Real.*
   Perception is the consciousness of an appearance (prior to all concepts)

⎫
⎬ Mathematics
⎭

3. Analogies of Experience
4. Postulates of Empirical Thought in General

} *Physiologie* { 1. *Physical*
                 2. *Metaphysical*

Sensation not beyond experience.
(R LXIV, 23:28)

In this table, Kant clearly undermines the distinction between mathematical and dynamical principles by suggesting that the principles of *applied* mathematics – precisely what the so-called mathematical principles were, on his most reasonable account – are "*dynamik.*" Further, given the sort of thing Kant typically means by the distinction between "formal" and "real," this table suggests that the line between the principles concerning mere intuition and the principles concerning existence is to be drawn between the axioms of intuition and the anticipations of perception themselves, rather than between these two principles together, on the one hand, and the analogies of experience on the other – exactly as I have just argued. In other words, Kant at least considered retracting almost everything he had argued about the general organization of the system of principles in the *Critique* as published.

All of this confusion provides additional evidence for the suggestion that the architectonic organization of the *Critique* by means of the separate deduction, schematism, and system of principles is a possibly late and certainly ill-digested addition to the basic theory of time-determination which really underlies Kant's theory of experience. Detailed examination of the two "mathematical" principles will further confirm this view.

The axioms of intuition

In the "Axioms of Intuition," Kant clearly wishes to prove a thesis which the original transcendental theory of experience supposed could be derived directly from the pure form of intuition without invoking any of the "titles of the understanding," the thesis that all external objects of knowledge have a determinate magnitude. Kant's discussion of this thesis in the *Critique* seems straightforward but is not. Several of the confusions to which it gives rise may be resolved with material from other parts of the *Critique* or elsewhere. But in some cases the attempt to supplement the argument in this way will only make even clearer the fragile connection between the principle of the axioms of intuition and Kant's underlying theory of time-determination.

Confusion begins with the title of the section. It is plural, but Kant goes on to enunciate only a single principle, the principle (as stated in the first edition) that "all appearances are, in their intuition, extensive magnitudes" (A 162).[3] The confusion engendered by a plural title for a single principle can be resolved by the same consideration which explains another difficulty. This second difficulty is that Kant here seems to suggest that there is one or more axiom about the nature of intuition which is properly to be included in transcendental philosophy, yet later explicitly asserts – in line with his view in the 1770s – that "since philosophy is simply what reason knows by means of concepts, no principle deserving the name of an axiom is to be found in it" (A 732 / B 760). How can Kant use the plural term "axioms" to designate a *single* principle which is also explicitly *denied* to be an axiom?

The answer to both questions is that the principle of the axioms of intuition is not so called because of its own status but rather because of its function. What it does is to address the problem of applied mathematics by justifying the application *of* the axioms of the mathematics of extensive magnitudes *to* empirical intuitions and the empirical objects which they represent. So Kant says retrospectively:

In the Analytic . . . I have indeed thought of certain axioms of intuition; only the principle introduced in this connection was not itself an axiom, but rather served only to provide the principle of the possibility of axioms in general, and [was] itself only a principle from concepts. For even the possibility of mathematics must be shown in transcendental philosophy. Philosophy therefore has no axioms and is never permitted to offer its *a priori* principles as such, but must comfort itself with justifying their authorization with a thoroughgoing deduction.

(A 733–4 / B 761–2)

The principle of the axioms of intuition is not itself intended to be an axiom, let alone more than one; it is intended to be the principle which licenses the empirical *use* of the genuine axioms of intuition more properly so called, which are none other than the axioms of the relevant portion of mathematics itself.[4]

Nevertheless, a problem about the singularity of the principle remains. This is that there are three *categories* of quantity – unity, plurality, and totality (A 80 / B 106) – yet, again, only the single *principle* that all intuitions and appearances are extensive magnitudes. What does this imply about the relations between the categories and the principle which is supposed to be linked to the schematism of those categories? Is the principle derived from the categories at all, or even a condition for their application of any obvious kind?

Kant himself suggests no explicit answer to this question. Perhaps he just assumes that if the *logical* functions of quantity are to be usable, if we are to have use for judgments about both single objects and groups of objects, then we must have concepts of objects under which either one object or determinate numbers of objects greater than one can be subsumed – concepts of objects conforming to the categories of quantity – and then makes the further inference that this requires that we be able to carve up what is given in empirical intuition into determinate units. He could then further assume that this can be accomplished only by representing the objects of our judgment as discrete from one another by virtue of their occupation of distinct regions of space and time, which themselves are represented by numerical measures of extensive magnitude.[5] Such an argument, at least, would bring the argument that is actually offered in the present section into connection with the official structure of the argument of the *Critique*. Moreover, it would not be implausible. Nevertheless, it must be noted that Kant himself does not make such an argument explicit. Perhaps he is so ill at ease with his official hierarchy of categories, schemata, and principles that he does not use it even when it would clearly work.

Let us turn from Kant's principle to the argument he does offer in its behalf. This argument is simple. The last paragraph of the section gives it in just two steps: "Empirical intuition is possible only through the pure intuition (of space and time); therefore what geometry says of the latter holds without exception of the former" (A 165 / B 206). Whatever geometry (and, Kant should have added, chronometry) tells us about the measurement of space and time in pure intuition must also be applicable to the measurement of particular spaces and times occupied by particular empirical objects.[6]

The argument is put slightly more elaborately in the opening paragraph of the section, with the desired conclusion made explicit. Appearances or empirical objects have to be perceived or "taken up in empirical consciousness" in accordance with the *a priori* forms of space and time. This implies that the representation of any "determinate space or time" will take place through a "combination of homogeneous parts and the consciousness of the synthetic unity of this manifold" of homogeneous parts (B 202–3).[7] But consciousness of the unity of a whole represented by means of separately given parts is precisely consciousness of that whole by means of the representation of its "extensive magnitude," or by the assignment to it of a number which represents its parts: "I entitle an extensive magnitude that in which the representation of the parts makes possible the representation of the whole (and which therefore necessarily precedes the latter)."

And this applies to all empirical objects, whether their spatial extent or temporal duration is concerned: "Even the perception of an object, as appearance, is possible only through the same synthetic unity of the manifold of the given sensible intuition as that through which the unity of the combination of a manifold of homogeneous parts is thought through the concept of a magnitude (*quanti*)" (A 162 / B 203), or "All appearances are accordingly already intuited as aggregates of antecedently given parts" (A 163 / B 204). So in the case of space, "I cannot represent any line to myself, no matter how small, without drawing it in thought, that is, without gradually generating all its parts from a single point," and similarly, any period of time, no matter how brief, can be thought "only through the successive advance from one moment to another, whereby through all the time-parts and their addition a determinate time-magnitude is finally generated" (A 162–3 / B 203–4). Both determinate spaces and times, therefore, are represented by extensive magnitudes, that is, numerical measures representing the existence of separate or at least separable parts, and the empirical objects of judgment, which must be both determinate and given in intuition, are therefore also represented as having extensive magnitude.[8]

Before we consider the problems with this argument, we may note that the conception of an extensive magnitude as representing the enumeration of antecedently given parts does *not* commit Kant to a view of space and time as *discrete* or atomistic rather than *continuous*. Quite the contrary. As Kant made clear in 1784–5, the concept of an extensive magnitude is itself a *generic* concept which does not specify whether the parts to be enumerated themselves *exist* independently of one another, or are discrete, rather than being *introduced* only by means of limits in a continuous existent; nor does it settle whether the parts in any given measurement are themselves simple or else capable of further, even infinite, subdivision:

Numerus est, Multitudo numerando distincte cognita [number is the enumeration of a distinctly cognized multitude]. ... – For the concept of magnitude *numerus* an required. ... – Every *quantum* is either *continuum* or *discretum*, a continuous [or] an aggregated magnitude. A continuous magnitude is: *cujus partes omnes possibiles sunt, quanta* [one whose parts are all possible quantities], and we call it so because it does not arise through the completed addition of an aggregate but rather through a continuous addition. A *quantum discretum* is one the parts of which are considered as units, and one the parts of which are once again considered as aggregates [*Menge*] is called a *continuum*. And a *continuum* can also be considered as a *discretum*, if we think of it first as unity and only afterward as a group; e.g., I can think of a minute as the unit of an hour, but also in turn as a group which itself contains units, namely sixty seconds ... (*Metaphysik Volckmann*, 28:423)

In other words, as long as magnitude is represented as composed of *distinct* parts, it is an extensive magnitude; whether the parts are discrete or continuous, themselves indivisible or capable of further division into parts of their own, are further questions. And indeed, so far is Kant from inferring the discrete rather than continuous nature of space and time from the fact that determinate spaces and times are represented as extensive magnitudes that he is clearly committed to the opposite in the *Critique* itself. For Kant says that *even the smallest* determinate space or time must be represented as an extensive magnitude, by means of the separate generation of its parts and the subsequent representation of the synthetic unity of these parts by means of a number, thus implying that no matter how small the space or time may be, it is capable of further division, indeed cannot be represented as determinate except by means of such further division. This of course means that there are no smallest and discrete units of space or time, regardless of what units we choose for any particular measurement.

This conclusion raises the fundamental problem for Kant's argument, but we shall defer the consideration of this problem until two subsidiary ones have been mentioned. First, many commentators have seen an incompatibility between Kant's present claim that the representation of any determinate space or time must take place by an enumeration of antecedently given parts and his claim in the "Transcendental Aesthetic" that space and time are each *given* as a unique, all-embracing whole, the parts of which cannot precede it "as being, as it were, constituents out of which it can be composed" (A 25 / B 39) but can instead "be determinately represented only through limitation" of an antecedently given whole (A 32 / B 48).[9] But there is not a direct contradiction between the two claims. The argument of the "Aesthetic" is that space and time must be *a priori* forms of intuition, and this conclusion is partially grounded on the ontological claim that space and time are unique and infinite wholes, the parts of which are created only by introducing limits or ideal boundaries between continuous regions of the whole. The argument in the "Axioms of Intuition" does not turn on any such ontological supposition, however, but rather makes only the point that the *measurement* of *determinate* regions of space and time, and thus of the empirical objects that occupy them, requires the selection of some region or duration as a unit and the generation of the determinate magnitude to be measured out of repetitions of such a unit so that a numerical value can be assigned to it.[10] There is no contradiction between this epistemological claim about measurement and an ontological claim about what kind of existence the parts of space and time enjoy. Indeed, one might even suggest that Kant's present assurance that any space or time, *no matter how small,* can always be represented as an extensive magnitude of even smaller units *depends* on his belief that space and time are infinite given wholes into which ever smaller parts can always be introduced by an even finer delineation of limits. Thus there is no contradiction between the "Axioms of Intuition" and the "Transcendental

Aesthetic," though the argument of the former may have to be supplemented by that of the latter to be fully comprehensible.[11]

There is yet another problem with the argument, however. This is that even on the official program for the "Analytic of the Principles," *all* of the principles of judgment are supposed to be principles of time-determination, yet the "Axioms of Intuition" offers more than a principle of time-determination. Its rule for the measurement of determinate magnitudes of time is only an instance of a more general rule, which has a rule for the measurement of determinate magnitudes of space as its other instance. Such a rule could thus be instantiated – and thereby schematize the categories of quantity – without any reference to time at all. The general rule that empirical intuitions must have determinate extensive magnitudes does not seem to have an essential connection with the "time-series." Thus, the official architectonic of Kant's argument seems to break down in the first case to which it is applied.[12]

Kant's only solution for this problem is his dubious theory that number itself is essentially temporal. Perhaps his need for this theory to preserve the argument of the schematism, combined with the theory's obvious implausibility, explains Kant's wavering attitude toward it. After his separate statements that both determinate spaces and determinate times must be measured by an enumeration of their parts, Kant continues by tacitly introducing a temporal dimension to *both* of these forms of measurement: "Since the mere intuition in all appearances is either space or time, every appearance as intuition is an extensive magnitude, in that it can be cognized only through successive synthesis (from part to part) in apprehension" (A 163 / B 203–4). What Kant is implying is that whether or not the units *to be counted* in any measurement are themselves temporal units, the *process of counting* is a temporal process. Thus, extensive magnitude, whether of space or of time, turns out to be essentially connected to the time-series after all.

Kant refrains from making this implication explicit in his published text and does not always assert that there is an essential connection between counting and time.[13] But a marginal note in his own copy of the *Critique* takes a very strong position indeed by *deriving* the principle of extensive magnitude *from* the temporal nature of all synthesis:

Since we can arrange all perceptions only through apprehension in time, but since this is a synthesis of homogeneous parts, which in the unity of consciousness corresponds to the concept of magnitude, the objects of outer and inner sense cannot be known in experience other than as magnitudes ...

(R LXVII, 23:28)

Any manifold, whatever the nature of its contents, must be successively synthesized, Kant suggests. But to successively synthesize is to count parts; therefore the manifold of objects extended in space as well as time must have enumerable magnitudes. In fact, in this argument the antecedently established status of space and time as *forms of intuition* is virtually irrelevant, for the argument does not turn on an inference from pure to empirical intuition. Instead, mathematics is introduced as a *consequence* of the nature of synthesis in general. In such an argument the inference would be from the nature of *empirical* intuition, as the object of synthesis, to the necessity of mathematics, rather than from mathematics to the nature of empirical intuition. Such an argument would thus have the form suggested by the *Prolegomena* and the *Metaphysik Volckmann,* namely a demonstration that the nature of the empirical manifold justifies the use of a certain system of *a priori* concepts, although in this case it would be mathematical rather than logical concepts that were so justified. Unfortunately, Kant did not include this argument in the *Critique.*

Perhaps he did not do so because the connection between counting and time may have appeared more intuitive to Kant than it does to us. Thus, one commentator has suggested that Kant may have thought of counting as including calculus, and then understood the latter, as Newton did, as involving infinitely small but flowing periods of time (fluxions): "The generation of reality has a moment, that of an extensive quantity an element: *differentiale.* (This is to be regarded as the line which describes a surface in time)" (R 5582, 18:239). Yet such historical explanation of Kant's thought[14] does not seem enough to make the extensive magnitude of *spatial* regions or objects a genuine *time*-determination, for what would be determined, what measured, would not itself be any passage or relation of time. Even if the fact that regions of space must be measured by a successive synthesis of parts, which takes time, were sufficient to justify the application of the mathematics of extensive magnitudes to empirical objects, in other words, the connection of the principle of the axioms of intuition with time-determination by means of the time-series seems tendentious.

The claim that all representation of space or time involves a synthesis, thus that all such representation involves a succession and consequently an extensive magnitude, brings us to the basic problem with Kant's argument. Norman Kemp Smith advances an objection to the principle of the axioms which is independent of his claim that the arguments of the "Axioms of Intuition" and of the "Transcendental Aesthetic" are "directly opposed." According to Kemp Smith, the principle of extensive magnitude rests on the assumption that "it is impossible to apprehend a manifold save in succession. This assumption is, of course, entirely false (at least as applied to our empirical consciousness), as has since been amply demonstrated by empirical investigation."[15] The objection appears to be that as a matter of psychological fact we sometimes perceive stretches of space or time without any synthesis and that Kant's argument that *all* spaces or times must therefore be represented as extensive magnitudes, since it rests on the assumption that all spaces and times are represented by successive syntheses, is undermined by the counterexample of nonsuccessively perceived stretches of space or time. As an objection from empirical psychology, if that is what it is intended to be, Kemp Smith's criticism does not seem overwhelming. One could reply on Kant's behalf that spaces or times perceived in the way Kemp Smith adduces could be assigned an extensive magnitude nevertheless, which would just happen to be the extensive magnitude 1. As long as Kemp Smith could not prove that any particular amount of space, a region of particular size, was *necessarily* perceived instantaneously rather than successively – and of course no "empirical investigation" could establish such a necessity – one could hold that this was just the context-relative perception of a unit for measurement that Kant's remarks, especially in his lectures, lead us to expect. Or one could reply that Kant was not concerned with the ordinary *phenomenology* of perception at all but with the theory of *measurement*, and then argue that the facts of "empirical consciousness," as attested by the "empirical investigation" to which Kemp Smith is alluding, do not preclude the theoretical possibility of assigning a nonunitary extensive magnitude to any space or time, even if it is phenomenologically a *minimum sensibile*.

But it is precisely as a theory of the *measurement* of empirical objects that Kant's principle seems open to a more telling objection. Kant's argument seems to be that "even the smallest" space or time must still be represented by parts and thus assigned a nonunitary extensive magnitude, as an infinitely divisible object which in any given case can, indeed must, be subdivided at least once more. But whereas Kant's *task* has from the outset seemed to be that of *justifying* the application of the relevant branch of pure mathematics to empirical objects, his *argument* ultimately seems to *assume* the applicability of the mathematics of extensive magnitudes, complete with infinite divisibility, to empirical objects. Instead of pursuing the clue suggested in his marginal emendation to the *Critique*, when all is said and done Kant seems to beg his own question about applied mathematics and to settle the age-old question of whether empirical reality is really or only ideally submissible to mathematics (including that of potentially infinite extensive magnitudes) by fiat. Or, at least, he renders a special theory of measurement otiose by simply presupposing a theory of empirical perception which itself, however, settles such questions merely by assuming that the properties of the *a priori* forms of intuition are necessarily and fully instantiated by empirical intuition as well.[16]

The anticipations of perception

The argument of the "Axioms of Intuition," as we have seen, does little to advance Kant's general theory of time-determination. We must now consider whether his argument in the "Anticipations of Perception" is any more intimately connected with this underlying concern. But here again we shall find only an uncertain connection between the theory of measurement and the general theory of time-determination.

The title "Anticipations of Perception" is again a plural title which subsumes only a single principle. Thus we must again infer that the title does not refer directly to a group of principles but to the function of a single principle in justifying certain repeatable "anticipations" or predictions about the nature of our perceptions. These anticipations are predictions that our sensations will always have some particular degree or "intensive magnitude" and that the empirical but real objects which we take to correspond to our sensations and to be represented by them will therefore also have an intensive magnitude in addition to the extensive magnitude already assigned to them. But even this general statement immediately raises three questions. First, what is the relation between sensations and empirical objects which Kant has in mind here? Second, what precisely does Kant mean by an "intensive magnitude"? Third, what does he mean by "anticipations"?

Kant clarifies his position on the first of these issues in the revision of the *Critique*. In the first edition, the principle of the anticipations is that "in all appearances, sensation, and the *real*, which corresponds to it in the object (*realitas phaenomenon*), has an *intensive* magnitude, that is a degree" (A 166). This suggests that there are sensations, and real objects which correspond to them, and that both have intensive magnitudes, but it leaves somewhat unclear where in this picture the term "appearance" is to be applied. In fact, it makes it seem as though the sensation is a *constituent* of the appearance, so that an appearance is an empirical intuition *constituted* from a sensation and something else (spatiotemporal form, of course), to all of which something "real" and numerically distinct somehow corresponds. The statement in the second edition is clearer. Here Kant writes: "In all appearances the real, which is an object of sensation, has intensive magnitude, that is, a degree" (B 207). Here appearances are more clearly empirical *objects,* which are not composed of sensations, even in part, but *represented* by them, though of course only in part (the formal structure of the empirical intuition of which sensation is only the material also functions in the representation of the empirical object). Empirical intuitions do not compose but represent empirical objects, but because the sensations which are components of empirical intuitions have intensive magnitudes, the empirical objects which these intuitions represent are also assigned such magnitudes.[17] So the appearances to which intensive magnitudes are assigned are ontologically distinct from the sensations on the basis of whose intensive magnitudes the appearances are assigned theirs.[18]

This consideration may also make the relation between the principle of the anticipations of perception and the categories which are supposed to be schematized, the categories of quality, clearer than was the case with the axioms of intuition. Here Kant makes it at least tolerably clear that he means to be arguing that reality is affirmed or denied of empirical objects by virtue of the presence or absence of sensation, and that because of the intensive magnitude of sensation there is a qualification of degree in the exemplification of the category of reality that is not to be derived from the logical contrast between being and nonbeing alone, which of course does not permit of any continuum of degree. The basic form of Kant's argument is to give the categories of reality and negation empirical sense by connecting them to sensation, and then to show that this creates scope for differences of degree in the use of these categories:

> Now what corresponds to sensation in empirical intuition is reality (*realitas phaenomenon*); what corresponds to the lack thereof is negation = o. But now every sensation is capable of dimunition, so that it can decrease and gradually disappear. Therefore between reality in the appearance and negation there is a continuum of many possible intermediate sensations ... (A 168 / B 209–10)

And that there might be such a continuum of degrees between reality and negation is at least not precluded by the fact that the logical functions of affirmation and negation, from which the categories of reality and negation are supposed to be derived, are functions in a two-valued logic between which no intermediary is possible. For there is already a gap between the affirmative and negative as logical values of *propositions* and reality and negation as qualities of *objects* which allows one to treat any amount of a property greater than nothing as a degree of the reality which is the ground of an affirmative assertion about an object, even though there is no room for differences of degree in the contrast between affirmation and negation itself. Indeed, the whole argument of the anticipations might be viewed as an illustration of the distinction between logical and real opposition with which Kant had been concerned since his 1763 essay, *Negative Quantities*. Precisely because reality and negation *in objects*, though the basis for affirmation or denial of judgments of those objects, are not themselves logical contradictions but rather real states which may be in physical opposition, the differences between them may admit of degrees.[19]

Of course, the question of how Kant argues that qualities in objects must admit of degrees is another problem entirely, but we are not yet considering that. Rather, what must next be considered is precisely what Kant means by an "intensive magnitude" or degree.

At one level, what he means is clear enough. An extensive magnitude is a numerical measure the units of which represent actual parts of the whole being measured; an intensive magnitude, on the contrary, is a numerical measure the units of which do not represent actual parts of the particular instance of the quality being measured.[20] Instead, the unit in a measurement of intensive magnitude represents some possible manifestation of that quality – less intense than the instance being measured, if the degree assigned to the case at hand is greater than 1, but more intense if the instance being measured is assigned a numerical measure less than 1 – which might be manifested in some other exemplification of the quality but is not an actual part of the particular exemplification being measured. Intensive magnitudes of a given quality intermediate between the unit amount and the particular instance being measured would then represent other possible manifestations of the quality, but again not actual parts of the latter. In other words, intensive magnitudes are numerical comparisons, rather than measurements in terms of parts. For example, 5 feet of plank are literally part of my 8-foot bookshelf, even if I would have to use a saw to introduce a physical limit between those 5 feet and the remaining 3; but 60 degrees of heat are not literally *part* of today's temperature of 90 degrees: There is no way in which I could separate them from the remaining 30 degrees. Rather, they represent the temperature of a cooler day, with which today is being compared by means of a numerical ratio. In Kant's terms, an extensive magnitude is one which measures a "successive synthesis proceeding from parts to the whole representation"; but anything the apprehension of which is instantaneous – an assumption he makes about sensation in order to get this argument going – cannot have parts, thus admit of a measure of its parts. So it can have only an intensive magnitude, "a magnitude which is apprehended only as a unity, and in which the multiplicity can be represented only by an approximation to negation = o" (A 168 / B 210).

Kant clarified this somewhat obscure explanation in some of his classroom lectures, but only at the price of raising a problem for his theory. In the *Metaphysik Volckmann,* extensive magnitudes are clearly defined as those which constitute a measure of actual parts: "The quantity which is represented by the aggregate of that which is contained in the thing is *extensive.* ... Some [things] are quanta because they contain a group of parts. ..." But intensive qualities or magnitudes are magnitudes which are not literally aggregates of parts: "There are objects in which no parts can be distinguished ... and which are intensive. ... [These] are not considered ... like a group of homogeneous parts." Yet Kant's completion of this contrast also seems to undermine the argument for the principle, as given in the *Critique.* That argument is that because the sensation which is a component of our representation of an empirical object has a degree of intensity, the object itself, or the real in the object – its matter as opposed to its form – must also be assigned a degree. But the elaboration of the distinction between extensive and intensive magnitudes in Kant's lectures defines intensive magnitude in a way which appears to block this inference. For Kant claims that the degree of intensity *in the sensation,* although not itself a matter of parts, is the effect of the *number of parts* in the object which is its cause. This means that intensive magnitude must be confined to sensation alone, both form *and* reality or matter in the *object* of the sensation being measurable as *extensive* magnitudes. Or so at least it seems when we look at the whole passage from which I have just quoted extracts:

Every magnitude (quantity) can be considered [as] either extensive or intensive. The quantity which is represented by the group of that which is contained in the thing is *extensive.* And the quantity which is represented through the group which is posited through the thing is *intensive.* Some [things] are quanta because a group of parts is contained in them, and some are quanta through which a group [of parts] is posited as ground. For instance, the illuminative power of a wax candle is greater than that of a tallow candle, for with the first we can read at a distance of 2 feet and with the second only at 1 foot; the former is therefore the ground of a greater effect, and the latter the ground of a lesser, or better: If I take a kettle and a thimble full of warm water, then the former is extensively greater than the latter, but if the water in the kettle is only lukewarm and that in the thimble boiling, then the latter is in this case intensively greater than the first. There are objects in which one cannot distinguish any aggregation and which must yet be considered as parts and which are intensive – this is called a degree; in the case of others I can see the aggregation [of parts], which is then an extensive magnitude. The former is not considered as a group of homogeneous parts but rather as a unity of greater effects.

(Metaphysik Volckmann, 28:424–5)

In part, this is not only consistent with Kant's exposition in the *Critique* but even an improvement on it. The doctrine of the *Critique* is that the intensity of a sensation can be measured only by what is essentially a comparison to other possible instances of the same sort of *sensation,* which may be less or more intense; then since an intensive magnitude is assigned to the *object* represented by the sensation corresponding to the degree of intensity of that sensation, the sensation is seen as a greater or lesser effect of a cause with greater or lesser intensity. This is also what is suggested by Kant's example of the kettle and the thimble. The example of the wax and tallow candles, however, suggests that (at least sometimes) we can measure intensive magnitudes more easily than by the putative comparison of different instances of the same sort of sensation, which cannot be carried out directly, since we cannot have two sensations of the same sort at once. Instead, we can measure and compare the intensive magnitudes of sensations and their causes by differences in the *extensive* magnitudes of the effects, for instance the *distance* at which they produce the same level of the brightness of light-producing objects are differences of degree, but they can be measured by the differences in the *extensive* magnitude of their effects, for instance the *distance* at which they produce the same level of illumination. Or at least – since the recognition of the same level of illumination presupposes some comparison of sensations – the extensive magnitude of the distance can be used to arrive at the numerical value of the ratio between the intensities of the two sources of light.

Thus Kant's examples in his lecture refine the position of the *Critique.* Nevertheless, the more abstract remarks with which Kant opens the paragraph undermine it, for they suggest that whereas in the case of an intensive magnitude the degree of the quality does not, to be sure, represent a multiplicity of parts in the *sensation,* it *is* correlated with, indeed produced by, a multiplicity of parts in the *object* causing the sensation: "Some are quanta, through which a group [of parts] is posited as ground." Here the degree of the sensation is not correlated with a *degree* of quality in the cause but with a *number of parts* in the cause. But to assume that this is so is precisely to contradict the inference of the *Critique,* which assumes that if a degree of intensity is assigned to a sensation, *only* a degree of efficacy can be assigned to the reality which produces it. If the causal power of the object in producing a sensation of a certain degree can be reduced to a multiplicity of parts, then intensive magnitudes in sensations are caused by extensive, and not intensive, magnitudes in reality. The principle of intensive magnitude would not appear to be a necessary principle for empirical knowledge of objects, and therefore would not seem to be an indispensable condition for the use of the logical functions of quality.

Since Kant's lecture antedates the *Metaphysical Foundations of Natural Science* by only one year, we could conjecture that he intended his classroom discussion of intensive magnitude to be reconciled to the exposition in the *Critique* by the use of the theory of matter expounded in the new book (though also anticipated in the *Monadologia Physica* of 1755). That is, given Kant's physical theory that the occupation of any determinate extent of space is not due to the presence in that region of a number of determinate atoms but is rather due to the balance in that region between the intensity of the attractive and repulsive forces there centered, we might conjecture that Kant held that at the most fundamental level of physical theory extensive magnitude really reduces to intensive magnitude, even if the opposite seems to be the case at some more superficial level. That is, whereas, say, in optics the intensity of illumination might seem to depend on the number of illuminated objects or their distance from a light source, in more basic physical theory such measurements would themselves depend on the intensity of attractive and repulsive forces which have no parts. Thus the apparent contrast between the *Metaphysik Volckmann* and the *Critique* would not be a contradiction after all. It must be noted, however, that if the two passages were reconciled in this way, then the principle of the anticipations of perception in the end would rest not on purely *a priori* conditions of the possibility of experience – whether deriving from intuitions, or from concepts, or from the intersection of the two – but on a considerable amount of physical theory, theory which on Kant's own account is at least partly empirical. In other words, if the claim of this principle to a place in a transcendental theory of experience is saved by a theory that matter consists of forces with intensive magnitudes and that the logical concept of reality can therefore be applied only by degrees, then the claim of such a theory to include only synthetic *a priori* judgments is endangered.[21]

This already suggests difficulties about the character of Kant's argument for the principle of intensive magnitude, but before we turn to explicit consideration of this argument, we must deal with one last point about the meaning of the principle: namely, what Kant intends by the term "anticipations" itself. What Kant says in justification of his use of this term is that if "there is something which can be known *a priori* in every sensation, as sensation in general (without a particular being able to be given), then this can be called an anticipation in an exceptional sense" (A 167 / B 209). In other words, Kant says that we can know *a priori* that every sensation (and corresponding reality) will have some degree or other, although we will not know *a priori* what the particular degree of any sensation is, yet that this is enough to justify the use of the term "anticipation." And so it is. But this certainly makes clear, as I argued in the first section of this chapter, that Kant undercuts his own classification of the principle of intensive magnitude as constitutive rather than regulative. As we saw, such a judgment as that the sun is 200,000 times as bright as the moon can hardly be considered determinable by any *a priori* means, for it follows neither from any *a priori* principle alone nor from the kind of construction in pure intuition by which it might be proved that the interior angles of a triangle add up to exactly half the interior angles of a rectangle. And with his explanation of the title "anticipations" Kant says the same thing. Kant himself concedes that all we can know *a priori* is that there must be *some* determinate value for the equation "The sun is n times as bright as the moon" or for any other comparison of any two objects producing sensations in the same sensory mode ("Aspartane is n times as sweet as granulated sugar"). That is all that we can anticipate, though of course quotidian experience and laboratory experiments generally allow us to solve such equations by supplying specific numerical values for the comparisons of intensity.

We may now turn to Kant's argument for the principle of intensive magnitude. Kant's original account of the connection between the intensive magnitude of sensation and the general theory of schemata as time-determinations seemed extremely tenuous, and although it is clear that he means his subsequent argument to close the gap between the two by making, in Kemp Smith's words, "all apprehension, even that of simple sensation, a temporal process,"[22] this task is exceedingly difficult.

In his initial account of the intensity of sensation as the schema of the category of reality, Kant emphasizes that "every sensation has a degree or magnitude whereby, in respect of its object otherwise remaining the same, it can fill out one and the same time, that is, occupy inner sense more or less completely, down to its cessation" (A 143 / B 182). On this account of sensation as "time-content," there seems to be no more connection between the structure of time and the fact that what fills it, namely sensation, comes in different degrees than there is between, say, the structure of wine bottles and the fact that what fills them comes in different vintages. Sensation could be what fills time, whether any kind of sensation admitted of even infinite degrees of variation or whether it came in only one boringly uniform intensity. As he proceeds, Kant tries to draw a closer connection between the fact that sensations fill time – are the basic contents of all empirical representations of outer and inner sense – and that they have a degree, but his argument encounters numerous difficulties.

The problem that Kant faces in assimilating his theory of intensive magnitude into the theory of time-determinations is posed precisely by what, as we have already noticed, Kant takes as the *premise* of his theory, that "apprehension by means merely of sensation occupies only an instant" (A 167 / B 209). This means that whatever magnitude is assigned to sensation cannot be the kind of magnitude generated by the successive apprehension of distinct parts of an object over time – that is, extensive magnitude. Nevertheless, Kant appears to argue, there is a connection between the measure of sensations and the structure of time, because

AXIOMS AND ANTICIPATIONS

individual sensations of a given quality, *though themselves instantaneous,* can be thought of not merely as members of classes of possible instances which vary in intensity and can be compared to each other, but also as members of potential *series* of instances of the same kind of sensation, which *are* undergoing an increase or decrease of intensity over time. A measure can be assigned to an individual and instantaneous instance of sensation, then, which would represent the *amount of time* it would take to reach it if such a potential series were actually occurring. Thus, although "apprehension merely by means of sensation fills only an instant" (A 167 / B 209), every sensation is also "capable of a diminution," and there is a continuous series of degrees between such a sensation and the absence of any sensation which can be represented as if it were occurring over a period of time. This series would generate the determination of the magnitude of time that would be required for the particular sensation to be reached if it were actually part of a continuous occurrence (which it is not), and the measure of that time, which is itself extensive, can be assigned to the sensation, though only as intensive: The length of the temporal duration it would take to reach the given degree of sensation when traversing such a series would represent the intensity of the particular instance of the sensation which is actually given in an instant. However, the supposition on which this argument turns, namely that any given sort of sensation can come in a continuous variation of intensity even though it actually occurs in an instant, is either without *a priori* justification or else can be justified only in a way that conflicts with the first premise, that all sensation is instantaneous.

On the one hand, in the opening paragraph added to the second edition, Kant tries to ground the premise of variability by saying that "from empirical consciousness to pure, a steplike alteration is possible, since the real [in empirical consciousness] can disappear, leaving behind only a purely formal consciousness (*a priori*) of the manifold in space and time; therefore there is also possible a synthesis of the generation of the magnitude of a sensation from its beginning, in pure intuition = 0, up to any particular magnitude" (B 207–8). But surely this *a priori* argument for the principle of degree proceeds only by committing the very error with which Kant was always taxing his predecessors, namely that of confusing a difference of *kind* with a difference of *degree* (e.g., A 43–4 / B 60–2; *Critique of Judgment,* §15, 5:228). The formal and material components in empirical intuitions – that is, the spatial and temporal forms and the sensory matter – are not different *degrees* of some one thing that can be gradually transformed into the other but are intrinsically different. Considering a geometrical figure is not examining an empirical object from which the matter has gradually been evacuated, but is examining in pure imagination the form of a possible object, without consideration even of the possibility of matter which might produce the sensation required for an empirical intuition of the object. But if this is so, then Kant surely cannot draw upon the distinction between pure and empirical intuition to defend the principle of intensive magnitude.

On the other hand, Kant's presentation of his thesis in the first edition does not even seem to rest on a (fallacious) *a priori* argument but only on an empirical claim. That is, the claim that "between reality and negation there is a continuum of possible realities and of possible smaller perceptions" (A 169 / B 211) seems to be asserted as a simple matter of fact; it may be true, but there is nothing inconceivable in the alternative assumption that any given sort of sensation can come in only one strength.[23] And Kant seems only to strengthen this impression by refusing to draw a general conclusion about the continuity of change from the (alleged) fact of the continuity of the degrees of sensation:

Now if all appearances, considered in their extensive as well as their intensive aspects, are continuous quantities, then the proposition that also all alteration (transition of a thing from one state to another) is continuous would be able here to be proved easily and with mathematical evidence, if only the causality of an alteration in general did not lie outside the borders of a transcendental philosophy and presuppose empirical principles. (A 171 / B 212–13)

But surely if the continuity of *alteration in general* rests on an empirical principle, then so must the continuous variability of sensations. Thus the principle of intensive magnitude seems to lack any *a priori* basis, let alone a clear place in Kant's theory of time-determination or even in the official schematism of the categories.

Kant did not always reject the possibility of connecting the principle of intensive magnitude with a general thesis of the continuous nature of change in time. In the passage just considered Kant did reject a derivation of the latter thesis *from* the variability of sensation. But on at least one occasion during the period including the composition of the *Critique,* Kant contemplated the opposite tack – directly deriving the principle of intensive magnitude from the continuity of change in time itself, with the latter clearly assumed as an *a priori* rather than empirical principle. Recall this remark, quoted at the beginning of this chapter:

Principium of the mathematical cognition of appearances: All appearance has as intuition its extensive magnitude and as sensation its degree. For (as far as the latter is concerned) every sensation arises from nonbeing because it is modification. Therefore through alteration. But all alteration proceeds from o to a through infinitely small steps. (R 5585, 18:241)

Here Kant does indeed derive the principle of intensive magnitude from an intrinsic feature of time itself: Time is continuous, he clearly assumes, so all change is continuous, but all sensation is the result of a change from the nonexistence of that sensation to its existence through a continuum of intermediate degrees of that sensation. Therefore any particular sensation at any moment can be assigned a degree on some scale of intensity.[24]

There are two problems with this argument, however. First, it works only by rejecting the premise of the published argument for the principle of intensive magnitude, that sensation is instantaneous. And by so doing, it again reduces the difference between extensive and intensive magnitude: Sensation has intensity because it occurs over a period of time, but that comes very close to saying that it has intensive magnitude because it has *extensive* magnitude. Second, its inference that because *time* is continuous *change* must be continuous is not reconciled with the *Critique*'s unqualified assertion that the continuity of change is only an empirical matter. Thus, even if the present argument were allowed, its place in a transcendental theory of experience – like the possible place in such a theory of Kant's theoretical conversion of extensive into intensive magnitude – would again be questionable.

Though Kant's principle of intensive magnitude undoubtedly had deep roots in his study and teaching of physics, it does not have a clear place in his transcendental theory of experience. Kant's confusion here is surely further evidence of the difficulties he faced in attempting to construct a general theory of categories with a deduction and schematism independent of the theory of time-determination and the justification for the three categories of relation which the latter could offer. Nevertheless, the implication of R 5585 that no mental event, not even the simplest sensation, can be conceived except as happening during a period of some temporal duration reminds us of the claim which was supposed to be the fundamental premise of the transcendental deduction but was not actually exploited there, namely the claim that a manifold of representations can itself be represented only by the representation of a temporal succession of impressions. We have now reached the point where we can consider how Kant exploits this premise, first in an apparent contrast between the necessary conditions of objective and subjective time-determinations, and then at last in an integrated theory of the necessary conditions for subjective as well as objective time-determinations. The first of these stages is contained in Kant's analogies of experience, and the second underlies the ultimate completion of his critical epistemology in the refutation of idealism.

8

The general principle of the analogies

The analogies of experience, in the *Critique of Pure Reason*, are the heirs to the analogies of appearance which constituted Kant's original transcendental theory of experience. The analogies of experience thus constitute both the historical and philosophical heart of Kant's theoretical philosophy as that existed prior to 1787 – prior, that is, to Kant's addition of his ultimate argument for the objective validity of the categories of the understanding in the form of his refutation of idealism. Seen from this ultimate perspective, the analogies are an indispensable but also incomplete part of an epistemological theory of the necessary conditions of time-determination. They show us that certain principles are required in order to ground temporal determinations about objects. But they assume that we can and must make such determinations, and it is only in the refutation of idealism that Kant attempts to defend this assumption by showing that temporal determinations about objects distinct from our own representations of them are themselves necessary conditions of the temporal determinations of our own representations considered merely as such. In other words (to return to the strategic terms used in the discussion of the transcendental deduction), the analogies of experience might seem to suffice for an answer to an empiricist, who supposes that we can make objective judgments about objects in time but without the benefit of any *a priori* concepts or principles; however, the conclusions of the analogies could not be forced on a skeptic (such as Hume on causation) who is also willing to doubt that we have knowledge of external reality at all. For this purpose there would be required the further argument of the refutation of idealism that subjective time-determination itself presupposes objective time-determination. But the relation between the analogies of experience and the refutation of idealism, or what I have earlier referred to as the two stages of Kant's theory of time-determination, the objective and the subjective, is even closer than that suggests. For although Kant's exposition in the text of the "Refutation of Idealism" proceeds as if the completeness of his argument in the text of the "Analogies of Experience" can be assumed, the real argument of the analogies, especially the second analogy's argument for a principle of universal causation, depends on the fundamental premise underlying the refutation of idealism – the implication of A 99 that even merely subjective sequences of representation are not directly given in passive apprehension alone. Only this premise will save the analogies from the customary charge of fallacy. Thus, although Kant first offers what appears to be a self-contained theory of the conditions necessary for making determinate judgments about the temporal relations of objects, their properties, and the events they figure in, and then goes on to offer the further argument that even the mere ability to make determinate judgments about temporal relations of representations in the self also presupposes the ability to make such judgments about the objective world, and all the conditions that entails, the first stage of his theory is not actually completed except by a vital premise which is explicitly employed only in the second.

Of course, Kant himself did not expound the analogies of experience in such a provisional tone – and he did not even make clear the existence of the second stage of the theory of time-determination until the second edition of the *Critique*. Instead, by the time he reached the analogies, Kant took the necessity of knowledge of objects already to have been established by the transcendental deduction (even though, as we saw, many of Kant's tactics for the deduction merely presupposed that we are entitled to claim objective knowledge of empirical objects). So Kant formulated the arguments in the "Analogies of Experience" as if the necessity of the application of the categories of relation to objects beyond our own representations of them had already been established, and as if what remained to be done was only to determine what principles can be inferred from the further fact – alleged by the "Schematism" – that this application must be by means of representations given successively in time.

This conception of the status of his argument is naturally reflected in Kant's statement of the general principle of the analogies and in his general account of the premises of the arguments to come which he gives at the start of the section. But although the general content of these pages is therefore somewhat predictable, there are a few details about Kant's exposition that are definitely worth notice. The difference between these pages in the two editions of the *Critique* is particularly revealing.

In the first edition, Kant writes that the "general principle of the analogies is: *All appearances, as far as their existence is concerned, stand* a priori *under rules of the determination of their relation to one another in one time*" (A 176–7). This is very naturally read as though it has already been established that appearances are subject *a priori* to rules, and as though what must be demonstrated now is only that these rules are rules for the determination of the temporal relation of these appearances. And in a way, this statement of the principle is preferable to the statement which Kant substituted for it in the second edition ("Experience is possible only through the representation of a necessary connection of perceptions" [B 218]), precisely because it contains this explicit reference to time-determination.[1] Such a reference is omitted from the new statement, and that makes it appear as though the principle of the analogies contains no advance at all over what has (supposedly) been established in the transcendental deduction. But there is also a subtle but important way in which the second statement of the principle is preferable to the first. The first-edition statement speaks of *appearances*, and, given that by "appearance" Kant frequently means "empirical object," one might take this to mean that Kant thinks that the basic principles for judgments that subjective representations signify independent objects and events have been established prior to the arguments for the analogies, and that what the latter are intended to do is only to ground certain *special* judgments, about certain *special* temporal determinations or aspects of objects or events already judged to be objective – for instance, judgments about *how long* given objects or events have endured or what the relative *order* of two given events is. But such an interpretation of Kant's intentions would be radically mistaken, even on Kant's own conception of the progress of his argument. Kant's reformulation of the general principle of the analogies for the second edition makes this clear. Here Kant speaks of the necessary connection of *perceptions,* and this suggests that without the principles of the three analogies there can be no well-grounded judgments about *objective* entities or events at all. The analogies are not intended to *supplement* some principles for judgments about objects which have been established prior to them. Rather, they *are* the basic principles for judgments about objects, although now formulated with reference to the specifically temporal form of our empirical intuitions and their objects, rather than purely in the logical terms originally furnished by the metaphysical deduction. Without the analogies, there can be no justification for the interpretation of our *empirical intuitions* as representing *objects and events in time* at all. Deprived of these principles, we would not be able to judge that we encounter objects and events and merely be unable to measure their duration or order them all on a single, perpetual calendar; we would not be able to determine that our unceasing succession of fleeting representations stands for any external objects and events at all.

The consequences of this point will become clearer when we turn to the details of the first and second analogies in particular, but it is worth emphasizing it further now by looking at the opening paragraphs following the general statement of principle. In the first edition, Kant starts by saying that there are three "modes of time," namely *"duration, succession,* and *coexistence,"* and that there must therefore be "three rules of all time-relations of appearances, according to which the existence of each appearance can be determined in respect of the unity of all time" (A 177). Kant elaborates this by presenting the argument for the analogies as the natural extension of the argument of the deduction: "There is a necessary *unity* of apperception, in respect of all possible empirical consciousness," and since the form of all empirical consciousness is temporal – "Original apperception stands in relation to inner sense (the sum of all representations), and indeed *a priori* to its form" – that means that "in the original apperception all this manifold must be united as far as its time-relations are concerned." Of course, since, as we saw, there is no successful argument that the unity of apperception requires *a priori* rules which is *independent* of this very claim that "the manifold must be united as far as its time-relations are concerned," the analogies cannot depend on a prior proof that the unity of apperception, more abstractly conceived, requires *a priori* rules; the present claim is really the only possible *premise* for a transcendental theory of experience. Nevertheless, Kant writes as though a general requirement of the transcendental unity of apperception is now being combined with the temporal form of our representations of objects to give rise to "the law: that all empirical time-determination must stand under rules of universal time-determination" (A 177–8).

Kant does describe what is grounded on this law as "*synthetic unity* in the time-relations of all perceptions" (A 177), so even in the face of his ambivalence about the independence of the transcendental deduction from the analogies of experience it should be clear that from the outset his intention is to establish what principles are required to judge that our representations represent objects at all, given that our representations, and consequently their objects, are in temporal form. Nevertheless, Kant's apparent contrast between "empirical time-determinations" and "universal time-determinations," combined with his emphasis on the parallel between the unity of apperception and the uniqueness of time *as a whole,* might give rise to the impression that by this point in the argument the conditions for the representation of objects have already been taken care of and that what is now needed is only certain *additional* principles for relating already given objects and events to a complete and unique temporal order, the whole of time – perhaps by grounding unique and unequivocal determinations of the relative duration and order of objects and events already recognized *to be* objects and events. But Kant's new opening paragraph in the second edition makes it clear that such an interpretation of his intentions would be mistaken. For here Kant's emphasis is clearly on the *contrast* between objects and perceptions, and what he argues is that the analogies of experience are needed to make any judgments at all about the "necessary" rather than "accidental" temporal order of perceptions, and by that means to judge that they represent *objective* states of affairs.

Thus, Kant commences the second-edition exposition by suggesting that the analogies of experience are the conditions of empirical knowledge itself, "that is, a cognition which determines an object through perceptions" (B 218). What is necessary for empirical knowledge, which Kant here also calls "experience" itself, is "the synthetic unity of the manifold [of perception] in one consciousness ... which constitutes the essential in a cognition of *objects* of the senses, that is, of experience (not merely of intuition or sensation of the senses)." So it is to permit us to judge that subjective representations represent objects at all that the analogies of experience are needed.

Kant's explanation of this claim might be taken to recapitulate the argument of the transcendental deduction but may also be seen as first exploiting one of its basic strategies while assuming little more than a prior contrast between subject and object, the accidental and the orderly. Principles are needed to ground experience or empirical knowledge of objects, because "in experience" (by which Kant plainly means precisely the *opposite* of what he meant a line earlier – namely, mere apprehension, the uninterpreted given or raw material for experience in the stronger sense) "perceptions are juxtaposed only accidentally, so that no necessity of their connections is revealed by the perceptions themselves, nor can be revealed, since apprehension is only a juxtaposition of the manifold of empirical intuition and yields no representation of the necessity of the connected existence of appearances ... in space and time" (B 219). Representations themselves come in a temporal order, and so must the objects they are to represent (that was made explicit by the schematism, but according to A 99 it was also supposed to lie behind the deduction all along), but there is no basis for assuming that the apparently entirely accidental succession of *representations* as such bears any determinate relation to the determinate temporal structure of the *objects or events* beyond them. Yet for experience, now again in the strong sense of empirical knowledge of objects, it is precisely the latter claim to knowledge which is required: "Experience is a cognition of objects through perceptions, consequently a cognition of the relation in the existence of the manifold, not as it is [merely] juxtaposed in time, but as it is objectively in time." So it is to ground the interpretation of subjective states as representing any objects at all that the analogies are required. Kant then concludes his new introductory paragraph with a statement of why the principles of the analogies are the only ones which can serve this purpose. This is as hasty as it is pregnant: "Since time itself cannot be perceived, the determination of the existence of objects in time can take place only by means of their connection in time in general, thus only through *a priori* connecting concepts" (B 219).

Kant's saying that "time itself cannot be perceived" has already concerned us; his reason for thinking that this entails that "*a priori* connecting concepts" are needed to make judgments about objective existence in time will be the subject of the detailed examination of the three analogies of experience. But before turning to those we might raise the question of why there are suddenly three principles here, when in the "Axioms of Intuition" and "Anticipations of Perception" there was only a single principle in each case. Or rather we might ask, *are* there really three independent principles here? Do the three analogies of experience literally yield three different principles for empirical judgment of three different temporal features or relations?

As we have seen, Kant does claim that there are three different modes of time – duration, succession, and coexistence – and does distinguish three corresponding analogies. It seems natural to conclude that each one of these analogies is meant to yield a principle which suffices to ground determinations in one of the three modes of time: the first to ground determinations of duration; the second, objective relations of succession; and the third, objective relations of coexistence or simultaneity. That is, one might assume that each of the three principles is intended to function independently of the other two in grounding its particular objective time-determination – that the principle derived from the first analogy is meant to ground determinations of duration independently of the use of the principles derived from the second and third analogies, and so on.[2] But other statements which Kant makes belie such a supposition. Thus, the opening paragraph of the first-edition text of the first analogy says that "all appearances are in time. Time can determine the relation in their existence in a *twofold* [my emphasis] way, either as *they succeed one another* or as they *are simultaneous*" (A 182). The next paragraph, retained in both editions, similarly says that "simultaneity and succession are the only relations in time" (A 182 / B 226). There is an apparent conflict here, and thus a question about the independence of the three analogies.

In fact, the initial expectation raised by the mention of the three "modes" of time is misleading. Except for one unfortunate line of thought in the first analogy, what Kant actually argues is (1) that the basic distinction to be made in placing an objective interpretation on representations, which are as such always successive, is whether they are to be taken as representing successive or coexistent states of affairs – change or the absence of change – and (2) that to judge either that there is any objective change at all or that there is objective coexistence requires the presupposition of enduring, indeed ultimately permanent objects governed by laws of causation and interaction. There are not *three* different "modes" of time which can be judged of independently of one another; in a way, it is almost misleading to speak of even *two* different relations of time, as if they could be judged of independently (and indeed Kant sometimes suggests that succession is the only purely temporal relation; see A 31 / B 47). Rather, there is a basic distinction to be made between the alternative temporal possibilities for the objective states of affairs represented by any two successive perceptions. Although the representations can only succeed each other, the objective states may either succeed one another or coexist with one another. To decide which of these is the case will always require *both* the presupposition of an enduring object or objects *and* the postulation of laws fully governing the action and interaction of such objects.[3]

The interdependence of both the *use* of the principles of the analogies and, as we shall also see, the *arguments* on their behalf becomes evident when we consider the three *categories* which Kant relates to the three modes of time rather than the three modes themselves. These categories are, of course, substance, causality, and community or reciprocity. Kant frequently makes it clear that the concept of substance is never one which can be used to furnish any information about objects by itself. He explicitly attacks what he takes to be the Lockean idea of substance as a substratum distinct from accidents: "Locke in his essay on human understanding says: We represent substance to ourselves as the *portitor* (bearer) of accidents. ... But the accidents are not particular things that exist, rather only particular ways of considering existence; they therefore do not need to be borne, but rather signify only the manifold determination of one and the same thing" (*Metaphysik Volckmann*, 28:429; see also R 5861, 18:371). But he also suggests that the manifold determinations of one and the same thing include not just those predicates traditionally called accidents, namely monadic predicates, but also relations of causality and reciprocity as well: "In substance there is 1. The relation of inherence (*accidens*); 2. of causality (Force); 3. of *commercii* (Influence)" (R 5680, 18:371). Another fragment does not bother to list the relation between substance and accident at all but emphasizes only that the concept of substance is used in conjunction with the two categories of relation: "2. Substance as cause, 3. As part of a whole in community" (R 5292, 18:145). And this note was written next to a paragraph in Baumgarten's *Metaphysics* which obviously drew Kant's attention by identifying the inherence of accidents in substance with force (*vis*) (§197, reproduced at 17:68):

1. *Substratum* (inherence). 2. *Principium Caussalitatis* (consequence). a. *ratio realis, sive synthetica. Caussalitas substantiae quoad accidentia est vis. primitativa, derivativa. Actio, passio, Influxus.* 3. *Commercium. Reciproca actio. Triplex unitas, cuius functiones sunt a priori, sed non nisi a posteriori dari possunt* (*construi*).

[1. Substratum (inherence). 2. The principle of causality (consequence). a. real or synthetic reason. The causality of substance as well as of accident is force. primitive, derivative. Action, passion, influx. 3. Commerce. Reciprocal action. A triple unity, whose functions are *a priori*, but cannot be given (constructed) except *a posteriori*.] (R 5289, 18:144)

This marvelous note, which Adickes could date only as written sometime between 1772 and 1778, already makes perfectly clear Kant's mature position that such concepts as causality are *a priori* concepts, yet also concepts which can be utilized only on the basis of material given *a posteriori*, and it draws a close connection between the two apparently independent concepts of accident and causality. But what is most revealing about it is simply the phrase *"Triplex unitas."* This suggests that although substance, causality, and community are three separate concepts, they can be *used* only in conjunction with one another. And in fact this is clearly stated in the *Critique* itself:

... Causality leads to the concept of action, this to the concept of force, and thereby to the concept of substance. ... I leave the detailed exposition of such concepts to a future system of pure reason. ... Only I cannot leave unmentioned the empirical criterion of a substance, insofar as it appears to manifest itself better and more readily through action than through the permanence of appearance.

(A 204 / B 249)

The empirically applicable concept – or schematized category – of substance may be the concept of something which lasts through time, but this concept itself can be applied only with the assistance of causal judgments. And indeed the detailed study of Kant's three analogies will demonstrate his realization that empirical judgments about what endures can be made only in connection with empirical judgments about what causes what and what interacts with what; the three categories of relation are used interdependently. The same will also turn out to be true of the three arguments contained in the "Analogies of Experience." My task now is to determine what these arguments are and to discover what they show about the interdependent use of concepts of substance, causation, and even interaction.

9

The first analogy: substance

Kant had intended to construct three analogies of experience since his first conception of a transcendental theory of experience. Perhaps this explains why we shall find a higher degree of clarity and uniformity in the arguments for the universal applicability of laws of causation and interaction in the second and third analogies than we find in the case of arguments which Kant had hardly invented before publishing – that is to say, of course, the transcendental deduction and, as we shall see, the refutation of idealism. But we also saw that Kant's original theory appealed to three "analogies of appearance" without delivering arguments for or from them, and we shall now see that in the case of the first analogy Kant's long search for an argument for the necessity of permanent substance as a condition of time-determination did not result in the formulation of a single argument with a clearly defined structure. Instead, the text, as Kant published it in the first edition of the *Critique* and emended it in the second, conflates at least three different arguments. After a comment on Kant's two versions of the "Principle of the Permanence of Substance" itself (A 180 / B 224), I will analyze these three styles of argument.

In the first edition of the *Critique*, Kant states the principle as "*All appearances contain the permanent (substance) as the object itself, and the changeable as its mere determination, that is, a way in which the object exists*" (A 182). In the second edition, Kant substitutes this: "*In all change of appearances, substance endures, and its quantum in nature is neither increased nor diminished*" (B 224). The first statement might seem preferable because it could appear to suggest only that (1) some substance must be invoked in any given case of change, or that in *any* change there is *some* substance which endures through *that* change, without implying (2) a principle of the perpetual conservation of a uniform quantum of substance which persists through all changes, no matter how many nor how drastic – that is, that there is *one* particular substance or set of substances which endures through *all* changes. This might seem preferable, because the principle (1) that there must be some substance for any change is typically seen to be a more conservative, and therefore more plausibly provable, philosophical principle than the substantive physical principle of the conservation of matter (2).[1] A correct analysis of the arguments Kant actually makes, however, rather than hypotheses about what sorts of considerations might lead a philosopher to argue for the necessity of some concept of substance, will show that the transition from the apparently weaker principle (1) that a substance which is possibly only relatively enduring must underlie any given change of properties to the stronger principle (2) that truly permanent substance is conserved throughout all change is no mere slip or confusion but a natural consequence of three main arguments which Kant deploys on behalf of the principle of the permanence of substance. The arguments we shall now examine will be seen to lead directly to principle (2), so, although it will hardly be obvious that these arguments (especially the first that we shall consider) are sound, they are hardly invalid derivations of the conservation of substance which merely confuse this with some more conservative conception of a thing which has qualities. On the contrary, Kant argues directly for the necessity of permanently enduring entities, or at least directly for the impossibility of empirical knowledge of the creation or cessation of any object *ex* or *in nihilo,* and only indirectly identifies the permanent objects thus introduced with substances in the merely relatively enduring sense of that which endures through some change of accidents.[2]

The substratum of time itself

The first form of proof which Kant deploys in both editions would, if sound, directly establish the permanent conservation of genuine substance, and not just the relative endurance of particular substances through particular changes. Unfortunately this argument is also the most problematic of Kant's three defenses of the principle of permanence of substance: It rests on an epistemic principle which he elsewhere disavows, and on an ontological equivocation.[3]

This first argument may be represented in four steps.[4]

(1) Kant begins by maintaining that although the succession of both moments of time and states of affairs and the coexistence of states of affairs (not, of course, different moments of time) are the only forms of *relation* in time ("simultaneity and succession are the only relations in time" [A 182]) permanence is, on the contrary, a property of time itself, the whole in which both succession and coexistence occur. Insofar as succession and coexistence are relations of moments of time and/or states of affairs in time, and time itself is permanent, succession and coexistence are modifications of that which is permanent. Thus,

All appearances are in time, in which, as substratum (as permanent form of inner intuition), *simultaneity* as well as *succession* can alone be represented. Time, therefore, in which all change of appearances is to be thought, remains and does not change, since it is that in which successive as well as simultaneous existence can be thought only as modifications. (B 224–5)

Or, as he puts it in the first edition, "Permanence, as the abiding correlate of all existence of appearances, of all change and of all concomitance, expresses time in general. For change does not affect time itself, but only appearances in time"; otherwise, paradoxes of more than one time (not just more than one moment of time) would result (A 183). Thus, permanence is introduced into this argument not as a property or determination of any *objects* in time, but of *time itself.*[5]

(2) Kant's next step is to invoke the general principle of the argument of the analogies, namely that "time itself cannot be perceived" (B 225). What he means by this here is the limited point that even if the *succession* of moments of time can be directly given in apprehension, there is nothing in apprehension itself, which, without further interpretation, can count as perception of the *permanence* of the time-series itself. "For in the mere succession alone existence is forever disappearing and recommencing, and never has the least magnitude" (A 183). We are *given* merely successive moments of time, not a *duration* of any magnitude, let alone a duration as long as that of permanent time itself.

(3) But, Kant continues, there must be something by means of which the permanent duration of time itself is represented, or "which represents time in general," and this must be found "among the objects of perception, that is, among the appearances" or empirical objects which are in time (B 225). Moreover, whatever it is among the appearances *in* time which functions to represent the permanence *of* time – and which, because of this representational function, Kant calls the "substratum which represents time in general" – is assumed to be itself permanent: "Time cannot be perceived in itself; therefore [the] permanent in the appearances is the substratum of all time-determination" (A 183).

(4) Kant next equates that which is the substratum *of time,* in the sense of the representation of the permanence of time, with "the substratum of all that is real," that is, *substance* in the traditional sense of the ultimate bearer of objective qualities. He thus assumes that because the substratum of time must be permanent, so must be the substratum of qualities, or substance in this traditional sense: "Consequently the permanent, in relation to which alone all time-determinations can be determined, is substance in the appearance, that is, the real is that which as substratum of all change always remains the same" (B 225). In other words, the permanence of substance as object or bearer of qualities is inferred from the need for a permanent substratum of time itself. On such an account, of course, the conservation of substance is not inferred from the traditional concept of substance by any inadvertent sliding from one concept of substance to another but is demonstrated before the traditional concept has been introduced into the argument at all.

This is not to say that Kant's argument is sound. It is open to fundamental objections, but before considering those it will be useful to consider what Kant's argument is not even attempting to prove. One recent interpreter, accepting Kant's suggestion that the first analogy offers a self-sufficient principle for the determination of duration as a "separate mode of time" in a particularly strong form, has taken Kant's claim that "the permanent" is that through which "*existence* in the different successive parts of the time-series acquires a *magnitude,* which one calls *duration*" (A 183) to mean that Kant is arguing for the permanence of substance on the basis of considerations concerning *measurement*, or the assignment of numerical values to the duration of particular objects and events or processes in time.[6] On this account, Kant's argument is that because the duration of such an object or event (the completion of one orbit of a celestial body, for instance) is not given in any direct observation, it must be determined by selecting one enduring but also periodically changing object, the periods of the behavior of which can be used as the units to measure the endurance or the change of other objects or processes. For example, the period between the reappearances of the enduring sun at a given point in the sky (the period, say, between the vernal equinoxes) can be used as the measure (one year) in terms of which the orbits of other planets can be measured. It is then objected, of course, that such an argument does not establish the endurance of *all* substances, but only of whatever substance happens to be chosen to function as the clock for others, and that it does not even establish the true permanence of *that* substance, since a consistent and continuing system for measuring duration could be operated using several different and successively existing clocks (or objects functioning as such), as long as the periods of these were correlated during periods of overlapping existence prior to the cessation of the existence of one clock but subsequent to the commencement of the next.

Such objections might be valid against the argument suggested, but this is not Kant's argument. Kant's argument has nothing to do with the measurement of the duration of specific objects or events *in* time; it concerns only the permanent duration *of* time itself, and even then has nothing to do with the assignment of any numerical magnitude to this permanence. The only place where Kant purports to offer a theory of the assignment of numerical measure to periods of time within the main body of the "Analytic of Principles" is in the "Axioms of Intuition," not in the discussion of the first analogy of experience. To be sure, the theory expounded in the earlier passage would certainly imply that a numerical measure could be assigned to a period of time, as to any other extensive magnitude, only by the selection of some unit period, such as the single orbit of a particular celestial body or the time it takes a determinate amount of sand to slip through a given orifice, but in fact Kant makes no explicit reference in the "Axioms" to a possible need for substances in order to specify the units of measurement for time. Only in the passing remark of the second-edition text of the transcendental deduction that "we must derive the determination of lengths of time or of points of time from the changes which are exhibited to us in outer things" (B 156) does Kant explicitly suggest a role for external objects in the determination of the extensive magnitude of periods of time, but here, it must then be noted, there is no explicit suggestion that it is in virtue of their *permanence* that external objects play this role. Perhaps merely relatively enduring objects would suffice to serve as clocks for the measurement of duration, or perhaps, on the contrary, even in this earlier passage Kant already supposes

218

that the conception of permanence is included in the concept of an external object – but if the latter is the case, then that would be a synthetic *a priori* proposition, to be proved by nothing other than the first analogy, and here, again, there is no explicit mention of the measurement of time.

One can only suppose that an interpretation of this sort arose from the tacit supposition that the analogies concern some *special* determinations of the temporal relations of objects, the more basic temporal relations of which are grounded in categories already secured – an assumption, for instance, that the analogies concern the metrical but not topological relations of time.[7] But Kant's argument is not intended to provide a special condition for the special purpose of assigning definite measurements to periods of time; it is rather intended to establish a general condition of representing objects as *succeeding* or *coexisting* in time at all, given that succession and coexistence are both relations *in* time whereas time itself is permanent, indeed has to be permanent, since it neither succeeds upon nor is succeeded by any other time.

There are serious objections to the argument which Kant does offer, however, which must now be considered. The primary locus of the problems with this argument is the claim that the permanence of time requires something permanent among appearances or empirical objects to represent it. Two objections could be raised to this thesis. First, one could question whether it is really sensible to predicate permanence of time itself. Kant's basis for this prediction is his argument that since change takes place *in* time, time itself must be changeless, hence permanent. But one could argue that just as saying that time changes is false, so calling it permanent would be equally misleading – that, as the framework for both duration and change, time itself neither changes nor lasts.[8] However, the theory of meaning by which such charges of meaninglessness would have to be adjudicated is controversial, as well as totally unexplored by Kant, and it is not clear what insight into Kant's argument could be gained by pressing this kind of objection.

More obviously problematic is the supposition, which one might call an epistemic principle or principle of representation, that permanence in something imperceivable must be *represented* by permanence in something perceivable. This is the spring of Kant's first argument: There must be permanence in what is actually perceived – empirical objects – because the permanence of time itself is imperceivable and needs to be represented by something which is both perceivable and permanent.

This premise, however, is deeply questionable. First of all, it is belied by Kant's own statement elsewhere in the *Critique*. In the footnote to the preface to the second edition which further elaborates on the new "Refutation of Idealism," Kant remarks that "the representation of something *permanent* in existence is not identical with [a] *permanent representation;* for [the representation] can be very transitory and change-able, as are all of our representations, even those of matter, and yet be related to something permanent. . . ." (B xliii). This implies that there is *no* general principle that the temporal properties of what is represented must be mirrored by what represents them, *a fortiori* that there is no general principle from which it can be inferred that if time is permanent, then what represents time, even what represents its permanence, must itself be permanent.

And as a matter of fact, the penultimate clause of the last quotation raises a further doubt about the plausibility of Kant's argument. By stating that even representations of matter are themselves transitory, in spite of the permanence which we ascribe to matter, Kant implies that the permanence of matter itself – that is, permanence in empirical objects, rather than of time itself – must be inferred rather than directly perceived. But if that is so, then it is less than obvious why the detour through the permanence of matter or substance is needed to infer the permanence of time itself. If permanence can be inferred in the one case, why cannot it be inferred equally directly, without further justification, in the other case, the case of time itself?

In the notes in his own copy of the first edition of the *Critique,* Kant apparently tried to forestall this sort of objection. At A 183 he wrote:

The perception of duration is not possible through the perception of determinations succeeding one another and of the relation of their series to time, also not through the relation to the determination of another series, wherein the first occupies a region of time [*Zeitraum*]; rather [it is possible] through something the existence of which is not a series of successions, but which includes this in itself as its determinations; consequently [it is possible] *per durabilitatem* of substance.

This proof, like all synthetic [proofs], is proved only from the possibility of perception. Where the perception cannot be perceived apart from its alterations, it holds, but where I cannot perceive it except through these alterations themselves, it does not hold, and I can estimate its duration and in general the time of its alteration only through outer things, as I, since I think, think my own existence; my permanence is therefore not proved. (R LXXXIII, 23:31)

The second paragraph of this seems to anticipate the "Refutation of Idealism" by arguing that since in my own case I perceive only successive states – alterations – but not my own substance, I must estimate my duration by reference to something permanent outside me. The first paragraph seems to suggest that this will work because, although in the case of some objects (such as myself) I perceive only successive states, in the case of another I somehow *perceive* the actual endurance of its existence, of which alterations are just the changing states. But this is precisely what was rejected by Kant's statement at B xliii.

The second main objection to Kant's opening argument is that it does in the end also seem to involve an equivocation on the concept of substance. As we saw, this is not the equivocation charged by commentators such as Bennett, namely, the substitution of the concept of the sempiternal (substance$_2$) where only the concept of a bearer of properties (substance$_1$) has legitimately been introduced. Rather, it is precisely the opposite: Kant seems to move illegitimately from the concept of something which is a substratum, in the special sense of functioning to *represent* the permanence of time, to that of something which is a substratum in the traditional sense of that which is a bearer of properties. At the very least, Kant too hastily asserts a connection between the two concepts which may only be contingent. That is, it may be natural to suppose that if there must be something permanent in the field of appearances or empirical objects, then this must be what bears properties rather than any given property, and thus be substance in the traditional sense, for surely properties of even the most stubborn sorts of substances, even igneous rocks of the hardest and most ancient kinds, are constantly changing. But if this is true, then it is so contingently and is only an empirical truth. There is hardly any *a priori* reason why the properties of objects and thus their predicates must be transitory, and thus no *a priori* reason why the permanence of time, if it needs to be represented by anything at all, could not be represented by a permanent property of substance rather than by substance itself. Of course, if there were such a property, then one might argue that there is *a fortiori* at least one permanent substance itself – namely, the one that bears that property – but in any case the connection between the permanence of time and the permanent substratum of properties seems very much more complicated than Kant's hasty completion of his argument suggests.

The analysis of alteration

Since the argument from the substratum of time is not merely implausible but also difficult to reconcile with some of Kant's own clearly expressed epistemological presuppositions, we may now turn to the second kind of argument which he deploys in behalf of the principle of permanence. Here Kant appears to reach his conclusion by what is essentially just an *analysis* of the *concept* of alteration which defines an alteration as a change in the state of something. On such an analysis, application of the term "alteration" thus presupposes the continued existence of that which changes through at least the two moments occupied by the alteration, if not longer. It is at least possible to read Kant as proffering such an analysis toward the end of the section:

On this permanence is grounded also the correct understanding of the concept of *alteration*. Coming to be and ceasing to be are not alterations of that which comes to be or ceases to be. Alteration is a manner of existing which succeeds another manner of existence of the very same object. Therefore everything which alters *persists,* and only its *condition changes*. Since this change therefore concerns only the determinations which can cease or resume, we can say, in a somewhat paradoxical-appearing expression: Only the permanent (substance) is altered; the changeable suffers no alteration but only a *change,* since some determinations cease to be and others commence.

Alterations can therefore be perceived only in substances ...

(A 187–8 / B 230–1)

Now, if we read past where I have broken off this quotation, we might conclude that Kant does not mean to *argue* for the principle of permanence yet but is only offering some definitions which are then to be supplemented by a further argument or used to add terminology to the argument already offered. That is, Kant might mean to define an "alteration" as a change in the state of a continuing substance, as contrasted with a change in general, which might involve the substitution of one state of affairs for another without the persisting existence of anything,[9] but to argue independently of this definition that as a matter of fact we can have cognition only of alterations and not of changes in the unrestricted sense. And perhaps that is really Kant's intention. But his use of "therefore" (*daher*) in the last line quoted suggests that he was at least tempted – in spite of his own conception of the problem of justifying a *synthetic a priori* judgment – by the idea that the mere *analysis* of the concept of alteration could lead to the conclusion that substance is permanent.

In any case, other evidence from the years immediately after 1781 shows that Kant sometimes succumbed to this temptation. Thus, an analytic argument for the endurance of substance is certainly present in this fragment from 1783 or 1784:

We can cognize things only through predicates, therefore [we can cognize] origination and cessation only as predicates; one can have no concept of something as a predicate without a subject, therefore the subject remains in the case of whatever ceases; otherwise we could not cognize cessation itself through experience. (R 5873, 18:373)

Even more evidently analytic is an argument from the *Metaphysik Volckmann*. After a brief statement that without the principle of sufficient reason the objects of sense would yield no experience, Kant went on to tell his students that

... to experience belongs further the principle that the substances remain: If this were not so, then no connection according to universal rules would take place. The philosophers have not even attempted to prove this proposition, although many volumes have been written about it; they have not even dared, because they immediately foundered, and yet the proposition that *vicissitudo* pertains only to *accidentibus* but that the subject must not be submitted to this is of the utmost importance. If there are to be alterations, then one presupposes an object in which the predicates follow one another, for if the subject itself were to change [*wechselt*], then it would not be altered [*verändert*], rather then it would already be something else; the permanence of substance is therefore always presupposed while the determinations change among themselves, and this is called alteration ...
(28:430)

An alteration is a change in the state of some one thing, rather than a change from one thing (or event) to another, so of course if there is an alteration then there must be some thing which changes; and if all changes are alterations, then there can be changes only in the states of things which always persist, but nothing which counts as the creation or annihilation of a thing itself. In other words, if all changes are alterations, then even the conservation of substance would follow.

But the problem not only with this strong argument but even with a weaker one merely for the continued existence of substances in some cases of change (namely alterations) is just that while defining the *concept* of alteration, it begs all questions concerning the scope of application of the *principle* of permanence. By assuming that some, let alone all, changes *are* alterations, Kant simply presupposes rather than proves the very point at issue, namely the endurance of substance in any form (unless this argument *just* adds terminology to the preceding argument about the substratum of time). The key to Kant's synthetic method, after all, is that from concepts alone no synthetic proposition can be demonstrated, yet surely the presupposition that there are alterations in the states of enduring substances, and not, for instance, just changes in total states of affairs without any continuing entities, is a synthetic proposition which can be presupposed by some analytic argument but never proved by one.

At least one commentator has attempted to salvage something from this line of argument by conceding that the principle that a change of predicates involves a continuing substance *is* analytic and arguing that a synthetic principle emerges only when it is added that a *change* of predicates requires a *succession* of predicates in time, for the principle that *different* moments must be *successive in time* is itself synthetic.[10] At the very deepest level, Kant's claim to produce synthetic a priori principles must indeed rest on the synthetic but in some sense *a priori* restriction of our experience to time and the uniqueness of the conditions by which we can determine temporal relations. But it is not clear that the connection between the difference of moments in time and their succession is not analytic, and, in any case, it seems premature to appeal to the ultimately synthetic truth of the temporality of our experience to defend Kant's argument for the principle of substance when, as this commentator himself notes, there is yet one further and quite distinct form of argument for the principle of permanence remaining in Kant's quiver. It seems better to let a comment Kant made at least a decade after the first publication of the *Critique* stand as his own judgment on the present form of argument:

In every alteration the substance endures, for alteration is the succession of the determinations of one and the same thing. This is a merely logical proposition according to the law of identity. But it does not say that in general substance does not come to be or cease to be, rather only [that it remains] during an alteration.

(R 6403, 18:706)

In other words, *if* one supposes that one has a case of alteration, then it follows by logical laws alone – given the definition of alteration – that there is an enduring substance, but this is only because alteration is defined precisely as a succession of determinations in a persisting thing. The definition alone cannot establish that any given change *is* a case of alteration, let alone that every change is. A "logical proposition" therefore cannot suffice to prove the permanence of substance.

Empirical knowledge of change

Fortunately, Kant suggests yet one more kind of argument for the principle of permanence, one which involves neither the ungrounded – or even rejected – epistemological presuppositions of the argument from the substratum of time nor the merely analytic propositions which plague the argument from the definition of alteration. Kant's exposition of this idea in the *Critique* is far from clear, but we do have at least one piece of evidence from outside the *Critique* itself for the ascription to him of what follows.

Unlike the argument just considered, but in accord with the general principle of the analogies, Kant's final argument in the first analogy is an epistemological argument which demonstrates a condition of the possibility of experience – a necessary condition for a certain form of claim to empirical knowledge. The argument concerning the substratum of time was also, in a sense, an epistemological argument: It claimed to demonstrate the knowledge of permanence in one case (substance in appearance) was a condition for knowledge of permanence in another case (the permanence of time itself). But it was doubtful whether time itself can even coherently be conceived as permanent and, if so, whether the permanence of substance in appearance could conclusively be shown to be a necessary condition of knowledge of the permanence of time. The present argument is not open to these objections, because it is *not* – in spite of what might have been suggested by Kant's original reference to the three "modes" of time (A 177 / B 219) – an argument about the necessary conditions *for* knowledge of permanence at all. Rather, Kant now argues that knowledge of *alteration in an enduring substance, a fortiori* knowledge of the existence of enduring substance, is itself the necessary condition for knowledge of *any change* at all. Only by treating any putative case of *change* as an *alteration* in the states of a continuing substance can we have evidence for the occurrence of any form of change, or, in terms suggested by Arthur Melnick, can change become "empirically verifiable."[11] But then, we must also note, the principle of the first analogy becomes interdependent with that of the *second* analogy, for what is there argued is that knowledge of the necessity of a succession according to a rule is *also* a condition for empirical knowledge of the occurrence of *any change* in objective states of affairs.

In other words, the principle of the permanence of substance and that of causation are not independent principles for the determination of independent aspects or modes of time or temporal relations, but are rather both necessary conditions for making any determination that objective change has occurred. And, in fact, since the principle of the *third* analogy, the principle of the reciprocity of action among coexistent substances, is a principle which grounds empirical knowledge that two or more states of affairs are coexistent when the representations or perceptions of them can be only successive, we might say that all three principles function together to make possible what is essentially the single decision whether successive representations represent change or coexistence among the states of empirical objects. This is just to say that all three analogies together function to provide the necessary conditions for deciding whether change or succession in representations – all that we are ever given, or passively apprehend – represents change or stability in the objective realm, in what is represented, at all. It is in precisely this sense that *all* of these principles constitute the necessary conditions of "a cognition which determines an object through perceptions" (B 218), rather than rules for some *special* time-determinations which presuppose that the necessary conditions for a more basic knowledge of objects have somehow already been supplied.

This is the primary sense in which the three analogies of experience are interdependent: They *function* conjointly as the necessary conditions for empirical knowledge of succession and coexistence. As we proceed, we shall also see that the *arguments* on behalf of these principles are interdependent: In the case at hand, considerations from the third analogy will have to be brought in to complete the third form of argument intimated in the first analogy. But at this point we must ask, what is this third argument?

If we now consider the whole paragraph the first line of which was previously read as the conclusion of Kant's analytic argument for the principle of permanence, we see that although Kant was tempted by that analytic argument, he also presented a quite distinct – though also obscure – argument for the conclusion that the postulation of permanent substance is a necessary condition for the empirical knowledge of objective change:

Alteration can therefore be perceived only in substances, and pure coming or ceasing to be which does not concern the determination of that which endures cannot be a possible perception at all, since it is this very enduring thing which makes possible the representation of the transition from one state to another, and from nonbeing to being, which can therefore be empirically known only as change in the determinations of that which persists. If you assume that something simply begins to be, then you must have a point of time in which it was not. But to what will you attach this if not to that which already exists? For an empty time, which could precede, is no object of perception, but if you attach this coming to be to things which previously were and which persist until this coming to be, then the latter would be only a determination of the former, as that which endures. It is just the same with ceasing to be: for this presupposes the empirical representation of a time in which an appearance no longer exists.   (A 188 / B 231)

In conjunction with this passage from the *Critique* we should also consider this note, apparently from the period of the composition of the *Critique* itself:

We can notice change only in that which endures. If everything disappeared, then the disappearance itself could not be perceived. The experience of coming and ceasing to be is therefore possible only by means of that which endures. Therefore there is something in nature which persists (neither comes nor ceases to be), and this is substance. Only the *accidentia* change. *Principium* of the possibility of experience. Place designates the substance. In different places there are different substances; what pertains to that which endures in a place and distinguishes itself from that which endures is *accidens*.   (R 5871, 18:373)

The last two sentences of this note are deeply revealing, but first we must consider the premise and main thrust of Kant's argument. I can depict these in three broad strokes.[12]

(1) I begin with Kant's claims that "an empty time ... is no object of perception" or that "disappearance itself could not be perceived." What these remarks (which clearly represent the application of the general premise that "time itself cannot be perceived," in the present context) must mean is that there is nothing which can count as the *direct perception* of the *absence* of any given state of affairs. That is, if we consider some state of affairs S which exists at some time t_1 and which is supposed to have originated after t_0 or to have ceased to be prior to t_2, there is nothing which can count as simply the direct perception of moment t_0 or t_2 devoid of state S. This is because moments of time are not themselves possible objects of direct perception; all that can be perceived is the *presence* of some state of affairs or other at a given moment of time. This means that we cannot directly perceive the absence of S at t_0 or t_2, but can perceive only the presence of some *other* state of affairs, an S' in some way distinct from S, at one of those moments.

(2) Kant's next assumption is not stated in the present passages but is obviously required, as well as ultimately revealed to be a fundamental premise of the refutation of idealism (B xli), and is thus a point at which the argument of the analogies depends upon the final stage of Kant's theory of time-determination. This premise is that since all *representation* is fleeting and transitory, whether or not there is any change in the *objects* of perception, the mere occurrence of, say, a *representation* at t_1 with the apparent content S, followed by a *representation* at t_2 with the apparent content S' (what we would expect in the case of the cessation of S), or, in other words, the mere occurrence of an S-like representation at t_1 followed by an S'-like representation at t_2, will not itself be sufficient evidence for the occurrence of any kind of objective change from S to S'. For there is always the possibility of this kind of succession in representations, whether or not there is any objective change in what is being perceived; even if S and S' are coexisting states of affairs, the perception of them will be successive. Only if there is some kind of incompatibility between the objective states of affairs S and S', such that S' cannot be perceived without S having ceased to exist (*mutatis mutandis* for the case of coming rather than ceasing to be), will the occurrence of one sort of representation followed by the occurrence of the other provide evidence for the occurrence of an objective change. Otherwise, the perceiver could merely be undergoing a change in perceptual state – a change in which of two objectively coexistent states of affairs is being perceived – without any change occurring among the objects of perception.

(3) But how does Kant get from the requirement of incompatibility between what is perceived at one moment and what is perceived at another to the conclusion that the changing states of affairs must both be determinations of some single, enduring substance? As will become clearer in the exposition of the second analogy, Kant must be assuming that S and S' are not simply *logically* contradictory or cannot be determined to be incompatible by laws of logic alone. Rather, there must be a *synthetic* rule according to which S and S' can occur only in succession and not in coexistence. But, we might suppose, this rule cannot be of the broad form "S and S' cannot coexist *tout court*," for S and S' will typically be states of affairs, such as being black and being red, being hot and being cold, being hard and being soft, or, to use Kant's own example, being wooden and being ashen (A 185 / B 229), which can be instantiated many times over – indeed, they may have to be repeatable states of affairs if we are to have empirical, and therefore inductive, knowledge concerning them. In any case, we certainly cannot have rules which say that hot and cold, red and black, simply cannot coexist. There is no difficulty in imagining that while one ingot is cooling off in one part of the mill (changing from hot and red to black and cool), another is being heated (changing from black and cool to red-hot). So the rules which enable us to infer from the succession of an S'-like representation after an S-like representation an objective change from state S to S', and not just a change in which one of the simultaneously existing states S and S' is being perceived, must be of the form that *one object* cannot be in both of the incompatible states at the same time. The rule must be of a form which entails that some x which is S at t_1 cannot also be S' then, but only at some other time such as t_0 or t_2. And that is just to say that we cannot have evidence for the occurrence of any objective change at all unless we postulate an object which can endure through the period of our successive representations of it and have properties such that the simultaneous exemplification of two different properties *in that object* is impossible. Only then can inferences be made that the successive occurrence of S- and S'-like representations represents an objective change from S to S'. Only if S and S' are changing determinations of a single enduring object, and not just successive states of affairs *simpliciter,* can we have evidence for their succession on the basis of our successive representations of them.

Arthur Melnick's interpretation of Kant's epistemological argument is similar to the one just offered, but emphasizes the role of *space* in the argument in a way in which I have not (although the first step of Melnick's argument is implicit in my examples of how "incompatible" properties can be instantiated in several cases, that is, places, at the same time). The gist of Melnick's interpretation (modifying his symbolism to accord with what has just been used) is that we cannot conclude that some state S came into being at a time t_1 just by having failed to observe S at a previous t_0, for there is always the possibility that S was just *somewhere else* at t_0. That is, what we actually perceive is the presence of S *at some place* p_1 at t_1, and there is always the possibility that S was just at some other place p_i at t_0, or else that we were just looking at some place other than p_1 at t_0 and *began to notice* S only when we turned to p_1 at t_1. Melnick then argues that because space is infinite there is an infinite number of other places p_i where S could have been exemplified at t_0. We cannot, of course, inspect an infinite number of such places in the finite time allotted to us for the conduct of our always successive acts of empirical synthesis.[13] So, given the nature of our cognitive capacities, the only way in which we can empirically verify that S was not the case at t_0 is to postulate that there was a *continuing object* at p_1 (or some other determinate place) which was in some state S' incompatible with S and which has now just come to be S.[14] Or at the very least, Melnick says, we must postulate laws about the behavior of states of affairs *at regions of space* which are of the form "that if the state of affairs obtained anywhere at the previous moment then it had to be at a particular place."[15] This will allow us to make inferences of the form that if S, which is observed at t_1 at p_1, was not at p_1 (or some other determinate p) at t_0, because some incompatible S' was, then S must have come into being between t_0 and t_1; then the new *perception* of S really represents a *change* in the objective world. Melnick then concludes that the concept of substance is essentially identical to the concept of "spatial law-governedness."[16]

This seems a plausible reconstruction of what Kant might have thought. Indeed, we could even take it to be precisely what was meant by the final remark in R 5871, that "place designates substance" (a remark which Melnick does not, however, adduce): This could be taken to mean that it is essentially by identifying regions of space that we identify substances, and that therefore what we are actually doing when we postulate a change in an enduring substance is postulating a change in which states of affairs are instantiated in a region of space over a period of time. Moreover, given Kant's ultimate theory that matter – that is, the substance of at least physical objects – consists not of atoms but of differing degrees of attractive and repulsive forces at different regions of space, there is further reason – though this time from physical theory, and thus not obviously *a priori* – for interpreting Kant's argument as ultimately resting on the necessity for postulating incompatible states of affairs at particular regions of space in order to determine that a change in representations represents any objective change at all.

But I think that these are not the sorts of consideration which Kant had in mind in the present argument. Rather, I think that Kant's intentions in this argument of the first analogy can be more accurately rediscovered by bringing in evidence from elsewhere in the text of the "Analogies of Experience," namely from the *third* analogy. For what Kant suggests there is that *absolute space is no more directly perceivable than absolute time,* consequently that position in space is no more immediately given than position in time, and that particular positions in space can themselves be determined only by associating them with enduring substances. In Kant's words, without a "dynamical community" of the kind that exists only between interacting substances (or forces which endure), "even local community (*communiio spatii*)" – which must certainly mean the relative location of positions in space – "could never be empirically known." Even more clearly, "We cannot empirically alter position (perceive this alteration) without matter everywhere making possible the perception of our position" (A 213 / B 260). Only by positing dynamical interactions between simultaneously existing physical objects, Kant will argue, can we even determine that they are in different positions in empirically perceived space, and thus we presuppose the existence of substance in empirically determining the spatial position of anything. In this way, we shall see, the empirical use of the concept of substance indeed presupposes the principle of interaction, and empirical knowledge of spatial position in turn presupposes substance.

We thus arrive at the following interpretation of Kant's argument. Given that we perceive even potentially objective states of affairs as displayed in space, there are at least three different possibilities in the interpretation of any given succession of representations. We could be successively observing (a) the successive existence of two different states of affairs in one and the same place, and thus a change in objective existence. Or we could be observing (b) the result of a change of place in two otherwise unchanging objects, that is, the presence of first one and then another object in the same place. This would also be an objective change, of course, though perhaps not so dramatic a change as type a. Finally, we could be observing (c) nothing but the result of changing the focus of our own act of perception: Nothing in the objects being perceived is changing, but the direction of our attention has been changed. However, we have no basis for making empirical determinations of the position of anything in space except by associating places with enduring objects, so there is no way we can distinguish among any of these possibilities except by postulating the continued existence of substances. Even to determine (b) that otherwise unchanging objects have merely changed places, in other words, or (c) that we ourselves have just changed places, we need enduring objects: in case b, at least a third external object around which the first two can be determined to have revolved, and in case c at least our own body and its motions, in addition to the two objects of perception.

Kant's argument for the epistemic priority of substances over regions of space cannot be fully examined until our examination of the third analogy. And Kant's exposition of this third, and most promising, form of argument in the first analogy is so brief that any attempt at providing further details would now certainly overstep any conceivable bounds of historical interpretation and become assistance rather than interpretation. So I shall now just consider several consequences of Kant's argument, and then consider one major objection to it.

We may first consider an explicit but obscure consequence which Kant himself draws from his argument. In the penultimate paragraph of the section on the first analogy Kant writes:

Substances (in appearance) are the substrata of all time-determinations. The coming to be of some and the ceasing to be of others of them would itself suspend the sole condition of the empirical unity of time, and the appearances would then be related to two different times, in which existence flowed side by side; which is absurd. For there is only *one* time, in which all different times must be posited not simultaneously but in succession to one another.   (A 188–9 / B 231–2)

What Kant means by this cryptic argument has never been clear.[17] The present interpretation, however, suggests at least one way to read it. On my account, the basic premise of Kant's argument is that the mere succession of different representations of putative states of affairs leaves it undetermined whether what has been perceived is an objective change or not; only by counting two qualitatively distinct representations as representations of incompatible and successive states of a single object do we obtain any ground for judging that any objective change has occurred. But if we try to imagine that a given change is a case of substantial *creation* or *annihilation,* we omit the postulation of a continuing substance necessary for empirically determining that a change has taken place; yet such a substance is necessary for empirically determining that a change has taken place at all. Hence it must remain undetermined whether the change *has* in fact taken place. This could be expressed by saying that we would not after all have any ground for choosing between two different stories about the duration of the substance concerned; one on which it does indeed cease to be at the time of its alleged annihilation, and one on which it does not in fact cease to be at that time, but, if at all, then only at some later and undetermined time. Two different histories of the objective states of affairs would then be possible, one including an event constituting the cessation of the substance in question, the other not including such an event; in fact, an infinite number of histories would become possible,[18] since the object in question could cease to exist at an infinite number of times. Perhaps this is what is meant by time's flowing in two – or an infinite number of – different streams.

The conservation of substance

A further consequence of Kant's last argument is not explicit but is more obvious than this. It is that this form of argument, even more clearly than the first two arguments suggested in the first analogy, directly implies the necessity of a strong principle of conservation, namely that, as far as can be empirically verified, *all* substance is truly permanent and not merely enduring through some given change or changes. This is because there is simply nothing that can count as *empirical recognition or verification* of the annihilation of any genuine substance. This inference, it should be noted, would *not* be a fallacious inference from misplaced quantifiers, that is, from what may sometimes be the case to what must always be the case. In other words, Kant would *not* simply infer that because in any given change there must be *some* substance which endures, there is therefore some *unique* substance or set of substances which persists through *all* changes. Rather, his argument directly implies that there is nothing which can count as empirical *evidence* for the cessation of the existence of *any* substance. From this it certainly follows that, as far as what may be empirically verified is concerned, no true substance can be known to be destroyed, or that all true substances can be known only to endure. As far as possible experience goes, then, in all change of appearances the quantum of substance is neither increased nor diminished (B 224).

This point can easily be missed – and usually is – if the nature of Kant's argument is not properly understood. Again, if Kant is thought to be worrying about the *measurement* of time and to be arguing that there must be some enduring object by which to *date* all events – which are assumed to be simply given *as* events – then it would certainly not follow that any objects other than that one must endure for any determinate period, or even that any *one* substance must permanently endure. All that would follow, as Arthur Melnick puts the customary objection, is that *particular* "substances, employed as substrata, cannot come into existence or go out of existence during the time intervals for which they serve as such a substratum for the determination of time magnitude." [19] But, as we saw, even in the argument from the substratum of time Kant was not considering the use of any enduring objects for time-*measurement,* and in his argument from the conditions for the empirical knowledge of change, where his point does not concern the measurement of time but a necessary condition for the *perception of change at all,* there is surely no room for this objection. If *no* substance can be empirically verified to commence or cease existing *tout court,* then all substances, whether or not they happen to be employed as clocks or to have any of the features such as periodicity which would empirically fit them for such use, can be *known* only as enduring.

The point is also missed if it assumed that what Kant is talking about is just the idea of a background of a *relatively high degree* of stability against which our *general practice* of talking about change and continuance will seem *reasonable* – or, phenomenologically speaking, a *horizon* of expectations against which particular changes will be foreseen or not[20] – but which offers no basis for excluding the possibility of individual, inexplicable occurrences of disappearance, creation, and so on. Thus, for instance, Peter Strawson writes that "what must be conceived as absolutely permanent and abiding" is "the spatio-temporal framework of things at large," and that this in turn requires *only* "that we should *perceive* some objects *as* having a permanence which our perceptions of them do not have." [21] But this conclusion just misses Kant's point, for it depends upon Strawson's underlying assumption that what Kant's argument in the "Analytic" as a whole concerns is only the sufficient conditions for giving *sense* to the *concept* of the objective or the *general contrast* between subject and object, rather than the conditions for actually confirming *particular judgments* or claims to empirical knowledge. Kant is not simply trying to give sense to the concept of objective change by a contrast between the arbitrary and the rule-governed; he is trying to demonstrate the conditions which must be employed to determine in any case that an objective change has taken place.

I will emphasize this point by considering an example which is offered by Jonathan Bennett instead of Strawson, but which is meant to press the same kind of objection. Bennett asks us to imagine a porcelain pig in an airtight glass case. This pig is resting on one arm of a highly accurate balance inside the case and is precisely balanced by the weights suspended on the other arm of the balance. All of a sudden the pig disappears, and the weights on the balance drop to the floor of the case (in ghostly silence, of course), but nothing seems to leak from the case, nor is any explosive conversion of matter into energy observed. Bennett then asks, "does not [this scene] describe the existence-change of a physical object?"[22] Is it not a case in which some amount of substance – namely, the porcelain comprising the pig – simply ceases to exist? Now, Bennett correctly points out that Kant would not deny the logical possibility of such an event. For Kant's principle of the permanence of substance is not a logical principle entailing the logical impossibility of substantial annihilation. Nor is it a psychological principle, which would be belied by how well Bennett has had us imagine a case of substantial annihilation. Rather, Kant's principle is a synthetic, epistemological principle,[23] and what it asserts is that we can never, even in the case which Bennett describes, have sufficient *evidence* to *judge* that the substance which comprised the pig has disappeared. For what Kant's principle implies is that if we cannot now produce *that* substance, currently characterized by some determinations or properties incompatible with its continuing to comprise a porcelain pig, then it must simply remain undetermined whether the substance has ceased to exist or has just been moved or has even just been removed from our attention in some other way. Kant's argument is certainly not that we need some enduring object by which to *date* the disappearance of the pig, a condition which could be satisfied by the continued existence of the *other* objects involved in Bennett's thought experiment (perhaps there was also a clock inside the case). Kant's argument is that there can be *no* adequate evidence for the *occurrence* of any objective change at all unless we can produce some substance now in a state incompatible with the continued existence of that which is alleged to have been annihilated. That can be only the same substance in another state.

Of course, Kant would not treat something such as a porcelain pig as a genuine substance. This is precisely because, even without considering a made-up case like Bennett's, we would never think of something such as that as anything other than a relatively enduring object. Epistemologically speaking, it is ordinary empirical knowledge that such an object can be brought into being by baking kaolin paste at the appropriate temperature (in spite of how hard it was for Europeans to learn how the Chinese did this), that it can be pulverized to some dust having a predictable chemical constitution, that this dust can in turn be broken down into certain elements, and so on. What *is* a substance in the case of the porcelain pig, or anything else, is precisely *whatever* it is that endures through all such transformations, whether that be earth, air, fire, and water (on one, to be sure, no longer very attractive empirical theory) or quarks (on another theory). This is evident in Kant's own example:

A philosopher is questioned: How much does smoke weigh? He answers: Subtract from the weight of the wood that was burned the weight of the ashes that remain, and you will have the weight of the smoke. He therefore presupposes as incontrovertible: that even in fire, the matter (substance) does not cease to be, but only suffers a transformation of its form.   (A 185 / B 228)

Neither wood nor ash nor smoke are themselves substance as such; they are only a variety of forms which some substance common to them all can take on – on nineteenth-century chemical theories, a certain combination of carbon, hydrogen, and oxygen; on more recent theories, a variety of atomic or subatomic particles. They are therefore nothing but determinations of substance, which can begin or cease to be, but the substance itself must remain through all such transformations, as a condition of our knowledge of the occurrence of any actual transformation.

At this point, it might be objected that Kant's argument has been undermined by scientific developments.[24] For we now know that in such a case as Kant considers there is *not* an absolute conservation of *matter;* rather, a small – very small, since we are considering a fire and not a nuclear explosion – amount of the matter of the wood must be transformed into the energy which we sense as the heat of the fire, and so, as a matter of fact, the weight of the smoke and the ashes does not precisely equal the weight of the original wood. But this is not really an objection to Kant's argument. For although Kant typically seems to assume an identity between substance and matter (as in this very example), his argument does not commit him to a principle of the conservation of matter as part of some particular physical hypothesis. This is *not* because as a (somewhat apriorist) physicist Kant himself ultimately interprets matter as energy. It is rather because as a transcendental philosopher he employs *endurance* as the primary *criterion* of substance – indeed, perhaps even *endurance of action* (see again A 204 / B 249). Thus, it is simply *whatever* is ultimately determined by empirical theory to endure – or act enduringly – through any empirically discoverable change that is properly identified as substance. *If* matter endures, then matter is substance, but if it is only a constant quantum of matter-cum-energy which endures, then from the philosophical point of view *that* is what must be regarded as substance. That substance endures, and that all that exists is ultimately reducible to substance, are philosophical points; the question of what substance actually is is a scientific question.[25]

This may not be made clear in the *Critique* itself, but Kant does make it quite plain elsewhere. This note from the late 1770s emphasizes the criterial role of endurance:

Between substance and accident the logical relation is synthetic. The subject is itself not a predicate, ... but only that which is no further predicate is called a substance: 1. since no further subject is thought for it; 2. since it is the

233

presupposition and *substratum* of the others. This can be inferred only from endurance, insofar as the other changes. It therefore belongs to the essence of a substance that it is perdurable. If one assumes that the substance ceases to be, this cessation proves that it is no substance ... (R 5297, 18:146)

Something's status as a substance is *inferred* from the fact of its endurance. Or, as Kant elsewhere puts it, "We do not sense outer substances, ... rather we think them" (R 5358, 18:160). That is, what is to *count* as a substance is not simply given by any obvious mark but is to be inferred from our discoveries about what really endures. If our beliefs about what really endures change, then so must our conception of what is actually a substance. Thus, the scientific substitution of the principle of the conservation of matter plus energy for the conservation of matter alone is not an objection to Kant's philosophical theory of substance; it is rather an *illustration* of the role of endurance – or conservation – as the "essence" or criterion of substance.

Another way of making this point would be to recall that all of the dynamical principles are supposed to be *regulative* principles (A 180 / B 222–3). This implies that our conception of what counts as substance at any given time is always open to revision, though subject to regulation by the assumption of permanence. This is again made clearer in places other than the *Critique*. As early as 1769, Kant identified the concept of substance as a *"conceptus terminator"* (R 4039, 17:394), a term he also used of other concepts, such as that of something absolutely necessary and of the limits of the world, which were later to be treated as ideas of reason that also function as regulative ideals. Closer to the period of the *Critique* (1778?), Kant included a revealing treatment of substance in his metaphysics lectures. He made the natural identification of the substance in a physical object with the parts which endure through all its transformations, and then made clear that the notion of physical parts is a *comparative* notion, one which represents an approximation to an ideal but cannot itself be taken to be final at any given stage of knowledge:

The *partes constitutive* of the universe as absolute first parts are simple parts or substances. – We cannot assume absolute first parts in matter or in the material world. A whole of matter has no *partes constitutives absolute primas*. The primary simple parts are called elements; matter therefore has no elements. To be sure, we call something in matter in respect of its division an element, comparatively speaking, but ... matter is possible only insofar as it fills space; therefore every part of it must fill space, because it is between two limits, and therefore matter does not consist of simple parts. Matter is also no substance, but only a phenomenon of substance. That which persists in appearance, what lays at the basis of the manifold in bodies, we call substance. Now since we find in bodies substances which we call substances only *per analogiam,* we cannot conclude that matter consists of simple parts ... (*Metaphysik L1*, 28:209)

In this passage Kant – or the student who transcribed it – mixes up considerations about the infinite divisibility of space itself with claims about the nature of substance, but the conclusion is clear. The notion of what endures in an object can be equated with what remains in it after all division; but since no *a priori* limits can be placed on the division of matter – indeed, if Kant's dynamical theory of matter as the filling of space by force is accepted, it can be determined *a priori* that there are no limits on its division – then the idea of reaching ultimate parts of matter must always be an ideal, and whatever is treated as substance at any given point in the division must always be so only "comparatively speaking" or *per analogiam*. But this is just to say that the concept of permanent substance is a regulative ideal, and thus always open to revision in light of our actual progress in the *a posteriori* employment of our *a priori* principles – that is, in light of scientific progress.

Many interpreters have failed to appreciate this point. Bennett, for instance, does so when he objects to the assumption that "anything which underwent an existence-change and so failed as a substance$_2$" (something absolutely permanent) "would also lose the right to the substantial treatment which is definitive of substance$_1$" (a bearer of properties) as "an extravagant conclusion."[26] It might seem extravagant indeed, if the deduction of the categories from the logical functions of judgment were really independent of their role as the conditions of possible empirical knowledge. But if we assume that the categories can be deduced only from their role in time-determination, or even, as the official program of the schematism would have it, that they derive their empirical sense from this role, then the only "rights" that can be assigned to them must be those discovered by the exploration of the conditions of empirical knowledge. If what this shows is that empirical knowledge of changes can be justified only on the basis of the assumption of truly permanent substances, then only the truly permanent is a fully satisfactory candidate for the category of substance. There are no independent considerations of what Bennett would call "conceptual efficiency" to appeal to,[27] even though Kant's own view is that our employment of the idea of truly permanent substance is regulative rather than constitutive in specificity. Just as he said in the *Duisburg Nachlass*, after all, the analogies of experience provide "*analoga* of axioms," but not axioms that themselves determine the unique solution to empirical problems, and it is experience, not any abstract consideration of conceptual efficiency, which will show what it is that actually endures through time – or at least through as much of time as is in reach of our scientific experiments.

10

The second analogy: causation

The second analogy is the single argument intended both to replace the rationalists' fallacious derivation of the principle of sufficient reason from laws of logic alone and to refute Hume's skepticism that causal connections among distinct states of affairs can be known by human thought at all. Kant's rejection of a merely logical proof for the principle of sufficient reason was evident by the early 1760s, although even before then he had already pressed against Leibniz the argument that the principle entailed rather than precluded the genuine, causal action of one substance on another.[1] Kant's obsession with Hume's attack on causation, of course, is manifest in his famous statement that it was this which first awoke him from his dogmatic slumber, and indeed that the *Critique of Pure Reason* itself was the result of nothing less than his attempt to put Hume's problem in its widest possible form (*Prolegomena*, 4:260–1). But the centrality of Hume's problem to Kant's thought is even more than usually evident in this passage from the *Metaphysik Volckmann*, which immediately precedes Kant's statement of the transcendental deduction in those revealing lectures:[2]

Ratio realis is: *quo posito ponitur aliud sed non secundum principium identitatis* [A real ground is something which, when posited, something else must also be posited, but not according to the principle of identity], this relation of ground to consequence is therefore: *si ponitur aliquid realiter diversum* [if something really distinct is also to be posited], but the logical ground is: *quo ponitur aliquid logice, sed non realiter diversum* [that which is to be posited is logically but not really distinct]. ... *Logice opposita sunt quae sibi contradicunt, e.g., A et non A* [logically opposed are those which contradict each other, e.g., A and not A], learned and unlearned, which are given to me *per principium contradictions*. ... In the concept of a real ground a synthetic nexus is forthcoming, in that of a logical ground only an analytical nexus. [H]ow the latter is possible requires no explanation since it is possible by means of the principle of contradiction. But there is great difficulty in understanding the possibility of the connection between a real ground and its consequence. It is synthetic, because it goes beyond the concept, thus the question arises: Do I not therefore have it from experience? That which contains the real ground for a consequence is called cause, therefore I ask whether I do not have the cause from experience? Many who would avoid breaking their heads have also asserted this, but it will not do, for the concept of necessity is contained therein, and no one can understand the latter from experience. ... Only the category of causality yields the connection of ground and consequence. ... We must therefore undertake a deduction, a derivation from the sources, and if we do not wish to arrive at obvious

237

difficulties we must ask: How do we come by [this concept]? Hume therefore grounded an entire skeptical philosophy on the question: How do we come by the concept of cause? Cause is that which contains the real ground of something else, and is fully identical with the real ground, e.g., the wind is the cause of the motion of the ship; now how does it come about that if the wind is posited something quite different – namely, the motion of the ship – also follows? What sort of connection does the wind have with the motion? According to his allegation, all concepts of cause and effect would come from experience, and the *necessity,* he says, would merely be something imagined and a longstanding habit; he therefore saw no other way but to assume that the concept of a real ground is an empirical concept. His opinion, however, can be grounded only [on the supposition] that [the concept] must be taken from experience or experience from it.

(Metaphysik Volckmann, 28:403–4)

In this passage, Kant virtually identifies the problem of synthetic connections in general with the problem of causation, and as we saw in our earlier examination of this passage, he also virtually identifies the transcendental deduction of the categories with the solution to this problem. And then he makes the nature of his program even clearer by explicitly connecting the proof of the principle of sufficient reason to the conditions of time-determination: "The principle of sufficient reason is really a fundamental principle on which rests the possibility of experience, and indeed [the principle] for the determination of succession in time" (28:408). Experience is equivalent to knowledge of determinate relations in time, and the principle of sufficient reason, in spite of Hume, can be justified as a condition of the possibility of such experience, although, in spite of Leibniz, Wolff, Baumgarten, and even the Kant of 1755 himself, it can be justified *only* as such a condition of possible experience.

So the centrality of the argument of the second analogy to Kant's entire theoretical philosophy is obvious enough. Is the nature of Kant's argument for the principle of sufficient reason as a condition of the possibility of experience equally obvious? As a matter of fact, unlike almost every part of Kant's *Critique* that we have considered so far, Kant's exposition of the second analogy does not seem to contain an unresolved variety of stratagems evolved over a long period of time.[3] Insead, in this crucial case Kant seems to have arrived at a fairly clear form of argument without a great deal of trial and error. We cannot tell exactly when he arrived at it, for though the idea of associating the proof of the principle of causation with the concept of analogy, and both in turn with the problem of time-determination, had clearly emerged by the period of the *Duisburg Nachlass,* no sketch of any actual argument which Kant might have considered prior to the first edition of the *Critique* has survived. Further, and again unlike the case with so many of his other arguments, Kant seems to have been satisfied with the results of his efforts in the text of 1781, for there is neither any substantial change in the argument in the edition of 1787 nor any evidence of additional extended work on the argument among Kant's surviving papers from after 1787.

That means that there is also little of the kind of supplementary evidence for the interpretation of Kant's intentions which I have been able to use elsewhere in this study. Fortunately, in this case such additional evidence is not necessary, for Kant makes his intention for this argument as clear as he ever makes anything, by repeating each of its basic considerations several times over.

The intended conclusion of the second analogy can most readily be stated by combining the versions of the principle from the two editions of the *Critique*. In the first edition, what is to be proved is that "everything that happens (begins to be) presupposes something from which it follows *according to a rule*" (A 189). In the second edition, the principle is that "all alterations take place according to the law of cause and effect" (B 232). The second edition's reference to "all alterations" is preferable to the first edition's mention of "everything that happens (begins to be)" for two reasons.[4] First, the first analogy has already argued that the only *empirically cognizable* sorts of happening are changes in the states of enduring substances, or alterations: The second edition's statement makes this prior step explicit, but that of the first edition does not. Second, the first edition refers only to commencements but not to cessations of states of affairs, whereas a truly universal application of a principle of causation will surely entail the existence of causal explanations of cases of cessation as well as commencement. However, the first edition is superior to the second insofar as it does not simply invoke the unanalyzed concepts of cause and effect but conveys the key component of these concepts: To say that two things are related as cause and effect is to say that one follows from the other according to a rule. Thus, the two statements together suggest that what is to be demonstrated is that all cases of empirically recognizable alterations in substances must *also* be successions of states of those substances according to rules. The second analogy thus does *not* concern a *different* "mode of time" from the first; it concerns an *additional condition* necessary for the empirical judgment of objective change, the condition that empirically recognizable changes must be not only alterations but also rule-governed.

Two observations about this proposition must be made before we can continue. First, it is easy to read Kant as saying that any two states which can be determined to constitute an objective succession or event must be related by a rule which says the *earlier* state is itself the cause of the *later* one. Many of Kant's own statements certainly suggest this. Thus, the "rule, by which we determine something according to the time-series, is: that the condition under which the event always (i.e., necessarily) follows is to be found in what precedes" (A 200 / B 245–6), and "The relation of appearances (as possible perceptions) according to which that which succeeds (what happens) is determined as to its existence in time necessarily and according to a rule by something which precedes, thus the relation of cause to effect, is the condition of the objective validity of our empirical judgments" (A 202 / B 247). But this is surely open to the objection that states of affairs can be determined objectively to succeed one another which are not the cause and effect *of each other*: In the pungent language of Arthur Schopenhauer, "In fact even the succession of day and night is undoubtedly known to us objectively, but they are certainly not *regarded* as cause and effect of each other." [5] But this objection threatens only Kant's looser formulations of his principle. More precisely stated, what his principle maintains is just that one state of affairs can be determined to succeed another, and thus that the two together can be judged to constitute an event comprising the change from one state to the other, only when there is a causal law according to which the latter state *necessarily succeeds* the former: It is *because of its cause* that the latter state must succeed the former, but the former state need not *be* the cause of the latter. Thus, in one place Kant says that "if therefore we experience that something happens, then we presuppose that something precedes it on which it follows according to a rule" (A 195 / B 240). This says that the latter state must be determinable to follow, this is, succeed, the former state, by a rule, but not that it must literally follow *from* the former state. It must have *some* cause which dictates that it must follow rather than precede the prior state, but this is not to say that the prior state *is* that cause.

In fact, we shall later see that although Kant is not always careful to draw this distinction, it not only captures the actual conclusion of his argument but is also the basis for the solution of one of the most vexed problems in his treatment of causation, namely, the problem of reconciling *simultaneous causation* with Kant's apparent identification of cause and effect with prior and successive states.

This will occupy us later; for now, I make only the second preliminary observation that although Kant defines causality in terms of succession according to a rule, he does not say anything explicit about the precise degree of universality required of a law of nature. That is, though it is natural to assume that universal laws of causation must be completely deterministic universalizations, it is not part of Kant's argument that the kind of rule according to which one state can be determined to follow another must be fully deterministic, as opposed to, say, merely probabilistic. The possibility that the laws of nature might be statistical rather than fully deterministic would *not* undermine Kant's account of their role in empirical knowledge. [6] Of course, the force of the causal laws employed in time-determination would limit the force of the conclusions they ground: That is, if the causal laws used to ground judgments about the temporal order of states of affairs are only highly probable, then our judgments that some states succeed others will themselves be only highly probable rather than completely certain. But nothing Kant ever says commits him to the certainty of empirical time-determinations. If anything, Kant's general position on empirical knowledge assumes the *uncertainty* of all such judgments and would receive support – though undoubtedly unforeseen support – from a nondeterministic conception of the force of natural laws.

In the *Critique of Judgment,* it might be objected, Kant does assert that individual causal laws must be able to be conceived of as necessary truths:

These rules, without which no advance from the universal analogy of a possible experience in general to the particular would take place, must be thought as rules (that is, as necessary), for they would otherwise constitute no order of nature, even though their necessity cannot be cognized or ever understood.

(*Critique of Judgment,* 5:184)

He argues that such laws must be seen as embedded in a *system* of natural law precisely to lend them at least a claim to necessary truth. Two things should be noted here, however. First, even here Kant does not explicitly argue that a probabilistic law could not be necessarily true, though he undoubtedly never considered such a possibility. But more important, it must be remembered why this thesis is saved for the *Critique of Judgment* rather than asserted in the *Critique of Pure Reason*: precisely because it is only a requirement of reflective rather than determinant judgment, or part of our *ideal* of scientific knowledge but not a *necessary condition* of empirical knowledge. Perhaps it is just because the latter requires only that individual sequences of states of affairs be seen as necessitated by causal laws but not that the latter themselves be necessarily true that Kant studiously avoids including in the first *Critique* the claim made in the third.[7]

Causation and objective time-determination

Following Erich Adickes, Norman Kemp Smith claimed to find no fewer than six distinct arguments in Kant's text for the second analogy.[8] More charitable commentators have followed A. C. Ewing in identifying two, or at most three, distinct arguments in Kant's exposition.[9] But common to all these commentators is the recognition of an alleged *a priori* argument from the structure of time as a pure form of intuition to the existence of rules for the determination of empirical objects in time. Because the identity of one moment of time is determined by that which precedes – for example, 1924 is necessarily the year which follows 1923 – Kant is supposed to argue that the content of the first moment of time must fully determine the content of the succeeding moment. (This argument is supposed to be found at A 199–200 / B 244–5.) What distinguishes the two schools is whether they find in the remainder of the exposition five discernibly different epistemological arguments to the general conclusion that objective events or successions can be recognized only by means of causal laws or else just five different expositions of a single argument. In fact, Kant advances only a single, epistemological argument that the existence of causal connections is the presupposition of objective time-determination, though he reiterates its main point numerous times and on some occasions, of course, more clearly than others. What appears to be the separate, *a priori* argument which both the Adickes and the Ewing schools agree in identifying (and soundly criticizing) is nothing but a somewhat elaborate way in which Kant states the *conclusion* of his argument, after four tries at it but prior to its final exposition.

The thesis of Kant's single argument about causation is that causal rules are needed to determine the succession of objective states of affairs in time and thus to judge that any objective events have transpired. This thesis is clearly stated in one of Kant's very rare anticipations of the second analogy from the period between the *Duisburg Nachlass* and the *Critique*:

Principium rationis is the principle of the determination of things in the time-series; for they cannot be determined through time, rather the latter must be determined in the understanding through the rule of the existence of appearances.

Therefore it is not possible to determine the position of things in time without the presupposition of this principle, through which the flow of appearances is first made uniform ...   (R 5202, 18:116)

The basis of the principle of sufficient reason is not logic; instead, its basis is to be found in its role in determining the order of states of affairs in time, or their position in the time-series, which cannot be done on the basis of any intuition of time alone. But the principle of the permanence of substance was also demonstrated by its role in determining the position of things in the time-series. What is the relation between that and the present principle?

What is virtually Kant's only other surviving note on this subject from the period between 1775 and 1781 makes it clear that both principles function in the *single* task of making objective time-determinations of the order in time of states of affairs:

Everything which happens happens according to a rule, is determined in general, can be cognized *a priori*. Thereby do we distinguish the objective from subjective play (fiction), truth from illusion. The appearance has an object when it is a predicate of a substance, that is, when it is one of the modes of cognizing that which endures; therefore the appearances belong to the representation of something which endures only insofar as they are connected with each other and have unity through something universally valid. Something can of course appear to us without the ground therefore appearing to us, but we cannot then cognize it, without the cognition presuming a ground, since it would otherwise be no cognition, that is, objective representation.

That is therefore a condition of the cognition of objects, thus of the objects them- selves, for mere appearance does not yield any object. It is, to be sure, not a con- dition of apprehension, for this is directly concerned with appearance without knowing its ground. But the appearance belongs to a whole of time, and in this it can be connected only when it flows from the universal. Things are not connected through time, but in time by means of the universal in their determinations ...

(R 5221, 18:122–3)

This brings out several points. First, as I have already emphasized, the principles of the analogies do not serve to ground some special determina- tions about the behavior of what are already, in some more basic way, judged to be objects; they are the basis for any empirical judgment of objects at all. They are what we must add to mere apprehension, structured by the forms of intuition alone, in order to make confirmable claims to empirical knowledge.[10] Second, although the principle of causation (here characterized simply as the presumption that the objects of cognition have "grounds") functions to place the objects of appearance in the whole of time, it does not do so by itself. There is, rather, a twofold function which must be performed on potential representations of successive states of affairs comprising objective events. First, they must be assigned to enduring objects, as their *states*; second, their temporal *order* must be determined on the basis of their "flowing" from or being subsumed under universal laws of some kind.

This same point is made in the opening paragraph added to the exposition of the analogy in the second edition of the *Critique*. First, Kant reminds us that objective "appearances of succession in time are one and all *alterations*" (B 232), or that it is *one* necessary condition of judging that any two representations of states of affairs represent an objective change that they represent "one and the same object as existing with two opposed determinations" (B 233). But second, he holds, to determine *which* of such determinations precedes *which*, or *what* the order of the opposed states is – that is, if we are to determine *what* alteration it is that is taking place in the states of one or more substances – not only must we suppose that the change in question is an alteration in an enduring substance, but we must also "subject the succession of appearances, and therefore all alteration, to the law of causality" (B 234).

However, Kant's initial explanation of this second condition, in the text of B 233-4 as well as in R 5221, is not particularly clear. The note says merely "Things are not connected through time," but rather that they must be connected *in* time by means of their subsumption under universal laws, which have something to do with their grounds; the statement in the second edition of the *Critique* says that "time cannot be perceived in itself, and what precedes and what follows cannot, therefore, by any relation to it, be empirically determined in the object" (B 233). Kant then just asserts that there must be some basis for such a determination in "a pure concept of the understanding" and apparently simply assumes that this must be the "concept of the *relation of cause and effect*" (B 234). Is there a basis for such assumptions?

To answer this, we should turn to the initial formulation of the argument from Kant's first edition. Here Kant clearly explains the problem which can be solved only by the employment of the relation of cause and effect. The problem arises from the following circumstance: "The apprehension of the manifold of appearance is always successive. The representations of the parts follow one another. Whether they also follow each other in the object is a further point for reflection, which is not contained in the first" (A 189 / B 234). That is, any pair or series of distinct *representations*, whether they *represent* states of affairs which coexist but are successively perceived or states which succeed one another and thus comprise the several states of an actual event or alteration, *themselves* succeed one another. So the fact that the represented *states of affairs* succeed one another in a determinate order – that an alteration or event is taking place in the *objects* of perception and not just in the *subjective* series of representations itself – where there are, of course, *always* changes taking place – cannot be inferred from the successive occurrence of the *representations of* those states of affairs themselves.[11] The underlying premise of Kant's argument, then, is precisely that time cannot be directly perceived, or that, at the very least, *objective* temporal relations are not simply given in passive apprehension. In fact, this premise really comprises three distinguishable assumptions. (1) Representations as such *have* a temporal order, but nothing about the temporal order of *what they represent* can be inferred from their own temporal order, just because the temporal order of the representations themselves is always precisely the same – successive – whether or not they represent any objective change. (2) And of course *individual* representations taken in isolation reveal nothing about the relations of their possible objects to any extended time (relative or absolute): Unlike images from sports telecasts, they have no digital timers in their corners.[12] And this means that the successive states of affairs which may – or may not – be represented by successive representations cannot be judged to be successive on the basis of separate perceptions of the temporal positions of each. As Kant puts it, "This determination of position cannot be derived from the relation of appearances to absolute time (for that is no object of perception), rather the reverse, the appearances must themselves determine their positions in time for each other" (A 200 / B 245). (3) But the temporal order of the objective states of affairs cannot be determined by any direct access *to the objects* either, for it is of course only *by* the representations that the objects are given. Thus, the first two assumptions imply that representations themselves can determine the order of the states of affairs they represent neither in isolation nor by their own order; and the third assumption, which must hold on any representative theory of perception,[13] entails that we have no other and no more direct access to objects. So the determination of the temporal order of the represented states must be grounded on something other than *either* the order of the representations (even supposing *that* to be directly apprehended – although it is ultimately crucial to Kant's argument that it is not) *or* the order of the objective states themselves.

This is the moral of Kant's famous contrast between the successive perceptions of the parts of an unchanging house and the successive perceptions of the locations of a moving ship:

For example, the apprehension of the manifold of a house which stands before me is successive. Now the question is: whether the manifold of this house in itself is also successive, which to be sure no one would assume. ... That something happens, that is, that something, or a state, begins, which previously did not obtain, cannot be empirically perceived where no appearance precedes which does not contain this state in itself; for a reality which should follow an empty time, thus a coming-to-be which is preceded by no state of things, can just as little be apprehended as empty time itself. Every apprehension of an occurrence is therefore a perception which follows some other. But since this is the case in every synthesis of apprehension, as I have indicated above in the case of the appearance of a house, [the perception of an occurrence] does not distinguish itself from other [perceptions] by this means.   (A 190–2 / B 235–7)

Kant follows this statement of his problem with what is both the most detailed account of his solution that he offers and also the one that has caused the most confusion about his theory:

But I also notice that, if in the case of an appearance which contains a happening I call the preceding state of perception A and the succeeding one B, B can only follow A in apprehension, whereas the perception A cannot succeed B but only precede it. For example, I see a ship descending downstream. My perception of its position downstream follows the perception of its position higher up in the course of the river, and it is impossible that in the apprehension of this appearance the ship should first be perceived downstream and only afterward higher up in the stream. The order in the succession of the perceptions is here determined, and to this order the apprehension is bound down. In the previous example of a house, my perceptions in its apprehension could begin with the roof and end at the ground floor, but could also begin beneath and end above; likewise [I could] apprehend the manifold of empirical intuition from the right or from the left. In the series of these perceptions there was therefore no determinate order which made it necessary [where] I must begin in the apprehension in order to connect the manifold empirically. This rule, however, is always to be found in the perception of that which occurs, and it makes the order of successive perceptions (in the apprehension of this appearance) necessary.   (A 192–3 / B 237–8)

Such a rule is supposed to be a causal law:

In our case I must therefore derive the *subjective succession* of apprehension from the *objective succession* of appearances, since the former is otherwise entirely undetermined and distinguishes no appearance from any other. The former [succession] alone proves nothing about the connection of the manifold in the object, because it is entirely arbitrary. The latter [succession] will therefore consist in the order of the manifold of appearance according to which the apprehension of the one [state] (that which happens) follows on that of the other (which precedes) *according to a rule*. Only by that means can I be justified in saying of the appearance itself, and not merely of my apprehension, that in it a succession is to be found, which means as much as that I cannot order the apprehension otherwise than in this very succession.   (A 193 / B 238)

Note Kant's remark that the function of such a rule is that of *justifying me in saying* (or judging) of an empirical object that it contains an objective succession. Here – and almost nowhere else – Kant precisely delineates just what it *means* to call a principle such as that of causation a principle of the possibility of experience. It is not to say that such a principle is one which constitutes an empirical object in any ontological sense, nor that it is one which is somehow a psychological precondition of the occurrence of a representation, even a propositional representation of – a belief about – an object. Rather, to call a principle a condition of the possibility of experience is to say no more and no less than that it is a necessary condition for the *justification, verification, or confirmation* of the judgments about empirical objects that we make on the basis of our representations of them – to whatever degree of confirmation they actually admit. It is in this sense, that of constituting the framework for our epistemic practice of judging about objects, rather than that of constituting either the objects themselves or the psychological processes by which we come to have images of or beliefs about them, that Kant means his statement that the business of the understanding "is not that it makes our representations of objects distinct, but that it makes the representation of an object possible at all" (A 199 / B 244).[14]

This is a point of tremendous importance. But here we must try only to understand why Kant thinks that the epistemological task which is presented by the fact that representations are always successive can be accomplished only given knowledge (or at least presumption) of causal laws determining that the states of represented objects must succeed one another in a determinate order. The initial statement of the argument added in the second edition offers some help by providing a succinct though abstract statement of the task to be addressed, the premise which creates the problem, and the conclusion to be drawn. First, the objective is to show how I can ground a judgment that "appearances follow one another, that is, that a state of things obtains at one time the opposite of which existed in the prior state" (B 233). But, second, it is presupposed that I cannot directly determine that any two represented states actually exist at different times because neither absolute time nor absolute temporal position is directly a part of the content of any single representation, *and* because "I am conscious only that my imagination sets [the representation of] one state before the other, not that one state precedes the other in the object; or, in other words, the *objective relation* of successive appearances remains undetermined on the basis of mere perception" (B 233–4). Finally, Kant draws the conclusion that "for this [relation] to be known as determined, the relation between the two states must be so thought that it is thereby necessarily determined which state must be set first and which in succession, and not vice versa." This Kant takes to imply that, since necessity is required, there must be a pure concept of the understanding, and that it must be that of *"the relation of cause and effect"* (B 234).

Since we now understand the problem to be addressed, two things remain to be explained. First, we must understand just what follows from the supposition that I am conscious merely that my *imagination* sets the representation of one state before the other. Second, we must explain why Kant assumes that we can ground a judgment of the *determinateness* of a sequence of states of affairs only on the supposition of a law which entails the *necessity* of the occurrence of that sequence; for it would seem that the utterly contingent commencement of one state of affairs after the cessation of another would be just as *determinate* a succession as any sequence which was also necessitated by some law dictating its occurrence under the proper circumstances. In connection with this, moreover, we must more closely investigate Kant's transition from the need for some pure concept to the particular concept of cause and effect.

The case of the house and the ship will start – but only start – us on these problems. First, this discussion suggests that the significance of the claim that I am conscious merely that my imagination sets the representation of one state before the other, but not that one state succeeds the other, is that the mere fact of the successive occurrence of representations of two states of affairs is not sufficient evidence to exclude the simultaneous coexistence of the represented states of affairs themselves. This is because the mere occurrence of such a sequence of representations is not incompatible with the possibility of the occurrence of precisely the opposite sequence of representations – I can see the roof before the ground floor, or the ground floor before the roof – and this possibility is presumably to be explained precisely by the *simultaneous existence* of the objects of both representations. Thus, the evidence furnished by the mere fact of a succession of representations is compatible with the possibility that there is simply a changing perception of a complex object, rather than any change in the object at all.

But, Kant now supposes, if one state of affairs actually succeeded rather than coexisted with the other – if there were an actual occurrence – then, *ceteris paribus* (and this is a matter of some significance), such indifference between the possible orders *of their perceptions* would not be possible. If there were an actual event, thus if one state of affairs did succeed the other, then the *perception* of the one would not only succeed that of the other but would *have to* succeed it. "In the case of an appearance which contains a happening ... B can only follow A in apprehension, but the perception of A cannot succeed B but only precede it" (A 192 / B 237).

At this point, however, we must be very precise about just what Kant's argument is. The fact that in the case of an event the *perception* of one state of affairs can only succeed but not precede another is *not* itself what *constitutes* the event we are interested in, a change in the object. Nor is it itself what must in the first instance be explained by a rule. To be sure, a change in representations is itself an event, and judgment about such an event may even have its own necessary conditions (this is of course precisely what the second stage of Kant's theory of time-determination will show). But the present problem is only that of distinguishing an event occurring among represented states of affairs from the event of a change in representations themselves, knowledge of which may – for the moment – be taken for granted. Thus, the significance of the irreversibility of a sequence of representations, in the present context, is only that such a fact would be a *consequence* of the occurrence of an event in what is being perceived, which *could* be used as a *symptom*[15] of the occurrence of the event *if* it were directly given to consciousness.[16] But what Kant's underlying assumption means is precisely that such a modal fact about the sequence of perceptions is *not* given to consciousness by apprehension alone.[17] This is, in turn, of course nothing but a consequence of Kant's most fundamental assumption that experience "to be sure tells us what is, but not that it must necessarily be so and not otherwise" (A 1). No necessities of any kind, whether in the objective realm or even in the subjective arena of representations themselves, are ever given by uninterpreted apprehension. At best – and we shall subsequently see that even this is not the whole story – unaided apprehension or "imagination" indicates only that one representation succeeds another, not that it *necessarily* does so. And of course the necessary succession of one representation after another, even if this were what we were primarily interested in, could not at this stage be inferred from a judgment about the succession of one *objective state of affairs* after another, for that is precisely the type of judgment the grounds for which must still be discovered. So Kant's idea is that no alternative remains but that the occurrence of an event be inferred by *adding* to the omnipresent succession of mere representations a *rule* from which it can be inferred that in the circumstances at hand *one state of affairs* could *only* succeed the other, and *therefore* also that one *representation* could only succeed the other. In Kant's clearest words, "It is therefore only in respect of a rule according to which appearances in *their* succession, that is, as *they* occur, are determined by the preceding state that I make my subjective synthesis (of apprehension) objective, and it is only under this presupposition that the experience itself of something that happens is possible" (A 195 / B 240, emphasis added). Only from a rule which says that one of the represented states *must* succeed the other can it be inferred that it *does* succeed the other. For the temporal positions of the objective states themselves are not directly given, and though their succession *could* be inferred from the *necessary* sequence or irreversibility of the representations of them if such irreversibility *were* – since the irreversibility of their representations *would* be a genuine consequence of the sequence of the represented states of affairs – the necessity of the sequence of representations is also *not* directly given to consciousness. So nothing remains but to invoke a rule from which it follows that one objective state can only succeed and not coexist with the other, from which it *also* follows – again, *ceteris paribus* – that the *representation* of the one state not only does but also only could succeed the representation of the other.

Or, in another of Kant's formulations, his claim is that if *in addition* to merely *having* a succession of representations I *also*

... presuppose that in this succession there is a relation to the preceding situation, from which the representation follows according to a rule, then I represent something as an event, or as what happens, that is, I cognize an object which must be placed in a particular determinate position in time which, in view of the preceding state, cannot otherwise be assigned. (A 198 / B 243)

And a rule which dictates that in a given situation one state of affairs must succeed another is just what Kant means by a causal law. Thus, judgments that events occur are possible only if the states of affairs which comprise them are linked by causal laws.

Objections to Kant's argument

This argument is quite abstract, and of course Kant's conclusion has engendered a great deal of resistance, even outright scorn. The most efficient way to provide some more detail to Kant's argument will be if we now consider some of the chief objections to it, specifically to his inference to causal laws governing relations *among states of objects*.

(1) We may begin with what is not itself an objection, but an interpretation which quickly produces one. This interpretation is that the argument of the second analogy proceeds essentially by *analyzing* the *concept* of an event. This of course produces the objection that the question whether such a concept has objective validity is then begged. But more important, it fails to explain the crucial requirement of *causal* laws. Graham Bird's version of this interpretation displays exactly this failure. According to Bird, "The Second Analogy may ... be understood as an analysis of the concept 'event'."[18] On this analysis, an event is comprised of "two different characteristics, or states" of a single object,[19] and these two "constituent states of the object" must also be "regarded as irreversible." It is to follow from this that in the case of any given event there is a purely "logical necessity" that the states which comprise that particular event occur in the order in which they do; otherwise, those states would comprise not *that* event but some other event. The necessity in the event of a ship's sailing from a point upstream to a point downstream, for instance, would be the "logical necessity that to apprehend a ship's sailing downstream is, necessarily, to apprehend an event in which the ship's position downstream followed its position upstream. The order of *this* event is a necessary order, not because it is impossible for ships to sail upstream, but because if the constituent states had been reversed the event apprehended would have been a different event." And to introduce a role for causal laws into this analysis, Bird then argues that if what we mean by the concept of a particular event is just that one state of affairs must follow another, "then it presupposes the notion of a reason or ground for the constituent states of an object being in such a determinate order."[20] Thus it follows that any event has a cause.

Now some passages, such as Kant's final exposition of his argument, could be taken to offer an analysis of the concept of an event:

But if this synthesis is a synthesis of apprehension (of the manifold of a given appearance), then the order is determined in the object, or, to speak more precisely, there is therein an order of successive synthesis which determines an object, according to which something must necessarily precede, and if this is posited the other must necessarily follow. Therefore if my perception is to contain the cognition of an occurrence, namely that something really happens, it must be an empirical judgment in which one thinks that the succession is determined, that is, that it presupposes another appearance ... on which it necessarily follows ...

(A 201 / B 246–7)

This could be read to argue that the *presupposition* that a given sequence of representations represents the occurrence of a particular event entails that the states represented must follow one another in the order in which they do, and that the rule which is employed is just the rule that the identity of any particular event requires that the states comprising it *must* succeed each other in the order in which they do in order to comprise *that* event.

But though this rule is true, indeed trivial, it cannot be the rule which Kant's argument introduces. For it does not justify the assumption of a *causal* connection between the states comprising an event, at least by any argument which Kant himself would have accepted. This can be seen at once. Kant, of course, agrees with Hume in conceiving of a causal connection as a universal connection, one "where all the objects resembling the [cause] are plac'd in a like relation of priority and contiguity to those objects, that resemble" the effect.[21] But there is no reason why the analytically "necessary" connection which follows from the identity of a particular event must be a *universally valid* rather than completely *unique* connection. If a particular event is that of a ship's sailing downstream, then it follows analytically that its being downstream succeeds its being upstream. And as a matter of fact we also believe that there are causal laws which explain this sequence. But if my station wagon were to up and fly away, it would follow with equal "necessity," from the very description of the event, that the moment in which it started to fly succeeded the last moment in which it behaved as an earthbound car. Yet we would call this event a miracle and suppose that there is no universally valid law which explains it, without in any way altering our description of it. (Of course, we would not, on the view of either Hume or Kant, ever accept such an explanatory failure, but that is another matter.) Or, in Kant's terms, a "logical ground" for a predicate of an object or event in the concept of the latter is not a "real ground": It may follow by analysis of the concept of being chilled that my body temperature has been lowered, "but if in saying that in being chilled I also posit that I will catch a cold, then this is an entirely different concept of being chilled" (*Metaphysik Volckmann*, 28:403) – not an analytical concept of a type of event at all, that is, but a synthetic conception of possible consequences of such an event.

Bird does try to justify his introduction of causal laws by the following supplement to his "analysis":

What we mean by 'event' is ... a determinate temporal order of two states in the same object. But the idea of a determinate order between two states presupposes that of something which determines it; and this idea of a determinant or reason for such an order is that of a cause. ... Kant has, therefore, some ground for saying that the concept of a cause is required for our discrimination of a time order in phenomena.[22]

But it is simply incredible to attribute such an argument to the author of the *Critique of Pure Reason,* for it is no more and no less than the *rationalist's* argument for the principle of sufficient reason by means of the equation of logical grounds and real explanations, the rejection of which was one of the fundamental motivations for Kant's entire mature theoretical philosophy. To *assume* that just because logic's principle of noncontradiction requires that an object be characterized by (at most) one of two opposed predicates there must also be a sufficient *explanation* for the selection of the predicate that does correctly apply is to commit the same error which Wolff displayed in his classical statement that "nothing is without its sufficient reason, why it is rather than is not, that is, if something is posited then something else is also to be posited from which *it can be understood* why the former is rather than is not."[23] To be sure, although in 1755 Kant cast doubt upon the equation of *rationata cognoscendi,* or sufficient conditions for knowing the identity of a thing, and *rationata existendi,* or sufficient conditions for explaining the existence and characteristics of a thing, as we have already seen he did not then understand the distinction sufficiently well to avoid making an argument for the principle of sufficient reason which does simply assume that the logically necessary determinants for the identity of a thing include its explanation.[24] But by his seminal *Attempt to Introduce Negative Quantities into Philosophy,* of 1763, which represents his decisive break with rationalism, Kant had clearly hammered out the distinction between logical and real relations:

I understand very well how a consequence can be posited through a ground, since it is found to be contained in it through the analysis of the concepts. Thus necessity is a ground of invariability, composition a ground of divisibility, infinity a ground of omniscience, etc., and this connection of the ground with the consequence I can clearly understand, since the consequence is really identical with a partial concept of the ground. . . . But how something flows from something else but not according to the law of identity, that is something which I would gladly be able to make clear to myself. I call the first kind of ground a logical ground, since its relation to the consequent can be understood logically, namely clearly according to the law of identity; but I call the second kind of ground a real ground. . . . Now as far as this real ground and its relation to the consequent is concerned, I put my question in this simple form: How shall I understand it, that, *since something is, something else is?* . . . [A logical ground] I clearly understand by means of the law of contradiction, and I understand how, if I posit the infinity of God, the predicate of mortality is thereby suspended, namely since it contradicts the former. But how, through the movement of one body, the movement of another can be suspended, that is another question.   (2:202–3)

By 1763, then, Kant had clearly rejected the idea that the relationship of logical opposition which grounds an analytical judgment of identity also necessarily explains what it grounds. As we saw in the quotation from the

Metaphysik Volckmann at the beginning of this chapter, Kant had hardly altered his understanding of this distinction two decades later; he had only deepened his conviction that the distinction between logical and real grounds is the key to the problem of synthetic *a priori* judgments.

If Bird's interpretation rested just on historical ignorance, it would not be worth mentioning. But it is worth mentioning, because it also involves a radical misunderstanding of Kant's conception of our epistemic situation in attempting to distinguish between merely subjective and genuinely objective successions. For Bird's account seems to presuppose that we are actually *given* knowledge of events, and can then use our knowledge that there *is* a determinate succession to infer further conclusions, such as that there is a cause for that succession. But this is precisely the opposite of what Kant assumes. Kant's idea is that we are *not* given knowledge of objective successions but that we must infer *that* from something – namely, nothing less than a law which *explains* why, in the given circumstances, one succession rather than another should obtain. In other words, on Kant's theory causal laws are not logical consequences of determinacy but the epistemological preconditions of knowledge of determinacy.

We can illustrate this in the case of the ship's sailing downstream. Bird claims that "the order of *this* event is a necessary order, not because it is impossible for ships to sail upstream, but because if the constituent states had been reversed the event apprehended would have been a different event. It would have been the event of a ship's sailing upstream." Plausible as this sounds, it misses the point of Kant's argument. For Kant's claim is that, given only two successive *observations* of positions of the ship, which in imagination can be set in either of two orders, it can be determined that they represent (for example) the ship's sailing downstream only if, in the circumstances which are being assumed, it *would* be impossible for that ship to be sailing upstream. Kant's theory is precisely that it is only if we are in possession of causal laws which dictate that in the relevant circumstances – that is, not in general, but in the particular circumstances of wind, tide, setting of the sails, and so forth, which are assumed to obtain – the ship could *only* sail downstream that we actually have sufficient evidence to interpret our representations of it to mean that it *is* sailing downstream.[25] Bird's derivation of the necessity of a cause *from* the identification of the event begs Kant's question of just *how* we can identify the event.[26]

(2) Connected confusions underlie two more illustrative objections to Kant's argument. According to the first of these, Kant can show that knowledge of *some* determinate relations among states of objects is an epistemological precondition of recognizing events, but not that *causal* relations are. This is because the recognition of an event requires the assumption that the two relevant states of affairs are *opposite* or *incompatible* states of affairs (cf. B 233: "that appearances are in succession, that is, that a state of things exists at one time whose opposite [*Gegenteil*] existed in the preceding state"), but this already answers the question: If the two states

are incompatible, then of course they cannot exist at the same time, so there must be an event, namely that constituted by the change from one of the incompatible states to the other. Nothing *in addition* to the presupposition of incompatibility is needed to judge that there is an event.[27]

But there are two problems with such an objection. First, it too fails to appreciate Kant's distinction between logical and real opposition, for it overlooks the fact that the kind of incompatibility which will typically be involved in an event is not *logical* incompatibility derivable from mere concepts of the states of affairs concerned, but *real opposition*. And although Kant does not mention the fact in the text of the second analogy or do more than allude to it elsewhere in the *Critique* (see, e.g., A 265 / B 320) (perhaps just because he had already stated it so clearly in *Negative Quantities*), *real opposition is engendered by nothing other than causal laws.* Kant's "ground rule" for "real opposition" is that "real repugnance occurs only insofar as of two things as *positive grounds* one suspends the consequence of the other"; for instance, "Let a motive force be a positive ground: then a real opposition can take place only insofar as another motive force in relation to the first suspends its consequence. ..." (2:175–6). A state of affairs which can have this kind of effect on the consequence of another, however, is nothing less than a cause of that suspension of consequence – a state from which, according to a rule, another, in this case the absence of something expected, follows. Kant makes this explicit: "In nature there are many [changes] from the conflict of two efficient causes [*wirkenden Ursachen*], of which one suspends the consequence of the other through real opposition" (2:184). So for at least a large variety of cases, our knowledge that a thing cannot be in two different states at the same time cannot be derived from logical opposition between contradictories, but itself depends upon knowledge of what the causal powers of things are. For instance, our knowledge that something cannot be both hot and cold at the same time, so that our perception of it as both hot and cold must constitute a perception of its change from one of these states to the other, is itself knowledge of what the causal powers of objects are: knowledge that one object cannot cause another to melt but can cause yet a third, otherwise similar to the second, to gel in similar circumstances, or can cause us to have two different sorts of sensations in the same sensory modality at the same time. And if this is so, the need for causal laws is not *obviated* by the way Kant's argument is set up; rather, it is almost immediately *implied* by the way the argument is posed.

Second, even if the incompatibility of two states of affairs could be known independently of any knowledge of causation, it could tell us only that *some* event has taken place, but not *which*. That is, if A and B are mutually incompatible states of affairs, then we know that the perception of both A and B must represent some event, but we cannot know on that basis alone whether it represents the change from A to B or that from B to A. In order to make the latter determinate, what is required in addition to the incompatibility of A and B is precisely a law of the form that, for example,

B can only follow A, from which it can then be inferred that the particular event being perceived can be only the alteration from A to B.[28]

This has not been obvious for the simple reason that advocates of the present objection (and almost everyone else) have assumed that the *order* of two incompatible states of affairs *can* be determined by the order of *perception* alone. They assume, that is, that if it is given that A and B are incompatible states, then the further fact that they constitute, for example, the change from A to B is directly determined by the fact that the succession of my *perceptions* is a perception of A followed by a perception of B, that is, by the fact that whereas I am now perceiving B, I previously perceived A. For if A and B are incompatible and if the one of them which I am now perceiving is B, then the event which I have been perceiving can be only the change from A to B. Thus C. D. Broad wrote, "If I perceive that *x* is now in a certain place and I remember that it was in a different place, I know, without any appeal to causation, that it must have changed its place."[29]

This assumption seems natural enough; why is it wrong? Commenting on Broad's version of the objection, D. P. Dryer hints at an answer. Dryer says that Broad fails to realize that his contention "that in order for someone to know that a certain change has taken place in an object, it is sufficient for him to observe it in a certain state and remember that it was previously in an opposite state" is "analytically true," because "when someone is said to 'remember' that any object which he observes was previously in an opposite state, what is meant is that he knows, from what he recalls having observed, that it was previously in an opposite state," and because this knowledge requires the use of causal laws.[30] This points in the right direction, but what has to be emphasized is Kant's fundamental and *synthetic* claim that in any situation in which we seem to recall being successively conscious of two states of affairs, "imagination can connect these states in two ways" (B 233). That is, *at any moment* in which we reflect on what is apparently a present perception plus a memory of a prior one, *it is not actually given which is the present perception and which is the prior one.* For all that can be given in one moment is a *present representation* of the contents of two (or more) possible perceptions, but not both the present *and the past representation* itself. *Which* is the present representation and which the past is something *which itself* must be judged. And what Kant's argument ultimately supposes is that this inference requires precisely a law of the form that one *state of affairs* can only succeed the other, which would then entail, other things being equal, that the *perception* of the one can only succeed the *perception* of the other and thus must be the present, as opposed to the past, representation.

In other words, the ultimate premise of Kant's argument is not actually mentioned in his exposition of the second analogy itself, but is nothing other than the alleged key to the transcendental deduction, the premise that "every intuition contains a manifold in itself, which, however, would not be represented as such if the mind did not distinguish the time in the succession of impressions one after another: for as *contained in one moment* no representation can be anything other than absolute unity" (A 99). As we saw in the discussion of the transcendental deduction, this means that we are never at one moment in an epistemically qualified position to judge that a sequence of representations at earlier moments has occurred merely by virtue of the fact of the earlier occurrence of those representations itself; rather, we must interpret the content of what is always just our *present* representational state *as representing* such a sequence of earlier representations culminating in our present state, though this conclusion does not become clear until the refutation of idealism is accomplished. So, as I suggested at the outset, the second analogy does not stand by itself, but requires both the deduction and the refutation of idealism for its completion. However, I will say more about the underlying consideration just revealed, but only after expounding a second objection which fails in part for the same reason.

(3) This objection is Strawson's famous charge that Kant's argument "can seem legitimate only if the critical faculty is numbed by the grossness of the *non sequitur*."[31] Simply put, the charge is that Kant confuses "causal transactions or dependencies relating objects of subjective perception to one another ... with the causal dependencies of subjective perceptions themselves upon their objects."[32] In somewhat more detail, the argument is this. Kant is supposed to hold that "lack or possession of order-indifference on the part of our perceptions is ... our criterion ... of objective succession or co-existence."[33] So, for two objective states of affairs, A and B, and two representations of them, A_r and B_r,[34] if A_r and B_r are irreversible or lack order-indifference – had to come in that order rather than in the order B_r then A_r – it can be judged that they represent the event A-then-B, whereas if the representations possess order-indifference, they must be taken to represent the coexistence of A and B and not the event A-then-B. But for the distinction between irreversibility and order-indifference *of perceptions* to be made, Strawson charges, all that is required is the supposition of causal laws relating the states of affairs *to the representations of them* – that is, laws linking A to A_r and B to B_r respectively. This is because *if* it is known (1) that A_r preceded B_r *and* (2) that both A_r was caused by A and B_r by B by the same method of transmission or "mode of causal dependency," where that sameness is defined by the fact that no time lag is present in the one case which is absent from the other, *then* (3) it can be inferred that just as A_r preceded B_r, so A preceded B. In Strawson's words (but my symbols), *if*

(1) ... A and B are objective states of affairs of which A preceded B in time, this succession constituting a single event (the event of A's being succeeded by B), (2) [A_r] is a perception of A and [B_r] of B, (3) there is no relevant difference in the modes of causal dependency of [A_r] on A and [B_r] on B (a relevant difference being any which affects the time taken by the causal process whereby the object (A or B) produces its effect ([A_r] or [B_r]) to complete itself), then there follows, with *logical* necessity, the consequence that [A_r] precedes [B_r]. The substitution for (1),

however, of the supposition that A and B are coexistent leaves it a logically open question which, of [A$_r$] and [B$_r$], comes first. The necessary order of perceptions in the one case, their order-indifference in the other, reduce, it seems, to just this logical necessity and this logical indifference.[35]

But, he claims, Kant just confuses the necessity that A$_r$ and B$_r$ occur in that order, given the order of A and B and the isomorphic mechanisms of perception, with the necessity that *A and B* occur in that order, and it is only by such a confusion that any causal laws regulating the order of A and B are smuggled into the argument.

But the fallacy is Strawson's, not Kant's. Strawson confuses the means and the end: That is, he takes for granted knowledge of the order of A and B and uses it to infer the irreversibility of A$_r$ and B$_r$, whereas it is precisely the order of the objective states of affairs which *cannot* be made a "supposition" but which must somehow be established on the basis of the – insufficient – evidence furnished by the order of perceptions. And this is not Strawson's only misconstrual of Kant's conception of our epistemic situation. Like the incompatibility theorists, he takes for granted that the order of *perceptions* is known independently of anything else, whereas the underlying premise of the transcendental deduction undermines precisely this assumption. Further, Strawson's conception of our situation assumes that causal laws relating perceptions to their objects could be known independently of laws regulating the behavior of the objects themselves, whereas everything points against this assumption as well.

Let us consider these points in turn. Strawson concedes that *if* the irreversibility of the sequence A$_r$ then B$_r$ could be known, then it could legitimately be inferred that this sequence represents the occurrence A-then-B. And he does not, certainly, misunderstand Kant to say that the *irreversibility* of a sequence of representations can ever be directly given. Rather, what he supposes is that if it is directly known simply (1) what the *sequence* of the representations is, and (2) that each representation stands in the same temporal relation to its object, then (3) it can be inferred that the objective states of affairs are indeed ordered as are the representations of them and so constitute an event. But Kant's argument for causation among the states of objects turns precisely on the rejection of the two premises of such an inference. As far as direct knowledge of the determinate order *of representations* is concerned, Kant's transcendental deduction and refutation of idealism proceed precisely by rejecting the – admittedly natural – supposition that merely having the representation A$_r$ prior to the representation B$_r$ is sufficient for *knowing* that one has experienced A$_r$ prior to B$_r$. Again, what Kant assumes – although Strawson does not – is that "every intuition contains a manifold in itself, which, however, would not be represented as such if the mind did not distinguish the time in the sequence of one impression upon another: for as *contained in one moment* no representation can be anything other than absolute unity" (A 99). Or, as the analogy itself says, "Imagination can connect ... two states in two

256

ways" (B 233). What these imply is that in the case in which I in fact have A_r prior to B_r, what is present to me at *the time of B_r* is nevertheless a *single* representational state, which, to be sure, has both A-like and B-like content but which must be *interpreted* to count as a *present* experience of B_r plus a representation of a *prior* subjective state A_r rather than as, say, a *present* representation of both A and B. And Kant's view is that this can be accomplished only by relating the *content* of the present representational state to a sequence of states *in the external world* which dictates that the only way in which I could, at the time of B_r, be representing both A-like and B-like content is if I am *then having* B_r and *remembering* having previously experienced A_r. That is, so far from the sequence A then B being directly inferrable from the sequence A_r-then-B_r, the sequence A_r-then-B_r itself must be inferred from the sequence A-then-B. And, of course, since the sequence A-then-B itself is not directly given, *it* can be inferred only from a law which dictates that, in the given circumstances, B *must* have succeeded A. Here is a law which does indeed link A to B and not just A_r to A and B_r to B; and here is the true sense in which "we must derive the *subjective succession* of apprehension from the *objective succession* of appearances" (A 193 / B 238).

The second point to be made is this. The *non sequitur* charge claims that the event A then B could be inferred from the sequence A_r then B_r combined with knowledge of how A_r is caused by A, and B_r by B; in particular, knowledge that they are caused with the *same* time lag – for instance, the production of A_r has not been delayed by any medium or mechanism such that A_r succeeds B_r even though B succeeds A. But it is difficult to understand how knowledge of the laws relating A to A_r and B to B_r could be acquired without knowledge of the order of A and B. How could it be confirmed that, say, B_r was being produced with a delay not present in the transmission of A_r *unless* it were also known that A actually preceded B? Or how could it be tested that A_r and B_r were actually being produced by isomorphic mechanisms unless it were also assumed that in the test case the objects stood in the same temporal relations as the perceptions? In other words, causal laws governing the mechanisms of perception could not be confirmed independently of determinate knowledge about the order of objective states of affairs – so those sorts of laws could not be acquired independently of laws from which the sequence of the objective states of affairs themselves could be derived. Hence, it is not a fallacy for Kant to introduce the latter as well as the former kind of laws into his argument.

A slightly different way of making the same point may be found in a famous passage from Schopenhauer, which Schopenhauer took to be an objection to Kant but which I take as an illustration of the position which Kant ultimately strove to express.[36] Discussing the contrast between the sequence of perceptions of a moving ship and the changing perceptions of an unchanging house, Schopenhauer wrote:

... I maintain that the two cases are not different at all, that both are events, the knowledge of which is objective, in other words one of changes in real objects that are known as such by the subject. *Both are changes in position of two bodies relatively to each other*. In the first case one of these bodies is the observer's own organism ... and the other is the house; with respect to the parts of the house, the position of the eye is successively changed. In the second case, the ship alters its position relatively to the river [and the unmoving eye], and so the change is between two bodies. Both are events, the only difference is that in the first case the change starts from the observer's own body. ... Yet this body is nevertheless an object among objects, consequently is liable to the laws of this objective corporeal world ...[37]

Kant's efforts at completing the refutation of idealism after 1787 reveal that in the end this was precisely his own position; what the refutation suggests apropos of the present case is that there is no way in which knowledge of the laws explaining the perceptual effects of changing eye positions could be obtained independently of laws explaining the behavior of the bodies being looked at. How could it be confirmed that it is the changing position of the eye which is causing the succession of perceptions of the house unless it is assumed that the house is not changing – or that it is the changing position of the ship which is causing the succession of perceptions of it unless it is assumed that the eye is still? But if this information about the objects is not given directly on the basis of mere representations, whence can it come except from exactly the sort of laws which Strawson thinks are only fallaciously introduced by Kant?

At this point, of course, the reader may well wonder whence knowledge of these objective causal laws itself is supposed to derive. After all, Kant specifically denies that individual causal laws are known *a priori* (cf. A 196–7 / B 241–2, or more generally B 142). Yet on the only model of the acquisition of causal knowledge which Kant could have accepted – Humean inductivism without its skepticism – empirical knowledge of causal laws is surely derived from induction on repeated *experiences*. Does this not make Kant's entire theory incoherent?

My view is that it does not, as long as Kant's theory of judgment – or time-determination – is understood not as a psychological model of the generation of beliefs but as an epistemological model of the confirmation of beliefs. If Kant were supposed to be explaining how given instances of belief in the occurrence of events are generated, then he might be faced with the problem of explaining how the belief in the event could be generated on the presupposition of knowledge of causal laws when even generation of belief in a sequence of representations, which might furnish evidence for such laws, also itself requires them. But – unlike the transcendental deduction, where the postulation of transcendental acts of synthesis is actually a premise of Kant's argument (see this volume, Chapter 5, argument IIA) – the argument of the second analogy is entirely free from any reference to real or imagined psychological processes for the generation of particular representations and beliefs. As we have seen, Kant is dealing strictly with the principles that would have to be appealed to in the justification of empirical claims to knowledge. Such justification is not a psychological process that has to take place at the same time as the actual generation of a representation or belief; for the most part, indeed, such justification is never represented by an actual psychological process at all. But in such a purely epistemological framework, there will be no problem about appealing to causal laws to justify claims about the order of objective and even subjective states, on the one hand, yet appealing to such states in order to confirm claims to knowledge of causal laws on the other, as long as it is supposed that in any given case of actual confirmation of a judgment – say a case of testing a hypothesis about a sequence of representations – one and the same sequence of representations is not *both* being derived from a particular causal law about objects *and* being employed as evidence *for* the validity of the causal law. This point will be considered further in the discussion of Kant's refutation of idealism.

The causal principle and simultaneous causation

The exposition and defense of Kant's argument for his principle of causation is now complete. It remains only to consider the question mentioned at the outset of this chapter, about the precise content of the principle which Kant is defending. The crux of Kant's argument is that an event can be determined to have occurred only if there is a rule which entails that one of its constituent states must have succeeded the other. Many take Kant to mean that an event can be posited only where the first state is taken to *be* the cause of the second. This is not surprising, since Kant often writes in just this way. For instance:

When therefore I perceive that something happens, in this representation there is contained, first, that something precedes, since only in relation to this does the appearance acquire its time-relation, namely, to exist after a preceding time in which it is not. But it can acquire its determinate position in this relation only if something is presupposed in the preceding state on which it always follows, that is, follows according to a rule: which then implies ... that, if the state which precedes is posited, this particular occurrence follows necessarily and without exception.

(A 198 / B 243–4)

Or:

... if my perception is to contain the cognition of an occurrence ... it must be an empirical judgment in which one thinks that the succession is determined, that is, that it presupposes another appearance ... on which it necessarily follows, or follows according to a rule. ... Therefore the relation of appearances ... according to which the successor (that which happens) is necessarily determined by something which precedes and according to a rule in time, thus the relation of cause and effect, is the condition of the objective validity of our empirical judgments ...

(A 201–2 / B 246–7)

But the supposition that in any cognizable event what precedes must be the cause and what succeeds the effect is untenable. As Reid and Schopenhauer charged, we think that night follows day without being *caused* by day. Moreover, as Kant himself observes, we often think that the effect is *simultaneous* with, rather than subsequent to, its cause.

There is really no problem here, however, for the statements we have just considered are only imprecise statements of the conclusion to which Kant's argument leads. All that Kant's argument actually entails is that in order to determine that perceptions of two states of affairs represent the occurrence of an event, we require a rule which suffices to assign a temporal position to one of the two states – that judged to be the later in a sequence, "which, in view of the preceding state, cannot be otherwise assigned" (A 198 / B 243). We cannot, he says, "ascribe succession to the object . . . and distinguish it from the subjective [succession] of our apprehension unless there is a rule which necessitates [one] order of perceptions rather than another" (A 196 / B 241–2). But to satisfy this general condition, all that is required is a rule from which it can be deduced that, *of the two states comprising the event at issue,* the later of them can only have obtained after the earlier, or the earlier can only have preceded the later.[38] Yet such a determination could be grounded in at least *two* different ways. Given two states, we could judge that one of them must succeed the other (1) because the earlier one *is or contains* the cause of the latter – the situation which Kant typically envisions – or (2) precisely because the earlier state *lacks* a sufficient condition for the occurrence of the later state, and *that* cause or condition instead has to be *added* to the earlier stage of the event at issue in order to produce the later one. In the second case, the desired result that the later state could occur *only* after the earlier state would follow precisely because the cause of the second state, *not* being present in the first state, is itself assumed only to have succeeded that first state. (Of course, *this* temporal determination – that the cause of the second state succeeded the existence or commencement of the existence of the first state of the event – will be no more simply given in apprehension than any other time-determination and will itself have to be grounded by some other applications of causal laws. But Kant certainly never suggests that any act of empirical time-determination is *self-contained.* Rather, the ideal of confirming our empirical judgments about temporal relations is a regulative idea which imposes upon us a never-ending series of judgmental tasks.[39]) Again, *either* (1) a judgment that one state must succeed another because states of the later type *are* caused by and always follow states of the earlier type *or* (2) a judgment that the later state can only succeed the earlier because it must await the *addition* of its cause to a state which lacks it would suffice to ground the general claim that there is a necessary and irreversible order to the *two states comprising the event at issue.*

Thus causation is necessary to determine that one state succeeds another, but not necessarily causation *of the succeeding state by the preceding one.* To be sure, Kant did not see this clearly. Thus, he glosses the requirement of a rule which necessitates a particular assignment of the relative temporal position of two states of affairs thus:

If therefore I perceive that something happens, then in this perception there is contained first: that something precedes, since only in relation to this does the appearance obtain its time-relation, namely, that of existing after a preceding time in which it was not. But it can obtain its determinate time-position in this relationship only if in the preceding time something is presupposed, on which it always follows, that is, follows according to a rule: which then yields, first, that I cannot reverse the sequence, and place that which happens prior to that on which it succeeds: second, that if the state which precedes is posited, this determinate occurrence unavoidably and necessarily follows. (A 198 / B 243)

But this conclusion does not follow from a careful conception of what is required to determine that an order of objective states of affairs is irreversible, or that one state can only succeed the other. If indeed that time-determination is derived from the judgment that the first stage of the event is *itself* the cause – actually, in Cartesian terms, the complete and total efficient cause – of the second, then indeed it will follow not only that the sequence cannot be reversed but also that a state of the second kind will occur whenever a state of the first kind does. But if in fact the second state is determined to have succeeded the first only because a necessary condition for the existence of the second state was *absent* from the first state of affairs and itself only succeeded that state, then of course it will *not* follow that a state of the second kind will always follow a state of the first kind.[40] Perhaps it can follow *only* a state of the first kind, but it need not actually follow unless its appropriate cause – not in fact identical to the first state of affairs – also occurs.

Kant's confusion also explains the apparent problem concerning simultaneous causation, about which he creates unnecessary difficulty because he does not recognize the easy solution which a proper statement of his own necessary condition for determination of objective succession would afford. The problem about simultaneous causation which Kant raises, after his basic argument has been completed, is that in many if not most cases of physical causation the effect does *not* appear to succeed its cause but is simultaneous with it. This seems to be the case where cause and effect are both processes, as in Kant's case of a fire which is warming a room, but also in cases where at least the cause is a discrete event, as in the case in which placing a lead ball on a previously well-plumped pillow appears to cause immediately the existence of a hollow in the pillow (A 202–3 / B 247–8). Kant tries to explain this problem away by invoking the possibility of a "vanishing" quantity of time which can make the time *lag* between cause and effect indiscernibly small without disturbing the time-*order* according to which the cause precedes the effect (A 203 / B 249). But this expedient is not necessary,[41] precisely because Kant's basic principle does *not* require that an event – or alteration – can be determined to occur only if the first stage of the event is itself the cause of the second stage which succeeds it as its effect. All that is required is that the second stage be determined by its cause only to succeed the first stage, whether that cause is itself identical to the first state or is instead some third state of affairs. Thus, an event can also be determined to occur, or one state to precede another, if the cause of the succeeding state is simultaneous with *it*, but succeeds the earlier state of affairs which constitutes the initial state of the event – though again, of course, it will be a separate time-determination that that cause does succeed the first stage of the event at issue. And this is just the situation that obtains in Kant's examples. For in these cases the events which are determined to occur are *not* the event of a fire's burning and then a room's being warm or the event of a ball's being placed on a pillow and then the pillow's being dented, but rather *the room's change from cold to warm* (the event of its becoming warm) or *the pillow's change from plump to dented* (the event of its becoming dented).[42] In each of these cases, the event *so described* can be determined to obtain just because a cause *absent* in the initial condition *intervenes* to produce the succeeding condition, even though the commencement *of that intervening cause* is simultaneous with the commencement of its effect; the commencement of the effect is still subsequent to the existence of the *first stage of the change* from cold to warm or from plump to dented.

In other words, the cause may have to precede its effect where we have only *two* terms, one of which must succeed the other; but sometimes we may consider a *threefold* relation among preceding state, succeeding state, and cause of the latter, in which case the third state of affairs might be simultaneous with the second but successive to the first. And indeed Kant himself allows for precisely this possibility when he says that "if I lay the ball on the pillow, the dent follows upon the previously smooth form; but if the pillow [already] had a dent (from I know not where), a leaden ball would not follow" (A 203 / B 248). What this assumes is just that in one case but not in another, two states of affairs may be ordered because there is a causal law according to which the cause of the second state is in fact a third state of affairs which, in the given case itself, happens to succeed upon the first: Laying the ball on the pillow is a state of affairs distinct from both the pillow's being plump and its being smooth. Kant does not clearly realize that a third state of affairs can be used to order the relation of two others as long as there are suitable relations of causality,[43] but indeed this is enough to save him from the fuss about vanishing quantities of time. As long as Kant maintains only the general position that two states can be ordered only if there is *some* applicable relation of cause and effect and does not slip into the excessively restricted conclusion that states can be ordered only if the former is the cause of the latter, there is no problem about simultaneous causation.

The second analogy and phenomenalism

Many commentators have thought that Kant's problem in the second analogy arises from his distinction between appearances and things in themselves, and in particular because of his alleged *reduction* of empirical objects to collections or aggregates of perceptions themselves.[44] Indeed, this seems to be suggested by Kant's words in some crucial presentations of the problem. Thus, immediately preceding the comparison of the perception of something unchanging, such as a house, with that of something changing, such as a moving ship, which poses the problem of how to distinguish between them, Kant makes the general statement:

Insofar as [appearances], merely as representations, are also objects of consciousness, they are not to be distinguished from the apprehension, that is, their reception in the synthesis of imagination, and one must therefore say: The manifold of appearance is always generated in the mind successively. If appearances were things in themselves, nobody could determine from the succession of the representations of their manifold [states] how the latter are connected in the object. For we have to do only with our representations; how things may be in themselves (without respect to the representations through which they are given to us) is entirely outside the sphere of our cognition. Now, although the appearances are not things in themselves, and yet are all that can be given to us for cognition, I am to indicate what sort of connection in time pertains to the manifold in the appearances itself even though the representation of it in apprehension is always successive.

(A 190 / B 235)

And after saying that even the perception of the manifold parts of a house is successive, Kant comments: "That which lies in the successive apprehension is considered as representation, yet the appearance which is given to me is considered as the object of that representation, notwithstanding that it is nothing more than the content [*Inbegriff*] of these representations" (A 191 / B 236). Some have taken this final comment, in particular – especially since *Inbegriff* can also be translated, as it was by Kemp Smith, to mean a *sum*, or literally an aggregate of parts – to mean that Kant's problem is posed by *phenomenalism*[45] – that is, by a *reduction* of empirical objects to actual aggregations of representations as such.[46] The problem of *knowing* empirical objects then becomes one of *constituting* them out of aggregations of representations, or adding to the latter some further content (as it turns out, of course, necessary connection) which will make it meaningful to speak of *objects,* as opposed to mere representations.

If that were what Kant had in mind, what would be problematic to him would not be Hume's problem about *causation,* but rather his predecessor's problem about *continued existence*: that is, how we come to know *unchanging* objects on the basis of ever-*changing* representations; how we *avoid* carrying over the successiveness of our representations into the objects which are nevertheless supposed to be literally constituted out of them. But if that were Kant's problem, it would hardly be natural for him to begin by asking after an additional condition for the representation *of alteration.* Moreover, it is not what Kant's argument implies. Kant's use of the distinction between appearances and things in themselves is meant only as an additional argument for the thesis that we have no access to empirical objects except by means of our always successive representations of them. If we thought that the proper objects of our knowledge were things in themselves, then of course we would not even think of carrying over the successiveness of our representations into the states of those objects, because we would know that there is no necessary connection between the features of such objects and the means by which we represent them – of course, we should know in particular that there can be no connection of any kind between those objects and the *temporal* features of our representations of them. But appearances – empirical objects – are not things in themselves, that is, not things which are detached necessarily from *all* features of our representations of them, and they *are* what we are given by means of the representation of them. Yet nevertheless we still do not carry over to them *all* features of our representations of them, including the successiveness of our representations. So, Kant asks, on what basis do we then reasonably decide *only sometimes* that the objects of successive representations are themselves successive states of affairs, more particularly successive determinations of substances?

Many other formulations of Kant's question make it even clearer that the problem to which the principle of causation is the answer is this problem about the way we are *given* empirical objects, and not one posed by the literal *reduction* of such objects to aggregates of representations. In these other formulations, Kant clearly draws a distinction between representations and appearances, clearly equates the latter with empirical objects, and then clearly asks, not how we can *constitute* empirical objects out of representations, but rather simply how we can *distinguish* between change and coexistence in empirical objects, when the data for judgments about such objects which we are actually given, namely representations, are in *all* cases strictly successive. Things in themselves are never even mentioned after the one passage quoted (on which so many commentators have based their interpretations), because of course no one would even raise the question of how we might make distinctions about *their* determinations on the basis of the determinations of inner sense.

Thus, the opening of the argument in the second edition proceeds without the use of such ontological categories as appearances and things in themselves and uses only the epistemological distinction between representations and their objects:

> ... Time cannot be perceived in itself, nor can what precedes and what follows in objects be determined as it were empirically in relation to it. I am therefore conscious only that my imagination sets one [state] before, the other after, not that the one state precedes the other in the object; or, in other words, the *objective* relation of successive appearances remains undetermined by means of perception.
> (B 233–4)

Here what is claimed is that though we may assume that there *is* an objective relation – which will be either of coexistence or succession – between two objective states of affairs, the order of our perceptions or representations *of* those states cannot determine which relation obtains, since that order is always successive.

Similarly, the paragraph which concludes the discussion of the unchanging house and the moving ship contains no hint of reductionism:

In our case I must therefore derive the *subjective succession* of apprehension from the *objective succession* of appearances, since the former is otherwise entirely undetermined and distinguishes no appearance from any other. The former [succession] alone proves nothing about the connection of the manifold in the object, because it is entirely arbitrary. The latter [succession] will therefore consist in the order of the manifold of appearance according to which the apprehension of the one [state] (that which happens) follows on that of the other (which precedes) *according to a rule.* Only by that means can I be justified in saying of the appearance itself, and not merely of my apprehension, that in it a succession is to be found, which means as much as that I cannot order the apprehension otherwise than in this very succession. (A 193 / B 238)

There is no suggestion here that appearances are in any sense the *same* as what is directly given in apprehension, namely representations. Kant is merely arguing that because appearances can be known only by *means of* representations, and the latter, taken by themselves, have the same kind of order whether they represent an event or occurrence or not, the additional factor of a rule must be brought to bear to make the necessary distinction.

Kant's next statement of his problem takes the form of a *reductio*:

If one supposes that nothing preceded an occurrence from which it must follow according to a rule, then all succession of perception would be only in apprehension, that is, merely subjective, but it would not be objectively determined thereby which among the perceptions must be the preceding and which the succeeding. In such a case we would have only a play of perceptions, which would not be related to any object: That is, through our perceptions no appearance would be distinguished from any other as far as its time-relation is concerned, since the succession in the apprehending is always of the same sort and there is therefore nothing in the appearance which determines it so that thereby a particular succession would be made objectively necessary. I would therefore not say that two states succeed one another in the appearance, rather only that one apprehension follows the other, which is something merely *subjective,* and determines no object, thus which cannot count as the cognition of any object (even in appearance). (A 194-5 / B 239-40)

Again the claim is clearly just that the purely successive order of apprehension as such – which is nevertheless all that we are ever directly given as evidence of the existence of empirical objects – cannot suffice to distinguish an occurrence from an absence of change, so that a rule determining that one state of affairs *must* succeed another must be added to the successive order of the perceptions themselves to do this.

Finally, let me adduce one similar but briefer statement of the principle of the proof:

... Even in experience we never ascribe to the object the succession (of an event, of something happening that previously was not) and distinguish it from the subjective [succession] of our apprehension, except when a rule is the ground which *necessitates* that we observe this order of perceptions rather than another; indeed, it is really this necessitation itself which first makes possible the representation of succession in the object. (A 196-7 / B 241-2)

Again, no reduction of empirical objects to sums of representations is suggested. Kant just claims that we need something in addition to the succession of representations which we are always given, namely a rule, in order to interpret that succession as the representation *of* succession in the empirical object.

Of course, all of these passages presuppose that it is coherent for us to posit objects numerically distinct from our representations of them, even if we are never directly *given* anything but those representations. That such an antiphenomenalistic assumption is not only coherent but necessary is precisely what Kant shows in the refutation of idealism. Before we can turn to that, however, we must examine Kant's defense of a principle of universal interaction in the third analogy, for that is not merely the last of the three synthetic *a priori* propositions which Kant always had in mind to defend but also, as we saw, an indispensable support for the argument of the *first* analogy as well.

The third analogy: interaction

The argument of the third analogy can be expounded briefly. This does not reflect its lack of importance in Kant's transcendental theory of experience, however. Quite the contrary: Although many recent commentators have given short shrift to this argument,[1] it is necessary to complete the argument of the first analogy and the interdependent theory of the analogies as a whole. More broadly, the third analogy is of fundamental importance for Kant's picture of physical science, because it is clearly intended to demonstrate that in the absence of direct perceptions of positions in absolute *space* (up to this point, of course, Kant has emphasized only the implications of the impossibility of any direct perception of *temporal* positions) spatial positions can be empirically determined only within the context of a system of complete interaction among the occupants of those positions. Kant thus takes the opportunity offered by a discussion of the necessary conditions for determinate judgment about the third "mode" of time, simultaneity (a temporal relation often assumed to be directly perceivable, and thus to have no special conditions of possibility at all),[2] to sketch (or barely sketch) an argument for the fundamentally Newtonian, and profoundly anti-Leibnizian, thesis of universal interaction among numerically distinct substances, resting his argument on nothing other than the equally basic Leibnizian premise that the perception of spatial position must always be relative rather than absolute. Thus, the third analogy must be seen as the culmination of Kant's lifelong effort to provide foundations for Newtonian science, while rejecting both Newton's metaphysics of absolute space independent of the subject of experience and Leibniz's metaphysics of utterly independent rather than completely interacting substances.

The profound centrality of the principle of interaction in Kant's effort to connect the most essential elements of the Newtonian world-view to the most basic features of empirical time-determination was indeed recognized by the older generation of Kant scholars. Thus Ernst Cassirer described "Newton's law of gravitation [through which] the spatial position and motion of every member of the cosmos is explained as a function of all the rest, and these in turn as a function of it, ... this total reciprocity, which ... constitutes for us the objective whole of physical space itself," as Kant's "essential archetype of all natural knowledge,"[3] and H. J. Paton wrote that Kant recognized "that the concept of interaction is the most fundamental concept of science. Scientific laws are not expressed in the form 'A is the cause of B', but in the form of equations; and the world as known to science is not a series of causal successions parallel to, and independent of, one another, but is rather a *system* of functional relations between measurable quantities."[4] However, the utterly anti-Leibnizian impetus of Kant's replacement of the idea of a community of substances severally dependent on an external cause (which he himself still accepted even as late as the inaugural dissertation of 1770) with a community entirely dependent upon thoroughgoing interaction among the several substances which comprise it has not been noted as often.[5]

To be sure, the fundamental scientific as well as metaphysical significance of the third analogy is hardly made plain by Kant's brief exposition of his argument.[6] In particular, the role of this analogy in the determinations of spatial position essential for physical theory is not brought out in the statement of its principle in the first edition of the *Critique*. This statement of the "Principle of Coexistence" or "Simultaneity" [*Zugleichseins*], in accord with the program of the schematism and indeed of Kant's underlying theory of time-determination, emphasizes only the temporal: "All substances, so far as they are simultaneous, stand in thoroughgoing community (that is, interaction) with one another" (A 211). Space enters into the formulation of the principle only in the second edition:[7] "All substances, so far as they can be perceived to be simultaneous in space, are in thoroughgoing interaction" (B 256). The statement in the first edition may be preferable because it states a more general principle, from which the principle of the second edition follows as an instance. But given that space as a form of intuition is a synthetic but necessary condition on *our* perception of external objects, and that we do not have anything that counts as direct perception of mental rather than physical substances beyond our own cases, and thus have no possibility of direct perception of interaction among nonspatial substances, the actual extension of the more general statement is no larger than that of the more specific statement. Further, the statement of the principle in the second edition might be preferred because it clearly displays the epistemological character of Kant's argument.[8] There is no logical or metaphysical necessity that independent substances interact;[9] instead, what Kant argues is only that cognitive subjects like us, who cannot simply read off the temporal relations of represented objects from the temporal relations of our representations of them – because, once again, all representations as such are successive – can only confirm judgments that represented objects *coexist* on the basis of knowledge that they *interact*. And the extension of the argument to the specific case of objects in different positions of space has precisely the same epistemological character: Since the *perception* of such objects, even if they coexist, can be only successive, the belief that they coexist can be grounded only by the assumption that they interact. Belief in interaction is epistemically necessary "in order that the succession which is always in the perceptions as apprehensions will not be ascribed to the objects, rather that these can be represented as existing simultaneously" (A 214 / B 261).

The crux of Kant's argument has obviously escaped some commentators. Thus Strawson thinks that just as the second analogy rested on a fallacy about causation, so the third results from a fallacy about simultaneity:

Just as in the second Analogy the necessary order of perceptions is equated with the causal determination of objective change, so in the third the order-indifference of perceptions is equated with the mutual causal influence of coexistent objects. The thought that at the very moment at which we are actually perceiving the object A we might instead be perceiving the object B and vice versa is held to contain implicitly the thought that the two objects are in reciprocal causal interaction.[10]

There is one statement in the third analogy which might seem to contain the same kind of confusion between necessary connection among representations and necessary connection among the objects they represent which is the gist of the *non sequitur* charge made about the second analogy. Immediately preceding the last line quoted in the preceding paragraph (A 214 / B 261), what Kant says must be the case if we are not to ascribe succession in representations to the objects themselves, or what is required to believe that a "subjective community" of representations rests on an "objective ground," is that "the perception of one [object], as ground, make possible the perception of the other, and vice versa" (A 214 / B 261). But in spite of this one confusing statement, Kant's intentions in the third analogy are clearer than almost anywhere else in the "Analytic of Principles."

The task of the third analogy is to explain how we can be justified in judging that states of affairs coexist, on the basis of our necessarily successive perceptions of them. Since the second analogy has shown that states of affairs can be judged to *succeed* one another only if they are connected to causal laws which dictate that, in the circumstances, they must, it might be thought that judgments of coexistence could be arrived at by a simple process of exclusion, simply in view of the *absence* of a causal law. But this would not do: In general, because it is clearly Kant's intent to show that there is *nothing* in the natural world that is free of the rule of causality, and, in particular, because in any given case the *apparent* absence of a causal law of the appropriate kind could always be interpreted as mere *ignorance,* mere failure to have so far discovered the relevant law, and so it would leave undetermined whether or not the represented states of affairs coexisted or not. We can no more directly discern the absence of any applicable causal law than we can directly perceive the absence of a given state of affairs at an empty point in time. Rather, judgments of coexistence require a foundation of their own which cannot be confused with mere ignorance of the kind of causal connection on which knowledge of succession depends. In fact, this condition is more, rather than less, demanding than the condition of the possible experience of succession, for it requires that objects properly judged to coexist must be known to stand in interaction or a relation of mutual causation, and not just that one be the cause (or a prior condition which is lacking the particular cause) of the other.

Kant's argument is basically this. In the case of succession, it has been shown that the occurrence of an event dictates an irreversible sequence in the perceptions of its constituent states. So the absence of such an irreversible sequence, reversibility or the possibility of having a sequence of representations in the opposite order from what actually occurs, must be a necessary condition (i.e., consequence) of the coexistence rather than succession of two states of affairs. But two problems stand in the way of any immediate inference from reversibility to coexistence. First, as Kant emphasizes in the new first paragraph of the analogy which he supplies in the second edition, we are no more directly given the *reversibility* of a sequence of perceptions than we are directly given its irreversibility. "The synthesis of imagination in apprehension would yield only that one of these representations is in the subject when the other is not there," but it would reveal nothing more about their possible reversibility, for "time itself cannot be perceived in such a way that we can deduce from things being set in the same time that the perceptions of them could follow each other reciprocally" (B 257). As always, we are simply given successive representations, and we are *given* nothing about their *modality* from which their possible objective significance could be deduced without further information.[11] Second, although this is not quite as clear, Kant also seems to be suggesting (and certainly should suggest) that even if we did somehow know that a given series of *representations* could occur in the opposite order, this would not be a *sufficient* condition for judging that the *objects* represented by them coexisted: We would still have to exclude the possibility that the represented objects were succeeding each other in precisely the same reversed order as their representations would be under the assumption that the sequence of the latter is reversed.[12]

A certain imprecision in Kant's opening paragraph in the original exposition of the argument may obscure this point. What Kant says here is that

Things are simultaneous insofar as they exist in one and the same time. But on what basis does one know that they are in one and the same time? If the order in the synthesis of the apprehension of this manifold is indifferent, that is, can go from A through B, C, D, to E, or also vice versa from E to A. For, if they were successive to one another in time (in the order which commences with A and ends in E), it [would be] impossible to begin with the apprehension of E and proceed backward to A, since A belongs to past time and can no longer be an object of apprehension.

(A 211 / B 258)

Let us simplify matters by dealing with two states of affairs instead of five. What Kant is saying is that if the *perceptions of* states of affairs A and B (which will again be symbolized as "A_r" and "B_r") represent coexisting rather than successive states of affairs, then they must be able to occur in either of two orders – A_r-then-B_r or B_r-then-A_r – whereas if they represent the event A-then-B they can occur only in the order A_r-then-B_r (and, *mutatis mutandis,* if they represent B-then-A). But we have no direct evidence of the reversibility of a sequence of perceptions, any more than of its irreversibility. Even if we had what could seem to be the best sort of empirical evidence for such reversibility that we could imagine – that is, a series like A_r-then-B_r-then-A_r, we would still lack direct evidence for the *coexistence* of any objective states of affairs. For – and this is what Kant's example does not make completely clear – we cannot have the actual *reversal* of any particular series of representation *tokens,* even if such a thing would allow us to directly infer the coexistence of their objects. That is, a series we might be tempted to describe as A_r-then-B_r-then-A_r does not really involve just *two* representational states, referring directly to two objective states of affairs which must coexist so that A_r can recur after B_r. For remember, again, that *particular representations* as such are always fleeting and transitory; thus the same representation cannot recur after some interruption of its first occurrence, although a qualitatively similar representation – another representation of the same type, that is to say, with similar content – may. Thus a series of the type described is actually a series of *three tokens of two types* of representations: that is, A_r' followed by B_r' followed by A_r'', or A_r-at-t_1 followed by B_r-at-t_2 followed by A_r-at-t_3. But from this it does not follow directly that we *could* have had a representation of the *type* B_r followed by one of the *type* A_r at that moment of time when we in fact experienced the *tokens* A_r' followed by B_r', let alone that the *objective* states of affairs A and B coexist through that span of time (t_1 through t_2) or through the longer span of time (t_1 through t_3) occupied by all three tokens in the series of representations that seemed to constitute an actual reversal. Because representations are fleeting and transitory, we never have the same *tokens* even of representations of the same type twice, so it does not follow directly that the same *object* exists simultaneously with a series of tokens of the same type, let alone during the intervals occupied by tokens of representations of *another* type. Therefore, coexistence cannot be inferred *directly* from any immediate knowledge of the reversibility or even actual reversal of representations. As in the case of irreversibility, the reversibility of representations would be a *consequence* of coexistence and might therefore be a symptom of it – but for the fact that it is not directly given.

There must therefore be some sort of rule from which the coexistence of represented objects *and* the reversibility of the representations of them can be inferred.[13] This requirement Kant expresses by saying that

In addition to the mere existence [of A and B] there must therefore be something through which A determines the position of B in time, and vice versa also B that of A, since only under this condition can the intended substances be empirically represented as *existing at the same time.* Now something determines the position of another in time only if it is the cause of it or of its determination. Therefore every substance must ... contain in itself the causality of certain determinations in the other ...   (A 212 / B 259)

What is the basis of this conclusion? Kant must be reasoning thus: If both A and B are to coexist through the whole period of time t_1 to t_2 in which I have, for instance, a succession of representations of the type A_r-then-B_r, and if *a fortiori* I am to know that instead of that sequence I could then have had representations of the type B_r-then-A_r, then I must know that at the time t_1 when I was perceiving A – that is, having representation A_r – I *could have* been perceiving B (having B_r) instead. But my only basis for believing this must be the belief that the state of B at t_1 "determines the position" of A as also existing at t_1. This is because (1) since I am having A_r at t_1, my mere representation at t_1 gives me no direct evidence for the existence of B at t_1. (2) Since I have actually had a representation of type A_r at t_1, there is no way for me to actually have a representation of type B_r *at t_1* and in that way to obtain direct evidence for the existence of B at t_1. Even if I really undertake the experiment of reversing my sequence of representations, the most I will achieve is a representation of type B_r at some *later* moment entirely, such as t_3, and this will have no direct bearing on the state of affairs at t_1. Finally (3) no causal relation in which the state of A or B at some time determines the other at a *succeeding* time will provide any evidence for their simultaneous existence. Thus, (4) only a relationship between A and B such that the state of A at t_1 is necessarily connected with the state of B *at t_1* will provide me with the evidence necessary to judge that, although it was A that I was perceiving at t_1, B also existed at t_1 and *a fortiori* could have been perceived by me then. That is, although I am having A_r at t_1 because I am perceiving A then, the existence and state of A at that time must also imply the simultaneous existence of B. The *ground* for such an inference, in turn, would have to be that the state of A at that time either actually depends on the simultaneous existence of B or else that it must produce it: that, for one reason or the other, the state of the one is a necessary condition of the state of the other, thus that the state of one object at one moment must be either necessary cause or necessary effect of the state of the other at that moment. Further, Kant might also be supposed to have inferred that, since B exists when I am having A_r, and I could therefore (at least as far as the objects are concerned) be having B_r instead, then if I *were* to be having B_r I would still have to know that A exists to make my judgment of the simultaneity of A and B, and would therefore also have to have reason to believe that when I can perceive B, I *could* also perceive A – and the only basis for this would be that B in fact depends on A. So, Kant concludes, a judgment of simultaneity requires mutual causation or interaction between the simultaneous objects.

As will have been noted, there is a problem here about the transition from *causal* relations to *interactions*. What Kant's argument requires is simply that the existence of one object in one state at one moment necessitate the existence of another object in another state at that same moment, so that it may be inferred that both objects actually exist at the same moment and *a fortiori* that either could be perceived then. But this logical relation of necessitation will be satisfied if one object *either* depends upon *or* produces the state of the other at that moment; it is therefore not obvious that each state must be *both* cause and effect of the other. Yet that is what Kant seems to suppose when he says that "only that which is the cause of another, or of its determinations, determines the position of the other in time" (A 212 / B 260). Thus, although Kant's more abstract definitions of "influence" or "reciprocity" would seem to be satisfied by necessitation dependent upon production in either direction – "the relation of substances in which the one contains determinations of the ground of the other is the relation of influence, and when each reciprocally contains the ground of the determinations in the other, the relation is that of community or reciprocity" (B 257–8) – his conclusion that "each substance must . . . contain the causality of certain determinations in the other, and at the same time contain in itself the effects of the causality of the other" (A 212 / B 259) seems to go beyond what he has proved. This is only that in order to judge two states of two objects to exist simultaneously, given the always successive nature of our representations, those two states must be linked by a law which dictates that they *must* exist simultaneously, but although it might, such a law need not imply that there is some way in which each state actually produces the other.

This problem might have been avoided if Kant had restricted the definition of causality to the production by one object of a *successive* state of another; then it would be necessary to introduce an alternative name for the simultaneous dependence of the state of one object on that of another, and any of Kant's terms such as "community" or "reciprocal interaction" might be selected for that purpose. As we saw, however, Kant excluded that easy solution precisely by allowing for the possibility of simultaneous causation.[14] But perhaps, as Kemp Smith at least suggested,[15] this problem is not really a very deep one. Kant has shown that in order for us to be able to make determinate judgments about either the successive or coexistent states of separate substances, we need to be able to call upon – or at least presuppose – *laws* which entail – or in this sense necessitate – successive as well as simultaneous relationships among the states of those objects, for neither the mere succession of representations alone nor any indication of absolute temporal position by such representations can ground such judgments. This is a major accomplishment. Further suppositions about which states "produce" which, or rather "flow" from which, may merely be remnants of premodern thinking about natural laws, involving notions of agency, rather than just entailment, that may have no place in modern science and that are in any event not justified by the character of Kant's own argument for laws of succession and simultaneity. In any case, Newton and Hume had already disposed of such elements in their accounts of natural laws, and it would certainly have been enough for Kant's defense of Newtonian science against Humean skepticism and Leibnizian metaphysics if he had shown that it is an epistemological necessity and neither just a psychological habit nor a confused perception of divine harmony that we employ laws of nature necessitating both successive and simultaneous relationships among the objective states of affairs that we place in time. As Paton has suggested, as long as Kant has demonstrated that the objective world must be comprised of "substances in interaction, and cannot consist of substances whose states succeed one another (according to causal law) in complete independence of all other substances and all other similar successions" – or that we are not reduced to "a streaky view of causation" – "then manifestly his doctrine is of importance."[16] Given the requirement of laws with both kinds of consequences, the particular details of definitions of "causation" and "interaction" are not of much significance.[17]

Let us now consider how Kant intended the argument to be applied to the specific case of objects supposed to coexist at different points in space. Kant claims that "empty space," or absolute space, is not a possible object of perception (A 214 / B 261). Thus we cannot perceive that objects coexist at different points in space simply by perceiving their positions in absolute space. Their spatial positions, as it were, are not directly marked on our several perceptions of them. From this it follows that we cannot judge that two objects are in different positions in space except by judging them to interact with each other. For we do not have *simultaneous representations* of objects in different regions of space, of course; we have only successive representations of them. But if their spatial positions are not marked in the individual perceptions of them, by a self-evident relation to position in absolute space, then the very fact that they *are* in different regions of space – that they are not just different objects or states of affairs in one and the same place but existing and being perceived at different times – can be grounded only in the judgment that what is being perceived at one time *depends* upon the continued existence of the other object in another part of space, and vice versa. Conversely, if we supposed that objects separated in space had *no* causal relationship to each other, then "the perception which advances from the one to the other in time would, to be sure, determine their existence by means of a successive perception, but would not be able to distinguish whether the one appearance objectively follows on the other or is rather simultaneous with it" (A 212 / B 259). Very simply, Kant's argument is that since we cannot perceive at a single moment states of objects which exist simultaneously but which are in two different places, we can determine that perceptions really do represent objects in two different places only by judging that the perception of one is dependent on the continued existence of the other in a different place, and vice versa. Absolute space not being available for perception, dynamical interaction among objects in space is necessary in order to explain how we can even have empirical knowledge of the difference of positions in space.

Since empirical confirmation of simultaneous existence will require the continued existence of objects – at least if the actual reversal of series of perceptions is a necessary, even if not sufficient, condition for empirical judgments of simultaneity – the third analogy adds further grounds for the existence of enduring substances to those provided in the argument of the first analogy. In fact, enduring substances are necessary not just to determine the occurrence of objective *change* but also to perceive the variety of *place*. This of course means that enduring substances are necessary to perceive motion, but they are also necessary even for the possibility of observed stability in a multiplicity of places. And all of this works only if these objects are also in interaction, which is in turn an extension of causal connection. Thus, all three analogies are ultimately interdependent. And they show that determinations of temporal relation and spatial position are intimately linked: The determination of change presupposes that of endurance, which in turn requires knowledge of spatial positions; but knowledge of spatial position, in turn, requires knowledge of interactions, which are themselves temporal relations among spatially distinct objects. The determination of the apparently simplest temporal relations actually requires an indivisible network of relations of space, time, and natural law, indeed at least the regulative ideal of a fully determinate system of nature.[18]

Of course, all of this has thus far been argued on the supposition that we *are* entitled to make claims about the temporal relations of *objective* states of affairs as opposed to merely subjective ones. Would the entire edifice of enduring substances governed by natural laws that has just been erected collapse if that assumption were omitted from its foundation? The answer to this question is to be found in the next stage of Kant's theory, apparently discovered only in the final revision of the *Critique* and hardly worked out even there – namely, the new "Refutation of Idealism" of 1787. Here, Kant will argue that even temporal determinations about our own mental life, unwittingly assumed by even the most skeptical philosophers to be immediately given and to require no framework for justification at all, do stand in need of a framework in which they can be confirmed – and that this is the very framework of law-governed enduring substances which has just been erected. In other words, although the assumption that we can make objective as well as merely subjective time-determinations might seem a gratuitous even if natural habit, the fact is that without objective time-determinations – and their necessary conditions – even merely subjective time-determinations, taken for granted by even the most rabid skeptic that Kant could imagine, would be impossible.

The "Refutation of Idealism" is the only argument of major significance contained in the final section of the "Principles," the "Postulates of Empirical Thought." Otherwise, the section just gives empirical sense to the abstract concept of possibility by interpreting it as consistency with the formal conditions of sensibility, that is, with the structure of space and time; to the concept of actuality, by interpreting it as requiring both consistency with space and time and satisfaction of the "material condition of experience," that is, sensation; and to the concept of necessity, by holding that its empirical exemplification "is determined in accordance with universal conditions of experience" – that is, just the kind of natural laws which have been shown to be necessary in the analogies (A 218 / B 265–6). This means, of course, that there is little difference between the *extension* of the empirically actual and the empirically necessary – nothing is given by sensation which is not also subject to the principles of substance, causation, and interaction. So there is nothing actual about which determinations of empirical necessity cannot also be made, and although laws about substance, causation, and interaction may sometimes carry us beyond what has actually been sensed, they imply at least the possibility of appropriate sensations in suitable circumstances. So the bounds of empirical necessity do not exceed those of empirical actuality. There is little that requires explanation about these claims, except perhaps the tacit *withdrawal* of the earlier schematization of necessity as "existence of an object at all times" (A 145 / B 184). This withdrawal may not only show the tenuous connection between the official program of the schematism and Kant's underlying argument, but, more important, it suggests that there is no place for claims of necessity in Kant's transcendental theory of experience except in particular claims of causal or interactive necessitation. Thus, the conclusion of the "System of Principles" does not just tacitly withdraw Kant's earlier schematization of the category of necessity but undermines the supposition of his separate transcendental deduction of the 1780s: The category of necessity cannot really be used to license the claims to *a priori* knowledge that served as the premises for Kant's preferred forms of the deduction but can, rather, be applied only in conjunction with the empirical judgments of time-determination whose conditions have now been – so painfully – revealed. This conclusion has significant implications not just for the assessment of Kant's transcendental deduction but also for the evaluation of his transcendental idealism. Before we consider the latter, however, we must examine the second and completing stage of Kant's theory of time-determination, his refutation of idealism.

IV
The refutation of idealism

12
The problem, project, and premise of the refutation

In the preceding part, we examined Kant's arguments that objective states of affairs could be assigned determinate relations of succession and coexistence in time, and ultimately even determinate relations of position in space, only if interpreted as altering or coexisting states of enduring substances thoroughly subject to laws fully determining their successive and simultaneous occurrence. Of course, the *a priori* validity of such principles of objective time-determination presupposes that we *are* entitled to make empirical judgments about the properties and relations of objects distinct from our own representations of them, in spite of the obvious fact that our access to such objects is always through these representations. Thus the demonstration of the objective validity of the *a priori* concepts by means of their role in empirical time-determination cannot accomplish Kant's original objective of proving against both empiricist and skeptic that the understanding can "construct for itself entirely *a priori* concepts of things, with which the things are necessarily in agreement" (letter to Marcus Herz, 21 February 1772, 10:130–1) without a justification of the practice of objective time-determination itself. Further, we have now seen that there is an even more intimate connection between the objective and subjective stages of Kant's theory of time-determination. Kant's central argument for the principle of causation can be saved from the traditional objection of fallacy only by the recognition that determinate knowledge of even the merely subjective succession of experiences is not the product of passive acquaintance with successively apprehended representations but itself depends on empirical judgment connecting these representations to the realm of enduring and rule-governed objects. The actual accomplishment of the several goals of Kant's deduction of the categories thus requires an argument that it is necessary for us to make empirical judgments about enduring objects governed by laws of causation and interaction precisely because such judgments are themselves the conditions of the possibility of determinate consciousness of the temporal relations of even subjective states. It is just such an argument which Kant ultimately tried to supply with the refutation of idealism which he added to the second edition of the *Critique*. Of course, given his natural attachment to the architectonic he had finally created, particularly to the idea of a direct inference from *a priori* certainty of apperception to its transcendental ground, Kant hardly makes explicit the absolutely central role of his new refutation which completes the painstaking demonstration that even merely empirical judgments about the self require the objective validity of the categories. Instead, he just inserts it as a comment on the "postulate" that connection to perception by natural law is the schema of the modal category of actuality.

The problem of the refutation

Kant's intentions in his refutation of idealism have been no more self-evident to his readers than they were to himself. To be sure, Kant's announcement of the thesis of the refutation and of its basic premises could hardly be more emphatic. The thesis that will finally save philosophy from scandal (B xl) is the bold claim that "*the mere, but empirically determined consciousness of my own existence proves the existence of objects in space outside me.*" The argument for this thesis is supposed to turn on the equally bold claims that "all time-determination presupposes something *permanent*[1] in perception" and that "perception of this permanent is possible only through a *thing* outside me and not through the mere *representation* of a thing outside me" (B 275; see also B xl). But these boldly asserted claims nevertheless raise two serious problems of interpretation. (1) First, in spite of the stress Kant places on the contrast between a "thing outside me" and a "mere representation," it is not obvious what this contrast *means*. Thus, exactly *what* thesis the refutation is supposed to prove is unclear. (2) Second, nothing in the published text of the refutation explains *how* its conclusion is supposed to be reached. It offers no argument at all for the premise that something permanent is needed to make temporal determinations, and only a woefully schematic one for the thesis that whatever satisfies this function must be something distinct from the self and any of its own representations in whatever way is in fact intended.

(1) It is easy to explain *why* the intended conclusion of the refutation must be obscure in spite of Kant's strongly voiced distinction between a thing outside me and the mere representation of such a thing: Kant's discussion of idealism in the first edition of the *Critique* had claimed that the very "expression *outside us* is unavoidably ambiguous." In the fourth of the "Paralogisms of Pure Reason," as presented in the edition of 1781, Kant had argued that a reference to a thing "outside us" might be understood to signify "what as *thing in itself* exists distinct from us," that is, what is conceived as ontologically independent of ourselves, but could also be taken to mean just "what belongs solely to outer *appearance*," that is, what has the phenomenological form of things "which *are to be found in space*," *without* being conceived as "external in the transcendental sense," that is, ontologically independent of us (A 373).[2] Moreover, the Kant of 1781 did not merely diagnose this ambiguity. Rather, he argued that the problem of "skeptical idealism," the incapacity to prove the existence of external objects (A 377) because of the necessary inconclusiveness of any attempt to infer to their existence as the cause of our representations of them (A 368, 372), could be solved only by his own "transcendental idealism," *understood precisely as* "the doctrine that appearances are to be

regarded as being, one and all, representations only, not things in themselves" (A 369). That is, Kant did not merely contrast the concepts of ontological and phenomenological externality, or numerical distinctness from the self and any of its states, on the one hand, and the mere form of spatiality on the other; he also argued that objects with spatial form *had* to be reduced to what are ontologically merely states of the self, in order to render them safe from doubt. He held, of course, that there was a phenomenological difference between representation of inner states and of external objects but insisted that "external objects (bodies), however, are mere appearances, and are therefore nothing but a species of my representations, the objects of which are something only through these representations" (A 370). "Matter and corporeal things" are "merely appearances, that is, mere kinds of representation, which are never to be met with save in us, and the reality of which depends on immediate consciousness, just as does the reality of our own thoughts" (A 372). Reductionism did not play a central role in Kant's proof of the principle of *causation* in 1781 or at any other time, but it did in fact constitute his – obviously Pyrrhic – answer to skepticism about objective reality itself. But if in 1781 Kant held that external objects could be ontologically reduced to a variety of our own representations yet still be described as "outside us," then it can hardly be self-evident that when he claims in 1787 that the temporal determinations of self-consciousness require "objects in space outside us" he means to prove the independent existence of things numerically distinct from the self and its states. He could just mean to add an argument that we must have representations with the form of spatiality, as well as ones without it. And indeed Kant's prefatory amplification of the refutation claims that the new addition is "one affecting the method of proof only" (B xxxix). So unless there is additional evidence about Kant's intentions in the refutation of idealism, it must certainly remain unclear that this argument is meant to constitute a decisive break with the reductionism of 1781 and to furnish instead the key to metaphysics sought since 1772 – a proof that concepts which are known *a priori* and therefore must have a source in the constitution of our own minds can nevertheless be known to apply to objects which exist independently of ourselves and our representations of them.

The majority position on the interpretation of the refutation has indeed been that it is intended to be entirely consistent with the ontological reduction of external objects to groups of representations advocated by the fourth paralogism of 1781. This is what has been argued by a long line of distinguished Kantians such as Hans Vaihinger, Edward Caird, Robert Adamson,[3] H. J. Paton,[4] and Gerhard Lehmann.[5] Only a scorned minority party of such figures as Benno Erdmann, Henry Sidgwick, Arthur Balfour,[6] and H. A. Prichard[7] have clearly defended the view that the argument of 1787, whether so intended or not, requires a radical departure from the position of 1781. When the alternative to the reductionism of 1781 is understood to be that in knowing things in space *we know things as they are in themselves,* the reason for this scorn is obvious. The assumption on which this traditional debate about the refutation of idealism revolves is that Kant must either advocate the reduction of external objects to subjective states of mind or permit knowledge of things as they are in themselves. What will be argued here, however, is that this assumption conflates *ontological* and *epistemological* conceptions[8] of independence – as indeed did Kant himself in 1781 – and thus misses the force of Kant's position in 1787. For what Kant argues in 1787 is that for purposes of even subjective time-determination we must employ the intuition of space to represent objects which we conceive as existing independently of ourselves, even though for independent reasons he also insists that we must addition-ally acknowledge that the intuition of space (and for that matter even of time) does not represent those independent objects *as* they are in them-selves. The Kant of 1787 advocates epistemological subjectivism but ontological realism.[9]

In fact, the conclusion I will ultimately suggest is even stronger than this compatibility thesis. The participants in the traditional debate have divided over the question of whether the refutation of idealism is intended to prove the existence of things in themselves. The answer to that question is obviously no – if, by "things in themselves," that is, one already understands entities entirely inaccessible to the grasp of the human forms of intuition and, in particular, entities to which temporal predicates cannot apply. For the point of the refutation is precisely to prove that we must be acquainted with enduring objects in space, and endurance is, of course, an essentially temporal predicate. But to insist that the refutation is an argument either about appearances or about things in themselves is simply to prejudge the actual outcome of the argument. In fact, the refutation does not employ transcendental idealist premises,[10] so it provides no internal reason to interpret its conclusion at anything other than face value – thus, as the conclusion that we are indeed justified in claiming to know that objects other than our own representations exist, and that these objects endure through time and are in space as well. Any grounds for taking this conclusion at other than face value must come from outside the argument. Of course, Kant did have reasons for taking the conclusion of this argument at less than face value, and the question can certainly be asked whether the conclusion obviously implied by the refutation of idealism is incompatible with these other views or can be reconciled with them. By using the distinction between the independence of a thing's existence from us and the independence of its characterization from our forms of intuition, which Kant at least sometimes suggests, we can see how to reconcile the realist implications of the refutation with some versions of Kant's transcendental idealism, but Kant also states versions of his transcendental idealism which are incompatible with the implications of the refutation. As we shall see in the concluding part of this book, however, this issue is not terribly important, for the simple reason that although Kant's argument in the refutation of idealism is cogent, his separate arguments for the nonspatiality and nontemporality of things as they are in themselves are not. There is thus certainly no reason to reinterpret the conclusion of the refutation of idealism in order to accommodate transcendental idealism.[11]

(2) It is also unclear *what* argument Kant intended to use to accomplish the objective of the refutation. As I mentioned, the published text simply assumes that something permanent is required for the determination of time and proffers only the most perfunctory argument that such an object cannot be the self or anything in it. Yet if we look to the argument for the connection between permanence and time-determination on which Kant obviously means to rely – that is, of course, the first analogy of experience – we will find nothing which makes it self-evident why determinate judgments about the temporal structure of self-consciousness require claims to knowledge of objects which are external to the self *either* as merely phenomenologically spatial *or* "in the transcendental sense," that is, numerically distinct from the self and independent of its representations for their own existence. As we saw, the first analogy contains three distinct arguments for the thesis that time-determination requires something permanent, but none of these obviously entails that the permanent substance required for the representation of alteration cannot itself be an enduring self or subject of successive *mental* states rather than something which is *spatial* as well as (possibly) ontologically distinct from such a self.[12] Thus, even if it is taken for granted that time-determination requires something which endures, it is not obvious why this cannot be an enduring self.

Kant's argument (1) in the first analogy was that since time itself "remains and does not change" or is the "permanent form of inner intuition," but also "cannot by itself be perceived," its permanence must be represented by something permanent in perception which is its "substratum," and that this substratum must be "substance in appearance" (B 224–5). But as we saw, the assumption on which this argument turned, that the representation of something permanent must itself be permanent, flew in the face of Kant's own claim that "the representation of something *permanent* is not the same as *permanent representation*" (B xli) and thus really could not prove that the permanence of time required a permanent substratum after all. But even waiving that objection, there would still be no obvious reason why such a substratum would have to be a substance which is either spatial in form or ontologically independent from the self. Why should an enduring self not be an adequate substratum for the permanence of time, especially since time itself is apparently nothing more than the form by which we represent "ourselves and our inner state[s]" (A 33 / B 49)?

Kant also suggested the analytical argument (2) for the existence of substance. According to this argument, alteration is not so much a "mode" of time itself but is rather necessarily a feature of enduring objects in time, so that only something which itself endures can even be described as altering its state. But as we saw, without an independent argument that all

283

changes must be *alterations* as so described, this argument had to beg the question of the objective validity of the schema of permanence; a definition alone could not exclude the possibility that all that exists is just simultaneous or successive bundles of states of affairs without anything in which to inhere, whether these disconnected states be conceived of as somehow objectlike or instead as representations, like impressions in a Humean bundle. And in any case, applying the merely analytical requirement that altering states be conceived of as successive states in a single enduring subject to the case of mental states could surely yield only the result that an alteration in *mental* state requires an enduring *mental* substance. An analytical argument from alteration to permanence could hardly prove that subjective time-determination requires something spatial, let alone something ontologically independent of an enduring self.

Even Kant's most persuasive argument in the first analogy, the epistemological argument (3) that changes "can be empirically known only as changing determinations of that which endures" (A 188 / B 231), also fails to make it obvious why an enduring self would not be a sufficient condition for the empirical representation of change of subjective state. According to this argument, there is no way of distinguishing between, on the one hand, two successive perceptions that represent two successive states of affairs, and, on the other hand, two successive perceptions that represent merely a change in which of two coexistent states is being perceived, except by invoking in the first case an object which has a history of change such that the two perceptions can *only* represent successive rather than coexistent states of it, and which of course must endure in order to have such a history. But why should the enduring *self* itself not be the kind of enduring and law-governed substance which permits such discriminations to be made? And indeed, when we are not considering observations of *external* objects, where the issue of *changing* as opposed to merely *different* but not themselves changing objects arises, but are instead dealing with changing *representations* themselves, why should any special condition for empirical determination of succession be required at all? If the representation of something enduring is required to discriminate between a change in objects and a mere change in representations, it is not obvious after all that anything permanent is needed merely to represent the changing representations themselves. The fundamental question first raised by the argument of the *Duisburg Nachlass* – Why does self-knowledge require rules? – still remains to be answered.

So neither the published refutation of idealism nor the first analogy of experience to which it alludes makes obvious either the exact metaphysical import of the conclusion which Kant meant this refutation to reach or the argument by which he intended to defend his conclusion. However, Kant must have recognized almost immediately the inadequacy of his new refutation, at least the insufficiency of its actual argumentation, for even before the revisions of 1787 were ready for the press Kant added two emendations which attempt to provide additional support for its conclusion. Yet neither of these passages succeeds in putting beyond doubt the intended thesis or argument of Kant's new attack on skeptical idealism.

(1) A long footnote to the second-edition preface contains the first (at least in order of appearance) of these emendations. The initial objective of this note is to improve upon the blunt assertion of the main refutation that the enduring object required for the time-determination even of self-consciousness "cannot . . . be something in me, since it is only through this permanent thing that my existence in time can itself be determined" (B 275). For this statement, Kant tells us, the following should be substituted:

But this permanent cannot be an intuition in me. For all grounds of determination of my existence which are to be met with in me are representations, and as representations themselves require a permanent distinct from them, in relation to which their change, and so my existence in the time wherein they change, may be determined.

(B xxxix)

Moreover, at the end of the note, Kant remarks that *all* of our representations, "not excluding that of matter" itself, are "very transitory and variable" (B xli). These remarks can be taken to add two premises to the argument of the refutation. First, they lay down the premise that all representations regarded as such – in Cartesian terms, in their formal rather than objective reality – are to be regarded as themselves enjoying only momentary rather than enduring existence.[13] Second, they suggest that the empirical self is presented only by means of such transitory representations, or that determinations about *its* temporal structure can be based only on determinations about *their* temporal relations, and so is not itself available as a permanent object of perception, by reference to which the temporal features of its own representational states may be made determinate. These premises do seem to imply that *if* something permanent is needed in order to make some indispensable determination about the temporal relation of transitory representations, *then* this permanent thing must indeed be something other than any *representation*. But unless it is explained why the impermanence of representations should also imply the nonendurance of the empirical self itself – and after all, Kant's reference to "matter" can mean only that the impermanence of the states of an enduring *physical* substance do not themselves imply the nonendurance of that object – it will still not be apparent why we require knowledge of anything external to the self for subjective time-determination.

Moreover, this note still does not explain *why* something permanent is required for the special purpose of recognizing subjective successions of representations, as opposed to making determinate contrasts between such merely subjective successions and actual objective changes. Kant's emendation does make clear *what* temporal feature of representations a permanent thing is supposed to be necessary to determine, namely, their *change,* or their succession one upon another. But it remains unclear why anything more than mere *acquaintance* with representations which in fact succeed one another in otherwise uninterpreted experience, or anything other than the mere *occurrence* of such representations, should be necessary for one to *judge that* there has been such a succession, if this is what Kant intends. Indeed, as we saw, Kant's *second* analogy of experience is ordinarily understood to assume precisely that one *is* immediately aware "that the manifold of appearances is always generated in the mind successively" (A 190 / B 235) and to argue that the interpretation of one's own representations by reference to objects external to them is necessary *only* to determine whether a succession of representations *also* represents succession rather than coexistence in the states *of such objects.* Just as the permanence of substances seems necessary to make determinate *contrasts* between subjective and objective changes, so does the subjection of external objects to laws of nature. But then it is still obscure why Kant should think that an enduring object, even if necessarily distinct from any representation, is required in order to determine that there is change *in mere representations.*[14]

(2) However, this note to the second-edition preface does not even mention the *spatiality* of the external objects alleged to be necessary for time-determination. To complete the argument for spatiality is apparently the purpose of Kant's other emendation of the refutation, the "General Note on the System of the Principles" (B 288–94) added at the end of the chapter into which the new refutation had already been inserted. Here, Kant again makes two claims.

First, accepting the conclusion of the first analogy that time-determination requires something permanent, he argues that to perceive such an object "we require an intuition in space (of matter)," because "space alone is determined as permanent, whereas time, and therefore everything that is in inner sense, is in constant flux" (B 291). This assertion is utterly opaque, however: For one thing, as we have seen, the first analogy prominently features an argument turning on nothing less than the premise that time *is* permanent, even if not itself perceivable; for another, the endurance of *space* itself is hardly an obvious consequence of Kant's own – and still Leibnizian – definition of space as the form of intuition by which two or more *coexistent* objects may be presented (cf. A 23 / B 38).[15] To be sure, Kant argued in the *third* analogy that only enduring and interacting objects could be empirically determined to occupy distinct positions in *space,* but unless diversity of *spatial* position is shown to be a necessary condition of empirical *time*-determination, the relevance of this conclusion to the conditions of empirical self-consciousness would not be apparent.

Second, Kant claims that the perception of space is a necessary condition of the perception of alteration itself. He argues that reason alone could not comprehend the "combination of contradictorily opposed determinations in the existence of one and the same thing" (B 291) but instead requires an intuition as an example of how such "opposed determinations" can constitute a *change* rather than a *contradiction.* He then asserts that

The intuition required is the intuition of the movement of a point in space. The presence of the point in different locations (as a sequence of opposite determinations) is what alone first yields to us an intuition of alteration. For in order that we may afterward make inner alterations likewise thinkable, we must represent time (the form of inner sense) figuratively as a line, and the inner alteration through the drawing of this line (motion), and so in this manner by means of outer intuition make comprehensible the successive existence of ourselves in different states.

(B 292)

But again these claims are puzzling. First, Kant's claim that it is the motion of an object in space which gives us the idea of alteration is unargued, as is his further claim (in the second-edition text of the transcendental deduction and in the second note to the main refutation itself) that it is only by observing *regular* motions in space ("for instance, the motion of the sun relative to objects on the earth" [B 277]) that we can do anything like assign determinate *magnitudes* to "lengths of time" (B 156). If true at all, these claims would thus seem empirical and contingent, and in any case, we saw in Chapter 9, the assignment of numerical *magnitude* to durations is not obviously involved in Kant's argument for enduring substances. Even less is it a self-evidently necessary condition of empirical *self*-consciousness: It is hardly obvious that making determinate judgments about the *order* of one's representations, for instance, requires that one also have a numerical measure of their *duration*.[16] Second, Kant's present claim seems inconsistent with the suggestion of an earlier passage of the "Principles" chapter that *time* is sufficient to avoid the reduction of opposed determinations to an actual contradiction – that is, that the sheer fact of *succession* suffices to make what would otherwise be contradictory predicates compatible: There is no problem about being both young and old, as long as two different times are at issue (A 152–3 / B 191–2).[17] Unless Kant also has an argument that space is in turn a necessary condition for any representation of time, it is not obvious that he can show space to be a necessary condition for the representation of any kind of change at all. Finally, Kant's claim that the perception of motion in space is necessary even to render *thinkable* the "successive existence of ourselves in different states," which is to say, any succession in representations at all, seems to contradict not only the apparent assumption of the second analogy that rule-governed objects are necessary only to judge *objective* successions but also common sense: How can we become conscious of motions in outer objects without already being capable of recognizing changes in our own representational states as such?

So Kant's initial attempts to improve upon the refutation of idealism do not throw much additional light on the argument he might have had in mind. Fortunately, there is other evidence which can clarify both the thesis which Kant ultimately wished to defend against skeptical idealism and the tactics by which he thought he could attain his goal. For Kant's dissatisfaction with his newly published refutation did not yield only the additional remarks in the preface and "General Note" of 1787; in fact, Kant continued to work at the task of refuting idealism for at least half a dozen years after 1787. His surviving *Nachlass* includes no fewer than ten lengthy fragments from the years 1788 to 1793 which, in view of their titles, form, and content, could only have been intended as improved versions of the argument first attempted in 1787, and thus as efforts to fulfill the intentions of that argument.

As published by Erich Adickes in 1928,[18] these additional attempts at the refutation of idealism are as follows: R 5653–4 (18:305–13), written in the period after 13 October 1788; R 5709 (18:332), dating from some less determinate time in the late 1780s; R 6311–17 (18:606–29), written in conjunction with the visit of Kant's disciple J. C. E. Kiesewetter to Königsberg in the fall of 1790, and R 6323 (18:641–4), from the period of April to August 1793. That these notes represent a continued effort to clarify or accomplish intentions already clearly formulated when Kant published the first refutation of idealism in 1787 cannot of course be established decisively by any single piece of verbal evidence. Nevertheless, the similarities between the titles Kant gave to various of these fragments and the title of the original refutation strongly suggest that in writing them Kant must have conceived of himself as attempting to improve upon what he had only begun in the revision of the *Critique* – a monumental task, after all, that must have been hastily sandwiched in between Kant's equally monumental labors on the *Metaphysical Foundations of Natural Science* of 1786 and the *Critique of Practical Reason* of 1788. Some of these captions, so close to the published title *Widerlegung des Idealismus* of 1787, are: *Gegen den (materialen) Idealism* (R 5653); *Wieder den Idealism* (R 5654); *Widerlegung des problematischen Idealismus* (R 6311); *Wieder den Idealism* (R 6313); *Ueber den Idealism* (R 6314); *Vom Idealism* (R 6315); *Wieder den Idealism* (R 6316); and (a subheading) *Idealism* (R 6323). Far more important than any such terminological similarities, however, is the simple fact that these fragments show Kant struggling to provide answers to precisely the kinds of question about the published refutation that we have just been considering.[19]

And indeed these fragments contain vital clarifications of both the thesis which Kant wished to maintain against idealism in 1787 and the argument – or, as should be no great surprise by now, arguments – by which he thought he could defend this thesis. First, both by their arguments and by certain specific turns of phrase they strongly suggest that in spite of the ambiguity he analyzed in 1781 Kant *did* intend his refutation of 1787 and after[20] to establish the legitimacy of our claim to know of the existence of objects which are ontologically independent of, and not just phenomeno-logically external to, ourselves. In spite of Kant's claim merely to provide a "new method of proof," his new refutation of idealism was meant to break with his reductionism of 1781.[21] Second, Kant's post-1787 versions of the refutation of idealism throw light on the means by which he intended to justify the claim to knowledge of objects conceived of as ontologically independent of the self. Specifically, they contain arguments considerably

288

amplifying the assumptions of Kant's two emendations of 1787, the assumptions that there is a direct connection between the determination of time and *spatial* form and that there is a direct connection between the determination of time and the positing of *enduring objects* other than the self. Neither of the arguments Kant finally suggests is complete in itself, for each ultimately requires appeal to the premise, stated only in the first-edition text of the transcendental deduction, that even the representation of a manifold of intuition as such requires more than a passive synthesis of apprehension. Nevertheless, it is one of these newly expounded arguments which at last suggests what should be done with this fundamental premise of A 99. Finally, these fragments attempt something else which was left undone in the published text. At least some of them explicitly attempt to show how an argument for the thesis that we can know that there are objects independent of ourselves – a position which Kant himself calls "dualism" (R 5653, 18:310), as well as "realism" (R 6315, 18:620) – can be reconciled both with his original analysis that skeptical idealism is due to the inconclusiveness of any causal inference to external objects and with his own transcendental idealism on at least one interpretation of that fluid metaphysical position. For this reconciliation to be effected, we shall see, transcendental idealism must be understood not as the ontological thesis that outer *objects* are themselves reducible to representations but rather as the merely epistemological thesis that *space and time* are only forms for our representation of outer objects and indeed of ourselves, which cannot necessarily be ascribed to those things as they are in themselves – or indeed which necessarily cannot be so ascribed.

As has already been suggested, the failure of Kant's arguments for transcendental idealism may make the task of reconciling the results of the refutation of idealism with that doctrine unnecessary for the contemporary philosopher. But the very fact that Kant himself, who of course accepted transcendental idealism, nevertheless suggested the method for such a reconciliation is one more piece of evidence for the assumption that he himself recognized the ontologically realistic implication of his new refutation of idealism. The issue of transcendental idealism, however, will be reserved for the final part of this book. In the present part, the ontological implications of the refutation, and the method of its arguments, will be considered without further discussion of this reconciliation or its necessity in the first place.

The project and the premise of the refutation

In this section, we shall first consider the evidence offered by its post-1787 versions that the refutation of idealism was meant to justify our claims to knowledge of ontologically independent, and not just phenomenologically spatial, objects. We shall then consider a clarification of the concept of the empirical self which these notes suggest and which is essential to Kant's ultimate justification of this claim to knowledge.

Independent objects

Some of the notes in Kant's *Nachlass* clearly imply that the representation of an object in space is the representation of something numerically distinct from the self without employing any explicitly ontological terms of art. Thus this passage from the first new refutation of 1788 emphasizes that treating the self as itself an object of knowledge requires relating it to something which is represented as outside the self *because* it is represented as *other* than the self:

> That if I make myself into an object space is not in me but (yet) is in the formal subjective condition of the empirical consciousness of myself, that is time, proves that something outside of me, that is, something which I must represent in a different manner [*auf eine andere Art*] than myself, is connected with the empirical consciousness of myself, and the latter (is) at the same time consciousness of an external relation, without which I could not empirically determine my own existence. (R 5653, 18:309)

The nonreductionist implications of this passage lie in the fact that an object in space is said to be represented in a different way than the self is represented. This is hardly a natural thing to say of something which is merely a *state* of the self. Further, such an object is said to stand in an external relation to the self, which is again not a natural thing to say of something which is nothing but a modification of the self (especially for someone writing against the background of the Leibnizian denial of extrinsic relations).[22] The same conclusion seems to be implied a few lines later when Kant says of space itself, rather than of an object in space, that it "is not a representation related to the self (as object)," that is, it does not represent the self, "but is rather immediately *related* to something as existing distinct from the subject" and is *thus* "the consciousness of the object as a thing outside me." Here the phrase "a thing outside me" is virtually glossed as something which is numerically distinct from me.

Other passages emphasize a distinction between an external object and our representation of it. This one, from Kant's second fragment from 1788, is not very clear because it tends to confuse the objective content *intended* by a thought of something independent of the self with the mental status of the *thought* itself, thereby undermining the intended independence:

> ... Every object signifies something distinct from the representation, which, however, is only in the understanding; thus the inner sense itself, which makes ourself an object of our own representation, is related to something distinct [*etwas ... verschiedenes*] from ourself (as transcendental object of apperception). If we did not therefore relate our representations to something distinct from ourself, they would never yield knowledge of objects. (R 5654, 18:312)

Kant's lack of clear terminology for the difference between thought and its intended object – he avails himself neither of Descartes's distinction between formal and objective reality nor of any of the terminology of intentionality revived by Brentano a century after he wrote – obviously hampered him throughout his discussion of idealism. Much clearer, however, is the distinction between a representation and its object invoked in this explict endorsement of realism from 1790:

My representations cannot be outside me, and an external object of representations cannot be in me, for that would be a contradiction. It could well be, however, that although the representation is in me its object is yet without contradiction outside me, or else that the representation together with its object is in me. On idealism it is asserted that it is not possible to decide that the object of a representation is not in me along with its representation, even when the latter is represented (in intuition) as existing outside me. – The realist, on the contrary, asserts of outer intuition that this is possible, and indeed correctly ...   (R 6314, 18:620)

Here Kant explicitly sides with the "realist" and aligns himself precisely with the position that we can know that in addition to our representations objects numerically distinct from them exist – even though this was just what he denied by his equation of appearances or empirical objects with representations in 1781.

The most revealing passages of all, however, are those in which Kant uses his own ontological terminology to assert explicitly that what we know when we know that something exists outside us is that something other than our representations exists *in itself*. Thus, a different fragment from 1790 maintains that the ground of the possibility of a temporal determination (in this case that of simultaneity) "lies in the relation of representations to something outside us, and, indeed, to something which is not in turn merely inner representation, that is, form of appearance, thus, to something which is something in itself [*sache an sich*]" (R 6312, 18:612). And Kant's last effort at the refutation contains this explicit rejection of the reduction of that which serves as the condition of time-determination to any representation *or* succession of representations:

The impossibility of determining [our] existence in the succession of time through the succession of representations in us, and yet the actuality of this determination of [our] existence, [requires] an immediate consciousness of something outside me, which corresponds to these representations,* and this intuition cannot be mere illusion [*Schein*] ...)

*(and which does not exist merely in my representation (rather (as thing) in itself) ...   (R 6323, 18:643)

If we read this as contrasting "something outside me" with any *succession* of my representations and take the latter to include possible as well as actual successions of representations, then this passage precludes the phenomenalist reduction of the contrast between object and representation in general to that between possible sequences of perceptions and particular perceptions with which Kant has so often been charged since 1782. Kant's new method of proving outside objects as the condition of time-determination thus seems intended to secure knowledge of things ontologically independent of ourselves.

Again, the question of how Kant intended to reconcile such an at least relatively robust form of realism with the continued assertion of any form of transcendental idealism, or whether he even needed to do so, will be reserved for the final part of this book. The next item on our agenda is Kant's clarification of the fundamental premise for this justification of realism.

Transcendental and empirical consciousness

In the first of the three notes which follow the 1787 refutation Kant suggests that the underlying premise of the argument is that "inner experience" or "empirical knowledge" of the self – "not indeed the consciousness of my own existence, but the determination of it in time" – requires intuition as well as "the representation 'I am,'" or the mere "thought of something existing" (B 277). But this condition taken by itself which is merely Kant's requirement that empirical judgment involve intuition as well as a concept, would seem to be satisfiable by inner intuition alone. It is therefore not sufficient to generate an inference to anything independent of the self, for it does not explain why mere inner intuition – passive apprehension of representations – is not only *necessary* but at the same time *insufficient* for empirical knowledge of the self. One of Kant's fragments from 1790, however, employs a more complex and suggestive division of the way in which the self is presented. Though the rest of Kant's notes follow the text of 1787 in making explicit only a twofold distinction between "the transcendental consciousness of the self" and "empirical consciousness of myself" (e.g., R 5653, 18:306),[23] this note implies that the refutation of idealism requires a *threefold* distinction between

[1] the transcendernal consciousness of my existence in general. (2) my existence in time, thus only in relation to my own representations, insofar as I determine myself through them. This is the empirical consciousness of myself. (3) The knowledge of myself as a being determined in time. This is empirical knowledge.

(R 6313, 18:617)

The distinction of "empirical consciousness" from *both* the mere *concept* of self-existence and any actual *knowledge* of the self's history in time suggests that there must be a difference not only between the mere concept of the self (or even an undated recognition of self-existence, such as the Cartesian *cogito*) and actual self-knowledge, but also between the mere succession of representations which constitutes the raw material of consciousness, on the one hand, and, on the other hand, the recognition *of* the temporal relations of such representations which constitutes empirical knowledge *of* the history of the self which is comprised by such a succession of empirical consciousness.[24] Gerhard Lehmann, who has also discussed this fragment,[25] sees it as an anticipation of the doctrine of *Erscheinungstufe* ("levels of appearance") which Kant was attempting to develop in the *Opus*

292

Postumum. If we think of an "appearance" as the *object* of an empirical intuition, however (see A 20 / B 34) – "undetermined," to be sure, insofar as it is thought of *only* in connection with empirical intuition, but determinate insofar as concepts and judgment are brought to it – there would seem to be no need to think of two kinds or stages of appearance as being involved here. "Empirical consciousness" would simply designate the *undetermined* intuitions by which the self and its history are presented, and "empirical knowledge" of the self would designate *determinate* knowledge of the "appearance" which is the object of those intuitions – namely, the empirical self. This in turn would suggest that knowledge of outer objects is the condition by which the transition is made from undetermined empirical consciousness to empirical self-knowledge, from the mere occurrence of successive representations to the recognition of their succession and its history.

With his usual terminological fluidity Kant makes the same distinction in another paragraph in the very same fragment by contrasting the mere "form of representation in time" with "empirical consciousness," now meaning by the latter precisely what the paragraph just quoted called "empirical knowledge." Here Kant claims that idealism

... can be refuted [first] by showing that the representation of external things must not lie merely in the imagination, but in an outer sense, because the *form* of representation in time would make possible no empirical consciousness of one's own existence in time, thus no inner experience, unless supplemented with [the form of representation] in space. (R 6313, 18:613)

If we take the form of representation in time to consist simply of the successiveness of all representations in time (the manifold of inner sense, of which time is "nothing but the form," "constitutes a series of one dimension ... the parts [of which] are always successive" [A 33 / B 49–50]), then this too implies that the mere fact of the successiveness of representations is not sufficient for empirical knowledge *of* their relations in time and that for some reason the representation of space or objects in it is also necessary for this purpose.

But although these remarks make clearer than the published text what Kant's fundamental premise must be, our key question still remains: *Why* is the successiveness of consciousness insufficient for its own recognition, and why should spatial, let alone independent objects be necessary for this purpose? This question has haunted us since our discussion of Kant's original transcendental theory of experience. In the years after 1787, however, Kant finally made some headway with it. In fact, what Kant tries to do in the new attempts at the refutation of idealism from these years is to improve upon the two alternative tactics unsatisfactorily attempted in the two emendations to the refutation already published in 1787. On the one hand, Kant attempts to improve upon the bald assertion that the representation of time and of alteration in it requires the representation of space and motion. He does this by developing an explicit – if not persuasive –

argument that the determination of temporal relations, even among purely subjective states, requires the representation of *space,* and by then supplying further grounds for inferring from the representation of space to the existence of enduring objects ontologically *independent* of the self. On the other hand, Kant also attempts to improve upon the bare suggestion that the change of representations themselves requires representation of something permanent, which could not explain why this object had to be other than an enduring self. He attempts this by developing an argument that goes from the assumption that we can determine the sequence of our own representations to the requirement of enduring objects which cause the sequence of subjective representations and which therefore must be conceived of as distinct even from the enduring self which is constituted by the succession of such representations. Only subsequent to its proof that such time-determination requires *independent* objects does this argument add that such objects must be represented *spatially.*

Both these tactics represent epistemological analyses of the conditions under which judgments of time-determination can be made. Some passages in Kant's notes, however, suggest that such epistemological arguments are not sufficient to imply the ontological conclusion ultimately intended by his refutation of idealism. This may not be immediately apparent when Kant writes that the type of argument called for by the first paragraph of R 6313 (just quoted) must be followed by a second step, in which it is shown

... that the *matter* of representations in space would not possibly occur in the mind without an outer sense. For the imagination can create a representation of the external only if it [is] affect[ed by] the outer sense, ... and there would be no material for external representations in the imagination if there were not an outer sense. (18:613)

But as we shall later see, what this actually describes is a metaphysical argument assuming premises not just about the conditions under which representations may be *judged* but also about the substances which can *produce* them. Such an argument is deeply problematic. Fortunately, we shall also see that it is not in fact required by both of the tactics by means of which Kant attempts to execute his ultimate refutation of idealism. It is not required by the argument which goes directly from time-determination to the necessity of enduring objects, and only thence to their spatiality; and this, we shall see, is Kant's most persuasive argument for the refutation of idealism, and thereby for the completion of the theory of time-determination and proof of the objective validity of the categories. And this additional metaphysical argument is not even required by all of the forms of the argument which goes directly from the representation of temporal succession to the representation of space, but only by an incomplete form of this argument which does not go on to show that the existence of enduring objects is an *epistemological* condition of the perception of space. Rather, all that is required in these cases is a review of the argument already offered to remind us that an ontological commitment to objects other than the self is a condition of the possibility of time-determination. Thus, the problems that arise when Kant adds a second stage to the refutation need not undermine it.

13
The central arguments of the refutation

We shall now consider the two forms of argument just proposed. First we shall examine Kant's argument that the representation of succession in time requires the representation of space, which in turn involves the existence of enduring objects distinct from the self and its representations. This argument will be more elaborate than any of the hints in that direction included in the *Critique*, but ultimately no more successful. Then we shall consider Kant's argument that subjective successions can be made determinate only if they are regarded as caused by objects conceived to exist independently of the self and its states, which are represented as spatial precisely because that is how we can represent the independence we ascribe to them. This argument will represent nothing less than Kant's final attempt to solve the puzzle about the objective validity of the *a priori* concepts of understanding first discovered in 1772.

Displaying time in space

As we saw, neither the refutation of 1787 nor the first analogy contains any obvious ground for the conclusion that an enduring object must be *spatial*, and Kant's attempt to reach this further conclusion in the second note to the refutation (B 277–8) and the "General Note" rests on the undefended assertion that the empirical intuition of motion in space is necessary to measure or even to represent succession in time. One of Kant's tactics in the subsequent years was clearly to attempt a direct argument to the necessity of space for time-determination which would remove the arbitrariness of these earlier suggestions and, indeed, obviate the difficulty of having to establish the connection between time-determination and endurance as a prior step of the argument.

The first of Kant's fragments from 1788 begins with the simple assertion that change can be recognized only by comparison with something which endures and then infers that this something must be spatial by using both a simple argument by exclusion and the additional assertion that space is intrinsically permanent. Thus, Kant first writes:

For in space alone do we posit that which endures; in time there is unceasing change. Now, however, the determination of the existence of a thing in time, that is in such a change, is impossible unless its intuition is connected to that which endures. This must therefore be intuited outside us as the object of outer sense.

(R 5653, 18:307)

This simply assumes that the perception of change requires the perception of something enduring, and since time does not furnish the latter perception it must be space which does. But Kant also attempts to buttress this indirect argument by a more direct statement, namely:

Permanence is intrinsic to the representation of space, as Newton said. The permanence of the form of our mind is not the same (for the form of time is just as permanent); rather [the representation of space is] the representation of something permanent, to which we subsume all time-determination and therefore represent as permanent, and thus cannot represent as the spontaneity of self-determination.

(R 5653, 18:308)

None of this improves upon the ungrounded assertions of 1787. However, Kant's next paragraph intimates a possible argument:

The representation of space is the ground of time-determination on account of permanence (insofar as only in space can one acquire a representation of time as a magnitude through a line which I draw [even] while I am conscious of my synthesis merely in my subject). (R 5653, 18:308-9)

This starts by repeating that it is permanence which is the premise for the necessity of space, which would require that there already be an argument for the principle of permanence as a necessary condition of time-determination; however, what follows then suggests that there is some connection, in which permanence plays no direct role, between space and the synthesis of a representation of the duration of time. Still, this is not very different from several remarks already made in 1787 (B 154) or even 1781 (A 33 / B 50). What new argument is intended by this reference to "synthesis"?

The notes of 1788 do not explain this, but one from 1790 finally suggests what sort of argument Kant had in mind for a direct connection between time and space:

We cannot represent any number to ourselves except through successive enumeration in time and then through collecting this multiplicity together in the unity of a number. This latter, however, cannot occur otherwise than by my placing [the units of the multiplicity] beside one another in space; for they must be thought of as given *simultaneously*, that is, as collected together in one representation, for otherwise this manifold [*Viele*] constitutes no magnitude (number); simultaneity, however, cannot possibly be cognized unless if in addition to my act of placing the manifold together I can *apprehend* (not merely think) it as given both forward and backward. Therefore an intuition must be given in which the manifold items are represented outside of and next to one another, that is, the intuition which makes the representation of space possible must be given (in perception) in order to determine my own existence in time; that is, an existence outside me is the ground of the determination of my own existence, that is, the empirical consciousness of myself. Therefore I must be just as conscious of the existence of outer things as I am of (my) existence in time, though, to be sure, only as appearances yet as real things.

(R 6314, 18:616)

Kant's argument appears to be that to determine the magnitude of any duration of time is to assign a numerical value to this duration, and that such an act of enumeration, like any other, requires in addition to the successive apprehension of the individual moments of time a single act which we can count as their collective representation as well. In the language of the first-edition text of the transcendental deduction, a synthesis of reproduction as well as of apprehension is required, for although intuition "does indeed offer a manifold," this "manifold can never be represented as a manifold, and *as contained in a single representation,* save in virtue of such [a further act]" (A 99).[1] Such a single act of representation is interpreted as the simultaneous representation of the successive moments of time themselves, and this is then conceived of as a spatial display of these items, because it is only in space that things can be represented as numerically distinct yet available for a form of perception – one in which the coexistent items may be indifferently perceived in either of two orders – which provides evidence of their coexistence. Thus, the ability to represent spatial extension is held to be necessary in order to have a single representation of even a temporal succession.

How could this argument be supposed to justify a further inference from the necessity of spatial objects to the existence of *enduring* objects, which have not so far been mentioned explicitly? One possibility would be that which appears to have hovered before Kant in the quotation previously cited from R 5653, namely that spatiality is necessary for a single representation of temporal succession because it is the only way in which coexistence can be represented, and that endurance is then implied simply because space itself, "as Newton said," is permanent. Yet as we have seen, this just rests the argument on an assumption not otherwise entailed by Kant's more Leibnizian conception of space. However, an alternative way of continuing the argument may already be implicit in the quotation just considered and is explicitly suggested in two other notes from 1790. On this alternative, once the epistemological necessity of space as the form of a simultaneous representation of a manifold has been shown, it is then argued that the existence of enduring objects is itself the *epistemological* condition of the recognition of such simultaneity – an argument, by the way, which would make explicit a point left unstated in the argument of the third analogy.

That there is an epistemological necessity that in order for objects to be recognized as having spatial form they must be recognized to be enduring, and therefore not just mere representations, is first argued in R 6312:

How do we recognize the simultaneity of things, since all our representations succeed one another in apprehension? By means of the fact that we can represent the manifold in such a case both forward and backward. Now since in inner sense everything is successive, thus nothing can be taken backward, the ground of the possibility of the latter must lie in the relation of representations to something outside us, and indeed to something which is not in turn just inner representation, that is, form of appearance, but which is something in itself. ... – Thus the representation of something which endures must pertain to that which contains the ground of time-determination, but not in respect of succession, for in that there is no permanence; consequently only in that which is simultaneous must that which endures lie, or in the intelligible[2] which contains the ground of appearance.

(18:612)

Here Kant's argument would be the complement to the third analogy. There Kant argued that interaction between objects, assumed to endure, is necessary to represent the diversity of their spatial position; now he turns to the justification of the assumption that such objects do endure. Spatiality is necessary to represent simultaneity, itself necessary for a single act of reproduction of representations, but the *recognition* of simultaneity is possible only in the case of objects which endure at least long enough so that we can obtain perceptions of pairs of them in either of two orders. This is made even clearer in a passage (which is part of a larger argument) in Kant's next fragment:

The simultaneity of A and B cannot even be represented without something which endures, for all apprehension is really successive. But insofar as the succession can take place not only forward from A to B but also (as often as I want) backward from B to A, it is necessary that A endure [*fortdaure*]. The sense-representations A and B must therefore have a ground other than in inner sense, but yet in some sense, therefore in outer sense; therefore there must be objects of outer sense (and as far as dreaming is concerned, this object, which causes the illusion of the presence of several outer objects, is the body itself). (R 6313, 18:614)

As I stated in my earlier discussion of the third analogy, no reversal of sequences of representation types would be *sufficient* to imply the simultaneous coexistence of the represented objects; that is precisely why interaction between observed and unobserved states of those objects at the same moment is required. But here Kant seems to assume that the actual reversal of sequences of representations is at least *necessary* empirical evidence of simultaneity. Thus, he suggests that in order for representations of two objects, A and B, to be determined to be representations of coexistent and thus spatial objects, rather than just successive states of affairs, one if not both of A and B must be supposed to endure long enough to allow the perception of it in two different sequences. This argument is not sufficient, nor, as Kant's use of the word *fortdaure* may suggest, is it intended to imply the strong conclusion of the permanent conservation of any particular object. But it does seem to imply that objects *actually perceived* to be spatially related must endure longer than a single representation does, and this is enough to imply that they cannot be equivalent to representations, which are fleeting by nature. So the determination of time requires the representation of space, and this in turn requires the positing of objects which endure and are therefore distinct from any representation of them.

Of course, there are serious problems with this argument.

(1) It apparently depends on an assumption that we must be able to assign *numerical* magnitude to the *duration* of our own experience, yet, as I have frequently emphasized, there is no obvious reason why a "skeptical

300

idealist" must concede such an ability. This appearance, however, seems misleading. In spite of Kant's metrical language, the present argument does not really poach on the territory of the axioms of intuition. Kant is not really assuming an ability to *measure* the passage of time but only the ability assumed from the outset of the transcendental deduction, namely the ability simply to *distinguish* between a single present experience and a multitude of experiences, past and present, and thereby to represent a manifold of intuition even as such (see again A 99). And such an ability is not merely presupposed by Kant's own theory of threefold synthesis; it is difficult to imagine any serious skeptic – surely any known to Kant – who could put it in doubt. Even prior to his proof of the divine guarantee of external reality, for instance, the skeptical *persona* of the Cartesian meditations does assume that he is justified in the claims to "perceive that I now exist, and remember that I have existed for some time; moreover, I have various thoughts which I can count"; indeed, Descartes – admittedly a very imperfect skeptic – even goes on to add that "it is in these ways that I acquire the ideas of duration and number which I can then transfer to other things." [3] A successful argument that the ability even to count thoughts already presupposes knowledge of external objects would stand at least Cartesian skepticism on its head.

(2) But the idea that there is any necessary connection at all between the ability to reproduce representations of counted items and the *spatial* representation of them still seems problematic. On the one hand, such a connection seems inadequately defended: When in the "Transcendental Aesthetic" Kant *illustrates* the reproduction of intuitions in a synthetic operation of addition by reference to such spatial objects as "our five fingers" or "five points" (B 15), we may be inclined to let it pass; but when he asserts that *only* spatial separation can represent temporal succession, we may wonder why, for instance, different *qualitative* features of a present representation, such as different feelings of pain or temperature, could not be employed to represent past representations. Yet on the other hand Kant's connection may be too strong: Would it not make the succession of inner states determinable only by assigning *all* of them distinct spatial positions, and would this not then mean that we could prove that we know external objects *at all* only by proving that we know *only* external objects and *no* nonspatial feelings, thoughts, and so forth? But surely Kant would accept this conclusion no more than anyone else; indeed, he explicitly asserts that "not everything which is in time is also in space, e.g., my representations" (R 5653, 18:309).

(3) Finally, and what would seem most damaging, Kant's argument appears to be circular. It holds that a succession of time can be known only if spatial coexistence can be recognized, but then adds that spatial coexistence itself can be recognized only through a series of representations "backward and forward." Yet surely recognition that one is having such a series presupposes that one can recognize temporal ordering independently of spatial relation.

Objection 2 seems insuperable. Nevertheless, Kant's attempt to argue directly from the ability to enumerate subjective representations to the necessity of representing space does make plain the centrality of the allegedly fundamental – but then not utilized – premise of the deduction to his present enterprise of refuting idealism, and perhaps this premise could be used to construct an argument that avoids this objection as well as objection 3. This is, of course, nothing other than the claim that even in the temporal determination of self-consciousness a synthesis of reproduction as well as apprehension is required. That is, at any given moment in which knowledge of a succession even of mere representations is claimed, it must not merely *have been* the case that these subjective states successively occurred; it must also *be* the case that there is something which *presently* counts as the representation *of* them. For "if I were always to drop out of thought the preceding representations (the first parts of the line, the antecedent parts of the time period, or the units in the order represented) ... a complete representation would never be obtained" (A 102). To be sure, Kant does not explicitly mention this premise in the notes we have been discussing, and in originally introducing it in the transcendental deduction what he was concerned with was the case in which we must recognize the identity of something over time *given* the diversity of our successive representations of it. What he argued there was that such reproduction is necessary because "if we were not conscious that what we think" – the object of our thought, that is – "is the same as what we thought a moment before, all reproduction in the series of representation would be useless" (A 103). But the reason Kant adduced for this claim – that without a concept of the identity that it contains such a reproduction of previous representation "would in its present state be a new representation which would not in any way belong to the act whereby it was to be gradually generated" – is relevant to the present argument as well, for on Kant's own conception of representation a present one always *is* a new representation which cannot be linked to past representations, to represent *either* their diversity *or* their continuity, without some interpretation. Again, such a condition on the recognition that a succession of representations *is* a succession is the key consequence of Kant's fundamental assumption concerning any recognition of the unity of a manifold:

Every intuition contains in itself a manifold which can be represented as manifold only insofar as the mind distinguishes the time in the sequence of one impression upon another; for each representation, *insofar as it is contained in a single moment,* can never be anything but absolute unity. (A 99)

In its merely formal reality, that is, a single representation signifies (or logically implies) nothing beyond itself. But Kant's premise that all representations are fleeting and transitory means that *in fact* no more than one representation ever is present to us; the manifold of successive representations is not in fact before one's mind at the moment of its recollection in the way in which a dozen eggs can be before one's eyes. And what this all means is that for us to have any knowledge of even a subjective succession of representation – a manifold even apart from any objective significance it may have – *some form of interpretation* by (extralogical) rules or concepts must be placed on our present representation in order to allow it to represent such a multiplicity.[4] Without such an interpretation the present representation is simply a *new* representation without any connection to a temporally extended – or "gradual" – act of representing, or a succession of representations. Yet representation of such a succession is surely the minimal condition of any empirical determination of the self and its history in time.[5]

The nature of my claim might be made even clearer by a contrast with Jonathan Bennett's deeply suggestive interpretation of the transcendental deduction.[6] Bennett summarizes Kant's argument as follows: "Self-consciousness, then, involves whatever intellectual capacities may be required for the establishment – sometimes by empirical synthesis – of the truth of statements about one's past mental states. To verify such a statement requires more than just a group of criteria for mental identity . . ., but all that Kant needs at the present stage of his argument is that it does involve that much."[7] He then objects, however, that although criteria may be needed to establish the identity of the self *over* time ("identifying-rules"), none are needed to establish its identity *at* a time ("counting-rules"), so that Kant cannot establish the applicability of the categories (or "criteria") in every case in which he wants to (including the case of the present unity of the mind).[8] Indeed, Bennett takes the thesis of A 99 to be a tacit (or grudging) recognition of this *restriction*.[9] But he fails to see that Kant's point is that there is no question of the diversity (and thus identity) of the self's representation at all *unless* temporal succession is recognized, or that the unity of apperception itself – certainly any recognition of the diverse contents of empirical consciousness of the self – is always understood by Kant as a unity of temporally diverse constituents. Thus, to return to Bennett's terms, categorically-based "identifying-rules" *are* a necessary condition of any meaningful recognition of the unity of a subjective manifold at all.

Of course, it would be absurd if the act of interpretation of a present representational state by which the fact that it actually represents a temporally diverse manifold of representations were understood as a mental act by which, at a given moment, temporal order is *first generated* out of some kind of diversity (or potential diversity) which is before the mind in some kind of nontemporal way – if, to use Kantian terminology, the *synthesis of recognition* by which at any given time the manifold of representations is reconstituted were confused with the *synthesis of apprehension* by which the manifold is indeed first given in temporal succession. Whatever Kant may have thought – and we will see in Part V that he did indeed have some unfortunate thoughts on this score – his theory of the necessary conditions for the recognition of the manifoldness as well as the unity of the empirical manifold of self-consciousness does not imply a transcendental psychology according to which the mind somehow *generates* a temporal succession from some kind of nontemporal manifold. Insuperable questions about whether the transcendental act which generates temporal order is itself located either at a point in time prior to any moment which it recognizes or subsequent to any such point – in both of which cases all sorts of nasty regresses will arise – or else not located in time at all – in which case it will become unintelligible – need never be considered.[10] For Kant's premise concerns not the psychological process by which the temporal succession of data is given, but the epistemic conditions under which the occurrence of such a succession can be recognized, or, perhaps better, the conditions under which *beliefs* about the contents of the manifold of representation, however generated, can be *confirmed* or *justified*. What Kant's argument requires, indeed what the use of his own distinction between syntheses of apprehension and recognition should allow us to see, is not the transmutation of a nontemporal manifold into a temporal one by a mysterious act of a transcendental self, but just the transmutation of mere beliefs into claims to knowledge. The interpretation of our present manifold must therefore not be thought of as a psychological *event* in which a sense of its succession is first generated, but as something more akin to the kind of *argument* – that, of course, will often remain unstated – by which our *judgments* about the temporal order of even subjective states of affairs, even mere representations, can be confirmed. And even if such a process of justification is ever consciously undertaken, there is no reason why there should be any mystery about its own temporal structure and location. It will not occupy any limbo, temporal or not, but will simply be both extended in time and later than the time of the particular judgment which it is to confirm.

Some writers, presumably cowed by the general rejection of verificationism *as a theory of meaning,* try to reject the idea that Kant is describing conditions for verifying or confirming empirical judgments, in this case judgments about the self. Thus, for instance, Allison writes, "This does not mean, however, that Kant, in proto-Wittgensteinian fashion, is concerned with the conditions of the justification or verification of particular knowledge claims about the self and its states. His concern is rather with the conditions of the possibility of making such judgments (judgments of inner sense) at all."[11] I fail to understand the intended distinction. Although I can certainly admit the difference between a procedure entirely *sufficient* to ensure the certainty of empirical judgments and a framework of basic assumptions *necessary* to have any procedure for confirming such judgments at all[12] and do not suppose that Kant intends his refutation of idealism to furnish the former, I do not see in what sense a principle which is not a psychological factor in the production of a form of *belief* can serve as a condition of the possibility of a form of *judgment* except by furnishing the basic framework for the *justification* of beliefs. Clearly Kant does not treat claims to the knowledge of the existence of external objects as a psychological condition in the refutation of idealism; indeed, psychological conditions of knowledge are blissfully absent from Kant's entire discussion of the principles of empirical knowledge. So I see no alternative but to assume that Kant's condition of the possibility of making judgments of inner sense at all is indeed a necessary condition for the verification of such judgments.

A clear grasp of this point undercuts objection 3, for as long as the correlation with diverse spatial positions is not thought of as a psychological event which first generates temporal order, but only as a method by which judgments of temporal order can be confirmed, there is no problem in the fact that the perception of space itself takes time. However, the problem of objection 2, that there is no convincing direct connection between the reproduction of counted units and *spatial form*, remains. Can Kant circumvent this problem by employing the underlying premise just examined to construct a connection between the representation of subjective temporal succession and *enduring* objects, then only subsequently showing that these objects must be spatial as well?

External objects and subjective succession

An inference from subjective time-determination to enduring objects, and only thence to the spatiality of the latter, is precisely what is attempted in the alternative tactic for the refutation which Kant tried out after 1787.

A number of passages attempt to link the perception of even subjective change or succession of representations with the existence of an enduring object, but many of these contain no notable advance over the text of 1787. For instance, R 6311:

In our inner sense our existence is determined in time, and the representation of time itself is therefore presupposed; in time, however, the representation of change is contained; change presupposes something enduring, against which it changes and which allows the change to be perceived. Time itself is, to be sure, enduring, but it cannot be perceived by itself; consequently there must be something which endures, against which one can perceive change in time. This enduring thing cannot be our self, for precisely as object of inner sense we are determined through time; that which endures therefore can only be posited [*gesetzt*] in that which is given through outer sense. Thus the possibility of inner experience presupposes the reality of outer sense . . .[13] (18:611)

However, the same R 6313 on which I have already drawn in several places contains these two paragraphs:

Since the imagination (and its product) is itself only an object of inner sense, the empirical consciousness[14] (*apprehensio*) of this condition can contain only succession. But this itself cannot be represented except by means of something which endures, with which that which is successive is simultaneous. This enduring thing, with which that which is successive is simultaneous, that is, space, cannot in turn be a representation of the mere imagination but must be a representation of sense, for otherwise that which lasts would not be in the sensibility at all.

And then, after the intervening paragraph, already quoted, in which it was

305

argued that the endurance of simultaneously existing objects is a condition not of their simultaneity itself but of the perception of it, Kant continues:

Since we therefore could not perceive succession in ourselves, and thus could not order [anstellen] any inner experience, if we could not also become empirically conscious of simultaneity, but since this latter is possible only by means of an apprehension ordered both forward and backward, which does not occur in the case of the objects of inner sense, thus even inner experience can be thought only by means of the relation of our senses to objects external to us. (Inner sense would otherwise have to be represented as outside us, etc.)   (R 6313, 18:614)

The starting point of this argument is clearly that the mere occurrence of a succession of representations or inner states is not sufficient for the representation or recognition *of* this succession. But Kant's further claim that such recognition can be grounded "only on something which endures, with which that which is successive is simultaneous" can then mean only that successive representations in one's own experience can be judged to be successive only if they are judged to be severally simultaneous with the severally successive states of some enduring object. That is, in order for the present representation, which is all that one actually possesses at a given moment, to be interpreted as a representation of several past and present representations that have succeeded each other in some determinate order, a correlation must be posited between such a succession and the successive states of an enduring object which is distinct from the succession of subjective states, such that the various representations which *now* seem to have previously occurred *could* have occurred only simultaneously with the successive states of that object. For only thus can it be judged that the subjective states *must* have occurred successively. But that means that it is only if one's *present* representation can be understood to include a representation of such an enduring object and evidence about its history that it can be interpreted to provide evidence for a belief in a succession of past representations.[15]

Let me spell the argument out. Consider two possible objective states of affairs, A and B, and two qualitative aspects of mental states in virtue of which they can at least potentially represent A and B – that is, by means of which they are suited to represent objects of types A and B under some imaginable circumstances or other; we can designate these mental states as "being appeared to A-ly" and "being appeared to B-ly." (For instance, if A and B are a desk and a chair respectively, then being appeared to "deskishly" and "chairishly" would mean having sensory contents that could under some suitable circumstances count as representations of a desk and a chair respectively.) As we know well by now, Kant assumes that time cannot be perceived by itself. Further, unlike Hume, he never suggests that there is any phenomenological feature such as degree of vivacity[16] which could automatically mark one appearance as, for instance, a present impression and another as a mere memory. In addition, following the Baumgartian equation of the "possible" and the "representable,"[17] as well as his own definition of the empirically possible, he must also assume that the faculty of representation itself is capable of representing anything consistent with the laws of logic and the forms of sensibility and does not *itself* place any further limits on the potential contents or complexity of given representations. Alternatively, though at a less abstract level of argument, since there is no room for a science of the soul or psychology independent of physics, there is no possibility of natural laws governing the sequence of subjective states in total independence of any laws governing the sequence of physical states (see *Metaphysical Foundations of Natural Science*, 4:471). But on these assumptions there would be no way of telling whether a present representational state which on either interpretation would not contain a logical or spatiotemporal impossibility or violation of the postulate of empirical possibility – that is, an outright contradiction of the laws of logic or forms of intuition – is then to be taken to signify just (a) *now* being appeared to both A-ly and B-ly or else (b) *now* being appeared to A-ly and (*now* remembering) *previously* having been appeared to B-ly – unless the *objective states of affairs A and B* themselves place some constraint on the possible sequence of representations of them.

For example, neither logic nor the form of space and time preclude either that a desk and a chair not actually occupying the same position are in a room at the same time or that they are there successively, the chair being carried in only as the desk is removed, and thus they alone cannot suffice to dictate that a present state which might be described as one of being appeared to both deskishly and chairishly should be interpreted as (b) a present perception of the chair combined with a memory of the desk, rather than (a) a present perception of both. Only the objective fact that the chair was not brought into the room until after the desk had been removed can dictate the interpretation of the present representational state along the lines of (b) rather than (a). In other words, it will be possible to determine that one's present representational state is itself a representation of a succession of representations – (b) rather (a) – only if A and B are themselves successive states of enduring objects, rather than, say, simultaneous states of affairs.

Such an argument, suggested by the first of the two paragraphs from R 6313, does not follow Kant's earlier tactic in threatening to identify inner states with objects in space; it only *correlates* them for the purpose of assigning them a determinate temporal sequence or confirming the judgment that such a sequence obtains. Two questions now remain, however. First, we need to clarify the inference by which Kant finally makes it clear that the permanent object involved in subjective determinations of time cannot be just the *enduring* self itself. Second, we must ask, how does Kant introduce *spatiality* into this argument at all?

The empirical self and enduring objects

Kant has argued that the determination of the proper sequence of successively experienced representational states requires claims to knowledge of enduring objects, the objective order of whose states can be used to reconstruct the determinate order of previously experienced but no longer present subjective states precisely insofar as the latter are interpreted as perceptions of the former. Clearly we must conceive of such objects as numerically distinct from any particular representations, since representations by their very nature do not endure. But we can now see further that the enduring object which functions in subjective time-determination must also be numerically distinct from the empirical self as a whole. As we saw at the outset of this chapter, this conclusion by no means followed from argument (1) of the first analogy, concerning the substratum of time itself, or from argument (2), which required that any alteration of states take place in a continuing substance, for there was no obvious reason why an enduring self contrasted to its own fleeting representations could not play the conceptual role of a substratum of time or a substance for subjective alterations. However, Kant's present argument that the epistemological conditions for determinate judgment of even subjective sequences of representations require the correlation of the latter with successive states of enduring objects entails that those objects are objects *acting on* the self and must therefore be numerically distinct from it. It is precisely because enduring objects are conceived of as agents of the empirical succession of self-consciousness, and not because of any analytical relation between endurance and change, that they must also be conceived of as numerically distinct from the self. In other words, Kant's present argument really is the epistemological heir to the ontological refutation of idealism with which he began his philosophical career in 1755. In the *Nova Delucidatio*, it will be remembered, the principle of sufficient reason had yielded the "principle of succession" that no change or succession of states could occur in any substance without interaction with another, since all self-contained reasons or "internal determinations" for the properties of a substance would be present in it from the start and therefore incapable of producing change (Proposition XII, 1:410). A simple application of this general doctrine about substances to the special case of minds had yielded Kant's first proof of the "real existence of bodies": Since no substance contains the grounds of its own changes entirely within itself, neither do mental substances; therefore the "internal changes" of a mind cannot arise "apart from a connection with other things [which] must be present outside the mind" (1:411).[18] By 1788 or 1790, Kant no longer supposed that the principle of sufficient reason could itself be demonstrated except as a synthetic condition of the possibility of experience and was generally – although, as we shall shortly see, not always – more wary about venturing ultimate *explanations* about the nature of thought. But he was willing to argue precisely that there could not be sufficient ground for making *determinate judgments* about the sequence of changes in the empirical self except by correlation of those changes with objects acting on the self, and that just as the successive states of those objects are numerically distinct from the subjective states they are employed to order, so must the objects whose states they are be numerically distinct from the empirical self on which the objects act.

Kant may not make this inference entirely plain. He emphasizes the more abstract, and therefore possibly less persuasive point that cognition or recognition of the empirical self is nothing but another interpretation of one's present representational state as representing a succession of previous representations of the sort which requires some other enduring object for its construction. As he puts it,

> I cannot know time as antecedently determined, in order to determine my own existence therein. (Therefore [I can determine it] only insofar as I connect my own alterations according to the law of causality.) Now in order to determine that empirically, something which endures must be given, in the apprehension of which I can cognize the succession of my own representations and through which alone the simultaneity of a series, of which each part disappears when another comes into being, can become a whole. Wherein I posit my existence.   (R 6313, 18:615)

In other words, my whole existence as an empirical self is simply the limiting case of the kind of succession of representations which is never actually before me but which must be reconstructed out of my present state, so it is not itself available as the ground for such a determination. Because the enduring self itself can be represented only on the basis of an interpretation of the succession of subjective states, Kant therefore suggests, the enduring object necessary for time-determination must be other than the empirical self as well as any of its particular states.

However, emphasis on the role of the *agency* of enduring objects in subjective time-determination makes the point more clearly. For what Kant's argument depends on is not just the fact that knowledge of the history of the empirical self must be reconstructed out of its representational state at any given time, but the fact that this reconstruction – or, less misleadingly, possible confirmation of judgments about the empirical self – depends on the *causal* relation of the successive states of the enduring objects to the sucessive states of the self. The states of the self are judged to have a unique order just insofar as they are judged to be caused – whether by ordinary perception or less directly – by the successive states of enduring objects. It is because they must stand in a causal relation to the empirical self, not just because the latter is itself a construction from the succession of subjective states, that the objects which function in subjective time-determination must indeed be external to or independent of the self, objects conceived of as ontologically distinct from the self.

This realization will also allow us to answer another question that may have been suggested by Kant's own remark about the conditions under which I can "determine my own existence." It will be remembered that an objection to Kant's argument that the permanence of time required a permanent substratum in substance was drawn from his own remark that "the representation of something *permanent* in existence is not the same as a *permanent representation*" (B xli). But then, one could ask, what difference is there between an enduring self, knowledge of which must somehow be reconstituted out of a mere succession of its momentary states, and an enduring object distinct from the self, which, after all, is also not simply *given* as permanent but must instead be *interpreted* as permanent on the basis of representations – perceptions of it – which are not themselves permanent?[19] If the transitory nature of the individual glimpses of an external object are no bar to the representation of it as enduring, after all, then why should there be any problem about simply representing an enduring empirical self on the basis of the fleeting and transitory subjective states out of which it is actually constituted? The answer to this should now be clear. Objects distinct from the empirical self are not necessary to justify determinate judgments about the succession of states in the latter because those objects are actually *given as* permanent in some way in which the empirical self is not; rather, they are necessary because their *causal* role in determining the sequence of representations of them (and other representations in turn related to those[20]) can be fulfilled *only* by objects distinct from the self. It is the epistemological function of objects conceived to be distinct from the self but capable of acting on it, rather than any direct intuition of their permanence, that makes such objects indispensable for subjective time-determination. Indeed, given Kant's view that the permanence of genuine substances is only a regulative ideal of systematic empirical knowledge, it is hard to see how any other conclusion would be possible.

The spatiality of enduring objects

We may now return to the question of how Kant finally intended to reach the conclusion that the external objects of subjective time-determination must be spatial. After all, the notion of an object numerically distinct from oneself and that of a physical object in space are hardly analytical equivalents. As has been noted, a Leibnizian who accepted the *Nova Delucidatio*'s argument that there must be genuine interaction between substances would simply think that one mental substance is acted on by other *minds*; as a matter of fact, Kant sometimes characterizes idealism as nothing but the "assertion that there are none but thinking beings" (*Prolegomena,* §13, Remark II, 4:288). So it is not obvious that a requirement which would be satisfied merely by interaction among multiple thinking beings would constitute a refutation of idealism. Even a dualist would hold that there are mental as well as physical substances numerically distinct from my own empirical self and so would not immediately infer spatiality from ontological independence. And we have already rejected Kant's direct inference from time-determination to spatiality. However, I think that Kant entertained three distinct ways of adding to the present line of thought the requirement that the objects for time-determination be represented as in space.[21]

(1) The first of the two paragraphs from R 6313 with which the present

section began seemed to infer the necessity of space directly from the necessity of positing something enduring in order to determine time. This may have seemed arbitrary, but in fact the premise necessary to complete such an inference would have seemed natural to Kant. For the argument we have been considering emphasizes that enduring objects play their role in subjective time-determination just by being regarded as agents of change in the empirical self which are numerically distinct from the latter, and Kant would have inferred the further conclusion that such objects must be represented spatially simply by adding the further premise that space is the form of intuition by which we represent things other than ourselves and our states. When a commentator such as Strawson objects to the refutation of idealism that "there is, as usual, no independent argument to the effect that the objective order must be a spatial order,"[22] he fails to see that in a way the refutation of idealism is just the second step (to be sure, taken only after a laborious detour) to the argument begun in the "Transcendental Aesthetic"; having there as it were argued only that if we are to represent objects distinct from ourselves we must do so by representing them as having a different spatial location from ourselves – so that they must be *at least* physical, even if not *only* physical – Kant now adds that we must indeed represent such objects, and thus must indeed have intuitions with the form of spatiality.

That spatiality is our form for representing that which is ontologically independent of ourselves seems to have been a premise to which Kant had long subscribed.[23] Indeed, only by interpreting it to assert precisely such a synthetic *a priori* proposition can we render nontautologous the opening claim that the "Transcendental Aesthetic" will prove that "by means of outer sense, a property of our mind, we represent to ourselves objects as outside us, and all without exception in space" (A 22 / B 37)[24] or the claim, made in 1777, that "space ... is the form of the mind's ability to perceive things as external" (R 4673, 17:640–1). But it is a claim to which Kant gives special prominence in the refutations of idealism written after 1787. Thus, R 5653 claims that it is "through space that the representation of an object as outside me (in intuition) first acquires reality" (18:307); that if I must place myself in a relation of genuine distinction to "a correlate to my condition" then "the sensible, but real representation of this external relation is space" (18:309); and, finally, that the very "proof of dualism" is based on the fact that for the determination of our existence in time we must have "a perception of the relation of our subject to other things and regard space as the mere form of this intuition" (18:310). So if I must think of myself as standing in relation to something which is ontologically distinct from my empirical self and my representations, then I must represent this thing – or more precisely the fact of its independence from me – by representing it as separated from me in space. (Of course, to say that spatiality is that by which we represent the ontological independence of an object is *not* to say that it *has* its spatial properties independently of us; but again, I defer the discussion of transcendental idealism to Part V.)

This inference to the spatiality of enduring objects may seem disappointingly trivial or at least unduly dependent on the "Transcendental Aesthetic." But if the polemical context of Kant's refutation of idealism is kept in mind, it will be realized that this argument is an appropriate response to the Cartesian or "skeptical idealist." For his doubt, unlike that of the Berkeleian or "dogmatic idealist," is not addressed to the *spatiality* of external objects but *only* to their ontological status of independent existence. If it is independence that is the target of skepticism, then Kant's argument has already addressed that, and the skeptic who has come this far will not balk at this final step to spatiality as merely the form in which independent existence is represented.

(2) Nevertheless, Kant does suggest two more considerations by which the spatiality of enduring objects may be even further entrenched in his refutation. The first of these depends on the fact that, as R 6313 says, the method for time-determination just described requires that we can "become empirically conscious of simultaneity," since we must be able to judge that various representations are simultaneous with various states of the enduring external object. But as R 6313 has also argued (see the preceding section), the empirical consciousness or recognition of simultaneity requires objects coexistent in space; only spatial separation creates the possibility of alternative sequences of perceptions necessary to confirm the judgment of simultaneity.

This point may create a difficulty. If two objects, A and B, can be confirmed to coexist only if it is possible to go from the perception of A to that of B and then from another of B to another of A, and if, say, A is to be an external object and B itself a representation, it might seem as if both A and B must endure, thus undermining the assumption that B, *qua* representation, is necessarily momentary. Perhaps this is why in the paragraph from R 6313 quoted in the preceding section of this chapter Kant suggests only that it is necessary to be able to go from A to B and back to A, and thus that only A must endure: This allows for A to be an enduring object and B a nonenduring representation. It is not obvious, however, that Kant had sufficiently thought through the idea he is presenting to have seen this problem, and thus not clear that he intended this solution.

An apparently more pressing problem is that Kant's conditions for the possibility of determinations of simultaneity seem to require that *both* of two items to be judged to exist simultaneously have spatial location, for this would imply that a representation judged to be simultaneous with a state of an object in space must itself have a spatial location – which, as in Kant's direct argument from time to space, would collapse the distinction between a *representation of* something in space and a spatial object itself. In this context, however, the problem can be solved by holding not that representations must themselves *be* spatial, but that they must be given a spatial location by being assigned to an object in space as their bearer – namely, the body of the perceiver. But since this radically anti-Cartesian conclusion is also implied by Kant's final point in the present argument, its further discussion will be deferred for a moment.

(3) The last link in Kant's complete justification of "objects outside us in space" turns on the fact that the correlation between a succession of representations in the self and of states in an enduring object requires that both the relations among the state of external objects and the relations between those states and the representations of them be rule-governed; otherwise the inferences by which judgments of succession are to be confirmed could not be drawn. But this is just to say that time-determination even of subjective successions is possible only if all representations are part of a thoroughly causal order. As we have seen, this is precisely what Kant has said in claiming that to determine my existence in time I must "connect my own alterations according to the law of causality" (R 6313, 18:615), and it is indeed the key to Kant's inference that the permanent object necessary for subjective time-determination is not merely the empirical self. However, if Kant's remark in the *Critique* that "in order to exhibit *alteration* as the intuition corresponding to the concept of *causality*, we must take as our example *motion*, that is, alteration in space" (B 291; see also B 156) were taken to mean not that it is the idea of alterations in outer sense which first makes alterations in inner sense *thinkable* (B 292) but rather that it is the former which first makes the latter *determinable according to rule*, there would then be an argument that the necessity of causal laws for time-determination also implies the necessity that enduring objects be perceived in space.

This last step might seem arbitrary, and is certainly not explicitly defended by Kant. Nevertheless, there is an argument for it – namely, the consideration, already mentioned, that precisely because representations regarded merely as such must be regarded as potentially capable of representing anything which is possible, the constraints on their actual representational content must be imposed from several sources. Logic provides the most minimal such constraint, and space must provide the next constraint. It does this by precluding "contradictorily opposed determinations" (B 291) from existing in the same place at the same time. In other words, although the general argument outlined in this section presupposes that the mere form of spatiality is not a sufficient condition for the interpretation of the objective significance of representations and thus even for their mere subjective sequence, space is in fact a necessary condition for such interpretation. (This is again an illustration of the significance of the postulate of possibility.)

Like the claim that verifiably simultaneous states of affairs must all have spatial location, the claim that causally connectable states of affairs must have spatial form also suggests that representations as well as their objects must have spatial location and must thus be associated with an *embodied* perceiver.[25] Though Kant failed to mention this corollary of his argument in the text of 1787, he did not fail to note it in his notes from the subsequent years. Thus, in 1788 Kant drew the conclusion that "since time cannot be externally perceived in things, insofar as it is only a determination of inner sense, so we can determine ourselves in time only insofar as we stand in relation to outer things and consider ourselves therein" (R 5654, 18:313) – that is, consider ourselves as standing in the same network of relations which relates outer things to one another, or space. The same conclusion is drawn even more strongly in a note from 1790: "We are first *object of outer sense* to ourselves, for otherwise we could not perceive our *place* in the world and thus intuit ourselves in relation to other things" (R 6314, 18:619), or "I am myself an object of outer intuition and without that could not know my position in the world" (18:620). But to say that I must perceive myself in a place in space is to say that I must have a body and that my representations must be assigned the spatial location of this body. Kant implies this in concluding from the last remarks that "the *soul* as object of inner sense *cannot perceive its place within the body* but is in the place in which the person [*Mensch*] is" (18:619; cf. 18:620). For the reason why the soul – the bearer of representations – cannot be a particular part of the body is that it must be assigned the location of the body as a whole for the system of time-determination to function.

As Karl Ameriks points out,[26] this is an anti-Cartesian conclusion directed against the specific location of the soul in the pineal gland. As such, it is surely stated too broadly: It might well be possible to exclude some parts of the body as the site of the soul by showing them to be completely dispensable for the time-determination of the empirical self without thereby narrowing down the possibilities for the location of the soul as far as Descartes would have liked. But the most crucial part of Kant's observation is his recognition that although embodiment may well not be "logically necessary" to our existence,[27] it is most clearly *epistemologically necessary*: Only as a perceiver of external objects by means of its own physical organism can the empirical self arrive at determinate knowledge of its own mental life.[28] In the end, Kant has created an epistemological argument for the thesis of Baumgarten – himself far from an orthodox Leibnizian – that "*the human soul* is the faculty of representation which represents the world according to the situation of the human body."[29]

This corollary of Kant's refutation might appear to undermine it, for as an enduring object in space one's own body could be held to be not merely a necessary but also a sufficient condition for subjective time-determination, and then the conclusion that there must be an object independent of the self would appear to be in danger. But this would be a misguided objection, for at least in modern skepticism[30] – one need only think of Descartes's first *Meditation* – one's own body is not *excepted* from the objects of unreliable perception and doubt but is rather the *paradigm* of an object independent of one's consciousness or inner sense. It is precisely one's own body which is made of flesh, though one might think it made of glass, or which is upstairs asleep even while one thinks it downstairs before the fire. By inferring the necessity of embodiment from his final refutation of idealism, Kant has confirmed rather than undermined its antiskeptical impact.

Rather, the more serious objection to be considered at this point is analogous to objection 3 considered in the preceding section. This is the charge that insofar as Kant's final refutation of idealism turns on the necessity of causal inferences in subjective time-determination it involves a vicious circle, for it requires that empirical consciousness of subjective succession depend upon knowledge of the causal powers of external objects but also, presumably, assumes that such causal knowledge must be generated by an induction from subjective successions, since it is not itself *a priori* (B 165).

I have already touched on this issue several times, but now its importance will be even more evident. Kant's argument would certainly imply a vicious circle if both his refutation of idealism and his acceptance of an empiricist model for the knowledge of particular causal laws were meant to describe the psychological processes through which the consciousness of subjective time-order and of objective causal laws respectively are *generated*, for they would then jointly describe an incoherent psychological process. Causal laws would have to be learned from particular experiences but, in order to individuate and order these experiences themselves, would also have to be known already. If, however, Kant's argument does not describe the generation of particular occurrences of belief about both the self and the external world but rather the perhaps ideal conditions under which such beliefs, however they actually arise, may be confirmed or made into justified members of a system of empirical knowledge – if, in other words, Kant's argument describes the conditions which *restrict* empirical knowledge, rather than a process which imposes structure on some formless matter – then it involves no circularity. Even a mere justification of an empirical knowledge-claim, of course, would be circular if a particular belief about a subjective sequence were used to confirm a causal belief about a particular external object but were also confirmed only by that same belief itself. But as long as the former belief is not the only evidence for the latter, and as long as any other belief about subjective successions for which that particular belief about external objects has functioned as evidence could then also be revised or supplied with additional evidence, and vice versa, there will be no difficulty for Kant's theory in the supposition that any particular belief about external objects might be accepted or rejected on the basis of some belief about a subjective succession of representations.

In other words, Kant's refutation of idealism must be construed as an argument in epistemology rather than in empirical psychology, if the role of beliefs in external objects and their causal relations in the determination of self-knowledge itself is not to present any vicious circularity. As we have already seen, the argument suggested by the refutation must also be distinguished from a theory in a putative "transcendental psychology," according to which the transcendental self creates time from a nontemporal manifold; it does not itself imply such a metaphysical thesis, though it would encounter insuperable difficulties if it did. Thus, the refutation of idealism ultimately fulfills Kant's original promise of a transcendental theory of experience with an epistemological theory that is an exercise in neither empirical nor transcendental psychology. It is far from clear that Kant always recognized this distinction; indeed, it is clear that he sometimes failed to make it. Yet we also saw that at the very outset of his efforts toward his theory of experience Kant did propose the interpretation of what he then called the "analogies of appearance" – the forerunners of the two-staged theory of time-determination of his mature philosophy – as "restrictions" on possible experience (R 4678, 17:611). To be sure, even in the 1770s Kant found it difficult to choose between that interpretation and one according to which the mind imposes its laws on unformed nature, and his new transcendental deduction of the 1780s moved him decidedly toward the view that the mind literally imposes order on nature. But what we now see is that the ultimate argument of Kant's mature transcendental theory of experience, the theory of subjective time-determination which fulfills the original promise of the *Duisburg Nachlass*, requires only the *conditional* necessity that we be able to claim knowledge of a law-governed realm of empirical objects interacting with the self whenever we are able to claim determinate knowledge of the latter, without including any suggestion that there is an absolute necessity that we always have such knowledge of the self. Moreover, the theory of time-determination can be coherently expounded only if this, rather than the alternative interpretation of the force of this theory, is adopted.

14
The metaphysics of the refutation

Kant's efforts in 1788 and the following years thus produced at least the outline of one sustained argument from epistemological considerations alone for the conclusion that we must know enduring objects in space in order to determine the succession of our own representations. On this argument these objects must be regarded as ontologically independent of these representations and the empirical self represented by them, because they are enduring but also agents of change which must be conceived of as independent of the self upon which they act.

Completing the refutation?

Kant's notes, however, also contain a further attempt to argue for such an ontological conclusion from patently metaphysical premises. This is an attempt to offer a general *explanation* of our possession of the *spatial form of representation* itself by means of objects independent of ourselves, rather than an argument that particular judgments about the subjective succession of experiences can be justified only by the correlation of such experiences with external objects. Such a metaphysical explanation is in profound tension with the strictures on speculation characteristic of Kant's more critical moments. Fortunately, such an additional step also seems to be required to supplement only the most schematic version of Kant's first tactic for the refutation, which carried the argument from time to the spatial form of the manifold of intuition but not beyond. A separate inference from spatiality to ontological independence would be otiose where the primary inference is from succession in time directly to enduring objects, for in any argument of that general form, spatiality is introduced only to represent the already established independence of such objects. Thus, the problems which infect this separate metaphysical stage of one form of Kant's refutation need not destroy the whole.[1]

Kant's first fragment from 1788 contains passages which expound this additional metaphysical argument as well as others which seem designed only to clarify the ontological commitments already contained in his more purely epistemological argument. At first, Kant's exposition is ambiguous:

The intuition of a thing as outside me presupposes the consciousness of a determinability of my subject, whereby I am not myself determinant, which therefore does not belong to [my] spontaneity, since the determining object is not in me. And indeed I cannot think of space as in me. Therefore the possibility of representing things in space in intuition is grounded on the consciousness of a determination through other things ... (R 5653, 18:307)

This could just mean that in inferring the history of my own representations from the history of an independent enduring object, I am of course thinking of that independent object as responsible for the sequence of my representations rather than vice versa, and that it is because of the need to represent such an object as independent of myself that I must also represent it as in space. This analysis would clarify the ontological commitments of Kant's second tactic for the refutation without introducing any new premises into it. And both in later passages of R 5653 and in subsequent notes as well, Kant does make remarks which can bear such an interpretation. The immediate continuation of the discussion in R 5653, however, proceeds instead as if this passage introduced an *explanatory* inference from our possession of representations with phenomenologically spatial form to the existence of ontologically independent objects. Such an account could be based only on the metaphysical premise that the resources of the self as it really is – and not just the contents of its representations – are incapable of *producing* spatial representations unless affected by something other than itself, with respect to which it is passive. The argument would then contend not that the employment of spatial representations for the epistemic purpose of time-determination requires the interpretation of them as representing something other than mere representation itself, or that we conceive of our representations with spatial form as representing independent objects, but rather that the *explanation* of our mere possession of spatial representations, whatever their use, implies the existence of objects distinct from a passive self but capable of affecting it.

Kant, indeed, glosses the last line of the passage just quoted by explaining the possibility of spatial representation as due to external action on a passive faculty of the self rather than to a spontaneous capacity of the self:

Thus the possibility of representing in intuition things in space is grounded on the consciousness of a determination through other things, which signifies nothing other than the original passivity of myself, with respect to which I am not active. That dreams produce the illusion of existence outside me proves nothing against this, for there must always have been preceding external perceptions. Originally to acquire a representation of something outside me without in fact being passive is impossible. (R 5653, 18:307)

That it is possible to be wrong about the existence of the objects of particular representations, "as in dreams and delusions," without that undermining the broader claim that "inner experience in general is possible only through outer experience in general" was of course one of the anti-Cartesian conclusions of 1787 (B 278–9) and seemed attractive indeed: a reasoned ground for setting aside Descartes's worry that the possibility of error with respect to any member of a class of judgments must undermine the authority of the class as a whole would be a powerful antidote to skepticism.[2] But its attraction will surely be diminished if it must be grounded on the assumption that because of the mind's *incapacity* to produce representations with spatial form by itself, the occurrence of even nonveridical instances of such a form of representation can be *explained* only by a prior action of independently existing objects on the passive self. Yet further passages in both R 5653 and elsewhere emphasize precisely such an explanatory claim.

Thus, the next paragraph of R 5653 reiterates that the passivity of the self requires an external agency to explain the mere possession of the representation of space, "for if we were affected only by ourselves, yet without noticing this spontaneity, only the form of time would be found in our intuition; and we would not be able to represent any space (an existence outside us)" (18:308). As a *consequence* of this metaphysically explained lack, of course, the epistemological function of spatial objects would also be impossible: "Empirical consciousness as the determination of my existence in time would be caught in a circle and presuppose itself – but would obviously be impossible, since even the representation of that which endures would be lacking . . ." – but this is not the *premise* of Kant's present argument. The next note from 1788 also makes the ultimate premise of the refutation the explanatory thesis that

. . . if there were not an external sense, that is, a capacity to become immediately conscious (without an inference of reason) of *something* as outside us and of ourselves, on the contrary, in relation [to it], then the representation of outer things as such, space itself, would not even possibly belong to our intuition. For inner sense can contain nothing but the temporal relation of our representations.

(R 5654, 18: 313–14)

Similarly, some passages from 1790 claim both that the representation of the external in general is inexplicable without an actual experience of it and that specific nonveridical representations of the external cannot be explained except by reference to the ontologically independent. In particular,

It is possible to take an image of external objects for perception (to dream), but only on the presupposition of an outer sense, that is, on the presupposition that our outer sense relates to objects which are really to be found outside us. (R 6315, 18:618)

And in general,

. . . In the realism of outer sense nothing is asserted except that not even imagination could make any things at all representable as objects of the senses outside us as such, unless there really were such a sense; thus we do not distinguish the latter as a capacity distinct from the imagination by sensation [*Empfindung*] alone, but by a certain inference [*sicheren Schluss*] . . .   (R 6316, 18:622–3)

As these last words make clear, the present attempt to complete the argument of the refutation of idealism depends on nothing less than an explanatory inference to the cause of our possession of spatial representations *in general*. That is, it does not argue merely that our determinations of successions within inner sense must be made on the basis of *particular* causal inferences from independent objects, which for us *happen* to be represented spatially; rather, it attempts to give a causal explanation of the very *general* fact that we possess the *spatial* form of sensibility at all. Yet in the transcendental deduction itself Kant had declared that it is simply impossible to explain "why space and time are the only forms of our possible intuition" (B 146). Thus this metaphysical completion of the refutation of idealism would appear to overstep the strict limits on levels of explanation that are at the heart of the critical philosophy, which teaches precisely that *within* the intuitional and categorial framework of empirical knowledge *everything* is explicable, but that beyond – or beneath – it *nothing* is. Moreover, such an argument *against* idealism would seem to lay *itself* open to the objection that Kant made to skeptical idealism not only in 1781 but throughout the period subsequent to 1787 as well – namely that attempting to ground the independent reality of external objects on the mere contents of our own representations by means of a causal inference must lead to skepticism, because such an inference can never be conclusive. This objection to idealism is frequently reiterated in these notes (e.g., R 5653, 18:306; R 5654, 18:312; and R 6311, 18:610) but nowhere more strikingly than in one which then lays itself open to the very same criticism:

Idealism is the opinion that we immediately experience only our own existence but can only infer that of outer objects (which inference from effect to cause is in fact uncertain). However, we can only experience our own existence insofar as we determine it in time, for which that which endures is required, which representation has no object in ourselves. This representation also cannot be grounded on the mere imagination [*auf der blossen Einbildung*] of something enduring outside us, because something merely imagined for which no corresponding object can be given is impossible. It is that which gives the object in intuition, and our representation, insofar as it belongs merely to the consciousness of ourself, has no object of that sort. (R 5709, 18:332)

The idealist is criticized for trying to secure the reality of external objects in general by a causal inference, but Kant then goes on to infer such reality from an argument which itself involves a causal explanation of the availability to the imagination of a certain form of image.

Perhaps Kant thought that his association of the forms of inner and outer sense with active and passive powers of the self respectively could allow him to overcome the indeterminacy which infects the ordinary attempt at a causal inference to the external. But he provides no account of how we know these powers of the self or assign to them the ancient Aristotelian labels "active" and "passive." In fact, his argument rests on a metaphysical assumption no more secure than the alleged insight into the essence of a thinking substance which is supposed to teach the Cartesian meditator that intellect is an active faculty of the soul but imagination not, so that given the nondeceitfulness of God the clear and distinct ideas of corporeal objects furnished by the imagination must be due to the active agency of such bodies rather than of the self.[3] Indeed, Kant's argument is essentially the *same* as that of Descartes and rests our knowledge of external existence on a premise which is, in Kant's own words, "valid merely as a hypothesis" (R 5654, 18:312).

But this relapse into Cartesianism does not really affect the cogency of the refutation of idealism. For the ontological commitment to the independent reality of external objects is already implicit in Kant's second main tactic for the refutation, which derives the spatiality of objects only from the prior proof of their endurance. This commitment is also implicit even in that form of his first tactic which goes directly from time to space but then adds that endurance is a condition of the possible perception of space. Therefore, Kant's attempt at a metaphysical completion of the refutation is just as unnecessary as it is unpersuasive. And, as I mentioned earlier, even R 5653 itself contains passages which do not try to *explain* the origin of our spatial representations but only *analyze* the ontological commitments of our use of them for time-determination. This one, for instance, merely describes how we must *regard* the representation of an object in space if we use it for this purpose:

That if I make myself an object, space is not in me but (yet) in the formal subjective condition of the empirical consciousness of myself, that is, in time, proves that something outside me, that is, something which I must represent in a manner other than myself, is connected with the empirical consciousness of myself, and this is at the same time the consciousness of an external relation without which I could not empirically determine my own existence.   (R 5653, 18:309)

Here the representation of space is significant not because of its own explanation but only because it is what is used to represent what is *already posited* as distinct from the self. Then the most that is needed to complete Kant's argument is a reminder that if we are to use our representations of spatial objects for purposes of time-determination we cannot also fall back into the ontological attitude in which they are regarded as *merely* representations with no content referring beyond themselves. It is at least plausible to read what Kant says next as just such a reminder:

It comes to this, that I can become conscious of myself in an external relation through a special sense, which is, however, requisite for the determination of inner sense. Space proves to be a representation which cannot be related to the subject (as object), for otherwise it would be the representation of time. That it is not, but is rather immediately *related* as existing to something distinct from the subject, that [is] the consciousness of the object as a thing outside me.   (R 5653, 18:309)

It is possible to read this to mean only that *whatever* the explanation of their origin, if spatial representations are regarded merely as inner states without independent referents, then they can be assigned only the same purely temporal status as any inner states regarded merely as such – that is, transitoriness rather than endurance – but this then destroys the epistemological usefulness of representations of objects in space.

It is even more natural to read this last paragraph of R 5653 as arguing that the ontological reduction of objects in space to mere representations undermines their usefulness for time-determination even while it is still assumed that as inner states they *can* themselves be ordered in time:

The proof of dualism is based on the fact that the determination of our existence in time by means of the representation of space would contradict itself if one did not consider the latter as the consciousness of a relation quite other than that of representations in us to the subject, namely, as the perception of the relation of our subject to other things and of space as the mere form of this intuition. For if the perception of space were grounded merely in ourself without an object outside us, it would at least be possible to become conscious of these representations as containing merely a relation to the subject. But since by the latter only the intuition of time ever results, the object which we represent to ourselves as spatial must rest on the representation of something other than our own subject. However, that we can be conscious of an external relationship, without being able to cognize the object itself, but only the form of this relationship of our self to its presence, occasions no difficulty. (R 5653, 18:310)

I will return in Part V to the final claim that "there is no difficulty" in the interpretation of space as only the form by which we represent the ontologically independent; my concern now is only the argument that it is contradictory for us to think of spatial representations as just like any other representations. Kant's claim is that in so doing we in fact continue to assume that we can become conscious of their determinate temporal relations but also limit ourselves to the mere "intuition of time," which is to say that we regard these representations as merely successive, and thus fleeting and transitory. Or, as another commentator has put it, "It will not do in this connection to say that I could get by with no more than the *apparent* experience of external things, by *seeming* to perceive something outside me, for this would merely land me with extra items of inner experience (with more 'representations')." [4] We would thus deprive ourselves of the function of spatial representations necessary for the determination of time, as opposed to the mere intuition of time, namely their representation of endurance. We contradict not some *metaphysical explanation* of spatial images but simply the ontological commitments of an *epistemic procedure* to which we have no alternative.

Such an analysis is also contained in some passages from 1790. One note supports its inference that the spatial representation "through the outer sense" of something enduring which allows us to perceive change must be thought of as ontologically distinct from any mere representation by this argument:

Thus the possibility of inner sense presupposes the reality of outer sense. For suppose one wanted to say that even the representation of the enduring object which is given through outer sense is only a perception given through outer sense by the imagination; it would yet still be possible in general (even if then not for us) to become conscious of it as belonging to inner sense, but then the representation of space would be transformed into a representation of time (according to one dimension), which contradicts itself. Therefore outer sense has reality, since without it inner sense is not possible. (R 6311, 18:611–12)

Since even at his most metaphysical the mature Kant never argues that we would not *have* any representations in inner sense unless we possessed representations of outer sense – the ontological refutation of the *Nova Delucidatio* has, after all, been replaced with an epistemological argument – the last line can mean only that the *determination* of inner sense is not possible without the interpretation of spatially represented objects as enduring objects independent of the self, or without the ascription of "reality" to "outer sense." But perhaps even clearer than this passage is another, from the last of Kant's refutations of idealism from 1790, in which Kant argues that the representation of an object in space

... is a special kind of representation in us, which cannot represent that which is in us, thus what exists in the flux of time, for then as a mere representation it would be capable of being thought only in relations of time; therefore such an intuition must stand in a real relation to something outside us, and space really signifies something, which it is possible to represent in this form of intuition only by means of a relation to a real thing outside us. ... Thus the refutation of skepticism, idealism, Spinozism, even so of materialism, predeterminism.

(R 6317, 18:627–8)

All of the alternatives[5] to Kant's own realism, in other words, are finally held to fall before the argument not that thinking of spatial representations as mere representations makes their actual form or occurrence *inexplicable,* but rather that so thinking of them would, by assigning them to the mere flux of time, make them entirely transitory and thus undermine their *function in "the determination of our own existence in time"* (18:627). This requires no metaphysical premise but is merely the analysis of the ontological commitments contained in the second of those arguments and even in the more complex version of the first. And, indeed, if Kant attempts to explain why we possess space as a form of intuition (either in addition to time or in contrast to some other conceivable – though of course unimaginable – form of outer intuition) he must damage his entire project. If, however, Kant confines his refutation to the epistemological argument that if we can make determinations of subjective time-order then we must possess some form for outer intuition, our only candidate for which just happens to be space, then his argument will have a legitimate as well as indispensable place in his critical philosophy.

Presupposing realism

The exposition of the constructive argument of the refutation of idealism, and indeed therefore of Kant's ultimate argument for the *a priori* principles of a transcendental theory of experience, is now complete. Kant has argued that we can make determinate judgments about the temporal course of our own subjective states only if we interpret such states as representations of our law-governed interactions with a realm of enduring physical objects distinct from these representations and our empirical selves. Thus even

323

empirical self-consciousness comprises ontological commitments to objects which we can conceive only as existing independently of us. To have self-knowledge, we must also be realists of some sort. Yet ascribing any form of ontological realism to Kant obviously raises difficult questions. First, Kant appears strongly committed to the view of his times that we are never *directly acquainted* with anything but our own representations (A 104), yet also maintains the principle that our knowledge of the independent existence of external objects in general cannot be understood as a causal inference from the form of our own representations, even though in practice he sometimes lapses from this principle. But if our knowledge of objects ontologically independent of us can be obtained neither from direct acquaintance nor from causal inference, then what kind of knowledge is it? Second, of course, although Kant has argued that knowledge of objects in space is necessary even for subjective time-determination, he also affirms the doctrine of transcendental idealism, which insists that "space does not represent any property of things in themselves" (A 26 / B 42). Indeed, he argues that precisely *because* time-determination depends upon space, time too is not a real property of things: Even "in what concerns inner sense we cognize our own subject only as appearance, not according to that which it is in itself" (B 156). Then how can Kant argue for "dualism" (R 5653, 18:310) or be a "realist of outer intuition" (R 6315, 18:620) without surrendering every shred of this "transcendental idealism"? How can he argue that outer objects really are ontologically distinct from ourselves even while adhering to his established line that "if our knowledge of external objects had to be knowledge of them (and of space) as things in themselves, we would never be able to prove their reality from our sense-representations of them (as outside us)" (R 6313, 18:614–5)?

Again, I shall defer until Part V the issue of whether Kant really needs to answer the second of these questions. But one long passage from 1790 suggests Kant's own answers to both of them. As if in answer to the first, Kant writes:

Whether the objects (outside us) or their representations affect us ... can be decided thus. We need space in order to construct [*construieren*] time, and therefore determine the latter by means of the former. Space, which represents the outer, therefore precedes the possibility of time-determination. Now since in respect of time we are affected only by representations, not by outer things, no alternative remains but that in the representation of space we must be conscious of ourselves as affected by external things. We do not know this through an inference, but it is grounded in the way in which we affect ourselves in order to construct time as the mere form of the representation of our inner condition, whereby there must yet always be given to us something other, not belonging to this inner condition (that is, something external, the construction of which also contains the intuition of time and is its ground).

And then, as if in answer to the second, Kant continues:

In order that something can appear to be outside us, there must really be something outside us, though not constituted in the way we have the representation of it, since other kinds of sense could afford other ways of representing the same thing. For otherwise the representation of something outside us could never come to be thought, since we would only be conscious of our representations as inner determinations and for their object would have only inner sense, which we yet carefully distinguish from outer sense.　　　　　　　(R 6312, 18:612–13)

The second of these paragraphs gives Kant's own reconciliation of the refutation of idealism and transcendental idealism in a nutshell. But for now we shall consider only the answer Kant suggests to the first question, namely, how is our knowledge of the existence of external objects to be understood if it is *not* to be interpreted as the result of a causal inference from some general feature of our representations, such as their spatial form?

This question is not as easy to answer as the other. For in both the published text of 1787 and many of the fragments from 1788 and 1790 Kant creates considerable difficulty for himself by tacitly assuming that there is an exhaustive distinction between *immediate* and *inferential* knowledge. Thus he is inclined toward the presupposition that our knowledge that there are independently existing objects must fit one or the other of these models, even though he has himself offered objections against each, so when he tries to force the result of his actual argument into these two categories he is bound to distort it. Thus we saw that in spite of his own diagnosis of the source of "skeptical idealism" Kant was still tempted to argue that the distinction between mere imagination and outer sense can be known by means of a "correct inference" (R 6316, 18:622). Yet in spite of his adherence to the customary view that we are never directly acquainted with anything but our own representations, Kant also asserts that his refutation shows our knowledge of external objects to be immediate rather than inferential. Thus the published "Refutation" concludes with nothing less than the claim that "the consciousness of my existence is at the same time an immediate consciousness of the existence of other things outside me" (B 276), and this claim is repeated in 1788:

The mind must be immediately conscious of a representation of outer sense as such [a representation], that is, not through an inference from the representation as the effect to something external as a cause. . . . If there were not an outer sense, that is, a capacity to be conscious of something as outside us immediately (without an inference of reason) and to be conscious of ourselves on the contrary as in relation to it, then the representation of external things as such would not even possibly belong to an intuition.　　　　　　　(R 5654, 18:312–13)

The claim of immediacy is also raised in 1790: The alternative to ascribing to spatial representations "only the form (and dimension) of time" is that spatial form "must not be thought but intuited, that is, immediately related to an object" (R 6315, 18:618), ("*even if,*" as Kant continues, "*we also do not know what this is in itself* but only how it appears to us" [18:618–19]).

Yet even had Kant not ruled out from the start the possibility that we might have direct acquaintance with external objects, there would still be a problem with the claim that our knowledge of external reality is immediate as well as with its alternative. I do not refer to the problem that Paton points to – the fact that this claim of immediacy is the conclusion of an elaborate argument which Kant himself describes as requiring a climb "through difficult subtleties to the peak of principles." After all, Kant himself also observes that the point of this argument is not so much to prove something which "the healthy understanding could not attain without all this falderal, but rather to deprive entirely of their force all the sophisticated subtleties which are raised against it" (R 5654, 18:313). That is, it could perfectly well be the case that our knowledge of something is immediate, whereas our *further* claim that this knowledge is immediate itself requires considerable defense from some ultimately (although not self-evidently) groundless objection to it. Rather, the problem is that Kant's refutation of idealism contains no premise which requires that our knowledge of external reality be immediate. If an argument is to entail that one form of knowledge which is the condition of another form of knowledge is immediate, it would seem, then the argument must include either a premise that the latter form of knowledge is itself immediate or at least an explanation of why this latter form can rest only on immediate knowledge. Yet Kant cannot claim that the empirical knowledge of subjective time-determination for which knowledge of external objects serves as a condition is *itself* immediate, for the distinction between the unconditioned, transcendental consciousness *that* I exist and the conditioned, empirical knowledge of *how* I exist in time, on which his refutation of idealism (and thus his entire transcendental theory of experience) ultimately depend, implies precisely the opposite. In Kant's own words, "The transcendental consciousness of ourselves, which accompanies the spontancity of all acts of our understanding, but which consists in the mere 'I' without the determination of our existence in time, is certainly immediate, but the empirical consciousness of myself, which constitutes the inner sense ... by no means occurs immediately" (R 5653, 18:306).[7] So the "empirical consciousness of myself," which is the premise of the refutation as a whole, is not itself a premise for the immediacy of our knowledge of the external. Yet the only obvious alternative, namely an argument that our knowledge of external objects must be immediate because they justify (without, in turn, being justified by) mediate claims of self-knowledge will also fail, for, as we saw, Kant's refutation can be saved from circularity only by the assumption that although a particular claim of self-knowledge cannot be used to justify the very same judgment(s) about external objects which are used to confirm it, such a claim could be used to justify some *other* claim about external objects. On this account, however, judgments about external objects are no more immediate than determinations about self-consciousness. Thus we must conclude that the claim of immediacy is not directly supported by the argument of the refutation itself. At the most, it can be successfully maintained only if read simply to mean that the supposition that knowledge of the external *in general* is inferential leads to skeptical idealism.

METAPHYSICS OF THE REFUTATION

However, what the first of the two paragraphs with which this section began can now be seen to suggest is that Kant realized, at least once, that the very assumption that our knowledge of external objects must be *either* immediate *or* inferential was misleading – that neither of these alternatives is suitable for describing the status of a *presupposition* which must be brought to bear on the raw material of experience in order to make *any* determinate judgment whatever about that data.[8] Instead, Kant saw that the concept of endurance and the belief in its representation of an independent object has to be brought to the data of sense, in order to "construct" time – a term which we may best understand to connote not a literal (phenomenalist) construction but rather a *construal*, an *interpretation* of the subjective through a network of judgments about temporal relations for which there is, in turn, some method of justification. By this account, the presupposition that there are external objects would be neither immediate nor inferential. For these are terms appropriate for classifying the status of particular claims *within* a system of justified beliefs, yet the supposition that there *are* some external objects, just like the supposition that there are some subjective states, is part of the interpretative framework within which individual efforts at justification can proceed.

That neither the existence of the self nor the existence of objects are individual items of empirical knowledge but that they are, rather, presuppositions for the determination of any empirical belief to which designation as immediate or inferential applies is also implied in the words following Kant's express denial that empirical consciousness is immediate:

... The consciousness of other things outside me (which, as intellectual, must also be presupposed and which is thus not a [mere] representation of them in space but rather can be called intellectual intuition, through which we have no knowledge of things) and the determination of their existence in space must be simultaneous with the determination of my existence in time; therefore I [know] my own empirically determined existence no more than that of things outside me (which, what they are in themselves, I do not know).   (R 5653, 18:306)

It is surprising for Kant to characterize the knowledge that external objects exist as "intellectual intuition," since by that phrase he ordinarily means something that is, of course, not possible – knowledge attained by the intellect from concepts *alone* – and since he has indeed invoked nothing less than the *impossibility* of intellectual intuition of the self in this sense as the very basis for the refutation of idealism (B xl). And it is clumsy of Kant – as we shall see in Part V, a relapse into an unnecessary dichotomy – to say that this "intellectual intuition" provides *no* knowledge of things, when, as even the last line of this extract makes clear, he means to deny only that we know these things *as* they are in themselves. But what Kant is trying to say seems clear enough and might have been caught by a phrase such as "intellectualized intuition." Kant's point is that the *mere occurrence* of intuitions with either temporal properties or even the phenomenological form of spatiality is not itself enough to provide empirical knowledge of the temporal relations of these representations; for this purpose the presupposition that at least some of these represent enduring objects, including one's own body, is an essential element of the *interpretation* that must be placed on the sensory content of the representations. An interpretation must be placed on intuition before such intuitions can be used for the empirical determination of one's own experience, thus before questions of immediate or inferential status can even properly arise.

Language of intentionality not available to Kant might have helped him to avoid giving misleading impressions here, but even without it he has pointed to something important. In fact, it was correct for Kant to contrast himself to the "skeptical idealist" by denying that our knowledge of independent reality in general is inferential. For on the Humean model of particular causal inferences which Kant himself appears to have accepted, the premise for any causal inference must be logically independent of the conclusion to be inferred. But the potential premise for such an inference to the existence of external objects is our knowledge of our own temporally discrete representations, and, on Kant's final account, knowledge that external objects exist is already implicated in this premise. At the same time, it was also correct for Kant at least to suggest that knowledge that external objects exist might not usefully be described as immediate. For such a description could be taken to mean that such knowledge is simply given in intuition, when in fact intuition by itself yields no knowledge of anything. Rather, the knowledge that external objects exist is a presupposition which must be brought to bear on intuition. Confusing as it may be, the language of "construction" or "intellectual intuition" is, at any rate, an improvement on the misleading dichotomy between immediate and inferential knowledge.

So although he can himself state it only with considerable difficulty, the lesson of Kant's refutation of idealism and thus of his only successful strategy for achieving a transcendental theory of experience is that any form of self-consciousness beyond entirely passive apprehension depends upon a realist interpretation of what we are given in experience. We must now consider how this conclusion is to be reconciled with Kant's transcendental idealism – or even whether it really needs to be. As has already been suggested, Kant himself suggests how to reconcile the refutation of idealism with his own version of idealism when he stresses the distinction between the ontological independence of external objects – which Kant accepts in his mature discussion of the refutation – and the epistemological dependence of the way in which we represent them on our own cognitive constitution, to which Kant sometimes confines his statements of transcendental idealism. But we shall also reach a blunter conclusion. Although as historians we must obviously try to reconstruct Kant's own chain of thought accurately, as philosophers we must also be prepared to subject his inferences to our own critical scrutiny. Since the refutation of idealism has not employed transcendental idealism among its own premises, there is no intrinsic reason to weaken its conclusion that we must presuppose the existence of things independent from us until proved otherwise. All of Kant's elaborate and treasured argumentation in behalf of transcendental idealism fails to provide any compelling reason to deny that the independent objects of experience are indeed spatial and temporal. This simple conclusion – although it will take many pages to prove it – will save us from needless subtlety in attempting to reconcile all of the details – and diversities – of Kant's transcendental idealism with the realistic implications of the refutation of idealism.

V
Transcendental idealism

15
Appearances and things in themselves

In the 1960s, Kant's doctrine of transcendental idealism was only an embarrassment to those who were returning to the critical philosophy for refreshment as the springs of ordinary language and Wittgensteinian philosophy seemed to run dry. "Descriptive metaphysics"[1] might be rehabilitated, but it hardly needed to be burdened by the "picture of the receiving and ordering apparatus of the mind producing Nature as we know it out of the unknowable reality of things as they are in themselves."[2] But philosophy is no less subject to the whims of fashion than other human activities, and since the late 1970s transcendental idealism has come to seem to some not merely a harmless but indeed a salubrious recommendation of epistemological modesty. In characteristic words, for instance, Graham Bird has written that "to assert the existence of . . . objects beyond our capacities is to underline the modesty with which we should view our own frameworks of belief"; transcendental idealism, he asserts, "indicates a kind of subjectivity which is not . . . that of an individual's private sensory experience but is rather that of a certain relativism associated with a system of belief."[3] However, Kant's transcendental idealism is not any heir to ancient skepticism's healthy reminder, against all forms of dogmatism, that our views and theories may be only one way of looking at reality. That form of epistemological modesty always requires that a theory or conceptual framework subjected to skeptical doubt be no more demonstrably *false* than demonstrably *true,* but what Kant sets out to demonstrate under the name of transcendental idealism is that a spatial and temporal view of things as they really are in themselves, independent of our perceptions of them, would be *demonstrably false.* Transcendental idealism is not a skeptical reminder that we *cannot be sure* that things as they are in themselves *are* also as we represent them to be; it is a harshly dogmatic insistence that we *can be quite sure* that things as they are in themselves *cannot be* as we represent them to be. Space and time are the indispensable elements in all of our intuitions and judgments, yet transcendental idealism is nothing other than the thesis that things in themselves, whatever else they may be, *are not* spatial and temporal. Kant does not use the qualified language of a true skeptic when he writes that "space represents no property whatever of any things in themselves, nor does it represent them in their relation to one another, that is, any determination which attaches to the objects themselves and which would remain, even if one abstracted from all subjective conditions of intuition" (A 26 / B 42), or that "time is

333

nothing which would subsist by itself or attach to things as objective determinations, thus remain if one were to abstract from all subjective conditions of intuition" (A 32 / B 49), or that "this space together with this time, and together with both all appearances, are not in themselves any *things*, rather they are nothing but representations, and cannot exist outside of our minds" (A 492 / B 520).

On traditional interpretations of these remarks, Kant has been taken to assert the existence of two realms of objects, to postulate a mysterious realm of things in themselves numerically distinct from ordinary empirical objects such as tables, chairs, and (nowadays) keyboards, which objects somehow – though of course not spatially – lie behind the more ordinary ones. As evidence against such an interpretation, perhaps most colorfully expressed by Schopenhauer's image of appearance as the "veil of Maya" drawn before the impenetrable will in itself, some recent commentators have emphasized Kant's remark that the *Critique* "teaches [us] to name the object in a *twofold significance,* namely as appearance or as thing in itself" (B xxvii). According to this, it is argued, Kant does not advocate an *ontological* duplication of realms of objects but a *conceptual* or *semantical division*: not two sets of objects, but two ways of thinking of or describing one and the same set of objects. Thus, it is supposed, one and the same object – an ordinary desk or chair – may be described and conceived in terms of the features in which we experience it or it appears to us, among which, of course, its spatial and temporal characteristics will be foremost; in that case, it will be "considered" as "appearance." Alternatively, we may for some reason need to describe or consider such a thing in abstraction from those features in virtue of which we actually experience it, in which case it is "considered" as "thing in itself." But in neither case, it is argued, is any mysterious object being imagined to lie behind the ordinary realm of tables and chairs; rather, those ordinary objects are being described or considered in two different ways or from two different points of view.[4]

However, denying that Kant means to postulate a second set of objects in addition to the ordinary furniture of the universe, or asserting that he merely means to distinguish between conceptions of that single realm of objects which include their spatial and temporal features and conceptions which do not, is of little avail in the face of Kant's firm announcements that things in themselves *are not* spatial and temporal. He does not just say that there is a *conception* of ordinary things which does not include their spatiality and temporality. He says that there are *things* which are actually not in space and time or possessed of spatial and temporal form. Of course, that the *concepts* of such things will not include spatial and temporal predicates *follows* from the fact that the things themselves lack spatial and temporal properties, but it is clearly Kant's view that the concept of a thing in itself lacks such predicates precisely because a *thing in itself* must lack any such properties. And it is no help to claim that Kant does not postulate a second set of ghostlike nonspatial and nontemporal objects in addition to the ordinary referents of empirical judgments. Indeed he does not, except in the special cases of God and the soul, which clearly are intended to be objects numerically distinct from any encountered in ordinary experience. But he does something just as unpleasant – namely, *degrade* ordinary objects to mere representations of themselves, or *identify* objects possessing spatial and temporal properties with mere mental entities. Kant does not need to postulate a second set of objects beyond the ones we ordinarily refer to in order to strip space and time from things as they are in themselves, and not just from our concepts of them, because the ontology from which he begins *already* includes two classes of objects, namely things like tables and chairs and our *representations* of them. Kant does not have to add a *third* set of objects to these; to deny that the things we ordinarily assume are spatial and temporal really are so, all he has to do is *transfer* spatiality and temporality from objects to our *representations* of them or *confine* assertions of spatiality and temporality to the latter. Evidence that he does not create an *additional* set of objects – what Hegel called an "inverted world" – thus simply fails to count against clear evidence that he affirms that spatiality and temporality *are not* genuine properties of things as they are in themselves. And what I will maintain in this part of the book is that Kant is led, not to skeptical doubt, but to the dogmatic assertion that things in themselves *are not* spatial and temporal by a rich budget of arguments that in spite of the necessity of space and time for any empirical knowledge of self or objects – indeed, ultimately *because* of that very necessity – space and time cannot really be properties of the things to which we ultimately intend to refer.

Yet even those who do not deny the evidence of Kant's dogmatic assertions that things as they are in themselves are not really spatial and temporal have always been quick to spy a paradox here. The concept of a thing in itself, they argue, is nothing other than a concept of a thing of which nothing can be known; yet even a negative assertion – that a thing is *not* really spatial or temporal – is a definite claim to knowledge. So doesn't Kant maintain both that nothing can be known about things in themselves yet that something is known, namely that we *do* know that things in themselves are not spatial and temporal even if we know nothing else about them? Aren't we then involved in a paradox, as F. H. Jacobi said even before Kant could get out the second edition of the *Critique*, since *without* the presupposition of the thing in itself I "cannot enter into the system, yet *with* this presupposition I cannot remain in it"?[5]

In the final analysis, this objection need not worry us, for Jacobi's first assumption is false. One can enter the critical philosophy, or at least the transcendental theory of experience, without the presupposition of the thing in itself, because none of Kant's arguments for the nonspatiality and nontemporality of things in themselves, certainly none of his arguments from legitimate claims of the transcendental theory of experience, succeeds. Thus one can accept the transcendental theory of experience finally expounded in the analogies of experience and the refutation of idealism without any commitment to dogmatic transcendental idealism.

(So in the last analysis we are also delivered from worry about the reconciliation of transcendental idealism and the refutation of idealism, even though Kant shows us how to effect such a marriage.) Nevertheless, it is worth pausing over this objection just because it depends on confusion about what the overall structure of Kant's argument for transcendental idealism is. Kant does not begin by introducing the concept of a thing in itself as that of a thing about which nothing whatever can be known and then violate such a conception by going on to claim that he does know that things in themselves are not spatial and temporal even if he does not know anything else about them. Instead, what he does is offer a number of arguments that things – not initially designated by any special concept – cannot really be spatial and temporal and *only then* introduce a specific concept, that of a thing in itself, meaning thereby a thing about which nothing can be known by intuitions of space and time and by the application of pure and empirical concepts of the understanding to such intuitions. Since such a concept is introduced only as a *result* of the prior proof that things in themselves are not really spatial and temporal, it can hardly be intended to undermine that previous result. Our (alleged) knowledge that things in themselves are not spatial and temporal is philosophical knowledge by means of argument, not first-order synthetic *a priori* knowledge by means of intuitions and concepts, and thus not *prima facie* incompatible with Kant's position that synthetic *a priori* knowledge always requires intuitions of space and time.[6] Of course, we will see that Kant's arguments for transcendental idealism often founder exactly where they run afoul of well-founded elements of his synthetic *a priori* theory of experience, but that is, as it were, a problem of practice rather than principle.

Since my interpretation of Kant's transcendental idealism will seem harsh even while my rejection of the charge of paradox seems generous, it may be useful to contrast the interpretation which I shall offer to one which averts the charge of paradox by interpreting transcendental idealism as an anodyne recommendation of epistemological modesty employing a non-spatiotemporal *conception* of things but no denial of the spatiality and temporality of *things* themselves. This is the interpretation that has recently been offered by Henry Allison.[7] Allison also rejects the ancient criticism that Kant is inconsistent in positively asserting both that things in themselves *are not* spatial or temporal but also that we can *know nothing at all* about things in themselves. Rather, Allison claims, the very *concept* of things in themselves is a concept of things which are not spatial and temporal, so although Kant would be inconsistent in asserting any *synthetic* proposition about things in themselves, for him to assert only that they are not spatial and temporal is just for him to assert an innocuous *analytic* proposition, essentially to reiterate their definition.[8] I have already accepted the claim that Kant makes the general statement that things in themselves are unknowable because of his prior acceptance of the premise that they are not spatial and temporal. But Allison's explanation of how

Kant arrives at the premise that things in themselves are not spatial and temporal is erroneous and obscures the substantive grounds for Kant's adoption of transcendental idealism – which are serious (though unpersuasive) arguments rather than harmless definitions.

Actually, Allison attributes two different arguments to Kant and does not carefully distinguish between them. Each argument turns on the concept of an "epistemic condition" (which is defined as a condition "that is necessary for the representation of an object or an objective state of affairs"[9]) but makes a different use of this concept. In both his original article and in the initial presentation of his view in his book, Allison truly tries to make the nonspatiality of things in themselves a matter of definition. (As in most discussions, Allison limits himself to the case of space.) Basically, he argues:

(1) By showing that external objects can be represented only by means of the representation of space, the "Transcendental Aesthetic" shows space to be an epistemic condition, a necessary condition for the representation of objects.
(2) The concept of a thing in itself is, however, precisely a *conception* of a thing which excludes any epistemic conditions necessary for the representation of objects.
(3) Therefore, things in themselves are conceived without reference to space.
(4) Things in themselves cannot be spatial.

In the words of his book, Allison puts the argument thus:

Kant affirms the transcendental ideality of space and time on the grounds that they function as *a priori* conditions of human sensibility, that is, as subjective conditions in terms of which alone the human mind is capable of receiving the data for thought or experience. He terms these conditions "forms of sensibility." Things in space and time (empirical objects) are ideal in the same sense because they cannot be experienced or described independently of these sensible conditions. Correlatively, something is real in the transcendental sense if and only if it can be characterized and referred to independently of any appeal to these same sensible conditions. In the transcendental sense, then, mind independence or being external to the mind (*ausser uns*) means independence of sensibility and its conditions. A transcendentally real object is thus, by definition, a nonsensible object or noumenon. . . . Correlatively, to speak of things in themselves transcendentally is to speak of things insofar as they are independent of these conditions. (p. 7)

So bluntly stated, such an argument simply confuses claims about a *concept* with claims about *things*. That is, the key inference (the step from 3 to 4) is just an inference from the absence of the *predicate* "spatiality" in a certain *concept* of things to the absence of the *property* of spatiality from those things themselves. If the conclusion of the argument is really supposed to be 4, that there are *things* which are nonspatial, and not just 3, that we have a way of *conceiving* of things which abstracts from their spatiality, then the

337

inference is no more valid than, say, an inference from the description of someone in an equal employment opportunity compliance document as a "person" to the conclusion that the person is sexless, neither male nor female. Allison seems to interpret the concept of the transcendentally ideal as merely an expression of the fact that our knowledge is subject to epistemic conditions, that it is possible for us to experience objects only under certain conditions. "Thus the doctrine that we can know things only as they appear, not as they are in themselves, can be regarded as equivalent to the claim that human knowledge is governed by such conditions" (p. 9). But surely the epistemologically interesting but metaphysically neutral fact that we can know objects only if they conform to certain conditions does not imply that those objects or any other objects do *not* in themselves conform to those conditions, even if for some reason the fact of their conformity can or even should be omitted from certain *conceptions* of those objects. In any case, it is very puzzling simply to suppose that the existence of epistemic conditions should be expressed by the formation of a concept of things which omits precisely *those* conditions in the first place.

To put this point clearly: To choose to *abstract* from a certain property of a thing in some particular conception of it is just to choose to *ignore* that property. To be sure, we sometimes have good reasons to ignore even incontrovertible facts. Thus, in the example concerning equal employment opportunity, moral, political, and/or legal goals may lead us to introduce a characterization of candidates for a position which omits their sex (in the hope that this will get us to ignore sex when the hiring decision is made). Or, in another case, we may have to ignore the general fact of determinism in going through the process of making a decision, both because our going through that process is part of what determines the outcome and because, in any case, we lack adequately detailed knowledge of the influences on our choices to make decisions in any other way. Thus, we may have good reason to introduce a conception of voluntary action which simply ignores the fact of determinism. But these abstractions do not change any facts about the world, and we also have good reasons for introducing them. How could abstracting from the conditions under which we can represent objects imply any absence of properties from those objects, and, even more puzzling, why would we acknowledge the fact that there *are* such conditions by introducing a conception of objects which *lacks* them? That is the opposite of our usual procedure in abstraction, where we abstract from those conditions we wish to ignore, not those we wish to acknowledge.

The argument of Allison's original paper, and indeed all attempts to interpret Kant's transcendental idealism as an anodyne conceptual analysis, thus seem open to a simple but fatal objection. However, the more extended argument which Allison's book goes on to offer seems intended to escape this objection, for it employs what is clearly intended to be seen as a more substantive consideration to ground the inference from the premise that space and time are epistemic conditions to the conclusion that they cannot be properties of things as they are in themselves. Since similar assumptions could be shown to underlie many traditional accounts of Kant's transcendental idealism, it will be worth pausing to examine Allison's account.

According to this interpretation, Kant begins his argument in the "Transcendental Aesthetic" by showing first that space is a necessary condition for the representation of objects because we cannot represent objects as distinct from ourselves or from each other except by representing them as separated from ourselves or each other in space; space can therefore be regarded as an epistemic condition. Allison, however, sees Kant as proceeding not merely from the *definition* of a special concept of things in themselves but rather from a *substantive premise* that an epistemic condition necessarily represents the structure of the epistemic subject *instead* of the structure of the object of knowledge:

> ... Behind Kant's formal idealism ... lies a principle that is implicit in the *Critique* as a whole, but is nowhere made fully explicit: that whatever is necessary for the representation or experience of something as an object, that is, whatever is required for the recognition or picking out of what is "objective" in our experience, must reflect the cognitive structure of the mind (its manner of representing) rather than the nature of the object as it is in itself. To claim otherwise is to assume that the mind can somehow have access to an object (through sensible or intellectual intuition) independently of the very elements that have been stipulated to be the conditions of the possibility of doing this in the first place. This involves an obvious contradiction.[10] (p. 27)

With this substantive premise, it follows from the two suppositions that there are objects of knowledge and that spatiality is the ineliminable condition of our representations of these objects that space must be a feature of our representations rather than of these objects.

There are still insuperable difficulties, however, with such an argument. Most generally, any such argument obviously begs the question of transcendental idealism by assuming from the outset that any necessary condition of knowledge is subjective rather than objective, even if this subjective status will be dignified by the title "transcendentally ideal" to signify that it is an indispensable rather than an arbitrary aspect of subjectivity. More specifically, Allison's description of the contradiction that allegedly arises from the denial of this principle is itself incoherent. He says in the passage quoted that *rejecting* the principle that epistemic conditions reflect the structure of the mind rather than of the object leads to the incoherent supposition that the mind can somehow have access to objects which do not conform to the necessary condition of the mind's access to objects. In fact, it is only the *acceptance* of this principle, not its rejection, which leads to the idea that there *are* objects which lack the structures which are the necessary conditions of our access to objects. The contradiction lies in using the principle to deny spatiality to objects but continuing to assume that we have access to such objects even when spatiality is a necessary condition of our knowledge.

Allison's initial presentation of the principle on which Kant's argument is supposed to turn makes it sound as though there will be a more extensive demonstration of the principle later on. But Allison makes only one further defense of the principle, and this seems just as confused as the initial allegation of a contradiction. The problem with the supposition that "our idea of space is derived from the experience of ... 'real things' and represents a property and condition of them," Allison claims, is that

... by assuming that the representation of space is somehow derived from our experience of things as they are in themselves, this formulation denies the possibility that space can function as a condition of the possibility of the experience of things. As was already suggested, there is a contradiction involved in the assumption that the representation of something that is supposed to function as a condition of the possibility of the experience of objects can have its source in the experience of these objects. This is contradictory because it entails that experience be possible apart from something that is stipulated to be a condition of its possibility.

(p. 110)

But the rejection of Kant's alleged principle entails no such thing. The contrary of the principle that Allison is imputing to Kant is that something which is a necessary condition of knowledge may reflect the structure of *both* the epistemic subject and the object of knowledge, rather than of the former *instead* of the latter. But then to suppose that knowledge takes place, thus that *this* principle is satisfied, hardly supposes that experience is "possible apart from something that is stipulated to be a condition of its possibility," for it does not suppose that the alleged condition of possibility is absent *anywhere*. Quite the contrary: On the rejection of Kant's supposed principle, knowledge takes place precisely when what is determined to be a necessary condition of experience, presumably by some form of reflection on the nature of the subject, is *also* satisfied by the object. The contrary to Kant's supposed principle does not suppose that either subject or object lacks the condition of the possibility of experience; thus it hardly "stipulates" that experience ever takes place in the *absence* of the condition of its own possibility. Again, it seems to be the alleged principle which stipulates that, not the rejection of the principle.

Finally, it must be emphasized that the principle which Allison imputes to Kant is "nowhere made fully explicit" in the *Critique* for the very simple reason that Kant does not use it in any of his primary arguments for transcendental idealism in his chef d'oeuvre.[11] Invoking such a principle does nothing but obscure the fact that the claim that space and time *merely* reflect the structure of the mind rather than that of real objects of knowledge is not the *premise* of Kant's chief arguments for transcendental idealism either in the "Transcendental Aesthetic" or elsewhere in the *Critique* but is, rather, the *conclusion* of these arguments.

To be sure, Kant does accept a principle like that which Allison assigns him. Even in the *Critique* he sometimes quickly draws a connection between something's being a *form* of appearance and its having a subjective origin: "That in which alone the sensations can be posited and ordered in a certain

340

form cannot itself be sensation, and therefore, although the matter of all appearances is given to us *a posteriori* only, its form must lie ready for the sensations *a priori* in the mind" (A 20 / B 34). And earlier he had even offered an explicit argument for such a general principle. Thus, in the inaugural dissertation of 1770 he had written:

In this way whatever in cognition is sensitive is dependent upon the special character of the subject to the extent that the subject is capable of this or that modification by the presence of objects, and these modifications can differ in different cases according to variations in the subjects. But whatever cognition is exempt from such subjective conditions has regard only to the object. Consequently it is clear that things which are thought sensitively are representations of things *as they appear,* but things which are intellectual are representations of things *as they are.* . . . The *form* of the . . . representation is undoubtedly evidence of a certain respect or relation in the sensa. But properly speaking it is not some adumbration or schema of the object but only a certain law implanted in the mind by which it coordinates for itself the sensa which arise from the presence of the object.

(ID, §4, 2:392–3)

Like most of us, Kant was loath to surrender any argument he had once made. But it should be evident that the argument here offered is neither identical to the argument adduced by Allison nor, more important, one which Kant could have used in the *Critique of Pure Reason* with any consistency. The argument makes no mention of any contradiction of the kind described by Allison. Much more important, its crucial inference is from the *variability* of a feature of a representation to its subjectivity – yet this is a ground for transcendental idealism which Kant explicitly *rejects* in the *Critique of Pure Reason.* Kant expressly abjures any comparison between the subjectivity of secondary qualities, the variation of which had traditionally led to the rejection of any claim of objective validity in their behalf, and the ideality of space and time themselves:

With the sole exception of space, there is no subjective representation . . . which could be entitled [both] objective [and] *a priori.* This subjective condition of all outer appearances cannot, therefore, be compared with any other. The taste of a wine does not belong to the objective determinations of the wine, not even if by the wine as an object we mean the wine as appearance, but to the special constitution of sense in the subject that tastes it. Colors are not properties of the bodies to the intuition of which they are attached but only modifications of the sense of sight, which is affected in a certain manner by light. Space, on the other hand, as condition of outer objects, necessarily belongs to their appearances or intuition. Tastes and colors are not necessary conditions under which alone objects can be for us objects of the senses. They are connected with the appearances only as effects accidentally added by the particular constitution of the sense organs. Accordingly, they are not *a priori* representations . . . whereas, since space concerns only the pure form of intuition and therefore involves no sensation whatever, and nothing empirical, all kinds and determinations of space can and must be represented *a priori.*

(A 28–9)

The key to Kant's most fundamental, direct arguments for the transcendental ideality of space and time is not the "variations in the subjects" mentioned in the argument of the inaugural dissertation but the fact that space and time are supposed to be *necessary invariants* in all human experience. Any interpretation of transcendental idealism which failed to emphasize this would obviously be false, and although Allison would surely agree with this, it is far from obvious that the subjectivity of necessary features of representation is self-evident or even that Kant thinks that it is. Instead, a principle that necessary features of knowledge can be only subjective is completely counterintuitive, and Kant clearly expects us to accept it only as the conclusion of his arguments for transcendental idealism, not as their premise.

In the end, an interpretation such as Allison's actually obscures the character of Kant's own most fundamental arguments for transcendental idealism, which derive the nonspatiality and nontemporality of things in themselves from several premises, but most prominently from the absolute *necessity* of both intuitions of and certain judgments about space and time in our experience. Allison represents Kant as arguing, either from the definition of the concept of a thing in itself or from the alleged principle about epistemic conditions which we have been examining, that space and time cannot be properties of things in themselves *because* they are subjective forms of representation. But what Kant argues is exactly the opposite of this: namely, that space and time can *only* be mere forms of representation because they *cannot* be properties of things as they are in themselves.[12] And in so arguing, Kant is far from simply assuming that anything which is shown to be a necessary condition for representations is thereby automatically shown to reflect the structure of the mind rather than of the object represented. Instead, his primary concern is to *argue* that what is a necessary form of representation, and which for that reason may have to be *at least* a structure or subjective condition of the mind, is *at most* such a condition or is a *merely* subjective condition of representation.

Further, we shall see that Kant's arguments that what is necessary must also be subjective turn on a very strong assumption about the kind of necessity which can be claimed for the *a priori* features of both our intuitions and our judgments about space and time. Neither Allison nor other commentators have cared to examine the exact nature of Kant's link between apriority, necessity, and subjectivity; perhaps they have even thought that they could be spared such a detailed investigation by the kinds of argument we have just considered. But, as we shall see, Kant's transcendental idealism is nothing other than the heir to the "imposition" view of the rules of thought which he had originally rejected in behalf of the "restriction" view of the conditions of thought but was subsequently seduced into preferring by several very bad arguments. So, although Kant naturally believes that there are sound arguments for this position, we shall see that there is not a single sound argument in his mature philosophy which can prove that the forms of intuition and judgment which we know *a priori* are *imposed* on otherwise formless objects of experience, rather than being forms which those objects do possess on their own and in virtue of which *they* thereby satisfy the necessary conditions for our own experience.

The following discussion of Kant's arguments in behalf of transcendental idealism, understood as the restriction of spatial and temporal features to our representations of objects rather than to those objects as they are in themselves, will be divided into three main sections, for there are three arenas in which Kant intends to offer separate defenses of his doctrine. Kant's new preface for the second edition of the *Critique* makes this threefold division of the argument for transcendental idealism clear. In a footnote on the famous Copernican analogy, Kant says that transcendental idealism "will be proved, apodictically not hypothetically, from the nature of our representations of space and time and from the elementary concepts of the understanding" (B xxii); this implies the existence of two separate direct arguments for transcendental idealism, one from the forms of intuition and one from the theory of judgment. Kant also says that only the distinction between appearances and things in themselves can avoid metaphysical contradictions (e.g., B xx); this is intended to yield an indirect proof for transcendental idealism. As we shall see, then, Kant's overall argument for transcendental idealism takes the following form.

First – and chronologically earliest as well, since this part of Kant's argument is already present in the dissertation of 1770 – the ideality of space and time is supposed to be a consequence of the fact that they are the forms of intuition, or the necessary conditions for our even being given any data for experience of objects or self. In this part of his case, Kant draws on metaphysical and even theological considerations,[13] but what is clearly most prominent is an epistemological argument that we have *a priori* knowledge of space and time, but that *a priori* knowledge of the properties of objects as they are in themselves is impossible, therefore that space and time cannot be properties of objects in themselves. It has long been obvious that Kant's metaphysical or theological considerations can have little interest outside of their immediate historical context. It is far from obvious, on the other hand, that the epistemological portion of his argument turns on an interpretation of the necessity of what is known *a priori* about space and time which is equally dubious.

The second main part of Kant's case is connected with his theory of the conditions for conceptualizing and judging what is given to us by means of the forms of intuition, and so it is offered in (or at least in connection with) the "Transcendental Analytic" rather than the "Transcendental Aesthetic." That is, this part of Kant's case for transcendental idealism is offered in connection with the transcendental theory of experience which has been expounded here. In part, of course, the "Transcendental Analytic" merely incorporates results of the "Transcendental Aesthetic" or parallels the epistemological argument offered there by arguing that because we have *a priori* knowledge of the objective validity of the categories or even of the necessary unity of apperception itself, the categories must be imposed on the objects we ultimately experience rather than being derived from them.

But Kant also offers a new argument, which is very peculiar indeed. This new argument, unique to the theory of judgment, tries to show that a contradiction would arise if the self that makes temporal judgments were itself in time, so that the real self (and *a fortiori* real objects?) cannot be temporal.

Finally, Kant's last stand for transcendental idealism is what he describes as the indirect argument for it offered as the solution to the "Antinomy of Pure Reason" in the *Critique*'s "Transcendental Dialectic." This is the argument that when the claims of reason are added to the claims of sense and understanding, contradictions arise which can be resolved only by the supposition that sense and understanding characterize the appearances of things but not those things as they are in themselves.

I will argue that none of these arguments succeeds. Kant's epistemological arguments for transcendental idealism from our *a priori* knowledge of the forms of sense and judgment presuppose a conception of the necessary truth of what is known *a priori* which Kant never succeeds in establishing, indeed barely even attempts to establish, and the indirect argument in the "Antinomy" works only by violating one of the cardinal rules of Kant's own mature methodology. Kant generates its conflict between the claims of sense and understanding, on the one hand, and the claims of reason, on the other, only by tacitly interpreting the latter in the very way which he abjured when he rejected what he called a positive conception of the noumenon as an actual object of knowledge by means of reason alone in behalf of a purely monitory or limiting conception of the noumenon. By means of the latter conception, Kant did indeed recommend a salubrious dose of epistemological modesty, but when he argued for transcendental idealism, what he swallowed was not the antidote but the poison. Thus, the transcendental theory of experience which we have gleaned from Kant's writings (both published and unpublished) can be accepted without automatic commitment to the doctrine that space and time do not represent genuine features of reality, because that dogma follows neither from the conclusions of the transcendental theory of experience nor even from any premise successfully employed within it.

16
Transcendental idealism and the forms of intuition

Kant presents the "Transcendental Aesthetic" as a theory equally about space and time. But it is clear that in this part of his work his views about space were fundamental and that the argument for the transcendental ideality of time proceeds only by parallels (often strained) to the example of space. This is not to say that Kant was any less committed to the transcendental ideality of time than to that of space. His fierce defense of his theory about time in the face of the criticisms of Lambert, Sulzer, and Mendelssohn[1] shows how committed to the transcendental ideality of time Kant was, and in the arguments derived from the theory of judgment rather than intuition we shall see that it is time rather than space which is foremost in Kant's thought. But the derivative nature of the theory of time in the "Transcendental Aesthetic" does mean that I can focus my exposition of Kant's arguments there on the case of space, as indeed most commentators do.

The amount of commentary generated by Kant's views on space may be a better reflection of the interest of philosophers in this subject than of the intrinsic merits of Kant's own theories. In any case, it is not my intention to add to the already enormous literature yet another general discussion of the "Transcendental Aesthetic" but only to consider the specific means by which Kant proposes to argue from the conclusion that space and time are indispensable forms of intuition to the further result that they are therefore only features of representations rather than features of things as they are in themselves. For this purpose, a brief account of Kant's notorious arguments for the first conclusion – that space and time are the indispensable forms of intuition – will suffice. These arguments comprise what in the second edition of the *Critique* Kant named the "Metaphysical Exposition of the Concept of Space" and of time.[2]

The indispensability of space and time

In the first edition of the *Critique*, Kant simply advances five claims about space and about time which are listed without any further classification (A 22–5, 30–2) and which are collectively supposed to ground the further conclusions in which the transcendental ideality of space and time are asserted (A 26–30 / B 42–5, A 32–6 / B 49–53). The first two arguments in each of these sets are supposed to establish that space and time are the pure, and therefore *a priori, forms of intuition,* that all data for judgment are given

345

only as representations of states of affairs in space and/or time. The third argument in each set is supposed to show that the "apodictic certainty of all geometrical propositions" (A 24) and of an allegedly parallel body of "apodictic principles concerning the relations of time" (A 31) entail *a priori* knowledge of the properties of space and time themselves. The last two arguments in each set are supposed to show that we have *a priori* knowledge of the uniqueness of space and time themselves, or that our representations of space and time are *pure intuitions* as well as *pure forms of intuition,* representations of two extraordinary particulars as well as forms for the representation of all more ordinary particulars. In the second edition, Kant introduces his distinction between "metaphysical" and "transcendental expositions" or between arguments which simply exhibit a "concept *as given a priori"* (B 38) and arguments which show that a representation must be *a priori* because it is "a principle from which other *a priori* synthetic cognition can be understood" (B 40). He then segregates out the third argument – about geometry and the putatively parallel mathematical science of time – for "transcendental" expositions.[3] This distinction is supposed to reflect the fact that the argument for our *a priori* knowledge of space from geometry explicitly presupposes the prior classification of the propositions of geometry as synthetic *a priori* (and *mutatis mutandis* for the case of the science of time), whereas the other four arguments are supposed to prove that space and time are both pure forms of intuition and pure intuitions without any such prior concession. In fact, we shall see, this division is a clue that the inference from the role of space and time as indispensable conditions of intuition to their transcendental ideality can be made only by means of an additional assumption about the *necessary truth* of propositions about space and time, which is most obvious in Kant's conception of geometry.

The arguments included in the "metaphysical expositions" may be described as follows. First, Kant offers two reasons why space and time should be considered *a priori forms of intuition,* that is, forms for the presentation of particular objects or states of affairs which we know independently of our experience of any of the particulars so presented. Argument 1 about space is that the representation of space cannot be derived from experience of particular objects because objects can be represented as in different locations from each other and from myself only by virtue of a prior representation of space (A 23 / B 38). The argument sounds tautologous – objects cannot be represented in space unless they are represented in space – but comparison with the version of the argument in the inaugural dissertation suggests that what Kant means is that objects cannot be represented as *distinct* from each other or the self *at all* except by being represented as having *diverse* spatial locations.[4] Contrary to what is supposed by empiricists such as Locke, then,[5] the representation of space cannot possibly be acquired by induction from experience of particulars but is presupposed by any experience of particulars whatever: "The possibility of external perceptions as such *supposes* the concept of space and does not *create* it" (ID, §15A, 2:402). Even the inaugural dissertation does not so readily suggest a nontautologous interpretation of the parallel argument about time, which Kant claims cannot be "derived from any experience" because "simultaneity or succession would not enter into perception at all if the representation of time did not lie *a priori* at its ground" (A 30 / B 46; compare ID §14.1, 2:399). But as we have already seen, Kant is certainly committed to a synthetic proposition that we cannot conceive of *diversity of experience* at all except as *temporal succession of representations* (A 99, of course), and perhaps with that in mind he here means to argue that since the representation of time could not be derived by induction from anything otherwise recognized as a multiplicity, it can be only an *a priori* form of representation itself.

These first arguments are obviously intended as purely epistemological arguments about the conditions under which particulars can be recognized for any possible inductions or empirical concept-acquisitions at all and are not meant as psychological observations about the genesis of representations. The status of Kant's second pair of arguments is less clear. Here Kant argues (2) that space must be a form of representation with which we are acquainted *a priori,* because although one can easily "think that no objects are to be met with" in space, "one can never represent that there is no space" itself (A 24 / B 38–9). The parallel claim is that one can easily think of the removal of all appearances from time but can never "suspend time itself" (A 31 / B 46). As psychological claims, these are of dubious import: Even if space and time were empirical representations acquired only through acquaintance with more particular objects, one could imagine them becoming so well entrenched that they could not be imagined away, even if any particular object could be. As epistemological claims, it is far from obvious how they are to be reconciled with what we have come to see to be Kant's most fundamental premises that positions in space and time can never be perceived except by means of causally and dynamically related objects.

But in any case it would not advance our purposes to worry about the precise character of Kant's first two arguments about space and time. Even if we concede his claims that we must have the representations of space and time in order to represent particulars at all, and suppose that some interpretation of these claims can be found on which they assert neither merely logical tautologies nor merely psychological facts, it would still be far from obvious how they would imply the nonspatiality and nontemporality of things in themselves. They might imply that we must have *a priori* acquaintance with the *representations* of space and time, for we could not otherwise derive *representations of objects* at all, but this would just be a thesis about the *representations* of space and time: It would not automatically imply that space and time themselves *are* representations, or that they *cannot* be features of things as they are in themselves. Some additional argument would clearly be needed to reach such a conclusion.

The same conclusion applies to Kant's last two arguments about the cases of space and time. These arguments 3 and 4 are intended to show that space and time are *pure intuitions* rather than *pure concepts* – that is, that instead of being characteristics of indeterminate extension they are actually particulars which are, however, represented *a priori*. Argument 3 maintains that "diverse spaces" – particular points or regions in space – are always represented as subdivisions of a unique and all-embracing space and, moreover, that they are not given antecedently to that single larger space but can be represented only by the introduction of limitations or boundaries within it (A 25 / B 39); likewise, "different times are only parts of one and the same time" (A 31–2 / B 47). Since space and time are conceived as particulars rather than as types, they are intuitions rather than concepts; since the representation of them as particulars must precede the representation of their several parts, they cannot be acquired *a posteriori* from the experience of particular spaces or times but can be only *a priori*. The particularity of space and of time is also emphasized in argument 4: Here Kant claims that "space is represented as an infinite *given* magnitude" (B 39–40) and that "the original representation *time* must be given as unlimited" (A 32 / B 48). What is explicitly asserted in this pair of arguments is that since space and time are thus conceived of as particulars of unlimited extent, rather than as types with indeterminate extension, they must be intuitions rather than concepts; concepts do not specify the scope of their own application in such a way, but that is precisely the role of intuition. It is not explicitly asserted that this knowledge of the scope of space and time is *a priori*, but clearly Kant does not think otherwise, and so again the conclusion follows that space and time must be pure intuitions as well as the pure form of all other intuitions.

It will again be obvious, however, that these arguments depend upon characterizations of the *representations* of space and time: What they assert is that space and time are *represented* as particulars of infinite extent which contain, rather than subsume, all more restricted regions of space and time. One could certainly argue that it remains an empirical question whether space and time themselves must *be* as they are thus represented to be, and thus that it is an empirical question whether space and time are unique and infinite. But even without stepping into such controversial terrain, one can raise doubts about the significance of arguments 3 and 4 for a proof of transcendental idealism. Kant's claim that we have *a priori* representations of space and time from which we can derive our *a priori* knowledge of the uniqueness and infinity of space and time can be conceded, but the reduction of space and time to mere representations, the identification of them with pure intuitions rather than with the *objects* of such singular representations, will hardly follow without an additional argument that apriority entails subjectivity or transcendental ideality. Even if the metaphysical expositions of space and time as a whole establish that we have *a priori* knowledge that particulars can be given only in space and time and that space and time themselves are given as particulars (which is just to say represented without the use of general characteristics or concepts), it will not immediately follow that "this space and this time, and together with them all appearances, are not in themselves any *things;* rather they are nothing but representations and cannot exist outside of our mind" (A 492 / B 520).

The same conclusion applies even more obviously to the "transcendental" expositions of space and time. Here Kant offers his classical "regressive" argument: Beginning with the assumption that "geometry is a science which determines the properties of space synthetically and yet *a priori*" (B 40), and likewise that there are synthetic *a priori* judgments about time, he argues that such cognition must depend on an "original intuition." For synthetic propositions cannot come from a "mere concept" (B 41), and as *a priori* knowledge "these principles cannot be drawn from experience, for this would not yield either strict universality or apodictic certainty" (A 31 / B 47). Yet even if we concede Kant's claim that such synthetic *a priori* knowledge can be explained only by *a priori* representations of space and time which reveal connections beyond those contained in mere concepts of spatial figures or temporal relations, it is clear that a further argument is needed to prove that space and time themselves are nothing but these *a priori* representations. Kant may well present the final step to transcendental idealism as if it were unproblematic: "Now how can there reside in the mind an outer intuition, which precedes the objects themselves and in which the concept of the latter can be determined *a priori*? Obviously not otherwise than insofar as it has its seat only in the subject ... therefore only as the form of outer *sense* in general" (B 41). But the justification for Kant's conclusion that space and time are *only* representations or forms of representation, therefore *not* things in themselves or properties or relations thereof, is far from obvious. Once again, what is to exclude the possibility that we can indeed have *a priori* knowledge of spatial and temporal relations because we are acquainted with a feature of our own minds which *restricts* us to the experience of objects which are themselves spatial and temporal? Even if we know it *a priori* – indeed, just because we know it *a priori* – why isn't the necessity that our experience be spatial and temporal decisive evidence that whatever objects we do in fact experience are themselves in compliance with this restriction or are experienced at all just *because* they are spatial and temporal? Why doesn't the indispensable role of space and time in our experience prove the transcendental realism rather than idealism of space and time themselves?

What I will argue is that Kant's deepest reason for this conclusion lies in his conception of the nature of *a priori* knowledge, specifically in an interpretation of *necessary truth* as absolute rather than conditional which is incompatible with the otherwise natural assumption that our minds' restriction to spatial and temporal representation is good evidence for the actual spatiality and temporality of what we experience. In Kant's view, our *a priori* knowledge of space and time thus requires the denial that things in themselves really are spatial and temporal, and from this it follows that space and time are *merely* forms of intuition or representation.

349

However, Kant also entertained metaphysical and even theological considerations which inclined him toward the denial that space and time are genuine constituents of ultimate reality, and these must be at least briefly mentioned.

The metaphysics and theology of space and time

The metaphysical argument

Kant's purely metaphysical argument for transcendental idealism arises in his discussion of the great philosophical and scientific controversy of the previous generation, namely the controversy between the absolutist and relativist conceptions of space and time championed by Newton and Leibniz respectively. Although Kant thought that the Newtonian conception of space and time as all-embracing containers which exist independently of whatever they contain could serve to ground the mathematical content of Newtonian physics, which of course he accepted without reservation – and which indeed was all that Newton himself claimed was certain (with his famous reservation *"hypotheses non fingo"*) – he clearly thought the concepts of absolute space and time were otherwise untenable. We have already seen that Kant's view that positions in absolute space or time cannot be immediately perceived is nothing less than the ultimate epistemological premise of the transcendental theory of experience. But Kant also thought that the metaphysical conception of "two eternal and infinite self-subsistent nonentities ... which are there (yet without there being anything real)" (A 39 / B 56) was absurd; as he put it as early as 1770, such a conception is an "empty fabrication of reason" which "pertains to the world of fable" (ID, §15D, 2:404). And of course the possibility that space or time could themselves be a property of any single thing is not even mentioned; no one since Parmenides had imagined that all of space or time was filled by any single object. So from the metaphysical point of view, the only alternative is some form of the Leibnizian conception, namely that space and time are some kind of relation or system of relations.

It is clear that Kant's most fundamental objection to the Leibnizian theory of space and time was epistemological and not metaphysical. In the Dissertation he argued that the Leibnizians

... throw geometry down from the summit of certitude and thrust it back into the rank of those sciences whose principles are empirical. For if all the affections of space are merely borrowed by experience from external relations, there is only a comparative universality present in the axioms of geometry, of the kind that is obtained by induction, that is, extending as far as it is observed.

(ID, §15D, 2:404)

And in his foremost discussion of the controversy between "mathematical" and "metaphysical students of nature" in the *Critique,* what he argues

350

against the Leibnizians is that because they conceive of spatial and temporal relations as "abstracted from experience" and thus "confusedly represented," they must "controvert the validity or at least apodictic certainty of *a priori* mathematical doctrines in regard to real things (e.g., in space)" (A 40 / B 56–7). As we have seen, however, it is not self-evident that *a priori* knowledge could not be grounded in pure intuition yet also characterize things as they really are, and indeed, Kant basically follows this criticism of the Leibnizians with his most detailed exposition of the epistemological argument for transcendental idealism.[6]

However, in the second edition of the "Aesthetic" he also tacks on a purely metaphysical argument from the premise that space and time can only be relations. In fact, like his empiricist predecessors as well as the rationalists themselves, Kant harbored a prejudice against the ultimate reality of relations. Leibniz himself was led to deny that monads are really in space by, among other things, his own prejudice against relations: Since a typical spatial relation, such as that between two lines of different length, "is indeed out of the subjects; but being neither a substance, nor an accident, it must be a mere ideal thing, the consideration of which is nevertheless useful."[7] And Locke, for instance, also held that relation cannot be "contained in the real existence of Things, but is something extraneous, and superinduced."[8] Similarly, as I noted in my discussion of the transcendental deduction, Kant himself seems to have derived some part of the impetus for his transcendental idealism by simply assuming at the outset of the "Transcendental Aesthetic" that *if* something could be shown to be a "*form* of appearance" – that is, something which allows a multiplicity of data to be "ordered in certain relations" – then it would follow immediately that "it must lie ready *a priori* in the mind" (A 20 / B 34). But to the conclusion of the "Aesthetic" Kant also added an explicit argument from the metaphysical premise that relations are not real:

Now a thing in itself [*Sache an sich*] cannot be cognized through mere relations; therefore it is well to judge that since nothing can be given to us through outer sense except mere representations of relation, this can contain nothing but the relation of an object to the subject in its representation, and not anything intrinsic which pertains to the object itself. This is likewise the case with inner sense.   (B 67)

Just because space and time are constituted by the relations among their parts (even if they can be represented antecedently to those parts, as the metaphysical exposition requires), yet relations are never intrinsic properties of things as they are in themselves, therefore space and time cannot be features of things in themselves. But since these relations must have *some* foundation, Kant concludes that the forms of intuition must "express only the relation of an object to the subject," though nothing true of either object or subject by itself.

Though he did not state this explicit inference from the relational character of space and time in the *Critique* until the second edition, Kant had long held the general form of this argument. Thus the *Nova Delucidatio*, in spite of its anti-Leibnizian treatment of causation, had included a typically Leibnizian argument against the existence of any possible interaction among the constituents of a single world, apart from their common causation by an extramundane God. This argument turned on the supposition that "since relation is a relative determination, i.e., not intelligible in a being considered absolutely, the relation, and likewise its determining reason, cannot be understood through the means of the existence of a substance whose existence is affirmed in it" (Proposition XIII, 1:413). However, this argument surely turns on nothing other than simply equating considering a thing absolutely, in the sense of considering it in its ultimate reality, with considering it absolutely in the sense of *considering it in isolation* – thereby, of course, insuring that none of its relations will count among its genuine characteristics. A similar equivocation infects Kant's later application of this line of thought to the special case of space and time. If the metaphysical expositions sufficed to establish that space and time are nothing but systems of relations, and if Kant were entitled to the metaphysical premise that relations are not ultimately real, then he would have a sound metaphysical argument for transcendental idealism. Of course, it would now be hard for us to take the metaphysical premise seriously. After Frege and Russell succeeded in clarifying the logic of relations, a metaphysical prejudice against relations could certainly derive no comfort from their earlier logical obscurity, and so this metaphysical argument could hardly be persuasive today. But Kant produces no metaphysical title to the claim that relations are not real. For either he just confuses the idea of a thing which lacks relation *to us* with a thing which lacks *all relations whatever*[9] – certainly making a hash of the case of *inner* sense in the process, since the real self of which time is only an apparent property could hardly be conceived to be without relation to ourselves to begin with – or else he just assumes from the outset that space and time merely represent relations to ourselves, which is supposed to be the conclusion of the argument. His argument must therefore simply presuppose the unsupported metaphysical premise that relations are not real in order to yield the conclusion that space and time are not properties of things in themselves, which in turn implies that they must be mere forms of our own representation of things.

The theological argument

Kant also added to the second edition of the *Critique* a theological argument against the ultimate reality of space and time. This is even less persuasive than the metaphysical argument just considered, but since it manages to grip Kant even during the period of his most intense effort on the refutation of idealism it must at least be described.

Kant claims that any conception of space and time as "forms of things in themselves, and indeed ones which, as *a priori* conditions of the existence of things, would remain even if one removed the things themselves" (B 71) is incompatible with natural theology. This is not for the reason one might expect, namely that the genuine spatiality and even more so temporality of things would make it hard to comprehend God's eternal omniscience, but rather because on such a conception of space and time "as conditions of all existence in general they would also have to be conditions of the existence of God." That is, on the assumption of the ultimate reality of space and time, God would not merely have to *perceive* spatiotemporally but would have to *be spatiotemporal,* and this is obviously absurd.

On the face of it, such an argument is simply fallacious. It seems to confuse the supposition that space and time are genuine properties of *some* things in themselves – namely, the ones we can also perceive – with the supposition that they are properties of *all* things as they really are, and this seems entirely groundless. Even if we suppose that the *universality* of a property which both genuinely pertains to its object and can be known to do so *a priori* derives from the *necessity* that the property pertain to the object, it would not follow that the property necessarily pertains to *all* beings, even a being which is itself necessary (*per hypothesis*). Even if we concede that whenever any object necessarily has some property *F* then *all* objects of some particular group must also be *F*, we do not thereby suppose that *all objects whatever* must be *F*. Rather, we presuppose some other property *G* and the premise that all *G*'s are *F*, from which we infer that some particular object, being *G, must* also be *F*. But then Kant's argument would fail if the property which fills in *G* when *F* is spatiotemporality is something which some or even all other objects have but which God lacks. From a theological point of view, of course, the property of *being created* might fill this bill very neatly: It might perfectly well be a consequence of an object's genuinely being created that it is genuinely spatiotemporal without it thereby being required that God be spatiotemporal.

It may be hard to imagine that Kant could have committed such an elementary error. And in fact, he probably did not but was instead worried about the possibility that God and the objects which we perceive in space and time *would* share some property which would entail that God himself was spatiotemporal if the other objects were genuinely so as well. This property is none other than infinitude:

Besides, space and time are such necessary *a priori* determinations of the existence of things that if they were determinations of things in themselves, then not only would they along with all the consequences that pertain to them have to be made into conditions of the existence of divinity [*Gottheit*], but, on account of their infinitude, absolute necessity, and necessity [*sic*], they would even have to be made into divine properties. For if one has once made them into determinations of things in themselves, then there would be no reason why they should be limited to finite beings. If theology is not to contradict itself, it sees itself as necessitated to make both mere form[s] of our sensibility ... (R 6317, 18:626)

Kant clearly thinks that precisely because space and time are themselves infinite (perhaps even our only ways of representing infinitude), yet, because God himself is also conceived as infinite, then if space and time are thought to be genuine they might also be thought to pertain to God as consequences of his infinitude. Perhaps Kant even thought that Newton, following Henry More, had already committed such an error in identifying God's *immensitas* with infinite space and his *aeternitas* with infinite time. But of course there would clearly be a fallacy in affirming that because space and time are infinite, all that is infinite is spatiotemporal, and even if Kant's idea were only that because we can only *represent* infinitude spatiotemporally there is a danger that we will so represent God, traditional theories of the equivocal or analogical nature of divine predicates – or, in Kant's own words, "divine properties" – would suffice to avert such temptation. Transcendental idealism would not be required.

This paragraph also mentions "absolute necessity" as a property which spatiotemporality and God himself seem to share. This would seem an even more dubious common property, for surely an absolute necessity that God *be* is not equivalent to an absolute necessity that he or anything else *be spatiotemporal*. And in any case it is hardly self-evident why there would have to be an absolute necessity that things in themselves be spatiotemporal just for them to be genuinely spatiotemporal at all. We shall now see, however, that Kant's argument that our *a priori* knowledge of space and time entails that space and time are not properties or relations of things as they are in themselves depends on nothing other than an assumption that our *a priori* knowledge of space and time entails an absolute necessity: the absolute necessity that the objects of such knowledge be as they are thereby represented, rather than the merely conditional necessity that *if* we perceive any particular objects then they must indeed satisfy the restrictions on our possible experience which we know to hold *a priori*. Obscure as it may be, therefore, Kant's theological argument for transcendental idealism contains a clue to the character of his epistemological argument.

Transcendental idealism and necessary truth

Before describing his metaphysical and theological arguments for the transcendental ideality of space and time, I claimed that Kant's most fundamental argument for transcendental idealism is to be found in his understanding of the conditions of possibility of *a priori* knowledge, thus in his epistemology. As Kant interprets the necessary truth of what is known *a priori*, the objects of such knowledge cannot actually be things as they are in themselves or properties they have independently of their relation to us, and it is precisely *because* space and time cannot be properties of things in themselves that they must be *mere* forms of representation, not vice versa. In order to sustain this claim, two steps are required. First, I must show that Kant's key inference is *from* the nonspatiality of things in themselves *to* the merely subjective status of space as a form of representation, and not vice versa. Second, I must explicate Kant's inference from the necessary truth of the contents of our knowledge about space to the nonspatiality of things in themselves.[10] In the end, we shall see that this assumption about necessary truth on which Kant's argument ultimately depends is not merely intrinsically controversial, but also – just as Kant's early jottings about philosophical claims to necessity suggested[11] – could not possibly be grounded by Kant's own transcendental method. This will be our first decisive evidence that a necessary condition for the possibility of experience is not *eo ipso* transcendentally ideal.

From nonspatiality to subjectivity

First, that Kant's inference is from the nonspatiality of things in themselves to the subjectivity of the necessary forms of representation, rather than vice versa, is evident from prominent passages in Kant's published work as well as from several key passages in his unpublished remains.

The passage in which Kant draws his conclusions from the "Metaphysical" and "Transcendental Expositions" of the "concept of space" should itself be sufficient to establish the outline of Kant's argument, since it is the very first place where Kant introduces the concept of the thing in itself into the body of the *Critique*.[12] This passage begins with the outright assertion that things in themselves *are not* spatial, not with any suggestion that their nature is undecidable or that we are ignorant of it. This certainly suggests that it is precisely the nonspatiality of things in themselves which is the fundamental content of Kant's transcendental idealism, not some abstract conception of a totally unknowable order of things, the nonspatiality of which would itself also be unknowable. Further, the passage concisely displays the order of Kant's inference *from* the nonspatiality of things in themselves *to* the merely subjective nature of space, as well as the claim about knowledge of necessity on which the premise of this inference itself depends. Thus:

(a) Space does not represent any property of things in themselves, nor does it represent them in their relation to one another. That is to say, space does not represent any determination that attaches to the objects themselves, and which remains even when abstraction has been made of all the subjective conditions of intuition. For no determinations, whether absolute or relative, can be intuited prior to the existence of the things to which they belong, and none, therefore, can be intuited *a priori*.

Kant denies that things in themselves are spatial – or more precisely, that they are spatial in any of the ways permitted by metaphysics: That space itself is a substance has already been held to be absurd (A 39 / B 56), so it is now more to the point to deny that it can be either a property or relation of substances as they really are. This assertion is itself *derived* from the alleged incompatibility of such a supposition with the apriority of our knowledge of space – and though Kant hardly explicates this assumption here, this is where his interpretation of the necessary truth of our knowledge of space will ultimately play its fatal role. Only then does Kant draw, from what is

355

therefore the intermediate premise (a) that space is *not* a feature of things in themselves, the *conclusion* that space can be *only* a subjective form of representation:

(b) Space is nothing but the form of all appearances of outer sense. It is the subjective condition of sensibility, under which alone outer intuition is possible for us. (A 26 / B 42)

Thus, the premise that as a necessary condition for the representation of objects space must reflect the nature of the knowing subject *rather* than of the object known, which Allison, Strawson, and others have identified as the fundamental assumption of Kant's argument, is not the "fundamental" premise of Kant's most prominent argument for the nonspatiality of things in themselves. It is clearly the conclusion of Kant's argument.

The chief task, then, is to explain the final sentence of premise a, that is, the assertion that *a priori* knowledge entails the nonspatiality of things in themselves. First, however, we will examine further evidence for the assertion that the nonspatiality of things in themselves is the basis for Kant's introduction of the concept of things in themselves, rather than a consequence of the latter. Another clear piece of evidence for this interpretation can be found in the prize essay, *What Is the Real Progress Which Metaphysics Has Made in Germany since the Time of Leibniz and Wolff?,* a work which we have already seen to reveal even Kant's mature thought in its most elemental form. Here again Kant first derives the nonspatiality of things in themselves from the requirements of *a priori* knowledge and only then draws the additional inference that space is therefore merely a feature of the "natural constitution of the subject":

But it is not the form of the object as it is constituted in itself, but rather the form of the subject, namely what manner of representation its sense is capable of, which makes possible *a priori* intuition. For if this form were to be taken from the object, then this would first have to be perceived, and we could be conscious of its constitution only in this perception. But that would then be an empirical *a priori* intuition. We can quickly be convinced whether such a thing could exist or not when we consider whether the judgment which attributes this form to the object is accompanied with necessity or not, for [only] in the latter case is it merely empirical.

The form of the object, as it can be represented in an *a priori* intuition alone, is therefore grounded not on the constitution of this object in itself, but rather on the natural constitution of the subject which is capable of an intuitive representation of the object, and this subjective [element] in the formal constitution of sense, as the receptivity for the intuition of an object, is alone that which makes possible *a priori,* that is, preceding all perception, intuition *a priori. . . .* (20:266–7)

This passage is even clearer than the passage from the *Critique,* since it makes explicit that the real premise of the argument is not just a general claim about the conditions for *a priori* knowledge but a specific claim about the conditions under which *judgments of necessity* can be known. It again confirms that Kant first argues for the impossibility of things being spatial in themselves and only then asserts the alternative that space must be a

merely subjective form of representation. Kant's overall argument clearly
takes the form of an argument by exclusion: Space might be either a
property of things in themselves or of the constitution of the subject, or
both, but it cannot be a property of things in themselves, because of the
problem (yet to be explicated) about necessity; therefore it can be only a
feature of the constitution of the subject.

The same pattern of inference appears in a number of Kant's notes. One
note is from the same period in which Kant was preparing the essay on the
progress of metaphysics. Like the passages we have considered so far, this
passage makes it clear that it is a claim about the possibility of *a priori*
knowledge which leads to the denial that space is a property of things in
themselves, although, unlike those considered so far, this passage specifically mentions the propositions of mathematics, thus suggesting that the
necessary truth of mathematics is, or is connected with, the ultimate
premise of Kant's transcendental idealism. I shall return to this point later;
for now I want to emphasize only that this passage too makes clear that the
key to Kant's overall argument is the *denial* that space and time can be
properties of things in themselves, and that it is this which implies that our
a priori knowledge can be explained only by the theory that space is a
merely subjective form of representation:

That synthetic *a priori* propositions are real, therefore that they are also possible,
is proved by mathematics. But that these [propositions] are not possible by means
of the perception of objects as things in themselves is clear from the fact that they
would otherwise be empirical and would contain no necessity, which is characteristic only of *a priori* cognitions. That they therefore express only the subjective
constitution of our sensibility, which yields the form of intuition before everything
empirical, (therefore) *a priori* ...   (R 6349, 18:674)

In other words, the first thing that must be done to explain the *a priori*
knowledge of mathematics is to reject the reality of space; then it can be
inferred that space is merely a form of representation, such a form, of
course, being a sufficient condition for explaining *a priori* knowledge.

Perhaps even blunter is a passage from a set of student lecture notes from
the winter semester of 1783–4, that period of intellectual ferment in which
Kant was trying to clarify so much about the *Critique* in the face of the
hostile reviews which its first edition had finally received after a year of
silence:

Space and time give us *a priori* cognitions prior to all experience; therefore they
cannot be derived from experience. – We recognize *a priori* propositions by their
necessity; we have such propositions in geometry, e.g., two times cannot be
simultaneous. [Space and time] therefore cannot be properties of things in
themselves. Since [space and time] are not determinations of objects, therefore they
must be determinations of the subject – therefore the forms of our sensibility. –
Space is the form in which we perceive external things, time the form in which we
perceive ourselves. What we cognize through inner and outer sense is mere
appearance, not things in themselves.   (*Metaphysik Mrongovius*, 29:832)

Again, Kant's argument takes the form of a choice between two alternatives. Space may be either a property of things in themselves or else just a merely subjective condition and feature of our representations of things other than ourselves. But if it is the former, then *a priori* knowledge of it – again, knowledge which is exemplified by our knowledge of mathematical propositions – is impossible. Therefore, it must be the latter.

A few further reflections put Kant's subscription to this form of argument beyond doubt. First,

Since the conditions of space and time, which lie at the ground of all representations of experience, are accompanied with necessity, thus lie *a priori* in the faculty of representations of the senses, this cannot occur except insofar as they lie in the subject and its sensible form of intuition; for this alone is given prior to experience.

If it were assumed that we know the objects of the senses as they are in themselves when we are immediately conscious of them, then this would not be *a priori* knowledge but mere perception, which is not accompanied with any necessity, but would reveal only that it is so, and not that it must necessarily be so.

(R 6346, 18:671)

And

That synthetic *a priori* propositions are possible only through the subjective form of sensibility, consequently that their objects can be represented only as appearances, is to be recognized from the fact that they are accompanied with necessity, but not from concepts by means of analysis. – For if it were assumed that we could perceive things *in themselves,* then necessity and universality would be missing from such propositions. But if [the objects] are mere appearances, then we can know *a priori* how they must appear to us, for [we] can have no other intuitions than those permitted by the subjective constitution of our senses. – But this has nothing to do with the fact that in the case of colors everyone may have his own manner of sensing. For that is sensation, therefore not objective, rather only subjective and carries with it no universality and necessity.

(R 6355, 18:681)

Far from reflecting uncertainty about the objective validity of the most basic elements of our conceptual framework, Kant's idealism derives precisely from his assurance that we have *a priori* knowledge of the necessity of space and time as the unique conditions of the representation of objects. It must now be clear that his argument has the following form. That we have access to a feature of our representations which is known *a priori* by means of access to something which lies within us or which is a feature of the "natural constitution of the subject" is a *necessary* condition for *a priori* knowledge; thus it is at least *part* of the explanation of how we could have knowledge of objects independently of experience of them. But this is not *sufficient* to prove that such a feature is *merely* a subjective form of representation. For here there are two alternatives: that *in addition* to somehow lying in the natural constitution of the subject, the feature concerned is also a genuine property of objects, or else that it is *only* an aspect of the natural constitution of the subject. Thus, for the second alternative to be established, it must be established that the feature is *not* a property of

358

things as they are in themselves in addition to being a property of our representations of things. This first alternative is, however, excluded by the fact that we have *a priori* knowledge of the feature, for this involves necessity – and properties that attach to things in themselves could at best be known to do so *contingently but not necessarily.* So, to return to the case at hand, space certainly does reflect the structure of our form of representation, but, more important, it *cannot* represent the structure of things as they are in themselves, given that our knowledge of it is *a priori.* Therefore it is merely a subjective form of representation.

Space and geometry

Our fundamental question then becomes: What kind of necessity underlies Kant's inference from apriority to subjectivity? But before we turn to that, we must briefly consider the issue of exactly *what* body of (allegedly) *a priori* knowledge about space it is on which Kant's argument is intended to turn. As we have seen, some of Kant's expositions of his argument make only the general assertion that "the conditions of space and time ... are accompanied with necessity, thus lie *a priori* in the faculty of representations of the senses" (R 6346), whereas others refer specifically to the synthetic *a priori* propositions of mathematics (R 6349) or geometry (*Metaphysik Mrongovius*). Indeed, the latter passage not only refers specifically to the *a priori* propositions of geometry, it also uses the example that between two points only one straight line is possible; that is, it specifically assumes the truth of euclidean geometry. This naturally raises the question, is Kant's entire epistemological argument for transcendental idealism predicated on the necessary truth of euclidean geometry, and does it thus fall immediately to the objection that euclidean geometry is contingently true, if indeed true at all (or true of more than a small region of space, etc.)? Or is Kant's argument dependent only upon some more general claims about space, such as that space, whatever exactly its particular form may turn out to be, is the necessary condition for our representation of ontologically distinct objects, or that individual spaces can be recognized only by the introduction of boundaries into an otherwise continuous and unique space, again whatever its precise geometrical form turns out to be?

In spite of the fact that he may have known of the logical possibility of consistent alternatives to euclidean geometry,[13] it seems clear that Kant assumed the necessary truth of euclidean geometry and only euclidean geometry. Kant's commitment to this assumption is sometimes questioned on the basis of his remark that "there is no contradiction in the concept of a figure which is enclosed within two straight lines, since the concepts of two straight lines and of their coming together contain no negation of a figure" (B 268). This is supposed to reflect his recognition of the possibility of alternatives to a fundamental theorem of euclidean geometry. However, as Gordon Brittan has suggested,[14] this sentence is meant to illustrate only the *syntheticity* of geometrical propositions, not their *contingency*: As we saw in Chapter 7, Kant tends to equate mathematical truth with the valid application of a proposition of formal mathematics to an object which may be presented in intuition, and what he is arguing here is clearly that this theorem can neither be derived from the definitions of the terms included in it nor be proved to have such objective validity by logical analysis of definitions alone, *not that there may actually be alternatives to it*. Kant not only assumed that mathematical *proof* requires intuitions as well as definitions and logic (a view to which he may have been reasonably inclined by the fact that there was no logic available to him adequate for axiomatizing truths about a continuous space[15]) but also adopted a theory of mathematical *truth* which would not, in any case, count even consistent but merely logical possibilities as any form of truth.[16] For a proposition to be known to be a truth (*a fortiori* a necessary truth), Kant always supposed that it must *describe an object*. Thus,

The possibility of experience is, then, what gives objective reality to all our *a priori* cognitions. . . .
Although we know *a priori* in synthetic judgments a great deal regarding space in general and the figures which productive imagination describes in it and can obtain such judgments without actually requiring any experience, yet even this knowledge would be nothing but a playing with a mere figment of the brain were it not that space has to be regarded as a condition of appearances which constitute the material for outer experience.

(A 157 / B 196; see also A 239–40 / B 298–9)

Without an object, on Kant's view, there is no knowledge of mathematical truth at all, yet when space, as the object of pure and empirical intuition alike, is presented, it clearly confirms only euclidean geometry. Indeed, as was suggested in my discussion of the transcendental deduction, much of Kant's battle with rationalism can be understood as the result of his attempt to distinguish between *logical* and *real* relations, and it is clearly his view that in mathematics as well as physics the merely logical consistency of a system of concepts does not suffice to establish its objective reality. Intuitions are needed for that, and our intuitions, he obviously supposes, confirm the truth of euclidean geometry alone.

Nevertheless, some defenders of transcendental idealism have tried to drive a wedge between Kant's commitment to *a priori* knowledge of spatiality in general and his commitment to *a priori* knowledge and thus the necessary truth of euclidean geometry in particular.[17] Thus, Allison has asserted that "the argument from geometry only moves to ideality by way of an appeal to the *a priori* and intuitive character of the representation of space," which is provided in the metaphysical exposition of space without reference to the synthetic *a priori* propositions of geometry, and has concluded "therefore, that the argument for ideality can bypass completely . . . any considerations about the nature of geometry."[18] However, this is misleading. For one thing, it overlooks the fact that Kant clearly felt that

360

the necessary truth of euclidean geometry was more evident and more persuasive than the necessary truth of the more general synthetic *a priori* propositions about space demonstrated in the metaphysical exposition, and could thus be used in the popular presentation of his theory by the "regressive" method in the *Prolegomena*. But (and this is much more important) the supposition that general truths such as that space is a necessary condition of representation, that it is unique and does not consist of parts, and so on, could be known to be necessarily true without any specific geometry which describes the structure of this space also being known to necessarily true seriously misrepresents that conception of necessity which underlies Kant's inference from necessary truth to transcendental idealism – an absolute necessity which must be imposed on reality, rather than a conditional necessity which reality may happen to satisfy. That is, if it were merely Kant's view that, for some reason having to do with our "natural constitution," it is a subjective condition for any successful perception that we can perceive objects only *if* they are in space or are spatial, then we could imagine that we might be able to perceive objects with any of a variety of particular spatial forms, that is, satisfying any of a variety of geometries. For instance, certain topological constraints might be indispensable if space is to serve its role of enabling us to represent the distinctness of objects from each other and ourselves by their spatial separation, but a large amount of metrical variation might be compatible with such a function. But it is not Kant's view that we know merely the conditional necessity that if we are to perceive things external to ourselves they must be spatial. Rather, it is Kant's view that what we perceive is *necessarily spatial* in an absolute sense, and that the existence of this absolute necessity can be explained only by the supposition that we actually *impose* spatial form on objects. But it is difficult to conceive how we could impose spatial form on objects without imposing some *particular* spatial form on them – for the simple reason that although we can *state a requirement* on our cognition (or anything else) without being fully determinate about the properties of any object that will satisfy it, we cannot *make an object* (to satisfy such a requirement) without making it determinate. Conditions are like *concepts,* thus not fully determinate, but objects are always fully determinate. Or, in his own terms, precisely because Kant conceives of space as an *intuition* not a concept, a particular rather than something general, he must also suppose that even as a purely subjective form of intuition *it must be fully determinate.* But that means that if we impose spatial form at all we must impose some particular spatial form, and if it is necessarily true that we impose some spatial form, rather than just necessarily true that if we are to perceive things they had better be spatial, then it must be necessarily true that we impose some particular spatial form on things. But this means that the necessary truth of euclidean geometry – or, if Kant is wrong about the facts, then the necessary truth of some other particular geometry *instead*[19] – is not an eliminable feature of his transcendental idealism. Rather, it is an obvious reflection of Kant's basic

361

assumption about the necessary truth of *a priori* propositions, which leads to his denial that things in themselves can be characterized by such truths and his conclusion that the conditions necessary for the truth of such propositions must instead be imposed on our representations of things.

Thus, the issue of the role of the *a priori* knowledge of geometry in Kant's argument for transcendental idealism brings us to its heart, Kant's interpretation of the necessity of *a priori* knowledge and the reason for his inference from the very necessity of spatiality to the nonspatiality of things in themselves. So we may now return to that inference.

From necessity to nonspatiality

As we saw before the last digression, the crucial premise of Kant's argument for transcendental idealism is that whatever is known *a priori* cannot be a property of things in themselves. The basis for this, in turn, is his supposition that properties of things in themselves could not be known *a priori* because they could not be known to be necessary. Kant's subscription to this premise is at the heart of his Copernican revolution:

> If intuition must conform to the constitution of the objects, I do not see how we could know anything of the latter *a priori*, but if the object (as object of the senses) must conform to the constitution of our faculty of intuition, I have no difficulty in conceiving such a possibility as this. (B xvii)

And the same assumption is the explicit premise for the unambiguous conclusion that "space does not represent any property of things in themselves":

> ... Space does not represent any determination that attaches to the objects themselves and that remains even when abstraction has been made of all the subjective conditions of intuition. For no determinations, whether absolute or relative, can be intuited prior to the existence of the things to which they belong, and none, therefore, can be intuited *a priori*. (A 26 / B 42)

To have *a priori* knowledge of a property of objects is to know that it attaches to objects (in some class) universally and necessarily. But to know that it attaches to objects (in that class) universally and necessarily is to know that it attaches to any particular object (in the class) independently of experience of that object, thus even prior to experience of it. But, Kant assumes, it is not possible to know independently of experience of it that an object genuinely has, on its own, a certain property. Therefore, space and time, which are known *a priori*, cannot be genuine properties of objects and can be only features of our representations of them.

That Kant's argument turns on this premise, thus on the inference from necessity to idealism, is obvious in the end, and it is difficult to see why anyone should suppose that an argument which does not employ the premise that the *a priori* knowledge of a determination is incompatible with its independent existence could represent Kant's thought. But why does

Kant assume this premise, when it is *not* in fact self-evidently impossible to know that an object must have a certain property prior to experience of it? On the contrary, it seems at least possible to imagine that we could know, *because of certain constraints on our ability to perceive,* that any object we perceive must have a certain property: We can perceive only objects that *do,* and so we can know that whatever objects we perceive *will.* But then it would seem natural to explain our actual perception of any particular object as due to the very fact that it *does* have the property in question. In the contemporary terms also used in our discussion of the transcendental deduction of the categories, it would be a *de dicto* necessity of any object described as experienced by us that it satisfy the necessary conditions of the possibility of our experience, but it would not be a *de re* necessity that any particular object satisfy such conditions. Why does Kant assume precisely the opposite?

To put this question in the traditional terms going back to the nineteenth-century debate between Adolf Trendelenburg and Kuno Fischer,[20] Kant assumes that space and time must be features *either* of our representations *or* of objects but not both, rather than that space and time may be either properties of objects or *both* necessary constraints on our perception of objects *and* genuine features of the objects we do succeed in perceiving. However, contrary to what Trendelenburg supposed, Kant hardly *overlooked* this last alternative. Obviously he meant to *exclude* it on the ground that it is incompatible with our *a priori* knowledge of space and time, particularly with the necessity of this knowledge. Again, "no determinations ... can be intuited prior to the existence of the things to which they belong." But why does he think that this alternative is *excluded* by the necessity of spatiality? Why does he suppose that the genuine spatiality of things in themselves is *incompatible* with our *a priori* knowledge of spatiality rather than being our *best explanation* of it, given our *a priori* knowledge that spatiality is a *necessary condition* on our perception of objects?

As I have suggested, the answer to this question lies in Kant's interpretation of the necessity inherent in our knowledge of space. My formulation of the alternative to the assumption that independent existence is incompatible with *a priori* knowledge depends on expressing the conclusion of Kant's argument that spatiality is a necessary condition on our perception of objects as a *conditional necessity.* That is, this formulation supposes that Kant's argument is intended to yield a result of the form, "It is necessary that *if* an object is perceived by us it must be perceived in space" (or even in euclidean space). It is indeed natural to explain perception of an object understood as satisfaction of this *conditional* necessity by the assumption that any object actually perceived *is* spatial (and euclidean) independently of our perception of it. But this is not how Kant interprets the necessity implicated in our *a priori* knowledge of spatiality and euclidean geometry. Kant interprets this necessity as *absolute necessity* and believes that knowledge of absolute necessity is incompatible with the independent existence of the object in question. That is, Kant assumes that what we know *a priori* is not this proposition:

(1) Necessarily, if we are to perceive an object then it *is* spatial and euclidean.

but rather this proposition:

(2) If we perceive an object, it is *necessarily* spatial and euclidean.

He then assumes, reasonably enough, that this cannot be known of objects that are spatial independently of us, for of such objects we could at best know that they are spatial, but only *contingently* rather than *necessarily* so. So instead he concludes that we can know any object to be *necessarily* spatial only if it is, in the end, an object of our own creation: "We can know things . . . *a priori* only so far as we make them ourselves" (R 6342, 18:667).

That it is on the alleged incompatibility of the necessity of *a priori* knowledge and the independent existence of the properties known *a priori* that Kant's fundamental argument for transcendental idealism depends is, as we have seen, evident in many passages. But the exact assumption about necessity which Kant must be making in order to be led to this argument is not revealed as often. Indeed, sometimes Kant even writes as though he did assume a merely conditional necessity:

Since we cannot make the special conditions of sensibility into conditions of the possibility of objects, but only of their appearances, we may well say that space comprehends all things which may appear to us externally, but not all things in themselves, whether they are intuited or not . . .   (A 27 / B 43)

However, such a cautious statement simply fails to explain the inference which Kant draws from it, which is not that agreement with the special conditions of our sensibility is a *contingent* property of the objects that possess it, but that it is an *ideal* property – that is, "nothing, as soon as we leave out the condition of the possibility of all experience, and assume it is something which pertains to the things in themselves" (A 28 / B 44). But Kant does reveal his interpretation of the necessity of spatiality, indeed of euclidean geometry, and thus does explain this otherwise inexplicable conclusion, in one central passage in the "Transcendental Aesthetic." This is the first of his "General Conclusions," in which, "to avoid all misapprehension," he proposes to "explain as clearly as possible, what our view is regarding the fundamental constitution of sensible knowledge in general" (A 42 / B 59). Given this introduction, it seems reasonable to assume that what follows is indeed a precise statement of Kant's argument.

Kant insists that what will lend the argument of the "Aesthetic" "that certainty and freedom from doubt which is required of any theory that is to serve as an organon" (A 46 / B 63) is his explanation of the fact that in regard to both space and time "there is a large number of *a priori* apodictic and synthetic propositions," such as the "propositions of geometry," which are incompatible with the supposition that "space and time are themselves objective" (A 46 / B 64). Kant adduces as examples of the propositions he has in mind the propositions that "two straight lines cannot enclose a space, and with them alone no figure is possible" and that "given three straight lines, a figure is possible" (A 47 / B 65). He then rehearses his explanation that because these propositions are synthetic – that is, cannot be derived from the *concepts* of the objects mentioned – their confirmation requires intuition. The nature of Kant's assumption about the exact nature of such geometrical propositions is revealed, however, in his further argument that this intuition must be *a priori,* and that this apriority requires in turn that space be a *merely* subjective condition of sensible intuition:

> But of what kind is this intuition? Is it a pure *a priori* intuition or an empirical intuition? Were it the latter, no universally valid proposition could ever arise out of it – still less an apodictic proposition – for experience can never yield such. You must therefore give yourself an object *a priori* in intuition and ground upon this your synthetic proposition. If there did not exist in you a power of *a priori* intuition, and if that subjective condition were not also at the same time, as regards its form, the universal *a priori* condition under which alone the object of this outer intuition is itself possible; if the object (the triangle) were something in itself, apart from any relation to you, how could you say that what necessarily exist in you as subjective conditions for the construction of the triangle must of necessity belong to the triangle itself? You could not then add anything new (the figure) to your concepts (of three lines) as something which must necessarily be met with in the object, since [on the rejected hypothesis] this object is given antecedently to your knowledge, and not by means of it. If, therefore, space (and the same is true of time) were not merely a form of your intuition, containing conditions *a priori,* under which alone things can be outer objects to you, and without which subjective conditions outer objects are in themselves nothing, you could not in regard to outer objects determine anything whatsoever in an *a priori* manner. It is therefore, not merely possible or probable, but indubitably certain, that space and time, as the necessary conditions of all outer and inner experience, are merely subjective conditions of all our intuition ...
>
> (A 48–9 / B 65–6)

The final sentence of this extract makes it indeed "indubitably certain" that Kant does *not* think that something's being an ineluctable constraint on our perception and its reflecting merely a subjective condition of our own constitution instead of a property of the objects represented are *analytically* equivalent. Instead, that a necessary condition of our intuition is *merely* a subjective condition is precisely what has to be demonstrated. That is, Kant does intend to exclude Trendelenburg's missing alternative, but not as a logical consequence of the mere concept of a condition necessary for our perception. Instead, Kant's exclusion, thus his argument for transcendental idealism, depends on the assumption that spatiality, indeed the specific features of euclidean geometry alluded to, are not merely necessary *if* we are to perceive objects, but must be *necessarily true* of whatever objects they are supposed to be *true* of. This is why Kant introduces *two* references to necessity, or asserts that "what necessarily exist in you as subjective conditions for the construction of a triangle" *must also* "of necessity belong to the triangle itself" or "must necessarily be met with in the object." It is not enough for him that our *representations* of objects are necessarily spatial – which will be true as long as space is *at least* a necessary form of intuition – but he also requires that the *objects* which we represent as spatial are *necessarily* spatial – which they will be only if we make them so, or if they are reduced to our necessarily spatial representations. Thus, although "subjective conditions for the construction" of a figure could be understood as conditional necessities which must be satisfied if you are to succeed in perceiving figures of that sort, Kant's argument depends precisely on the assumption that his claims about space and geometry do *not* just reveal necessary conditions which objects must satisfy if we are to perceive them. Conditions of this sort could be satisfied even if the objects were *contingently* spatial and euclidean, but Kant explicitly asserts that if we perceive objects at all, then it is *necessarily true* of them – *de re* – that they are spatial and euclidean. Only this last assumption requires that the form of the object be "nothing at all" apart from its relation to us, that our subjective condition of intuition also be the condition under which the form of the object *is itself* possible, or even that we must make the objects of *a priori* knowledge.

To slightly formalize this contrast, we can now see that Kant's argument indeed depends, not on the assumption

(1) Necessarily (if x is an object and we perceive x, then x is spatial [and euclidean]),

for this could *easily* be explained on the assumption that since we can perceive only euclidean spatial objects, whatever objects we *happen* to perceive *happen* to satisfy these conditions. Instead, Kant's argument depends on the assumption that

(2) If (x is an object and we perceive x), then necessarily (x is spatial [and euclidean]),

for only this requires not just that we have some *evidence for the truth* of, for example, the statement "Two straight lines cannot be perceived by us to enclose a space" but rather that we have an *explanation* of the *de re* necessity that two straight lines cannot enclose a space. And this explanation is precisely what Kant offers by denying that spatiality is a property of things as they are in themselves and is instead only a feature of our constructive representations of them. Only the assumption of the absolute necessity expressed by assumption 2 instead of the merely conditional necessity expressed by assumption 1 gives rise to an argument for transcendental idealism by excluding Trendelenburg's missing alternative. Or, as Kant's argument suggests, on the excluded alternative the synthetic propositions at stake would be necessarily true of our *representations* of them but only *contingently* true of the objects themselves, but given the coextensionality of universality and necessity (B 4), this would undermine the necessity and thus the apriority of these propositions. On Kant's conception, spatiality cannot be necessarily true of some objects (representations) and contingently true of some others (things in themselves), for then it is not necessarily true of any objects at all; if it is to be necessarily true of any objects at all, it must be necessarily true of all objects of which it is true. Since we cannot assert that spatiality is necessarily true of things in themselves – but can assert that it is necessarily true of some objects – it thus follows that it is not true of things in themselves at all.

Now, of course, the question must arise whether Kant was *entitled* to an assumption of the form of 2 – to his assumption that, for instance, euclidean properties "of necessity belong to the triangle itself" and not just to our representations of triangles. For if he were entitled to it, then his argument for transcendental idealism, though far from an anodyne conceptual necessity, might still be defended; but if he were not, then the denial of spatiality to things in themselves seems groundless. To this question the immediate answer must be that *assumption 2 is not a logically valid consequence of assumption 1*, and thus the absolute necessity of the truths of geometry or of the more general truths about spatiality hardly follows from the conditional necessity that objects must conform to the requirements of our geometry if we are to succeed in perceiving them.[21] Yet a conditional necessity of the form of assumption 1 would seem to be the only kind of necessity that we could ever arrive at by any investigation construed, in Lockean fashion, as *an exploration of the limits of our own cognitive faculties* – which is to say, by a Copernican revolution as Kant apparently intended that to be understood. Discovering by some sort of examination of it that our cognitive constitution limits us to perception of objects satisfying some constraint C can surely reveal to us only that whatever objects we do perceive must satisfy C, not that there is some stronger sense in which they *necessarily* satisfy C. So nothing understood as an investigation of the conditions of our perception alone could yield the result that any property "must of necessity belong to the triangle itself." Thus the argument for transcendental idealism could proceed only by means of an *independent assumption* of the necessary truth of geometry – as indeed is suggested by Kant's "regressive" argument in the *Prolegomena* and is also reflected in the additions to the preface of the second edition of the *Critique* and the separate title for its "Transcendental Exposition" of space. Kant's own transcendental method cannot ground the unconditionally necessary truth of propositions about objects in space, so this necessary truth must be an independent axiom of Kant's argument if transcendental idealism is to follow. Far from being a mere popularization, the regressive style of argument in the *Prolegomena* represents the only form of argument from which transcendental idealism follows – an argument from the outright assumption of the necessary truth of geometry and the more general propositions about spatiality. As with Kant's own preferred tactics for a separate transcendental deduction itself, his argument for transcendental idealism depends on a claim to knowledge of necessary truth. But of course this is shaky ground to stand on, and certainly not a necessary assumption of the transcendental theory of experience described in parts III and IV of this book.

There would seem to be one alternative to this conclusion. As Ross Harrison points out,[22] an absolute necessity of the form "Necessarily (p)" may validly be derived from a conditional necessity of the form "Necessarily (if j then p)," if the *other* premise of the argument is not in fact just "j" but rather "Necessarily (j)." Thus, the necessary truth of unconditional propositions about objects in space might follow from the conditional necessity that we can perceive objects only in space if there were an additional necessity involved. But to exploit this possibility would mean that Kant would have to begin with an assumption such as "Necessarily we perceive objects," yet, as we saw in Part II, it is hard to see how Kant could successfully defend this proposition if it is itself understood as an absolute necessity, or what could possibly explain this, other than an initial assumption to the effect that we make the objects in question. But this would just be an initial assumption of idealism and would make the argument for transcendental idealism from the *a priori* knowledge of geometry circular.

But it must be clear by now that Kant's assumption of absolute rather than conditional necessity in the argument of the "Transcendental Aesthetic" is not an isolated occurrence. As we saw in our examination of the transcendental deduction (argument IIA) and shall see again in the next chapter, it is precisely such an assumption that there is an absolute rather than conditional necessity that we experience external objects which underlies one of Kant's chief arguments for transcendental idealism from the theory of judgment rather than from the forms of intuition. This is why Kant offers his own explicit rejection of the missing alternative objection as a concluding comment on the transcendental deduction:

A middle course may be proposed between the two mentioned above, namely that the categories are neither *self-thought* first principles *a priori* of our knowledge nor derived from experience but subjective dispositions of thought ... so ordered by our Creator that their employment is in complete harmony with the laws of nature ... – a kind of *preformation-system* of pure reason. ... There is this decisive objection against the suggested middle course, that the *necessity* of the categories, which belongs to their very conception, would then have to be sacrificed. The concept of cause, for instance, which expresses the necessity of an event under a presupposed condition, would be false if it rested only on an arbitrary subjective necessity, implanted in us, of connecting certain empirical representations according to the rule of causal connection. I would not then be able to say that the effect is connected with the cause in the object but only that I am so constituted that I cannot think this representation otherwise than as thus connected. This is exactly what the skeptic most desires. (B 167–8)

The difference between "self-thought first principles" of knowledge and subjective necessities "implanted in us" can only be the difference between rules of thought which we are capable of imposing upon objects – and which are thus "self-thought" – and requirements of thought which objects must satisfy if we are to successfully represent them but which we cannot impose upon them merely by our own thought. But Kant simply has no basis for claiming that the *a priori* forms of intuition as well as conceptualization are such "self-thought first principles" instead of mere subjective necessities, unless he makes the additional assumption of the absolute rather than conditional necessity of the premises of his argument. Without such an assumption,[23] Kant has no ground on which to exclude a "preformation-system" of either pure reason (that is, understanding) or pure intuition, or, in other words, to reject an argument of the form that since we can perceive external objects only if they are spatial and euclidean, the best explanation of our perception of any given object is just that it happens to be spatial and euclidean, and nothing more. That it is something more – namely necessarily so – is the additional assumption required to generate transcendental idealism, but, as we saw, one for which Kant has no sound basis. If this is what it takes to refute skepticism – a proof that any suspect predicate of an object is, unconditionally, *necessarily* true of it – then Kant would hand the skeptic an easy victory indeed.

To be fair, we should note that Kant has somewhat more motivation for his exclusion of the preformation system in the case of causality than in that of geometry. As was noted earlier, Kant assumes not merely that particular causal connections must be necessary *relative* to causal laws under which they are subsumed but also that the causal laws themselves must be *necessarily true*.[24] However, as we saw, Kant also concedes in the *Critique of Judgment* that the lawlikeness or necessity of particular causal laws can be established only as what we might call a quasi-necessity by *reflective* rather than *determinant* judgment (see especially 5:183–4). Yet to concede this is to acknowledge that the investigation of the conditions of the possibility of determinant judgment – the alleged project of the *Critique of Pure Reason* – can yield only conditional and not absolute necessities.

Thus, Kant's argument for transcendental idealism from his theory of the forms of intuition does not express epistemological modesty but is rather the consequence of an exceedingly immodest interpretation of the necessity of synthetic *a priori* propositions. We shall now see that a similar assumption is involved in Kant's derivation of transcendental idealism from his theory of judgment, although that also involves both use of the prior results of the "Aesthetic" and a new – and most peculiar – argument about the special case of time.

17
Transcendental idealism and the theory of judgment

My claim that the transcendental theory of experience does not itself imply transcendental idealism would be undercut if Kant could successfully argue from his theory of empirical judgment itself – that is to say, from his theory of subjective and objective time-determination – to the conclusion that things as they are in themselves are not really spatiotemporal. There are several places in which Kant tries to argue for the general thesis that the activity of the understanding can be understood only as the imposition of rule-governedness on objects which cannot be subject to the rules they appear to satisfy independently of our judgment of them, as well as for the particular thesis that special features of the intellectual activity of time-determination require the nontemporality of the real self and, apparently, of the objects which the self represents through the medium of its only apparently temporally successive representations. This chapter will show that these arguments fail.

As we have seen, Kant's transcendental theory of experience ultimately turns on the argument that judgments about the temporal relations of even inner states depend on their correlation with the rule-governed states of objects independent of the self, which are represented as independent of our representations of them precisely by being represented as in space. Sometimes Kant simply infers that because the *spatiality* of the objects which serve as evidence for judgments of time-determination does not represent a feature of those independent objects as they are in themselves, neither can the *temporality* of the self be a real feature of the self.[1] Just because "for all inner perceptions we must derive the determinations of lengths of time or points of time from the changes which are exhibited to us in outer things," he asserts, "the determinations of inner sense have therefore to be ordered in precisely the same way in which we order those of outer sense in space." So if in making spatial determinations we deal with the mere appearances of objects, then "so far as inner intuition is concerned, we know our own subject only as appearance, not as it is in itself" (B 156).

As must be clear by now, Kant has no sound argument for the premise that space does not represent any feature of things as they are in themselves and has likewise failed to provide any sound direct argument for a similar conclusion about time. But even if we were to concede the transcendental ideality of space, Kant's present inference from the case of space to that of time would still not automatically follow. For in addition to the premise of the transcendental ideality of space, this argument would also require the further premise that all features of the epistemic status of the *evidence* for a type of judgment necessarily characterize the *judgments* they support as well. Such a principle could not be derived from logic, of course, where a false statement is permitted to entail a true one. But what is more important is that it cannot even be maintained as a general principle of epistemology itself. To be sure, in many or even most cases for judgment, if there is anything misleading or false about our data for an inference then our conclusion will probably be misleading or false, and we might even allow a general principle that misleading or false evidence can never suffice entirely by itself to *justify* a claim to knowledge. But neither of these points means that it is epistemologically necessary that a conclusion even from false premises *must* be false. I might draw perfectly good conclusions from the testimony of an inveterate liar, for instance, if I know that he is a liar and know how to correct for his lies, perhaps by supposing to be true precisely what he says is false – thus drawing my inferences from his statements supplemented by that supposition. In such a case, certainly, I could not arrive at veridical conclusions about the nature of reality from evidence which considered in itself does not give a veridical picture of reality. Nevertheless, without special reasons to prove that the relation between spatial premises and temporal conclusions might not be one in which false evidence can be corrected by an additional assumption, Kant cannot assume that the transcendental ideality of space automatically implies the transcendental ideality of time and thus of all judgments of the understanding as well. So the burden of Kant's argument for the transcendental ideality of time will have to be borne by independent arguments for the transcendental ideality of time or for the principles of empirical knowledge employed by understanding and judgment more generally. We shall therefore now consider arguments by which Kant does indeed attempt to prove that time and even the entire empirically recognizable world order are transcendentally ideal rather than real.

The act of time-determination

Again, the key to Kant's transcendental theory of time-determination is the argument that the mere apprehension of successively occurring representations is not tantamount to knowledge of the determinate succession of such representations. At any given time, the justification of a claim to knowledge of the determinate order of even merely subjective representations would require defense of that ordering by appeal to a rule-governed realm of enduring objects, interaction with which could have produced only that order of experiences. Kant frequently expresses this theory with the traditional metaphors of mental *action* and *passion*: The *passive* reception or apprehension of representations in the form of inner sense – temporal succession – must be supplemented by the *active* exercise of understanding and judgment in order to complete the synthesis of recognition necessary even for empirical self-consciousness. This metaphor causes a great deal of confusion, for although Kant sometimes writes as though this nontemporality of the self is entailed by the fact that time-determination, or empirical judgment more generally, results from a mental *action,* he also sometimes writes as though it were the *passivity* of apprehension in inner sense which requires transcendental idealism.[2] The latter train of thought is most evident in some of his notorious comments on the idea of an inner sense itself. Thus, in one of the sections of the second-edition text of the transcendental deduction devoted to this delicate topic, Kant writes:

> Now since for *cognition* of our self besides the act of thought, which brings the manifold of every possible intuition to the unity of apperception, there is also requisite a determinate manner of intuition, by means of which this manifold is given, therefore my own existence is not, to be sure, appearance (let alone mere illusion), but the determination of my existence can occur only in accordance with the form of inner sense according to the particular manner in which the manifold, which I connect, is given, and I have accordingly no *cognition* of myself *as I am,* but only as I appear to myself. (B 157–8)

The section as a whole is concerned to argue that self-knowledge cannot stem from the mere *concept* of a self but also requires *intuition*; in the passage quoted, however, Kant actually suggests that just because the manifold of intuition furnished by inner sense is, after all, a kind of intuition, what results is not really knowledge of the self as it really is but only knowledge of how it appears. This seems to rest just on the assumption that forms of sense, as passive, are necessarily ideal, and would thus really represent another, this time even more direct, application of the alleged result of the "Transcendental Aesthetic" to the *materials* for the act of time-determination. Kant at least once obscures this point by introducing activity rather than passivity, but this central passage from the "Transcendental Aesthetic" still makes essentially the same point that because temporality is the form of intuition for inner sense it must be transcendentally ideal. This occurs in Kant's attempt to apply the metaphysical argument against the reality of relations to the case of the self, where the operative assumption of this argument in the case of space – that relations *to the self* cannot represent real relations of objects *among themselves* – cannot be used, and so a more general premise must be employed instead:

> Now since through mere relations a thing in itself is not cognized: It is therefore well to judge that since through the outer sense nothing but mere representations of relation are given, this can contain only the relation of an object to the subject in its representation, and not that which is intrinsic, what pertains to the object in itself. The case is precisely the same with inner intuition. Not merely because the relations of *outer sense* really constitute the material for it, with which we occupy our minds, but rather because time, in which we place these representations, which itself precedes the consciousness of them in experience, and which as the formal condition of the way in which we place them in the mind lies at their basis, already contains [only] relations of succession, simultaneity, and of that which is simul-

taneous with succession (the enduring). Now that which, as representation, can precede all action of thinking something, is intuition, and, if it contains nothing but relations, it is the form of intuition which, since it represents nothing except insofar as something is placed in the mind, cannot be anything other than the manner in which the mind is affected by itself through its own activity, namely this placing of its representation, thus an inner sense as far as its form is concerned. Everything which is represented through a sense is to that extent always appearance, and an inner sense must therefore either not be allowed, or else the subject, which is the object of such a sense, must be able to be represented by it only as appearance ...

(B 67–8)

Here Kant begins by applying to the case of time an argument already made about space – since time consists entirely of relations, it is not real – but then continues, to be sure quite obscurely, to suggest that just because the temporal form of inner sense is something which the mind *creates* for itself or with which it *affects* itself, it cannot be a genuine feature of the mind at all. Here the underlying assumption would perhaps have to be that anything which could characterize the purely *passive* mind might characterize it as it really is, but that somehow cognizance of even its own activity could give only a distorted picture of the passive mind. It is, of course, difficult to imagine what could recommend such an assumption. But the general form of Kant's argument remains clear enough: Forms of intuition cannot represent real properties of objects; therefore, even the form of intuition of the self cannot represent the self as it really is.

But Kant also suggests an independent argument that the act of temporal judgment or time-determination, rather than the temporal form of inner sense, directly implies the non-temporality of the real self. To be sure, our discussions of the transcendental deduction and refutation of idealism have already suggested that Kant's theory of time-determination cannot be understood as a psychological theory, of either empirical or transcendental nature, about mental acts by which the consciousness of time is generated but should instead be interpreted as an epistemological theory about the kinds of principles that would have to be appealed to in order to justify or confirm claims to knowledge about subjective time-determinations, whether or not such justification ever actually occurs in a mental act, conscious or otherwise. We might well hope that Kant's metaphor of mental action and passion would not lead to results incompatible with such an interpretation of his theory of time-determination. But we shall find that Kant suggests an argument for the nontemporality of the real self which turns on the assumption, stronger than anything yet seen in Kant's bouts of transcendental psychology, that time-determination is not merely an activity but a *single act*. Since such a unique act cannot readily be associated with any particular moment in the ordinary history of an empirical self, Kant seems to infer, it cannot really be in time at all, and thus neither can the real self, whose most fundamental act is, after all, time-determination. This argument must be displayed in all its unfortunate glory before it can

374

be fully appreciated just how confused Kant's thesis of the transcendental ideality of time really is.

The text of the *Critique* contains only an obscure adumbration of this argument. It is buried in a footnote which is even more mystifying than the remainder of the second edition's discussion of inner sense on which it comments:

> The "I think" expresses the act of determining my existence. Existence is therefore already given through it, but the way in which I am to determine it, that is to place in myself the manifold which belongs to it, is not yet thereby given. For that is required self-intuition, which has as its basis a form given *a priori*, that is, time, which is sensible and belongs to the receptivity of the determinable. Now since I do not have yet another self-intuition, which gives the *determining* in me, of the spontaneity of which alone I am conscious, prior to the act of *determination*, as *time* does in the case of the determinable, I cannot determine my existence, as that of a self-active being, but I can only represent to myself the spontaneity of my thought, that is, of my determining; and my existence always remains determinable only sensibly, that is, as the existence of an appearance. (B 157–8n)

As in the second-edition deduction's §25 as a whole, Kant begins simply by contrasting the abstract thought of the self with the inner intuitions needed to achieve empirical knowledge of the self. But then he goes on to suggest an argument which appears to have the following form. Any empirical determination of my own existence – that is, even a mere judgment of the form that I am now in some particular representational state, although I was at some determinate previous time in some other, requires two things: (1) not only a passive apprehension of states which are temporal in form, and which are thus actually given successively and are at least susceptible of a subsequent determination of their order, but also (2) an act of determination of the proper order of this manifold of data, carried out by the understanding in accordance with its categories and principles. Now, Kant apparently suggests, such a *particular* act of myself as a "self-active being" by which such a temporal determination is made cannot itself be assigned a determinate position in time. First, its own position in time would have to be marked by yet another intuition, in addition to all those the positions of which it itself makes determinate, although those already include all the intuitions I might have. Second, its position would also have to be determined by yet another act of the understanding, although it is itself the only such act. These conditions are obviously incoherent, so it seems that the act of understanding which provides determinate empirical knowledge of temporal relations cannot itself be assigned a temporal position and thus cannot reasonably be characterized as temporal at all. At the same time, however, Kant also seems to suppose that the act of time-determination, since it is, after all, the fundamental activity of the understanding, must be more fundamental to the self as it really is than the temporal relations which characterize what is merely the material for this activity, from which it follows that temporal relations must not characterize the real nature of

375

the self. The temporal self of empirical self-knowledge must be a mere appearance of the self as it is in itself, and since time enters into empirical objects only through the representation of them, all that is temporal must be mere appearance.

Such a conclusion might seem open to the objection that although any account of the *spatial* representation of external objects must intend a numerical distinction between the external objects and the representations which represent them, so that there is at least conceptual space for the ascription of features to the latter which are not ascribed to the former, there is no such gap in the case of self-awareness; here, instead, the *representations* of the self must be numerically identical with the *acts* they represent, so the latter cannot lack properties – such as temporality – which the former possess. Such a natural objection seems to have been behind the earliest objections to Kant's original assertion of the transcendental ideality of time. Thus Mendelssohn objected to the inaugural dissertation that "succession must at least be a necessary condition of the representations of finite spirits. Now finite spirits are not only subjects, but also objects of representations. ... Thus succession is also to be regarded as something objective," and "we must ascribe succession to representing beings and to their alterations" (25 December 1770, 10:115). This argument turns precisely on the fact that the successive representations of creatures like us are themselves objects of representations, yet as such objects must also include at least all those properties they have *qua* representations; thus, if our representations are temporally successive, then it must be an objective fact about us that we exist through their temporal succession.

However, Kant is not unaware of this natural objection (he is constantly trying to defuse it with his claims that he does not mean to degrade the temporality of representation to a mere illusion; e.g., B 69); rather, his position is that the intuitive attraction of the natural assumption on which it rests must give way before a philosophical argument. But the problem is with his argument itself: It rests on a fallacy of misplaced concreteness or a confusion of types with tokens. For Kant's argument depends entirely on an equation of a *singular description* of a (putative) *type* of act of the understanding with a *single act* of the understanding. That is, although it may seem natural to Kant to cast his description of the role of the understanding in making temporal determinations in grammatically singular terms – to talk of the "activity" or even the "act" of the understanding – there is nothing in his deduction of the categories to imply that this is more than a description of a *type* of act or, to be more exact, of general features which a certain type of act would have to satisfy if it ever occurs at all. As I noted in my criticism of the transcendental deduction, nothing in the transcendental theory of experience implies the existence of some single act of transcendental synthesis which the understanding gets to perform just once – except perhaps the utterly unfounded assumption of the *a priori* certainty of (a synthetic principle) of the transcendental unity of apperception, which we have already rejected. Kant certainly has no independent reason to identify the fundamental activity of the cognitive self with a single action which, if it cannot coherently be assigned to one position in time, cannot coherently be assigned to the temporal realm at all.

Kant's basic theory of time-determination does not presuppose a single act of the understanding which is itself performed prior (but not temporally prior) to all other mental events yet which orders them all once and for all, even if some of his characterizations of transcendental apperception as an act of the understanding make it sound like such an act. Rather, Kant's theory of the conditions under which judgments about the temporal relations of objective and subjective states may possibly be confirmed simply requires that *any* judgment which does in fact determine the order of some other mental events be subject to confirmation in conformity to certain rules or "restrictions." And that surely does not mean that any particular act of time-determination which might actually occur cannot itself be assigned a perfectly determinate – and perfectly ordinary – place in time, even if the determination of *its* temporal position might require a *further* particular act – that is, *token* – of judgment. To be sure, such a regress might mean that there is no one time in which any cognitive subject possesses a complete determination of the time-order of its experiences, whether subjectively or objectively considered, but rather that as psychological subjects we can at best engage in an indefinitely extendable series of time-determinations. But there would be nothing vicious in such a regress. Rather, it would be precisely the kind of never-completed empirical synthesis of intuitions which Kant's exposition of the "Antinomy of Pure Reason," which we shall shortly consider, insists is the paradigmatic form of empirical knowledge. It would also be an accurate if rather abstract reflection of the open-ended nature of human experience. As we saw earlier, the complete determination of the temporal structure of our experience can be regarded only as a regulative ideal for our cognitive conduct.[3]

It might seem as though I have used slender evidence to ascribe to Kant an argument open to such harsh criticism, for the note which I quoted might just mean to say that the spontaneity of the mental activity of time-determination is a matter of philosophical rather than empirical knowledge. But Kant expressed the assumption I have criticized in an even more explicit argument. This is found in a little sketch that he wrote, after the publication of the second edition of the *Critique,* entitled "Answer to the Question, Is It an Experience That We Think?" (R 5661, 18:318–19).[4] Kant begins this argument by describing a *perception* as involving an "empirical representation," *empirical knowledge* as knowledge which involves such perception, and *experience* as the judgment which expresses such knowledge (318). He then illustrates this classification by saying that an *a priori* judgment about the pure construction of a square is not an experience, since it involves no empirical perception, although a judgment about a square actually drawn in some medium is an experience, since it does yield sensory perception. And then the argument that interests us

377

commences, for Kant next claims that the first kind of judgment cannot indirectly be *made* into an experience in the sense defined, by treating our consciousness of the figure in pure intuition as itself an empirical perception, and thus as the subject of an experience. "Neither is the consciousness of having such a thought an experience, just because the thought itself is not experience and consciousness in itself is nothing empirical" (319). But why is the *consciousness* or *representation of* even a pure *content* not itself something empirical, something which as an intuition of inner sense could be assigned a determinate place in time? Kant's answer is this:

My consciousness when I *order an experience* is the representation of my existence insofar as it is empirically determined, that is, [is determined] in time. But now if this consciousness were itself in turn empirical, then the same time-determination as is contained under the [first] time-determination of my condition would again have to be represented. Yet another time would therefore have to be thought, *under* which (not *in* which) the time which constitutes the formal condition of my inner experience is contained. Therefore there would have to be a time in which, and yet simultaneously with which, [another] time flows, which is absurd. Therefore the consciousness of ordering an experience or of thinking in general, is *transcendental consciousness*, not experience. (R 5661, 18:319)

Again, the conclusion seems to be that since contradictions arise if we think of our act of determining time as occurring in the same temporal sequence which it makes determinate, that act, and the real self whose fundamental act it is, cannot really be temporal at all.

But, as before, the argument fails. Kant's claim seems to be that an *act* of judgment which makes a temporal determination must have both the same yet different temporal properties as its content, and that this is contradictory.[5] But there would be no reason to assume that an act of judgment could not have different temporal properties from another act about the temporal properties of which it judges unless there were in fact just one act of transcendental time-determination. In this case it would indeed have to be assumed either that this single act of judgment which once and for all determined all the temporal relations which one could ever judge about could have a temporal position isomorphic to that of only one of the acts about which it judges, or, even worse, that it could not have a temporal position identical to that of any of them, which would leave it without temporal position at all, since the states of the empirical self about which it judges exhaust the contents of inner sense. But, as we have already seen, Kant has no reason to postulate the occurrence of any such unique act of time-determination.

In fact, even if Kant intends only that there is some contradiction in *particular* judgments about temporal determinations themselves taking place in time – that any judgment of the form "At t_1 I experienced a" must actually be made both at t_1 and yet at some subsequent t_2 (which is, of course, absurd) – his argument still fails. For there is simply no reason in Kant's basic theory of time-determination why I should *ever* have to make any judgment of the form "At t_i I experienced x" at t_i as opposed to any subsequent time t_j; it might well be the case that such judgments can be made *only* at t_j. Of course, this might mean that my evidence for such judgments must always be indirect – it must consist of present beliefs about past states and not consist of directly accessible present states – and thus that such judgments, basic as they may be to human mental life, must always remain uncertain. But Kant certainly could not object to that, for – leaving aside his fatal relapse into Cartesianism in the transcendental deduction – one of the most fundamental theses of his own rejection of the underlying Cartesianism of both his empiricist and rationalist predecessors is the thesis that judgments about inner states are just as empirical as judgments about outer objects, and therefore just as liable to uncertainty (B 278–9).

Thus, neither the role of space in time-determinations nor anything true of time-determination independently of the role of space entails that the self which may judge of its own temporal structure is not as temporal as it appears to be. In that case, of course, the transcendental ideality of time cannot be carried over from the self as it is in itself to any other things as they are in themselves. It now remains to be seen whether any more general features of Kant's theory of empirical judgment entail transcendental idealism.

The legislation of nature

At the most general level, independent of specific premises about the ideality of space and time, Kant argues that the lawlikeness of the objects of empirical knowledge itself proves that they are merely appearances. From this it could presumably be inferred that the most characteristic features by virtue of which such objects are subsumed under law – of course, their spatial and temporal relations – are ideal. Though it does not use the transcendental ideality of the forms of intuition as a premise, however, Kant's argument for this view – the view that the understanding actually imposes its legislation on nature or that it creates a transcendental "affinity" – has the same form as his fundamental epistemological argument for the transcendental ideality of space. That is, it depends on the assumption that the laws of nature are absolutely necessary of the objects which they characterize, rather than just conditional necessities which objects must satisfy if we are to have empirical knowledge of them or even of ourselves. And the argument is open to the same objection as the other: Kant's transcendental method for discovering the conditions of the possibility of experience cannot really yield the requisite sort of necessity.

Kant's parallel between his fundamental argument for the transcendental ideality of the forms of intuition and that for the principles of judgment is evident in a passage such as this:

Now it is no more strange that the laws of appearances in nature must agree *a priori* with the understanding and its *a priori* form, that is, its capacity to *connect* the manifold in general, than it is that the appearances themselves must agree *a priori* with the form of sensible intuition. For laws exist just as little in the appearances, rather only relatively to the subject in which the appearances inhere, as appearances exist in themselves, but rather only relatively to the same being insofar as it has sense. Their own lawfulness would necessarily pertain to things in themselves independently of an understanding which cognizes them. All appearances are only representations of things which, as far as what they may be in themselves, are unknown. But as mere representations they are not subject to any laws of connection at all except those which the connecting capacity prescribes. (B 164)

The key to this passage lies not in a prior reduction of empirical objects to mere representations, although Kant undoubtedly felt safe in assuming such a reduction by this stage in his text and, indeed, career. Rather, what is crucial here is the double use of *"a priori"* in the opening sentence: Kant does not merely assume that we know *a priori what* laws objects must satisfy if we are to have experience but also that we know *a priori that* they satisfy these laws. Even if things are subject to laws independently of us, we could not know *a priori* that they are, but of our own representations we can know *a priori* that they are subject to the laws of our cognitive faculties. Since Kant assumes that we know *a priori* that nature is subject to the laws of our understanding, it then follows that nature must be identical to our representations.

It may sometimes seem as though Kant does argue for the transcendental ideality of nature as a whole on the basis of the sort of purely conceptual consideration favored by some recent commentators – that is, from a definition of nature as essentially equivalent to our *conception of* the lawfulness of empirical objects. Kant does draw a distinction between "material" or "substantive" and "formal" conceptions of nature, the first being the "sum of all objects of experience" (R 5607, 18:248), the extension of any conception of the natural world, and the second the conception itself of the *"nexus* of determinations" (R 5406, 18:174).[6] He can then suggest that since nature (*formaliter*) is equivalent to our conception of the laws that bind together the objects of experience, of course it is itself a product of the understanding rather than something which exists independently of the understanding. Thus, this note from the early 1780s apparently begins by suggesting such an argument:

All possible objects of experience have their nature, partly their particular nature,[7] but partly that which is common with other things. Nature taken substantively signifies: the sum of all objects of experience. Nature rests on forces (fundamental forces) and is in general the lawfulness of appearances. . . .

Things are not appearances in themselves but only because there are beings which have senses; in the same way they belong to a nature because we have understanding. For the word "nature" does not signify anything in things in themselves, rather only the ordering of the appearances of them by means of the unity of the concepts of understanding or the unity of consciousness, in which they can be connected.

We do not have understanding, because there is a nature; for we could never know the rules (laws) of such a nature from experience; their necessity consists precisely in that they can be cognized *a priori*.

For just that reason can we have *a priori* cognitions not only of appearances but also of the nature in which they are connected, for the form of our sensibility grounds the former as principle of possibility and the form of our understanding the latter.

To say, "We can determine the constitution of things *a priori*," and yet at the same time, "These things have such a constitution independently of our capacity to determine them," is a contradiction; for then whence would we derive our [*a priori*] knowledge? (R 5607, 18:248–9)

Kant begins by suggesting that the concept of nature *is* the concept of our *ordering* of appearances in the unity of consciousness, or our *conception* of their lawfulness; this would make the transcendental ideality of nature a conceptual necessity. But as he continues it becomes clear that it his explanation of *a priori* knowledge which is at work, ultimately his assumption that there is a *contradiction* between the assumption that we have *a priori* knowledge of the laws to which things conform and the assumption that those laws also express the constitution which those things have in themselves. That is, this argument too rests on the rejection of the hypothesis of a "*preformation-system* of pure reason" (B 167) or of an apparently contingent congruence between the constitution of things and the conditions which things must satisfy – and which we can know *a priori* they must – if we are to successfully experience them. But is there really a contradiction here? There is none, as we have seen, if a transcendental theory of experience yields merely knowledge of the conditions which must be satisfied for experience to take place; it is only if it is assumed that we know *a priori* that objects *must* satisfy these conditions – that *a priori* knowledge is knowledge of an absolute or *de re* necessity in the objects of knowledge themselves – that this contradiction arises, and thus that it becomes necessary to reduce nature to representations to explain *a priori* knowledge.

The role of Kant's assumption of absolute or *de re* necessity, but also its groundlessness, are both apparent in Kant's exposition of the doctrine of transcendental or objective "affinity" in the first-edition text of the transcendental deduction. Kant's conception of the necessity implied by apriority is clear in this famous passage:

The order and rule-governedness of appearances, which we entitle *nature,* we therefore introduce ourselves, and would also not be able to find there unless we, or the nature of our mind, had not originally introduced it. For this unity of nature is to be a necessary, that is *a priori*, certain unity of the connection of appearances. But how should we be able to bring about *a priori* such a synthetic unity if the original sources of cognition in our mind did not contain *a priori* subjective grounds of such unity, and if these subjective conditions were not also objectively valid, in that they are the grounds of the possibility of cognizing an object of experience in general[?] (A 125–6)

Again, Kant's language reveals what is really a double assumption of necessity: We do not merely know *a priori* what the subjective conditions of experience are, which could be satisfied by a conception of such conditions merely as restrictions on the possibility of our experience; we also know *a priori* that we will always find these conditions to be satisfied, which of course can be explained only if the objects of our experience are mere appearances on which the requisite rule-governedness can always be imposed. The assumption that objects necessarily satisfy the conditions of the possibility of our experience, not merely that we know what conditions must be satisfied, is also evident in Kant's own marginal comment on this passage:

That the laws of nature really have their origin in the understanding, and just as little as space and time are to be found outside it, is already demonstrated by the otherwise acknowledged assertion that we cognize them *a priori* and as necessary, although we could cognize them as contingent only if they had to be derived from outside. (R LI, 23:26)

It is only if the laws of nature must be assumed to be necessarily true, not merely true if experience is in fact – or contingently – to occur, that we must explain them by reducing nature itself to a subjective connection of mere appearances.

But what could possibly explain such an assumption of necessary truth? Nothing other than an assumption that the occurrence of experience is not itself something contingent upon the satisfaction of certain conditions for our understanding by objects beyond our control, but something which is itself necessary. And this is what Kant does assume in his justification of the doctrine of affinity, although, as we have already seen in Part II, he does not have an adequate basis for doing so:

Now if this unity of association did not also have an objective ground, so that it would be impossible for appearances to be apprehended by the imagination otherwise than under the condition of a possible synthetic unity of this apprehension, then it would also be something entirely contingent that appearances are fit for a connected whole of human cognition. For although we would then have the capacity to associate perceptions, it would remain in itself entirely undetermined and contingent whether they were also associable; and in the case in which they were not, then a crowd of perceptions and even an entire sensibility would be possible, in which much empirical consciousness would be to be met with in my mind, but separated and without belonging to a consciousness of *my* self, which is, however, impossible. For only if I assign all perceptions to one consciousness (of original apperception), can I say in the case of all perceptions: that I am conscious of them as mine. (A 122)

But this argument does *not* prove the impossibility of a "separated" manifold of consciousness, or of states of consciousness which are insusceptible to self-consciousness; rather, Kant begs the question of the necessity of apperception itself, for to appeal to the conditions necessary to *say* or judge that I am conscious of a given representation is to concede the possibility of self-consciousness or apperception of it and thus of its satisfaction of the conditions of possibility of experience. Nothing Kant says proves that a "separated" consciousness is absolutely impossible, thus that apperception is absolutely necessary. Thus he also offers nothing to prove the absolute necessity that the objects of experience satisfy the conditions we require to have determinate experience, and the necessary lawfulness of nature which can be explained only by its transcendental ideality is never really proved.

We have now seen that Kant's attempts to prove that things as they are in themselves cannot be spatial and temporal directly from special considerations about space and time, as well as from general considerations about forms of sensibility and forms of judgment, fail. It now remains to consider whether the indirect proof of transcendental idealism which is supposed to be the heart of his "Transcendental Dialectic" fares any better.

18
Transcendental idealism and the "Antinomy of Pure Reason"

Kant claims that an indirect proof of transcendental idealism is furnished by the "Antinomy of Pure Reason," the second of the three "Dialectical Inferences of Pure Reason" (A 338 / B 396), the discussion of which comprises the bulk of the "Transcendental Dialectic" of the *Critique of Pure Reason*.[1] On the assumption that things as they are in themselves really are spatial and temporal, he argues, reason is necessarily ensnared in paradoxes, certainly those concerning the upper and lower bounds of spatial and temporal extent, the infinite, and atoms, which had plagued philosophers since Zeno and which had been pressed with renewed vigor in Kant's time by Bayle and Hume, but also the paradoxes about causality and freedom, both human and divine, which had given Leibniz such trouble. But on the assumption that space and time are merely features of our representations of objects but not of the objects themselves, Kant claims, and only on this assumption, these paradoxes can be avoided. As he puts it in the preface to the second edition of the *Critique,* the pretension of traditional metaphysics to transcend the limits of possible experience

... yields just the experiment to check the truth of ... this assessment of our *a priori* knowledge of reason, namely that it concerns only appearances and, on the contrary, lets the thing in itself lie, as, to be sure, real for itself but unknown by us. For that which necessarily drives us to go beyond the limits of experience and all appearances is the *unconditioned,* which, to complete the series of conditions for all that is conditioned, reason necessarily and with complete right demands in things in themselves. But now if it is found that if one assumes that our empirical knowledge directs itself to objects as things in themselves, then the unconditioned cannot *even be thought without contradiction,* but that if one assumes that our representation of things as they are given to us is not directed to these as things in themselves but rather that these objects, as appearances, instead conform themselves to our method of representation, then *the contradiction disappears:* Then this shows that what we initially assumed only on trial is grounded.   (B xx–xxi)

However, Kant's proud claim to have found the *experimentum crucis* for transcendental idealism in the "Antinomy of Pure Reason" also fails. The resolution of the antinomies requires the positive assertion that things in themselves are not spatial and temporal only on assumptions about truth and knowledge which Kant does not defend and, given his own methodological stance, could not defend. This is so in spite of the fact that all of Kant's treatments of the antinomies of pure reason *prior* to the publication of the *Critique* showed how to avoid the paradoxes he worried about with

385

methodological restrictions on the claims of sense and reason, rather than by *metaphysical* dogma. In these earlier versions of the dialectic, Kant does indeed deploy the kind of methodological rather than metaphyiscal doctrine which so many contemporary commentators have attempted to find in his transcendental idealism; unfortunately, the indirect proof in the *Critique* itself attempts to prove nothing less than the metaphysical proposition that things as they are in themselves really cannot be spatial and temporal.

In barest outline, the "Antinomy of Pure Reason" argues as follows. Valid arguments seem to prove that the world is finite in both spatial and temporal extent (first antinomy) and composed of finitely small atoms (second antinomy), but also that it is infinite in spatial and temporal extent and composed only of infinitely divisible constituents. The truth of both of these sets of conclusions would be contradictory, but on the doctrine that space and time are merely features of representations and not of things as they are in themselves, it can be seen that the opposed propositions are all false. As indefinitely extendable and divisible, representations and thus space and time are neither finite nor infinite, and things in themselves are unconditioned, but not spatially or temporally so. Valid arguments also seem to prove that there must be an uncaused cause but also that everything has yet another cause (third antinomy), and that a necessary being must exist but also that no absolutely necessary being is possible (fourth antinomy), but these pairs of conclusions are also contradictory. Here Kant argues that transcendental idealism avoids contradiction, not by showing that both theses and antitheses are false, but rather by showing that both may be true but of different objects. Whereas in the spatio-temporal world of appearances everything has another cause but nothing is absolutely, as opposed to merely relatively, necessary, in the nonspatio-temporal world of things in themselves there can be uncaused and absolutely necessary causes.

However, Kant's argument that spatial and temporal representations cannot represent things which truly are spatial and temporal fails. Either it *assumes* a principle that limits on what can be *empirically confirmed* about objects must also imply limits on what can be *true* of those objects – for only thus could it be concluded that just because the spatial and the temporal cannot *be perceived* to be either finite or infinite, they can only be indefinite and can therefore be only series of representations, since no other objects or series of objects could be indefinite. Yet such a principle is unwarranted. Or else Kant *derives* this principle from a prior identification of the spatial and temporal with mere representations, from which it could indeed be inferred that what cannot be *represented* of the spatial and temporal cannot be *true* of them at all. But this would be inferred only at the cost of rendering Kant's *experimentum crucis* circular.[2] Further, Kant sometimes even seems to assume that what can be *conceived to be true of some possible objects* by reason must in fact *be true of some actual objects,* for only this can yield the conclusion not merely that objects must be *either* conditioned *or* unconditioned – which might be assumed to follow from the logical law of bivalence alone – but that there must be objects which are actually *unconditioned*, with which the always conditioned objects in space and time cannot, therefore, be identical.

We shall see that Kant does employ both of these principles in constructing his overall argument that if there are limits on what can be confirmed about objects by the senses which do not match what can be conceived to be true of them by reason, then there must in fact be separate objects of sense and of reason – the former characterized by spatiality and temporality, the latter, though nothing else may be known of them, characterized by the absence of these two properties. But in assuming a general principle that the limits of confirmability imply the limits of truth, Kant assumes a general theory of truth which he nowhere defends and from which even the most committed verificationist would shy away; and in suggesting that we can know not only that things must be either conditioned or unconditioned but that we can know that there must be some things which are unconditioned, Kant violates his own rule against confusing the concept of things in themselves with that of noumena, in a "*positive* sense of the term" (B 307) – that is, things actually known to have some feature or other by reason alone.[3] Yet without such assumptions, the antinomies do not in fact necessitate the denial that things are really temporal and spatial, though they may certainly show that there are limits on what we could confirm *about* the spatiality and temporality of things.

The antinomies in the 1770s

Indeed, such a truly modest conception of purely epistemological limitations is exactly what Kant suggested during the 1770s. Throughout this period, his conception of the solution to the antinomies of space and time which had furnished so much of the impetus for ancient and modern skepticism was primarily methodological: To avoid the snares of paradox, basically one must just not expect to find confirmation where the limits of sensibility will not allow it. This is a skeptical solution to the antinomies, of course, in the sense that the truth-value of certain propositions must go unknown, but it is not skeptical in the worrisome sense of undermining anything which was thought to be known with any good reason. This modest approach may not be obvious in the inaugural dissertation with which Kant commenced the 1770s, precisely because that work's explicit theory that sensibility and intellect are two separate faculties of knowledge is itself an assumption which, tacit but still active in 1781, helps produce the dogmatic transcendental idealism of the *Critique of Pure Reason*. But it is worth noting that even in the dissertation, so fateful for Kant's later thought because of its anticipation of the "Transcendental Aesthetic," Kant does not actually argue that the *antinomies* can be exploited to produce any additional support for idealism (not yet named "transcendental"), which is derived entirely *independently* from the supposition of a *priori* knowledge of space and time. And in any case, in many passages written later in the decade Kant at least suggests a purely methodological solution to the antinomies, on which the limits of sensibility are shown to leave the truth of certain propositions *undecidable,* without any implication that there is either an alternative basis on which to decide their truth – that is, reason – or incompatible truths which must therefore describe two separate realms of objects.

1770

In the inaugural dissertation Kant had already arrived at the view that the apriority of our knowledge of space and time implies the subjectivity of these forms of intuition, and he also unabashedly held that there was a real use of the intellect, or what he later called reason, which could give insight into the substances of the world and, in particular, into their dependence on a single necessary being (ID, §16–22). So it was certainly not his view at this point that there were questions about the ultimate constitution of things which were necessarily undecidable. Rather, what plays the role of the later "Transcendental Dialectic" in this work is an argument that paradoxes arise when the assumption is made that truths which can be known by reason alone must also be capable of representation in the forms of human sensibility, spatiality and temporality. In other words, confusion arises if one thinks that propositions which can be confirmed by reason alone can *also* be confirmed by sense. To assume this is to adopt what the dissertation calls a "subreptic axiom," and the lesson of the paradoxes is simply that subreptic axioms – which are nothing less than principles of epistemological immodesty – must be avoided. Of course, there is an ulterior motive to this – the danger is that if one assumes that at least in principle whatever can be known by reason can also be confirmed by sense, one will then confuse the inevitable limits of sensibility with entirely unnecessary limitations on *reason.* Thus, "great care must be taken *lest the dogmatic principles of sensitive cognition transgress their boundaries and affect things intellectual"* (ID, §24, 2:411). But there is no suggestion that the theory of subreptic axioms itself *yields a proof* of the difference between the sensible and the intellectual world. That difference is simply assumed at the stage in the exposition of the dissertation at which the subreptic axioms are introduced.

Kant's analysis of the general "PRINCIPLE OF REDUCTION for any subreptic axiom," the principle that "*if of any intellectual concept whatsoever there is predicated generally anything which pertains to the relations of* SPACE AND TIME, *it must not be enunciated objectively, and it denotes only the conditions without which a given concept is not cognizable sensitively"* (ID, §25, 2:412–13), is, as a matter of fact, presented against the background of a peculiarly abstract form of verificationism which does in a way anticipate one of the assumptions of his later treatment of the antinomies. Alive as he already was to the difference between real and merely logical possibility, and therefore already committed to the critical thesis that real possibility cannot be established by the internal consistency of a concept alone, Kant says that we "rightly suppose that *whatever cannot be cognized by any intuition at all is thereby not thinkable* and so is impossible" (2:413). However, he allows that this general constraint may be satisfied by the mere possibility of some form of intuition of an object other than our own, even an intellectual intuition, and then proceeds to make his main point: that we should not confuse what can be confirmed by *our form* of sensibility with what may be confirmable more generally, which, in fact, we can *assume* to be confirmable by some other possible intuition *precisely because* we come at least remarkably close to knowing it to be true, and therefore confirmable, on the basis of reason alone. Then, although Kant's underlying concern is to prevent damage from being done to the claims of reason by the limits of sensibility, he emphasizes the positive, that is, argues that we must not assume that what *is* known to reason can *also* be represented in the characteristic manner of our senses.

Kant reduces to "three species" "all the illusions of sensitive cognitions passing under the guise of cognitions that are intellectual," depending on the three unjustified or subreptic axioms that

1. The same sensitive condition under which alone the *intuition* of an object is possible is the condition of the *possibility* itself of the object.

2. The same sensitive condition under which alone *the things given can be collated with one another to form the intellectual concept of the object* is also the condition of the possibility of the object.

3. The same sensitive condition under which some *object* met with can alone be *subsumed under a given intellectual concept* is also the condition of the possibility itself of the object. (ID, §26, 2:413)

These three general grounds of illusion clearly anticipate Kant's four later antinomies: The second principle is obviously concerned with the two "mathematical" antinomies about both *extent* and *divisibility* in space and time, whereas the first and third axioms somewhat less clearly address the topics of the two "dynamical" antinomies, the disputes over whether or not the *existence* and *possibility* of objects are to be constrained by the sensory conditions of intuition or can be represented intellectually as well. For present purposes, however, we may focus on what Kant calls the "prejudices" (ID, §28, 2:415) arising from the second subreptic axiom.

These prejudices concern the extent and the composition of the world, the questions whether or not it is finite and whether or not it is composed of simple substances. Kant's basic concern is that we should not let the difficulties in obtaining a *sensory representation* of the infinitude of the universe, on the one hand, and of the simplicity of its parts, on the other, obscure the clear deliverances of *reason* on these matters. It is a prejudice in favor of *sensibility*, Kant argues, to suppose that because it is a constraint on sensibility that manifolds be represented numerically, and a constraint on the synthesis of numerical magnitudes that only finite syntheses can be completed, therefore a constraint on sense that it can represent only finite magnitudes, it must thus *also* be true that "*every actual manifold can be given numerically* and so every quantity is finite" (2:415). This cuts two ways. Although reason tells us that the world must have some kind of limit, it is a mistake to infer that this limit must also be representable as a finite numerical quantity, therefore that a sensory representation of the limit of the universe must be possible; but then again, it would be another mistake to suppose that because such a *sensory* representation is not forthcoming the *intellectual* conclusion that the world must be limited is endangered. And although it would be a mistake to infer that because reason tells us that every composition must have simple elements these must be capable of sensory representation, it would be yet another mistake to infer in reverse that because simples are not given in space and time – infinite divisibility being a characteristic of the forms of sensibility – reason must err when *it* tells us that the ultimate constituents of reality are simple. The claims of reason and the claims of sense need not match: There is no reason to suppose that what is yielded by reason must be confirmable, at least by our kind of sensibility, nor that the *limits* of sensibility undermine the claims of reason:

... That the quantity of the world is limited (not the highest quantity), that it recognizes a principle for itself, that bodies are composed of simple things, these can be known by a sign of the reason that is perfectly certain. But that the universe in its mass is mathematically finite, that its past duration can be given according to its measure, that there is a definite number of simple things constituting any body whatsoever, these are propositions which openly proclaim their source in the nature of sensitive cognition, and however much they can be treated as true in other respects, they suffer none the less from the undoubted blemish of their origin.

(ID, §28, 2:416)

Against a background which is unabashedly dualistic, committed to the view that space and time characterize the sensible but not the intelligible world, Kant's approach to the antinomies themselves is nevertheless purely methodological: He tries to avoid false views about the nature of sensibility by denying that we should assume that what is given by reason must also be confirmed by sense, but he is even more concerned to prevent any undermining of the metaphysical deliverances of reason by his insistent denial that the limits on sensory confirmation imply any limits on reason itself. Yet there is no suggestion that the danger of subreptic axioms leading to prejudices in itself *proves* the split between the sensible and the intelligible worlds. There is no argument that *without* this distinction *paradoxes* ensue. There is merely advice on how to avoid danger to conclusions which follow merely if this distinction is already in place – the metaphysical claims of completeness and simplicity which are licensed merely by the prior assumption that reason is a self-sufficient faculty, or at least a faculty adequate to prove the possibility of a form of intuition with which we are not ourselves acquainted.

In the inaugural dissertation, then, the material of subreptic axioms preserves metaphysical results arrived at by other means but is not itself exploited for deductive support of these results. Even more revealing than this limited conception of the future dialectic, however, is the kind of solution to the antinomies which Kant sketched in a variety of passages from the creative central period of the 1770s. Here what seems to be suggested is a purely methodological doctrine for the avoidance of paradoxes, without any reference to idealist metaphysics, even as something already presupposed.

A half dozen extensive sketches of the eventual "Antinomy" – sketches for the first time introducing such titles as "Dialectic of Sensibility" (R 4756, 17:699), "Antithetic or Apparent Antinomy of Pure Reason," and just plain "Dialectic" (both of these examples from R 4757, 17:704) – survive from the period 1775–7 (R 4756–60, perhaps also R 4762). In these sketches, there are but one or two passing suggestions that conflicts between the limits of sensibility and the unconstrained ideas of reason reveal the subjectivity of the former, and even these do not intimate that these conflicts *prove* the distinction between mere appearance and metaphysical reality, but employ such a distinction only as already given (R 4756, 17:702, lines 1–2; R 4757, 17:704, lines 3–5). On the contrary, Kant's general argument in these notes is that it is only the principles of the "exposition of appearances," that is, the principles expressing the limits of sensory representation – principles which consistently anticipate the *antitheses* of the later antinomies – which are "objective"; the "principles of rationality or comprehension," those principles anticipating the later *theses,* are *only* "subjectively necessary as principles of the use of reason in the whole of knowledge" (R 4759, 17:709–10). What makes these principles "subjectively necessary" is not entirely univocal: They may simply manifest the spontaneous inclination of reason to carry syntheses to completion, and thus function similarly to the later regulative ideals of reason; but there is also some suggestion that they are "practically necessary" (see again 17:710), and they may thus anticipate Kant's later theory of the postulates of pure *practical* reason. But in any case, the overriding claim is that the *principles of reason* have merely subjective validity, as contrasted to the principles characterizing the constraints on sensibility; thus, the precursors to the later *antitheses* alone are constitutive, objectively valid principles, whereas the precursors of the *theses* of the later antinomies are not:

The transcendental principles are principles of the subjective unity of knowledge through reason, that is, of the harmony of reason with itself.
Objective principles are principles of possible empirical employment.

(R 4758, 17:706)

The meaning of this contrast appears to be that it is only *one* set of principles, those derived from sensibility (joined with understanding) for the exposition of empirical appearances, which have any claim to yield knowledge of objects. Thus, it follows that although there may be *tension between two inclinations* within human thought, there is no genuine *conflict between incompatible ontological principles* which could be resolved only by distinguishing between two separate sets of objects or between genuine and merely apparent properties of objects. It is rather the *conflict* itself which is a merely "apparent antithetic." Thus, R 4759 says that "the partiality of sensibility and the totality of reason conflict subjectively in the determination of knowledge: the conditions of empirical use in the exposition of appearances; the conditions of rational use in the comprehension of appearances" (17:710). *Both* the empirical and the rational uses mentioned here seem to concern *appearances*; there is no suggestion that these two uses concern two different kinds of objects. And Kant's next note makes clear that a "subjective" conflict is no real contradiction at all, precisely because no genuine ontological import can be attached to the pretensions of *reason*, whatever internal impetus to these principles there may be. Here Kant writes:

> The ground of the antinomy of reason is the conflict: 1. All empirical synthesis is conditioned, the mathematical as well as the dynamical. . . . On the contrary 2. The transc[endent] synthesis (through pure concepts of reason) is unconditioned *but also takes place through merely intellectual concepts; there is therefore really no antinomy.* (R 4760, 17:711; emphasis added)

The implication seems to be that "merely intellectual concepts" do not provide *any* knowledge of objects, so no distinction of kinds of objects or their properties is required to dispel the tension between reason and sensibility. What is required to avoid the antinomies is only a clear contrast between the limits of empirical *knowledge* grounded in sensibility, on the one hand, and, on the other, the *ideas* of pure reason connected to no intuitions at all. The latter, whatever other roles they may play in our intellectual or moral life, *do not claim knowledge of objects at all.*

We may now examine Kant's treatment of the antinomies in the mid-1770s in some detail.

R 4756 is a remarkable document, in which Kant gave one of the most extensive outlines we find for the emerging structure of the *Critique* and subsumed even more under the term "dialectic" than he was to do later. The outline is divided into four sections: a "Dialectic of Sensibility," which goes over the same ground as the later treatment of the antinomies; a section entitled "Dialectic of Understanding. Transcendental Theory of Magnitude," which emphasizes the continuity of space and time; another entitled "Transcendental Theory of Appearance. Reality and Negation," which again emphasizes the continuity of space and time; and finally the "Transcendental Theory of Experience," discussed in Chapter 2, in which Kant asserts the four central theses that substance neither originates from nor disappears into nothing, that every state of the world is the consequence of another, that all appearances together constitute a single world, and finally that all of these properties "belong to real objects (against idealism)" (R 4756, 17:699–702). But what is most remarkable of all about this note is that in spite of the twofold use of "dialectic" in its headings, it contains virtually no suggestion of *actual conflict of principles*.

The first section does mention Kant's thesis that space and time are not real (pp. 699–700, where the controversy between Leibniz and Clarke is explicitly mentioned), but this and the next two sections are primarily concerned to advance the thesis that space and time are continuous, or that all spaces and times are parts of spaces and times themselves. Kant takes this to imply both the indefinite extendability of space and time – no matter how big a space or time has been measured, it is still part of a larger one – as well as the indefinite divisibility or absence of simple parts in empirical objects – no matter how finely any spatial or temporal region has been divided, it can be still further divided into regions which are themselves spaces or times: "All appearance consists in turn of appearances; no sensation is simple" (701). But Kant mentions no theses which *conflict* with these conclusions. Indeed, even in the final section, the "Transcendental Theory of Experience," where Kant does associate the assertion that "every state of the world is a consequence, for in the continuity of alteration everything is starting and ceasing, and each has its cause" with the "antithesis: Then there would be no first cause" (702), no *thesis* opposed to this "antithesis" is mentioned.

Only in the section of R 4756 entitled "Dialectic of Understanding" is a conflict even intimated. Here, after stating that space and time are continuous, Kant remarks that "infinite is greater than any number. The allness or totality (the all) is not to be understood in a series, not to be conceived in the aggregate" (p. 700). This might seem to suggest that there is a conflict between the task of representing "the all" and the means which sensibility actually furnishes for the representation of magnitudes, namely series or aggregates. But even this passage does not explicitly hold that the faculty of reason legitimately claims knowledge of totality in genuine conflict with the limits of sensibility. The remark does not seem to describe an antinomy, but rather seems simply to dismiss any thought of transgressing the limits of empirical series or aggregates.

Kant's next few sketches do clearly describe a conflict between incompatible principles, but they also suggest a resolution of the conflict independent of any ontological distinction between appearances and things in themselves or between apparent and genuine properties of objects.

The first of these sketches, R 4757, clearly anticipates the structure of the published "Antinomy," differing only by collapsing the first and second antinomies into a single contrast. But it also prefaces its presentation of the conflict with the suggestion that although the "principles of the empirical use of the understanding," on the one hand, are principles for the representation *of objects,* the "principles of the pure use of reason," on the other, have a purely *internal* significance. Like what Kant later called "regulative" ideals, they aim at unity among our *cognitions* but do not directly characterize *objects* at all. This is the preface:

The principles of the possibility of experience (of distributive unity) are at the same time principles of the possibility of the objects of experience. 1. (Unity) of Intuition (Appearance), 2. Of the giving or existence of appearances (of experiences).

Immanent principles (space and time are conditions of appearance) or transcendent ones (there are not any).

The former of the empirical, the latter of the pure use of reason. Harmony of reason with itself in its entirety.

The former needs (has) no *a priori* first, only *a posteriori*, and from there *progressus* or *regressus in infinitum*. (R 5757, 17:703)

Kant's telegraphic style here obviously precludes certainty about his intentions. But it seems fairly clear that he is suggesting that although the immanent principles of empirical knowledge of objects are of course subject to the constraint of incompleteness intimated in the final sentence, the deliverances of reason are either not genuine principles at all (the second statement of the quotation) or else are only principles of the internal organization of the intellect (the third statement).

It is within this framework, apparently, that we are to understand the first explicit presentation of the antinomies, which now follows:

Immanent principles of the empirical use of understanding.
  1. There is no limit in the composition and decomposition of appearances.
  2. There is no first ground or first beginning.
  3. Everything is mutable and variable, therefore empirically contingent, since time itself is necessary but nothing necessary attaches to time.

Transcendent principles of the pure use of understanding.
  1. There is a first part, namely the simple as the *principium* of composition, and there are limits on all appearances together.
  2. There is an absolute spontaneity, transcendental freedom.
  3. There is something necessary in itself, namely the unity of the highest reality, wherein all the multiplicity of possibilities can be determined through limits, as forms are in space and states in time, and thereby all existence.
(R 5757, 17:703–4)

In this display of the conflict of principles, Kant treats the issue of whether or not there is a limit to the composition and decomposition of substances – that is, of their extent or duration, as well as their division into parts – as a single issue, though he divides this into two separate antinomies not only in the later *Critique* but also elsewhere in these notes (e.g., R 4759, 17:709). And when he comes to the final antinomy, he alludes to the decade-old "only possible proof" of the existence of God as the ground of all possibility much more clearly than he does in the published fourth antinomy. But apart from such details, the set of antinomies he portrays is clearly identical with that displayed in the *Critique*.

That is why it is so significant that at this point Kant makes no suggestion that the metaphysics of transcendental idealism is required to solve these conflicts. Instead, what Kant provides are "rules" for the "dialectic" which are clearly designed to enable us to *avoid* the formation of misleading conclusions in the first place:

1. not to judge according to rules of appearance that which does not belong to appearance, e.g., God with space and time.
2. not to subject to its conditions what does not belong to outer appearance, e.g., spirit [*Geist*].
3. not to hold as impossible that which cannot be conceived (and which cannot be represented in intuition: the totality of the infinite or infinite division. The infinitude of a series, the finitude of that which is derived without the *substratum originarium*).

Further, the principles of the absolute unity of reason are not to be mixed up with those of empirical unity.

a. Simplicity of the thinking subject.
b. Freedom as the condition of rational actions.
c. *Ens originarium* as *substratum* of all connection of one's representations in a whole.
d. Limitation [*Einschrankung* (sic)] of the world as far as its origin and content are concerned [is] not to be confused with its bounding [*Begrenzung*].

(704–5)

Here Kant's position is similar to that of the inaugural dissertation. He does assume that there are certain objects of reason, namely God and souls, which no one would ever even consider to be numerically identical with any objects we might encounter in ordinary experience. So when he then suggests that we can avoid arriving at false beliefs by not assuming that the limits of sensible representation apply to objects such as God and the soul, Kant is not introducing any distinction between appearances and things in themselves which lie behind them; he is trying to preserve the purity of our knowledge of objects which are from *no* point of view objects of experience at all. Nor does Kant suggest that the antinomies themselves yield evidence for the existence of such objects of reason. The rules of dialectic are simply rules to avoid the miscegenation of sense and reason, not rules which themselves generate any ideas of the objects of reason and which thereby might themselves contribute to ontology.

What is the status of the principles of reason themselves? The present note again stresses the two obscurely connected ideas that the principles are *internal* principles for the unity of cognition, on the one hand, and that they are *practical* principles or postulates on the other:

We must have principles of the original unity or systematic unity of our cognitions – that is, of their spontaneity – insofar as we act independently and will practically and originally determine appearances or ourselves among the appearances.

They are principles for the self-determination of reason or of the unity of the whole among our determinations of reason. (704)

But they are not, so far as anything in this note suggests, principles that yield *theoretical insight into objects* which could be reconciled with the content of our "empirical use of understanding" only at the cost of transcendental idealism.

Finally, it is precisely Kant's clearest anticipation of the published "Antinomy of Pure Reason" which concludes with his explicit statement that the principles of reason are *merely* subjective and practical, so that the very conflict between theses and antitheses is merely apparent. R 4759 lays out the conflict thus. On the one hand,

Principles of the exposition of appearances presuppose that these are entirely *conditioned,* therefore that nothing is posited unconditionally [*schlechthin*].
1. no absolute totality ... of composition, thus *progressus* is infinite ...
2. no absolute totality of decomposition, thus nothing unconditionally simple ... (Infinite progress cannot be conceived, and the unconditioned cannot be intuited.)
3. no absolute totality of the series of generation, no unconditioned spontaneity.
4. no unconditioned necessity ...

"All of these propositions," Kant states, "as principles of empirical use are (objectively) certain although they are counter to reason." Opposed to them, reason asserts its

Principles of rationality or comprehension ...
1. Unconditioned all of the (dependent) whole. World-origin.
2. Unconditionally simple.
3. Unconditioned spontaneity of action.
4. Unconditionally necessary existence.   (R 4759, 17:709–10)

But it is precisely these last principles which Kant describes as merely "subjectively necessary as principles of the use of reason." They are conceded no pretense to objective significance. Therefore, no ontological contradiction arises which could be solved only by an ontological distinction between the real and the apparent.

Indeed, at this point in his career Kant decisively drives a wedge between the methodological lessons of his discussion of the "apparent dialectic" and ontology, by asserting explicitly that nothing about the possible or the impossible follows from the limits of human comprehension. "The totality of the infinite and the parts of the finite ... [are] impossible for the human understanding, but not in themselves" (R 4675, 17:721). So then the question becomes, How does Kant arrive at the view that the antinomies can be resolved only by transcendental idealism?

1778–1780

We have just seen that in the mid 1770s Kant demoted the principles which he later presented as the theses of the antinomies to merely subjective principles. This treatment is certainly preserved in his later theory of the regulative ideals of theoretical reason and the postulates of practical reason, but it does not itself contain any "indirect" proof of transcendental idealism. How, then, did Kant arrive at the view that there are actually antinomies which are inevitable except on the assumption of transcendental idealism, indeed which even on that assumption remain "*natural* and inevitable *illusion*[s]" (A 298 / B 354) that, like optical illusions, can be explained away but not actually prevented from occurring?

He certainly did not arrive at this view immediately. In the few years following the period just considered, Kant's view is even more emphatically that the ideas of reason which overstep the bounds of sense have a purely practical significance which occasions no conflict within theoretical philosophy. This marginal note in his copy of Baumgarten's *Metaphysica* perhaps shows Kant moving closer to the idea of a genuine rather than apparent antinomy, but it also makes clear that reason's impetus toward the infinite, which gives rise to such a conflict, arises solely from "practical laws of our reason":

Infinity is the absolute impossibility of a complete synthesis (not of the completeness of the object) in the composition or decomposition of a given object. The appearance is infinite, and the division of it continues infinitely. This infinity concerns the dynamical as well as the mathematical synthesis. On the contrary, the synthesis is complete in the intellectual [realm], but the condition for cognition of this completeness *in concreto* is sensible (a first or outermost). Reason therefore demands independence from the sensible, but the determination of its concept can be only sensible (antinomy). The omnisufficience of reason seen as determining is, in respect of its origin in us, a practical law of our reason, which necessarily presupposes completeness as a hypothesis. (R 4780, 17:725)

Kant initially creates confusion by failing to draw his later contrast between the *infinite* and the merely *indefinite* – he seems both to deny yet to assert that there can be a *completed* synthesis of the infinite in sense, whereas what he obviously means is only that sense can provide an indefinitely extendable representation of magnitude but not a completed representation of the infinite. Nevertheless, the gist of Kant's argument is clear enough. The antinomy arises because reason demands what it has no right to, namely a sensory confirmation of its ideas, a representation of its conception of totality *in concreto,* and its impetus toward such an assumption derives from some practical rather than theoretical objective.

But *what* practical law of reason is it that requires the representation of anything unconditioned? This has not been made clear in anything so far considered. It begins to become clearer in some further remarks – in a form, however, which contains no obvious ground for a distinction between appearances and things in themselves.

R 4849, written sometime between 1776 and 1779, is highly illustrative. It begins with one of Kant's first clear statements that metaphysics serves the dual purpose of grounding the laws of experience but also freeing practical reason from the constraints contained in those very same laws:

The purpose of metaphysics: 1. To make out the origin of synthetic *a priori* knowledge. [2.] To provide insight into the restricting conditions on the empirical use of our understanding. 3. To show the independence of our reason from these conditions, thus the possibility of [its] absolute use. 4. Thereby to extend our use of reason past the borders of the sensible world, that is, to do away with the obstacle which reason makes for itself (out of the principles of its empirical use). 5. To show the condition of the absolute unity of reason, that is, of the harmony of the sum of all purposes. (R 4849, 18:5–6)

Exactly what the practical significance of a harmonious summing of purposes would be is not made clear. But if we suppose that it represents some sort of constraint on the rationality of one's actions by requiring their compatibility with, or even advancement of, the harmonious achievement of the aims of all, thus an anticipation of the conception of the categorical imperative as a universal law of nature, we shall see that Kant is shortly to suggest that the ideas of reason characterize necessary conditions for such rationality. It is crucial to note, however, that before going any farther Kant once again expresses a constraint on the *ontological* significance of the ideas of reason:

The dogmatic use of our reason beyond the bounds of (possible) experience cannot be objectively determinant, and no new synthesis takes place; rather it is only a harmonization of the theoretical with the practical unity, since the practical use is led beyond the bounds of the pragmatic, thus also past the present world, in analogy with empirical use but in relation to the conditions of a complete unity, and thereby the business of our reason is completed *a parte priori* and *posteriori*.

(R 4849, 18:6)

In other words, there is still no suggestion that we have an ontological conflict, that is, competing views about the actual constitution of objects which can be reconciled only by transcendental idealism.

And when we finally see why it is that the requirements of practical reason lead beyond the "bounds of the sensible world" we can also see why transcendental idealism must be invoked. Here is Kant's derivation of the ideas of reason, as stated in this same note:

The principles of the completion of our knowledge, that is (of the absolute unity of the use of reason) of the absolute whole of knowledge are *synthesis* [sic] of reason.

They contain conditions of wisdom, that is, of the harmony of all our purposes in one sum. . . .

The determination of all objects through mere reason is therefore the completion of our knowledge of understanding (*in progressu* of my existence).

    ı. In respect of the self-knowledge of reason. Completion in *progressu.*

       a. I belong in a world-whole.

       b. [I] am simple.

       c. Free. intelligence.

       d. My existence is not externally dependent (on body) nor contingent . . .

Here I consider myself not as soul but as intelligence. The *synthesis* is here merely negative, namely to separate the conditions of sensibility from myself as intelligence.

And the ground of this synthesis is the freedom of reason from the restricting conditions of sensibility, which is a negative *principium* of morality, therefore of wisdom.

398

2. Completion *in regressu* from the conditioned to the unconditioned. There is an
   ens originarium,
   a. which is omnipotent and unique,
   b. simple,
   c. free cause (intelligence),
   d. necessary according in its nature.
These are the conditions of the complete unity of all objects and therefore knowledge. This unity, however, is the condition of the harmony of everything practical.

(R 4849, 18:6–7)

What practical reason requires for its abstract objective of a harmonious
sum of all purposes is the idea of the freedom of human action and the
intelligent creation of the world, which is, of course, the theater of human
action. The conception of these conditions goes beyond the bounds of
sensible representation and is also unconditioned and complete. But it is
again crucial to note that even such thoughts of free human and divine
agency do not require transcendental idealism's completely *general* distinction between things as they appear and *those same* things as they really are
in themselves. These requirements of practical reason can be satisfied by
adding to the furniture of quotidian reality two naturally unobservable
types of entities: a God who grounds the series of all empirical states but is
not himself part of the series, and a free soul in human beings which is, of
course, related to their observable actions but is not itself part in any sense
of observable reality. But nowhere does Kant suggest that time and space
must be *subtracted* from any of the ordinary objects of experience which
would have been thought to be spatial and temporal to begin with. At least
this is what Kant's claim that freedom attaches to the human being as
"intelligence" seems to suggest. Reason does not require the division of all
objects into appearance and the in-itself, or require that we look at one and
the same objects from two standpoints; it requires that we *add* to the
objects represented by sense additional objects: one divine intelligence and
numerous human intelligences. As we saw in Chapter 1, of course, this was
the original ontology of the inaugural dissertation.

A similarly clear expression of the limited ontological significance of the
disagreement between the ideas of reason and the limits of sensibility may
be found in a fragment probably written in the late 1770s or early 1780s:

... The concepts [of the understanding] can, however, be extended to all objects of
thought in general. But they yield no amplification of theoretical knowledge. In a
practical respect, however, where freedom is the condition of their use, practical-
dogmatic knowledge can obtain – God, freedom, and immortality (spiritual nature).
...

Applied to the intelligible, the categories can nevertheless ground practical-
dogmatic cognitions, namely if they are directed toward freedom and determine the
subject only in relation to that; for then we know God only according to the analogy
with the subsistence of a thing through all alteration of its accidents through time;
freedom according to the analogy with causality in the connection of force with

399

effects in the time-series; immortality in analogy with the connection of many things in one time ... (R 5552, 18:220-1)

Again, the idea is only that reason must introduce the additional ideas of God and freedom (now assigned to an immortal bearer), not that some special ontological attitude must be taken toward the whole realm of more ordinary objects of experience.

So the question still remains, how does Kant come to draw the broader ontological conclusion from the conflict between reason and sensibility? One answer is that the "practical-dogmatic" use of reason itself does, in the end, require transcendental idealism. The clearest expression of such an argument, of course, is found in the *Critique of Practical Reason*. There Kant argues that moral obligation or responsibility presupposes an ability to act independently of all prior determination, whether by external influences or even by previously established internal dispositions or traits of character, which is so radical that it can be conceived of only as an ability simply to break the grip of the past at any time. But since this possibility must be reconciled with the thoroughgoing causal determination of nature and cannot be grounded in the supposition of any anomalies within the natural realm, it can be understood only by seeing the whole natural realm – not merely internal character but also the external objects with which the agent interacts – as itself dependent on the free will of the agent. "If we were capable of an intellectual intuition of the same subject, we would then discover that the entire chain of appearances, with reference to that which concerns only the moral law" – which must include, however, anything that could figure as either a pathological influence on one's desires or an *object* of one's pathological desires, which is to say pretty much anything at all – "depends upon the spontaneity of the subject as a thing in itself" (*Critique of Practical Reason*, 5:99). And this in turn could be explained only if space, and more especially time, were not genuine features of *any* of the relevant objects at all, so that even the entire history of one's "sensible character is but a single phenomenon in the view of an intelligible consciousness of its existence."

This broader conclusion, at any rate, seems to be hinted at in this note:

It is a necessary hypothesis of the theoretical and practical employment of reason in the whole of our knowledge, consequently in relation to all purposes and an intelligible world, that an intelligible world lies at the ground of the sensible, of which the soul as intelligence is the subjective image, an original intelligence however the cause; that is, just as the *noumenon* in us is related to the appearances, so is the highest intelligence related in respect of the *mundi intelligibilis*; for the soul really contains the condition of all possible appearances in itself ...

(R 5109, 18:91)

Here the idea seems to be that for the practical use of reason the whole of the sensible world must be considered mere appearance to the real self, the free human agent, which must then itself be explained as only part of an intelligible world dependent on a highest intelligence. In this way a general distinction between appearance and reality flows from the dogmatic-practical use of reason.

But it is crucial to remember that in his published writings in practical philosophy Kant always characterizes the *theoretical* proof of the *possibility* of freedom as a *presupposition* of the *practical* proof of the *actuality* of freedom derived from the morally necessary conditions of responsibility or obligation. Yet this is to say that even if transcendental idealism is required as a precondition of moral obligation, it cannot itself first be proved by reflection on the practical alone. The argument from practical reason cannot stand on its own as the indirect proof of transcendental idealism, for Kant clearly recognizes that by itself the requirement of such a metaphysical dogma would be more likely to damage our natural but fragile recognition of the laws of morality than derive the necessary conviction from this delicate stem. In the end, instead, the question of how Kant can get from his merely methodological solution to the antinomies of pure reason to their use for an indirect proof of practical reason becomes even more pressing than before.

Toward the Critique

Why Kant's view of the antinomies changes may be impossible to explain, in the end, but in *what* the change consists can at least be clearly stated. The view so far described is one on which, because of the indefinitely extendable nature of sensible syntheses, neither the actual infinitude nor the actual finitude of the extent or parts of the sensible world can ever be sensibly presented, and so the choice between them remains *undecidable*. On the other side, ideas of totality or completeness, which *would* decide these issues, have a certain (though obscure) practical force but no theoretical truth-value. Transcendental idealism arises, however, when Kant adopts the position that, for instance, the proposition that the world of space and time is finite is not merely decidable but *false,* yet the proposition that reality is complete is not merely thinkable but *true.* This then creates a conflict which can indeed be resolved only by supposing that the objects we represent in space and time must be ontologically distinct from the realities known by reason. In other words, transcendental idealism arises from the dual assumptions that the limits of empirical decidability are also the limits of empirical truth, yet that the conceptions of reason also provide truths about reality; where the limits of empirical decidability and rational insight do not coincide, Kant then infers, the conflict can be resolved only by introducing two different objects of reference for these otherwise conflicting truths.

Or maybe the situation is even worse. Perhaps, instead of simply assuming the premise that empirical decidability and empirical truth (i.e., what may be decided about objects by empirical means and what may be true of them) necessarily coincide, Kant adopts such a theory of truth because transcendental idealism is already assumed in the arguments of the antinomies – in which case, of course, the "indirect proof" of transcendental idealism would beg the question. This would be the case if Kant were inferring that the limits of empirical decidability are also the limits of empirical truth just because he is – as he always claims to be – using the ordinary, correspondence conception of truth – that truth is the correspondence of thought to its object – but also simply *assuming* that empirical objects are *constituted* by the process of the representation of them. If this were so, of course, all that could be true of empirical objects is what is true of the representation of them, and anything else would be not merely undecidable but false. But to assume this, of course, would be to *assume* what is supposed to be *proved* by the indirect proof, namely that objects in space and time are mere appearances.[4] And in any case, Kant's complete contrast between appearances and things in themselves will still require the additional assumption that our unconditioned ideas of reason inform us of truths about things in themselves, truths incompatible with what is true by the earlier assumptions about empirical objects. This, of course, will be to identify things in themselves with noumena "in the *positive* sense of the term" – that is, objects supposedly known by means of unaided reason or "a special mode of intuition, namely the intellectual" (B 307) – in spite of Kant's explicit rejection of such an identification (B 309).

We shall see that these assumptions are at work in the published text of the "Antinomy of Pure Reason." Let me prepare the way for this by a last glance at some unpublished notes composed very close to the time when the *Critique* itself was being written. Even during this period, Kant is still capable of writing so as to suggest perfectly clearly that the antinomies arise directly from *confusing* issues of decidability with issues of truth:

The illusion first arises thus: that we represent to ourselves a progress in the field of experience according to mere laws of experience, which [however] is not an empirical progress but a mere idea which cannot be an experience. We remain in the sensible world and will be led by nothing but the principles of understanding which we employ for experience, but *we make our possible progress into an object in itself*, in that we regard the possibility of experience as something real in the object of experience.
The antinomy reveals itself here ...   (R 5642, 18:280–1)

Here there is a clear separation between limits of the possible experience of objects and any limits on what may be true of them, and certainly there is no suggestion that ideas of reason themselves reveal truths about things in themselves. To think that is exactly what Kant here claims gives rise to illusion. But this modest statement is in obvious contrast to some others from this period. Thus, R 5608 (from either the end of the 1770s or the first years of the 1780s) gives Kant's first clear statement of his characteristic later distinction between the first two antinomies and the last two in a way which commits him not merely to the *undecidability* of whether the world in space and time is finite or infinite but to the *falsehood* of any claim that it is complete and infinite, as opposed to merely indefinitely extendable:

The infinity or finitude of composition or decomposition must in both cases be assumed to be in the sensible world. But these ideas of absolute totality belong to the concepts of things in themselves; therefore they are both false. On the contrary, in the case of the concept of natural necessity and that of freedom: Of these the first pertains to the sensible world, the second to the intelligible, and the idea of totality belongs to the things themselves, of which [ideas of totality] the idea of freedom would be contradictory if it were ascribed to the sensible world; but now, as belonging to the sensible world, both [it and the idea of natural necessity as belonging to the sensible world] can be true. (R 5608, 18:250)

Now, the propositions that the sensible world is infinite or that it is finite are not merely undecidable but are both false, and "absolute totality" is no longer merely an idea of reason but something *true* of things in themselves. In this case, indeed the objects of the sensible world and things in themselves must be distinguished.

An even more explicit rejection of the epistemologically modest position that certain propositions might be undecidable but still possibly true of empirical objects, as well as evidence that the theory of the congruence of empirical truth with empirical decidability may come directly from begging the question of transcendental idealism, is found in this note that is also either from the end of the 1770s or the beginning of the 1780s:

If space and time were properties of things in themselves, then it would not follow that they are impossible from the fact that they are mathematically infinite, i.e., that the *progressus* in them insofar as they are given as infinite wholes is greater than any number, but only that they are incomprehensible for us. But now space and time are not things in themselves, and their magnitudes are not given in themselves but only through the *progressus*. Now since a *progressus in infinitum* that would be given in entirety is a contradiction, so an *infinitum mathematicum datum* [a given mathematical infinite] is impossible, but a *quantum in infinitum dabile* [an infinitely extendable quantity] is possible. But from that it also does not follow that space and time have boundaries in themselves, for that is also impossible; rather it follows only that they are simply not things in themselves and have instead only those limits where our thoughts and representations [currently] stand. (R 5903, 18:379–80)

But no such conclusion follows, unless it is already assumed that if space and time cannot be determined either to have specific boundaries or to be infinite then they cannot *have* boundaries or *be* infinite. And such an assumption could follow only either from a general principle that truth implies decidability (which Kant never defends) or else from a prior reduction of space and time to our representations of them. In the latter case there would be no indirect proof that space and time are mere appearances rather than things in themselves; that would simply be assumed in order to yield the conclusion that the propositions that space and time are infinite and that they are finite are both *false*.

This should make clear the type of argument that underlies the "indirect proof" of transcendental idealism furnished by Kant's antinomies, but perhaps before turning to the published text we can look at one more fragment:

The whole dialectic comes to this. One will hold the sensible world as a thing in itself, although it can be thought only in space and time. Now as a thing in itself, to be sure, there must be an absolute totality of conditions in it. But this is not possible in space and time, neither in composition nor in decomposition nor in origination ...   (R 5961, 18:400–1)

But there must be totality in things in themselves only if they are actually known by the ideas of reason – that is, are noumena in the positive sense; and absolute totality is genuinely impossible in space and time (not merely not to be represented or confirmed) only if it is already assumed that the limits of (empirical) confirmation and the limits of empirical truth are in fact congruent or that space and time are nothing but appearances. The latter assumption begs Kant's question, and the former is surely incompatible with the methodological prescriptions of the critical philosophy.

The antinomies in the *Critique*

As in much that we have just examined, there are places in the "Antinomy of Pure Reason" finally published in the *Critique,* especially at the beginning, which seem simply to counsel against the assumption that the unconditioned, as imagined by reason, must necessarily be capable of sensible representation. Thus, early on Kant says that "if we represent everything exclusively through pure concepts of understanding, and apart from conditions of sensible intuition, we can indeed at once assert that for a given conditioned, the whole series of conditions ... is likewise given," but then adds that "whether this completeness is sensibly possible is a further problem; the idea of it lies in reason, independent of the possibility or impossibility alike of our connecting it with any adequate empirical concepts" (A 416–7 / B 444). In other words, it does not follow from the fact that reason can conceive of the unconditioned that sense can represent it. Subsequently, Kant says that the "empiricist" denial that sense can *represent* the unconditioned can be understood as "a maxim urging moderation in our pretentions, modesty in our assertions, and yet at the same time the greatest possible extension of our understanding, through the teacher fittingly assigned to us, namely, through experience" (A 470 / B 498), but that such a denial is not to be confused with a denial of the possible *existence* of the unconditioned. He also seems to deny any ontological significance to his argument when he says that "the critical solution, which allows of complete certainty, does not consider the question objectively, but in relation to the foundation of the knowledge upon which the question is based" (A 484 / B 512). And this next statement too seems simply to warn against the careless assumption that reason's speculations can necessarily be confirmed by sense:

We have already ... shown that no transcendental employment can be made of the pure concepts either of the understanding or of reason; that the [assertion of] absolute totality of the series of conditions in the sensible world rests on a transcendental employment of reason in which reason demands this unconditioned completeness from what it assumes to be a thing in itself; and that since the sensible world contains no such completeness, we are never justified in inquiring, as regards the absolute magnitude of the series in the sensible world, whether it is limited or *in itself* unlimited, but only how far we ought to go in the empirical regress ...

(A 515–16 / B 543–4)

This certainly makes it seem as though Kant is indeed just counseling epistemic modesty, telling us that we have no ground to believe that sense can represent, for example, absolute magnitude, but not inferring from this the *impossibility* of such magnitude or anything else incapable of sensible representation or confirmation.

But whatever such passages may suggest in isolation from their immediate contexts, the Kant of 1781 does not rest content with this "maxim of moderation." On the contrary, he now claims to draw from the antinomies, especially the mathematical antinomies concerning the extent and composition of the world, an indirect proof of transcendental idealism understood as the doctrine that space, time, "and with them all appearances, are not in themselves *things*; they are nothing but representations and cannot exist outside our mind" (A 492 / B 520). Indeed, at one place he says, sounding like Schopenhauer, "Our object is in our brain" (A 484 / B 512). "This proof," he says, "would consist in the following dilemma":

If the world is a whole existing in itself, it is either finite or infinite. But both alternatives are false (as shown in the proofs of the antithesis and thesis respectively). It is therefore also false that the world (the sum of all appearances) is a whole existing in itself. From this it then follows that appearances in general are nothing outside our representations – which is just what is meant by their transcendental ideality.

(A 506–7 / B 534–5)

The question is, how does Kant make the transition from what has seemed to be his position, that we have no reason to expect that questions about the absolute finitude or infinitude of the world can be decided, or even from the stronger position that such questions are necessarily undecidable, to the second premise of the present indirect argument, which is that the propositions that the world is finite and that it is infinite *are both false*? Only the supposition that both are false requires that they be treated as dialectical opposites which can be reconciled only by a denial of the assumption on which they both rest – the assumption that the world genuinely has any magnitude at all (A 503–4 / B 531–2). If the world does have a determinate magnitude, then, by bivalence, it must be either finite or infinite, but if both of these are false, the world cannot have a determinate magnitude at all. But how does Kant derive the conclusion that these propositions are both false? What we have seen so far suggests only that they are undecidable.

In fact, Kant does not successfully argue from the undecidability to the falsehood of the opposed propositions about the extent or divisibility of the world. Kant's opposed arguments do not, after all, directly prove the *falsehood* of the antithetical conclusions; they remain only epistemological arguments which at best prove the undecidability of the opposed propositions. This can imply the falsehood of the antithetical statements only on the additional assumption that the undecidability of a proposition implies its falsehood. But either Kant just assumes this strong principle outright or else he arrives at it in a way that is even worse. This additional assumption could be derived in either of two ways. First, perhaps Kant himself commits precisely the error he has been warning against – that is, he assumes that the ideas of reason necessarily characterize things in themselves but also that these ideas must be representable in sense, which is to treat things in themselves as noumena in a positive sense, objects of knowledge by ideas of reason alone. Alternatively, Kant begs the very question at issue – that is, he already identifies objects in space and time with representations, from which it would indeed follow that there is nothing true of them which is not representable, or decidable, and that whatever cannot be decided about them cannot be true of them.

To defend this analysis, and the consequent rejection of Kant's "indirect proof" of transcendental idealism, I shall first show that the mathematical antinomies do "prove" their antithetical conclusions almost exclusively on the basis of epistemological considerations. From these the falsehood of these conclusions would follow only if it is also assumed either that things in themselves are necessarily knowable or else that the objects concerned are already reduced to representations and are for that reason, instead, necessarily knowable objects.

Kant finally organizes the discussion of the antinomies as disputes over four issues, which yield five pairs of opposed propositions: (1) the dispute over "absolute completeness of the *Composition* of the given whole of all appearances," which actually subsumes two disputes: whether the world is finite or infinite in elapsed history, and whether it is finite or infinite in spatial extent; (2) the question of "absolute completeness in the *Division* of a given whole in appearance," that is, the question of whether or not the world is ultimately constituted of simple atoms; (3) the problem of the "absolute completeness in the *Origination* of an appearance," that is, the question of whether or not natural causation is the sufficient explanation of all that exists; and (4) the question of "absolute completeness as regards *Dependence of Existence* of the alterable in appearance," that is, the question of whether explanation always proceeds from contingent to contingent or whether it must finally terminate in something necessarily existent (A 415 / B 443). The first two of these headings subsume what Kant calls the "mathematical antinomies," that is, the disputes over the extent of past time, the extent of space, and the divisibility of matter. The mathematical antinomies will receive the more detailed discussion in what follows, since Kant makes it plain that they must bear the burden of the indirect proof of transcendental idealism alone (see again, e.g., A 506–7 / B 534–5). This is appropriate, because only in their case does he argue that both mutually exhaustive propositions about space and time are false, so that space and time must be reduced to mere indefinitely extendable representations; in the case of the antinomies concerning freedom and necessity, he argues only that both sides *may* be true, which will not furnish an indirect proof of transcendental idealism but rather presupposes one (just as in the case of the postulates of practical reason, with which of course the third and fourth antinomies are intimately connected).

The first antinomy

The antinomies are not merely supposed to furnish an indirect proof of transcendental idealism but are also themselves constituted by indirect arguments. That is, in each antinomy the thesis and antithesis are both defended by what is supposed to be a valid refutation of its alternative. The first antinomy, then, proceeds as follows. The two theses are that the world has a beginning in time, or extends only finitely back from the present, and that it "is also limited as regards space," or is bounded and finite in spatial extent (A 426 / B 454). The argument for these theses pretends to undermine their contraries. First, the denial of the assumption that the world has a beginning in time is held to require "that there has passed away in the world an infinite series of successive states of things," but this is asserted to be impossible precisely because "the infinity of a series can never be completed through successive synthesis." Second, the denial that space can be infinite is impossible, because although an infinitely extended space would not itself have to be infinitely extended in time, "a magnitude ... can be thought only through the synthesis of its parts," and this means that "to think, as a whole, the world which fills all spaces, the successive synthesis of the parts of an infinite world must be viewed as completed" – but again, the synthesis of an infinite is precisely a synthesis which cannot be completed. So in neither case can the requisite synthesis be completed, and thus the denials of the finitude of past time and space cannot be sustained. Instead, the assertions of finitude must stand.

It is obvious that these arguments turn on purely epistemological conclusions, that is, on the claims that it is impossible to *represent* or, by means of sense, *confirm* the existence of infinite past time or infinite space. But from this it would follow that space and time cannot *be* infinite only if it is already directly assumed that only what can be decided or confirmed can possibly be so, or if one of the underlying assumptions from which this epistemological maxim would follow has been made: that whatever is true of things that really exist has to be knowable, or else that space and time are only representations, so that of course only what is representable can be true of them. But to assume the first of these would be precisely to assume that things in themselves must be knowable either by reason or (even worse) by sense, the very mistake which Kant had been warning against since the inaugural dissertation, and to assume the second would be to assume precisely what is supposed to *follow* from the indirect proof of transcendental idealism.[5]

The demonstration of the antithesis in the first antinomy is not so patently dependent on epistemological conclusions which can prove the metaphysical point at hand only by begging the metaphysical questions, but the character of the argument should still be evident on reflection. The antitheses to be proved are that "the world has no beginning, and no limits in space" but is, rather, infinite in both regards. Again, the arguments are intended to undermine the denial of these assumptions. As far as the contrary assumption that the world does have a beginning in time is concerned, then, Kant's argument is that "no coming to be of a thing is possible in an empty time, because no part of such a time possesses, as compared with any other, a distinguishing condition of existence rather than of nonexistence" (A 427 / B 455). This is, of course, Leibniz's argument against the beginning of the world at some particular point in absolute time, on the ground that God would lack sufficient reason to begin the world at that point rather than any other because of the qualitative identity of all points of absolute time.[6] But now remember that Kant cannot just be *describing* the argument of Leibniz: If his indirect proof is to succeed, Kant must be offering a *valid* argument from which the falsehood of the denial of its conclusion actually follows. But then we must ask, What is the status of the principle of sufficient reason in Kant's own philosophy? The key to Kant's transcendental theory of experience was nothing other than his transformation of this alleged ontological argument into a purely epistemological argument, so unless the entire result of the "Transcendental Analytic" and Kant's answer to both Leibniz and Hume is to be undermined, the principle of sufficient reason – that for every consequent there is a sufficiently determining antecedent – can only be an epistemological principle, a principle requisite insofar as we are to know or empirically determine the temporal position of any state of affairs, thus insofar as we are to determine the occurrence of any event. But this means that the epistemological necessity of the principle of sufficient reason, schematized as the principle of universal causation, precludes only the possibility of *knowledge* or *representation* of a first moment of time. And from this it follows that a first moment of time cannot *be* real only if it is either assumed that whatever is true of things in themselves must also be knowable, so that if time really began it would necessarily be knowable that it did, or else if it is already assumed that time is merely a feature of representations, so that knowability and truth again coincide. But as before, to assume the first of these is precisely to assume a "subreptic axiom" of the form that Kant had rejected since 1770, and to assume the second is to assume nothing less than what is supposed to follow from the indirect proof.

The argument against the supposition that space is bounded or finite is a bit harder to follow but perhaps also more obviously epistemological. Kant claims that if the world were limited in space, it would have to exist "in an empty space which is unlimited" – already a dubious interpretation of what it would mean for space itself to be limited. But since the world includes all objects, "the relation of the world" – the filled portion of space – "would be a relation of it to no *object*," and this seems to mean that the relation of the finite, filled portion of space to the rest *could not be perceived*, for Kant also says that on the supposition under attack the world would be "an absolute whole beyond which there is no object of intuition" – that is, nothing by relation to which the bounded portion of space could be perceived (A 428–9 / B 456–7).

This is evidently a conclusion about the conditions under which the limits of existence in space *could be known*, which could be transformed into a conclusion about the conditions under which limits in space could *exist*, and thus into a conclusion about the actual falsehood rather than mere undecidability of the thesis of the antinomy, only by means of the proscribed or circular assumptions already described. But in this case, Kant reveals his hand and shows that the argument for the falsehood of the thesis does indeed turn on begging the question at issue in the indirect proof. For Kant defends the supposition that the – impossible – relation of the world to an object in empty space would be necessary for the world to be limited in space by saying nothing less than that "space is merely the form of outer intuition," from which it follows that it is not itself "a real object which can be outwardly intuited." *From this* he concludes that from the attempt "to set space outside all appearances, there arise all sorts of empty determinations of outer intuition, *which yet are not possible perceptions*" (B 457, n. b; emphasis added). In other words, it is from the *prior* assumption that space is nothing but a form for perceiving objects that it follows that the limitation of objects by empty space beyond could not be perceived, and only from this does it follow that "such a relation, and consequently the limitation of the world by empty space, is nothing" (A 429 / B 457). It is from the prior assumption of transcendental idealism, in other words, that even the claim that empty space cannot be perceived is derived, and from this same assumption that it is also concluded that empty space could not exist. The falsehood of the thesis of the antinomy is anything but independent of the transcendental idealism which it is ultimately supposed to prove.

The second antinomy

In the second antinomy, it is the argument for the thesis rather than antithesis which is harder to follow, but this argument still appears to turn on an epistemological assumption, and the argument for the antithesis does so quite patently. This antinomy presents conflicting positions on whether anything genuinely simple can exist in the world, either in composition or in isolation. The thesis asserts that "every composite substance in the world is made up of simple parts," from which it follows that "nothing anywhere exists save the simple or what is composed of the simple" (A 434 / B 462). (It is not asserted in this that simple things are ever found apart from their combination into composites, but the antithesis contravenes both the assumption that composites are made up of simples and what is treated as a "second proposition" that anything simple exists at all; this is presumably to undermine the supposition that the *soul* is simple, since this would not naturally be thought of as part of a composite). The argument revolves on the claim that if, as on the assumption which is to be undermined, nothing simple exists, but also "if all composition be then removed in thought," nothing at all will exist. Exactly what this means is obscure, but if it is supposed to be a sound argument which proves the truth of its conclusion, thus the falsehood of its antithesis, it would seem that it would have to assume, first, that the process of decomposition in thought is necessarily a process which reaches a termination, which assumes that an idea of reason can necessarily be given a sensory confirmation, and, second, that the results of a thought experiment, the impossibility of terminating an exercise of decomposition without simple parts, necessarily represents an actual state of affairs, the impossibility of existence without simple parts. This again seems to assume a necessary congruence between what may be represented and what must be true.

The character of the argument for the antithesis is clearer. Here Kant argues that the supposition that composite things are made up of simple parts is undermined by the fact that "all external relation, and therefore all composition of substances, is possible only in space," for since spaces are always made up of further spaces, any simple would in fact be a further "composite of substances," that is, not simple at all (A 435 / B 463). This seems to depend on the assumption that because simple parts could not be *perceived* in space they could not exist, an assumption which must be derived either from the direct assumption that only what can be known can be true or, as is suggested by the note on the antithesis of the first antinomy, from the prior assumption that appearances are nothing but representations necessarily characterized by space as the form of intuition. In any case, the continuation of Kant's argument, in behalf of the more general claim that "nowhere in the world does there exist anything simple," turns on the explicit assertion that "the existence of the absolutely simple cannot be established by any experience or perception, either outer or inner; and that the absolutely simple is therefore a mere idea, the objective reality of which can never be shown in any possible experience ..." (A 437 / B 465). Obviously this can prove the falsehood of the proposition that something absolutely simple exists only if it is already assumed that the limits of possible experience are also the limits of possible truth. In Kant's own words, "The proofs are based upon insight into the constitution of space, insofar as space is in actual fact the formal condition of the possibility of all matter" (A 439 / B 467). This is indeed how the proofs work – but this "insight" is also what the antinomies were supposed to *yield,* rather than *presuppose.*

Thus, although the arguments for the theses and antitheses of the first two antinomies may successfully describe the limits on the *empirical decidability* of questions about the age, extent, and divisibility of the world, thus condemning us to the at best indefinitely extended pursuit of knowledge in these matters, they cannot imply the *joint falsehood* of dialectical opposites except by presupposing the ontological position – the identification of the world in space and time with merely indefinitely extended series of representations – for which such dialectical opposition is supposed to furnish an indirect proof. Since Kant himself explicitly claims only that the indirect proof is yielded by the mathematical antinomies, and since the remaining two "dynamical" antinomies tend to prove only the necessity of *adding* a nonsensible first cause and necessary being to the otherwise unchanged sum of ordinary objects, rather than that of positing a mysterious realm of things in themselves *lying behind* the objects of ordinary experience, we might well leave the issue of Kant's indirect proof of transcendental idealism at this point. However, since Kant's procedure in the third and fourth antinomies provides further evidence of his tendency in these arguments to infer ontology directly from epistemology, a few further words may be in order.

The third and fourth antinomies

Kant's position on the mathematical antinomies is that both theses and antitheses are false, and their joint falsehood proves the impossibility of the underlying assumption that space and time are real properties of objects at all. In the case of the second pair of antinomies, however, his position is rather that both sides at least may be true if predicated of the proper objects: The two antitheses correctly describe the realm of appearances, and the two theses put forth at least possibly true propositions about nonsensible realities.[7] On the side of the antitheses, there are no problems. In the case of the third antinomy, the antithesis of which asserts that "there is no freedom; everything in the world takes place solely in accordance with laws of nature" (A 445 / B 473), Kant explicitly asserts that "transcendental freedom" must be denied because "it stands opposed to the law of causality"; the anomalous "kind of connection which it assumes as holding between the successive states of the active causes renders all unity of experience impossible" (A 445–7 / B 473–5). This is an explicitly epistemological claim, but that is in order if what is to be inferred is not, in this case, an absolute ontological conclusion but only a limit on what can be known. Similarly, although the fourth antinomy states its antithesis in ontological form – "An absolutely necessary being nowhere exists in the world, nor does it exist outside the world as its cause" – yet draws on an epistemological premise, Kant claims that the supposition that there is a necessary cause in the world "conflicts with the dynamical law of all *determination* in time" (A 453 / B 481; emphasis added), which requires that everything determined in time be treated as contingent on some prior condition. This is, again, an admissible procedure if the final lesson to be learned is also itself only that of a limit on sensible representation.[8]

The arguments for the theses, however, are more problematic. In the third antinomy, Kant argues for the possibility of a "causality of freedom" independent of the normal chain of the "causality of nature" precisely on the ground that whereas the determination that something has taken place "presupposes, in accordance with the law of nature, a preceding state and its causality" (A 444 / B 472), it is also the case that the "law of nature is just this, that nothing takes place without a cause *sufficiently* determined *a priori*" (A 446 / B 474), which is supposed to require the termination of the series of causes in something which is itself first, and must thus be determined by something other than yet one more temporally antecedent cause. The difficulty is, first, as we have already seen, that the proof for the "law of nature" is explicitly epistemological. Second, it was *not* any part of what was proved in the proof of the general "law of nature" that there must be causation which is *sufficient* in the sense of *terminating*; this would follow from the argument of the second analogy (which, after all, turns on the necessary conditions of time-determination) only if it explicitly assumed that the whole series of states of affairs determined in time *could itself be placed in time,* which of course the argument of the second analogy leaves completely undecided. So the argument can only be understood as illegitimately transporting reason's idea of complete determinability into the realm of the sensible, thus misinterpreting the consequences of a law for the determination of sensibility under the guidance of reason. This would, of course, be an interpretation entirely in accordance with the original intentions of Kant's discussion of "subreptic axioms," but then it would not itself even so much as *suggest* the possibility of an ontological split of the kind on which both thesis and antithesis come out true. Thus, the third antinomy would not provide evidence of even the possibility of transcendental idealism, which could then be supplemented by other (e.g., practical) arguments in behalf of this position. Of course, Kant's later discussions of the positive practical argument for freedom assign just such a role to the third antinomy, but again, this practical postulate presupposes that transcendental idealism has already been proved; it does not itself provide even an indirect proof of it.

The argument for the thesis of the fourth antinomy, that an absolutely necessary being belongs to the world as either its part or its cause (A 452 / B 480), employs exactly the same sort of combination drawn from conditions of sensible knowledge – in this case, the claim that without the representation of a series of alterations, the "representation of serial time, as a condition of the possibility of the sensible world, would not be given us" (A 452 / B 480), the assumption on which the joint argument of the first and second analogies turns – with the overtly rational assumption that "every conditioned that is given presupposes, in respect of its existence, a complete series of conditions up to the unconditioned." Thus, this argument too gives us a perfect illustration of a "prejudice" that can be sustained only by a "subreptic axiom" and is admissible only if intended as such, but it would have no force even to suggest a thesis which is true if only predicated of the right sort of object. Thus it too fails to prove the possibility of transcendental idealism.

Postscript: Realism and idealism

This concludes my discussion of Kant's arguments for transcendental idealism. We have now seen that Kant's indirect proof of transcendental idealism from the paradoxes of pure reason is no more persuasive than his direct proofs of the denial of the spatiality and temporality of things in themselves. The results of the "transcendental theory of experience" are thus indeed properly separated from the metaphysics of "transcendental idealism." Nevertheless, Kant was clearly committed to some form of transcendental idealism, and even when his ultimate refutation of idealism finally pushed him to a form of realism, he clearly felt the need to effect some form of reconciliation between the two. I must thus conclude this part by returning to the strategy for such a reconciliation that Kant suggested in the versions of the refutation which he drafted after 1787 and which I examined in Part IV.

As we saw there, Kant's interpretation of transcendental idealism, in the fourth "Paralogism" of 1781, as requiring the reduction of spatial appearances to a species of our own representations depended on the assumption that the ontological and epistemological status of external objects must be isomorphic. We have now seen that the exposition of the "Antinomy of Pure Reason" (which remained unchanged after 1781, in spite of other changes in his views) depends upon precisely the same assumption. That is, Kant's proofs of transcendental idealism have assumed that if things numerically distinct from us *exist* independently of us, then the properties by which we *represent* them must be ones they can be known to possess independently of us, and, conversely, that if the properties by which objects are represented are known to depend upon ourselves in any way, then the objects themselves must also be dependent on us for their own existence. Thus the analysis in the fourth "Paralogism" defines the "transcendental realist" as one who "hypostasizes outer appearances and comes to regard them not as representations but as *things existing by themselves outside us, with the same quality as that with which they exist in us*" (A 386). Kant's own transcendental idealism – because, as he always continued to suppose, it had already established "that time and space are . . . only sensible forms of our intuition, not determinations given as existing by themselves nor conditions of objects as things in themselves" – was thought to require the ontological assertion that the objects represented by means of these forms, namely objects as appearances, "are to be regarded as being, one and all, representations only, not things in themselves" (A 369). But it was merely necessary for Kant to drop this single assumption in order for him to conclude that there is "no difficulty" with the idea that we could be conscious of a relation to something independent of ourselves "without being able to cognize the object itself, but only the form of [its] relationship [to] ourself" (R 5653, 18:310) or with the claim that I am "conscious of (my) existence in time, also of the

existence of external things, to be sure as appearances, yet as real things"
(R 6314, 18:616). Kant simply needed to drop the assumption that the
epistemological status of being an "appearance," or known through one of
our own forms of intuition, requires the ontological status of being a
"representation," an actual state or modification of the self, in order to
exploit the possibility that we could know that something *exists* independently of us without knowing *what it is like* independently of us. And even if
he made this move nowhere else, Kant clearly made it in the versions of the
refutation of idealism which he wrote after the publication of the second
edition of the *Critique*.[9]

Thus it was by this means that Kant could retain his arguments for the
transcendental ideality of space and time even while advancing his
argument for ontological realism, and assert that

... the idealism of space and time, which is merely formal, does not contain real
idealism, which asserts that in the perception of things in space no object at all
beside the representation is given; rather [it implies] only that the same form of
space does not pertain in itself to this object or these external objects (which of these
it is remains undecided) by means of which we intuit it or them, since this form
belongs solely to the subjective manner of our faculty of representation in
perception, which can be inferred from the fact that space contains nothing in itself
which could be a representation of a thing in itself or of the relation of (different)
such things to one another, and if it were considered as such a determination, as an
ens imaginarium it would be a *non ens*.   (R 6316, 18:621–2)

Or, to use again the note quoted in the final section of Chapter 14, the
rejection of the assumption of ontological and epistemological isomorphism allows Kant to say without self-contradiction that

in order that something can appear to be outside us, there must really be something
outside us, though not constituted in the way we have the representation of it, since
other kinds of sense could afford other ways of representing the same thing. For
otherwise the representation of something outside us could never come to be
thought, since we would be conscious of our representations only as inner
determinations and for their object would have only inner sense, which we yet
carefully distinguish from outer sense.   (R 6312, 18:613)

Because he could maintain the dependent status of the *form* by which we
represent external objects without implying that the *existence* of these
objects is dependent on us, Kant could rightly call his mature position
"formal idealism" rather than "real idealism": It is idealism with respect to
the *forms* but not the *objects* of intuition. As he put it in a letter to J. S. Beck
of 4 December 1792: "... Messrs. Eberhard's and Garve's opinion that
Berkeley's idealism is the same as that of the critical philosophy (which I
could better call 'the principle of the ideality of space and time') does not
deserve the slightest attention. For I speak of ideality in reference to the
form of representations, but they interpret this to mean ideality with respect
to the *matter,* that is, the ideality or the object *and* its very existence"
(11:395).[10] The charge of Berkeleianism had rankled Kant for ten years;

the argument of the mature refutation, unlike the reductionism which is explicitly asserted in the fourth "Paralogism" and tacitly at work in the indirect argument of the "Antinomy," is what finally made it unjustified *ex post facto.*

Indeed, once Kant dropped the simplistic dichotomy underlying the fourth "Paralogism" of 1781 he could even retain the position, unsuccessfully argued there, that our knowledge of the independent reality of objects in space can be secured *only* if we recognize that their spatiality, unlike their existence, cannot be independent of our representations of them. Thus the same R 6317 which contained Kant's final argument against skepticism, Spinozism, idealism, and all his other targets could also argue that

... reality can be secured for outer objects (as things in themselves) precisely insofar as one does not assume that their intuition is one of a thing in itself; for if it were this, and the form of space were the form of a thing which pertained to it even without the special constitution of our subject, then it would be possible that we should have the representation of such a thing without its existing.

(R 6317, 18:627)

Of course, the argument underlying this claim – that if the characteristics of space can be known only empirically rather than *a priori,* then there will be a lack of certainty to this knowledge which will also infect our knowledge of the existence of objects in space – is dubious. Even so, it should now be clear that the form of transcendental idealism which it requires is compatible with a realistic interpretation of the intended conclusion of the refutation of idealism. And in the absence of any convincing connection at all between the transcendental theory of experience and transcendental idealism, Kant can simply become a realist *malgré lui.* As Kant himself understands it, transcendental idealism is a metaphysical dogma, not a doctrine of epistemological modesty. But the real principles of his ultimate proof of the necessity of rule-governed enduring objects independent of ourselves need only subject our empirical self-knowledge to the natural limits of empirical decidability without degrading it to a transcendental illusion.

Afterword

In the work just completed, I have tried to discover, in all their multiplicity and complexity, Kant's own arguments on the issues in theoretical philosophy which he perceived as most important and to critically assess these arguments on grounds that Kant himself would have recognized as compelling. I have thus attempted to develop my interpretation and criticize Kant's arguments independently of explicit reference to contemporary preoccupations – although if philosophy as we know it is still practiced five or ten decades from now, a future reader of this book would undoubtedly have as little trouble dating the period of its origination as we have in dating Kemp Smith's *Commentary* or Strawson's *Bounds of Sense*. The last two decades, however, have witnessed an enormous effort (stemming in large part from Strawson's work) devoted to the "reconstruction" of "Kantian" "transcendental" arguments and to the assessment of the "antiskeptical" prospects of such arguments. Many of these arguments involve issues, especially about the conditions of the possibility of the meaningful use of *language,* which are quite distant from anything ever considered by Kant himself. In any case, the literature has become so extensive that a systematic survey of it would have to be as large again as the historical study which I have already presented. But at least a few suggestions about how the arguments Kant himself made fare with respect to several of the most prominent issues in this debate will be in order here.[1]

Kant seemed to give an unequivocal characterization of a "transcendental proof" when he asserted that such a proof

... does not show that the given concept (e.g., of that which happens) leads directly to another concept (that of a cause), for such a transition would be a leap which could not be made responsibly; rather it shows that experience itself, thus the object of experience, would be impossible without such a connection. Therefore the proof must at the same time show the possibility of attaining synthetically and *a priori* a certain cognition of things, which is not included in the concept of them ...
(A 783 / B 811)

Nevertheless, the arguments which he actually offered in attempting to fulfill his early promise of a transcendental theory of experience take two fundamentally different forms. On the one hand, as we saw in the discussion of the transcendental deduction in Part II as well as in the discussion of the "Transcendental Aesthetic" in Part V, many of Kant's

417

own "transcendental proofs" have the following underlying form (on the classification used in Part II, we may call these type A deductions):

(1) A premise which presupposes the validity of a claim to knowledge of a universal and necessary truth.

(2) An intermediate step in which we are reminded that ordinary experience can never justify any such claim (e.g., B 3–4) and that any such claim must therefore have an *a priori* basis of some sort: "All necessity, without exception, is grounded in a transcendental condition" (A 106).

(3) A conclusion in which a particular form of intuition, concept, or principle of judgment is asserted to be the only possible condition satisfying 2 in the case of the particular premise of form 1 at issue – which conclusion may be arrived at directly or through the further supposition that there must be some particular *a priori* act of or capacity for synthesis underlying the claim to knowledge in 1.

On the other hand, as we saw in the discussion of his theory of objective and subjective time-determination in parts III and IV, Kant also offers arguments – although he does not himself tend to label these as transcendental deductions – which have the following structure (using the earlier classification, we may label these type B arguments):

(1) An initial supposition that we are entitled to claim empirical knowledge of the relations, primarily temporal, of certain states of affairs – whether these are states represented as objective or representations as such.

(2) An intermediate step in which it is argued that since time itself and therefore temporal relations cannot be immediately perceived, the remaining materials available to us – spatial intuition and the concepts and principles of the understanding – must be sufficient to enable us to construct a framework for the confirmation of the claims to knowledge described in 1.

(3) A conclusion consisting in the display of the concepts and principles of the understanding which would actually do the job described in 2, and which must therefore be *a priori,* at least in the sense of not themselves being derivable by straightforward induction or abstraction from any judgments of form 1 conceived of as epistemologically secure independently of these *a priori* concepts and principles.

Kant himself describes the paradigmatic case of such an argument:

In the transcendental analytic, for instance, we have derived the principle that everything which happens has a cause from the unique condition of the objective possibility of a concept of that which in general happens: that the determination of an occurrence in time, thus [the determination] that this (occurrence) belongs to experience, would be impossible unless it stood under such a dynamical rule.

(A 788 / B 816)

It is evident that these two general forms of argument have profoundly different sorts of premises. They should therefore fare very differently in

418

face of the standard questions about "transcendental arguments." I shall now touch upon three of these issues.

(1) Several writers have asked what status the premises of Kant's arguments must have if they are to deliver synthetic *a priori* conclusions. Can such conclusions be derived from nothing but analytically true premises? That seems impossible, but there has been disagreement about the point at which synthetic premises must enter Kant's arguments. One view has been that Kant's transcendental arguments must begin from a premise which is synthetic *a priori* – such as the premise that we have experience at all – but then proceed to their conclusion by entirely analytical inferences – thus, for example, by analysis of the concept of experience. The requisite analyses may not be obvious – hence the difficulty of transcendental arguments, after all – but they ultimately show only the analytical consequences of the original synthetic premise, and thus transcendental arguments are at best unobvious analytical arguments.[2]

This characterization does not seem to fit either of Kant's basic models for a transcendental proof very well. Consider first proofs of type A. To be sure, the claim to necessary truth from which such an argument begins must indeed be a synthetic proposition itself, as is clear in the paradigmatic regressive argument from the synthetic *a priori* propositions of geometry and also, although this is more controversial, in the argument from the synthetic principle of apperception (see again A 117n). We find, however, that Kant does not always expound arguments of this type as though he understood them to begin from a synthetic premise; instead, as we saw in his many versions of the deduction from the concepts of an object and of a judgment, he proceeds as though the claims to necessary truth were derivable precisely from the analysis of these concepts. In such cases, then, the first premise of the deduction is actually associated with the analysis of a concept – although typically with the concept of an object or a judgment, rather than with a concept of experience itself (the deduction in the *Prolegomena*, which begins with the analysis of a *judgment of experience*, comes closest to breaking down this distinction and thus beginning with an analysis of the concept of experience itself). What is much more important, however – since it might well be argued that all of these arguments starting from analyses of concepts as inherently claiming necessary truth tacitly presuppose the additional synthetic premise that we know objects, make judgments of experience, and so on – the arguments of type A certainly do not proceed past their opening step by moves that are reasonably characterized as analytic. As my tripartite representation of such arguments suggests, they depend on the further premise that experience can never yield necessity, so any source of necessity must itself be *a priori*, and on the assumption that the particular transcendental ground which Kant adduces – be it an *a priori* form of intuition, an original and *a priori* synthesis of all the possible data for self-consciousness, or anything else – is the only available "transcendental ground" for the necessity which has been claimed. It is difficult indeed to conceive of these, especially the second type of assumption, as analytic. It may be hard to say what the status of these propositions is, but it seems most unlikely that they are obtained by the straightforward analysis of any known concept. The recognition that experience could never yield knowledge of necessity, after all, was secured only by difficult arguments first discovered by Hume; that there can be alternative grounds for claims to necessary truth at all can hardly follow from the analysis of any concept; and that the particular "transcendental ground" which Kant produces in any given transcendental argument is the sole ground for the claim to necessary truth which is the premise of the argument is an equally implausible candidate for analyticity. (We shall return to the problem raised by this last point later on.)

Of course, Kant's arguments proceeding from an initial claim to necessary truth, once unmasked, can be of little interest to contemporary supporters of transcendental arguments. His theories about the necessary conditions of empirical time-determinations, however, are of great interest indeed. But it is even more obvious that these cannot be conceived of as analyses of concepts. Such arguments start from the clearly synthetic premise that we are entitled to claim knowledge of certain empirical judgments about temporal relations, whether these be among states of objects or among our own representations. Such a synthetic premise might be thought equivalent to the synthetic premise that we have experience at all, although it is in fact more likely that assent could be gained for the proposition that we make a particular form of judgment about time than that we could reach agreement about what is actually contained in the "concept of experience," a controversial construct of philosophers if ever there was one. Thus the introduction of any general concept of experience into such arguments is probably an unnecessary detour: Acceptance of any concept of experience will be parasitic upon acceptance of the premise that certain kinds of judgments are made, rather than vice versa. What is again more important, however, is the problem with conceiving of the remaining premises of Kant's type B transcendental arguments as products of the analysis of any concepts. As we have seen, the vital steps in such arguments are the claims that time itself cannot be perceived and that instead the spatial application of concepts of substance, causation, reciprocal determination, and, ultimately, ontological independence itself is the only alternative means for grounding judgments of temporal relation. Although it might be suggested that it is part of (if not the whole of) the concept of time that its separate moments must be successive, from which it might follow analytically that temporal relations (at least among successive states of affairs) cannot be directly perceived, it would again seem that Kant's claim that temporal relations cannot be perceived directly is itself more intuitive than any alleged analysis of the concept of time – another philosophers' artifact, after all. Moreover, it would seem much closer to Kant's own view to think of this vital premise as one learned from the inspection of a form of intuition and for that reason synthetic – indeed, Kant's "transcendental exposition" of the concept of time includes among the "axioms of time" precisely the

420

claim that "different times are not simultaneous but successive" (A 31 / B 47). So even if this "axiom" itself logically implies that temporal relations among objects existing at successive moments cannot be perceived in any single representation, to regard the "axiom" and thus what it implies as analytic propositions would completely undermine Kant's own conception of the "Transcendental Analytic." Further, it is even less obvious how Kant's alternative to the direct perception of time, the conclusion that we must apply the categories and principles of judgments to objects in space in order to make temporal determinations, could be thought to flow from the analysis of any concepts. As Kant says,

But for the peculiarity of our understanding, that it can bring about *a priori* the unity of apperception only by means of the categories, and indeed only through this manner and number of them, a further ground may be offered just as little as for why we have these and no other functions for judging, or for why space and time are the sole forms for our possible intuition.   (B 146)

Kant's own view is clearly that it is not analytically true that space and time are our sole forms of intuition, not analytically true that temporal relations cannot be directly perceived, and therefore not analytically true that applying the principles of understanding to independent objects in space is the only alternative means for making temporal determinations.

If not analytically true, however, what is the status of Kant's fundamental premises that time itself cannot be directly perceived and that the application of principles of understanding to independent objects in space is the only alternative means available to us for any confirmation of temporal determinations? This is harder to say. After a lifetime of study, Lewis White Beck has concluded simply that propositions of this sort "are brutely factual yet in some not well-defined sense self-evident; they are factual but not empirical."[3] I am sure that in the brutal factuality of such premises we have reached the bedrock of human imagination, although less sure that anything other than a verbal victory for the synthetic *a priori* is gained by denying that these premises are empirical. I am prepared to concede that we might imagine some form of direct perception of temporal relations – a digital time-stamp on every one of our perceptions – and to rest the transcendental proof of causality and the other categories on my empirical assurance that no one – certainly not the skeptic – will claim that he has such an alternative means for confirming temporal determinations. If Kant's argument really showed that in the absence of the direct perception of temporal relations only causal judgments about interacting substances in space could confirm our empirical time-determinations, it would matter little whether the underlying premise that time is not directly perceived was itself empirical rather than *a priori*. It certainly is brutal enough.

(2) The claim that categorial judgments about objects in space are the only alternative to the direct perception of temporal relations brings us to a second line of criticism. Here it is argued that Kant has failed to show that

what are admittedly *sufficient* conditions for the possibility of certain forms of judgment are also *uniquely* sufficient, and therefore truly *necessary* conditions of the possibility of such judgments, and that his strategy of effecting a transcendental deduction by demonstrating the only possible conditions for the possibility of experience fails for that reason.

The best-known version of this criticism is Stephan Körner's. Körner distinguishes between a "method" and a "categorial schema" for the identification and differentiation of objects in an external realm. By a "method" he means something such as a particular theory about geometry, or dynamics, and so on, and by a "schema" he means the most general characteristics of a class of such theories, in particular its "constitutive attribute," or conception of what makes something an object at all (in Kant's schema, of course, this is substance) and its "individuating" attribute, or its criterion for the differentiation of one object from another (in Kant's schema, spatiotemporal location).[4] He then argues that in order to establish that a schema is unique – and thus a necessary condition of the possibility of experience, an *a priori* condition of knowledge which can be proved by a transcendental deduction – it must be shown not only that any proposed "method" for representing objects belongs to the schema but also that *all* possible methods belong to this one schema (p. 233). But such a "uniqueness-demonstration" – the need for which, he claims, Kant failed "even to *consider*" – is impossible (p. 236). This is because there are only three ways in which a schema for constituting and individuating objects might be shown to be unique, but none of them can work. These three means would be (1) "to demonstrate the schema's uniqueness by comparing it with experience undifferentiated by any method of prior differentiation"; (2) "to demonstrate the schema's uniqueness by comparing it with its possible competitors"; and (3) "to examine the schema and its application entirely from within" (pp. 233–4). But none of these three means can accomplish the desired end: The first is, of course, impossible from a Kantian point of view (we never experience raw sensations without already applying the forms of intuitions and categories to them); the second undercuts itself precisely by supposing that an alternative schema is available for comparison; and the third could at most show the internal structure of the schema under consideration, and nothing about any others (pp. 234–5).

But this highly abstract argument, which is conducted at enormous distance from any of Kant's own texts, is far from conclusive. It is indeed fair to bring it against Kant's type A deductions, where Kant makes a direct transition from the need for a "transcendental ground" for claims of necessary truth to a particular *a priori* synthesis or form of intuition or judgment, without any proof that the *a priori* structure adduced is the sole one available to us. Of course, the even more pressing problem with such arguments is the initial claim to necessary truth itself. But it seems unfair to bring these charges against Kant's type B arguments, concerning which neither Körner's objection 2 or objection 3 is obviously justified.[5] In general, Körner's argument seems to presuppose that to form any conception of an alternative to our own schema for experiencing objects is *eo ipso* to demonstrate the possibility of that schema. But this surely ignores Kant's fundamental distinction between merely logical and real possibility: To give a characterization of a schema sufficient to argue about it (or its inadequacy) cannot be thought sufficient to prove its real possibility. Körner's objections 2 and 3 both fail because of this assumption.

As far as objection 3 is concerned, Körner overlooks the possibility that we may not only be able to investigate the internal consistency of the schema that we do employ but may also be able to formulate a characterization of a proposed alternative to our schema which is sufficient for us to determine that it is internally inconsistent or else inadequate to objectives accepted even by a proponent of an alternative schema, without thereby ever assuming the real possibility of the schema which is to be rejected. One critic of Körner has argued that this is the logical form of Kant's refutation of idealism: Kant shows that a schema which does not include the posit of independent objects in space, though it may seem logically possible, falls short of accomplishing the task of time-determination accepted even by the proponent of the alternative schema.[6] If the refutation has this form, however, then it demonstrates the necessity of the Kantian schema not by reflecting on its own structure but rather by demonstrating the inadequacy of an apparently possible alternative schema – call it the Cartesian schema – for a purpose which the Cartesian himself accepts.

The interpretation of the refutation of idealism which has been offered in this work might be thought to have such a character: It shows that a Cartesian who tacitly assumes that his temporal determinations can be confirmed by a direct perception of temporal relations cannot accomplish his own objectives. It seems easier, however, to use the theory of time-determination which has been ascribed to Kant in this work to show that Körner's objection 2 is unfair, at least to Kant's intentions. It is hardly true that Kant simply failed to consider the problem of "uniqueness." Of course he considered it: The significance of his fundamental premise that time cannot be directly perceived is precisely to exclude all but one alternative schema for making empirical time-determinations. To be sure, one may object to his initial delimitation of the alternatives – that is, to his not quite explicit argument that space and time are the only forms of intuition, therefore that if temporal relations cannot be directly perceived their perception must in some way depend upon spatial intuition; one may argue that he has not adequately proved this limitation of the alternatives. One may not be satisfied with the brutally factual claim that we simply cannot explain why we have only these two forms of intuition. Further, one may argue with the supposition that there is no direct perception of temporal relations – the supposition on which the inference to the other alternative also depends.[7] But surely the strategy of Kant's theory of time-determination is nothing less than that of demonstrating that of the two imaginable bases for the determination of temporal relations, one, that they

423

are directly perceived – although it is describable and thus apparently a logically conceivable alternative – is not a real possibility, and therefore that the other supposition, that these determinations must be made as Kant argues, is the unique, and therefore necessary as well as sufficient, condition of the possibility of these empirical judgments. Kant's argument may fail, but surely it exploits the very strategy which Körner requires of it.

One other point about Körner's critique may also be noted. Körner seems to suppose that Kant overlooked the problem of establishing the uniqueness of his schema because he assumed the uniqueness of euclidean geometry and Newtonian physics, which, however, are just particular methods for applying the more general schema requiring differentiation of spatial regions and the existence of substance (and which might themselves also be subsumable under more than one schema).[8] As we saw, however, Kant is at least sometimes quite clear about the difference between a general requirement of his schema – such as the requirement of the conservation of *substance* – and a particular theory satisfying that general requirement – such as the conservation of *matter*. As became clear in my discussion of Kant's treatment of substance – if not in his treatment of geometry – Kant does recognize that even what he himself sometimes calls the "constitutive" concepts of the understanding offer only ideals for particular scientific theories and that the latter may well undergo revision without affecting the former. Although a detailed examination of any particular Kantian argument might show that it confuses "method" and "schema," certainly Kant was aware of the general distinction.[9]

(3) The most widely discussed criticism of "transcendental arguments," however, has been the claim that they depend upon verificationism as a theory of meaning, yet that this theory of meaning is both itself implausible and also renders the transcendental argument otiose, since the theory of meaning offers a refutation of the skeptic without any detour. The criticism, which owes its classical formulation to Barry Stroud,[10] is directed against Strawson's interpretation of the transcendental deduction. According to Strawson, the deduction turns on the supposition that in order to have a meaningful conception of oneself as a subject or possessor of experiences, one must also have a conception of objects with which experiences can be contrasted, or, as Richard Rorty reformulated Strawson's point, "One would not know what an experience was if one did not know what a physical object was."[11] According to the objection, however, to use such an argument as an antidote to skepticism assumes verificationism, that is, it assumes that because one can meaningfully use a concept ("experience"), one must in fact *know* that the conditions which would make that concept meaningful (the contrasting existence of enduring, rule-governed physical objects) must in fact obtain – when surely the most that could be derived from one's assumption that one's use of the term is meaningful is that one must at least *believe* that its truth-conditions *can sometimes* obtain.[12] Indeed, even that may be more than the argument proves, for the most that any plausible verificationist theory of meaning can

show is that if one is to understand a term, one must know what conditions would make a proposition using it *true or false,* and not that any propositions using it are in fact ever *true.*[13] Second, the objection charges that the acceptance of the verificationist theory of meaning required to make anything out of the conceptual contrast – although that theory is intrinsically dubious and, in any case, too weak to prove the desired result – also renders the transcendental argument itself superfluous. For the transcendental argument is supposed to proceed by showing that a proposition employing a certain concept is a member of some privileged class, and that propositions of this class are meaningful only because of a certain further concept, the conditions for the meaningful use of which defeat the skeptic; but verificationism allows the contrast argument to be run directly, without any detour through a privileged class of propositions.[14] In terms closer to Kant, the Strawsonian argument renders the role of the *unity* of experience in Kant's transcendental deduction superfluous. The need for knowledge of objects arises directly from the conditions for the meaningful description of any representation as an experience, and not from any special considerations about what is required for the representation of experience as unified;[15] and if verificationism is accepted, then one simply argues from the presumably meaningful use of the concept of experience to knowledge of the external objects with which experience is contrasted.

What is to be said about this charge? It is clear that the whole issue bypasses Kant's type A arguments completely. These arguments – for instance, the inference from the *a priori* certainty of apperception to the existence of *a priori* synthesis – involve no contrasts of meaning whatever. They do not suggest that the judgment about apperception, for example, involves a conceptual contrast with the nonself but only that it must have a "transcendental ground," which, to be sure, may have implications for the nonself as well as for the unity of the self. The contrast between ordinary experience, as an inadequate ground for a claim to necessity, and an *a priori* ground for such a claim, at any rate, on which this style of argument really turns, can hardly be thought to be a contrast implicit in the *meaning* of necessity. Again, however, these sorts of argument seem to offer little assistance against skepticism.

What about Kant's arguments from empirical knowledge-claims of temporal determination to knowledge of external objects and their essential rule-governedness (type B)? Here the issues seem more complicated. It does seem that these arguments would be superfluous if a theory of meaning could take one directly from one concept, such as that of a subjective succession of representations, to knowledge of the instantiation of the concept naturally contrasted to this, namely, that of an objective succession in appearances (empirical objects). Thus the second part of the charge against transcendental arguments – or at least against Strawson's reconstruction of Kant's deduction – seems justified. But what this suggests is precisely that Kant's arguments have nothing to do with the conditions for the meaningful use of concepts at all, but rather with necessary conditions for confirming characteristic forms of judgment, which (to be sure) use certain concepts but hardly assume that such concepts are justifiably used simply because they are understood.[16] Kant's argument is not that because we understand certain concepts, therefore certain judgments, employing concepts with which the first are to be contrasted, must be true. His argument is rather that because we take one set of judgments to be true, another set of judgments, which offer indispensable evidence for the former, must also be taken to be true. This argument has nothing to do with conditions for understanding at all: As far as it is concerned, we might by divine gift understand all our concepts innately in isolation. The argument is concerned, rather, with the conditions under which we might be able to justify empirical claims to knowledge. That is to say, the argument premises from the outset that certain judgments are true and never attempts to introduce claims to the truth of anything *via* the theory of meaning, but only by a specific model for the confirmation of the truths initially asserted. Both truth and knowledge are present in the argument from the beginning, and it is not a matter of transferring them from one concept to another but from one set of judgments to another.

Still, a version of the present objection might be pressed against this style of argument. Kant's theory of time-determination basically holds that because we take one class of empirical judgments to be justifiable (whether these are judgments about the temporal relations of external objects or of inner states) and discover that another class of judgments (whether these are judgments about the causal relations of external objects or about their temporal relations) furnishes the only means of confirming such judgments, we must therefore also take the latter types of judgments to be true – to be "experience," not mere "imagination." Of course, we may occasionally be mistaken about specific instances of the confirmation-lending judgments (B 278), in which case, however, we will just have to admit that we are mistaken about particular members of the class of judgments which are to be confirmed; Kant never supposes otherwise.[17] But cannot one just *believe* the propositions in the confirming class without actually *knowing* them? After all, false premises do not logically imply false conclusions. Or, even worse, cannot one just *believe* the propositions in the class for which evidence is to be provided, and therefore also just have adequate grounds for merely believing but not literally claiming to know judgments in the class which is to provide the evidence? What is one to say to these objections?

At one level, of course, it must be conceded that no argument by itself can ever prove more than that if one accepts one set of claims, then, at pain of logical inconsistency (and what kind of pain is *that?*) one must also accept another. Deny that one knows the premises, and nothing ever follows. But if skepticism just plays on that fact about the limits of argumentation, it is boring. And the logical point that the falsehood of a

426

premise does not itself imply the falsehood of the proposition which has been treated as its consequence is irrelevant; it has already been assumed that we are dealing with a class of judgments which provides the *sole* form of evidence for judgments of another class, and the question is only whether one can continue to take the latter as true while acknowledging that the former may as well be false. Here it seems that skepticism must trade on taking a third-person point of view, that is, a stance external to that of the subject whose claims to knowledge are being considered. For although it is easy to suppose that another may believe some, even very central propositions on the basis of unreliable evidence, or even that all of the subject's beliefs in the former of these groups are false, it is far harder to think oneself into this position. If one can really entertain the proposition that all of one's even subjective temporal judgments are false, of course one can do without commitment to another set of propositions which could provide evidence for these. But it is not easy to see how one could accept one's subjective time-determinations as true, acknowledge that judgments about objective time-determinations (as well as the causal and other relations of the external objects) are the sole evidence for such judgments, and yet seriously entertain the possibility that these further judgments are all, or mostly, false. Such a stance seems incoherent: It seems to collapse into that of perhaps verbally affirming one set of sentences and verbally rejecting another without actually believing anything at all, thus making no judgments at all. In such a position, of course, arguments can make no difference at all.

In the end, the skeptical suggestion that one might merely believe the sole evidence for judgments which one acknowledges to be true does not seem very threatening. The real question about Kant's arguments from empirical time-determination to *a priori* constraints on the knowledge of external objects – the only ones among his arguments which can sustain our contemporary interest in his theoretical philosophy – can be only the substantive issue which arises when we consider each of these three forms of criticism: What is the force of the fundamental premises of Kant's theory of time-determination itself? If Kant is wrong that temporal relations cannot be directly perceived, or at least directly perceived on the basis of representations regarded as such alone, and if, instead, enough information can be gleaned directly from introspection to ground reasonable beliefs about the temporal order even of subjective states – if "we still have no strong positive reason for supposing that knowledge of facts about *outer objects* is necessary in order to form justified beliefs . . . about the position occupied by an experience in my subject time-order"[18] – then his theory of time-determination cannot accomplish the goals of the transcendental theory of experience. If it might be the case that I can satisfactorily "use knowledge about *regularities among my experiences* in order to figure out the temporal order of a particular experience in my subject time-order,"[19] then Kant's attempt to entrench the fundamental assumptions of a scientific world-view in the most elementary fact of human self-consciousness, the barely controvertible fact that we make reasonable judgments about the temporal order of our own experiences as such, is a failure. My own view is that such an objection fails to acknowledge an insight which underlies Kant's theory of time-determination at the deepest level: the recognition that a genuine capacity for representation cannot be thought to be governed by regularities of its own – certainly not regularities in the sequence of its contents which are due to its own constitution rather than to the constitution of what it represents – for the simple reason that this would immediately undermine its use *as* a faculty of representation. Changes in its contents must be ascribable to changes in what it represents, or else it cannot be safely judged to represent change outside itself at all. Of course Kant has taught us that the mind cannot be a completely passive mirror of nature, that it may be constrained to represent nature as having a certain form (even if nature itself, contrary to Kant's supposition, may also have this form), and certainly that knowledge does not lie in the passive registration of sensation but requires the active enterprise of conceptualization and judgment as well. But the idea that a faculty of representation may have internal regularities in its changes adequate to ground judgments of subjective time-order and yet even potentially afford knowledge of an external reality seems incoherent: A faculty of representation must be sensitive primarily to what lies beyond it or give up its claim to representation. If this were all that Kant meant by his claim that it must be our "thought of the relation of all knowledge to its object" which "carries with it an element of necessity" and which "prevents our cognitions from being haphazard or arbitrary" (A 104), then he would have made an indisputable contribution to epistemology. As we have more than amply seen, Kant was frequently tempted to exploit this recognition for more than it is worth by his hasty inference from a claim to necessity directly to a transcendental ground. But we should not let this failure deter us from a serious consideration of the theory of time-determination which he offered us, true to his original inspiration, if not to his lingering desire for certainty.

Notes

Introduction

1 John Locke, *An Essay Concerning Human Understanding*, ed. P. H. Nidditch (Oxford: Oxford University Press [Clarendon Press], 1975), bk. I, ch. 1, §2. The only other philosopher Kant mentions at all is "the celebrated" Christian Wolff, "the greatest of all the dogmatic philosophers" (B xxxvi). But not only is Wolff not a major philosopher by our own standards; more important, although he furnishes much of the target for Kant's criticism of traditional metaphysics, he counts as a "dogmatic" philosopher precisely because he does not commence with any reflection upon the constitution and limits of human cognitive capacities themselves. Thus his philosophy, unlike Locke's, cannot even be compared with the constructive elements of Kant's own.

2 Thomas Reid, *An Inquiry into the Human Mind*, ed. Timothy Duggan (Chicago: University of Chicago Press, 1970), p. 91.

3 Arthur W. Collins, *Thought and Nature: Studies in Rationalist Philosophy* (Notre Dame: Notre Dame University Press, 1985), pp. 193–4.

4 J. N. Findlay, *Kant and the Transcendental Object: A Hermeneutic Study* (Oxford: Oxford University Press [Clarendon Press], 1981), pp. 19–20.

5 This denial is in his letter to Marcus Herz of 21 February 1772 (10:130), to which I shall return in Chapter 1.

6 See, for instance, Collins, *Thought and Nature*, pp. 194–5.

7 Kant's own term – *Lehrart* – could as easily refer to the style of exposition as to the underlying method of discovery.

8 That is, the fundamental concepts we employ in thinking of objects, rather than the essential forms by means of which we sense them; his basic theory about the latter, the forms of intuition, was already in place by 1770 – and unfortunately conforms to the model described in the preceding paragraph.

1. The problem of objective validity

1 An argument itself anticipated by Leibniz's objection that Descartes's ontological argument omits the necessary step of first establishing the real possibility of a being possessed of all possible perfections before drawing the desired conclusion from an analysis of the concept of such a being.

2 The defense of this proposition continued to preoccupy Kant into the last stages of his career, as in his controversy with the rearguard Leibnizo-Wolffian J. A. Eberhard.

3 For Leibniz's classical statement of this thesis, though a passage unknown to Kant, see "Discourse on Metaphysics," §14; for a less clear statement, although one known to Kant, see *New Essays Concerning Human Understanding*, bk. IV, ch. 10, §10.

4 Jill Vance Buroker has interpreted Kant's transcendental idealism as grounded largely in his solution to the problem of incongruent counterparts; see her *Space and Incongruence: The Origins of Kant's Idealism* (Dordrecht: Reidel, 1981), especially ch. 5, pp. 92–118. Kant's need to find a suitable metaphysical category for absolute space may have been his first reason for the description of it as transcendentally ideal, but, as we shall see in Part V, he later placed most emphasis on transcendental idealism as the solution to the epistemological problem of *a priori* knowledge, and this emphasis is already visible in the dissertation of 1770.

5 Translation from G. B. Kerferd and D. E. Walford, *Kant: Selected Pre-Critical Writings and Correspondence with Beck* (New York: Barnes & Noble, 1968), p. 113.

6 It should be noted that "analysis" and "synthesis" are not used here to connote logical operations on judgments and their constitutents, but are used instead to connote operations of decomposition and composition performed upon *objects* or their representations. "Synthesis" is thus used in the same sense as the German *zusammensetzen,* as in J. H. Lambert's *Anlage zur Architectonic* (1771), ch. 17, §§531–2.

7 Henry Allison makes such a principle the foundation of Kant's argument for transcendental idealism in the *Critique of Pure Reason* (*Kant's Transcendental Idealism* [New Haven: Yale University Press, 1983], p. 27). I will argue in Part V that Kant does *not* explicitly employ such a principle in the *Critique* and grounds his transcendental idealism on a number of very different assumptions, but there is no doubt that Kant does express such a principle in 1770, and it doubtless retained a continuing hold on him.

8 J. N. Findlay, in *Kant and the Transcendental Object*, p. 18, also notices Kant's peculiar assumption that "our passive subjection to affections stemming from things outside of us . . . is as much an expression – Kant would hold it to be even *more* of an expression – of our *own* inherent nature than of the nature of the things thus acting upon us."

9 However, as we shall see in Part V, he admits it more thoroughly in principle than in practice.

10 No distinction between constitutive and regulative functions is reflected in Kant's haphazard ordering of the principles, however, which is not the ordering just given.

11 See Part V, this volume.

12 Kerferd and Walford, *Kant,* p. 97.

13 Ibid., p. 106.

14 Ibid., p. 108.

15 See H.-J. DeVleeschauwer, *The Development of Kantian Thought* (1939), tr. A. R. C. Duncan (Edinburgh: Nelson, 1962), who also notes that Kant "oriented his meditations in another direction from that actually suggested by his critics" (pp. 57–8).

16 Ibid., p. 60.

2. The transcendental theory of experience: 1774–1775

1 A major piece of evidence for this dating is the fact that one of the lengthiest and most important of these notes is written in the blank spaces of a letter written to

Kant and dated 20 May 1775 (R 4675, 17:648); Kant apparently had the habit of using letters for scrap paper shortly after he received them. (The letter itself is just a social invitation; see 10:182.) Throughout, I have used the dating of these fragments established by Erich Adickes in the *Akademie* edition. Although scholars have questioned some of his conclusions, the dating of the *Duisburg Nachlass* is accepted by even the most skeptical; see DeVleeschauwer, *Development of Kantian Thought*, p. 65. Prior to Adickes's edition, these fragments were edited and commented upon by T. Haering, in *Der Duisburg'sche Nachlass und Kants Kritizismus um 1775* (Tübingen, 1910); the only discussion of them in English is in DeVleeschauwer, *Development of Kantian Thought*, pp. 62–75 (which summarizes the discussion in vol. 1 of his *La déduction transcendentale dans l'oeuvre de Kant*, 3 vols. [Antwerp: De Sikkel, 1934], vol. 1, pp. 173–87, 262–84).

2 See J. N. Tetens, *Philosophische Versuche* (1776), reprinted by the Kant-Gesellschaft (Berlin, 1911), e.g., pp. 96, 162, 255, 273.

3 Kant does not explicitly state this premise here, but it is an obvious inheritance of the Leibnizian and Baumgartian tradition and is explicitly asserted at A 205 / B 250–1.

4 As it will until the *Critique*, Kant's conception of this third category remains fluid, including both reciprocal interaction between distinct substances and composition of the parts of a single substance. Of course, if the premise that all genuine substances are simple were adopted, these two concepts would collapse into one, but this is just the kind of Leibnizian assumption which Kant proscribes from a mere analytic of the understanding as opposed to a proud ontology.

5 DeVleeschauwer sees the argument of the *Duisburg Nachlass* as culminating in the introduction of a "permanent and unvarying self" or "transcendental ego" as the "last substratum of the function of rules" (*Development of Kantian Thought*, pp. 73–4). This is misleading: Kant's revolutionary discovery is that rules are required to determine the proper temporal order of the *varying and successive* states of the self. Though such rules must obviously flow *from* an enduring self as agent, any suggestion that they serve to represent something permanent *in* that self would be wrong and would confuse the notion of apperception clearly employed in the *Duisburg Nachlass* with a more problematic conception introduced only in the *Critique*.

6 The terminology of this claim may imply a direct rejection of Crusius, although the latter's rejection of the analyticity of the principle of sufficient reason was a vital stepping-stone for Kant; see his *Entwurf der notwendigen Vernunftwahrheiten* (1745), §1.

7 DeVleeschauwer makes the ambiguous remark that by the year 1775, Kant "has mastered the doctrine of understanding, which is divided in the *Critique* into the Analytic of Concepts and the Analytic of Principles" (*Development of Kantian Thought*, p. 65). If by his second clause he means that the doctrine of understanding was *subsequently* divided into those two separate arguments, that is correct, but if he means that Kant already employed this distinction in 1775, it would be false. He must in fact mean the former, since he subsequently argues that the logical functions of judgment, and thus the metaphysical deduction, were not correlated with the categories and their transcendental deduction until after 1775 (pp. 75–80). This implies that in 1775 there was no deduction of the categories independent of the conditions of time-determination.

8 It did so seem, for instance, to DeVleeschauwer; cf. *Le déduction transcendentale*, vol. 1, p. 290.

3. The real premises of the deduction

1 One is not well advised to attempt to discern a historical order of composition in the lines which actually constitute the texts of the transcendental deduction, as did the original advocates of the classical "patchwork theory," Hans Vaihinger and Norman Kemp Smith. As Lewis White Beck once argued (in an oral presentation), any man capable of putting together inconsistent notes written over a number of years would also be capable of writing an inconsistent text in a single go – and this is even more obviously true when one recognizes that even the rewritten deduction of 1787, not only the original text of 1781, clearly contains a number of independent arguments. Rather, one must confine oneself to the claim that the texts of the transcendental deduction, whatever the history of their composition, do indeed express a patchwork of arguments. In this I agree with the statement made some years ago by Robert Paul Wolff (*Kant's Theory of Mental Activity* [Cambridge, Mass.: Harvard University Press, 1963], p. 83), though my own description of the various patches in Kant's quilt will of course be different from that which Wolff offered.

2 See, e.g., Leibniz, *New Essays on Human Understanding*, bk. I, ch. 1, §5; in the translation by Jonathan Bennett and Peter Remnant (Cambridge: Cambridge University Press, 1981), p. 162.

3 See Tetens, *Philosophische Versuche*, III, i, e.g. pp. 256, 266, 273.

4 Perhaps the clearest exposition of this interpretation is Patricia Kitcher, "Kant's Real Self," in Allen Wood, ed., *Self and Nature in Kant's Philosophy* (Ithaca: Cornell University Press, 1984), pp. 113–47, especially pp. 138–47. Another clear account is in Allison, *Kant's Transcendental Idealism*, especially pp. 144–8. See also Wolfgang Becker, *Selbstbewusstsein und Erfahrung: Zu Kants transzendentaler Deduktion und ihrer argumentativen Rekonstruktion* (Freiburg: Alber, 1984), p. 99, and Edwin McCann, "Skepticism and Kant's B Deduction," *History of Philosophy Quarterly* 2 (January, 1985):71–89, especially pp. 75–6.

5 Patricia Kitcher emphasizes this point in "Kant on Self-Identity," *Philosophical Review* 91 (January, 1982): 41–72, especially pp. 44–59.

6 The locus classicus for such objections is Jonathan Bennett, *Kant's Analytic* (Cambridge: Cambridge University Press, 1966), especially §§23 and 25.

7 See Kitcher, "Kant on Self-Identity," p. 56, and McCann, "Skepticism and Kant's B Deduction," pp. 76–8.

8 Allison, *Kant's Transcendental Idealism*, pp. 133–6, 158–64.

9 See Manfred Baum, *Deduktion und Beweis in Kants Transzendentalphilosophie: Untersuchungen zur "Kritik der reinen Vernunft"* (Königstein: Athenaeum Verlag, 1986), especially pp. 78–81. Baum argues that the deduction first establishes that if apperception must link a manifold of data, then it must do so by the categories (derived, according to Baum, from the necessary concept of experience as giving an object), and then that the specifically spatiotemporal form of human experience establishes that our data for thought is a manifold which must be synthesized, and to which the categories must therefore apply.

10 In this, the current commentators all follow the lead of Dieter Henrich's important article, "The Proof-Structure of Kant's Transcendental Deduction,"

Review of Metaphysics 22 (June, 1969):640–59 (available to most German readers as "Die Beweisstruktur vom Kants transzendentaler Deduktion," in Gerold Prauss, ed., *Kant: Zur Deutung seiner Theorie von Erkennen und Handeln* [Cologne: Kiepenheuer & Witsch, 1973], pp. 90–104). Among the many emendations of Henrich's interpretation, by far the most interesting is that of Manfred Baum. His argument (see n. 9) that the actual structure of the deduction is, first, a conditional proof that if consciousness requires synthesis it must use the categories, followed by a second step which shows that because of the spatiotemporal form of human intuition all human consciousness does require synthesis, is specifically directed against Henrich's account, on which the first step, a general demonstration that consciousness of the synthetic unity of a manifold requires the categories, can be followed only by the trivial reminder that since the specific form of human intuition is spatiotemporal, the categories must apply to everything in space and time.

11 The only significant exception to this generalization is Henrich's subsequent work, *Identität und Objektivität: Eine Untersuchung über Kants transzendentaler Deduktion* (Heidelberg: Carl Winter Universitätsverlag, 1976). This work, which has been of profound influence on my own, divides Kant's attempts at the deduction into those employing the concept of an object and those based on the premise of the numerical identity of the self. Henrich does not recognize Kant's assumption of synthetic necessary truth, in the former case, nor does he explicitly acknowledge that Kant's principle of apperception is actually a synthetic truth, but he does recognize that Kant's deduction from apperception is based on the premise that we have *a priori* certainty of the identity of the self.

12 E.g., Karl Ameriks, in "Kant's Transcendental Deduction as a Regressive Argument," *Kant-Studien* 69 (1978):273–87.

13 McCann, for example, in "Skepticism and Kant's B Deduction."

14 Compare B 14–18 with *Prolegomena* 4:268–9 and B 40–1 with *Prolegomena* 4:283–4.

15 Gordon Brittan also ascribes at least two fundamentally different argumentative strategies to Kant – one presupposing not only objective but synthetic *a priori* knowledge in the natural sciences – that is, what I call, a little later in this section, strategy IA, which he calls the "presupposition" method – and the other, ambiguous between what I call strategies IIA and IIB, "to the effect that the unity of consciousness entails the application of the Categories," which he calls the "necessary condition" argument – and then argues that the *Prolegomena*'s distinction between analytic and synthetic methods does not reflect an unequivocal distinction between the real arguments of the *Critique* and *Prolegomena;* see *Kant's Theory of Science* (Princeton: Princeton University Press, 1978), pp. 113–14.

16 Lewis White Beck, "Did the Sage of Königsberg Have No Dreams?" in Beck, *Essays on Kant and Hume* (New Haven: Yale University Press, 1978), p. 40.

17 See also Philip Kitcher, "How Kant Almost Wrote 'Two Dogmas of Empiricism,'" in J. N. Mohanty and Robert W. Shahan, eds., *Essays on Kant's Critique of Pure Reason* (Norman: University of Oklahoma Press, 1982), p. 220.

18 That is, the theory of science offered in the "Appendix to the Transcendental Dialectic" of the *Critique of Pure Reason* and in the first introduction to the *Critique of Judgment.*

19 These sections of the second-edition text of the deduction will be carefully examined in Chapter 4, under tactic IA. iii.

NOTES TO PAGES 84-97

20 See translator's introduction, in Immanuel Kant, *What Real Progress Has Metaphysics Made in Germany Since the Time of Leibniz and Wolff?* ed. and tr. Ted Humphrey (New York: Abaris Books, 1983), p. 13.

21 This argument will also be considered further in Chapter 4.

22 See Kant, *Metaphysical Foundations of Natural Science,* 4:475n.

23 Henrich, *Identität und Objektivität,* p. 70.

24 The argument of Part II of my book may thus be regarded as an elaboration of the criticisms of Henrich's interpretation first sketched in my review of *Identität und Objektivität* in *Journal of Philosophy* 76 (1979):151–67.

25 Kant actually writes, "In der reinen ... liegt der Grund der Moglichkeit [*sic*] aller empirischen Erkenntnis *a priori,*" which leaves it ambiguous whether "*a priori*" is to be understood adverbially as modifying "lies" or rather adjectivally as part of the expression "empirical knowledge *a priori.*" Since the latter seems oxymoronic, I have preferred the former, but it might also be that the present passage is another piece of evidence for the view, to be explored in the discussion of tactic IA, that even empirical knowledge explicitly contains some *a priori* content.

4. The deduction from knowledge of objects

1 This statement is also used to yield an independent and self-evidently fallacious argument for *a priori* rules; see the discussion of IB.i, later in this chapter.

2 This is indeed the gist of the argument to be examined in parts III and IV of this book.

3 A notorious review, written by Christian Garve but considerably altered by the editor J. G. H. Feder (*Göttinger Anzeigen von gelehrten Sachen,* 1782), aroused Kant's ire and called forth the *Prolegomena.* The original version of Garve's review appeared later (*Allgemeine deutsche Bibliothek,* 1783), but too late to placate Kant.

4 See *Critique* A 1–2, of course, but also, for instance, from nearly a decade earlier, "We have ... *a priori* judgments, which are yet synthetic and therefore cannot be derived from any experience, for in addition to clear concepts they contain a true universality, thus necessity, which can never have been created from experience" (R 4634, 17:617).

5 This could be evidence for my claim that at the most fundamental level Kant always identified the transcendental deduction with the argument for the objective validity of the categories of substance, causation, and interaction. But Adickes points out that we must also consider the possibility that Kant wrote this and several other sketches for the deduction at this point in his lecture-room copy of Baumgarten just because there was still enough blank paper left there (18:385n).

6 In terms of the language he uses later, that is, Kant leaves it unclear whether he is talking about "*objective*" or "*subjective*" universal validity" (*Critique of Judgment,* §8, 5:215); as he points out there and assumes in the *Prolegomena,* the logical or objective universal validity of a judgment (if true) also implies its intersubjectively universal acceptability, though the converse is not true, but this fact nevertheless leaves it unclear what the real function of the category is: Does it ground the *classification* of objects by logically universal concepts or rather the *epistemic acceptability* by all knowers of such classifications? This ambivalence has itself occasioned considerable diversity in the interpretation of

Kant's deduction; contrast, for instance, Henrich's interpretation of the "object" deduction, which focuses on the conditions for classification of an object (*Identität und Objektivität*, ch. 2) with the interpretation of the deduction offered only a year earlier by W. H. Walsh, which makes the argument turn on conditions for the intersubjective acceptability of knowledge-claims (*Kant's Criticism of Metaphysics* [Edinburgh: Edinburgh University Press, 1975], §10, especially p. 49).

7 An extensive discussion of how Kant arrived at this table may be found in DeVleeschauwer, *La déduction transcendentale*, vol. 1, pp. 210-50.

8 Here Kant has in mind, though, an epistemic feature of the status, thus a qualification on the assertability of a judgment, rather than an actual feature of its logical content representing an objective modality (which, in modern modal logic, would in any case be reduced to a feature of quantity in all possible worlds).

9 Kant, *Attempt to Introduce the Concept of Negative Quantitites into Philosophy*, 2:165-204.

10 It should be noted that on Henry Allison's account of the second stage of the transcendental deduction, this *is* precisely what the transcendental deduction (not very successfully) attempts to add to the metaphysical deduction; see *Kant's Transcendental Idealism*, pp. 158-72.

11 Here Kant at least clarifies one ambivalence, which we observed earlier in the discussion of R 5923 and R 5927: He does not mean that an (objective) judgment necessarily claims logical universality (what the *Critique of Judgment* calls "objective universal validity"), that is, necessarily makes some assertion about a whoie class of objects; rather, it claims "subjective" universal validity, or validity for any experience of the object, whether the relevant object itself be a particular or a group of individuals.

12 Kant says that the judgment "When the sun shines on the stone, it becomes warm" is a "mere judgment of perception" because "no matter how often I and even others have perceived this . . . perceptions are only usually found to be so connected" (*Prolegomena*, §20, 4:301n).

13 The most controversial treatment of the subject in recent years, and un-doubtedly the most elaborate ever, is that of Gerold Prauss, *Erscheinung bei Kant: Ein Problem der "Kritik der reinen Vernunft"* (Berlin: De Gruyter, 1971). Prauss tries to solve the problem by interpreting judgments of perception as "Theaetetan judgments" (named after Plato's *Theaetetus*) which do employ the categories but defeat the claim to objective validity which the categories would otherwise imply by the, as it were, tacit prefix "It seems to me that . . ." A judgment of such a form directs attention to the inner condition of the perceiver, rather than to outer objects, by alluding to the kind of perceptual response ordinarily associated with a certain objective state of affairs without asserting that the latter actually obtains. But this solution works only by assuming something that Kant never asserts, namely that there must be some way of *expressing* judgments of perception. This solution also ignores Kant's assumption that logical conceptions *suffice* for judgments of perception, which is precisely what entails that something more (namely, the categories) is required for universal and necessary validity. In other words, Prauss's interpretation works only by ignoring the actual argument of the *Prolegomena*.

14 Here it may be noted that the type of reconstruction of Kant's deduction which has been most popular during the last two decades essentially rests on the

supposition that the very idea of knowledge of an object introduces a *contrast* between the arbitrary representations of states of the self as such and the rule-governed representation of an object but does not note that in Kant's own account the rule-governedness of objective representations is immediately identified with universal and necessary validity and that Kant then simply infers the *a priori* validity of the categories directly from that equation. For the classical reconstruction of the deduction on the basis of the contrast between subject and object, see of course P. F. Strawson, *The Bounds of Sense* (London: Methuen, 1966), especially, pp. 89–93 (and for a valuable recent criticism of Strawson, see Becker, *Selbstbewusstsein und Erfahrung*, pp. 111–17). For a recent version of the (first step) of the deduction which is still essentially the contrast argument, see Baum, *Deduktion und Beweis in Kants Transzendentalphilosophie*, especially pp. 64–70, 104–18.

15 This paragraph is marked by Adickes as an emendation to the first draft of the note but one made at about the same time as the note's original composition.

16 There is a large literature on the proper definition of a Kantian intuition. Jaakko Hintikka, in particular, has argued that a Kantian intuition is essentially a singular representation, thus associating the concept of an intuition with the logical criterion of singularity alone; among his many essays on the subject, see especially "On Kant's Notion of Intuition (*Anschauung*)," in T. Penelhum and J. J. MacIntosh, eds., *The First Critique* (Belmont, Calif.: Wadsworth, 1969), pp. 38–53. On the other side, Charles Parsons and Manley Thompson have argued that the concept must be defined in terms of both the logical criterion of singularity and the epistemological requirement of immediacy. See Parsons, "Kant's Philosophy of Arithmetic," in S. Morgenbesser, P. Suppes, and M. White, eds., *Philosophy, Science, and Method* (New York: St. Martin's Press, 1969), pp. 568–94, and Thompson, "Singular Terms and Intuitions in Kant," *Review of Metaphysics* 26 (1972):314–43. The present passage certainly supports the latter interpretation.

17 R 6350 is a note on which Henrich places great emphasis in his exposition of the object-oriented deduction (*Objektivität und Identität*, p. 44). But this note leaves obscure Kant's reason for inferring the existence of *a priori* forms for such connection from the need for a connection of predicates. The abstractness of the result implied in R 6350 is also suggested by Allison, *Kant's Transcendental Idealism*, pp. 146–7.

18 Kemp Smith translates, "The unity of this apperception I likewise entitle the *transcendental* unity of apperception, in order to indicate the possibility of *a priori* knowledge arising from it." This would clearly indicate that Kant initially assumes only that the unity of apperception *leads* to some *a priori* knowledge, not that there is a sense in which it is *itself* known *a priori*. Unfortunately what Kant himself writes is a little less clear: He simply says that the name is given "um die Möglichkeit der Erkenntnis *a priori* aus ihr zu bezeichnen": ". . . in order to signify the possibility of *a priori* knowledge from" the unity of apperception. Perhaps the ambiguity of this remark explains how Kant can offer a kind of argument which does in fact suppose that the unity of self-consciousness is itself an object of synthetic *a priori* knowledge (tactic IIA).

19 Henry Allison tries to save the argument of §17 by arguing that the confusion between the unity of apperception as a necessary and as a sufficient condition for knowledge of objects is avoided when one recognizes that only a weak sense of object is intended, for the principle of apperception is already known to require

a concept of an object of knowledge in a suitably weak sense (*Kant's Transcendental Idealism*, p. 146). However, as we have seen, Kant has not yet established any link between apperception and rules for its representations, and his argument now proceeds precisely by attempting to derive rules for apperception from a strong conception of objectivity rather than *vice versa* – although this will of course raise the problem of how there can be self-conscious states which are not representations of objects, that is, how apperception *can* be a sufficient condition for knowledge of objects.

20 Manfred Baum tries to save the argument of §18 by suggesting that the transcendental unity of apperception is itself a universally valid requirement for all discursive intellects, who must thus always contrast a universally valid representation of their mental states – which can be achieved only by taking these states as representations of objects – with an idiosyncratic connection of them (*Deduktion und Beweis in Kants Transzendentalphilosophie*, p. 204). I am hard pressed to find any ground for the premise of this argument in §16 or §18, and it would still leave unproved Kant's supposition that a correct representation of the history of one's own mental states requires any rules at all, the point that is at issue in §18.

21 I am accusing Kant of committing the modal fallacy of confusing the necessity of a conditional with the necessity of its antecedent and of thus illicitly inferring the necessity of its consequent. The reader may find it hard to see Kant as capable of such an error, but it should be noted that Kant commits exactly the same kind of error when he argues that Descartes's *sum* cannot be the product of an inference from *cogito* through the premise " 'Everything which thinks, exists'; for then the property of thought would render all things which possess it necessary beings" (B 422n). But of course this premise does not have this consequence; it would have it only if, in addition to its being (1) necessary that if something thinks it exists, it were also (2) necessary that the thing thinks, which is not implied by 1. Thus here too Kant is insensitive to the difference between the necessity of a conditional and the necessity of its antecedent. In "Apperception and Section 16 of the 1787 Transcendental Deduction" (*Synthese* 47 [1981]:385–448), which is otherwise very careful, Robert Howell makes the undefended assumption that Kant is content to show the categories to be necessary just in the "necessity-of-the-conditional sense." This misses precisely the kind of assumption on which an argument like that of A 100–1 rests, and the problem with it. Ross Harrison shares my view that Kant is capable of this kind of modal confusion; see his "Transcendental Arguments and Idealism," in Godfrey Vesey, ed., *Idealism Past and Present*, Royal Institute of Philosophy Lecture Series 13 (Cambridge: Cambridge University Press, 1982), pp. 211–24, especially pp. 214–15.

22 This procedure has the same logical structure as the possibility which Harrison also canvasses and rejects in "Transcendental Arguments and Idealism."

23 We saw a clear assertion of this assumption in R 5926.

24 Patricia Kitcher's otherwise sensitive presentation of what I have described as the emerging current consensus about the transcendental deduction omits any mention of this problem (see "Kant's Real Self," p. 143). Ten years earlier, Arthur Melnick clearly raised the problem about the necessity of introducing any of the relational functions other than categorical judgment; see *Kant's Analogies of Experience* (Chicago: University of Chicago Press, 1973), pp. 52–3. He did not make clear, however, that the problem arises for any version of the

deduction in which the logical functions of judgment have a central role, even if only that of leading to the identification of the categories, precisely because of Kant's insistence on the distinction between categorical judgments, as atomic judgments connecting representations which are not themselves judgments, and the relational judgments, as higher-order judgments which link other judgments. It is this distinction which raises the question of why the relational forms of judgment *must* apply in any complete account of the combination of representations. The problem is also recognized by Lauchlan Chipman, who argues that Kant does not intend even the conjunction of the metaphysical and transcendental deductions to establish the necessity of all the categories but reserves this proof for the schematism of the categories; see "Kant's Categories and their Schematism," originally in *Kant-Studien* 63 (1972):36–50; reprinted in Ralph C. S. Walker, ed., *Kant on Pure Reason* (Oxford: Oxford University Press, 1982), pp. 100–16, especially pp. 102–3.

5. The deduction and apperception

1 See Henrich, *Identität und Objektivität*, pp. 12–13. The ascription of such an attitude to Kant can be supported by his remarks in the preface to the *Metaphysical Foundations of Natural Science:* "If it can be proved *that* the categories, which reason must make use of in all its cognition, can have no other use at all except only in relation to objects of experience . . . then the answer to the question, *how* they make those possible, is interesting enough in order if possible to *complete* this deduction, but in relation to the chief purpose of the system, namely the determination of the limits of pure reason, is by no means *necessary* but rather only *meritorious*" (4:474n).

2 The reader should be warned that my claim that Kant assumes a synthetic principle of apperception, first published in "Kant on Apperception and *A Priori* Synthesis," *American Philosophical Quarterly* 17 (1980):205–12, has been widely criticized; see Karl Ameriks, "Kant and Guyer on Apperception," *Archiv für Geschichte der Philosophie* 65 (1983):175–86; Allison, *Kant's Transcendental Idealism*, pp. 137, 353; McCann, "Skepticism and the B Deduction," pp. 73–4; and Becker, *Selbstbewusstsein und Erfahrung*, pp. 103–6. Rather than distracting the reader with detailed responses to criticisms of an earlier publication, however, I shall simply rest my case on the following, more detailed exposition of Kant's argument.

3 See Patricia Kitcher, "Kant on Self-Identity," pp. 57–8, and Becker, *Selbstbewusstein und Erfahrung*, pp. 108–9. The latter writes: "In a weakened sense, *a priori* synthesis can rather be understood in respect to empirical cognition, as meaning the possibility of an empirical synthesis of thinkable representations which stands under specific restrictive conditions."

4 On this connection between Kant and Hume, see Patricia Kitcher, "Kant on Self-Identity," pp. 41–53.

5 See Henrich, *Identität und Objektivität*, pp. 86–90.

6 Locke, *An Essay Concerning Human Understanding*, bk. I, ch. 2, §5.

7 This is the problem that undermines McCann's defense of the analyticity of Kant's principle of apperception; cf. "Skepticism and the B Deduction," p. 74.

8 Patricia Kitcher uses this letter for purposes opposed to mine. She argues that in it Kant really introduces two different senses of consciousness, animal consciousness and our own, and that in the case of the latter he maintains the

necessary connection between consciousness and self-consciousness ("Kant's Real Self," p. 141). On my account, that would mean that Kant persists in the error of his argument from *a priori* apperception (although Kitcher does not recognize this to be an error). Allison simply uses this letter as further evidence of Kant's basic distinction between the passive reception of empirical intuitions, which implies no conceptualization of them, and the need to add categories to them "even for a consciousness of our mental states" (*Kant's Transcendental Idealism*, p. 153). No one could dispute that use of the letter.

9 This seems to be recognized in Kemp Smith's reconstruction of the transcendental deduction; see his *Commentary to Kant's "Critique of Pure Reason,"* 2nd ed. (London: Macmillan, 1923), p. 284.

10 Henrich, too, seems to find something problematic in this kind of argument, but he does not seem to realize that this is Kant's ultimate support for the kind of interpretation (namely, as a genuine synthetic proposition) of the "Cartesian certainty" of apperception which Henrich thinks not only must but also can be employed in any successful reconstruction of Kant's deduction; cf. *Identität und Objektivität*, pp. 70–1.

11 This has also been recognized as the fundamental premise of the deduction by Patricia Kitcher; see "Kant on Self-Identity," pp. 53, 65.

12 Wolfgang Becker appears to accept (1) "the immunity of the use of 'I' from any false identification" and (2) the inference that this means that self-ascription must be criterionless, since criteria are always connected to the possibility of error (*Selbstbewusstsein und Erfahrung*, pp. 139, 144). But 1 seems to repeat Kant's ungrounded assertion of the *a priori* certainty of our numerical identity, and 2 to mistake the nature of Kant's argument from this premise, which is precisely that since self-knowledge is both certain *a priori* and yet requires criteria, these criteria (the categories) must also be known *a priori*.

6. The schematism and system of principles

1 For similar statements, see Chipman, "Kant's Categories and Their Schematism," pp. 105–6, Walsh, *Kant's Criticism of Metaphysics*, pp. 67–8, and Allison, *Kant's Transcendental Idealism*, pp. 174–6.

2 Bennett, *Kant's Analytic*, p. 141. See also Robert B. Pippin, *Kant's Theory of Form* (New Haven: Yale University Press, 1982), pp. 143–50.

3 Some commentators have supposed that Kant is still tempted by the empiricist view of concepts as essentially equivalent to images, even if pallid rather than vivid ones; see, e.g., Walsh, *Kant's Criticism of Metaphysics*, p. 67. But it seems clear that Kant's emphasis on rules is meant precisely to express the radically different nature of concepts from any particular mental entities such as images, and that even if he speaks of the "representation of a universal procedure of the imagination in providing an image for a concept" (A 140 / B 180–1) in order to make himself intelligible to his empiricist opponents, he is not using the term "image" in the narrow sense of a private mental object but is referring more generally to empirical instances of concepts, whether currently experienced or otherwise presented to the reproductive imagination. Contrast Bennett, *Kant's Analytic*, p. 141, with Chipman, "Kant's Categories and Their Schematism," pp. 112–13.

4 See Allison's contrast between "objective validity" and "objective reality"; *Kant's Transcendental Idealism*, pp. 134–5.

5 Chipman describes the pure categories as requiring "sensory components" ("Kant's Categories and Their Schematism," p. 104), and Allison, following C. I. Lewis and Lewis White Beck, refers to them as standing in need of "empirical meaning conditions" or "sense meaning" (*Kant's Transcendental Idealism*, pp. 174, 185–6).

6 They are evident especially if we read it as Kant wrote it, and not as Vaihinger and (following him) Kemp Smith emended (see Kemp Smith's translation, p. 180); Allison reads this passage as I do (*Kant's Transcendental Idealism*, p. 177).

7 Berkeley, *The Principles of Human Knowledge* (1710), Introduction, §10.

8 Note that Kant describes the rule as applying both to actually experienced objects and to images. Again, not only does Kant refuse to equate concepts with images; neither does he suppose that concepts are just rules for producing images (as Bennett seems to say) but treats concepts as rules for either the construction or classification of any manner of empirical intuition by which a given sort of object might be presented.

9 Chipman also agrees that Kant identifies empirical concepts with their schemata ("Kant's Categories and Their Schematism," p. 107) but argues that he goes too far in so doing. Whereas in the case of such familiar things as dogs, he argues, it is perhaps inconceivable that anyone could understand what one is without also being able to recognize it, in the case of other, less familiar empirical objects it is conceivable that one could assign empirical content to their concepts adequate to understand them without necessarily being in a position to recognize an instance if actually presented with one (pp. 108–10. Chipman uses the examples of tadpoles and bone marrow, but would probably do better with more refined scientific concepts such as genes or gravitational fields). There is justice to this criticism – one might indeed know that a tadpole is a developmental stage of a frog without knowing that it is a little thing with a tail and gills that does not, however, look quite like a minnow, and one might therefore fail a tadpole-identification test at summer camp although still having some idea of what one is. But this does not affect Kant's basic point, which is simply that empirical concepts are ipso facto rules connecting terms to empirically presentable properties (whether readily identifiable properties or not), whereas in the case of the pure concepts of the understanding the connection between their logical content and any intuitable content whatever has yet to be made out.

10 Chipman appears confused on the issue of the determinacy of empirically presentable properties. He describes Kant's problem of schematism as nothing other than "Plato's problem of giving an account of how it is possible to subsume a concrete particular under a thoroughly abstract universal" ("Kant's Categories and Their Schematism," p. 108), which is precisely that of recognizing both curly short fur and long silky fur as instances of the universal *fur*, or both a wavery figure in the sand and a fine etching on a copper plate as two instances of the universal *isosceles right triangle*, which neither of these figures quite perfectly exemplifies. He then takes it that by a schematism Kant intends a "mechanism of subsumption" which takes us from such general concepts to their numerous and infinitely variable instances, and concludes that although there must be rules for such subsumption, they must also, contrary to Kant, be incapable of explicit statement, precisely because of the unlimited variation of the cases to which they must apply (p. 107). But the transition from,

for example, the concept of an isosceles right triangle to this figure in the sand is precisely what Kant thinks requires not another rule at all but only "mother wit" or "judgment"; his conception of a schema is only that of a rule which links terms such as "dog" or "triangle" with empirically presentable properties such as being four-footed or a closed figure of three straight lines, and not that of rules which would themselves enable one to recognize concrete instances of four-footedness or three straight lines for what they are.

11 Berkeley, *Principles,* Introduction, §§13, 16.

12 Cf. Allison, *Kant's Transcendental Idealism,* p. 190.

13 This is the crucial thesis of the little understood third analogy of experience; see Chapter 11 in this volume.

14 The greater prominence of space in the second edition of the *Critique* has been noted by Michael Washburn in "The Second Edition of the Critique: Toward an Understanding of Its Nature and Genesis," *Kant-Studien* 66 (1975):277–90. Washburn does not comment on the relation of the new prominence of space to the "Schematism," however, or suggest that this prominence shows that we must see the "Schematism" as part of a larger argument but one which is *not* inconsistent with the more restricted argument of the "Schematism" itself.

15 See the letter to Johann Schultz of 25 November 1788 (10:556–7). The crucial passage is cited by Kemp Smith (*Commentary,* pp. 130–1), though his citation provides an incorrect page number.

16 Allison (*Kant's Transcendental Idealism,* p. 196) offers similar criticisms of the schematization of necessity, but then, following H. J. Paton, *Kant's Metaphysic of Experience,* 2 vols. (London: Allen & Unwin, 1936), vol. 2, p. 60, proposes to reconstruct the schema to mean not existence throughout all time but rather existence at some time which is determinate with respect to the whole of time. But this then raises the question, What is the difference between the schemata of actuality and necessity? – which is, however, a genuine question for Kant's account, and not just an artifact of its interpretation.

17 For a less generous statement of the same point, see Wolff, *Kant's Theory of Mental Activity,* p. 227.

7. Axioms and anticipations

1 If this were not a literal translation, perhaps we could say that these principles are the *foundations* for the (empirical validity) of the *propositions* of (pure) mathematics.

2 W. H. Walsh and Philip Kitcher both also suggest that the purpose of the axioms of intuition in particular is to ensure that the synthetic *a priori* propositions of mathematics which can be known by means of pure intuition also apply to the objects we encounter in empirical intuition; see Walsh, *Kant's Criticism of Metaphysics,* pp. 108–11, and Kitcher, "How Kant Almost Wrote 'Two Dogmas of Empiricism,'" p. 240. Neither of them mentions, however, that Kant makes this point by means of the clear distinction between pure and applied mathematics, as well as by means of the more obscure and inflated rhetoric used in the *Critique.*

3 The distinction here between "appearances" and "intuitions" suggests that appearances or empirical objects are ontologically distinct from our intuitions of them. This sort of realism is more typical of the second edition of the *Critique,* although as a matter of fact the restatement of the principle of the axioms of

intuition in the second edition – "All intuitions are extensive magnitudes" – does not itself express the emphasis on the ontological independence of appearances.

4 However, this passage must not be understood, as it is by R. P. Wolff, as meaning that "the principle stands to the axioms of a particular mathematical system as a meta-systematic assertion of their possibility" (*Kant's Theory of Mental Activity*, p. 231). Kant is not offering anything like a proof-theoretic demonstration of the consistency of a formal system; rather, he is equating the "possibility of mathematics" with that of *applied* mathematics, and arguing for the necessity of the *empirical* validity of a formal system, the *formal* consistency or soundness of which is not itself at issue in the present context.

5 Jonathan Bennett mentions in connection with his discussion of the "Axioms of Intuition" that the category of limitation in the original triad of the logical functions of quantity is "spurious" (*Kant's Analytic*, p. 165). This would mean that only the logical quantities of one and several have to be made applicable to empirical objects, and the single principle that by means of extensive magnitude empirical intuition can be carved up into discrete objects would suffice to ensure the application of both of these logical categories.

6 Thus, the substance of the interpretation to be offered here is somewhat similar to the interpretation of the "Axioms" offered by Gordon Brittan. His view is that the argument is meant to establish the possibility of applying a metric, or scheme for measuring determinate size, to objects of empirical intuition, where such a guarantee is contrasted to a guarantee that more purely topological mathematics can be applied to such objects, which would already be supplied by the "Transcendental Aesthetic" (*Kant's Theory of Science*, pp. 95–7). That is, on this account features of shape are already known to apply to empirical intuition, and it must now be added that empirical intuitions also admit of determinate measurement. However, as the generality of Kant's comment reveals, Kant himself does not draw the distinction between metrics and topology; it is just that what he argues in the discussion of the axioms actually concerns metrics rather than topology. Thus, the view of Walsh and Philip Kitcher that Kant simply intends a general proof that pure mathematics also applies to empirical intuition appears to capture Kant's own intention, whereas Brittan's view better describes Kant's literal accomplishment.

7 For a similar statement, see Philip Kitcher, "How Kant Almost Wrote 'Two Dogmas of Empiricism,'" p. 243.

8 As Brittan points out, a precise statement of Kant's principle should say that empirical objects must have determinate extensive magnitudes among their properties, not that empirical objects *are* extensive magnitudes; for of course empirical objects, as is proved in the "Anticipations of Perceptions," also have properties which are intensive magnitudes. Cf. *Kant's Theory of Science*, pp. 91–2.

9 Kemp Smith, for instance, claims that "the argument [of the 'Axioms'] ... starts from the formulation of a view of space and time directly opposed to that of the '*Aesthetic*'" (*Commentary*, p. 346), and Wolff claims that "this proof should come as something of a shock to the reader who has mastered the Aesthetic, for it is the direct contradictory of an argument offered there" (*Kant's Theory of Mental Activity*, p. 228). Further references are given by Brittan, *Kant's Theory of Science*, p. 90.

10 Thus one need not suggest, as does Wolff, that Kant simply *substitutes* one view

of the synthetic representation of space for another view, on which the representation of space required no role for the understanding (pp. 229–30). The situation is more subtle: On the one hand, the form of space is given, and parts can be introduced only by limitation; on the other, even parts separated in this manner must also be aggregated numerically to represent any determinate space.

11 This is suggested by Paton. His view (see *Kant's Metaphysic of Experience*, vol. 2, pp. 122–3) is that the argument for the axioms of intuition correctly reflects the need for a successive synthesis of space and time by the understanding, which was suppressed in the exposition of the "Transcendental Aesthetic," but that Kant's argument fails to acknowledge that this synthesis is guided by the antecedent conception – given by pure intuition – of space and time as infinite wholes which, as it were, set the terminus ad quem for this synthesis. On the account of the basis for Kant's assumption of the continuity of space and time which I have just suggested, Kant would be at least tacitly employing one aspect of the infinity of space and time in the argument for the axioms of intuition – that is, their infinite divisibility.

12 See Kemp Smith, *Commentary*, p. 347.

13 The assertion of this at *Prolegomena* 4:282–3 is not paralleled in the *Critique*.

14 See Michael Friedman, "Kant's Theory of Geometry," *Philosophical Review* 94 (October, 1985):455–506, especially pp. 477–81.

15 Kemp Smith, *Commentary*, p. 348.

16 The problem of infinite divisibility seems to be skirted in other accounts of the "Axioms." Thus, Philip Kitcher describes the essential steps of Kant's argument as, first, the premise that an empirical object must be represented as in space and, second, the premise that such space must be represented by means of homogeneous parts ("How Kant Almost Wrote 'Two Dogmas of Empiricism,'" p. 243) but makes no mention of Kant's additional assumption that the infinite divisibility of space in pure intuition also guarantees the application of the mathematics of infinite divisibility to empirical objects; thus he does not ask how this stronger assumption might be justified.

17 Kemp Smith writes that "in the section on Anticipations of Perception the phenomenalist tendencies of Kant's thought are decidedly the more prominent." "The phenomenalist tendencies" are defined, more clearly than Kemp Smith usually manages, as essentially consisting in the threefold distinction "between sensation as subjective state possessing intensive magnitude, spatial realities that possess both intensive and extensive magnitudes, and the thing in itself" (*Commentary*, p. 351). This seems correct as far as it goes, omitting only that sensations are literally components of empirical intuitions which also must have forms representing the spatial and temporal properties assigned to appearances or empirical objects.

18 Of course, on Kant's background assumption of transcendental idealism we cannot infer that the assignment of intensive magnitude to these distinct objects constitutes cognitions of properties they have entirely independently of us, any more than does the assignment to them of extensive magnitude, which is an obvious derivative of spatial and temporal form.

19 Thus, Walsh sees Kant's aim in the "Anticipations" as that of establishing simply that a continuum of degrees of sensation is indeed a possibility (*Kant's Criticism of Metaphysics*, pp. 121–2). But he does not explain that this claim has a point, namely, precisely that of showing the difference between the logic of

affirmation and denial, on the one hand, and the nature of external reality on the other. It also seems misleading to suggest that Kant's thesis is exhausted by the thesis that such a continuum of degree in sensation is a *possibility*; as we shall see shortly, Kant clearly wanted to argue that it is a necessity, as well as a possibility.

20 Cf. Bennett, *Kant's Analytic*, p. 171.

21 This is obviously not the place for a detailed discussion of Kant's conception of the apriority of physics. The most useful discussion of the relation between the *Critique* and the *Metaphysical Foundations of Natural Science* is Michael Friedman, "Kant on Laws of Nature and the Foundations of Newtonian Science," in *Proceedings of the Sixth International Kant Congress* (forthcoming).

22 Kemp Smith, *Commentary*, p. 353.

23 Cf. Bennett, *Kant's Analytic*, p. 172.

24 This is essentially the argument which Gordon Nagel presents in his interpretation of the "Anticipations" in *The Structure of Experience: Kant's System of Principles* (Chicago: University of Chicago Press, 1983), pp. 103–4.

8. The general principle of the analogies

1 A similar point is made by Walsh in *Kant's Criticism of Metaphysics*, p. 124.

2 This has certainly been the standard assumption; see, e.g., Paton, *Kant's Metaphysic of Experience*, vol. 2, p. 163; Walsh, *Kant's Criticism of Metaphysics*, p. 124; and Allison, *Kant's Transcendental Idealism*, p. 199. Kemp Smith, however, bluntly rejects this supposition; see *Commentary*, p. 356.

3 As Kemp Smith puts it, although Kant "might seem to imply that the three aspects of time can be separately apprehended, and that each has its own independent conditions," what he "really proves is that all three involve each other. We can only be conscious of duration in contrast to succession, and of succession in contrast to the permanent, while both involve consciousness of coexistence" (*Commentary*, p. 356). As we shall see, the suggestion that our temporal judgments are made by direct contrasts is far too simple, but the basic idea that we use the concepts of substance, causation, and interaction conjointly to confirm our judgments of succession and coexistence is correct.

9. The first analogy: substance

1 The major commentators of the 1960s all take this approach in one form or another. Thus, Wolff writes that "Kant ... moves from the concept of a substratum in the first edition to the conservation of matter in the second edition" and also claims that "neither version states with any exactitude a principle which can be proved in Kant's system" (*Kant's Theory of Mental Activity*, p. 250). Strawson does not explicitly comment on any difference between the two formulations of the principle but suggests that something like my principle 1 is more defensible than principle 2: He is willing to grant that Kant's argument legitimately "requires that our perceptual experience be such as is only adequately describable by the application of concepts of certain kinds ... (e.g., concepts of material bodies)" but asserts that "none of this implies any necessity for any absolute permanence either of particular objects or of any such quantitative aspects of matter as physicists once did, or now do, refer to under such names as 'mass' or 'energy'" (*Bounds of Sense*, p. 129). And Bennett, who

distinguishes in "the traditional concept of substance ... two main strands" which he designates as "substance$_1$," or the concept of "a thing which has qualities," and "substance$_2$," something which is "sempiternal" (*Kant's Analytic*, p. 182), seems to find both concepts present in each formulation of the principle of the permanence of substance (p. 183). He makes the same general charge when he claims that "substance$_2$ is supposed to be derived by schematism from substance$_1$ which is supposed to be derived in its turn from the table of judgments; and both derivations are faulty" (p. 184). Gordon Brittan also ascribes two different conceptions of substance to Kant, which he distinguishes as the "Aristotelian" or bearer of change and the "Cartesian" or invariant substance; see *Kant's Theory of Science*, pp. 143–4.

2 A similar conclusion is reached by Allison, *Kant's Transcendental Idealism*, p. 214.

3 The following analysis should thus be contrasted with those of Walsh, *Kant's Criticism of Metaphysics*, pp. 129–31, and Allison, *Kant's Transcendental Idealism*, pp. 202–3, where this argument is largely accepted without question (although Allison thinks it needs to be completed by steps equivalent to what I shall shortly describe as two independent arguments not resting on the conclusion of the present argument as a premise). Kemp Smith, on the contrary, recognized the present argument as unpersuasive but mistakenly supposed that it exhausted the argumentation of the first analogy, and thus arrived at an unduly negative evaluation of the section as a whole (*Commentary*, pp. 360–1).

4 See also Allison, *Kant's Transcendental Idealism*, pp. 202–3, and Paton, *Kant's Metaphysic of Experience*, vol. 2, pp. 190–1.

5 Both Kemp Smith (*Commentary*, p. 360) and Walsh (*Kant's Criticism of Metaphysics*, p. 130) suggest that Kant's premise is that all events can be uniquely ordered or dated in a single temporal order. Although Kant clearly does suppose that (he obviously presupposes it in the *reductio* argument at A 188–9 / B 231–2, to which we shall return), he does not explicitly suggest in the present argument anything about dating events. He simply supposes that permanence is a property of time itself, with no reference to events at all, and looks for something to represent that property of time.

6 Melnick, *Kant's Analogies of Experience*, pp. 58–71.

7 Such a supposition would certainly not characterize Melnick's very useful discussion of the analogies as a whole; that is why I suggest only that it may be a tacit assumption of the present argument.

8 This objection was pressed by Edward Caird, *The Critical Philosophy of Immanuel Kant* (New York: Macmillan, 1889), vol. 1, p. 541, and, both citing Caird, Kemp Smith (*Commentary*, p. 359n) and Wolff (*Kant's Theory of Mental Activity*, p. 251). Allison, who also quotes Caird (*Kant's Transcendental Idealism*, p. 202), defends Kant.

9 For further discussion of the several terms involved and their definitions, see Allison, *Kant's Transcendental Idealism*, pp. 204–5.

10 D. P. Dryer, *Kant's Solution for Verification in Metaphysics* (London: Allen & Unwin, 1966), p. 346.

11 Melnick, *Kant's Analogies of Experience*, pp. 71–7.

12 Sketchier suggestions of a similar interpretation can be found in Dryer, *Kant's Solution*, pp. 353–5, and Allison, *Kant's Transcendental Idealism*, p. 206. The development of the present interpretation, however, was primarily influenced

by Melnick, *Kant's Analogies of Experience*, pp. 71-3, but see the remarks about that interpretation later in the present chapter.

13 This is the premise, of course, on which Kant builds his arguments in the "Antinomy of Pure Reason."

14 Melnick, *Kant's Analogies of Experience*, pp. 71-2.

15 Ibid., p. 73.

16 Ibid., p. 72.

17 See, for instance, the account in Walsh, *Kant's Criticism of Metaphysics*, p. 132.

18 As Walsh points out, Kant's limitation of the alternative to two incompatible temporal sequences is completely arbitrary; *Kant's Criticism of Metaphysics*, p. 133.

19 Melnick, *Kant's Analogies of Experience*, p. 67.

20 As in the kind of interpretation suggested by Hansgeorg Hoppe in *Synthesis bei Kant* (Berlin: De Gruyter, 1983), §18, pp. 176-94.

21 Strawson, *Bounds of Sense*, p. 129.

22 Bennett, *Kant's Analytic*, p. 189.

23 This point is also emphasized by Walsh, *Kant's Criticism of Metaphysics*, p. 125, and Allison, *Kant's Transcendental Idealism*, p. 209.

24 See, for instance, Kemp Smith, *Commentary*, pp. 361-2, and James Van Cleve, "Substance, Matter, and Kant's First Analogy," *Kant-Studien* 70 (1979):149-61, especially pp. 160-1.

25 As Allison points out, Kant is not introducing an Aristotelian theory of some single kind of prime matter underlying all more obvious forms of matter (*Kant's Transcendental Idealism*, p. 210); rather, Kant introduces (1) a need for permanence, and (2) permanence as the criterion of substance, but leaves it up to empirical science to determine what it is that endures through all changes, indeed how many sorts of things might so endure, and therefore what it is that counts as substance.

26 Bennett, *Kant's Analytic*, p. 198.

27 See ibid.

10. The second analogy: causation

1 Kant, *Nova Delucidatio*, §3, Proposition XII: "No change can happen to substances except insofar as they are connected with others, their reciprocal dependence determining the mutual change of state" (1:410). In this work of 1755, however, Kant's argument for the principle of sufficient reason was still essentially rationalistic: He argues that the principle of contradiction implies that an object must be characterized by only one of two logically opposed predicates (which it does), and then infers that this suffices to prove the existence of a "determining reason" adequate to explain *which* of the opposed predicates applies (which it does not); see §2, Proposition V (1:393-4).

2 For the remainder of this quotation, see this volume, ch. 4, pp. 125-6.

3 Kemp Smith automatically assumed that because Kant's exposition is repetitive it must have combined texts written over an extended period of time (*Commentary*, p. 363). However, Kant left no documentary evidence outside of the *Critique* to support such a conjecture.

4 This view is contrary to that of Walsh, *Kant's Criticism of Metaphysics*, pp. 135-6.

5 Arthur Schopenhauer, *The Fourfold Root of the Principle of Sufficient Reason*, tr.

E. F. J. Payne (LaSalle, Ill.: Open Court, 1974), §23, p. 127; also cited in A. C. Ewing, *Kant's Treatment of Causality* (London: Routledge & Kegan Paul, 1924), p. 89, and discussed by Kemp Smith (*Commentary*, p. 378) and Allison (*Kant's Transcendental Idealism*, p. 230). Thomas Reid had earlier used the same example to object to Hume's regularity analysis of causation; see *Essays on the Active Powers of the Human Mind* (Cambridge, Mass.: M. I. T. Press, 1969), p. 334. Schopenhauer refers to Reid only in another context, but it is reasonable to suppose that he borrowed the example from him.

6 Contrary to the assumption of R. C. S. Walker in *Kant* (London: Routledge & Kegan Paul, 1978), p. 103.

7 Many commentators assume that Kant, essentially following Hume, accepts a simple regularity analysis of causation, thus that he drops the requirement that there be any necessary connection between cause and effect other than the entailment of the effect by the cause, given a generalization connecting them which is itself entirely contingent (see, e.g., Dryer, *Kant's Solution*, pp. 396–7, and Allison, *Kant's Transcendental Idealism*, p. 223; then contrast these with the far more sensitive discussion in Bennett, *Kant's Analytic*, pp. 153–63). The *Critique of Judgment* makes it clear that Kant does not think that such necessitation exhausts the nature of causation but assumes that causal laws must themselves be necessary truths. He just does not attempt to argue for such a strong refutation of Hume in the *Critique of Pure Reason*.

8 Kemp Smith, *Commentary*, p. 363; see also Paton, *Kant's Metaphysic of Experience*, 2:224–5.

9 See Ewing, *Kant's Treatment of Causality*, p. 73; Wolff, *Kant's Theory of Mental Activity*, pp. 262, 272–3; C. D. Broad, *Kant: An Introduction*, ed. C. Lewy (Cambridge: Cambridge University Press, 1978), pp. 165–75, especially p. 173; and Allison, *Kant's Transcendental Idealism*, p. 222.

10 The passage just quoted is misleading, however, in its suggestion that the principle of causation is used to distinguish "truth from illusion" or that it suffices to distinguish between true and false judgments of objects (and some commentators have followed Kant in this confusion; e.g., Walsh, *Kant's Criticism of Metaphysics*, p. 136). As we shall see, Kant's argument is that causal connections are necessary to make any judgments about objective events as opposed to mere subjective changes in representation, but not that causal laws are sufficient to distinguish between true and false judgments about objective events.

11 This description of the problem Kant is trying to solve should make clear that numerous commentators have simply misconceived it. Committing the general error of supposing that the analogies deal with some *special* time-determinations rather than with empirical judgments about the temporal structure of any objective realm at all, they have written as though the problem is that of *dating* individual items *already interpreted as events* in the larger calendar of reality, rather than that of determining that a sequence of representations *represents an event at all*. Examples of this error may be found in Kemp Smith, *Commentary*, p. 369; Bennett, *Kant's Analytic*, p. 225; Walsh, *Kant's Criticism of Metaphysics*, p. 136; and Walker, *Kant*, p. 101. The problems to which such an interpretation give rise are illustrated by Walker. If it is assumed that events must simply be dated relative to each other, it may seem that merely correlating them with some sort of clock to which they are not themselves causally related should be adequate. But of course Kant's point is precisely that a succession of

representations cannot be recognized to represent an event at all without causal connections among the represented states of affairs; the very premise of Walker's objection – that we can "just think of ourselves as directly aware of events" (p. 102) – is exactly what Kant has rejected. Commentators who avoid the error of the dating interpretation include Kemp Smith, *Commentary*, p. 370, and Allison, *Kant's Transcendental Idealism*, p. 229. Melnick's account is simply ambiguous: He speaks indifferently of ordering "events or states of affairs" (e.g., *Kant's Analogies of Experience*, p. 91), when of course an event is already comprised of two or more ordered states of affairs. But his account of Kant's argument, although sketchy, is not vitiated by this imprecision.

12 As Walsh says, though about whole events rather than the states of affairs that have to be judged to constitute an event, "Events do not come to us with objective dates upon them" (*Kant's Criticism of Metaphysics*, p. 138).

13 The third assumption does not hold only on a phenomenalist *reduction* of objects to representations, as is sometimes assumed; see the final section of this chapter. See also Allison, *Kant's Transcendental Idealism*, p. 227.

14 As Kemp Smith puts it, "Only an experience which conforms to the causal principle can serve as foundation either for the empirical judgments of sense experience, or for that ever-increasing body of scientific knowledge into which their content is progressively translated" (*Commentary*, p. 270). Kemp Smith's formulation may or may not make clear that Kant, unlike some twentieth-century phenomenologists, as well as ordinary-language philosophers, recognizes no epistemological difference in principle between quotidian and scientific judgments.

15 This term is also used by Walsh, *Kant's Criticism of Metaphysics*, p. 138.

16 But it is not; therefore, unlike Peter Strawson (see the discussion later in this chapter), I do not interpret Kant to mean that irreversibility is a criterion of the occurrence of an event.

17 This is the premise necessary to explain Melnick's correct statement that irreversibility is not itself "a criterion in terms of which we determine a succession as objective. We do not ascertain that what we apprehend is successive by ascertaining that our apprehensions are irreversible" (*Kant's Analogies of Experience*, p. 83; see also Allison, *Kant's Transcendental Idealism*, p. 225).

18 Graham Bird, *Kant's Theory of Knowledge* (London: Routledge & Kegan Paul, 1962), p. 153.

19 That the two states belong to a single object is supposed to follow from the first analogy, which in fact Bird treats as the first stage of the analysis of the same concept analyzed by the second analogy.

20 Bird, *Kant's Theory of Knowledge*, p. 155.

21 Hume, *Treatise of Human Nature*, ed. L. A. Selby-Bigge, rev. P. H. Nidditch (Oxford: Oxford University Press, 1978), bk. I, pt. III, §xiv, p. 172.

22 Bird, *Kant's Theory of Knowledge*, p. 161.

23 Christian Wolff, *Philosophia prima sive Ontologia* (Frankfurt, 1729), §70 (my emphasis).

24 Compare *Nova Delucidatio*, Proposition XI (1) (1:408-9), with Proposition V (1:393).

25 Kant's claim, of course, is not that ships can move only downstream, therefore that we can have representations only of ships downstream after having representations of them upstream; it is rather that in given circumstances we can

judge that a particular event has occurred only if there are causal laws entailing that in such circumstances the relevant sequence of states of affairs must have occurred. Given other initial circumstances – different conditions of wind and tide, for example – the same or other causal laws might entail an alternative sequence of states of affairs. On this point see also Ewing, *Kant's Treatment of Causality*, p. 81, and Melnick, *Kant's Analogies of Experience*, pp. 89–90.

26 Bird does not misconstrue Kant's objective of grounding our distinctions between events and nonevents by means of the principle of the second analogy (see *Kant's Theory of Knowledge*, p. 155). He must therefore be sharing the assumption, which will be discussed in the next few pages, that as long as it is known that some event is happening, the question of *which* event is happening is automatically settled by the mere fact that one of the two representations involved is a present representation, and the other is not. But this, as we shall next see, is not Kant's assumption at all.

27 This interpretation has recently been advanced by William Harper in "Kant's Empirical Realism and the Distinction between Subjective and Objective Succession," in *Kant on Causality, Freedom, and Objectivity*, ed. William A. Harper and Ralf Meerbote (Minneapolis: University of Minnesota Press, 1984), pp. 108–37, and by James Van Cleve, in "Four Recent Interpretations of Kant's Second Analogy," *Kant-Studien* 64 (1973):71–87.

28 This defense is most clearly put in Dryer, *Kant's Solution*, p. 436.

29 C. D. Broad, "Kant's First and Second Analogies of Experience," *Proceedings of the Aristotelian Society* 26 (1925–6):189–210, see p. 208; quoted in Dryer, *Kant's Solution*, p. 437.

30 Dryer, *Kant's Solution*, p. 437.

31 The ringing words are Strawson's (*Bounds of Sense*, p. 28; see also p. 137), but the substance of his objection goes back at least to Arthur Lovejoy ("On Kant's Reply to Hume," in Moltke Gram, ed., *Kant: Disputed Questions* [New York: Quadrangle Books, 1967], pp. 289–308, especially pp. 299–300) and H. A. Prichard (*Kant's Theory of Knowledge* [Oxford: Oxford University Press, 1909], pp. 288–91), and the objection was being made clearly by Broad in his Kant lectures, probably for many years, but certainly by no later than 1951 (*Kant: An Introduction*, p. 168). Most recently, Walker has repeated Strawson's account virtually unaltered (*Kant*, p. 101).

32 Strawson, *Bounds of Sense*, p. 136. Paton tried to save Kant from the charge that he confused object–perception causality with object–object causality by interpreting Kant as identifying objects and perceptions to begin with (*Kant's Metaphysic of Experience*, vol. 2, pp. 242, 264). Melnick has conclusively demonstrated the inadequacy of Paton's solution, which simply dissolves the problem Kant is attempting to solve: that of grounding the judgment of difference between perceptions and objects at the empirical level, even if from some transcendental point of view all objects of empirical knowledge are appearances rather than things in themselves (*Kant's Analogies of Experience*, pp. 80–1; see also Allison, *Kant's Transcendental Idealism*, pp. 233–4).

33 Strawson, *Bounds of Sense*, p. 134.

34 I replace Strawson's symbolism with that of Lewis White Beck, in "A *Non Sequitur* of Numbing Grossness?" in Beck, *Essays on Kant and Hume*, pp. 146–53.

35 Strawson, *Bounds of Sense*, p. 136.

36 As did Ewing, *Kant's Treatment of Causality*, pp. 89–90.

37 Schopenhauer, *Fourfold Root of the Principle of Sufficient Reason*, §23, pp. 124–5.

38 The generality of the principle Kant's argument implies has also been appealed to in other solutions to the day/night problem (see Caird, *Critical Philosophy of Kant*, vol. 1, pp. 571–2; Kemp Smith, *Commentary*, p. 378; Ewing, *Kant's Treatment of Causality*, p. 87; Walsh, *Kant's Criticism of Metaphysics*, p. 139; and Allison, *Kant's Transcendental Idealism*, p. 130), as well as the simultaneous causation problem (Kemp Smith, *Commentary*, p. 379, and Melnick, *Kant's Analogies of Experience*, pp. 97–101).

39 See Melnick, *Kant's Analogies of Experience*, p. 93.

40 This point is confused by Dryer, who writes as though Kant's argument requires laws to the effect that states of one sort must *always* follow states of another, rather than laws which determine that in suitable circumstances states of the one sort can *only* succeed states of the other (*Kant's Solution*, pp. 421–2).

41 It has, however, been accepted by some commentators, e.g., Walsh, *Kant's Criticism of Metaphysics*, p. 142.

42 Melnick makes the same observation; *Kant's Analogies of Experience*, p. 99.

43 Yet another case in which this would be true, suggested to me by Robert Fogelin, is that in which the third state of affairs is the cause of *both* of the two states being ordered as a particular event, but has to produce one of its effects prior to the other. This is the appropriate model not only for the case of a cause initiating a several-stage process, such as the lighting of a match which first burns a fuse which then ignites some powder, and so on, but also for the day/night case itself, where a single phenomenon, the rotation of the earth around the sun, can be viewed as the single cause of the sequence of night and day (at some given location).

44 For instance, Kemp Smith, *Commentary*, p. 368; Ewing, *Kant's Treatment of Causality*, pp. 76–7; and, most notably, Broad, *Kant: An Introduction*, pp. 166–8. Although himself a defender of a form of transcendental idealism, Allison makes clear that the problem faced in the second analogy has nothing to do with the transcendental distinction between appearances and things in themselves but arises entirely because of the non-self-evident differences in the temporal relations of empirical intuitions and empirical objects; *Kant's Transcendental Idealism*, p. 227.

45 It is not, though, phenomenalism in Kemp Smith's special sense, which is closer to what I will subsequently call a form of *realism*; in Kemp Smith's terminology, this passage expounds *subjectivism*, on which the only status for empirical objects alternative to the possibility that they are things in themselves is that they are literally conjunctions of subjective states.

46 Surprisingly, as has already been noted, Paton, at least, thought that a phenomenalist reduction of objects to representations was the *solution* to Kant's problem.

11. The third analogy: interaction

1 Older commentators, such as Caird, Kemp Smith, Ewing, and Paton generally recognized the importance of the third analogy to Kant's larger project of constructing a theory of empirical time-determination adequate to underlie his conception of the continuum of our knowledge from ordinary to scientific, even if their accounts of the argument were not particularly illuminating. (An

exception to the last remark is Paton, whose extended discussion of the third analogy in *Kant's Metaphysic of Experience*, vol. 2, pp. 294–331, although not perfect, is by far the most useful account in the older as well as more recent literature.) More recent commentators, however, have often seen no reason to discuss the third analogy at all; thus, among books cited in the preceding two chapters, those by Bird, Bennett, Dryer, Brittan, Walker, and Allison pass it by entirely. One recent commentator who does emphasize the importance of the third analogy is Gordon Nagel, in *Structure of Experience*, ch. 7. Unfortunately, he commits the opposite error of inflating its significance beyond reason by mistaking its argument for community among *objects* as an argument for community between *subject and object* and even among *cognitive subjects*. This makes the third analogy trespass onto the territory of the refutation of idealism and beyond.

2 Of course, Einsteinian relativity theory makes it perfectly clear that judgments of simultaneity are conditioned, and indeed conditional on position within or without the light-cone; but I think it would be fair to say that this has hardly undermined ordinary assumptions about the direct perceivability of simultaneity.

3 Ernst Cassirer, *Kant's Life and Thought*, tr. James Haden (New Haven: Yale University Press, 1981), p. 188 (this book was originally published in 1918).

4 Paton, *Kant's Metaphysic of Experience*, vol. 2, p. 324.

5 It is recognized, at least in passing, however, by both Caird (*Critical Philosophy of Kant*, vol. 1, p. 577) and Paton (*Kant's Metaphysic of Experience*, vol. 2, p. 245).

6 As Robert Paul Wolff observed, the section reads almost as if Kant had run out of energy after the exhausting task of writing the second analogy (*Kant's Theory of Mental Activity*, p. 284).

7 As is also observed by Paton, *Kant's Metaphysic of Experience*, vol. 2, p. 294.

8 This is what Paton means by the "Critical Character of the Principle"; *Kant's Metaphysic of Experience*, vol. 2, p. 294.

9 This point is made clear by Kemp Smith, *Commentary*, p. 382.

10 Strawson, *Bounds of Sense*, p. 139; here again Strawson is following Prichard in the charge that Kant's argument just rests on a confusion; see Prichard, *Kant's Theory of Knowledge*, pp. 304–7 (and, as in the case of the second analogy, Paton avoids Prichard's charge that Kant confuses relations among representations with relations among objects by the Pyrrhic strategy of simply identifying representation and object [*Kant's Metaphysic of Experience*, vol. 2, p. 306].)

11 This fundamental premise of Kant's argument has simply escaped many commentators, but has been recognized by Paton, *Kant's Metaphysic of Experience*, vol. 2, pp. 301–2, 305; see especially this note on p. 303: "We could not, in my opinion and I believe in the opinion of Kant, say (on the basis of sense-perception in abstraction from thought) even that the series was reversible. We could say only that it took place in the order in which it did take place …"; Wolff, *Kant's Theory of Mental Activity*, p. 290; and Melnick, *Kant's Analogies of Experience*, p. 94: "We do not determine that A and B are coexistent by determining that our perceptions of A and B are reversible. … Again, we derive facts about the subjective order of our perceptions (i.e., whether the order is reversible) from the objective temporal connection of the appearances that are perceived (whether they coexist)."

12 This point is noted by Kemp Smith, *Commentary*, p. 382, and Ewing, *Kant's Treatment of Causality*, p. 113.

13 Cf. Melnick, *Kant's Analogies of Experience*, p. 95.

14 In any case, this solution would not resolve another objection which is often alleged against Kant, namely that two states of affairs may also be judged to be simultaneous when they are both necessary consequences of some earlier third state and succeed it after the same interval; see, e.g., Ewing, *Kant's Treatment of Causality*, pp. 116–17, and Paton, *Kant's Metaphysic of Experience*, vol. 2, p. 314.

15 Kemp Smith, *Commentary*, p. 389.

16 Paton, *Kant's Metaphysic of Experience*, vol. 2, pp. 296–7; he borrows the expression "streaky view of causation" from A. D. Lindsay.

17 To be sure, any breakdown of the distinction between the concepts of causation and interaction will wreak havoc with Kant's correlation of those schemata with the logical relations of ground and consequence and disjunction, but since, as is often pointed out, Kant's connection of the real relation of reciprocal influence with the logical notion of an exclusive disjunction is the most tenuous piece of his metaphysical deduction of the categories, this is no loss.

18 For a similar conclusion, see Walsh, *Kant's Criticism of Metaphysics*, p. 146.

12. The problem, project, and premise of the refutation

1 Kant's word is *beharrlich*. It might be preferable to translate this as "enduring," since the first analogy's ultimate implication that empirical knowledge of alteration requires at least the regulative ideal of genuinely permanent rather than merely relatively enduring substances is not really required here. But since, as we saw, the ideal permanence of substance is in fact a legitimate consequence of Kant's argument from the conditions for the empirical confirmation of change, there will be no harm in retaining here the translation of *beharrlich* which in any case Kemp Smith has made canonical.

2 Thus, Kemp Smith's claim that the expression "objects in space outside me" in the thesis of the 1787 "Refutation" is "pleonastic" (*Commentary*, p. 309, n. 2) is true only if "outside me" is taken in the merely phenomenological rather than ontological sense distinguished by Kant in 1781. That this is *not* what Kant intends, however, is precisely what will be argued here.

3 For references to these figures see Kemp Smith, *Commentary*, p. 314; another catalog of traditional positions on this problem can be found in Moltke S. Gram, "What Kant Really Did to Idealism," in J. N. Mohanty and Robert W. Shahan, eds., *Essays on Kant's Critique of Pure Reason* (Norman: University of Oklahoma Press, 1982), pp. 127–56, see pp. 127, 151–2.

4 Paton, *Kant's Metaphysics of Experience*, vol. 2, p. 383.

5 "Kant Widerlegung des Idealismus," in his *Beiträge zur Geschichte und Interpretation der Philosophie Kants* (Berlin: De Gruyter, 1969), pp. 171–87.

6 See Kemp Smith, *Commentary*, p. 314, and Gram, "What Kant Really Did to Idealism," pp. 151–2.

7 See Paton, *Kant's Metaphysic of Experience*, vol. 2, pp. 378–80.

8 Gram intends a similar distinction, I take it, with his contrast between "ontological" and "criteriological" concepts of things in themselves ("What Kant Really Did to Idealism," pp. 135–6).

9 Kemp Smith's own position in the traditional controversy is unclear. He does

indeed think that the argument of 1787 "proves the *direct opposite* of what is asserted in the first edition, viz. that though outer appearances are immediately apprehended they must be existences distinct from the subjective states through which the mind represents them" (*Commentary*, p. 312), but since he then goes on to interpret this claim in terms of his obscure distinction between "subjectivism" and "phenomenalism" it is not evident whether he really has *ontological* distinctness in mind here. On balance, though, it would seem that he does incline against ascribing to the Kant of 1787 an outright reduction of external objects to groups of mental states which are characterized by a merely phenomenological form of spatiality.

10 This has also been observed by Gram, "What Kant Really Did to Idealism," p. 139.

11 Thus, Gram unnecessarily weakens the conclusion of his discussion of the refutation by stating that the argument "can be formulated all over again without assuming that there are things in themselves" ("What Kant Really Did to Idealism," p. 150); the point is rather that as far as the argument of the refutation itself goes, it contains no reason whatever to *deny* that there are things in themselves, if that just means things which exist entirely independently of us – and none of Kant's other reasons for denying that we know things as they really are are any good. Even though Gram also wishes to undercut the traditional debate, this formulation already concedes too much to it.

12 Gram is one of the few commentators who have made clear that one of the fundamental issues for the refutation is precisely that of the transition from enduring to spatial objects; indeed, he has emphasized that even if the argument proves the existence of objects *independent* from the self (or, more accurately, *oneself*), separate considerations must still be brought to bear to prove that such objects are also spatial ("What Kant Really Did to Idealism," pp. 130–1, 141, 147). Comment on his solution to this question will be reserved for the following chapter.

13 Kant's exposition may suggest that this is simply a brute but contingent fact about representations. It is not obvious that this would ultimately undermine the force of any argument employing this premise; however, D. P. Dryer's rather obscure remark that "the absence of continuance in what immediately presents itself to introspection is bound up with what differentiates introspection from outer observation" (*Kant's Solution*, p. 364) might be taken to suggest that the momentary existence of a representation is not a contingent feature of an entity which could conceivably last longer than a moment but rather a necessary feature of what should really be understood not as an entity at all but rather as an *act of attention*, with the brief duration such an act must have.

14 Ewing has argued that Kant's exposition of the argument of the analogies as if it depended merely on the conditions necessary to contrast subjective and objective states of affairs, instead of those necessary to make determinate judgments about *either*, is misleading and is connected to his misleading presentation of the transcendental deduction in the *Prolegomena* and similar passages (*Kant's Treatment of Causality*, pp. 126–9). This is certainly correct; the problem remains to show *why* determinate judgments about subjective as well as objective states do require rules of the kind suggested by the analogies of experience.

15 For Leibniz's definition of space purely in terms of coexistence, see, e.g., his "Third Paper" in reply to Clarke, §4: "I hold space to be something merely

relative, as time is: . . . I hold it to be an order of coexistences, as time is an order of successions. For space denotes, in terms of possibility, an order of things which exist at the same time, considered as existing together, without enquiring into their manner of existing" (*The Leibniz-Clarke Correspondence*, ed. H. G. Alexander [Manchester: Manchester University Press, 1956], pp. 25–6). See also Baumgarten, *Metaphysica*, §240: "Positis simultaneis extra se, ponitur spatium. . . . Positis succesivis, ponitur tempus . . ." (If simultaneous things are posited beside each other, space is to be posited. . . . If successive things are posited, time is to be posited . . .).

16 This point will be pressed further in the first section of the next chapter.

17 Kant also adds this point to the second edition of the "Transcendental Aesthetic" under the rubric "The Transcendental Exposition of the Concept of Time" (B 48–9), thereby suggesting that it is so fundamental as to be virtually self-sufficient for the proof that time is an *a priori* form of intuition.

18 They were published earlier, in a different arrangement, in Rudolf Reicke, *Lose Blätter aus Kant's Nachlass* (Königsberg, 1889).

19 These materials have received remarkably little discussion. In his initial catalog of Kant's various arguments against idealism, Kemp Smith refers, without any bibliographical citation, to one of the "*Seven Small Papers* which originated in Kant's discussion with Kiesewetter" – apparently a reference to R 6311, which, according to Adickes, is in the hand of Kiesewetter rather than of Kant and was printed as an independent essay in several nineteenth-century editions of Kant; but Kemp Smith then concludes his chapter on the refutation without either quoting or discussing this "paper." Lewis White Beck makes one reference to R 6311 in "Did the Sage of Königsberg Have No Dreams?" (p. 48); this reference, I am grateful to say, was what first drew my attention to these fragments. More recently, Michael Washburn has referred to these documents in "The Second Edition of the *Critique*: Toward an Understanding of its Nature and Genesis," *Kant-Studien* 66 (1975): 277–90, but he ascribes them to the period *between* the two editions of the *Critique* (pp. 279, 283) without providing any reason for departing from Adickes's dating, and says little about their content. Since the original publication of the article on which Part IV of the present book is based (1983), these fragments have been briefly referred to by Allison, *Kant's Transcendental Idealism*, pp. 294–304, and Eckart Förster, "Kant's Refutation of Idealism," in A. J. Holland, ed. *Philosophy, Its History and Historiography* (Dordrecht: Reidel, 1985), pp. 295–311. Neither of these discussions has led me to change any of my original conclusions. The only German discussions of these fragments remain Gerhard Lehmann, "Kants Widerlegung des Idealismus," and Wolfgang Müller-Lauter, "Kants Widerlegung des Materialen Idealismus," *Archiv für Geschichte der Philosophie* 46 (1964):60–82.

20 At this point I will begin to refer to the refutation without capitalization and quotation in order to indicate that I am referring to the whole project of refuting idealism represented by the texts of 1787–93, rather than to the specific text included at B 274–9 of the *Critique*.

21 The opposite conclusion is reached by Förster in "Kant's Refutation of Idealism." He does not, however, either explain away the verbal evidence I will consider or show how the arguments contained in these notes can be made to work without assuming that they posit the existence of ontologically independent objects. His argument that Kant returns to the reductionist tendencies of 1781 in his *Opus Postumum* of the late 1790s does not provide any direct

evidence that Kant did not entertain a diametrically opposed line of thought in the late 1780s.

22 Lehmann takes this very passage to reveal that Kant's ultimate refutation is still a "phenomenology of the consciousness of reality ... which has nothing to do with a 'proof' of external things" ("Kants Widerlegung des Idealismus," p. 183). This conclusion would appear to rest on the assumption that just by virtue of standing in relation to my mind, something must be a modification of it rather than an independent existence, but this is belied by Kant's most basic assumption that the very notion of an appearance – a relation in which something stands to me – implies the independent existence of something which appears: "Otherwise we should be landed in the absurd conclusion that there can be appearance without anything that appears" (B xxvi–vii); see also A 249: "For if the senses represent to us something merely *as it appears*, this something must also in itself be a thing ..."

23 As Beck points out, the phrase "transcendental consciousness" for the mere concept of self-existence is introduced only in Kant's *Nachlass*; this is the point of Beck's reference to R 6311 in "Did the Sage of Königsberg Have No Dreams?" p. 48. He does not discuss the passage I am about to quote, however, although it could only have buttressed his argument there.

24 The centrality of this threefold distinction among forms of presentation of the self has also been recognized as central to Kant's argument by Paton (*Kant's Metaphysic of Experience*, vol. 2, p. 384), Förster ("Kant's Refutation of Idealism," pp. 306–7), Becker (*Selbstbewusstein und Erfahrung*, pp. 248–61), and Allison (*Kant's Transcendental Idealism*, pp. 295–6). Allison argues that the refutation's use of this threefold distinction constitutes a fundamental critique of the Cartesian conception of self-knowledge directly constituted by the single act of the *cogito*, which it surely is, but he also seems to draw the peculiar inference that this means that the goal of the argument is *other* than that of refuting the skeptic "by demonstrating that the reality of 'objective experience' ... is a necessary condition of the consciousness of one's identity through time" (p. 294). Obviously there is no conflict between these two objectives: Kant shows that Cartesian skepticism is unfounded precisely by showing that the Cartesian image of self-knowledge is simplistic and omits its necessary dependence upon knowledge of external objects.

25 "Kants Widerlegung des Idealismus," p. 179.

13. The central arguments of the refutation

1 This quotation is drawn from the text of the "Synthesis of Apprehension in Intuition" (A 98–100), not from the "Synthesis of Reproduction in Imagination" (A 100–2). But as we saw, the latter section was largely occupied with the fallacious argument that there must be an *a priori* ground for the (absolute) necessity of the synthesis of reproduction, rather than with the nonfallacious argument that such a synthesis is (relatively) necessary for knowledge to occur; see ch. 4, argument IB.i.

2 "Intelligible" here would not seem to carry its usual connotation of accessible to reason alone but would instead seem to be another clumsy way of referring to an intentional object. However, Kant's use of this term, linked as it is to "noumenal" and thus in at least some contexts to things in themselves, *may* be an expression in his traditional terminology of his view in 1787 and after that the

455

enduring object of time-determination must be conceived of as ontologically independent of the self.

3 "Third Meditation," in *The Philosophical Writings of Descartes,* tr. John Cottingham, Robert Stoothoff, and Dugald Murdoch (Cambridge: Cambridge University Press, 1984), vol. 2, pp. 30–1.

4 That rules or concepts are required for this purpose means that the boundary between "the synthesis of reproduction in imagination" and "the synthesis of recognition in a concept" (A 103) dissolves when Kant's premises are fully understood. I take it that this does not constitute an objection to the present interpretation, however, but is rather just a reflection of the "preliminary" (A 98) and indeed superficial nature of the distinctions among the three forms of synthesis. It is of course paralleled by the fact that the very distinction between imagination and understanding tends to collapse in Kant's hands (e.g., A 119).

5 The only other recent commentator who comes close to explaining this real premise of the refutation of idealism is Wolfgang Becker. He argues that although "a subject can ascribe immediately given states of consciousness to himself without criteria," "past states of consciousness are [only] accessible to myself through their recollection in a present state of consciousness," which must be connected to these past states by some sort of criteria (*Selbstbewusstsein und Erfahrung,* p. 258). Although his account clearly implies it, he could state more explicitly that past representations cannot be immediately given and therefore need to be reconstructed from the present contents of consciousness for the simple and incontrovertible reason that they no longer exist when recalled; he also does not mention the crucial evidence of A 99 in his discussion.

6 Bennett's account has also influenced Becker; see *Selbstbewusstsein und Erfahrung,* pp. 257–60.

7 Bennett, *Kant's Analytic,* p. 119.

8 Ibid., pp. 120–2.

9 Ibid., p. 123.

10 For examples of such questions see Strawson, *Bounds of Sense,* pp. 38–9.

11 Allison, *Kant's Transcendental Idealism,* p. 297; see also Walsh, *Kant's Criticism of Metaphysics,* p. 194.

12 See also Bennett's distinction between what makes a judgment *possible* and what makes it *trustworthy; Kant's Analytic,* p. 209.

13 According to Adickes's note (18:607–10), this fragment is in the hand of Kiesewetter rather than of Kant, and although it could represent the former's attempt to transcribe an argument which Kant presented to him orally during their meetings in the fall of 1790, it is more likely that it simply represents Kiesewetter's attempt to reproduce what had been published in 1787, as a memorandum for his upcoming discussion with Kant.

14 Here "empirical consciousness" must be meant in the special sense of R 6313, 18:615, as the raw material for empirical self-knowledge, rather than such self-knowledge itself. Its association with *apprehensio,* the least interpreted form of synthesis, is evidence of this.

15 A slightly different statement of Kant's basic idea may be found in Becker, *Selbstbewusstsein und Erfahrung,* p. 262.

16 Hume, *Treatise of Human Nature,* bk. I, pt. I, §iii (Selby-Bigge, p. 8).

17 Baumgarten, *Metaphysica,* §8.

18 As Gram points out, the argument of the *Nova Delucidatio* does not establish the necessity of *spatial* objects but only *other* objects – thus, one mind could be

acted upon by another *mind,* as far as this argument is concerned ("What Kant Really Did to Idealism," pp. 128–31). Of course, Kant clearly supposes that we perceive other minds only by means of our perceptions of bodies, but a point that is more important for the present purpose, and which Gram does not mention, is simply that the argument of 1755 is a metaphysical rather than epistemological argument: It supposes that the principle of sufficient reason is a metaphysical truth rather than a principle of the possibility of experience.

19 See Walsh, *Kant's Criticism of Metaphysics,* p. 193, and Förster, "Kant's Refutation of Idealism," p. 304.

20 "Other representations": that is, dreams or other internal states which are not perceptions of external objects but must ultimately be related to the latter.

21 None of these answers is equivalent to that which Gram, who has so usefully insisted on the present question, ascribes to Kant. His view is that since in Kant's view time is a feature of representation in both inner and outer sense (whereas spatiality is a feature of representations of outer sense alone), Kant's "operative inference here is ... from the fact that temporality is also an essential part of what it is for anything to be material to the conclusion that the objectivity of the time order guarantees our ability to be directly aware of material objects external to us" ("What Kant Really Did to Idealism," p. 148). But this just confuses the fact that temporality is a *necessary* condition for the representation of objects in space with the supposition that representing time is thereby a *sufficient* condition for representing such objects. I see no evidence that Kant ever commits this particular non sequitur.

22 Strawson, *Bounds of Sense,* p. 127.

23 See, for instance, ID, §3, 2:392.

24 For a similar interpretation of this passage see Allison, *Kant's Transcendental Idealism,* pp. 83–6.

25 This vital point is noted by Walsh (*Kant's Criticism of Metaphysics,* p. 192) and Allison (*Kant's Transcendental Idealism,* p. 303); however, neither of these authors adduces the textual evidence offered here for this conclusion.

26 Karl Ameriks makes this point with reference to passages in Kant's lectures (28:225, 756), however, rather than the *Reflexionen;* see *Kant's Theory of Mind* (Oxford: Oxford University Press [Clarendon Press], 1982), p. 107.

27 A point on which Ameriks insists (ibid., p. 108).

28 Though Kant omitted such an argument for the (epistemic) necessity of embodiment in the *Critique,* he had prefigured this aspect of the mature refutation in a number of earlier works – for example, *Träume eines Geister-sehers,* 2:323–4, and ID, §30, 2:419.

29 This quotation is from G. F. Meier's German translation of Baumgarten, *Metaphysik* (Halle: Hemmerde Verlag, 1767), §545. See also Baumgarten's Latin *Metaphysica,* §§740–1.

30 That this is not so clearly true of ancient skepticism is suggested by M. F. Burnyeat in "Idealism and Greek Philosophy: What Descartes Saw and Berkeley Missed," *Philosophical Review* 91 (1982): 3–40, especially pp. 23–32.

14. The metaphysics of the refutation

1 It should be noted that the metaphysical argument about to be discussed, although first added to the refutation of 1787 by the notes of 1788, was not a new argument. Rather, it had been deployed by Kant as early as the inaugural

dissertation (§§10-11, 2:396-7). Perhaps, then, its occurrence in the later period should be explained away as another instance of Kant's unfortunate attachment to ideas which the development of his own thought had rendered anachronistic. If so, this makes infelicitous Müller-Lauter's negative assessment of the post-1787 refutation, since that assessment depends precisely on seeing this metaphysical argument as its dominant element ("Kants Widerlegung des materialen Idealismus," pp. 71-2). Förster also seems to regard the argument we are about to consider as Kant's "main contention" ("Kant's Refutation of Idealism," pp. 304-6). Allison, however, although he too criticizes this metaphysical argument –indeed, like me, regards it as a relapse into, rather than rejection of, Cartesianism – also recognizes that it is not Kant's sole strategy in the rufutation of idealism (*Kant's Transcendental Idealism*, pp. 300-2).

2 See Barry Stroud, "Kant and Skepticism," in Myles Burnyeat, ed., *The Skeptical Tradition* (Berkeley: University of California Press, 1983), pp. 413-34.

3 See the "Sixth Meditation," in *Philosophical Writings of Descartes*, vol. 2, pp. 54-5.

4 Walsh, *Kant's Criticism of Metaphysics*, p. 190.

5 See also Kant's list of rejected dogmas as B xxxiv.

6 E.g., Paton, *Kant's Metaphysic of Experience*, vol. 2, p. 382.

7 As Wolfgang Becker puts this point, "Empirical self-knowledge . . . is mediated through immediately given representations and, epistemically regarded, thereby corresponds to the cognition of external objects" (*Selbstbewusstsein und Erfahrung*, p. 264). But be it noted that although the representations of external objects may be given immediately, the *interpretation* of them *as* representations of enduring objects is *ipso facto* mediated.

8 Paton seems to be making the same point in his argument that the permanent is really presupposed rather than perceived on Kant's account. See *Kant's Metaphysic of Experience*, vol. 2, pp. 379, 204-7.

15. Appearances and things in themselves

1 This was Peter Strawson's title for the enterprise on which he embarked in his *Individuals* (London: Methuen, 1959) and for which he then sought historical backing in *Bounds of Sense* (1966).

2 Ibid., p. 22.

3 Graham Bird, "Kant's Transcendental Idealism," pp. 91, 90, in Godfrey Vesey, ed., *Idealism – Past and Present*, Royal Institute of Philosophy Lecture Series 13 (Cambridge: Cambridge University Press, 1982), pp. 71-92, especially 91, 90.

4 This interpretation was placed in the forefront of recent discussion by Gerold Prauss, *Kant und das Problem der Dinge an sich* (Bonn: Bouvier Verlag Herbert Grundmann, 1974). Other advocates have included Arthur Melnick, *Kant's Analogies of Experience*, especially §21 (pp. 151-6), Robert Pippin, *Kant's Theory of Form*, especially pp. 193-201, and most recently Henry Allison, *Kant's Transcendental Idealism*, especially chs. 1, 2, and 11. For a detailed discussion of these interpretations, see Karl Ameriks, "Recent Work on Kant's Theoretical Philosophy," *American Philosophical Quarterly* 19 (1982):1-24, especially §1.

5 F. H. Jacobi, *Werke* (Leipzig: Gerhard Fleischer, 1815), vol. 2, p. 304.

6 A similar position is suggested by Jill Vance Buroker, *Space and Incongruence,* pp. 111–13. There is indeed a problem about how philosophical knowledge itself is supposed to be fit into Kant's model of synthetic *a priori* judgment (see Lewis White Beck, "Toward a Meta-Critique of Pure Reason," in his *Essays on Kant and Hume,* pp. 20–37), but that is a *general* problem which creates no difficulties for Kant's negative claims that it does not create for his positive ones as well.

7 Allison's view was first expounded in "The Non-spaciality [sic] of Things in Themselves for Kant," *Journal of the History of Philosophy* 14 (July, 1976):313–21. It receives a revised treatment in his *Kant's Transcendental Idealism,* especially chs. 1, 2, and 5.

8 See Allison, "Non-spaciality of Things in Themselves," e.g., p. 320, or *Kant's Transcendental Idealism,* p. 7.

9 Allison, *Kant's Transcendental Idealism,* p. 10. Further page references are given parenthetically in the text.

10 In support of his position, Allison invokes Arthur Melnick, whose argument he interprets as turning "on the incoherence of construing an element that functions as a form of our cognitive relation to the world as a feature of the world in itself, that is, a feature of the world which pertains to the world in abstraction from our cognitive relation to it." I think Allison correctly describes Melnick's position, though that makes clear only that Melnick also confuses abstracting from a property in a *conception* of an object and actually supposing that the object *lacks* this property.

11 The following comments therefore also apply to Strawson, who similarly holds that the thesis that any perceptions which "are the outcome of our being affected by" things can produce "knowledge only of those things as they appear . . . and not of those things as they are in themselves . . . is a fundamental and unargued complex premise of the *Critique*" (*Bounds of Sense,* p. 250).

12 Buroker has also noticed this fact about the basic structure of Kant's argument; see *Space and Incongruence,* p. 95. As will become clear in the next chapter, however, my own view about which of Kant's reasons for denying that things in themselves are spatiotemporal is primary differs from hers.

13 Strawson's remark that "as far as the Transcendental Aesthetic is concerned, the doctrine of the transcendental subjectivity of space rests on no other discernible support than that provided by the argument from geometry" (*Bounds of Sense,* p. 277) thus overstates the case, although I shall argue that the link between necessity and subjectivity, which is clearest in Kant's account of geometry, is indeed his *chief* argument for transcendental idealism in the "Transcendental Aesthetic."

16. Transcendental idealism and the forms of intuition

1 Kant's emendations to the "Aesthetic" for the second edition (see B 69–71) show that as late as 1787 he was still smarting at the objections of Lambert, Sulzer, and Mendelssohn in 1770 that he reduced time to a mere illusion; see their letters at 10:98–111, or Kerferd and Walford, *Kant,* pp. 93–107, or Arnulf Zweig, *Kant: Philosophical Correspondence, 1759–99* (Chicago: University of Chicago Press, 1967), pp. 60–70.

2 Despite the passage of two decades, the most useful reviews of Kant's

arguments in the metaphysical expositions remain the discussions in Bennett (*Kant's Analytic*, chs. 2–6, pp. 15–67), and Strawson (*Bounds of Sense*, pt. II, ch. 1, pp. 47–71, and pt. V, pp. 277–92). Useful material will also be found in Gottfried Martin, *Immanuel Kant: Ontologie und Wissenschaftstheorie*, 4th ed. (Berlin: De Gruyter, 1969); Brittan, *Kant's Theory of Science*, and Allison, *Kant's Transcendental Idealism*, ch. 5, pp. 81–114. The most exhaustive commentary ever written on the "Transcendental Aesthetic" has to be vol. 2 of Hans Vaihinger's *Commentar zu Kants Kritik der reinen Vernunft*, 2 vols. (Stuttgart: Union Deutscher Verlagsgesellschaft, 1892), the 563 pages of which are devoted exclusively to the "Aesthetic." Since this ground is so well trodden, I will proceed in the following section without further mention of these and other commentators.

3 As a matter of fact, though, he just repeats the third argument about time under the title of a transcendental exposition without removing it from the metaphysical exposition.

4 Here I will mention the useful discussion of this argument in Buroker, *Space and Incongruence*, pp. 75–7.

5 See Locke, *Essay Concerning Human Understanding*, bk. II, ch. 12, §4.

6 Buroker's otherwise very useful treatment of Kant's metaphysical argument for transcendental idealism is misleading on this point. She does "not think that the analysis of synthetic *a priori* knowledge is Kant's only, or even his initial, basis for asserting the radical subjectivity of knowledge of space. For one thing, Kant draws that conclusion in the Dissertation, which contains *no* doctrine of synthetic *a priori* knowledge" (*Space and Incongruence*, p. 78). It is true that the epistemological argument is never Kant's only argument for transcendental idealism. But to deny that the epistemological argument is present in the inaugural dissertation because Kant has not yet adopted the *terminology* of synthetic *a priori* knowledge is to ignore the obvious implication of his contrast between "certitude" and "empirical knowledge" in that work.

7 Leibniz's Fifth Paper, §47, in *Leibniz-Clarke Correspondence*, p. 71.

8 Locke, *Essay Concerning Human Understanding*, bk. II, ch. 25, §8.

9 This point is well made by Allison, *Kant's Transcendental Idealism*, p. 164.

10 As usual, similar considerations are supposed to apply to time as well. But since Kant's most crucial illustrations of the epistemological argument do not even go through the motions of making a separate case for the transcendental ideality of time, I shall refer to space alone in the remainder of this chapter.

11 See Chapter 2, this volume.

12 This is a point which Allison notices, but he blunts the significance of it by presupposing an already defined "transcendental sense" for the expression "things in themselves" (*Kant's Transcendental Idealism*, p. 102). He is clearly supposing that the remark in the preface to the second edition that the *Critique* teaches "that the object is to be taken *in a twofold sense*" (B xxvii) is to govern the interpretation of the present passage. Since the passage now to be quoted was not only already included in the first edition, and thus temporally precedes that remark, but is also the first passage in the body of the text to speak of things in themselves, surely *it* must govern the interpretation of what is, after all, merely a prefatory and therefore promissory comment, not vice versa.

13 See Martin, *Immanuel Kant: Ontologie und Wissenschaftslehre*, §2, pp. 18–24.

14 Brittan, *Kant's Theory of Science*, p. 70.

15 See Friedman, "Kant's Theory of Geometry," 455–506.

16 See also Parsons, "Kant's Philosophy of Arithmetic," pp. 568–94.

17 See Nagel, *Structure of Experience*, ch. 2, especially p. 31.

18 Allison, *Kant's Transcendental Idealism*, p. 99.

19 It is, of course, possible that Kant correctly supposes that the true geometry is necessarily true but incorrectly identifies what the true geometry is; it is equally obvious that a mistake of this sort would cast significant doubt upon the justification for his claim that the true geometry is necessarily true.

20 This debate is chronicled at great length in Vaihinger, *Kommentar zu Kants Kritik der Reinen Vernunft*, vol. 2, pp. 290–326; and is reported on more briefly in Kemp Smith, *Commentary*, pp. 113–14.

21 Compare the similar statement by Ross Harrison in "Transcendental Arguments and Idealism," in Vesey, *Idealism Past and Present*, p. 215.

22 Harrison, "Transcendental Arguments and Idealism," p. 215.

23 As Allison fails to note in his passing endorsement of the "preformation" argument (*Kant's Transcendental Idealism*, p. 110).

24 This is why, although Harrison has clearly and correctly analyzed the character of the modal assumption in Kant's argument for transcendental idealism, his use of an example about causal laws, which I suppressed in my previous reference to his discussion, detracts from his otherwise persuasive argument ("Transcendental Arguments and Idealism," p. 215).

17. Transcendental idealism and the theory of judgment

1 Allison refers to this as the "materials argument" for the nontemporality of the real self; his criticisms of it are not identical to those offered here, but he agrees in rejecting it (*Kant's Transcendental Idealism*, pp. 264–5). This argument is omitted from Patricia Kitcher's otherwise useful catalog of Kant's arguments for denying the phenomenality of the real self (as she puts it) in "Kant's Real Self," pp. 113–47.

2 Allison has suggested that this confusion be understood as the result of the conflation of two different forms of self-*affection*: The effect of the temporal form of inner sense on the raw materials transmitted to the self is one kind of "affection," and the act of making determinate judgments *about* such temporally formed materials is another act of "affection." The implication would then be that Kant illegitimately associates the ideality of time, which allegedly follows from the fact that time is a form of inner intuition with which we "affect" the data given to us, with the further act of *judging* temporal relations as well (*Kant's Transcendental Idealism*, pp. 265–7). I will argue that Kant's inference that even the act of temporal *judgment* implies the transcendental ideality of time does not depend solely on this confusion – which is certainly part of the story – but that it involves additional confusions about the nature of this "act" of judgment as well.

3 See, again, Melnick, *Kant's Analogies of Experience*, p. 93.

4 This reflection is also discussed by Allison, who however places a weaker interpretation on it than I will. He takes it as merely another argument for the thesis that the "conceptual activity through which the mind represents an object ... cannot itself be given to it as an object," which is part of the general distinction between apperception and inner sense (*Kant's Transcendental Idealism*, pp. 276–8). But this point could be made without the argument we are about to see; the purpose of the threat of duplicate time-orders can only be to

take the underlying reality of conceptual *activity* out of time altogether.

5 This undercuts the interpretation of T. D. Weldon, who holds that Kant followed Tetens in treating acts of inner sense as awareness of *past* awarenesses only; see *Kant's Critique of Pure Reason*, 2nd ed. (Oxford: Oxford University Press [Clarendon Press], 1958), pp. 262–3. Weldon's interpretation of inner sense is also criticized by Allison (*Kant's Transcendental Idealism*, pp. 259–60).

6 He also distinguishes between both of these and the essential characteristics of an individual thing or type of thing; he sometimes calls the latter "essence," as at R 5406, but also sometimes confuses matters by calling the essence of an individual rather than the nexus of all entities "nature taken *formaliter*" (R 5608, 18:249); indeed, here he further confuses things by apparently *defining* nature *materialiter* as the "sum of appearances, in opposition to the intelligible world." This would make the transcendental ideality of nature a conceptual truth on either its formal or material interpretation.

7 "Their particular nature": That is, in the terminology of R 5406, their essence.

18. Transcendental idealism and the "Antinomy of Pure Reason"

1 The first and the third of the dialectical inferences – the "Paralogisms of Pure Reason," which concerns (the errors of) traditional rational psychology, and the "Ideal of Pure Reason," which concerns (the errors of) traditional rational theology – have no direct bearing on the indirect proof of transcendental idealism and will not be discussed here.

2 Henry Allison tries to defend Kant's indirect argument for transcendental idealism by claiming that both the "transcendental realist" and the transcendental idealist would accept the underlying assumption of the coextensiveness of what is and what is known and by then concluding that only the transcendental idealist has any explanation of this assumption (*Kant's Transcendental Idealism*, pp. 51–6). But this is not credible. In postscholastic times, at least, the classical concomitant to metaphysical realism is epistemological pessimism – Locke is the paradigmatic example. It is of course precisely to avoid skepticism about the outer reaches of our knowledge – that is, the position that we simply cannot reach a decision about such issues as whether the world is finite or infinite, that such matters exceed the weak candle we have been given – that Kant advocates transcendental idealism and its reduction of what can be true of space and time to what can be known about them.

3 As Kemp Smith puts this, *"The antinomies exist as antinomies only when viewed from the false standpoint of dogmatic rationalism.* Had [Kant] eliminated the rationalistic proofs, the conflict of the antinomies, in its strictly logical form, as the conflict of direct contradictories, would at once have vanished" (*Commentary*, pp. 482–3). Kemp Smith is rare among commentators in perceiving that Kant's loyalties in the "Transcendental Dialectic" (in the text actually published in 1781) are deeply split between what Kemp Smith describes as "Kant's more sceptical tendencies," on which the lessons of the "Dialectic" are purely cautionary, and a more "constructive" or even "idealist" tendency, which presupposes the "ultimate validity of the absolute claims of pure thought" (*Commentary*, pp. 426–9; see also pp. 519–21). We shall see in this chapter that the antinomies indeed do not work without presupposing such validity to the claims of reason; this will be all the more surprising given Kant's unequivocal

adherence to the purely "skeptical" conception of the dialectic through most of the 1770s.

4 Making this point with reference to the first antinomy, which I shall discuss later in this chapter, Jonathan Bennett says: "What creates the problem in the first place, by making these infinities look troublesome, is the mildly phenomenalist view that any statement about an infinity involves some thought of an infinite 'synthesis' or enumeration. ... Someone who allowed *no* connection between 'what there is' and 'what one could in principle discoverk' would not have the problem in the first place." So Kant's "indirect proof" of transcendental idealism is merely a case of "moving from half-hearted to whole-hearted phenomenalism" (*Kant's Dialectic* [Cambridge: Cambridge University Press, 1974], pp. 124–5).

5 For similar analyses see Kemp Smith, *Commentary*, p. 485, and Bennett, *Kant's Dialectic*, pp. 123–5 (see n. 4). Allison tries to defend Kant against the charge that his indirect proof is circular in the way just claimed by arguing that Kant is employing a special definition of the infinite as a "*totum syntheticum*," which does indeed imply the possibility of completing the synthesis (or representation) of it (*Kant's Transcendental Idealism*, pp. 43–4), but there is no reason to suppose that any realist would accept such a definition (contrary to Allison's assertion on pp. 53–5), and in any case Allison's defense of Kant seems halfhearted (p. 45).

6 See, for instance, Leibniz's Third Paper, §6, in *Leibniz-Clarke Correspondence*, pp. 26–7.

7 W. H. Walsh gives a useful explanation of the reason for Kant's different treatment of the mathematical and dynamical antinomies. In the case of spatial or temporal extent and divisibility, one is restricted to the homogeneous units of space and time: thus, one cannot represent a completed space by adding a nonspatial thing in itself to any spatial units. But in the cases of a first and necessary cause, one is not so restricted (Kant does not accept the principle of Berkeley that like must cause like): So there is no reason why a nonspatiotemporal free agent or necessary being cannot simply be *conjoined* to the series of ordinary spatiotemporal objects. This allows both thesis and antithesis to be (possibly) true in the dynamical antinomies. See *Kant's Criticism of Metaphysics*, pp. 200, 208–11.

8 The argument for the second disjunct of the antithesis, that a necessary being cannot exist outside the world, is a little less obvious. What Kant says is that the contrary supposition "contradicts itself, since the existence of a series cannot be necessary if no single member of it is necessary" (A 453 / B 481). The basis for this claim is not obvious, but if it means that nothing can be *known* to be necessary unless it is represented, yet that if it is represented it is in fact part of the series of appearances, then the argument is epistemological. In other words, he may be drawing on his earlier argument that the only empirically confirmable kind of necessity is the necessity of an event in a series of states governed by both the formal laws of intuition and also causal laws, that is, the argument of the "Postulates of Empirical Thought."

9 Not only the Kant of 1781 but also the majority school of his commentators, who see no doctrinal difference between the treatments of idealism in 1781 and 1787, have been misled by their failure to see that the epistemological dependence of that *by which* something is represented does not entail the ontological dependence of *what* is represented. An example is Paton: "On

Kant's view, however, the existence of permanent substances in space can never be proved unless these permanent substances are phenomenal substances dependent, like space and time, on the constitution of the human mind. Hence he is not departing in the slightest degree from his own doctrine" (*Kant's Metaphysic of Experience*, vol. 2, p. 380). What Paton fails to note is that Kant's argument in 1787 and after is that we must employ the *two* admittedly dependent forms of intuition – space and time – because we must represent objects which exist independently of ourselves as well as states which do depend on us.

10 Translation from Zweig, *Kant: Philosophical Correspondence, 1759–99*, p. 198.

Afterword

1 The literature on "transcendental arguments" has already generated a significant number of reviews and surveys about itself. Among these the reader might look at *Transcendental Arguments and Science: Essays in Epistemology*, ed. Peter Bieri, Rolf-Peter Horstmann, and Lorenz Krüger (Dordrecht: Reidel, 1979); Anthony L. Brueckner, "Transcendental Arguments I," *Nous* 17 (1983):551–75, and "Transcendental Arguments II," *Nous* 18 (1984):197–225; Reinhold Aschenberg, "Ueber transzendentale Argumente," *Philosophisches Jahrbuch der Görres-Gesellschaft* 85 (1978):332–58, and his *Sprachanalyse und Transzendentalphilosophie* (Stuttgart: Klett-Cotta Verlag, 1982); Eva Schaper and Wilhelm Vossenkuhl, eds., *Bedingungen der Möglichkeit: "Transcendental Arguments" und transzendentales Denken* (Stuttgart: Klett-Cotta Verlag, 1984); and Becker, *Selbstbewusstsein und Erfahrung: Zu Kants transzendentaler Deduktion und ihrer argumentativen Rekonstruktion*.

2 See Ralph Walker, *Kant*, pp. 18–21. Walker explicitly says that when Kant "himself actually presents transcendental arguments, such as the transcendental deduction of the categories, it appears that the steps in these arguments are supposed to consist of analytic propositions, propositions in which the concept of possible experience is analyzed" (p. 19). Jonathan Bennett also seems to accept the view that the intermediate premises of transcendental arguments are ultimately analytic: He labels a paper "Analytic Transcendental Arguments" and says in this discussion that Kant's transcendental argument turns on the fact that "a non-idle concept of the past needs a kind of ordered complexity which I cannot see how to get without also bringing objectivity-concepts into play," while apparently supposing that this fact is discovered by analysis of the concept of the past ("Analytic Transcendental Arguments," in Bieri, Horstmann, and Krüger, *Transcendental Arguments and Science*, p. 55). This sort of interpretation goes back at least as far as Ewing, who described the second analogy as "an analysis of the implications of objective sequence as a possible object of experience, i.e., an analysis of the concept of experienced, or 'experienceable,' objective sequence" (*Kant's Treatment of Causality*, p. 83).

3 Beck, "Toward a Meta-Critique of Pure Reason," in his *Essays on Kant and Hume*, p. 25.

4 Stephan Körner, "The Impossibility of Transcendental Deductions," in Lewis White Beck, ed., *Kant Studies Today* (LaSalle: Open Court, 1969), pp. 230–44; see especially pp. 230–1. Further citations to Körner in this paragraph are given parenthetically in the text.

5 Point (1) might seem to be necessarily true of any Kantian argument. However, Kant's suggestion at the beginning of the "Transcendental Aesthetic" that the pure forms of intuition can be discovered simply by abstracting away all contributions of sensation, on the one side, and understanding, on the other (A 22 / B 36), might entail the possibility of a direct and presumably "undifferentiated" experience of the pure forms of intuition themselves. But one would hardly want to defend the possibility of transcendental deductions on this ground.

6 See Eva Schaper, "Are Transcendental Deductions Impossible?" in Lewis White Beck, ed., *Kant's Theory of Knowledge: Selected Papers from the Third International Kant Congress* (Dordrecht: Reidel, 1974), pp. 5–6. It should be noted, however, that such a defense may fall afoul of Kant's claim that "transcendental proofs" must always be "direct or ostensive," never "apogogical," or an inference to the truth of an assertion from the truth of its consequences (see A 789–91 / B 817–19).

7 This tack has been taken in a number of recent works; see, for example, Brueckner, "Transcendental Arguments II," pp. 210–18.

8 Körner, "Impossibility of Transcendental Deductions," p. 237.

9 Even in the instance of euclidean geometry, where the case for supposing that Kant simply confuses the uniqueness of method and schema might seem best, we saw that the situation is more complicated than that. There, it will be remembered, I argued that the supposition that there must be a unique geometry was a natural consequence of the view that we *impose* spatiality on the objects of experience (although the latter theory itself depended upon unfortunate arguments). Even in that case, it is far from clear that Kant simply confused schema and method, and just mistook the uniqueness of the latter for that of the former. It is all the less obvious, therefore, that he does this in any argument which turns upon the "restriction" view of the rules of thought.

10 Barry Stroud, "Transcendental Arguments," *Journal of Philosophy* 65 (1968):241–56, most recently reprinted in Walker, *Kant on Pure Reason*, pp. 116–31.

11 Richard Rorty, "Strawson's Objectivity Argument," *Review of Metaphysics* 24 (1970):207–44; see p. 212.

12 See Richard Rorty, "Verificationism and Transcendental Arguments," *Nous* 5 (1971):3–14; see pp. 4–5, 9.

13 See Brueckner, "Transcendental Arguments I," p. 560.

14 Stroud, "Transcendental Arguments," in Walker, *Kant on Pure Reason*, p. 122.

15 See Rorty, "Strawson's Objectivity Argument," p. 219, in which Rorty tries to turn this into a virtue of Strawson's argument, and Brueckner, "Transcendental Arguments I," pp. 561–2.

16 Bennett attempts to suggest something like this while still remaining within the confines of his understanding of transcendental arguments as ultimately dependent upon the analysis of a concept of the self. He writes that whereas Strawson "argues that self-knowledge requires one to have a concept of 'person' ... Kant's insight [is] that self-knowledge involves intellectual activity: to know what one's inner states are like is to *make judgments* of certain kinds" ("Analytic Transcendental Arguments," p. 52).

17 Thus it is somewhat puzzling that Brueckner even considers the question of whether Kant's "anti-skeptical enterprise" might validate "any claims to

knowledge about particular physical objects" ("Transcendental Arguments I," p. 552).

18 Brueckner, "Transcendental Arguments II," p. 216.

19 Ibid.

Index of passages cited

This index includes all passages by Kant quoted or cited in this book. The location of the citation from Kant precedes the colon; the location in this book follows it. Citations from the *Critique of Pure Reason* are located by A and B numbers, as in the text. *Reflexionen* are listed by number only. Other citations are located by page numbers in the relevant volume of the *Akademie* edition.

Principiorum primorum cognitionis metaphysicae nova delucidatio (1755; volume 1)

393: 448
393–4: 446
408–9: 448
410: 308, 446

411: 308
411–12: 11–12
413: 352

Attempt to Introduce Negative Quantities into Philosophy (1763; volume 2)

175–6: 253
184: 253

202–3: 251

Dreams of a Spirit-Seer (1766; volume 2)

323–4: 457

De mundi sensibilis atque intelligibilis forma et principiis (inaugural dissertation) (1770; volume 2)

§1, 387–8: 13
§3, 392: 14, 15, 457
§4, 392: 15
§4, 392–3: 341
§5, 393: 16
§8, 395–6: 16
§9, 396: 17
§10, 396: 458
§11, 397: 21, 458
§14.1, 399: 347
§14.5, 400: 21
§14.7, 402: 36
§15.A, 402: 347
§15.D, 403–4: 12, 20, 21, 350

§16, 407: 17, 21
§19, 408: 17
§20, 408: 17
§23, 410: 18
§23, 411: 19
§24, 411: 388
§25, 412–13: 388–9
§26, 413: 18–19, 389
§27, 415: 19
§28, 415: 389–90
§28, 416: 390
§30, 418: 19
§30, 419: 457

Critique of Pure Reason (1781 = A, 1787 = B)

A ix: 1, 2
B xiii: 2
B xvi: 1, 3, 362
B xvii: 1, 3

B xx: 385
B xxi: 343, 385
B xxii: 3
B xxiii: 343

467

Prolegomena to Any Future Metaphysics (1783; volume 4)

Metaphysical Foundations of Natural Science (1786; volume 4)

Critique of Practical Reason (1788; volume 5)

Critique of Judgment (1790; volume 5)

Anthropology from a Pragmatic Point of View (1798; volume 7)

471

General index

abstract ideas and schematism, 158–9, 163–6

action as criterion of substance, 233

actuality and sensation, 275

Adamson, Robert, 281

Adickes, Erich: on dating of *Nachlass*, 288, 431, 434, 454, 456; on second analogy, 241

Allison, Henry E.: on analogies, 444; on first analogy, 445–6; on second analogy, 447–8, 450; on "Antinomy," 463; on apperception, 438; on consciousness, 439; on inner sense, 462; on refutation of idealism, 454, 455, 456, 457, 458; on schematism, 439, 440, 441; on transcendental aesthetic, 356, 360–1, 460–1; on transcendental deduction, 432, 436–7; on transcendental idealism, 336–42, 430, 458–9, 461–2; on verificationism, 304

Ameriks, Karl: on apperception, 438; on embodiment, 314, 457; on transcendental deduction, 433; on transcendental idealism, 458–9

alteration, analysis of, 221–4, 283–4; and causation, 239–59; as empirically knowable change, 224–30, 239

analogies between mind and object, 44–6, 63, 67–8

"Analogies of Experience," 207–76; and *Duisburg Nachlass*, 26–7, 35, 45–6, 61–70; general principles of, 168–9, 171, 207–14; interdependence of, 185, 211–14, 224–5, 239, 242, 267; and objectivity, 209–10; and principles of convenience, 19–20; as regulative ideals, 188; and transcendental time-determinations, 180–1; why so called, 62, 67–70

first analogy, 215–35; and alteration, 221–4; and conservation, 230–5; and empirical knowledge of change, 224–30; and measurement, 184; and official account of analogies, 70; and permanence of time, 216–21; principle of, 215–16; and refutation of idealism, 283–4, 286, 308; and third analogy, 224–5, 228–9

See also permanence; relational categories; substance

second analogy, 237–66; and analysis of events, 248–52; argument of, 241–69; epistemological not psychological, 258–9; whether a *non sequitur*, 255–9; objections to, 249–59; and phenomenalism, 262–6; premises of, 244, 246; principle of, 239–40; and refutation of idealism, 286–7; and simultaneous causation, 259–62; and third antinomy, 412; and time-determination, 238, 241–59. *See also* causal laws; causation; Hume; relational categories; succession of representations; time-determination

third analogy, 267–76; and first analogy, 224–5, 228–9; and official account, 70; principle of, 268; and refutation of idealism, 299–300; and simultaneity, 268–74; and spatial position, 274–5, 286; and substance, 274–5. *See also* interaction; relational categories; simultaneity

analytical method contrasted to synthetic, 6, 80

analytic judgments contrasted to synthetic, 28

"Anticipations of Perception," 196–205; and categories, 197–8; not constitutive principle, 201–2; and intensive magnitude, 198–200; whether mathematical or dynamical principle, 187–9; and matter, 201; principle of, 206–7; and realism, 184; and time, 202–5; and transcendental time-determinations, 174. *See also* intensive magnitude; sensation

"Antinomy of Pure Reason," 385–415; in inaugural dissertation, 388–90; in 1770s, 65, 387–404; in *Critique of Pure Reason*, 404–13; as indirect proof of transcendental idealism, 385–7, 401–2, 405–12, 463; methodological solution to, 387–401; organization of, 406–7

first antinomy, 386, 407–9

second antinomy, 386, 409–11

third antinomy, 386, 411–12

fourth antinomy, 386, 411–12

473

experience (cont.)
27–38, 55–6, 59, 75, 178–9, 245–6; as
empirical knowledge, 210–11; requires
time-determination, 35–6, 45; and transcendental arguments, 420; and transcendental ideality of time, 377–8. See
also "Analogies of Experience"; time-
determination; transcendental deduction
exposition: metaphysical contrasted to transcendental, 346; as time-determination,
52, 62, 63, 66. See also experience;
transcendental exposition
extensive magnitude, 190–6; and intensive
magnitude, 199–201, 205; and mathematics, 186; and matter, 201; in *Metaphysik Volckmann*, 192–3. See also
"Axioms of Intuition"
external objects: ambiguous conception of,
280–2; and time-determination, 305–16.
See also refutation of idealism

Feder, Johann Georg Heinrich, 434
Findlay, John N., 429, 430
Fischer, Kuno, 363
Fogelin, Robert, 450
form and transcendental idealism, 340–1,
351
forms of intuition: and "Axioms of Intuition," 64, 194–5; and categories, 51–2;
and geometry, 80; space and time as,
345–50; and time-determination, 33–8,
170–1; and transcendental idealism,
345–69. See also intuition; space, space
and time; time; transcendental idealism
Förster, Eckart, on refutation of idealism,
454–5, 457, 458
freedom in third antinomy, 400–1, 411–12
Friedman, Michael, 443, 444, 461

Garve, Christian, 434
geometry: and "Axioms of Intuition," 191–
2; and categories, 93–4; necessary truth
of, 80, 363–8; and transcendental exposition of space, 349–50; and transcendental idealism, 359–62. See also
euclidean geometry; space; space and
time
God: in inaugural dissertation, 17–18; and
necessity, 59–60; proof of, 394; as thing
in itself, 335, 352–4, 395, 399–400
Gram, Moltke S., on refutation of idealism,
452–3, 456–7

Haering, Theodor, 431
Harper, William A., 449

Harrison, Ross, on necessary truth, 368,
437, 461
Hegel, Georg Wilhelm Friedrich, 335
Henrich, Dieter, on transcendental deduction, 86–7, 432–3, 434, 436, 438, 439
Herz, Marcus, Kant's letters to, 13, 22–4,
44, 73, 142–3, 279, 429
Hintikka, Jaakko, 436
homogeneity and schematism, 163, 165, 169
Hoppe, Hansgeorg, 446
Horstmann, Rolf-Peter, 464
Howell, Robert, 437
Hume, David, 448, 456; on causation, 70,
105, 125, 128, 175, 237–8, 250, 328,
447; on continued existence, 263; on
laws of nature, 273; on necessary connection, 160, 166, 420; on self, 76, 137,
147; on substance, 175; on vivacity of
representations, 306
Humphrey, Ted, 434
hypothetical judgment, 98–9, 128. See also
judgment, logical functions of; metaphysical deduction

idealism, see skeptical idealism; subjective
idealism; transcendental idealism
images and schemata, 439–40
imagination: in deduction, 138; in Descartes, 320; in perception of causation,
246–8, 254, 256–7
immediacy of knowledge of external objects,
326–8
imposition: of categories, 53–61, 132, 144;
in geometry, 361–2. See also restriction
impossibility and incomprehensibility, 56–7
incompatibility of states of affairs, 226–7,
252–5
indiscernibility of moments, 37–8
infinite divisibility of space and time, 389–
90, 393, 409–11
infinite extension of space and time in "Antinomy," 402–3, 405, 406–11
inner sense: in *Anthropology*, 83; in deduction, 372–5; and refutation of idealism,
292–3; and representations, 83; and
transcendental idealism, 371–9. See also
forms of intuition; time
intellect: as active power, 54; dogmatic and
elenctic use of, 16–18; logical and real
use of, 16–18, 32, 38
intellectual intuition, 5, 327–8
intensive magnitude, 197–205; and category
of reality, 197–202; and continuity of
time, 186; and mathematics, 186; and
matter, 201; and measurement, 198–9;

in *Metaphysik Volckmann*, 199–201;
as regulative not constitutive, 188–9,
201–2; and schematism, 184; and time,
202–5. *See also* "Anticipations of Perception"
interaction, 267–76; category of, 431; and
causation, 272–4; and position in space,
170, 274–5; and simultaneity, 174, 268–
74; and substance, 212–14. *See also*
"Analogies of Experience"; relational
categories; simultaneity
intuition: and concepts, 13–14, 20, 105,
348; pure, 346–8; pure, and categories,
92–4; pure, in "Anticipations of Perception," 203; pure, in "Axioms of Intuition," 191–2; and self-knowledge, 151,
373–5. *See also* forms of intuition;
space; space and time; time
irreversibility in perception of causation,
245, 247–8, 255–7. *See also* "Analogies
of Experience"

Jacobi, F. H., 335, 459
judgment: deduction from concept of, 91,
94–102; and necessary connection, 119–
21; and transcendental idealism, 371–83
logical functions of: and categories, 30–1,
34–6, 66, 101–2, 111–12, 114, 120; and
metaphysical deduction, 97–99; in *Metaphysik Volckmann*, 124–9; and relational categories, 437–8; and schematism, 158, 162–3, 165; and temporal
relations, 166–7, 173–5; and transcendental deduction, 76–7, 124–9. *See also*
hypothetical judgment; metaphysical
deduction
system of principles of, 161–2, 176–81;
and categories, 176–81; in *Duisburg
Nachlass*, 62–5; general classification
of, 184, 189. *See also* "Analogies of
Experience"; "Anticipations of Perception"; "Axioms of Intuition"; "Postulates of Empirical Thought"
judgments of experience and judgments of
perception, 100–2, 117–19, 431
judgments of perception, *see* judgments of
experience

Kemp Smith, Norman: on "Analogies of
Experience," 444; on first analogy, 445–
6; on second analogy, 241, 446–50; on
third analogy, 273, 450–2; on "Anticipations of Perception," 202; on "Antinomy," 462–3; on apperception, 436;
on "Axioms of Intuition," 195–6, 442–

3; on patchwork theory, 432; on phenomenalism, 263, 443–4; on refutation
of idealism, 452–4; on schematism,
440–1; on "Transcendental Aesthetic,"
461; on transcendental deduction, 439
Kiesewetter, J. C. E., 454, 456
Kitcher, Patricia: on consciousness, 438–9;
on self, 461; on synthesis, 438; on transcendental deduction, 432, 437
Kitcher, Philip: on "Axioms of Intuition,"
441–3; on transcendental deduction,
433
Körner, Stephan, on transcendental arguments, 422–4, 464–5
Krüger, Lorenz, 464

Lambert, Johann Heinrich, on ideality of
time, 13, 22, 345, 430, 459
Lehmann, Gerhard, on refutation of idealism, 281, 292, 452, 454–5
Leibniz, Gottfried Wilhelm: on apperception, 32–3, 143, 146, 432; on causation
and/or interaction, 128, 175, 237–8; on
creation, 408; on metaphysics, 273; on
ontological argument, 429; on space
and/or time, 110, 267–8, 350–1, 393,
453–4, 461, 463; on sufficient reason
and indiscernibility, 37–8
Lewis, Clarence Irving, 440
Lindsay, A. D., 452
Locke, John, 429, 438, 460; on abstract
ideas, 158, 163–5; on consciousness,
141, 146; on origins of knowledge, 1–3;
on realism, 462; on relations, 351; on
space, 346; on substance, Kant's critique of, 212–13
Lovejoy, Arthur, 449

McCann, Edwin: on apperception, 438; on
transcendental deduction, 432, 433
magnitude: in "General Note," 169; and
refutation of idealism, 287; and space,
298–301; and time-determination, 173;
and transcendental deduction, 287. *See
also* extensive magnitude; intensive
magnitude; measurement; number
manifold of representations: necessarily temporal, 148–9; unity of, and transcendental deduction, 81, 89, 92–4. *See also*
representations; time-determination
Martin, Gottfried, 461, 462
mathematical principles, and dynamical,
183–90, 201–2
mathematics: and "Axioms of Intuition,"
190–1, 195–6; and categories, 93–4;

Schopenhauer (*cont.*)
second analogy, 240, 257–8, 259–60,
446–7, 450; on things in themselves,
334
scope of time, 172, 174–5
secondary qualities and transcendental idealism, 341–2
self, empirical: in refutation of idealism,
283–5, 292–5, 303–4, 307–10, 312–14;
and rules, 431; as nontemporal, 372–9
self-affection, 461
self-ascription, erroneous, 146–7
self-consciousness and consciousness, 141–4. *See also* apperception; self
sensation: and actuality, 275; and category of quality, 173–4; and intensive magnitude, 197–205
sensibility, faculty of: in inaugural dissertation, 13–16, 388–90; limits of, 388–90, 391–401. *See also* forms of intuition; intuition; space; space and time; time; "Transcendental Aesthetic"; transcendental idealism
Sidgwick, Henry, 281
simultaneity: in first analogy, 217, 219; in second antinomy, 409–11; empirical knowledge of, 267–75; and interaction, 174, 267–75; and relativity theory, 451; and space, 274–5, 298–303, 312; and succession, 247, 305–7. *See also* "Analogies of Experience"; interaction
simultaneous causation, 259–62, 273
skeptical idealism: and causal theory of perception, 320; in fourth paralogism, 280; and refutation of idealism, 289, 300–1, 312, 328
skepticism: and "Antinomy," 387; and fourth paralogism, 281; and refutation of idealism, 312–15, 318–19; and self-knowledge, 455; and time-determination, 168; and transcendental arguments, 421, 424–8; and transcendental deduction, 79–80, 99; and transcendental idealism, 333–5, 369, 462
soul: location of, 314; as simple, 409–10; as thing in itself, 335, 395, 399
space: absolute, metaphysically untenable, 350–2; absolute, not directly perceived, 170, 267, 274; and change, 286–7; as continuous, 192–3; and enduring objects, 310–14; whether finite or infinite, 407–9; as form of intuition of independent objects, 280–2, 286–9, 310–15, 317–21, 321–3; and interaction, 274–5; perception of position in, 168, 170, 267–8, 270–5; as permanent, 297–300;

and simultaneity, 298–303; and substance, 227–9, 234–5; and representation of time, 207–305; and time-determination, 152, 167–70, 268–9, 293–5, 321–3; and transcendental idealism, 12–13, 350–69, 371–2. *See also* forms of intuition; geometry; space and time; transcendental idealism
space and time: in "Antinomy," 406–11; as forms of intuition, 345–50; metaphysical exposition of, 346–9; transcendental exposition of, 349–50; as transcendentally ideal, 2–7, 12–13, 17, 20–1, 362–9. *See also* forms of intuition; geometry; space; time; transcendental idealism
Strawson, Peter F.: on first analogy, 446; on second analogy, 255–8, 448–9; on third analogy, 269, 451; on conservation of substance, 231–2, 444; on descriptive metaphysics, 333, 458; on refutation of idealism, 311, 456–7; on "Transcendental Aesthetic," 356, 460; on transcendental arguments, 417, 424–5, 465; on transcendental deduction, 436, 459
Stroud, Barry: on skepticism, 458; on transcendental arguments, 424, 465
subjective idealism, Kant's rejection of, 93. *See also* transcendental idealism
subreptic axioms, 18–19, 64, 388–90, 412
substance, 212–14, 215–35; and activity, 42; and alteration, 221–4; in third analogy, 274; and empirical knowledge of change, 224–30; and conservation, 230–5; Locke on, 212–13; and permanence, 174, 215–21, 223, 230–5; as regulative ideal, 232–5, and space, 227–9. *See also* "Analogies of Experience"; permanence; relational categories
succession: and causation, 239–59; and permanence, 217–19
succession of representations: contrasted to objective succession, 47, 171, 177, 211–12, 225–7, 229, 243–59, 264–6, 292–4, 302–4; and external objects, 305–16; knowledge of, 292–4, 372–3; and simultaneity, 268–75. *See also* time-determination
sufficient reason, principle of: epistemological not ontological, 308, 310, 408; in *Nova Delucidatio*, 308, 310, 446; in rationalism, 11, 251–2; and real possibility, 11–12; and time-determination, 37–8, 238, 242
Sulzer, Johann Georg: on ideality of time, 22, 345, 459

GENERAL INDEX

synthesis: and "Antinomy," 407–11; of imagination, 146; of recognition in a concept, 106–8, 303, 372–3; of reproduction in imagination, 92–4, 121–4, 299, 302, 455–6; as threefold, 106, 109. *See also* combination

synthetic *a priori* judgment: in *Duisburg Nachlass*, 27–38; principle of, 161, 176–81, 252; and transcendental arguments, 419–21. *See also* synthetic *a priori* knowledge; transcendental deduction

synthetic *a priori* knowledge: needs explanation, 11; and transcendental deduction, 77, 79, 85–7, 91–121. See also *a priori* knowledge; synthetic *a priori* judgment; transcendental deduction

systematicity: as principle of convenience, 19–20; as regulative ideal, 82

Tetens, Johann Nicolas: on apperception, 32, 74, 431, 432; on inner sense, 462

theology and transcendental idealism, 352–4

things in themselves: and "Antinomy," 385–7, 404–12; contrasted to appearances, 333–44; and geometry, 359–62; and necessary truth, 354–62; and refutation of idealism, 280–3, 290–2, 317–29, 413–15; and self, 372–9; and spatiality, 333–44, 344–69; and time-determination, 371–9. *See also* forms of intuition; space and time; transcendental idealism

Thompson, Manley P., 436

time: absolute, metaphysically untenable, 350–2; and "Anticipations of Perception," 202–5; and arithmetic, 37, 173; as continuous, 192–3; not directly perceived, 88, 167–72, 211, 217, 219–31, 226, 243–4, 246, 270, 283, 420–1, 423–4; multiple streams of, 230; and number, 194–5; permanence of, 216–21, 283; and self, 152, 372–9; spatial representation of, 297–305; and substance, 216–21; and transcendental idealism, 372–9; as universal form of intuition, 166–72; unity of, 48. *See also* forms of intuition; space and time; time-determination; transcendental idealism; transcendental time-determinations

time-content, 172, 174–5

time-determination: and "Analogies of Experience," 207–14; and "Anticipations of Perception," 202–5; and "Axioms of Intuition," 194–5; and categories, 77–8, 166–72, 176–81; in *Duisburg Nachlass*, 27, 33–8, 40–1, 45, 48–53, 62; and embodiment, 312–14; and empirical self, 292–5, 307–10; empirically uncertain, 240–1; and enduring objects, 305–16; epistemology not psychology, 153–4, 303–5, 315–16, 374; and events, 447; and interaction, 268–75; and theory of judgment, 70; and necessity of succession, 246–8; ontological presuppositions of, 321–3; and refutation of idealism, 279–95, 303–16; as regulative ideal, 260, 275, 377; and skepticism, 168; and space, 216–21, 224–30, 286–9, 293–5, 297–305, 321–3; and substance, 224–30; and synthetic *a priori* judgment, 176–81; and transcendental arguments, 420–1, 423–8; and transcendental deduction, 87–9, 133, 149–54; and transcendental idealism, 371–9; and transcendental synthesis, 136; two-staged theory of, 70, 158, 171–2, 177, 205, 207–8, 247, 279, 316. *See also* "Analogies of Experience"; time

time-order, 172, 175; and absolute time, 170; and relational categories, 174; and simultaneous causation, 261

time-series, 172–3, 179, 217; and causation, 242

"Transcendental Aesthetic": main arguments of, 345–69; and "Axioms of Intuition," 193–4; on counting, 301; and refutation of idealism, 311–12; and transcendental idealism, 345–69, 373–4. *See also* forms of intuition; geometry; space; space and time; time; transcendental idealism

transcendental affinity: in transcendental deduction, 132, 138, 144; and transcendental idealism, 379–83

"Transcendental Analytic," and *Duisburg Nachlass*, 64–5. *See also* "Analogies of Experience"; "Anticipations of Perception"; "Axioms of Intuition"; metaphysical deduction; "Postulates of Empirical Thought"; refutation of idealism; schematism; transcendental deduction

transcendental arguments: premises of, 419–21; and skepticism, 421, 424–8; and uniqueness, 421–4; and verificationism, 424–8

transcendental deduction of the categories, 73–153; ambivalence about strategies, 73–5, 85–7, 418; and "Analogies of